Women
of the
Medieval World

John H. Mundy

Women
of the
Medieval World

ESSAYS IN HONOR OF
JOHN H. MUNDY

EDITED BY
Julius Kirshner
AND
Suzanne F. Wemple

BASIL BLACKWELL

© Basil Blackwell Ltd 1985

First published 1985

Basil Blackwell Ltd
108 Cowley Road, Oxford OX4 1JF, UK

Basil Blackwell Inc.
432 Park Avenue South, Suite 1505,
New York, NY 10016, USA

British Library Cataloguing in Publication Data

Women of the medieval world: essays in honor
of John H. Mundy.
1. Women—Social conditions   2. Women—
History—Middle Ages, 500–1500
I. Kirshner, Julius   II. Wemple, Suzanne F.
III. Mundy, John H.
305.4′2′0902   HQ1143
ISBN 0–631–13872–2

Library of Congress Cataloging in Publication Data

Main entry under title:

Women of the medieval world.

Bibliography: p.
Includes index.
1. Women—Europe—History—Middle Ages, 500–1500—
Addresses, essays, lectures. 2. Mundy, John Hine,
1917–   . I. Mundy, John Hine, 1917–   .
II. Kirshner, Julius.   III. Wemple, Suzanne Fonay.
HQ1147. E85W66 1985   305.4′09′02   84–20342
ISBN 0–631–13872–2

Set in 11 on 12½ point Monotype Baskerville by
Gloucester Typesetting Services
Printed in Great Britian by T. J. Press Ltd, Padstow, Cornwall

Contents

Preface

The essays that follow are published in honor of Professor John H. Mundy. They are intended as a tribute to his distinguished career of teaching and scholarship at Columbia University spanning almost 40 years. With the exception of Professor Eugene Rice, all the contributors have studied with Professor Mundy at Columbia. Although the essays reflect varied research concerns and historiographic perspectives, they are united by a common theme which has engaged a number of the contributors in recent years; and by a common methodology based on a rigorous reading of texts which we first learnt in Professor Mundy's seminar. We hope these essays will be of interest not only to specialists in the history of women but also to those who profess a broad interest in the history of the Middle Ages.

We wish to acknowledge with gratitude the generous assistance we received in the preparation of this volume from James Grubb, Bernard McGinn, Charlotte Mundy, and especially Catherine Caballeira McGee for the many hours she contributed to this project.

JULIUS KIRSHNER *and* SUZANNE F. WEMPLE

Abbreviations

AD P-O	*Archives départementales de Pyrénées-Orientales*
AF	*Analecta Franciscana*
AFH	*Archivum Franciscanum Historicum*
ALKG	*Archiv für Litteratur und Kirchengeschichte des Mittelalters*
AM Perp.	*Archives municipales de Perpignan*
Annales, ESC	*Annales (Economies, Sociétés, Civilisations)*
AS	*Acta Sanctorum*
ASF	*Archivio di Stato di Firenze*
BF	*Bullarium Franciscanum*
BNB	*Bracton's Note Book*, ed. F. W. Maitland (3 vols, London, 1887)
Bracton	Bracton, *De Legibus et Consuetudinibus Angliae*, ed. George E. Woodbine, trans. with revision and notes by Samuel E. Thorne (4 vols, Cambridge, Mass., 1968–77)
BS	*Bibliotheca Sanctorum*
CCSL	*Corpus Christianorum, Series Latina*
Codex	*Codex* in the *Corpus iuris civilis*, eds T. H. Mommsen, W. Kroll, P. Krueger and R. Schoell (3 vols, Berlin, 1928–9)
CRR	*Curia Regis Rolls*
CSEL	*Corpus Scriptorum Ecclesiasticorum Latinorum*
Digesta	*Digesta* in the *Corpus iuris civilis*, eds T. H. Mommsen, W. Kroll, P. Krueger and R. Schoell (3 vols, Berlin, 1928–9)
EHR	*English Historical Review*
ELAR	*The Earliest Lincolnshire Assize Rolls AD 1202–1209*, ed. Doris M. Stenton (Lincoln Record Society, 1926)
Glanvill	*Tractatus de legibus et consuetudinibus regni Angliae qui*

	Glanvilla vocatur, ed. and trans. G. D. G. Hall (London, 1965)
HPM	*Historiae Patriae Monumenta*
JE	Jaffé – Ewald, *Regesta Pontificum Romanum*
MGH	*Monumenta Germaniae Historica*
MGH, Ep.	*MGH, Epistolae*
MGH, Poet.	*MGH, Poetae Latini Medii Aevi Karolini*
MGH, SRG	*MGH, Scriptores rerum Germanicarum*
MGH, SRM	*MGH, Scriptores rerum Merovingicarum*
MGH, SS	*MGH, Scriptores* (folio series)
Novellae	*Novellae* in the *Corpus iuris civilis*, eds T. H. Mommsen, W. Kroll, P. Krueger and R. Schoell (3 vols, Berlin, 1928–9)
PBKJ	*Pleas before the King or his Justices, 1198–1212*, ed. Doris M. Stenton (Selden Society, London, 1953)
PG	*Patrologia Graeca*
PL	*Patrologia Latina*
P&M	Sir Frederick Pollock and Frederic William Maitland, *The History of the English Law before the Time of Edward I*, 2nd edn, reissued with new introduction and select bibliography by S. F. C. Milsom (2 vols, Cambridge, 1968)
RCR	*Rotuli Curiae Regis*, ed. Francis Palgrave (2 vols, London, 1835)
X	The *Decretals* of Gregory IX in *Corpus iuris canonici*, ed. A. Friedberg (Leipzig, 1881)

John Hine Mundy:
An Appreciation

John Hine Mundy was born on 29 December 1917. His parents were musicians. His mother, Clytie Hine, was an opera singer from Adelaide, Australia. His English father, John Mundy, was a cellist who, before the war, played first cello in the Beecham Opera Company, but who when John junior was born, was a captain in the 7th Battalion, West Yorkshire Regiment, and in the trenches in France. A dispatch of Field Marshal Sir Douglas Haig mentions him for gallant and distinguished service.

After the war, in 1921, the family settled in the United States, where Clytie's parents joined them from Australia. During the absences of their mother and father on tour, John and his sister Meg lived with their maternal grandmother and grandfather, a retired jewelry maker and old-time socialist, in Spring Valley near New York City.

When the children were ready for school, they returned to their parents, who were by then permanently established in Manhattan. John went to the St Thomas School in midtown. He was musical and had a good voice, and from the age of nine until his voice broke was himself a professional chorister and, during his last two years as a soprano, solo boy. His extracurricular enthusiasm was for military miniatures, battle maps and campaign histories, interests he has retained. He received a sound secondary education at the Trinity School, a school he loathed.

The ambience at home was professionally musical and self-consciously British expatriate. John's father was cellist in the Vertchamps Quartet, in the CBS Radio Orchestra, and in due course became orchestra manager of the Metropolitan Opera Orchestra during the regimes of Edward Johnson and Rudolf Bing. After she retired from the operatic stage, Clytie Hine was a distinguished teacher who coached many opera and musical comedy singers. Among her pupils was the tenor Peter Pears, a connection that led to John's friendship with Pears and Benjamin Britten and, many years later, brought him invitations to lecture on love and war in the Middle Ages at the Aldeburgh Festival. Clytie's soirées in the thirties and forties attracted an entertaining cross-section of the New York musical and theatrical worlds. John's sister Meg grew up to be an actress and a great beauty. She created the title role in Jean-Paul Sartre's *La putain respectueuse* in its first American production, an early landmark in a long, active career.

In the meantime, John moved toward scholarship and the professoriate. His university training was at Columbia: BA (1940), MA (1941), PhD (1950), under Austin Evans and Lynn Thorndike. In September 1942, he married Charlotte Williams, a Columbia graduate student in American history from Oshkosh, Wisconsin. In the spring of 1943, he was drafted and sent to learn cryptanalysis at a US Army school in Virginia.

I met him a year later, on shipboard, as we sailed in convoy for England. My memory of him as a young man is sharp. His face was beautiful. He was extravagantly articulate (in the English accent taught him at home), exotic, elegant and radical in idea and gesture, full of wit and gaiety, irrepressibly shocking to provincial pieties. The *doctorandus* lurked behind the dandy. He read in French, German and Latin the books and articles Charlotte regularly mailed him overseas, remarking that the books *he* hoped to write would have one line of text on the page and the rest footnotes, an absurd exaggeration that yet tells us something useful about his later work and method: for although his special gift is for illuminating paradox and generalization, he reserves his best respect for technical expertise and his deepest affection for the *ipsissima verba* of the men and women of the past. My own wish to become a historian dates from that time and is owed to his example.

We had a safe and entertaining war, a pusillanimous crew in an inglorious service, enlisted men breaking simple German codes and cyphers of the kind used below divisional level (the point of the exercise was to identify the German units opposite us). The only member of our group with real talent for the work was a radio announcer from Shreveport, Louisiana, with a voice of modulated velvet. We crossed to France in July 1944, and moved in stages from an apple orchard in Normandy, to a hilltop near Verdun (with an excellent view, explicated by John, of a nucleated village and the open field system

still visible around it), to winter quarters in Falkenburg in southern
Holland (in peacetime a modest summer resort), then through bomb-
flattened northern Germany to the Elbe. In June, we withdrew to the
luxury of Spa. Soon after, John left for Shrivenham Army University
in England, where he taught history to GIs waiting to go home. He
was demobbed at Christmas and returned to postgraduate study at
Columbia.

A year in Toulouse, 1946–7, under the difficult conditions of the
postwar period in France (*pain au chocolat* and a flask of brandy in the
unheated archives), was to be the first of many campaigns and the
beginning of a permanent interest in the social and constitutional
history of that city. The first fruit of this research was his doctoral dissertation, published in 1954 by the Columbia University Press under
the title *Liberty and Political Power in Toulouse, 1050–1230*. He has followed the dissertation with studies of Toulouse's hospitals and lepro-
saria, the university, municipal brothels, monasteries, public charity,
family names and structures, usurers and heretics. All build toward a
meticulous, lively and continuing reconstruction of a twelfth and
thirteenth-century cityscape and urban culture, a telling example of
the power of a twentieth-century historian – when free of received
ideas, fresh of eye and disciplined by good judgement and good Latin
– to recover for the present some genuine understanding of a fragment
of the remoter past radically different in assumption, sensibility,
mentality, manners and taste from anything in our lived experience.
He has always known that the past is a foreign country.

With the degree and publications in hand, Mundy climbed the
academic ladder at Columbia: Assistant Professor (1950), Associate
Professor (1956) and Professor (1962). From 1967 to 1970, a time of
riot and divided loyalties in the university, he was Chairman of the
Department of History. 'The art of directing or commanding other
men does not require learning or even much practice', he was to write
a decade later and in a wholly different context, 'All it needs is intelligence, courage and decision.' This describes exactly his own qualities
during those testing months. He has taught briefly elsewhere – at New
York University, the New School for Social Research, Fordham
University and the University of Chicago. The institutions and foundations that patronize American humanistic scholarship have recognized
his merit and supported his research: the Council for the International
Exchange of Scholars (Fulbright Awards) (in 1958–9), the American
Council of Learned Societies (1958–9 and again in 1984–5), the
Guggenheim Foundation (1963–4 and 1977–8), and the National

Endowment for the Humanities (1970–1). He has twice been a visiting member of the Institute for Advanced Study. In 1975, he became a Fellow of the Medieval Academy of America, and in 1981 was elected a Fellow of the American Academy of Arts and Sciences.

Throughout his career, John Mundy has lectured on medieval urban history. He reshaped this material for a wider audience in *The Medieval Town* (1958) and in the Matthews Lectures delivered in 1965 at the Metropolitan Museum of Art under the auspices of the Columbia University School of Architecture. A parallel interest has been the history of political and ecclesiastical thought, this too reflected in published work, notably the essay on conciliarism with which he introduced the volume on *The Council of Constance* in the *Records of Civilization* series, published by the Columbia University Press in 1961. (Mundy was European editor of the series between 1956 and 1962.)

In seminars offered in alternate years, he trains graduate students in paleography and diplomatics and the close reading and interpretations of Latin texts and documents. The two-hour sessions are far from dull. I know because my office is across the hall from his: both students and professor rock with laughter and surprise. Out of these courses has come the first-hand acquaintance with the exceptionally broad and varied range of sources that undergirds his *Europe in the High Middle Ages, 1150–1309*, published in England in 1973, an exhilarating survey of Latin European society during its medieval apogee, a very personal book, with a tone and style which mirror vividly the man who wrote it. Few books that purport to be textbooks can be read with joy, even those written, as he puts it in the preface, for 'young men and women whose natural faculties have matured and who hope to acquire rather more learning than is needed by the mass of their peers.' This one can.

It is relevant to the theme of the essays assembled here to note that *Europe in the High Middle Ages* has more to say about women (and said it earlier and better) than any book of similar scope and ambition. Mundy is characteristically sympathetic and astringent. 'Women rarely went to war except to urge their men on, help them plan for it, and to bewail or rejoice in their departure.' The key word is 'rejoice'. He points out that the marriage sacrament was 'simply the free and voluntary agreement of a woman and a man before witnesses, something posing obvious difficulties for parents with nubile daughters.' Or on 'stolen freedoms', this: 'It is noteworthy that the poets did not bother to list the names or count the number of Iseult's children, and it is evident that what may be passed off as love among the rich and leisured is merely obvious and bare adultery among those of lesser means.' The thirteenth-century ideal was equality of lover and be-loved, of the man and the woman; but realities of superior male strength and of childbirth and their relationship to the holding and division of property and to contemporary notions about the power of family and lineage contradicted the ideal. On the other hand, the women of Latin Christendom were better off than Jewish and Islamic women, better educated, better protected from divorce on the initia-tive of a husband, and more active participants in religious life. Elderly men of substance often married young girls. 'Such marriages could lead to a kind of equality between the generous credulity or ignorance of the youthful bride and the sceptical carefulness of the experienced older husband. Besides, at the worst, there was always a propertied widowhood to be looked forward to.'

Medieval men were ambivalent about women; a good many modern men are too. Mundy likes women and writes justly about them. It is fitting that his former students, many of them women, have chosen to honor him with a book about medieval women. In the meantime, a lifelong New Yorker has returned to the city he knows best: his second book on Toulouse will appear more or less simultane-ously with this one.

I

Teste David cum Sibylla:
The Significance of the Sibylline Tradition
in the Middle Ages

BERNARD McGINN

In 1715 William Whiston, 'Sometime Professor of the Mathematiks in the University of Cambridge', wrote the following in his *A Vindication of the Sibylline Oracles*:

That common opinion of the Modern Criticks, as if the *Sibylline Oracles*, quoted by the most primitive Christians, were spurious, and forged by some among themselves, a little before the middle of the Second Century; and from such a forged Copy were alledg'd by those Primitive Writers for their Religion, is not only highly dishonourable to Christianity, but utterly False in itself, and Unsupported by any just Foundation in the World.[1]

Professor Whiston, who perhaps should have remained with 'the Mathematiks', was fighting a rearguard action. Dishonorable as it may have been to Christianity, by 1715 the century-long debate over the authenticity of the Sibylline oracles was well-nigh over and the victory was with the 'Modern Criticks'.[2] Those Sibylline *grande dames* who had had their portraits done by no less than Van Eyck, Michelangelo, Raphael and Pinturicchio, who had been hymned by Thomas of Celano as the equal of David, whom even the skeptical Augustine had numbered among the pre-Christian members of the City of God, who in their relative youth had prophesied the outcome of the Trojan War to Agamemnon and his troops, and led Aeneas through the

---

[1] W. Whiston, *A Vindication of the Sibylline Oracles* (London, 1715), p. 81.
[2] K. Prümm, 'Das Prophetenamt der Sibyllen in der kirchlichen Literatur mit besonderer Rücksicht auf der Deutung der 4. Ekloge Virgils', *Scholastik*, 4 (1929), pp. 498–533, gives a detailed but not exhaustive account.

Underworld, had come upon hard times. A slow fade into oblivion was well under way.

By 1715, of course, the Sybils, noted beauties in their day, were scarcely young, and hence they may well have preferred a decent obscurity to the harsh glare of public attention. Our first literary witness to the Sibyl is a well-known fragment of the Greek philosopher Heraclitus from about 500 BC: 'The Sibyl with frenzied lips, uttering words mirthless, unembellished, unperfumed, penetrates through a thousand years with her voice by the god.'[3] Heraclitus certainly did not invent the Sibyl. The origins of the female seer are lost in the prehistory of Greek religion, as is even the meaning of the name.[4] Like a number of famous women in antiquity, not the least of the Sibyl's charms was her aura of mystery; unlike many other beauties, however, the history of the Sibyl, at least until the seventeenth century, was not one of gradual unveiling, but of ever more complex and mysterious disguises. Today, many of these veils have been removed, but it would be foolish to think that none remains. My purpose here is to sketch the broad lines of the Sibyl's career between roughly AD 300 and 1500; but in order to understand the medieval Sibyl, it will be necessary to provide a prolegomenon on the seer's younger days.[5]

Female seers were known in the ancient Near East,[6] and the scanty sources we possess suggest that it was in Ionia where the Greeks were most in contact with the East that the Sibyl first became a part of Greek religion. We know, for instance, that a cave near Erythraea on the coast of Asia Minor facing Chios was associated with the Sibyl from an early period.[7] Such early witnesses as Aristophanes and Plato presuppose a single ecstatic seer who speaks for the god and foretells the future,[8] but as early as the mid-fourth century Heracleides

---

[3] Fragment 92, preserved in Plutarch, *The Pythian Oracle*, 397a.

[4] For a brief survey in English of some etymologies, see B. Thompson, 'Patristic use of the Sibylline oracles', *Review of Religion*, 16 (1952), pp. 118–20.

[5] There are many studies of the early Sibyllines. I mention here only those of C. Alexandre, *Excursus ad Sibyllina* (Paris, 1856); A. Rzach, 'Sibyllen', in Pauly-Wissowa (ed.), *Realencyclopädie der classischen Altertumwissenschaft*, ser. 2, 2: cc. 2073–183; and A. M. Denis, *Introduction aux Pseudépigraphes Grecs d'Ancien Testament* (Leiden, 1970), pp. 111–22.

[6] For a background sketch see J. Lindblom, *Prophecy in Ancient Israel* (Oxford, 1962), pp. 29–32.

[7] See Denis, *Introduction*, p. 112.

[8] Aristophanes, *Peace*, line 1095; Plato, *Phaedrus*, 244b. On the place of the Sibyl in ancient theories of inspiration and revelation, see E. Bevan, *Sibyls and Seers*

Ponticus lists several Sibyls.[9] Many subsequent lists of Sibyls were composed, the most influential on the later Christian tradition being the enumeration of ten made by the Roman scholar Varro and preserved in Lactantius.[10]

The important role that oracles played in the religion of the ancient Mediterranean world assured the Sibyls a remarkable diffusion in the Hellenistic period, not least of all in Italy. The stories of how a Sibyl came to Cumae are as confused and contradictory as most of the information we have received about the Sibyls, but no one who has ever visited that lonely height overlooking the Tyrrhenian Sea and explored the recesses of the Cyclopean cave in which the oracles were given can doubt that she chose an ideal spot. The eccentric landscape of the volcanic Phlegrean Fields and the brooding presence of Lake Avernus with its entrance to the lower regions form an ambience that it is difficult to imagine without a Sibyl, even today. The Cumaean Sibyl, immortalized by Virgil in the sixth book of the *Aeneid*,[11] became even better known than her Delphic sister.

The Sibyls acquired a notable official role in Roman religion. Pliny and Dionysius Halicarnassus are our chief sources for the well-known story of how the Sibyl sold three books of oracles to King Tarquin for the price of nine – an excellent illustration that the seer also had a good head for business.[12] However far back may go the Roman custom of collecting Sibylline oracles, entrusting them to a college of priests for safekeeping[13] and consulting them in times of crisis,[14] it is a sign of the increasingly important role that written Sibylline texts came to exercise in Rome. The Romans thought enough of these obscure

---

(London, 1928), especially pp. 135–8. More recently, H. Stumphol has studied the Sibyl's inspiration in 'Zur Psychologie der Sibylle', *Zeitschrift für Religions-und Geistesgeschichte*, 23 (1971), pp. 84–103.

[9] Heracleides in a fragment preserved in Clement of Alexandria, *Miscellanies*, 1.21.

[10] Lactantius, *Divine Institutes*, 1.6. The ten Sibyls are the Persian, Libyan, Delphic, Cimmerian, Erythraean, Samian, Cumaean, Hellespontic, Phrygian and Tiburtine.

[11] Virgil, *Aeneid*, 6.42–155. See R. J. Clark, 'Virgil, Aen. 6:40ff. and the Cumaean Sibyl's Cave', *Latomus*, 36 (1977), pp. 482–95.

[12] Pliny, *Natural History*, 13.88; and Dionysius Halicarnassus, *Roman Antiquities*, 4.62.

[13] First *Duoviri* then *Decemviri*, and finally *Quindecemviri* from the first century BC.

[14] For a list of the recorded consultations, see Alexandre, *Excursus ad Sibyllina*, pp. 198–209.

Greek hexameters to scour the Mediterranean world for replacements after a fire had destroyed the originals in 83 BC,[15] and Augustus later ordered a purging of the collection, probably to exclude anything that did not conform to his own religious and political program.[16] Under the Empire, consultation of the Sibylline verses stored in the Temple of Apollo on the Palatine was sporadic. Tiberius vetoed one attempt,[17] but Nero consulted them after the great fire of AD 64.[18] The last known Roman consultation was made by Julian the Apostate in AD 363,[19] and the books were destroyed by Stilicho about 408.[20]

Only a few fragments of the pagan Sibylline verses survive.[21] Perhaps we should not lament the loss of the rest unduly. Filled as she was by the god, the Sibyl was usually too distraught to write very well or even very intelligibly. Her literary productions were famed for their rough and obscure style, and we shall see that her art did not improve with age.

Despite the loss of the pagan Sibyllines, we do have the eight books of Greek hexameters attributed to the Sibyl that William Whiston defended with such vigor, books that had had a long and complex history by the time they were praised by the Cambridge don. They had been cited by both Greek and Latin patristic authors, and subsequently parts of them had been translated into Latin and used by many medieval and Renaissance writers. In the sixteenth century several editions of the Greek text and a full Latin translation had been made.[22] By the beginning of the seventeenth century, however, attacks on the claims of these verses to be the products of pagan prophetesses older than Homer had been expressed. The first unveiling of the Sibyl had begun.

These books are now known to be the products of Jewish and Christian authors, although they incorporate pagan Sibylline oracles

---

[15] Dionysius Halicarnassus, *Roman Antiquities*, 4.62.

[16] Tacitus, *Annals*, 6.12; Seutonius, *Augustus*, 31; Dio Cassius, *Roman History*, 54.17.

[17] Tacitus, *Annals*, 6.12.   [18] ibid., 15.44.

[19] Ammianus Marcellinus, *Histories*, 23.1.7.

[20] Rutilius Namatianus, *On His Return*, 2.52. See E. Demougeot, 'Saint Jérôme, les oracles sibyllins et Stilicon', *Revue des Études Anciennes*, 54 (1953), pp. 83–92.

[21] See the edition of H. Diels, *Sibyllinische Blätter* (Berlin, 1890), pp. 111–26; and the material in Alexandre, *Excursus ad Sibyllina*, pp. 118–37 and 242–53.

[22] The first edition of the Greek text was by X. Betuleius (Sixtus Birck) and appeared in 1545 in Basel. In 1555 S. Castellio issued a more influential edition which included a full Latin translation. The 1599 Paris edition of J. Opsopoeus (Koch) already expressed doubts about the authenticity of the verses.

in places.[23] It is generally agreed that they were written in various stages between the mid-second century BC and approximately AD 300, and that they were put together as a collection with a special introduction in the sixth century.[24] Cardinal Mai discovered four further books of Jewish origin in the nineteenth century, though since these appear to have been little known, they are not of moment for our story.[25]

The Greek travel writer Pausanius in the second century BC had spoken of a Palestinian Jewish Sibyl named Sabbe,[26] a fact which already hints at a connection between Judaism and the Sibyl. Adaptation of this originally pagan genre of literature by Jews in the Hellenistic world should not be surprising. The Jews of the Diaspora eagerly turned to the production of *Sibyllina* as effective apologetic and missionary tools. The witness of this most antique of seers (in the third book the prophetess announces herself as Noah's daughter-in-law who after the Flood migrated from Babylonia to Erythraea)[27] to the truth of Jewish monotheistic beliefs and to the superiority of the Jewish moral code was impressive in an era when antiquity was automatically equated with veracity. Her prediction of coming doom for immoral idolators was a salutary warning for many.

There are still debates about the order and dating of the eight books of the *Oracula Sibyllina*. Since the books have been much interpolated, edited and re-edited, what follows is only a general survey of current scholarly opinion. Book III is the oldest and most interesting of the Jewish oracles, being composed of various strata. The earliest parts (vv. 97–349 and 489–829) were drawn up in Egypt in the mid-second century BC, with later sections coming from the time of Cleopatra (51–30 BC).[28] Book IV is also predominantly Jewish, and was

[23] *Oracula Sibyllina*, III, 381–488; IV, 49–101, 174–92.

[24] The sixth-century introduction makes use of a late fifth-century summary on the Sibyls known as the *Theosophia*. See the edition and notes in A. Kurfess, *Sibyllinische Weissagungen* (Berlin, 1951), pp. 252–63.

[25] These four books are present in only some of the manuscripts and date from the first to the fourth centuries AD. As Book VIII is divided into three books in some manuscripts, Mai numbered his discoveries as Books XI–XIV. The fourteen books altogether contain 4230 hexameters.

[26] Pausanius, *Descriptions of Greece*, 10.12.9. The name Sabbe appears to be the source of the later medieval identification of the Sibyl with the Queen of Sheba.

[27] *Oracula Sibyllina*, III, 809–29.

[28] The fundamental work is still J. Geffcken, *Die Komposition und Entstehungszeit der Oracula Sibyllina* (Leipzig, 1902), pp. 1–17. The best recent discussion is that of J. Collins, *The Sibylline Oracles of Egyptian Judaism* (SBL Dissertation Series 13,

probably composed in Palestine in the late first century AD, as indicated by its use of the legend of the returning Nero (vv. 119–24 and 138–9) and various *vaticinia ex eventu*, or historical events disguised as prophecy.[29] Book V, also employing the Nero legend (vv. 28ff., 93ff., 139ff., 214ff. and 361ff.), is a group of oracles produced in Egypt after the destruction of the Temple and collected in the time of the Emperor Hadrian (*c.* 125).[30]

In the second century, Christian authors, or we might more correctly say Jewish–Christian authors, began to take an interest in the Sibyl. In the second vision of the *Shepherd of Hermas*, which appears to be as early as *c.* AD 100, Hermas sees an ancient lady whom he takes to be the Sibyl, but who turns out to be the Church.[31] Books I and II of the surviving *Oracula Sibyllina* are Jewish work, probably of the first century AD, revised in the next century by a Christian editor.[32] The earliest strata of the properly Christian Books VI–VIII also date from the second century. Jean Daniélou thought that Books VI and VII originated with Jewish–Christians in Egypt, the former early in the second century, the latter toward the mid-century,[33] but there is no real evidence for Egyptian provenance. Book VIII, the best known of the Christian *Sibyllina*, is composed of two parts: vv. 1–216, a Jewish survey of world history and coming doom reworked by a Christian editor, and *vv.* 217–500, Christian prophecies beginning with the famous poem predicting the return of Christ, whose initial letters spell out the acrostic Ἰησοῦς Χρειστὸς Θεοῦ υἱὸς σωτήρ σταυρός (*vv.* 217–50) or 'Jesus Christ, Son of God, Savior, Cross'.[34] The whole

---

Montana, 1974), cc. 2 and 4; but see also A. Momigliano, 'La portata storica dei vaticini sul settimo re nel terzo libro degli Oracoli Sibillini', in *Forma Futuri. Studi in Onore del Cardinale Michele Pellegrino* (Turin, 1975), pp. 1077–84. V. Nikiprowetsky, *La Troisème Sibylle* (Paris, 1970), has argued unsuccessfully that the book is a unified production of the time of Cleopatra.

[29] J. Collins, 'The place of the Fourth Sibyl in the development of the Jewish Sibyllina', *Journal of Jewish Studies*, 25 (1974), pp. 365–80.

[30] Collins, *Sibylline Oracles*, c. 5.

[31] Hermas, *Shepherd*, Vision 2. 1–4. The *Shepherd* was put together in its final form about AD 150.

[32] See J. Collins (ed.), *Apocalypse. The Morphology of a Genre* (Missoula, 1979), pp. 47, 97–8.

[33] J. Daniélou, *The Theology of Jewish Christianity* (Chicago, 1964), pp. 18–19. Geffcken, *Die Komposition*, p. 36, and Kurfess, *Sibyllinische*, pp. 313–14, also opt for the second century, while Rzach, 'Sibyllen', *c.* 2142, holds for the third.

[34] Many of the pagan *Sibyllina* were in acrostics, as Cicero tells us in *On Divination*, 2.110–11.

Book is violently anti-Roman and appears to date from the reign of Marcus Aurelius (*c.* 175).[35]

From the second century on, Christian ecclesiastical authors show a profound respect for the Sibyl as a prophetess of Christ, citing extensively from the surviving books and from lost materials.[36] Origen forms an exception in his coolness.[37] Justin, Athenagoras, Hippolytus and Tertullian all mention the Sibyl with respect;[38] Clement of Alexandria and Theophilus of Antioch are veritable gold mines of Sibylline materials,[39] and the *Divine Institutes* of Lactantius written *c.* 304–13 are so filled with the Sibyls that the prophetess is quoted more often than the Old Testament.[40] Lactantius was the great 'ecumenist' among the Latin Fathers, as was Clement among the Greeks. He summarized his desire to show the full agreement of all the ancient seers with the truth of the Christian religion as follows: 'Wherefore, since all these things are true and certain, being foretold by the unanimous annunciation of all the prophets, since Trismegistus, Hystaspes and the Sibyls have all foretold the same things, it cannot be doubted that all hope of life and salvation rests solely in the worship of God.'[41]

Lactantius' contemporary Eusebius also made use of the Sibyl,[42] and during later centuries a work ascribed to the imperial patron of both writers, the Emperor Constantine, provided an even more potent approbation of the Sibyl's prophecies of Christ. The *Oration to the Assembly of the Saints* purports to be a speech of the Emperor to a group of bishops, but recent study shows that it was more likely composed in the 360s as a part of Christian propaganda against Julian's revival of paganism.[43] This important piece of Christian apologetic cites the

---

[35] Collins (ed.), *Apocalypse*, p. 36.

[36] 'Patristic use of the Sibylline oracles', provides a useful, if not quite complete, survey. See especially the two appendices, pp. 130–6.

[37] Origen mentions the Sibyl only when responding to the attacks of Celsus in *Against Celsus*, 5.61, 7.53 and 56. Among the Latin Fathers, Arnobius, *Against the Peoples*, 1.62, seems to display an ambivalent attitude.

[38] Justin, *Apology*, 1.20 and 44, *Exhortation*, 16; Athenagoras, *Plea*, 30; Hippolytus, *On Christ and Antichrist*, 52; Tertullian, *To the Nations*, 2.12.

[39] Theophilus, *To Autolycus*, 2.3, 31 and 36; Clement, *Miscellanies*, 1.21, 3.3 and 5.14, *Exhortation*, 71.4.

[40] Forty-four times in all. For a list of citations, see Thompson, 'Patristic use of the Sibylline oracles', pp. 134–6; and Alexandre, *Excursus ad Sibyllina*, pp. 273–5.

[41] Lactautius, *Epitome*, 73.   [42] Eusebius, *Evangelical Preparation*, 9.15; 13.13.

[43] R. P. C. Hanson, 'The *Oratio ad Sanctos* attributed to the Emperor Constantine and the Oracle at Daphne', *Journal of Theological Studies*, 24 (1973), pp. 505–11.

acrostic poem of the Erythraean Sibyl from Book VIII as a 'foreign source' of testimony to Christ's divinity and couples this witness with that of Virgil's Fourth Eclogue.[44] Lactantius had already seen the Fourth Eclogue's Sibylline picture of a new Golden Age as a prophecy of the millennial kingdom,[45] but it remained for the pseudo-Constantine to identify the famous lines beginning 'Ultima Cumaei venit iam carmina aetas' as the Cumaean Sibyl's prophecy of the Virgin Birth of the Savior.[46] This interpretation was conveyed to Latin Christianity through Augustine's adoption of it in *The City of God*, 10.27, and elsewhere;[47] it was to be one of the crucial factors in the Sibyl's reputation in the Middle Ages and Renaissance.

Augustine's support of the Sibyl was not a foregone conclusion because he was firmly against forms of apocalyptic prophecy that purported to reveal either new details about or to give an exact timetable of the last events.[48] Although the bishop was sparing in his use of Sibylline material,[49] and he sometimes expressed a guarded position, his positive references gave potent support to the Sibyl's authority. Especially noteworthy was *The City of God*, 18.23, where he not only numbered the seer among the pre-Christian inhabitants of the City of God, but also quoted the famous acrostic in an improved Latin version.[50] Of equal weight in later centuries was the sermon

---

[44] *Oration*, 18–21.

[45] Lactantius, *Divine Institutes*, 7.24.

[46] The crucial passage is *Eclogue*, 4.4–10. Of the extensive literature on the Messianic interpretation of the Eclogue, I mention only D. Comparetti, *Vergil in the Middle Ages* (London, 1966, reprint of 1895 edn), c. 7; A. Kurfess, 'Virgils vierte Ekloge und die Oracula Sibyllina', *Historisches Jahrbuch*, 73 (1953), pp. 120–7; and the articles of K. Prümm, 'Das Prophetenamt der Sibyllen in der kirchlichen Literatur mit besonderer Rücksicht auf der Deutung der 4. Ekloge Virgils', *Scholastik*, 4 (1929), pp. 221–46, 498–533; and 'Die Heilserwartung der vierten Ekloge Virgils im Widerstreit neurer Ansichten', *Scholastik*, 6 (1931), pp. 539–68; and 7 (1932), pp. 239–57.

[47] See also *Letters*, 104.11, and 258.5; and the unfinished *Commentary on Romans*, 1.3.

[48] On this aspect of Augustine's thought, see B. McGinn, *Visions of the End. Apocalyptic Traditions in the Middle Ages* (New York, 1979), pp. 26–7, and the literature cited there.

[49] For a survey of texts where Augustine refers to the Sibyl, see B. Altaner, 'Augustinus und die Neutestamentlichen Apokryphen, Sibyllinen und Sextussprüche', *Analecta Bollandiana*, 67 (1949), pp. 244–7.

[50] Augustine's text lacks the σταυρός (cross) strophe. In the same chapter he also cites lines from *Oracula Sibyllina* VI and VIII that Lactantius had used in *Divine Institutes*, 4.18–19, as prophecies of Christ's Passion, Death and Resurrection. More cautious references to the Sibyl, along with other witnesses such as Hermes

Against the Jews, Pagans and Arians, universally attributed to Augustine until the modern era.[51] This influential, if tedious, work sets up a clear parallel between the Old Testament prophets who announced Christ to the Jews and the Sibyl who proclaimed him to the Gentiles, especially with her acrostic poem.[52] The pseudo-Augustinian sermon did not invent the theme of *Teste David cum Sibylla,* but it did much to convey it to the medieval audience.[53]

What were the characteristics and functions of the ancient *Sibyllina*? The pagan Sibylline texts belong to the genus of oracle collections, one that was popular, especially for political purposes, in the ancient world.[54] From the beginning, the Sibyl's gloomy voice was concerned with predicting changes of dynasties,[55] as well as coming disasters for cities and empires.[56] At times she also announced a more optimistic message of a returning Golden Age.[57] The Sibyl continued to give such messages under Roman aegis and she also added new elements to her religious functions. Not only did the Romans consult her oracles in times of political crisis, but they also used them as a warrant for the expansion of Rome's religious world through sanctioning of temples to Eastern deities and through approving new rituals.[58] The medieval

---

Trismegistus and Orpheus, occur in *Against Faustus,* 13.1–2, 15 and 17; and in *The City of God,* 18.46–7, where the stress is on the superiority of Old Testament prophecies. See also *On the Agreement of the Evangelists,* 1.28, and pseudo-Augustine, *Treatise on Five Heresies,* 3.

[51] Recent scholarship on this work attributes it to Quodvultdeus, a pupil of Augustine who died in 453. See P. Glorieux, *Pour revaloriser Migne* (Lille, 1952), p. 13.

[52] See especially the passage in *PL* 42, c. 1115. K. Young, *The Drama of the Medieval Church* (Oxford, 1933), vol. 2, pp. 125–71, studied the influence of this text on the medieval liturgy and on the *Ordo Prophetarum* Christmas plays.

[53] We should note that the Sibylline literature continued to be cited by the later Greek Fathers, e.g. Gregory of Nazianzen, *Hymn to Nemesius,* lines 241–6; and Sozomen, *Church History,* 2.1.

[54] See J. Collins, *Sibylline Oracles,* pp. 2–19, for an introduction.

[55] As in the case of Alexander the Great, see Strabo, *Geography,* 17.1.43.

[56] Plutarch, *The Pythian Oracle,* 398.

[57] As in Virgil's Fourth Eclogue and the Sibylline text that Servius refers to in his Commentary on the poem. See *Servii Grammatici qui feruntur in Vergilii Bucolica et Georgica Commentarii,* ed. G. Thilo (Leipzig, 1887), p. 44; and the discussion by Collins 'The place of the Fourth Sybil', pp. 370–5.

[58] For Greek and Roman consultation, see H. W. Parke, *Greek Oracles* (London, 1967), pp. 52–5; for new rituals, e.g. the approval of the *ludi saeculares,* see the texts in Alexandre, *Excursus ad Sibyllina,* pp. 248–52. On the function of the Sibyls in early Roman religion, see G. Dumézil, *Archaic Roman Religion* (Chicago, 1970), vol. 2, pp. 604–5.

Sibyls were never to lose the involvement with the fate of dynasties, and they, too, were avenues for the importation of exotic ideas and themes within more traditional religious horizons.

The Jewish Sibyllines have been called 'the Apocalyptic of Hellenistic Diaspora Judaism',[59] but this statement is in need of qualification. Even its author goes on to stress the difference between the inward-looking purpose of apocalyptic literature, 'designed to strengthen a particular community', and the more apologetic character of the Sibyllines as a part of 'the mission of Diaspora Judaism to the heathen'.[60] There are important differences in form, such as the fact that the Sibyl receives her revelation without the use of any mediating figure,[61] and in content, such as the usual lack of interest in the afterlife and in the heavenly realm,[62] that distinguish Sibylline verses from the genre apocalypse in the proper sense of the term. Without entering into the complex question of the definition of apocalypse as a genre and the relation of the genre apocalypse to apocalypticism as a particular form of eschatology,[63] we should note that it would be difficult to deny that the Sibyl was a blood relation of the apocalyptic seer and remained so throughout her career. The Jewish and Christian Sibyllines share with the major Jewish and Christian apocalypses and other early Christian apocalyptic writings such elements as reveiws of world history,[64] announcements of divine judgement in the form of imminent crisis and the destruction of the world by fire. At times they also contain hopes for a coming messianic figure, a monarch who will make all right with the world. This savior is sometimes preceded by an embodiment of evil, a wicked ruler who may take on the characteristics of the Anti-

---

[59] P. Vielhauer, 'Apocalypses and related subjects: introduction', in E. Hennecke and W. Schneemelcher (eds), *New Testament Apocrypha* (Philadelphia, 1964), vol. 2, p. 600.

[60] ibid., p. 601.

[61] Collins (ed.), *Apocalypse*, p. 46.

[62] Collins, ibid., p. 47; and *Sibylline Oracles*, p. 110. The latter point, however, needs some qualification in the light of the treatment of the resurrection of the dead in *Oracula Sibyllina*, IV, 179–82, and the elaborate battle of the stars, or conflict in heaven, found in *Oracula Sibyllina*, V, 512–30.

[63] I have tried to spell out some of these issues in B. McGinn, *Visions of the End*, pp. 2–14, 28–36; but see the critical remarks of M. Reeves, *Journal of Theological Studies*, n.s. 31 (1980), p. 637.

[64] In the *Sibyllina* this is frequently in terms of an enumeration of ten kingdoms, see Collins, *Sibylline Oracles*, p. 26. Reviews of world history, prominent in one group of Jewish apocalypses, are usually absent in another, and are rare in Christian apocalypses; see Collins (ed.), *Apocalypse*, pp. 13–19, 63–9. Schematization of world ages is also found in patristic literature, see McGinn, *Visions of the End*, pp. 17–18.

christ.[65] These are all themes that can also be found in the new Sibylline texts produced in the Middle Ages.

The Christian *Sibyllina*, of course, add a further element, the identification of the prophesied Messiah with Christ, both in his first coming and in his return in the *Parousia*. The element of Christocentric prophecy contained in the traditional texts forms the first strand in the history of the medieval Sibyl, what we may call the 'inherited' Sibylline tradition, because it was based upon materials handed down from antiquity and the patristic era. This inherited tradition was the primary source of the Sibyl's role in medieval and Renaissance art and literature.[66]

Knowledge of the *grande dame* of prophecy was conveyed to the medieval audience not only through the texts of Lactantius and Augustine, but also through partial translations of the *Oracula Sibyllina* into Latin.[67] The Sibylline prophecies regarding Christ's Passion, first found in Lactantius' *Divine Institutes*, 4.18–19, and translated in rearranged fashion in *The City of God*, 18.23, are found in an expanded version in several early medieval manuscripts under the title *Dicta Sibyllae magae*.[68] Another cento of Sybilline verses on Christ's Passion and his return at the Last Judgement beginning 'Veniet enim rex omnipotens' also originated in the early Middle Ages and first appears in manuscripts of the eighth century.[69] The third example are the variants on the acrostic of Book VIII. Augustine knew two versions of this most noted of Sibylline verses: an imperfect, scarcely intelligible one which did not keep the acrostic form and thereby marred the prophetic message, and a later version he was introduced to by his friend Flaccianus and which is the one cited in *The City of God*, 18.23. W. Bulst has edited a third version containing the σταυρός lines missing in Augustine's text. This last was apparently made by someone in the circle of Theodore and Hadrian in England in the late seventh century.[70] The acrostic was far and away the most popular Sibylline

[65] Collins summarizes these four themes in *Sibylline Oracles*, p. 113.

[66] In *The Gothic Image* (London, 1969), pp. 336–8, Emile Mâle pointed out that until late in the Middle Ages the Erythraean Sibyl was the only individual Sibyl found in art, a fact doubtless due to Augustine's identification of her as the author of the acrostic in his *The City of God*, 18.23.

[67] B. Bischoff, 'Die lateinischen Übersetzungen und Bearbeitungen aus den Oracula Sibyllina', in his *Mittelalterliche Studien* (Stuttgart, 1966), vol. 1, pp. 150–71.

[68] ibid., p. 151.   [69] ibid., pp. 152–4.

[70] ibid., pp. 154–5, citing W. Bulst, 'Eine anglo-lateinische Übersetzung aus dem Griechischen um 700', *Zeitschrift für deutsches Altertum und deutsche Literatur*, 75 (1939), pp. 105–11.

text of the Middle Ages. In the art of the period the Sibyl frequently holds a banner with the poem's incipit: 'Iudicii signum, tellus sudore madescit.'[71]

Bischoff edited another text, an obscure and at times unintelligible translation of large sections of Book VIII, that he tentatively identified with the original version of the acrostic seen by Augustine.[72] He also edited a Sibylline poem of 136 lines beginning 'Mundus origo mea est' which in the manuscript tradition is linked with the *Dicta Sibyllae magae*. No Greek original for this text survives, but it has the characteristics of the early Christian *Sibyllina* and appears to date from the fourth or fifth century.[73] It is difficult to determine how widely these texts were known, especially to later medieval authors; what were read and re-read were the witnesses to the Sibyl in Lactantius and Augustine.

Early medieval encyclopedists like Isidore of Seville[74] and Rabanus Maurus[75] provide summaries on the Sibyls, and they were well known to such other early authors as Aldhelm (d. 709) and the ninth-century Druthmar of Corvai and Freculph of Lisieux.[76] The eleventh-century Anglo-Saxon homilist Aelfric refers to the Sibyl's prediction of the life of Christ.[77] In most of the early references, the Sibyl and Virgil go together as pagan witnesses to the Incarnation. This traditional 'inherited' Sibyl, always closely associated with the history of the interpretation of Virgil's Fourth Eclogue, took on special vigor in the twelfth century. Abelard used the Sibyl not only as a prophetess of Christ but also as an argument to Heloise for the possibility of women leading a life of special religious dedication.[78] In a burst of enthusiasm

[71] For example, in the earliest surviving Western example of the portrayal of a Sibyl, that in the nave of San Angelo in Formis (*c.* 1080), and also in the fourteenth-century fresco in the Consistory Hall of the Papal Palace at Avignon.

[72] Bischoff, in *Mittelalterliche Studien*, pp. 155–63. The translation survives in two manuscripts from the early ninth century.

[73] ibid., pp. 164–71, for edition and commentary.

[74] Isidore of Seville, *Etymologies*, 8.8 (*PL* 82: 309–10).

[75] Rabanus Maurus, *On Everything*, 15.3 (*PL* 111: 420–1).

[76] Aldhelm, *Book of the Septenary and Meters* (*PL* 82: 172, 181), cites three verses from the Sibyl among his metrical examples, and uses the 'Anglo-Saxon' version of the acrostic. Druthmar, *Commentary on Matthew* (*PL* 106: 1427), and Freculph, *Chronicle* (*PL* 106: 980–1) also cite the seer.

[77] 'Christmas Homily', in B. Thorpe, *The Homilies of the Anglo-Saxon Church* (London, 1844), vol. II, 18.

[78] *Letter* 7, a passage repeated almost verbatim in *Introduction to Theology* and the *Christian Theology* (*PL* 178: 246–7, 1030–2 and 1162–3).

he even claimed that the Sibylline verses express the full total (*summa*) of Christian belief in the Savior.[79]

Other noted twelfth-century authors also praised the Sibyl. Otto of Freising cites the classic passages from Augustine and Lactantius,[80] and John of Salisbury noted the acrostic,[81] as did Peter of Blois in his *Against Jewish Unfaithfulness*.[82] The Cistercian Garnier of Rochefort counted the Sibyl as a prophetess of the Last Judgement,[83] and Philip of Hervengt dealt with the three main Sibyls in his *The Silence of Clerics*.[84]

Acquaintance with the inherited Sibyl, the prophetess of Christ, was so widespread in the later Middle Ages that it would be impossible to cite all the witnesses. Several examples must suffice for suggesting the way in which the traditional Sibyl was used during these centuries. Emile Mâle has noted that the role of the Sibyl in medieval iconography as the favored Gentile witness to Christ was widespread from the beginning of the thirteenth century.[85] The earliest portrayals were generally of the *Sibylla Erythraea* alone;[86] subsequently, groups of Sibyls were paired with Old Testament prophets as Gentile counterparts to Jewish predictions of redemption and coming judgement. In the famous fifteenth-century mosaic pavement of Siena Cathedral the ten Sibyls appear in the company of Hermes Trismegistus, as they had long before in Lactantius' writings.[87] The words of Thomas of Celano's great sequence perfectly capture this essential component of the medieval Sibylline tradition:

> Day of wrath, that day
> That will dissolve the world in flames,
> As David and the Sibyl attest.[88]

---

[79] 'Inspice singula Sibyllae dicta, et quam integre et aperte Christianae fidei de Christo summam complectitur' (*PL* 178: 247B).

[80] *The Two Cities*, 2.4.

[81] *Policraticus*, 2.15 (*PL* 199: 429–30).

[82] *PL* 207: 869–70.

[83] Sermon 31 (*PL* 205: 770).

[84] *PL* 203: 1001, 1020. Philip seems to have used Freculph's account (see note 77 above).

[85] See note 66 above.

[86] For the most recent summary of the iconography of the Sibyl, see G. Seib, 'Sibyllen', in E. Kirschbaum et al. (eds), *Lexikon der christlichen Ikonographie* (Rome, 1968–76), vol. 4, cc. 150–4.

[87] These portraits were executed between 1482 and 1488.

[88] Of the rich literature on the famous *Dies Irae*, I mention only F. Ermini, *Il 'Dies Irae'* (Geneva, 1928. Biblioteca dell' 'Archivum Romanicum'), vol. 11; and A. Kurfess, 'Dies Irae', *Historisches Jahrbuch*, 77 (1957), pp. 328–38.

Many sources contributed to the subsequent diffusion of this motif. Encyclopedists, like Vincent of Beauvais (d. 1264) in his *Mirror of History*, continued to provide handy summaries of knowledge of the inherited Sibyl.[89] In the fifteenth century the printing press helped spread both texts and illustrations. A block-book with illustrations of the individual prophetesses appeared in the third quarter of the century,[90] and in 1481 Filippo Barbieri's treatise, *Some Disagreements between St Jerome and St Augustine*, listed twelve Sibyls instead of ten (to provide a better parallel to the Prophets and Apostles), and described their appearance in ways that may have influenced such subsequent portrayals as those of Michelangelo in the Sistine Chapel (1508–11) and Raphael in the Chigi Chapel of S. Maria della Pace in Rome (*c.* 1512).[91] About 1550, selections from the Sibylline texts were even set to music by the young Orlando di Lasso with daring chromatic invention in his *Prophetiae Sibyllarum*.

The motive for this interest in the inherited *Sibyllina* was primarily theological, and it centered on the issue of revelation.[92] In the world of pre-Scholastic theology, it was enough to know that there was a Sibyl and that she had foretold the coming of Christ. Scholastic authors viewed the matter from a more technical perspective – what bearing did the Sibylline predictions have upon questions of the definition and extent of revelation, and upon the issue of what truths must be believed in order to be saved? Peter Lombard discussed pre-Christian revelation under the heading *fides antiquarum* in d. 25 of Book III of his *Books of Sentences* and thus provided a classic point of departure. The issue was not so much whether extra-Biblical revelation had existed before Christ, but rather what measure of faith was necessary for salvation, and particularly what kind of belief in the Redeemer. The Sibyl need not have worried about her own salvation – most medieval theologians, following Augustine's lead, were convinced that she knew enough to pass the test. Thomas Aquinas, to cite just one famous example, supports this view in his explicit references to the Sibyl.[93] His answer to

[89] *Speculum Historiale* (Douai, 1624), Book 2, cc. 100–102.

[90] There is a modern reprint edited by P. Heitz and W. L. Schreiber, *Oracula Sibyllina* (Strasburg, 1903).

[91] On the Renaissance pictures of the Sibyls in Italian art, see A. Rossi, 'Le Sibille nelle Arti Figurative Italiane', *L'Arte*, 18 (1915), pp. 427–58.

[92] This is not to deny Prümm's point that the Sibyl's role in debates over the theology of revelation was never a major one; see Prümm, 'Das Prophetenamt der Sibyllen', pp. 245–6.

[93] *On Truth*, q. 14, a. 11, ad 5; and *Summa of Theology*, IIa IIae, q. 2, a. 3, ad 7; q. 172, a. 6, ad 1.

the objection that the Gentiles who lived in the age of the Old Testament could not have known anything explicitly about Christ was: 'It is probable that the mystery of our Redemption had been revealed to the Gentiles for many generations before Christ's coming, as is evident from the Sibylline prophecies.'[94] When the cautious Thomas had gone so far, who could withhold approval?

Significant as the theological role of the inherited Sibyl was, the seer's most interesting career in the Middle Ages lay in other directions. The first of these we must examine is the broad area of legend, folklore and popular devotion. No less an authority than Pope Innocent III in his second sermon for the Nativity tells us: 'It is said that Octavian, the Augustus, at the manifestation of the Sibyl, saw the Virgin in heaven bearing her Son.'[95] It was Jacobus de Voragine (d. 1298) in his *Golden Legend*, one of the most popular works of the later Middle Ages, who spread the story far and wide of how the Tiburtine Sibyl had shown Augustus a vision in heaven of the Virgin Mary, the *ara caeli*, holding her child upon her bosom, that child who was greater than all mortal men, including the all-powerful emperor.[96] This Capitoline vision was the legendary basis for the foundation of the church of the *Ara caeli* on the same Capitoline hill. The vision was illustrated by P. Cavallini in a fresco in the church's apse, now lost, and in many later portrayals.[97] The origins of the legend, obviously connected with the pseudo-Constantinian interpretation of the Fourth Eclogue, are obscure. The earliest surviving appearance is Eastern, the *Chronicle* of the Antiochene John of Malalas from the sixth century.[98] How and when the story made its way to the West is not absolutely certain,[99] but it appears in an eighth-century chronicle and in the twelfth-century *Wonders of the City of Rome*,[100] and gained considerable circulation in subsequent centuries.

[94] 'Probabile est tamen multis generationibus mysterium redemptionis nostrae ante Christi adventum gentilibus fuisse revelatum, sicut patet ex sibyllinis vaticiniis.' *On Truth*, q. 14, a. 11, ad 5. See also the mention of the Sibyls *In III Sent.* d. 25, q. 2, quest. 4.

[95] 'Octavianus Augustus fertur in caelo vidisse virginem gestantem filium ad ostensionem Sibyllae' (*PL* 217: 456c).

[96] See under December 25 in *The Golden Legend of Jacobus de Voragine* (New York, 1969), p. 49, for a translation.

[97] On this and later portrayals of the theme, see 'Augustus' in E. Kirschbaum (ed.), *Lexikon der christlichen Ikonographie*, vol. 1, cc. 226–7.

[98] *PG* 97: 357AB. Here the Pythia rather than the Sibyl is mentioned.

[99] For an account of the legend, see M. Guarducci, 'Ara coeli', *Rendiconti di Pontificia Accademia de Arcaeologia* 23/24 (1947–9), pp. 277–90.

[100] *Wonders of the City of Rome*, c. 11.

There is another side to the legendary Sibyl, one not quite so respectable. In Italian folklore, at least from the fifteenth century, we have references to the Sibyl of the Appennines.[101] Near the accursed necromantic lake of Pilate in the Piceno area stands the Montemonaco with its cave of the Sibyl. It was said that the Cumaean Sibyl was imprisoned there until Judgement Day in punishment for having pridefully thought that she rather than Mary would be the virgin found worthy to bear God's Son.[102] In some accounts this Sibyl takes on the role of Venus in the Tannhäuser legend, that of a beautiful Queen of the Underworld who tempts handsome knights to enjoy a year-long orgy in her mountain retreat. Those who stay longer than the appointed year are trapped forever.[103]

The inherited and the legendary aspects of the medieval Sibylline tradition may seem far from the apocalyptic and political concerns of the original Sibyls, but there is a third strand in the history of the Sibyls in the Middle Ages that shows that these earlier interests were not abandoned. We possess a body of newly minted medieval Sibylline texts that are much concerned with the fate of kingdoms and dynasties, frequently in relation to the imminent end of the world. Many details of the history of these new texts are still obscure, but a general account of their contribution to the significance of the Sibyls in the Middle Ages can be given.

A number of the new political–apocalyptic Sibyllines have apparently not survived. Despite the destruction of the ancient *Oracula Sibyllina* by Stilicho, the reputation of the prophetess remained high in late antiquity. During the early stages of the Gothic siege of Rome in 537, Procopius tells us how some patricians brought out Sibylline oracles predicting that the Goths would cease to be a danger after July, a prophecy that proved incorrect in the light of the protracted

---

[101] The earliest written reference is in the Romance *Guerrin Meschino* of Andrea da Barbarino (*c.* 1400–30), where the Sibyl appears as both prophetess and temptress. In 1430, the Provençal knight, Antoine de la Sale, writes of the Sibyl as temptress alone.

[102] On the history of the legend, see F. Neri, 'Le tradizioni italiane della Sibilla', *Studi Medievali*, 4 (1912–13), pp. 213–30; and L. Paolucci, *La Sibilla Appenninica* (Florence, 1967).

[103] On the disputed question of the relation of the Italian and German legends, see Paolucci, *La Sibilla Appenninica*, pp. 35–52, who holds that the temptress aspect is originally non-Italian and is a subsequent grafting on the prophetic picture of the Sibyl.

siege.[104] These oracles were in Latin, as the fragment cited indicates, and they were apparently both fairly extensive and highly political in content. Procopius, who examined them personally, did not doubt the Sibyl, but wisely noted: 'in my opinion, it is impossible for a mortal man to discover the meaning of the Sibyl's oracles before the actual event.'[105] Were these texts Latin translations of ancient Sibylline material or new productions? We shall probably never know.

Subsequent centuries present other examples of Sibylline prophecies of political events that do not seem to be drawn from surviving texts. In the *Chronicle* of the pseudo-Fredegar of the mid-seventh century a Sibylline prophecy is applied to the blood-stained Queen Brunhild,[106] and in the tenth century Liutprand of Cremona saw political prophecies while on embassy to Constantinople which he claimed were in part Sibylline.[107] Paul Alexander has suggested that one of these Greek tracts, that ascribed to a Sicilian bishop named Hippolytus, was also translated into Latin.[108] From slightly later, we have a quotation from Bruno of Querfort of a Sibylline oracle he took to refer to the death of Otto III, and which Ernst Sackur thought might depend on a Byzantine imperial prophecy.[109] After the year 1000 there seems to be somewhat less evidence for wandering *Sibyllina* of this sort, though they never died out. In his noted *History of the Kings of Britain* (c. 1136) Geoffrey of Monmouth cites Sibylline oracles he

---

[104] Procopius, *History of the Wars*, 5.24. For an account of the siege, see J. Bury, *History of the Later Roman Empire* (New York, 1958), vol. 2, pp. 180–95 (p. 187, n. 3 on the oracle).

[105] τῶν γὰρ Σιβύλλης λογίων τὴν διάνοιαν πρὸ τοῦ ἔργου ἐξευρεῖν ἀνθρώπῳ οἶμαι ἀδύνατον εἶναι (Loeb Classical Library ed., vol. III, p. 236).

[106] *Chronicle*, 3.59 (*MGH, SRM* II, p. 109): 'Tanta mala et effusione sanguinum a Brunechildis consilium in Francia factae sunt, ut prophetia Saeville [*sic*] impletur dicens, "Veniens Bruna de partibus Spaniae, ante cuius conspectum multae gentes peribunt." '

[107] *Account of the Legation to Constantinople*, 39–43 (*MGH, SRG*, Hanover, 1915), pp. 195–8.

[108] Paul H. Alexander, 'The diffusion of Byzantine apocalypses in the Medieval West and the beginnings of Joachimism', in A. Williams (ed.), *Prophecy and Millenarianism. Essays in Honour of Marjorie Reeves* (Harlow, 1980), pp. 67–8.

[109] *Life of the Five Brothers* (*MGH, SS* XV, p. 724): 'Videtur autem in morte eius compleri vaticinium Cymanae Sibillae, quae de Salvatoris adventu, de redemptione et iudicio temporali cum plura vera cecinisset, inter Romana fata, ubi de regibus loquitur: "Rex in purpura natus ante portam civitatis in terra moritur non sua." '

applies to the reigns of Arthur and of Cadwallader that seem to have no source in the known ancient and medieval productions.[110]

The major new medieval Sibylline texts, or perhaps we should say 'textual traditions' because of their many variants, circulated under the two most popular Sibylline names, the Erythraean Sibyl whom Augustine had cited as the author of the acrostic, and the Tiburtine Sibyl whose location near Rome seems to have brought distinct advantages. There are in addition two shorter texts: the Cumaean Sibyl, usually found in conjunction with her Tiburtine neighbor, and the obscure Samian (sometimes called the Delphian) Sibyl.

The most popular of these new medieval oracles was the *Sibylla Tiburtina*, a medieval best-seller, since over 130 Latin manuscripts are known, about 30 before the thirteenth century.[111] In addition, there are Greek, Carshunic, Ethiopic and a variety of Arabic versions of the text.[112] Critical discussion of the *Tiburtina* is a century old, but we still have much to learn about its history and meaning.

In the best-known Latin version, that edited by Ernst Sackur in 1898,[113] the text proper begins with a brief description of the Sibyl,[114] the daughter of Priam and Hecuba, who wandered the world until invited to Rome by the Emperor Trajan. In Rome a hundred senators had had the same dream of nine suns in the heavens, and the Sibyl, who showed no signs of her age, was called in to interpret the sign. We are told that the Roman senators cried out in admiration at her beauty: 'Teacher and mistress, since your body is great and exceedingly beautiful in a way we have never seen in any woman but you, we ask you to interpret what the dream we all saw in a single night

[110] *History of the Kings of Britain*, 9.17, 12.18.

[111] D. Verhelst, 'La préhistoire des conceptions d'Adson concernant l'Antichrist', *Recherches de Théologie Ancienne et Médiévale*, 40 (1973), p. 99. In a footnote Verhelst lists the seven earliest texts, dating from the eleventh century.

[112] On the Oriental versions, see J. Schleifer, 'Die Erzählung der Sibylle', *Denkschriften der Kaiserlichen Akademie der Wissenschaften. Philosophisch-Historische Klasse*, 53 (1910), Abhandlung I (80 pp.). For newly discovered Arabic versions, see E. Ebied and M. Young, 'A newly discovered version of the Arabic Sibylline prophecy', *Oriens Christianus*, 60 (1976), pp. 83–94; 'An unrecorded Arabic version of a Sibylline prophecy', *Orientalia Christiana Periodica*, 43 (1977), pp. 279–307.

[113] E. Sackur (ed.), *Sibyllinische Texte und Forschungen* (Halle, 1898). Sackur made use of six manuscripts, as well as two printed versions, the one pseudonymously ascribed to Bede and printed in *PL* 90: 1181–6, and that found in Geoffrey of Viterbo's *Pantheon* (*MGH, SS* XXII, pp. 145–7).

[114] The text is preceded by a prologue describing the Sibyls taken from Rabanus Maurus, *On Everything*, 15.3.

portends for the future.'[115] Removing herself to the Aventine, a place unpolluted by pagan worship, the Sibyl revealed that the nine suns signified nine generations. The first two are good, but the third sees much fighting in Rome (probably a reference to the civil wars preceding the establishment of the Empire). The fourth generation is marked by the coming of Christ. The account of what has been called the 'Sibylline Gospel' given here contains some unusual doctrine, as well as a dispute between the prophetess and the *sacerdotes Hebraeorum*.[116] In the fifth generation Christ chooses two fishermen and sends them out to preach to all peoples, while the sixth generation is marked by a three-and-a-half year siege of 'that city' (Jerusalem), and the seventh by two kings who will make many persecutions in the land of the Hebrews. The eighth generation features apocalyptic woes on Rome.[117]

The nature of the text changes in the eighth and especially the ninth generations because here the transition from history cast as prophecy (*vaticinium ex eventu*) to true prophecy takes place. The picture is complicated due to the fact that subsequent editors who wished to update the text usually interpolated their own *vaticinia ex eventu* into the account of the ninth generation. True to the Sibyl's age-old political interests, much of what is presented under the ninth generation is concerned with rulers and their dynasties.

First mentioned are kings from Syria and Egypt, and then a king whose initial is C and who will reign for thirty years and build up God's Temple – usually seen as a reference to Constantine.[118] There follows a lengthy interpolation concerning Lombard and Salian rulers, each indicated by their initials.[119] Then there is what seems to be a return

---

[115] 'Magistra et domina, quoniam magnum et valde decorum est corpus tuum, quale umquam in feminis praeter te non vidimus, precamur, ut somnium, quod omnes nos in unam noctem vidimus, quid futurum premonstret aperias' (Sackur, *Sibyllinische Texte*, p. 179). The beauty of the Sibyl, at least in Italy, was a *topos*. G. Villani in his *Chronicle*, 4.20, notes that Tancred was said to have had a wife more beautiful than the Sibyl. Fame of the seer's beauty may have contributed to the popularity of the name from the twelfth century on, see U. Chevalier, *Repertoire des Sources Historiques du Moyen Âge. Bio-bibliographie* (New York, 1960), vol. 2, cc. 4235–6.

[116] Sackur, *Sibyllinische Texte*, pp. 179–80.

[117] ibid., pp. 180–1.

[118] ibid., p. 181. Sackur (pp. 156–7) took the reference this way, and most later interpreters have followed him.

[119] ibid., pp. 181–3, with the interpolations in italics.

to material from the original oracle,[120] followed by a second interpolation of lists of rulers.[121] Analyzing the meaning of these interpolations and dating their most recent historical references are crucial for
determining the history of the text; the problem is that the Tiburtine
Sibyl underwent so many successive changes that without a critical
edition of all the variants, our conclusions must remain at least
partially tentative.

The *Sibylla Tiburtina* concludes her account with a distinctive description of the events of the End, involving not only the signs of
imminent destruction but also the coming of the Last World Emperor,
Constans, who will reign for 112 (or 120) years, gain the whole world
for Christ, defeat Gog and Magog, and finally hand over the Christian
Empire to God the Father and Jesus Christ.[122] After that the Antichrist, already born but not yet manifested, will begin his great persecution, kill Enoch and Elijah, but then be slain by Michael the
Archangel. Sackur's text ends with a citation of the Sibylline acrostic,
an obvious sign of the interpenetration of the inherited Sibylline
material with the new creation.[123]

The first problem concerning the *Sibylla Tiburtina* is its origin. Ernst
Sackur advanced the case for a Greek original which he thought was
composed in the 360s and soon translated into Latin.[124] He claimed
that the early Latin translation, since lost, was the source for the medieval tradition. Basing himself on the interpolated regnal lists, he
thought the text he edited was composed in northern Italy in the early
eleventh century.[125] The problem of origin became more complex
when three manuscripts of a Greek version were discovered.[126] This
Greek text has been edited and studied in detail by Paul J. Alexander.[127] The general structure of the vision of the nine suns is the

[120] ibid., pp. 183–4.

[121] ibid., p. 184 (in italics).

[122] ibid., pp. 185–6. For an introduction to the Last Emperor myth and its rich
literature, see subject index of McGinn, *Visions of the End*.

[123] An earlier interpolation (Sackur, *Sibyllinische Texte*, p. 180) cites the Sibylline
predictions of the Passion found in Lactantius, *Divine Institutes*, 4.18.

[124] He did this largely on the basis of identifying the 'vir belligerator rex
Grecorum' (p. 183) as a *vaticinium ex eventu* of Constantius I who destroyed the temple
in Hieropolis in 360. See the discussion in Sackur, *Sibyllinische Texte*, pp. 158–61.

[125] ibid., pp. 134–5.

[126] The announcement was made by S. Mercati, 'É stato trovato il testo greco
della Sibilla Tiburtina', *Mélanges Henri Grégoire* (Brussels, 1949), pp. 473–81.

[127] P. J. Alexander, *The Oracle of Baalbek: The Tiburtine Sibyl in Greek Dress*
(Washington, DC, 1967).

same in the Greek text, but from the account of the fourth sun onwards considerable changes occur, especially in the lengthy and at
times confusing descriptions of various good and bad monarchs, which,
it should be noted, have nothing to do with the interpolated Lombard
and Salian lists of the Latin *Tiburtina*.[128] There is also no explicit mention of the Last World Emperor in the Greek version. On the basis of
dating by *vaticinium ex eventu*, Alexander argued that the surviving
Greek text, which he called the Oracle of Baalbek, was produced near
that city shortly after AD 500.[129] He also suggested, on more hypothetical grounds, that the original Greek *Urtext* was produced in the
time of the Emperor Theodosius about AD 380,[130] and that it did not
contain a reference to the Last World Emperor which the Latin versions appear to have taken over from the later Byzantine tradition,
since the earliest undisputed reference to the figure is found in the
pseudo-Methodius from the late seventh century.[131] Alexander's study
included a treatment of the later Latin versions that forms an important basis for subsequent research.[132]

Recently, David Flusser of the Hebrew University in Jerusalem has
reopened the question of the origin of the *Tiburtina* with a startling
proposal.[133] He claims that Sackur's Latin version, minus the obvious
medieval interpolations, is structurally simpler and therefore closer to
the original Greek *Urtext* than the inflated text of the Oracle of Baalbek.[134] This may well be so. Less convincing is the second part of his
thesis which argues that the original dream of the nine suns goes back
to a Jewish–Christian oracle of the late first century AD.[135] Flusser's

---

[128] Alexander compares these in parallel columns in *Oracle of Baalbek*, pp. 50–1.

[129] ibid., pp. 41–4.

[130] Alexander bases this both on a reference to 'a king who will be burned by
fire', which he takes to be a part of the original oracle and to be a *vaticinium ex
eventu* of the death of the Emperor Valens at Adrianople in 378, as well as on a
reference to Theodosius that he argues is not an interpolation. See Alexander,
Oracle of Baalbek, pp. 63–5.

[131] Alexander also puts this case forward in his article, 'Byzantium and the
migration of literary works and motifs: the legend of the last Roman Emperor',
Mediaevalia et Humanistica, n.s. 2 (1971), pp. 52–60, especially n. 35.

[132] See Alexander, *Oracle of Baalbek*, pp. 48–66; and subsequently 'The Diffusion
of Byzantine Apocalypses', pp. 56–9.

[133] D. Flusser, 'An early Jewish–Christian document in the Tiburtine Sibyl', in
Paganisme, Judaïsme, Christianisme. Mélanges offerts à Marcel Simon (Paris, 1978),
pp. 153–83.

[134] ibid., pp. 153–5.

[135] ibid., pp. 168–9, 176–8.

case, based both upon a search for historical events in the description of the first eight suns and also upon the detection of Jewish–Christian elements in the Sibylline Gospel, is ingenious but not totally convincing. His *vaticinia ex eventu* datings are open to question,[136] and his stress on the primitive character of the Jewish–Christian elements seems at times based on *a priori* exclusions as later interpolations of elements that do not fit his picture.[137] He has, indeed, shown that there are peculiar features to the Christology of the Sibyl, a fact also noted by Alexander;[138] but it is still easier to suppose that the Greek original was composed in the fourth rather than the first century, perhaps in an area such as Syria, where archaic Jewish–Christian elements long survived.

The subsequent history of the Tiburtine Sibyl, especially in the eleventh century when the major Latin versions were produced, is complex and difficult to unravel.[139] The twelfth century saw widespread use of the Latin text,[140] as well as the production of an Anglo-Norman verse translation made about 1140.[141] While the *Tiburtina*

---

[136] Flusser bases his argument (ibid., p. 163) on the supposition that the original oracle must have contained a balanced account of each of the nine generations, but this is by no means an invariable pattern in apocalyptic reviews of world history where the final age or ages frequently receive much more detailed treatment than the earlier ones. Even supposing that the nine generations should be given roughly equal treatment, it is by no means certain that the two persecuting kings of the seventh generation who lay waste Jerusalem (ibid., pp. 180–1) should be identified with Titus and *Domitian*, as Flusser claims on pp. 165–7, and not, for example, Titus and *Hadrian*, the two emperors under whom the city was destroyed.

[137] The stress on the virgin birth of him who will be *verus Deus et verus homo* (ibid., p. 179) does not look like a first-century feature. Flusser would exclude it on the *a priori* grounds that when it comes to Jesus' birth, 'all the versions and scribes have expanded the original according to their faith and fantasy' (ibid., p. 155, n. 3), but this seems too sweeping.

[138] Alexander, *Oracle of Baalbek*, pp. 69–74.

[139] I hope to give a more complete sketch of the textual history of the *Tiburtina* in a planned edition of one of the variants, that found twice in a manuscript originally from the Austrian monastery of Lambach and now in the Newberry Library in Chicago (Ryerson MS 3., ff. 198r–202v and 220r–224r). There is also a fragmentary copy of the same text in Munich, Clm. 17742, ff. 42r–51v.

[140] It was used in the twelfth century by such well-known authors as Honorius Augustodunensis, *The Gem of the Soul* (PL 172: 679); John of Salisbury, *Policraticus*, 2.15 (PL 199: 429); Geoffrey of Viterbo, *Pantheon* (MGH, SS XXII, pp. 145–7); and Peter Comester, *Scholastic History* (PL 198: 1454).

[141] *Anglo-Norman Texts. Le Livre de Sibile by Philippe de Thaon*, ed. H. Shields (London, 1979). On the dating and dedication, see pp. 24, 26. Shields' ascription to Philippe de Thaon seems open to question.

was generally employed to help understand the role of the German empire in world historical process (vernacular versions in German are known from the fourteenth century),[142] there is a reworking of the text from about 1220 which uses it as a prophecy of the glories of the French monarchy and its apocalyptic destiny as the line from which would arise the Last World Emperor, identified with Philip Augustus (1180–1223).[143] This francophile version of the *Tiburtina* had a predecessor at the time of the Second Crusade, when Otto of Freising in his *Deeds of Frederick Barbarossa* noted a prophecy 'declared by some to have been found in the Sibylline books' that many in France had applied to Louis VII.[144] This obscure text appears to be an independent Last Emperor oracle.

Sibylline prophecies owed a good deal of their continued popularity to a remarkable ability to keep up with the times. One of the crucial changes in the apocalyptic hopes of the high and the late Middle Ages was the new interest in the apocalyptic role of the Church – the delineation of the ages of the Church's history and of the role of ecclesiastical offices and events in the drama of the End of Time. This shift is also evident in some of the new Sibylline products of the twelfth century. In the *Vita* of the Gregorian bishop Altmann of Passau (1065–91), written about 1140, we have reference to a Sibylline vision of the Church as a great house supported by seven pillars representing seven ages.[145] The image of the house built on seven pillars is an obvious reminiscence of Wisdom's house in Proverbs 9:1; the distinction of the seven ages in terms of seven metals is unusual, but there is a possible prototype in Servius' reference in his *Commentary* on the Fourth

---

[142] For these texts, see F. Vogt, 'Über Sibyllen Weissagung', *Beiträge zur Geschichte der deutschen Sprache und Literatur*, 4 (1877), pp. 48–100.

[143] The text is found in Register E of the documents of the reign of Philip (*Arch. Nat.*, JJ 26, ff. 309 sqq.) and was edited about 1220 by Etienne de Gallardon. See E. A. R. Brown, 'La notion de la légitimité et la prophétie à la cour de Philippe Auguste', to appear in the papers from the CNRS 'Colloque Philippe Auguste' (27 September 1980).

[144] See *Ottonis et Rahewini Gesta Friderici I Imperatoris* (Hanover, 1884), pp. 8–9, and the translation and discussion in McGinn, *Visions of the End*, pp. 117–19. See also the *Annals of Corbei* (*MGH, SS* XVI, p. 14), and the *Annals of St James* (*MGH, SS* XVI, p. 641).

[145] *Life of Altmann* (*MGH, SS* XII, p. 234). For an introductory study, see B. Smalley, 'A pseudo-Sibylline prophecy of the early twelfth century in the life of Altmann of Passau', in P. Gallais and Y.-J. Riou (eds), *Mélanges René Crozet* (Poitiers, 1966), vol. I, pp. 655–61.

Eclogue to a Sibylline prophecy of four world ages also distinguished by metals.[146]

Again in the ecclesiastical vein, we have the brief cryptic oracle usually known as the *Sibylla Samia* (at other times as the *Sibylla Delphica*). O. Holder-Egger, who edited one version of this text, thought that it was from the thirteenth century;[147] I have argued elsewhere that it is a product of the late twelfth century, and that the first lines of the text refer to conflicts between the Pope and the Roman Commune, a frequent occurrence from the 1140s onwards.[148] This was certainly the way the text was understood by Joachim of Fiore, who wrote a commentary on it and also detailed the circumstances of its finding in the papers of Cardinal Matthew of Angers, who died in 1184.

The twelfth century ranks with the eleventh as the great age for the production of new *Sibyllina*. The most cogent proof is found in the second major new textual tradition, the *Vaticinium Sibyllae Erythraeae* or *Prophecy of the Erythraean Sibyl*. The patient researches of O. Holder-Egger, E. Jamison and P. Alexander have provided us with considerable information on the origins and growth of this text.[149] While not quite as complex as her Tiburtine sister, the Erythraean seer possessed many similar characteristics, especially the Byzantine connection and the mania for politics and dynastic gossip.

It was common knowledge from the encyclopedists that the Erythraean Sibyl had predicted the Fall of Troy to the Greeks. The *Vaticinium* begins with a reference to this legend:

[146] The Sibylline text used by Servius and noted above (note 57) distinguished four ages of gold, silver, bronze and iron, a tradition stretching back at least as far as Hesiod, *Works and Days*, ll. 109–201, and also at the basis of Daniel 2.

[147] O. Holder-Egger, 'Italienische Prophetieen des 13. Jahrhunderts', *Neues Archiv der Gesellschaft für ältere deutsche Geschichtskunde*, 15 (1890), pp. 177–8. For a listing of the eight manuscript versions and five appearances in thirteenth-century chronicles, see B. McGinn, 'Joachim and the Sibyl', *Cîteaux*, 24 (1973), p. 119.

[148] ibid., pp. 107–22. In this article, I edited the text from one manuscript (Padua, Bibl. Anton. MS 322, ff. 149^v–151^v). Since then several other manuscripts have come to my attention (e.g. Rome, Carmelite Archives MS III. varia 1, ff. 123^v–127^r; Wolfenbüttel, Extravagantes MS 259.1, ff. 44^r–47^v).

[149] O. Holder-Egger edited a long and short version of the *Sibylla Erythraeae* in his 'Italienische Prophetieen', *Neues Archiv*, 15 (1890), pp. 155–73; and 30 (1905), pp. 328–35. Though superseded in many details, the edition and Holder-Egger's remarks are still extremely valuable. E. Jamison, *The Admiral Eugenius of Sicily* (London, 1957), pp. 21–32, first proposed the earlier dating, a position seconded by P. Alexander, 'Diffusion of Byzantine Apocalypses', pp. 71–9, 87–93.

This book is taken from the book called *Basilographia*, that is, the 'Imperial Writing', which the Erythraean Sibyl of Babylon made at the request of the Greeks in the time of Priam, the king of Troy. Doxapater, a father of extraordinary skill, translated it from the Syriac into Greek. Then it was taken from the treasury of Manuel, emperor of the Greeks, and translated from the Greek into Latin by Eugenius, admiral of the king of Sicily.[159]

Since the surviving manuscripts of the text all demonstrate knowledge of thirteenth-century events through the medium of *vaticinia ex eventu*, the Erythraean Sibyl was long thought to date from this period and the entire introduction was therefore dismissed as an example of typical apocalyptical pseudonymity.[151] Jamison and Alexander, however, have shown that elements of the account appear to be true. Both scholars argue that the first and third parts of books of the surviving text roughly constitute a twelfth-century Greek text connected with Nicholas (or Nilus) Doxapatres, an official at the court of Manuel Comnenus who later appears as a monk in Sicily. This text, which 'Doxapater' apparently brought to Sicily, was then translated into Latin by the well-known scholar, diplomat and administrator, Eugenius, Admiral of Sicily, probably in the late 1190s.[152] Whether a Syriac original ever existed, and whether, if the work was originally Greek, Doxapater composed it himself or used an earlier Greek source, are difficult questions to answer given our present knowledge.[153]

The format of the text is a review of world history and its end supposedly delivered by the Sibyl to the Greek army after the Fall of Troy. The style is so deeply Hellenized and obscure, the animal symbolism so bizarre and complicated, that the text was assured an avid readership among the curious for centuries.[154] Book I begins with the Sibyl's *apologia* in defense of the divine source of her ecstatic prophecy and moves on to a sketch of Greek and Roman history presented

[150] 'Hic liber est extractus de libro qui dicitur *Vasilographo*, id est imperialis scriptura, quam Sibilla Erithea Babylonica condidit ad petitionem Grecorum tempore Priami regis Troie; quem Vedoxa peritissimus pater in Grecum transtulit de Chaldeo, tandem de erario Emanuelis imperatoris Grecorum eductum Eugenius regis [Jamison's reading, rather that the *regni* of Holder-Egger] Sicilie admiratus de Greco transtulit in Latinum' (Holder-Egger, 'Italienische Prophetieen', p. 155).

[151] ibid., pp. 149–51.

[152] See Jamison, *Admiral Eugenius*, pp. 21–32.

[153] Alexander, 'Diffusion of Byzantine apocalypses', p. 100, n. 78, is skeptical of a Syriac original.

[154] M. Reeves, *Prophecy in the Later Middle Ages* (Oxford, 1969), p. 519, lists 19 manuscripts, but many more have been cited in other studies.

through animal symbolism.[155] World dominion is prophesied to the Greeks, figured throughout as 'he-goats' (*hyrci*), until Troy revives in the founding of Rome. The careers of Alexander the Great (a *hyrcus terribilis*), Hannibal, Pompey, Caesar and Augustus are all set forth, and then Christ appears as the Lamb of the Book of Revelation.[156] At this point, Jamison argues that there are two interpolations in the original text, a pro-Byzantine account concerned with Constantine's conversion and the foundation of Constantinople, and an anti-Byzantine one containing a description of the Eastern Empire's troubles in the late twelfth century culminating in the Latin conquest of Constantinople.[157] This seems to be the case, because after these passages the text returns to a detailed account of Christ's life, a mysterious prophecy concerning 'a wonderful star and a prediction of 'a horrible beast coming from the East'. This last creature is a kind of Antichrist. Its seven heads associate it with the dragon of Revelation 12, and its 663 feet, or years of reign, with the apocalyptic number of Revelation 13:8. The beast is to be opposed by two stars and attacked by a mighty lion from the West who will check its progress but not destroy it, for the horrible creature will survive until the coming of the Abomination.[158]

Book II of the original text (now Part III) consists of an enumeration of the signs by which one can recognize the approach of the End.[159] Some of these portents are very general and echo the gloomy tidings that the Sibyl had delighted in announcing from the earliest stages of her career; others, such as the reference to the natural disasters which struck Sicily in 1169, were apparently added by the Admiral Eugenius.[160]

The key to the dating of the original oracle used by Doxapatres lies in the identification of the beast and the mighty lion mentioned in Part I. Without trying to give any final answer, there seems to be reason to see the beast as Mohammed, the classic enemy of the

[155] Book I is found in Holder-Egger, 'Italienische Prophetieen', pp. 155–63. Sections are translated in McGinn, *Visions of the End*, pp. 123–5.

[156] Holder-Egger, 'Italienische Prophetieen', pp. 156–9.

[157] ibid., p. 29. In Holder-Egger's text, the first interpolation begins on p. 160 (Venient autem dies . . .), the second is found on pp. 160–1 (Hinc Eneaden gloria . . . sicut inferius distinguemus). Cf. Alexander, 'Diffusion of Byzantine apocalypses', pp. 73–4, who argues that the first interpolation comes from Doxapatres because it contains a passage critical of Pope Silvester that would fit the Greek's published views concerning the papacy.

[158] Holder-Egger, 'Italienische Prophetieen', pp. 161–3. [159] ibid., pp. 170–3.

[160] ibid., pp. 172–3. See Jamison, *Admiral Eugenius*, p. 28.

Christian faith. The 663 years of his reign could be an addition by a thirteenth-century editor, since we have evidence of similar specula-tions in the thirteenth century concerning the duration of the Moslem threat.[161] The mighty lion may have been a reference to the Last World Emperor in a Syriac or Greek original; in the text as we have it, it appears to be a Westernized *vaticinium ex eventu* referring to Charlemagne.[162]

All the versions of the *Prophecy of the Erythraean Sibyl* found so far represent not the original translation of Eugenius, which was appar-ently little known, but an updating of the text performed in Franciscan Joachite circles early in 1249, as Paul Alexander has recently shown.[163] The additions include the second interpolation in Book I which ends by prophesying: 'No he-goat will bleat, no rooster crow, until the forty-four feet and nine-and-a-half thumbs measured out to it before-hand pass, the three-headed eagle flies back and forth, and the wedded he-goat is brought back to Byzantium . . .'.[164] This is apparently a reference to an expected return of Byzantine civil and ecclesiastical authorities to power in Constantinople made sometime during the Latin occupation. It cannot have been penned later than January of 1249, that is, 44 years and nine-and-a-half months after the conquest of 1204. The dating is confirmed by the whole of the interpolated Book II, a history of events in Sicily and the Mediterranean world from 1189 onwards, concentrating on the life of Frederick II.[165] This part of the text lets stand a prophecy of a 60-year reign for Frederick, an anomaly that would be difficult to understand had it been written after the emperor's death at the age of 56 in 1250.[166]

The revised Erythraean Sibyl shows its Joachite tendencies not only

[161] See McGinn, *Visions of the End*, Section 18, p. 155.

[162] A number of factors argue in this direction, e.g. the 50 feet, or years, of rule (close to the regnal dates of 768–814), and the checking of the Moslem power, i.e. Charlemagne's Spanish campaigns.

[163] Alexander, 'Diffusion of Byzantine apocalypses', pp. 71–93.

[164] '. . . hyrcus non balabit, gallus non cantabit, usque dum XLIIII pedes novemque polices semique premensurati discurrant, aquila triceps volet et revolet, hyrcus iugalis in Bicansiam reducetur . . .' (Holder-Egger, 'Italienische Pro-phetieen', p. 161). The translation is that of Alexander, 'Diffusion of Byzantine apocalypses', p. 73. The prophecy is repeated in Book II (Holder-Egger, 'Italie-nische Prophetieen', p. 165).

[165] Book II in Holder-Egger's edition is found in ibid., pp. 163–70.

[166] This prophecy is found in ibid., p. 165. See the discussion in Alexander, 'Diffusion of Byzantine apocalypses', p. 77. Book II contains the famous prophecy that circulated after Frederick's death '. . . sonabit et in populis: "Vivit, non

by its concern with the persecuting Hohenstaufen Emperors, but also by its prophecy of the two stars, or two orders of spiritual men, who will resist the evil final Emperor.[167] It is significant that the first author to cite the Sibylline prophecy of the two stars was John of Parma, the Joachite Minister General of the Franciscans, in an encyclical letter of 1255.[168] Paul Alexander argues that it was John of Parma himself, or someone in his immediate circle, who was responsible for the revised version, since John had been commissioned by Pope Innocent IV to head a mission sent to John III Vatatzes, the exiled Byzantine Emperor, to discuss reunion with Rome in exchange for repossession of Constantinople.[169] This would provide an excellent context for the production of the revised *Prophecy of the Erythraean Sibyl*.

The revised *Erythraea* circulated in a number of versions. As in the case of the *Tiburtina*, our conclusions must remain tentative until we are in possession of better editions. The Joachite propaganda machine assured the Erythraean Sibyl a wide subsequent diffusion. Within a few years, a work pseudonymously ascribed to Joachim of Fiore himself was in circulation commenting on the *Sayings of Merlin* (obscure poems describing the lives of Frederick I and II) and on the *Prophecy of the Erythraean Sibyl*.[170] It would certainly have taken all the ingenuity of the real Joachim to have unravelled the obscurities of both these dark prophetic writings. The *Erythraea* was known and used by a number of the major apocalyptic authors of the later Middle Ages. Arnold of Villanova cited it on the approaching end of the Moslem religion;[171] Angelo of Clareno found in it a prophecy of the career of the *pastor angelicus*, Celestine V;[172] and John of Roquetaillade frequently referred to it.[173] The interest continued well into the sixteenth century, where we have editions of the text printed in 1508, 1516 and

---

vivit" . . .' (p. 168). In later years this was influential in the growth of the legend of the Emperor's return, but E. Kantorowicz, in 'Zu den Rechtsgrundlagen der Kaisersage', *Selected Studies* (Locust Valley, New York, 1965), pp. 291–6, 305–7, has shown that it was originally an expression of dynastic continuity.

[167] Holder-Egger, 'Italienische Prophetieen', pp. 162–3.

[168] Partially translated in McGinn, *Visions of the End*, pp. 164–5.

[169] Alexander, 'Diffusion of Byzantine apocalypses', pp. 86–93.

[170] Reeves, *Prophecy*, p. 520, lists eight manuscripts. A translation of the Introduction to this text may be found in McGinn, *Visions of the End*, p. 184.

[171] See Reeves, *Prophecy*, p. 315.

[172] *Historia Septem Tribulationum*, ed. A. Ghinato (Rome, 1959), p. 134.

[173] J. Bignami-Odier, *Études sur Jean de Roquetaillade* (Paris, 1952), see Index. Jean also cites the *Sibylla Tiburtina*.

1522.[174] But to pursue the career of the Sibyl further into the fifteenth and sixteenth centuries is another story.

What I have tried to do in these comments on the history of the Sibyls, primarily in the medieval period, is to summarize the largely forgotten story of one of the more potent female images in Western religious tradition. These prophetesses were able to make a remarkable transition from paganism to Christianity largely because they were seen not only as foretelling the gloomy message of coming doom and the fates of kings, but also because they were reckoned the peers of the Jewish prophets in their announcement of the good news of the Savior's birth. Having made this adaptation from pagan prophetess to Christian seer, the Sibyl was not able to effect a similar transition to the modern world when the acids of historical criticism exposed the pious forgeries of the past. On the mythic level at least, the image of the Sibyl, the wise and beautiful old woman inspired by God, deserves our respect and consideration.

One of the ancient legends about the seer provides us with a fitting conclusion. In the fourteenth book of his *Metamorphoses*, Ovid retells the tale of how the virgin Sibyl was once offered any wish whatsoever if she would agree to submit to Apollo's advances. The god granted the maiden's desire to enjoy as many years of life as there were grains in a heap of sand. But the Sibyl then refused Apollo, unwisely, as the case turned out, because perpetual youth did not accompany her extended life, so that, as she says,

> The time will come
> When I shall shrivel to almost nothing,
> Weigh almost nothing, when no one seeing me,
> Would ever think a god had found me lovely.

That time has come for the Sibyl. But she has not totally vanished, as Ovid suggests by ending her speech with the poignant words:

> . . . Voce tamen noscar;
> vocemque mihi fata relinquent.
> (I am known by voice alone;
> my voice the Fates will leave me.)[175]

---

[174] *Divina Revelatio Erythree Sibylle* . . ., ed. L. de Tovar (Senis, 1508); *Abbas Joachim Magnus Propheta in Librum Beati Cirilli* . . . (Venice, 1516), ff. 52ᵛ–54ᵛ; *Opera Nuper in Lucem* . . . (Venice, 1522), unpaged.

[175] Ovid, *Metamorphoses* 14, ll. 149–53. I have used the translation of R. Humphries, *Ovid Metamorphoses* (Bloomington, 1955), p. 343.

2

A Legacy of Miracles: Hagiography and Nunneries in Merovingian Gaul

JO ANN McNAMARA

In the process of Christianizing Merovingian Gaul in the sixth and seventh centuries, a series of cults was established in honor of local saints. Wonderful events were attributed to their tombs and other relics which were recorded for commemoration on feast days and other important occasions. About a dozen women were 'canonized' in this manner. Through their *Vitae*, we have access to a history rarely mentioned in the chronicles of a warrior class. The saints upon whose lives this paper is based were not 'baptized' pagan deities. Their legends are not warmed-over folk tales from a prehistoric past. Nevertheless, their histories have consistently posed seemingly insoluble problems for the modern scholar. Hagiography was a literary form just developing in the early medieval period. Its purposes were liturgical and didactic. Hagiographers were fond of saying that God works wonders through his saints. Accordingly they set themselves to describe the wonders and the pious deeds of the women through whom they were accomplished. Only incidentally did they include information about the mundane secular world in which the saint moved before her apotheosis. Generations of historians have sought to formulate a method for separating the historical wheat from this fabulous chaff, but all have failed to do so.[1]

Must we, therefore, discard this biographical material with a sigh of regret? Most historians have not done so. They have labored to

---

[1] This has been a work of centuries for the Bollandist Society whose members have been editing the *Acta Sanctorum* (henceforward *AS*) since the seventeenth century. Their work and the critical contributions of B. Krusch and W. Levison who edited selected texts for the *Monumenta Germaniae Historica*, with more detailed critical essays, have been thoroughly surveyed by René Aigrain, *L'Hagiographie: ses sources, ses méthodes, son histoire* (Paris, 1953).

establish reliable indicators for its use by scrupulous textual criticism, checks of internal consistency and external conformity with information extracted from other sources. Material that appears to be reliable by these tests, material that intrinsically commands credit with the modern critic, has been cautiously included among the sparse historical records of an obscure age.[2] Unacceptable elements describing supernatural interventions have simply been cast by the wayside.

All these critical efforts, however, seem to lead to at least one conclusion regarding Merovingian hagiography. The miracles are not later, contaminating, material added to a base of authentic fact. They do not make up a separable penumbra around a solid core. They were there from the beginning and, without miracles, the saint's life would not have been considered worthy of interest. Some of these *Vitae*, miracles and all, were composed by contemporary witnesses.[3] Others are of unknown date but are generally believed to have been recorded within two or three generations of the saint's death. A final group represent revised editions of older texts, usually produced by Carolingian writers. Where successive lives have survived the vicissitudes of time, it is clear that later redactors are not the culprits who added fables of supernatural events to reliable Merovingian sources. In most cases, their contributions chiefly consist of repairing barbarities of literary style and embellishing the original with pious reflections and scriptural citations designed to heighten the didactic value of the story. Even where medieval hagiographers borrowed incidents from one another, or included large chunks of material foreign to the original work, they began with a tradition of miraculous events.[4]

One popular hagiographer of Carolingian times gave his readers some insight into his problems as an author. He had been commissioned to write the *Life of Rictrude*, an exceptionally active saint who

[2] This is the method followed by Suzanne F. Wemple in her survey, *Women in Frankish Society: Marriage and the Cloister 500 to 900* (Philadelphia, 1981).

[3] This was the case for the two lives of Radegund by her friend, Fortunatus and her fellow nun, Baudonivia, combined under the title *De Vita Sanctae Radegundis Libri Duo*, ed. B. Krusch, *MGH, SRM* II, pp. 364–95; for the *Vita de S. Monegunde Vidua Reclusa*, *AS*, 2 July, pp. 275–81, edited from Gregory of Tours, *De Vita Patruum*, 19; and for the accounts collected by Jonas of Bobbio of the lives of the disciples of Saint Columbanus, *Vitae Columbani Abbatis Discipulorumque eius Liber II*, ed. B. Krusch, *MGH, SRM* IV, pp. 113–52.

[4] See, for example, the *Vita Sanctae Balthildis*, ed. B. Krusch, *MGH, SRM* II, pp. 477–508, and the respective lives of Aldegund, *AS*, 30 January, pp. 649–70. The formative process of earlier hagiography has been carefully elucidated by Hippolyte Delehaye, *The Legends of the Saints* (New York, 1962).

continued to exert herself on behalf of her devotees until well into the twelfth century. He was reluctant to undertake the commission because he distrusted the source material initially at his command. He changed his mind when he was given access to earlier narratives written by persons whom he deemed worthy of respect and credence. The saint had many miracles to her credit but there is no reason to suppose that they came from the imagination of her Carolingian biographer.[5]

Simply put, the miracles are the whole point of the *Vitae* and the cults they served. Modern students of popular religion are only beginning to assess this material from the viewpoint of the people for whom it was written.[6] For the beneficiaries of the saint's largesse and for those dependent on her cult, the world was peopled by spiritual magnates as it was by earthly ones. Women who had been influential on earth and who had shown that they had the ear of a heavenly sovereign continued to be the focus of the hopes of their dependants when they had migrated to his court.

We have one settled and indisputable fact from which to proceed. The texts themselves exist. They were written by someone and they commanded a large and diverse audience. The *Vitae* were inserted into the liturgies associated with the saints' cults. They formed the basis of popular preaching and devotional literature. They were intended to provide inspiration and guidance, not data for the social historian. The saint's example could be directed to a variety of needs. It might demonstrate the power of God to the half-Christianized flocks of a barbarian age. It might lead other women into the ascetic life or it might inspire the miserable to appeal to the saint for assistance. The *Vitae* certainly served to recommend the saint's influence as a mediator for her earthly clients and to warn the predatory against provoking a powerful protectress. The cults of women saints were promoted chiefly by women in the monastic communities they left behind. At the best of times, these communities of unmarried women found it hard to survive in a world of violent and greedy men.[7] The patronage of a saint was an instrument, sometimes subtle and often blunt, in their struggle.

[5] Hucbald, *Vita Sanctae Rictrudis*, 1, *AS*, 12 May, p. 81.

[6] This is the approach taken by Patrick J. Geary, *Furta Sacra: Thefts of Relics in the Central Middle Ages* (Princeton, 1978); and Peter Brown, *The Cult of the Saints* (Chicago, 1981).

[7] I have considered some of the more immediate dangers to these communities in 'Living sermons', an article soon to appear in an anthology devoted to the female monastic experience by the Cistercian Publications of Kalamazoo, Michigan.

It was not an instrument that the nuns controlled directly. Many wealthy and noble women left the world, established convents and lived praiseworthy lives. They were even called 'holy' or 'saint' in the chronicles of the period. But they did not become saints in the sense that they had a cult of their own or a *Vita* circulated among its worshippers. One element in the progression to sainthood was probably the patronage of male prelates. Most of our saints had the protection and support of a bishop or an abbot, sometimes related to them by blood. For example, when the local bishop, Maroveus, either from jealousy or distrust of her motives, placed obstacles in the path of Radegund's plans to enrich her convent with relics from Constantinople, she could turn to Gregory of Tours for assistance and Gregory later provided important support for her claim to sainthood.[8] On the other side, however, the same bishop may have been instrumental in thwarting the hopes of Ingytrude of Tours, a holy woman who established a foundation in his own city. He seemed inclined at first to support her claims by recounting a miracle she performed under the auspices of Martin of Tours.[9] Later, however, he turned against her because of her persistent encouragement of her daughter to leave her husband and enter the convent and the subsequent quarrels of the two women which Gregory heartily condemned.[10]

Of those women who did receive the approval and support necessary to make the transition to sainthood (in Merovingian Gaul), all were foundresses or abbesses of monastic communities. Each began life in a noble family and came into possession of a substantial fortune. An examination of the dozen or so biographies available to us indicates that there were consistent principles at work in the creation of these saints. The miracles attributed to them reveal a pattern peculiarly suited to forwarding the purposes of the communities to which they had devoted their earthly influence and wealth. In death, as in life, the female saints were noble and wealthy; they were aristocrats in heaven, celestial courtiers busy with the patronage of the flock of nuns who promoted and benefitted from their cults.

Persons who embrace the ascetic way of life are generally supposed not to be greatly in need of material possessions. Those individual who live as hermits in forests or deserts probably have little difficulty

[8] Peter Brown, *Relics and Social Status in the Age of Gregory of Tours* (Reading, 1977).

[9] Gregory of Tours, *Historia Francorum*, 5, 21, ed. B. Krusch, *MGH, SRM* I/I, p. 229.

[10] ibid., 9, 33.

procuring nuts and berries, locusts and honey, to keep body and soul together. From their inception, however, the monastic movements of the West, particularly those intended to serve the needs of religious women, were communal in nature and required substantial amounts of money to feed, clothe and house the membership.

Caesarius of Arles, who wrote the first monastic rule addressed to a community of women, dealt with these material needs in some detail. He was aware that the establishment would cost money and, accordingly, bequeathed his own estates for the support of his sister and her companions. He further expected that their endowment would be supplemented regularly from donations by other postulants.[11] In addition, he urged the women to supply their needs as far as possible by their own labor. Similarly, Benedict of Nursia, whose rule was adopted by female as well as male communities, assumed that the members would work for their keep.[12] But for women, this was a more difficult problem than for their male counterparts. Their access to opportunities for profitable enterprise was as severely limited as their economic need was aggravated by the requirement for severe claustration imposed by most of their communal rules.

At the same time, female as well as male monasteries were becoming institutional necessities to the nascent civilization of Christian Frankland where they played a crucial role in providing both spiritual and material services for the greater community. All the *Vitae* emphasize the charitable endeavors of the saints and, indirectly, illustrate the crushing weight of the needs that prompted them. Radegund was perhaps the model for her successors in the monastic life, as her *Vita* was the model for future hagiographers. She was certainly the most spectacular of her contemporaries in the lavishness of the banquets she served daily to all who came to her door, giving her indigent guests not only food but baths, clean clothes and even money before sending them on their way.[13] Few people had the lavish wealth of resources available to this former queen, but all the saints were open-handed and, where necessary, God showed his approval of their charity in wonderful ways destined to appeal to future donors. For example, while the hagiographer criticized her prudent mother, he praised the open-handed Aldegund whose scanty supplies of money and clothing were multiplied as she gave them out to beggars at her door.[14]

[11] *Regula Sanctarum Virginum*, 5, ed. G. Morin, *Opera Omnia*, 2, 101–27.
[12] *Regula*, 48, *PL* 66.   [13] Fortunatus, *De Vitae Sanctae Radegundis*, 17–18.
[14] *Vita Aldegundis Auctore Anonymo E Veteribus Mss, AS*, 30 Janaury, pp. 651–5, 16.

These were not difficult wonders for God to perform, one supposes, but he did not perform them for the poor. No woman began a career of sanctity without the substantial material resources necessary to acquire a reputation for charity. Nobility and wealth were the first requisites. The hagiographers were unanimous on that point. The only possible exception was Balthilda, whose biographer claimed that she came of noble Saxon stock. In fact, her background was not verifiable. She had been captured and enslaved by a Frankish noble before she attracted the attention of the king who married her. But by the time she retired into the monastery she had founded at Chelles, she was a queen dowager and no one was likely to question her claim to nobility.[15] Nobility was important because influence was wealth and the family tie was not broken when a woman entered into the monastery. Even where the parents or husband of the future saint had opposed her initial vocation, they became willing participants in her cult once it began to take root. They furthered the community she founded with material benefits and, in turn, she acted as their patron in heaven.[16]

Each of these noble and wealthy women turned their beneficence to the advantage of female communities which varied quite widely in number, probably reflecting the relative wealth of the foundress. Monegund started as a recluse attended by a single servant who ran away in disgust at the hardship of her life.[17] After she came to the attention of the influential clerical establishment at Tours, however, the community grew, though never to large numbers.[18] Aldegund established a dozen nuns at her parents' grave.[19] She and her sister between them supported at least two other communities. Sadalberga was also responsible for two flocks: 100 women were at Langres,[20] of whom she chose about 30 to form the core of a new house when she

[15] *Vita Sanctae Balthildis*, 10.

[16] This aspect of the 'canonization' process has been studied from the point of view of the family by Friedrich Prinz, *Frühes Mönchtum im Frankreich* (Munich and Vienna, 1965).

[17] *Vita Monegundis*, 3.

[18] ibid., 6.

[19] Hucbald, *Aldegundis*, 15. The author of Aldegund's briefer, earlier *Vita* omitted the more detailed exposition of her donations provided by Hcubald, who probably drew on the *Testament of Aldegund*, dated 642 and witnessed by SS Ouen and Gertrude, as well as her two nieces whom she raised in her convent.

[20] *Vita Sadalbergae Abbatissae Laudunensis*, 12, ed. B. Krusch, *MGH, SRM* V, pp. 40–66.

migrated to Laon.[21] Gregory of Tours says that when Radegund died, she was mourned by more than 200 nuns whom she had converted by her preaching.[22]

These communities formed the core of the saint's cult. They depended on her for inspiration and guidance but also for immediate shelter and care. The wealth of the saint was used to support a number of women who might otherwise have starved to death had they attempted to follow the apostolic life unaided. Whether they had come into the monastery with nothing to offer but themselves or whether they had brought money for their maintenance, they had to be housed securely in a building suitable for their solitary pursuits and their common life. They had to be clothed and fed. Some of them grew old and required special care. Others were infirm from the beginning. The most extreme example, perhaps, was a woman who entered the convent with two daughters and her maids, all of whom were possessed by demons and had to be kept apart from the other sisters because of their periodic violence.[23]

Other women were able-bodied but financially vulnerable. Sadalberga's community supported both noble and servile women.[24] So did the monastery established by Eustadiola.[25] Puellemoutiers was founded by Bishop Bercharius as a shelter for six ransomed slave women.[26] Caesarius of Arles prohibited the sisters from using some of their number as personal maids.[27] But on the other side, Donatus of Besançon warned nuns of servile origin that they should not convert to the monastic life in the expectation of receiving a more comfortable life than they might otherwise have enjoyed.[28]

Children, too, were sheltered in the cloister and raised by the nuns, often to become members of the community in later life. They were often related to the sisters and brought money for their own support. Similarly women who, for one reason or another, could no longer live with their own families or their husbands, could generally be expected to bring some settlement for their subsistence.

[21] ibid., 17.
[22] *Liber in Gloria Confessorum*, 106, ed. B. Krusch, *MGH, SRM* I/II, pp. 364–6.
[23] *Vita Anstrudis Abbatissae Laudunensis*, 37, ed. W. Levison, *MGH, SRM* VI, p. 77.
[24] *Vita Sadalbergae*, 17.
[25] *Vita Sanctae Eustadiolae Viduae*, 3, *AS*, 8 June. This is a point also explored by Wemple, *Women in Frankish Society*, p. 164.
[26] *Vita Bercharius, AS*, 16 October.
[27] *Regula*, 7.
[28] Donatus Vesontionensis, *Regula ad Virgines*, 9, *PL* 87: 273–98.

The establishment of a convent, in brief, was much more than a matter of religious impulse. It was indispensable to a society committed to the care and protection of all these unmarried women. It is not surprising, therefore, that the grateful recipients were eager to elevate their benefactress to an exalted position in the next world. The proponents of monasticism did not always wait for divine inspiration to fall upon suitable candidates for this honor. They appear actively to have recruited girls of good fortune. Columbanus, for example, singled out Burgundofara while she was still a child in her parents' house. His successor, Eustatius, supported her resistance to her parents who wished to see her married. The rebellion was marked by periodic illness and timely miracles which later served as a lesson to anyone else who might attempt to prevent a wealthy young heiress from giving herself, with her worldly goods, to God.[29] Eustatius also used his miraculous powers to heal the young Sadalberga, who had been blind from birth, after she had declared her desire to join the ranks of consecrated women.[30] Without his continued presence, Sadalberga was unable to keep that promise until after she had been pushed into marriage by her parents. Eventually, however, she repaid her debt with interest: she brought her husband with her into the monastic life and eventually all her surviving children followed, as well as the disappointed suitor of her daughter Anstrude. The remainder of her parents' fortune was secured when her brother turned to a monastery, sending his wife Odila with a generous endowment into Sadalberga's house.[31]

Bishop Ouen was responsible for the recruitment of Bertilla for Jouarre, over her parents' objections.[32] Amand persuaded the widowed wife of Pippin, Mayor of the Palace for King Dagobert, to build a convent for herself and her virgin daughter Gertrude of Nivelles.[33] The same bishop helped the widowed Rictrude to evade the king's plans for her remarriage, diverting her to the monastic life.[34] Like Sadalberga, she added her husband's fortune to her own by bringing her son and her three daughters into the monastic life. Another woman from the circle of nobles around Dagobert, Aldegund, had a vision of

---

[29] Jonas of Bobbio, *Vitae Columbani* II 7.
[30] *Vita Sadalbergae*, 12.
[31] ibid., 18.
[32] *Vita Bertilae Abbatissae Calensis*, 1, ed. W. Levison, *MGH, SRM* VI, pp. 95–109.
[33] *Vita Geretrudis, MGH, SRM* II, p. 453.
[34] Hucbald, *Vita Sanctae Rictrudis*, 13.

Amand on his way to heaven surrounded by the rejoicing souls of the women he had brought to the conventual life.[35]

Perhaps the strangest story of recruitment of the wealthy daughters of the nobility is that of Rusticula, the only surviving child of a prominent Gallo-Roman family. She was kidnapped by an ambitious suitor while still a child. He entrusted her to his mother to raise as his future wife, apparently fully confident that he would be able to command her dowry and her inheritance when that time came. This nefarious plan was balked by the timely intervention of Caesarius of Arles from beyond the grave. The sainted bishop had endowed his sister's convent with his own wealth at the time of his death but it had probably been dissipated by the time of the fourth abbess, Liliola. In any case, he appeared to her in a vision revealing the kidnapping and the whereabouts of the heiress. With the assistance of the Bishop of Autun, Liliola rescued the girl from her abductor and secured her in the convent of Arles to be raised as a nun. Her hagiographer assured his readers that the girl was precocious in her sanctity as demonstrated by the miracles that marked her journey to Arles. He maintained that Caesarius himself had recruited her in a vision granted to her mother. None the less, her installation in the convent was in fact a second kidnapping and one which her grieving mother protested:

Give me hope for my child. Who now will care for my old age? She was the only one I had left. I seek my little sprout and cannot find her. Where can I run? Where to turn I do not know! I pray grace and call on God to witness that you should have mercy on me, struck with such sorrow and order the restoration of my only child in my widowhood.[36]

The bishop turned a deaf ear to the plea; the saint got his wish and the convent got the girl and her fortune.

Rusticula brought enough with her to build a new church for the convent at Arles.[37] Sadalberga used her paternal inheritance to establish her first convent while her second husband was still living.[38] For her second venture, she had also her widow's portion to contribute and

---

[35] *Vita Aldegundis*, 8.

[36] Florentius, *Vita Sanctae Rusticulae*, 3, ed. B. Krusch, *MGH, SRM* IV, pp. 399–51. Krusch was doubtful of both the date and the author of this work but both were vindicated by the careful research of Pierre Riché, 'Note d'hagiographie mérovingienne: *La Vita S. Rusticula*', *Analecta Bollandiana*, 72 (1954), pp. 369–77.

[37] ibid., 8.

[38] *Vita Sadalbergae*, 12.

ultimately both fortunes devolved upon her daughter, Anstrude, whose only surviving brother died after she had succeeded to her mother's place.[39] Similarly, Rictrude took the wealth she got from her husband to the church despite the desire of the king to divert it to a second husband of his choice.[40] It may seem obvious, but it is important to stress that these accounts found in the saints' *Vitae* are far more than empty pieties about the vanity of earthly things. God's work on earth needed money as well as holiness and the road to sanctity for the women of Merovingian Gaul was paved with their familial fortunes.

Even with these endowments, however, the communities appear always to have been in need. There was no end to the stream of indigent beggars who came to the convent doors or to the sick who crowded into their public places in the hope of a cure, miraculous or otherwise. The most commodious fortunes could not have lasted long in this atmosphere. Nor could very large sums ever have been raised by the industry of the community. Monegund's companions, for example, worked at weaving *mattas* of twigs and rushes, but these could never have commanded very large sums.[41] Donatus of Besançon's rule penalized any nun who wasted kitchen supplies, and was even harsher with those who tried to hide food and drink in bed so as to gain more than their share.[42] At Poitiers, the rebellious Basina complained of the poor quality of the food supplied by the Abbess Leubovera, who retorted that at least they always had enough to eat.[43]

Anxiety about the food supply is often reflected in the miracles recounted by hagiographers. Radegund was supposed to have a barrel of wine that always replenished itself when she served its contents to travellers.[44] When Sadalberga found that she had no wine to serve, she was obliged to save even her humble beer from spoilage by miraculously swelling the contents of the brewing sufficiently to drive out the contaminating air.[45] Sadalberga also counted it a miracle that she encountered a peddler with a large fish for sale just in time to provide dinner for an archdeacon who had been commanded by an angelic vision to go and learn a lesson in humility by watching the abbess cook. The practical biographer did not hesitate to point out that the visitor

[39] *Vita Anstrudis*, 4–5.
[40] *Vita Sanctae Rictrudis*, 14.
[41] *Vita Monegundis*, 6.
[42] *Regula*, 24 and 26.
[43] Gregory of Tours, *Historia Francorum*, 10, 14.
[44] Baudonivia, *De Vitae Sanctae Radegundis*, 10.
[45] *Vita Sadalbergae*, 20.

had thoughtlessly neglected to bring his own food.[46] The stories served to enhance the saint's reputation for influence with God while reminding the readers that it was well within their power to win her gratitude.

The scarcities inevitable in a community whose limited resources were committed to charity were aggravated by the constant threat of human predators and natural forces to their supplies. At Faremoutiers, the nuns were able to keep up their own vegetable patch.[47] But Sadalberga, who had moved her community within the security of the fortified walls of Laon, had to depend on a gardener outside the town who very nearly gave way to the temptation to steal her lettuce. He was prevented only by the reproachful voice of the abbess in his ear, though she was some miles away.[48] The needy and charitable nuns who guarded the miraculous cloak of St Martin supplemented their modest diet with honey. A thief who tried to steal their hives was stung to death when the protecting saint caused the bees to swarm.[49]

The cloistered nuns were obliged to depend on the charity or labor of others for their fish supply, and their stories made it clear that fishermen who served them would not regret it. Gertrude of Nivelles saved a fishing boat from attack by a giant whale.[50] Radegund sent a dove to calm the raging tempest that threatened her servitors.[51] Glodesind ensured the luck of a fisherman heading for her convent by causing a large fish to jump voluntarily into his net.[52] Aldegund kept a fish given to her community in a pond but it was threatened by crows when it accidentally beached itself. Happily, a peaceable little lamb, most unnaturally, defended it with tooth and hoof until the nuns could come to the rescue.[53]

After the death of Radegund, Gregory of Tours arrived to officiate at her funeral rites and found about 200 nuns distraught and weeping for the loss of their patroness:

To whom will you leave us orphans? To whom will you commend the desolate? We gave up our parents and goods and country and followed you. What do you leave us now but perpetual tears and never-ending

[46] *Vita Sadalbergae*, 23.

[47] Jonas of Bobbio, *Vitae Columbani* II, 17.

[48] *Vita Sadalbergae*, 22.

[49] Gregory of Tours, *Libri Octo Miraculorum: Liber de Virtutibus Sancti Martini Episcopi*, 17, ed. B. Krusch, *MGH, SRM* I, pp. 661–743.

[50] *Vita Geretrudis*, 5.

[51] Fortunatus, *De Vita Sanctae Radegundis*, 31.

[52] *Vita Antiquior Sanctae Glodesindis*, 33–4, *AS*, 25 July, pp. 203–10.

[53] *Vita Aldegundis*, 17.

sorrow? Behold, even now, this monastery is better to us than farm or city spaces. Where else could we have contemplated your face? Here we found gold and silver; here we knew flowering vines and leafy plants; here were fields flowering with riotous blossom. From you we took violets: you were the blushing rose and the white lily. You spoke in words bright as the sun and, as the moon against the darkness, you burned as a lamp with the light of truth. But now, it is all darkness with us and the place is strait where we can look no more upon your face. Alas, our sainted mother has deserted us! Happy are they who migrated before her from this world! We know you have joined the chorus of holy virgins with God in Paradise. This consoles us, but still we lament that we can see you no more with our bodily eyes![54]

These were not empty formalities of grief. Nor did their tears spring from affection alone, however genuine their love for their foundress. While Radegund lived, the nuns of her community could count on the bounty of her royal fortune. They lived on land she had received from her husband and the fortune she brought with her. Her presence had attracted other royal ladies whose endowments must have matched their disruptive temperaments. She had maintained her relationship with the ruling family and, with their assistance, had added a store of world-famous relics to the monastery which would attract pilgrims and their gifts for years to come. She protected them, also, from the hostility of the Bishop of Poitiers, Maroveus, who had opposed the installation of the relics in the convent church. His obstinate absence from her funeral services obliged the Bishop of Tours to come to the rescue and it was an ominous sign for the future of the community.[55]

Episcopal hostility was not an uncommon problem for monastic institutions. A similar attack was made on the property of Anstrude's convent at Laon by Bishop Madalgar which was thwarted only because the abbess was able to call on the powerful magnate Pippin for assistance against the bishop.[56] Radegund's community might well fear for a future without her powerful and protecting presence. Fortunately, however, the queenly saint had friends and supporters who would ensure that the community would not be entirely orphaned by her death. No less than three accounts promoted her cult in the following years, including the testimony of the influential Bishop of Tours who noted that her funeral was attended by a number of powerful persons who must have been profoundly shaken when victims of dia-

---

[54] *Liber in Gloria Confessorum,* 106.
[55] Baudonivia, *De Vita Sanctae Radegundis,* 13–16.
[56] *Vita Anstrudis,* 16.

bolical possession surrounded the company, their demons crying out against the power of the saint.[57] Baudonivia added that several miraculous cures were effected in the course of the procession.[58] The community could relax. The fame of the convent and its ability to attract patronage would only be enhanced by the death of its mother.

The practical uses of an edifying deathbed were not lost on other hagiographers. One of the advantages conferred upon saints was foreknowledge of their own deaths, which enabled them to make proper provision for their departure. Naturally, this included spiritual preparation and communal psalm singing and praying. It also gave the community a chance to invite outsiders to share the edifying experience, sometimes to the immediate benefit of the flock. The retired queen, Balthilda, a woman of considerable political skill, spent many hours in conference with her chosen abbess, Bertilla, planning a deathbed and funeral that would enhance the monastery's fame and fortune.[59] A nun of Faremoutiers named Willindane prophesied her coming death in plenty of time for the abbess to spread the news among some of the local magnates, including Aega, the guardian of the young King Chlodoveus, who had been usurping the lands of the convent for benefices to give his own followers. The abbess had tried in vain to prevent his incursions. Even as Willindane was proclaiming that she saw her deceased sisters coming to conduct her soul to heaven, she sensed his presence. Convulsively, she cried out from her deathbed that 'this piece of filth, this rubbish' be driven away. Needless to say, the potentate quickly repented of his errors and made immediate amends.[60] Likewise, Gertrude of Nivelles interrupted her prophesied death to denounce the depradations of the queen and her followers against the property of her monastery. Very soon they, 'so lately raptors, appeared as benefactors with all largesse and as defenders of benefices'.[61]

Sadalberga, as we have noted, had secured much of her brother's fortune to add to her own when she brought her sister-in-law, Odila, into her convent. However, it was only on her deathbed, prophesied a

[57] *Liber in Gloria Confessorum*, 106. The importance of the possessed as agents for the identification of the holy has been discussed by Brown, *Relics and Social Status*.

[58] Baudonivia, *De Vita Sanctae Radegundis*, 24.

[59] *Vita Sanctae Balthildis*, 12.

[60] Jonas of Bobbio, *Vitae Columbani* II, 17. For a further account of Aega, see Fredegar, *Chronicorum Liber Quartus cum Continuationibus*, 62, ed. and trans. J. M. Wallace-Hadrill (London, 1960).

[61] *Vita Geretrudis*, 6.

hundred days in advance to allow plenty of time for the event, that he was induced to confirm his deeds of gift for the estates he had promised to settle on the community.[62]

In brief, even on their deathbeds, the saintly foundresses were not unmindful of the material needs of their communities. They, and their hagiographers, reinforced their practical legacies with miracles and revelations designed to convince the reader that their deaths did not leave the nuns defenseless. Finally, the saint left her greatest legacy: her blessed body, its tomb and the subsidiary artifacts cast off at her death, a priceless endowment destined to produce miraculous interest.

Though hagiographers were always careful to state that God could perform what miracles he chose in any place and time, they stressed that he was often pleased to indicate his partiality for his favorites by channeling his wonders through certain relics they left behind. These relics were the prize possessions of the bereaved flock. It is rare that a biographer is as forthright as Baudonivia who stated baldly that a certain magnate, cured of an eye disease by the hair shirt of Radegund, gave the princely sum of 100 solidi to establish an oratory.[63] To be sure, the saint and her earthly admirers understood very well that it was a sin to ask for money in exchange for God's grace. One hagiographer remarked that whereas doctors took money from their patients and did not cure them, the saint performed the cure and made no charge.[64] However, their petitioners understood very well the importance of gratitude. Even the poor man in search of assistance knew that the saints would smile more sweetly on one who brought a fresh fish for the nuns.[65]

The tomb of a noted worker of miracles soon became the focus of numerous pilgrimages, sick persons camping out for indefinite periods of time. One such aspirant, a man with a putrescent affliction of his nose, considerately kept himself back from the tomb to avoid giving offense to the crowd installed there. Possibly the saint also found the stench hard to bear, for she acted quickly in his favor.[66] The nuns may have encountered difficulties with these crowds, or the tomb may have been placed outside the convent on a site inauspicious for the intended recipients of the saint's good will. Often some other relic supplemented or replaced the tomb as a carrier of the saint's virtue.

[62] *Vita Sadalbergae*, 29.

[63] Baudonivia, *De Vita Sanctae Radegundis*, 15.

[64] *Vita Antiquior Sanctae Glodesindis*, 22.

[65] ibid., 33–4.

[66] ibid., 26.

Most popular among these relics were cloth objects: clothing, funeral palls or gravecloths. Thus, in addition to her hair shirt, Radegund's funeral pall and even the water it was washed in proved to be vehicles of grace.[67] Aldegund's habit protected one of her nuns from a scalding, burns and concussion when she nearly fell into the fire with a pot of boiling water in her hands.[68] Dust from Anstrude's tomb provided the chief ingredient in a healing potion,[69] as did the washing water from Rusticula's tomb.[70] Dust and water of this sort, of course, were particularly convenient types of relics because of their infinite capacity for multiplication and their ready portability. Ingytrude of Tours, for example, made a start at sainthood by performing cures with water she used for washing Martin's tomb. Indeed, in a period of drought she was favored with a singular wonder: wine was turned into water so that the ablutions need not be missed.[71]

In two cases, pieces of furniture served as convenient agents of healing which could be kept under the control of the custodians. The chair in which Anstrude kept her nightly vigils proved to be beneficent.[72] So did the bed in which Gertrude of Nivelles died. So efficacious was the bed that a new church, separate from that which held her tomb, was built to house it.[73] When Nivelles sent out a new community, they sent a piece of the bed to the new daughter house.[74]

Gertrude was a saint whose powers may, in fact, have been stretched too thin over a period of time. Her first biography ended on a note of doubt and vindication. A matron who was in the habit of visiting the convent expressed a lack of faith in the saint's powers of advocacy. One of the nuns hotly defended her and promised that she would prove herself on her feast day. The matron, with her young son, attended the banquet on that day. While the party was still in the refectory, her restless son fell into a well while running about the cloister and drowned there. Happily he was restored to life by the power of the saint and amends were made to the community by his repentant mother.[75]

---

[67] Baudonivia, *De Vita Sanctae Radegundis*, 26 and 28.
[68] *Vita Aldegundis*, 19.
[69] *Vita Anstrudis*, 29.
[70] Florentius, *Vitae Sanctae Rusticulae*, 83.
[71] Gregory of Tours, *Historia Francorum*, 5, 21.
[72] *Vita Anstrudis*, 15.
[73] *Vita Geretrudis*, 6.
[74] ibid., 10.
[75] ibid., 11.

Perhaps it was because the doubts of the matron were widely shared and the cult of Gertrude fading that a second hagiographer took up the account of her miracles with the story of a sick girl who received a vision ordering her to go to Gertrude for a cure.[76] Certainly, it was many years after her death that she sent a fresh token to her flock through quantities of healing oil which flowed from her tomb.[77] Indeed, oil, which was already associated with the care of the sick, was a favourite relic. The mourning sisters of Monegund's community implored their resident worker of miracles to bless a quantity of oil and salt as she lay dying so that they might use it to relieve sick petitioners when she was no longer with them.[78]

The most aggressive and exacting of this company of saints was a young woman named Glodesind. She had established a community at Metz with the assistance of her sister, a nun at Trier. She had preserved her virginity through one marriage by the timely arrest of her husband on their wedding day and his subsequent execution. An angel assisted her flight from a second marriage. Then she died young while her community was still in the fledgling stage.[79] For some years, she lay quiescent in the episcopal cemetery. Then something must have occurred that gave an impetus for the establishment of a cult. The biography says that she began to appear to a nun in visions indicating that she did not like being buried at a distance from her community. She instructed the nun to establish a site for their cemetery by throwing stones from the city wall. Accordingly the bishop consecrated the ground and the saint was translated to the convent.[80] Even then, the saint was not at peace. She entered into another series of visionary demands, complaining that a mouse was gnawing at her great toe. The tomb was opened, the mouse ejected and the mousehole blocked up. But, still, she wanted a new tomb and was finally translated a second time.[81] Thereafter, however, she repaid all this trouble with multiple cures and an effusion of oil which spurted from the injured toe and overflowed the tomb in which she lay. It was gathered up reverently by an appointed custodian and kept in a special vase after it proved to be miraculous. The power of the oil, like the power of Glodesind's own body, was a gift that she intended only for her own

[76] ibid., Cont. 1.
[77] ibid., Cont. 2.
[78] *Vita Monegundis*, 9–10.
[79] *Vita Antiquior Sanctae Glodesindis*, 6–7.
[80] ibid., 14–16.
[81] ibid., 17.

community. When the generous custodian had agreed to share some with another convent, the vessel hid itself from her. When it was finally found, she persisted in her ill-conceived generosity and was punished by a severe illness which ceased only when all the oil was returned to its original vessel and safely housed in the convent again. Thereafter the site became a prosperous destination for pilgrims drawn by the miraculous properties of the oil.[82]

The modern reader is rarely inclined to give much credence to these wonderful stories of sanctified ladies and the marvels wrought through them or their remains. I hope, however, that this effort to systematize some of these accounts will demonstrate that these were not the foolish fantasies of idle and credulous tellers of tales. Saints and their miracles performed a number of functions in the religious life of Merovingian Gaul. Not the least of these was to procure protection, sustenance and often prosperity for the communities of consecrated women which spread and flourished in that violent and hostile environment. The legacy of miracles made the crucial difference to the survival of the community after the loss of the influential and wealthy patroness. Moreover, it was not a small miracle that communities of women could survive with relatively little threat of violence and rapine from the powerful and predatory men who surrounded them – and that, in such an environment, they could even thrive.

[82] ibid., 39–43.

3

Bishops as Marital Advisors in the Ninth Century

JANE BISHOP

People do not generally enter the religious life primarily in order to discuss sex, and this was presumably not the primary motivation in the ninth century. It is, therefore, with some amusement that one encounters evidence that members of the higher clergy in that century were devoting some of their time to solving marital problems of sometimes startling intimacy. As matter for grave public debate, for instance, consider this summary by a synod of bishops in 862 of the personal problems of their king:

> He asked very mournfully for divine and pastoral counsel, and made known his state of weakness in querulous tones . . . He brought out that he was incontinent, and asserted that without marital coupling he could not bear the ardour of his young age. He reiterated that we had [declared his wife ineligible for marriage] and commanded him to abstain from all concubines, and that it was extremely hard to remain thus in juvenile years . . .[1]

Or, as a question for a group of bishops to ask of a learned colleague, the inquiry of those who later attended the synod of 862 about the alleged conduct of the king's wife:

> Write back to us, on the authority of the Scriptures and the traditions of the Fathers, what the writings say about defilement and abortion, with the names of the authors and the titles of the books, so that we may know whether a woman can conceive in the way it is said she did, and after an abortion remain a virgin, as is said happened to this one.[2]

---

[1] Statement by the council of Aachen in 862; J. D. Mansi, *Sacrorum Conciliorum Nova et Amplissima Collectio* (Venice, 1759–98), vol. XV, col. 612.

[2] Hincmar of Rheims, the recipient, quotes this in his reply *De Divortio Lotharii Regis et Tetbergae Reginae*, in J. P. Migne (ed.), *Patrologiae Cursus Completus, Series Latina* (henceforward *PL*), vol. 126, col. 689.

The second example is the more notable for the way the man consulted, the famous Archbishop Hincmar of Rheims, answered it. Using the Bible as his main authority, he gave an astonishingly explicit description of how conception normally takes place, in terms which, in the words of his latest biographer, defy shame.[3] He then summed up as follows:

And it has never been heard in this world, nor is it read under this sky in the Word of Truth, that the vulva of a woman received semen and conceived without coitus, or that, her womb being closed, and her vulva not opened, she produced a living or aborted baby, with the sole exception of the uniquely happy and blessed Virgin Mary, who conceived not by nature, but by grace . . .[4]

From such passages as these it becomes clear that in this period, in a society dominated by a religion which has a modern reputation among certain literary persons[5] as having been a force for suppressing sexual openness, both laymen and churchmen felt free to discuss almost anything in public. And this was not because these particular churchmen were especially interested in marital problems, either by personal history or by predilection. Though it was still possible in the ninth century for married men to rise in the ranks of the clergy, most of those from whom we have these writings were known celibates.[6]

[3] Jean Devisse, *Hincmar, Archevêque de Reims, 845–882* (Geneva, 1975), vol. I, p. 377: Hincmar's language 'brave le pudeur'. His chapter V closely examines Hincmar's views on marriage and the situation in the Franklands in general, pp. 367–466; Hincmar's *De Divortio* is discussed and its format clarified on pp. 386–96.

[4] Hincmar, *De Divortio*, PL 126: 694. He then proceeds to go into detail about the Virgin Mary's special method of conception. It is without doubt this whole passage which so disgusted the nineteenth-century historian, Henry Hart Milman. In his *History of Latin Christianity* (London, 1855), Book V, c. IV, he states in a footnote, 'The questions submitted to the archbishop are only surpassed in their offensiveness by their absurdity. Hincmar discusses them with minute obscenity.'

[5] By 'certain literary persons' I am mainly referring to such *fin de siècle* figures as Swinburne and Anatole France, who is quoted as having said, 'I have but two enemies: Christ and chastity.' Such talk may seem old-fashioned, but new generations are constantly rediscovering it.

[6] For Hincmar, see *PL* 126: 695. Pope Nicholas I was almost certainly celibate (see J. Bishop, *Pope Nicholas I and the First Age of Papal Independence* (Doctoral Dissertation, Columbia University, 1980, p. 14, n. 1). Theodore the Studite, as a monk, was definitely bound to celibacy. Pope Hadrian II was a married man, but he was under so much pressure to follow the policies of his predecessor Nicholas that his status could not much affect his decisions.

Hincmar himself, after the clinical paragraph partially quoted above, apparently had second thoughts about the impression his knowledge would make, for he ended by asserting his own virginity. He also gave the true reason for the bishops' interest in the subject:

We bishops say this not because we want knowingly to reveal or ignorantly to make known the secret places of girls and women, which we know nothing of by experience; but because it is written, 'The thing I do not know I will diligently investigate', we will keep before our eyes what we see written in the teachers of the church, so that if anyone caught at such things comes to us, asking in penitence for the judgement of just judges, we can judge her without error.[7]

The passages quoted so far concern the case of King Lothar of Lorraine, a great-grandson of Charlemagne, whose attempts to divorce his wife Theutberga exercised the minds of the higher clergy of Latin Christendom from 858 to 869. Lothar, before his marriage, had loved and had children by one Waldrada; he married Theutberga for political reasons which soon became outdated, and she had no children. Wishing to be rid of her and marry Waldrada, Lothar chose to have Theutberga accused of premarital incest with her brother, which by the canon law accepted at that time would have made her incapable of being truly married. Theutberga claimed to be innocent of incest and took various steps to prove it. When the bishops of Lothar's realm, after consulting Hincmar and others, convicted her, she appealed to Pope Nicholas I, one of the dominating figures of his day. Nicholas decided in her favor and induced Lothar's bishops to accept this; Lothar's attempts to find other grounds to get out of the marriage then lasted until his death in 869.

Another case which demonstrates the free discussion of marital problems in church councils at this time was that of Count Stephen of Auvergne, who explained to a synod of 860 at great length and in very circumstantial terms why he had not consummated his marriage. His problem was that before his betrothal he had had an affair with a young woman who turned out to be a near relative of his prospective bride; to embrace the latter would therefore, by the rules of the day, have been incestuous. The bride's father, the powerful nobleman Regimundus, had apparently threatened Stephen with death when he showed signs of wishing to break off the engagement, so he had married her but left her untouched; Regimundus was growing wrath-

7 *PL* 126: 695. The quotation is from Job 19:16.

ful at this also, so Stephen now appealed to the bishops for advice. They seem to have ruled that the marriage was invalid and that both parties were free to marry again.[8]

These are only two of several very striking cases of marital discord of which the ninth-century Christian world has left us record. We have the facts of these cases, and we have the various ways in which the churchmen who were consulted about them dealt with them. As has been indicated already, the discussion was not much inhibited by considerations of propriety; it was an age in which not even the most austere leaders of the religious life minced words on any subject. It was not only that Pope Nicholas I habitually referred to extramarital intercourse as 'the vortex of fornication'; although the subject did not obviously seem to call for it, he was also in the habit of calling one of the Church's basic heresies what may be politely translated as 'the Arian ordure'.[9] We are therefore able to enjoy the incongruity of such subjects and language from such people. But more than this: we are able to examine the nature of the discussion, and draw some conclusions about ninth-century attitudes towards marriage, sex and the relations of the sexes.

Of course, clerics of the ninth century found themselves pondering intimacies far from their own way of life simply because the Christian church had claimed an interest in marriage from its beginnings. According to the mainstream Christian tradition, the sexual act itself is morally neutral, neither intinsically virtuous, as in a Dionysian religion, nor intrinsically vicious, as in a Manichaean one. But the Judeo–Christian requirement that people confine their sexual attentions either to no one or to one member of the opposite sex in a permanent bond raised endless ethical questions in other areas: the proper treatment of other people, justice for the weak, the keeping of promises. These were questions of morality in which the church was interested; Jesus Christ and the Apostle Paul, both of whom their sources and tradition depict as celibate, had made pronouncements on

---

[8] Stephen's case is discussed at some length, with quotations from his statement to the synod, by Hincmar in a letter which responds to the bishops' request for advice. He concluded that the marriage was invalid. The whole is in *Monumenta Germaniae Historica, Epistolae* (henceforward *MGH, Ep.*), vol. VIII[1], pp. 87–107. Stephen's own statement is p. 89.

[9] His letters are in *MGH, Ep.* VI. For 'the vortex of fornication' see, for instance, Jaffe–Ewald, *Regestum Pontificum Romanum* (henceforward JE) 2850, Letter 139 in the *MGH* edition. In JE 2796, Letter 88 *MGH*, Theodoric the Ostrogoth is described as 'haereseos Arianae fece pollutus'.

the ethics of marriage, and they had been followed and commented upon by churchmen in every century thereafter. The ninth century was no exception. Bishop Jonas of Orleans, in his *De Institutione Laicali*, devoted considerable space to that particular lay institution.[10] General pronouncements drawn from the Bible and patristic tradition about marriage were nothing unusual.

What was perhaps slightly unusual about episcopal marital advice in the ninth century was the nature of some of the individual cases. Advice given to individuals may often be different from general principles; abstract generalizations may break down when confronted with specific people. Tertullian, in the early third century, informed women in general that they were the Devil's gateway and ought to mourn eternally for having brought evil into the world; but he made no such pronouncements in his admiring letter to the individual women martyrs Perpetua and Felicitas.[11] We are here concerned not with ninth-century churchmen's opinions on marriage in isolation, but with how they applied them to the people they advised. And the situation in one important part of Christendom was such as to produce some peculiar cases.

The majority of ninth-century Christians lived in three places: Italy, the Byzantine Empire and the old Carolingian domains of north-western Europe.[12] Of these, Byzantium and Italy had been familiar with the Christian tradition on marriage since it had grown up in the old Roman Empire, But the Franklands, the increasingly fragmented remains of the Carolingian Empire, had a situation unique to this period. Though the Franks had been Christian for 300 years, their marital morals had not yet been brought effectively under the strict laws of the Roman–Christian tradition. The Merovingian kings of the sixth and seventh centuries had practised multiple concubinage and occasional polygamy. A form of common-law marriage known to modern scholars as *Friedelehe*, less formal and less binding than full marriage, was widespread in the Franklands well into the ninth century; Lothar's relationship with Waldrada may have been such a bond. Charlemagne repudiated at least one wife at will, and had several concubines in his old age; he also encouraged his beloved

[10] *PL* 106: 121–78; marriage is discussed in cols. 167–92, Book II.

[11] Respectively, *De Cultu Ferminarum* and *Ad Martyras*.

[12] Though by no means all; England and the unconquered remnant of Spain were, of course, Christian countries, and there were Christian minorities in the Islamic lands and in the parts of north-eastern Europe then in the process of conversion.

daughters to bear children more or less informally to men at his court
rather than marry formally and leave him. But in the period under
study here, this situation was changing. Charlemagne's son, Louis I,
was the first Frankish ruler who was truly committed to the strict
Christian view of marriage, and Frankish churchmen were encouraged to insist upon it. By the later ninth century, monogamy was
established in the Franklands, as an ideal if not as a consistent practice;
those who wished to evade it had to pay it homage (as it will be seen
that Lothar did) by putting forth arguments to prove that their conduct was really monogamous despite appearances to the contrary.[13]

And this era of transition gave rise to some of the *causes célèbres* which
made marital problems such a subject of concern among ninth-century
churchmen. There were also cases pertinent to this inquiry in lands
where strict Christian conduct had long been known and deviation
from it could be explained only by human frailty; but much of the fuss
is accounted for by the clash in the Franklands of old customs with new
ideals. Lothar of Lorraine had to explain to his bishops in such detail
his inability to contain himself because he needed ecclesiastical sanction to do what his great-grandfather had done with no word of objection even from the Pope.[14] That embarrassed virgin Hincmar was
called upon to write a long treatise dealing with, among other things,
whether a woman could conceive by sodomy and abort while remaining physically intact because, given the known facts of Lothar's past
conduct, this improbable assertion was the only way he could prove
the incest charge against his wife.[15] To some extent the bishops who
deliberated about marriage in this period were just conducting business as usual, but some of the circumstances were distinctively sharp
and lurid.

[13] For the process of change, see Suzanne F. Wemple, *Women in Frankish Society:
Marriage and the Cloister, 500 to 900* (Philadelphia, 1981) Part I, esp. c. 4, 'The
Ascent of Monogamy'.
[14] *Especially* from the pope, in fact. The marriage Charlemagne repudiated was
with a Lombard princess, and had been violently opposed, to the point of hysteria,
by a pope to whom the Lombards were the great enemies of Rome.
[15] Lothar had not said anything about Theutberga's premarital conduct for two
or three years after their marriage. Only when he no longer needed the alliance with
her brother for which he had married her did he start accusing her of not having
been innocent when they married. Since the obvious question was why he had not
made this objection after their wedding night, when he would presumably have
found it out, he had to assert that she had somehow maintained physical virginity
throughout her crimes with her brother, and that the deed had only come to light
when she told Archbishop Gunthar of Cologne in confession.

What are the issues we should bear in mind when assessing what kind of marital advisors these bishops made? There is one in particular. It is well known that part of the Christian tradition is not only egalitarian but actually abolishes the distinction between men and women: 'There is no male nor female, for you all are one in Christ Jesus.'[16] And when men and women renounce those things in which male and female roles unavoidably differ, they have always found it possible to be friends and equals. Even naturally misogynous churchmen who had a general idea that women were a separate and inferior class, from the Apostle Paul onwards, had individual women friends whom they treated simply as human beings.[17] But when sex outside monogamous marriage was regarded as a very great sin, the ability of men and women to be comfortable with each other depended to a large extent on the avoidance of sexuality. Frequently, especially in the early centuries of Christian history which produced what the Middle Ages regarded as definitive commentaries, celibate men, who resented the fact that men were tempted by women, took refuge in blaming the women for the temptation, and insisted on their subordinate, weak or evil nature. Since this is an issue that was present at many times in the history of the Church, it is instructive in the study of any given period to assess how much it was present at that time. The ninth century, with these fine examples of advice from churchmen to married people, can be illuminated by an examination of how its celibate clergymen actually reacted to the problems of married women, who had not removed themselves from sexuality and were therefore not 'safe'. How much or how little the idea of women as naturally or morally inferior to men entered into the attitudes of ninth-century marital advisors will be an ultimate question of this study.

In the ninth century, as in other periods, the tradition surrounding marriage and the Church was such that clerics were thought to be definitive problem-solvers. As Stephen of Auvergne said, 'Whatever advice you give me for my salvation before God, and for my reconciliation with and pacification of Regimundus and the safety and honour

---

[16] The words of St Paul, Galatians 3:28.

[17] See for this, and for the role of celibacy in making friendship between men and women possible, Rosemary Rader, *Breaking Boundaries: Male–Female Friendship in Early Christian Communities* (New York, 1983). The most notable examples after Paul were SS. Jerome and John Chrysostom; both wrote about the evil nature of women in general, but it is apparent from their letters that some of their best friends were women.

of the girl in the world, I am ready to obey in every way I can.'[18] People came to the Church in circumstances that were often desperate. Hincmar tells of a bishop in his metropolitan jurisdiction who was confronted by a parishioner who had been impotent for the entire two years of his marriage: 'he ran to him and said, in persuasive, pleading and menacing words, that unless the bishop let the marriage be dissolved, he would draw his sword on himself, and, if it could not be dissolved any other way, do it by homicide.'[19] Gunthar, Archbishop of Cologne, was involved (before he was deposed in 863 by Nicholas I for being overly and dishonestly concerned in the condemnation of Theutberga)[20] in the marital difficulties of Ingiltrude, wife of Count Boso in North Italy. This lady ran off with one of Boso's vassals in 856 and was ordered to return by Popes Benedict III and Nicholas I; the latter excommunicated her in 860 when she did not obey. At about this time she reached the diocese of Cologne and put her special problem to Gunthar, who consulted other bishops about it:

If the wife of Boso came to us and publicly confessed, saying, 'I am guilty, I committed adultery against my husband; and therefore, terrified by the fear of death, I fled to you, who are the vicar of God, that you might save me before God and free me from physical death, which hangs over me at the hand of my husband'; should I put a public penance on her and let her live, separated from her husband, in my parish to which she fled, or should I send her back to her husband, on the condition that he should by no means kill her, but receive her back as a wife after her penance? Because if he kills her, he should know that he will be trapped under churchly condemnation, because it is wicked for someone doing public penance to be killed by someone else.[21]

Ingiltrude's fear of being murdered by her husband if she returned to him was so strong that she apparently threatened 'that if they wanted to send her back, she would go to the Normans'.[22] This threat is an

[18] *MGH, Ep.* VIII, p. 90.

[19] In Hincmar, *De Divortio, PL* 126: 717.

[20] He had lent credence to the incest story in the first place by asserting in public that Theutberga had confessed it to him in secret. Hincmar pointed out that he was not supposed to reveal the secrets of the confessional even if true. He then controlled the council of 863 at which Nicholas' legates were supposed to judge the divorce case, allegedly suppressing dissent by force to produce a reaffirmation of Theutberga's condemnation.

[21] Letter of Hincmar in response, *MGH, Ep.* VIII, p. 82.

[22] The bishops of Lorraine relayed this threat to Hincmar, and he records it in *De Divortio, PL* 126: 754.

indication of the degree of alienation in the marriage; the Normans were not yet the Christian near-Frenchmen they would later become, but still the fierce pagan pirates and raiders who were regularly sacking the north of France and contributing to the breakdown of its public institutions. The threat of defection to them was used by several people at this time and was perhaps a convention, but one which expressed a state of extremity.[23]

The marriage of Lothar and Theutberga was already in difficulty by the time it first appears in the written sources. If Theutberga's innocence of the incest charge is assumed, which it was by everyone outside Lorraine itself and apparently should be,[24] the fact that this was the means chosen by Lothar to be rid of her argues the will to considerable cruelty on his part. With the single exception of the public ceremony in 865 in which Lothar obeyed the orders of Pope Nicholas and took Theutberga back as his wife, no scenes between the couple have been recorded, but there are hints of the rapid deterioration of their relationship in the successive declarations they made to various churchmen. Lothar, like Count Stephen, protested his trust in the judgements of the bishops of his kingdom when in 862 he pleaded that they relieve the passions which had driven him back to Waldrada after he had 'by your order' separated from Theutberga: 'What I afterwards committed either of necessity or of will because of the weakness of incontinence, it is yours opportunely and rationally to amend, and mine freely to obey.'[25] But his early expressions of obedience to their judgement depended on their complaisance in his desires. Secure in the knowledge that they would give him the order to separate that he wanted, he was able to protest that, as the 862 synod's statement summed it up, 'if she had been worthy of the nuptial bed, and were not contaminated by the deathly pollution of incest, and publicly condemned by oral confession, he would willingly have kept her.'[26] No

---

[23] Theutberga also threatened this (see note 31 below); so did Baldwin, Count of Flanders, when King Charles the Bald of France threatened to separate him from his wife, Charles' daughter Judith. We know this from a letter of Nicholas I successfully pleading for Charles's blessing on the marriage, JE 2703, Letter 7 *MGH*.

[24] Her innocence is most strongly argued by the fact that, with everything against her, she insisted on it. In a time when God's punishment for sin was a vital part of people's belief, if she had been conscious of guilt nothing would have been easier than to relieve her conscience and get away from a hateful husband by allowing herself to be relegated to a convent without a fight.

[25] His declaration at the Aachen synod, Mansi, *Sacrorum Conciliorum*, XV: 614.

[26] ibid., col. 612.

declaration survives to us by which Theutberga made known her feelings about Lothar, but her earliest known statements reveal her determination not to be driven out of the marriage on the grounds on which
Lothar had taken his stand. Nicholas I wrote in 862 that she had
'many times appealed to the apostolic see in tearful letters, in which
she stated in lamentable terms that she was pure and innocent of the
crime of which she is accused.'[27] And Nicholas later gave more details
of this appeal, showing that Theutberga was already aware that she
could expect no good from the husband whom honor demanded that
she try to keep:

Theutberga appealed again and again to the apostolic see, and said she was
unjustly deposed by the glorious king and forced by violence to accuse herself of the crime. For when she sent the statement of her appeal to the
apostolic see, not yet having confessed, she hinted that she would be forced
to commit a crime against herself, adding: 'If I am forced farther, know
that I will say what they want, not because it is true, but because I can do
no other, for fear of death and seeking to avoid it. But you will remember
that I made this known to you.'[28]

   Lothar, when it became apparent that the Church might not give
him his divorce after all, dropped the pretense that he was simply
obeying his bishops in separating from a polluted woman, and began
claiming that he had never willingly married her. One of his more
faithful bishops, Adventius of Metz, asserted in a document of 863 that
Theutberga's evil brother Hucbert had somehow bullied him into the
marriage:

In the very days when he was mourning his father, Hucbert the Headless
and his accomplices brought his sister named Theutberga to that most noble
adolescent the lord King Lothar, and associated her with him by fraud,
threatening the king with danger to his realm, and did not listen to his
protests. The king acquiesced, though, as he himself has witnessed, he did
not want to.[29]

---

[27] JE 2702, *MGH, Ep.* VI, p. 269.

[28] Nicholas's *Commonitorium* instructing his legates for his 863 council to review
the case; *MGH, Ep.* VI, p. 277.

[29] His *libellus* in favour of Lothar and Waldrada for the 863 council, *PL* 119:
1141–2. His reference to 'Hucbertus Acefala' alludes to the fact that Hucbert, the
abbot of a monastery, had been in severe trouble with the see of Rome for several
years for loose living and disrespect. It may have been his reputation which gave
Lothar the idea that the incest charge was plausible.

The situation changed when Pope Nicholas ordered Lothar to take Theutberga back as his wife and queen; Lothar had strong reasons for obeying the Pope, and did. But he still wanted to be rid of her, and he apparently treated her so badly that she agreed to plead for the divorce herself on more honorable grounds: sterility on her part, and an alleged previous marriage between Lothar and Waldrada. Nicholas' successor, Hadrian II, allowed her to come to Rome to put this case to him, and reported to Lothar; 'she said that, because of her body's infirmity and because she was not joined to you in legitimate marriage, she wanted to cease consorting with you, and leave the world's honour and glory for the love of God, submitting the head of her heart to the easy yoke of Christ.'[30] But a cry recorded by an unnamed bishop who heard Theutberga's plea evidently better expresses her true feelings in this, the last stage of her terrible marriage: 'she swore that she would rather flee among the pagans than see again the face of the glorious king Lothar.'[31] The cases presented to churchmen, then, were often of an extreme nature. Upon what premisses did they base their conclusions about them? These must now be examined.

At the heart of the Christian view of marriage in the ninth century was the assertion that it made a bond between two people which was less a partnership than an identity. Churchmen of this period quoted two Biblical texts in particular; based on these, the closest metaphor for a married couple would be, not two people chained together as in the modern cliché, but a pair of Siamese twins. The first of these passages was Jesus' saying (Matthew 19:4–6):

Have you not heard that He Who made man at the beginning made them male and female, and said, Because of this a man shall leave his father and mother and cleave to his wife, and the two shall be one flesh? Therefore they are no longer two, but one flesh. Therefore what God has joined together, let not man put asunder.

The other saying was St Paul's (I Corinthians 7:3–5):

Let the husband give her due to his wife; likewise the wife to her husband. The wife has no power over her body, but the husband. Likewise the hus-

[30] JE 2892, *MGH, Ep.* VI, p. 696.

[31] Lodovico Muratori, *Rerum Italicarum Scriptores*, vol. II, part II, p. 139. This is a record of the council held to discuss the matter. For why it was in fact a council of Hadrian II's in 868 rather than, as Muratori thinks, a council of Nicholas I in 864, see Bishop, *Pope Nicholas I*, p. 37, n. 1.

band has no power over his body, but the wife. Do not defraud each other, unless by [mutual] consent for a time for fasting and prayer; and then go back to each other, lest Satan tempt you with incontinence.

Every churchman of the ninth century who is on record as saying anything at all about marriage held that it was a mutual association of the flesh from which one partner could not draw back unilaterally. With this view in mind, it was to be expected, and was indeed the case, that almost every churchman who had to decide whether a marriage should be dissolved was very strongly inclined to perpetuate it. There was, however, another element which entered into the bishops' calculations. Possibly because it was the choice which they themselves had made, they heartily concurred in Paul's opinion on the relative values of celibacy and marriage:

I wish all people were as I am myself; but each one has his own grace from God, some one thing and some another. I say to the unmarried and to widows, it is good for them to remain as I am. But if they cannot contain, let them marry; for it is better to marry than to burn (I Corinthians 7:7-9).

That celibacy was the best way of life, and marriage was only second best, was agreed upon by churchmen from Byzantium to the Franklands. The prominent Byzantine monk, Theodore the Studite, praised his parents for their delay in consummating their marriage:

They lay in one bed for five whole years or more without knowing each other, which is extraordinary and hard to find; for how can fire lie next to rushes and not join with them, unless the event is supernatural? And if Boaz is praised for having Ruth sleeping by him untouched for one night, how much more praise must be given to both of them for temperance![32]

Abstention from sex, even for the married, was an ideal feature of penance. Both Nicholas I and Hincmar quoted Pope Leo I on this: 'According to true wisdom, nothing is more fitting for him who does penance than to persevere in chastity of mind and body.'[33] The attitude of the ninth-century church, in accord with that of most of the Middle Ages, may therefore be summed up as follows: marriage or celibacy, preferably celibacy, but if people did get married they were definitely one flesh, a unit rather than an association of two units.

---

[32] Theodore the Studite, *Oratio XIII, Laudatio Funebris in Matrem Suam*, in J. P. Migne (ed.), *Patrologia Graeca* (henceforward *PG*), vol. 99, cols. 885–8.

[33] Nicholas in JE 2787, among others; Hincmar in *De Divortio, PL* 126: 731.

Churchmen giving marital advice tried to operate by these principles, but they were, naturally, not operating in a vacuum. However much they tried to judge marital rights and wrongs by absolute Christian standards, political and emotional considerations weighed as much on them as on people of any other period. The commentaries on marriage with which they were working were so intricate and complicated that it was perfectly possible even for moral people to decide what result was wanted in a case and then to cite Biblical and patristic authorities in support.[34] And when political and emotional considerations became pressing, this is evidently what happened. It seems to have happened to the bishops of Lorraine when they gave Lothar his divorce. He was their king, and desired it. They were also very conscious that his two uncles, the kings of France and Germany, openly coveted his kingdom, and if the bishops really thought Theutberga was barren they must have deemed the legitimization of Lothar's children by Waldrada necessary for the survival of their country. They therefore acquiesced in a decision which went against the results of a trial by ordeal of Theutberga's innocence and which depended partly on Gunthar of Cologne's public revelation of what she allegedly confided to him in confession. It required the command of the pope, whom they sincerely recognized as their commander, to make them exonerate Theutberga and accept her as their queen. But even after they did this, their conduct was still partly dictated by their fear that Lothar would lose his kingdom to his uncles, this time because he was so reluctant to keep Theutberga that he was in danger of a papal anathema which would provide an excellent excuse for invasion.[35]

In the years after Nicholas' decision, they tried to convince the world that Lothar had in his initial attempts at divorce been led astray by the wicked: 'the king, at one time seduced by the changeableness

[34] Professor Robert Somerville tells of a modern case which also demonstrates this. A lawyer was handling the annulment of the marriage of a young Roman Catholic couple, and he consulted a respected canonist on the merits of the case. This canonist was a sincerely religious man and not a cynic; but his first question to the lawyer, asked perfectly seriously, was 'Now, do you want this marriage to be valid or invalid?'

[35] This, of course, was one of the main reasons Lothar obeyed Nicholas and took Theutberga back. The uncles in question were Charles the Bald and Louis the German; the bishops' fears of the former are amply demonstrated in the letter they wrote to his bishops in 866, viewing with alarm the awful rumor that Charles planned an invasion. In fact, Charles did invade Lorraine on Lothar's death in 869; Lorraine was thereafter a bone of contention between France and Germany up to our own century.

of adolescence and the astuteness of men, is now turned towards the better.'[36] One of them seems to have lied to the pope to shield his king. We have two letters of Adventius of Metz, one in 865 to Nicholas and the other in 866 to a fellow bishop who was then physically nearer the king than Adventius. In the first, he swears that Lothar has never touched Waldrada since Nicholas decided in Theutberga's favour; in the second, he implores his colleague to make Lothar stop his affair with Waldrada and be secretly absolved for it before the pope finds out and excommunicates him.[37] The Lotharingian divorce case, in fact, was a seething cauldron of extraneous motives. Nicholas himself, whose pontificate and life were devoted to establishing the papacy as the supreme power in the world, may have been moved to his vehemence against Lothar partly because Lothar ignored his right to decide his case when he formally married Waldrada just before the council Nicholas had called to settle the matter. Hincmar, for reasons too complicated to discuss here, spilled a good deal of ink explaining why his decision about Theutberga's secret confession could not be used as a precedent to challenge his own legitimacy as Archbishop of Rheims.[38] Political and personal considerations are clearest here because this is the case we know most about; they would undoubtedly be found for others if we had more information.

Ecclesiastical marital advisors are, of course, also influenced by elements peculiar to their own times. Lothar's first divorce attempt depended on the fact that, by the canon law of the day, two people who had committed incest together were thereafter forbidden to marry others (or, naturally, each other) while both lived. A man who had intercourse with two women who were related to each other was also, by the standards of the time, committing incest. Hincmar recognized that Stephen of Auvergne had done right to fear to sleep with his bride: 'The girl, though free from incest, would, if joined by coition to Stephen, have been made incestuous flesh; and Stephen, previously a fornicator, would after their joining have been incestuous,

---

[36] *MGH, Ep.* VI, p. 229, the letter mentioned in the previous note.

[37] ibid., pp. 233–5 and 232–3.

[38] To simplify greatly, Hincmar had succeeded to Rheims after his predecessor Ebbo had been deposed, largely on the basis of a secret confession he was alleged to have made. If this confession was, like Theutberga's, not admissible as evidence, Hincmar's enemies could have said Ebbo was not really deposed and therefore Hincmar was not really consecrated. The latter therefore had to argue in *De Divortio* that a churchman was judged by different standards than a laywoman.

which he was not yet, because he had slept with her relative.'[39] There was a sense among stricter churchmen that, in line with celibacy being desirable for penitents, an act of adultery should put an end to sexual relations within marriage. Photius, Patriarch of Constantinople, addressed a problem put to him by the Archbishop of Calabria: whether the wives of priests and deacons, captured by the 'barbarians' (presumably Arab pirates) and violated before being returned, could be fully taken back as wives. Photius carefully distinguished among three classes of women: those who had willingly slept with their abductors, those who had yielded to them 'mixing compulsion with consent', and those who had really been raped against their wills. The third class could return to their husbands, but the first two had to separate from them, and any husband of one of these who wanted her back had to give up his priesthood or diaconate.[40] This was a question of married people in holy orders, who were already restricted more severely than the laity (in the Latin part of the Church, sexual relations between a cleric and his wife were by this time prohibited from the subdiaconate up)[41] but laymen also incurred restrictions even within monogamous marriage. The ninth century in Byzantium began with a split among churchmen over whether to tolerate the Emperor Constantine VI's third marriage, to which the objection partly was that he had divorced his second wife without cause; it ended with a split among churchmen over whether to tolerate the Emperor Leo VI's fourth marriage, which that extraordinarily unlucky husband had felt impelled to make because his first three wives in rapid succession died without leaving him an heir. Multiple marriages were then frowned upon even if the prospective spouse's credentials were impeccable as a widow or widower.

In some areas, notably the Franklands, witchcraft was believed to be a factor affecting marriage. Hincmar's suffragan bishop who was confronted by the desperate, impotent husband inquired closely into his life, and concluded that he had been bewitched by devilish arts, so that 'to sleep with a former concubine for pleasure was possible, and with his legally chosen wife impossible'.[42] The bishop put an end to

[39] *MGH, Ep.* VIII, p. 95.

[40] *Letters of Photius*, Book I, *PG* 102: 777. He added that it would be desirable if even the third class of women did not go back to their husbands, to avoid even the appearance of wrongdoing.

[41] See Michel Andrieu, *Les Ordines Romani au Haut Moyen Age* (Louvain, 1943), vol. IV, pp. 140–7.

[42] *PL* 126: 717.

this situation by 'penance and churchly medicine' and reconciled the husband and wife, who lived happily ever after and had many children; the solution had, as Hincmar's modern biographer observes, some psychiatric validity, but it was given because the supernatural explanation was believed in. Supernatural forces were also accepted as valid in the case of Lothar and Theutberga. She, when first accused of incest, demanded a trial by ordeal to prove her innocence; it was held, and a champion who undertook to immerse himself in boiling water on her behalf came out unharmed. The bishops of Lorraine, who were then eager to get her convicted and divorced and were letting themselves believe in the evidence Lothar had procured of her guilt, professed their bewilderment at this result:

> Can it be true, as some say, that by the secret confession this woman made, as he who received it is witness, her substitute in the judgement escaped uncooked? But they also say that this woman thought of another name than that of her brother, when she sent her substitute into the judgement, and that is why in that judgement he was not cooked.[43]

Hincarm sternly refuted these attempts to evade the obvious and insisted on what, given the premiss, was the basic fact. The ordeal, he argued at great length, was an efficacious way of letting God show the truth; God's judgement could not be manipulated; and therefore, once Theutberga's champion had passed the test, her innocence was established.[44]

Indeed, given all the premisses discussed above – the sacramental view of marriage, the lesser supernatural forces which could enter into it, the primary importance of God's will – the ninth-century churchmen who inquired into marital rights and wrongs did so in a very sensible manner. Nicholas I, sending a fact-finding team to Lorraine in the early days before he decided the case, gave it instructions which are a model of sound practical and, by his lights, moral sense:

> First, inquire by diligent investigation, and if you find that the glorious king took Waldrada with prearranged dowries before witnesses according to law and ritual, as marriages are usually celebrated, and that she is admitted by public manifestations to be his wife, it remains for you to find out why she was repudiated and [Theutberga] admitted. But because the same glorious king says he took Theutberga through fear, you must remind him of the

[43] ibid., col. 659.
[44] His argument in ibid. 659–73.

Gospel, where the Lord says 'Do not fear those who kill the body,' and again, 'What shall it profit a man, if he gains the whole world and loses his soul?' . . . But if it is not proved that Waldrada is his legitimate wife . . . advise him not to react badly to being reconciled with his legitimate wife, if she is innocent.[45]

Both Nicholas and Hincmar picked just the right holes in the exceedingly flimsy story Lothar was trying to tell. 'We must add,' said Hincmar, after his explicit refutation of the idea that Theutberga could have come to Lothar as a virgin after conceiving by sodomy and aborting, 'that if the king found this woman to be a virgin, why did he agree to have her branded as having been defiled? But if he did not find her a virgin, why did he keep her for so long, and why did he accept the judgement of the trial?'[46] And Nicholas spotted Lothar's weak point when he answered a hypothetical question that obviously referred to the case:

We do not consent that divorce be made between those who are joined in the bonds of legitimate marriage and are made one flesh for any length of time. But if, when he first joined with her, finding her corrupted he voluntarily kept silent, and then kept her, even if not voluntarily, for a period of time, he shall keep her unwillingly, and abstain entirely from concubines.[47]

This was a case which needed all the common sense it could get. In a simpler one, Hincmar laid down a sensible rule of procedure, which shows that these bishops were not ignorant of some of the perversities of lay conduct. Noting Stephen of Auvergne's claim that he had left his bride untouched, he added that it was necessary to find out 'if the girl said the same thing as Stephen put forth; because we have often heard that, between men and women, what one says, the other denies.'[48]

Many pieces of ecclesiastical advice on marriage were affected by a mixture of a bias in favour of celibacy and a pragmatic recognition of human frailty. A number of concessions are on record in which churchmen allow people who were, by their standards, barely eligible for marriage to marry rather than burn. Hincmar's opinion about Stephen of Auvergne was that 'because he showed reverence for God,

45 *MGH*, *Ep*. VI, p. 277.
46 *PL* 126: 695.
47 JE 2697, *MGH*, *Ep*. VI, pp. 618–19.

and did not add incest to fornication, he should accept regular penance from his own bishop, who knows the canons . . . and after his
absolution, if he cannot contain . . . he should seek to join with a
legitimate wife, lest he fall again into the crime of fornication.'[49] It is
an indication of the ninth-century predilection for abstinence that
Nicholas I received many penitents whose local clerics had forbidden
them sex as part of their expiation; it is an indication of the recognition
of human weakness that Nicholas usually remitted this part of their
penance and allowed them to marry or continue their marital relations,
lest, in his words, they fall into the vortext of fornication.[50] In 862, the
bishops of Lorraine cited 'It is better to marry than to burn' as authority for the divorced Lothar to marry Waldrada. In general, marriage
was tolerated rather than eagerly advocated; as Hincmar quoted
Pope Leo I, 'We do not set up a rule, but estimate what is tolerable.'[51]
But, while yearning for the ideal, they accepted the real, as in this
decision of Nicholas's about partners in incest:

How much should those who voluntarily join and irrationally mingle be
subject to a fitting penance after they are separated, and yearn not for other
nuptials, but for chastity of mind and body from then on! But if one of the
partners in this unhappy mixing dies after the dissolution of the bond, and
the other who survives is still in adolescent years . . . if he complains that he
cannot contain, the remedy of marriage may be applied to him.[52]

Once people had married, the Biblical idea that they were almost
literally one flesh compelled churchmen to do everything they could
to maintain the bond. In cases that seem to be exceptions, it is clear
that the bishops involved thought that the association in question was
not a true marriage. Stephen of Auvergne and his virgin bride were
dismissed to marry others because a marriage whose consummation
would render two unrelated people incestuous was obviously invalid.
Sometimes there were conflicting views on the subject, especially with
regard to the transition to a strong ideal of monogamy in the Franklands. Hincmar excommunicated a man in the 850s for marrying after
his concubine or common-law wife went into a convent; he was taking
the semi-formal *Friedelehe* between the two as a true marriage and con-

[48] *MGH, Ep.* VIII, p. 91.
[49] ibid., pp. 105–6.
[50] As, for instance, JE 2849, 2852 and 2841.
[51] *PL* 126: 731.
[52] JE 2841, *MGH, Ep.* VI, p. 642.

demning the man's second marriage as bigamy. Pope Leo IV removed the excommunication; he was refusing to recognize this half-wedded state peculiar to the Franklands as more than simple fornication, after which a man, though reprehensible, could marry.[53] But despite stricter or looser definitions of marriage, it was universally agreed that the only acceptable alternatives were monogamy or nothing. The marital advisors of this period, therefore, went to extraordinary lengths to save every marriage they could, even in the most desperate cases of mutual loathing that were brought to them.

The most desperate of these was, of course, the case of Lothar and Theutberga. The mounting urgency of their pleas to separate has been noted. But even at the very end, when Theutberga was in Rome telling Hadrian II that she would rather defect to the Normans than see Lothar again, Hadrian was capable of writing a disingenuous letter to Lothar, as if the subject had never before arisen:

We were perturbed with no slight stupor, that she asked to separate from you for such causes, when it is written that the Lord said 'The wife is joined to the husband by God,' and again, 'Whom God has joined let not man separate.' Therefore, no matter how much your will may assent and give permission to her many supplications, we will in no way give our consent to this desire of hers.[54]

Hadrian was willing to hold a council on the issue of whether Lothar had been previously married to Waldrada when he took Theutberga, but he meanwhile instructed him to take the latter back and treat her as a loving wife. In this he was following his predecessor, who had gone very far indeed to see this marriage reconstituted. Nicholas I was determined not just that Theutberga should be vindicated, but that Lothar should take her back as his wife in every legal and emotional sense. In 865, when the latter capitulated to his decision, Nicholas sent a legate to lead Theutberga back to him; this man oversaw a ceremony in which she was formally reinstituted as Queen of Lorraine and twelve of Lothar's chief noblemen swore that he would treat her well from then on. And the bishops of Lorraine, obeying their pope, interested themselves in the carrying out of his orders to an extent which might have been painfully embarrassing to the couple even if they had loved each other. Adventius of Metz reported back to Nicholas:

[53] Known from a letter of Leo reproving Hincmar; *MGH, Ep.* V, p. 603.
[54] JE 2892, *MGH, Ep.* VI, p. 696.

Therefore Queen Theutberga, in the presence of our ruler, was seen to be treated as a king ought to treat a queen who is joined to him; namely that they were companions with equal honour at the divine office, and he likewise had her eating with him at the royal table, and, as rumour hints, he undertook joyfully [*hilariter*] to discharge his conjugal duty.[55]

Monogamy, then, was a basic principle of the bishops' advice, and one which was perhaps less tempered by recognition of human wants than the commitment to celibacy. But what did they advise when the enforcement of monogamy brought with it the real prospect of harm to one of the partners? It was the case in two of the known situations that the wife suffered from a genuine apprehension that her husband meant to kill her. Ingiltrude, as noted above, knew herself guilty of adultery and, either for that reason or because she knew her husband (we have no evidence as to his personality) feared that he would kill her if she returned to him. And Theutberga feared Lothar's intentions almost from the first record we have of her actions. In the early 860s, after she was pressured into a statement of guilt at a synod, she fled and took refuge with her brother; when she was brought back to Lothar in 865, fear of what he might do evidently played a part in her starting to plead with the pope for a divorce. Nicholas I, by the end of 866, was being informed that Lothar meant to kill her or else to get her reconvicted in a trial by single combat and executed.[56] Here, then, insistence on the union of husband and wife was put to a severe test.

In general, the bishops kept the principle intact. It is true that Gunthar of Cologne sheltered Ingiltrude in this diocese, apparently retaining the power to protect her even after Nicholas had deposed him as Archbishop.[57] It is also true that Hadrian II, though he told Lothar and Theutberga that they could not separate, then implicitly contradicted his own words by giving her permission to stop at a convent on the journey back to Lorraine 'to rest'; this tacit compromise resulted in a permanent *de facto* separation.[58] But these were exceptions;

[55] *MGH, Ep.* VI, p. 235.

[56] He relays the rumor to Charles the Bald in a letter of early 867: JE 2872, letter 48, *MGH*. Nicholas' ideas about trial by ordeal or combat were different from Hincmar's, and he condemns 'monomachiam' as unscriptural.

[57] It would be interesting to know what he himself made of the dichotomy between this conduct and his role in the persecution of Theutberga, towards whom he was at best the revealer of the secrets of her confessional and at worst the false accuser whose lies brought her ten years of misery.

[58] JE 2892, *MGH, Ep.* VI, p. 696, just after telling Lothar the separation could not take place.

Gunthar was defying public opinion and Hadrian was 'estimating what was tolerable' rather than setting up a rule. All other churchmen we know of insisted on Ingiltrude's return to Boso. Popes Benedict III and Nicholas I demanded it in synods, and Nicholas and John VIII in letters.[59] The bishops of Lorraine, after an initial period of acquiescing in Gunthar's policy, abandoned him to follow the pope after his synod of 863; Adventius of Metz wrote to Nicholas that 'since I heard the true report that [Ingiltrude] was wounded by an infamous act of adultery, I have avoided her like a death-bearing poison.'[60] And Hincmar of Rheims responded to Gunthar's proposal that Ingiltrude be absolved at a distance from Boso with a typical exposition of the sacramental view of a couple's identity in marriage. 'If you impose penance on this woman, who is part of the body of a man of another diocese, you go against ecclesiastical rules . . . And how can you judge a part of the body, that is of a man of another bishop and parish, without condemning him to penitential judgement?'[61] And as for Theutberga, Nicholas I continued and enforced upon others the papal policy of leaving her with her husband even after hearing the rumors of her danger; he refused to let her come to Rome to put her new case for the divorce to him because 'while Theutberga was going away [from Lothar], Waldrada would be fast approaching.'[62] Even a marriage bond which could bring mental or physical harm to one partner made the couple one flesh and must be maintained.

But not at all costs. No bishop who insisted on the union of people who physically endangered each other had any notion of tolerating the wife's maltreatment. Their inflexibility was in all cases based on their expectation that the Church could control the behavior of the husband. Nicholas had apparently made sure that Boso would neither kill nor maltreat Ingiltrude before he demanded her return, and had worked out a procedure to safeguard her. Hincmar had confidence in this procedure, and thus for him Ingiltrude's fears were not a relevant issue. The only point that really mattered was that Gunthar was defying the commands of the pope:

[59] The papal letters announcing this are JE 2673 (Benedict's), JE 2684, 2685, 2747, 2750 and 2874 (Nicholas'); and John VIII's letter of 872–3 reaffirming the anathema on her (*MGH, Ep.* VII).

[60] *MGH, Ep.* VI, p. 221.

[61] *MGH, Ep.* VIII, p. 83.

[62] JE 2873, *MGH, Ep.* VI, p. 323.

As Boso himself says . . . for the lord Pope and by his order he is prepared to forgive her; it remains for the king in whose kingdom he lives to bring her to her husband's presence . . . It is for you, the bishop in whose parish she is staying – because this is not the king's role – to ask . . . if there is the necessity, and obtain, security for her fair treatment by her husband, and after this the envoy of the republic will restore the wife who sinned by flight to her husband. And if the husband breaks his oath, and shows himself disobedient to the apostolic commands, the bishop to whose care he belongs will do canonical justice on him.[63]

Even Ingiltrude apparently had a moment of confidence in Nicholas' ability to protect her, for she met his legate in 865 and swore to follow him to Rome for the necessary penance and restoration. But she changed her mind and fled again on the way, and died without returning to Boso.[64] But the preparations made for her reception show that the bishops who were fighting for it were not naive. They did not expect this couple to be reconciled without trouble simply because they were one flesh; they had a clear idea of what might happen, and took steps to guard against it.

The same is shown by Nicholas' reaction to the rumors of Lothar's plans to cause the death of Theutberga. He called upon Lothar's uncles to oppose these plans, a shrewd political move considering that it was largely the fear of invasion by these uncles that was keeping Lothar in line; and he made it very clear in letters to both Lothar and Theutberga in 867 that no method the former could use would avail to get him out of this marriage and into the one he desired.[65] Lothar was doing no good for himself even by the milder course of pressuring his wife into the divorce:

Who is unaware that Theutberga has said these things against herself subjected to many pressures, and worn down by numberless ills, and indeed in fear of the danger of death, which she has often escaped only by God's protection? As we have said before, all the religious and noble men of Gaul

---

[63] *MGH, Ep.* VIII, p. 83.

[64] Nicholas' legate's only extant letter tells of this (Arsenius of Orta, in *MGH, Ep.* VI); Regino of Prum gives what purport to be the actual words of her oath in his *Chronicon, MGH, SS*, vol. I, pp. 573–4.

[65] JE 2870 and 2873, *MGH* Letters 45 and 46. He was extremely forthright in both. He informed them that, in his words to Theutberga, 'though you assert that you think you will always be sterile, this is brought about not by your body's infertility, but by your husband's iniquity.' He also called Lothar a packhorse wallowing in his own dung.

and Germany are witnesses to this; and she, who now writes, has fore-warned us of it many times by previous writings. But we will never receive this confession, which not will but violence has extorted, as a true confession. But whoever acts against Theutberga not only gravely harms the church of God, but also brings the apostolic see, whose judgements cannot be retracted, to move vehemently against him.

And if he thought of killing her, he would be no better off, which gave Lothar a good reason not just to spare her but actively to preserve her:

We think and feel that it is just and fair that, even if Theutberga were dead, you would not ever be able or permitted by any law or rule to take Waldrada as your wife. Therefore, if Waldrada should ever become your legitimate wife, the church of God would not fail to exact retribution for Theutberga. But we know one thing, that neither we nor the same holy church, made by God Who will judge adulterers, will let you go in any way unpunished if you ever go back to Waldrada, even if Theutberga dies.[66]

Having taken these steps, Nicholas was evidently sure Theutberga was safe. He wrote to her, 'We do not believe that Lothar, your husband, will stray into such wickedness as to consent in any way to plot against your life, since, if he falls into such a monstrous crime, he and his kingdom will suffer all the disasters no less than you.'[67] It is likely that Hadrian II, who neither was nor wished to be a man of Nicholas' firmness of command, allowed the separation in practice without admitting its legitimacy in theory because he was less certain than Nicholas of his ability to protect the injured woman.

The advice given by ninth-century churchmen to troubled couples thus far amounts to a preference for celibacy, a recognition that some people none the less have physical needs which call for marriage, and a determination that every marriage which is a true marriage be saved even if that calls for great efforts on the Church's part to protect one member of the couple from the other. But all of these things could have existed if the Christian tradition had never contained the slightest whisper of inequality between men and women. The view of marriage that led to the emphasis on monogamy stressed mutuality and reciprocal obligations; the main practical reason why husband and wife could not separate was that each had needs and desires which only the

---

[66] JE 2873, *MGH, Ep.* VI, p. 323.
[67] JE 2870, *MGH, Ep.* VI, p. 321.

other could legitimately satisfy.[68] And the Biblical texts most used in the ninth century to back marital advice were those two quoted above which implied a symmetrical reciprocal relationship. The Epistles of Paul, however, were authority not only for mutuality but to a large extent for inequality, for the subjection of the woman. 'Wives, submit to your own husbands as to the Lord,' wrote Paul (Ephesians 5:22–3), 'for the husband is the head of the wife, just as Christ is the head of the church.' This metaphor fits in with the description of husband and wife as one flesh, specifying more exactly which part of the flesh is which; it also makes the husband very much the superior. How did our advisors apply this part of the tradition when discussing the specific rights and duties of men and women in marriage? Were wives in fact told to submit to their husbands, and given fewer rights than the latter?

From some of the passages relevant to this inquiry, it might appear that this was the case. The husband's headship was certainly an issue to the churchmen under discussion. It often led to some peculiar flights of metaphor. 'How,' Hincmar asked Gunthar in the case of Ingiltrude, 'can the inferior part of the body of this man, who lives under another's [pastoral] care, separate and be held under penance? . . . If you put penance on her, and then she, the member, follows her head (for the husband is the head of the wife) into another province, how can she take penance from another bishop?'[69] Theodore the Studite, frowning like a good Byzantine citizen on second marriages, asserted that neither partner could be crowned in the Greek marriage rite even if only one had been married before: 'For if it is the man, the man is the head of the woman, and they are both in one body; shall the rest of the body participate and the head not?'[70] Pope John VIII, writing in 878, limited the rights of wives when he reproved some noblemen of Germany for holding lands given to them by Ingiltrude: 'She gave them after the judgement on her without the consent of her husband, which is wicked and against the authority of all law. For what can a wife do without the consent of her husband?'[71] And there

[68] Liutprand of Cremona, in his *Antapodosis*, a chronicle of events mainly in Italy in the mid-tenth century, tells (Book IV, c. 10) of a woman whose husband was captured by an enemy nobleman in the south of Italy. She successfully protested her husband's proposed castration on the grounds that his body belonged to her and she had done nothing to merit confiscation of her property.

[69] *MGH, Ep.* VIII, pp. 82–3.

[70] Theodore, *Letters*, Book I, *PG* 99: 1096.

[71] JE 3211, *MGH, Ep.* VII, p. 103.

was one ninth-century attempt to use the Pauline tradition to give husbands greater privileges than wives. This was the 862 synod which granted Lothar the right to marry Waldrada, and one of the ways the bishops backed this decision was to quote Ambrose of Milan's commentary on Paul. Paul had said that a woman who left her husband even for good reason had either to remain unmarried or to return to him, and Ambrose had claimed that the reverse was not the case:

But he does not come under what is said about a wife: 'If she leaves, let her remain so;' for a man is permitted to take another wife, if he dismisses a wife who sins. For the same law does not bind the man as binds the woman. For the man is the head of the woman.[72]

But these were the exceptions. The Synod of 862 was repudiated the following year even by its participants, and the cause for which the husband's superior privilege had been invoked was recognized as hopelessly tainted. John VIII took away nothing concrete from Ingiltrude, since he was writing after her death; and his argument was being made on behalf of two women, her daughters, to whom he wished the noblemen holding her lands to turn them over. Apart, therefore, from the loss of the ritual crowning for the virgin bride of a Byzantine widower, no known evocation of the husband's headship circumscribed the options of any known individual wife. And when Hincmar envisioned an inequality in male and female roles in marriage, it was to give the husband greater duties rather than greater rights. This is seen in his treatise on the divorce, in a passage which puts another nail in Lothar's coffin by asserting that a husband should not divorce even an adulterous wife.

But those husbands, who, as we have shown, are held by the same law and judgement before God as wives are, if they commit adultery, and are condemned to a graver penalty inasmuch as they are the heads and guides of the women, the weaker sex and the vessel of infirmity, should not presume to condemn their adulterous wives without judgement . . . Should there not be a greater and richer and fuller [goodness] between husband and wife, between man and spouse, between head and body? For, as the Apostle teaches, the husband is the head of the wife . . . Let a Christian man consider with how much care and consideration and advice from doctors, if a hand, or foot, or genital organ, or any other part of his body starts to putrefy,

[72] Quoted twice in the synod minutes: Mansi, *Sacrorum Conciliorum*, XV, cols. 613 and 616.

or be eaten by cancer, he will either care for it that it may be cured, or cut it off if it cannot be cured, and he should do the same for the part – also of his body – that is his wife.[73]

In fact, whatever may have been the theoretical opinion of ninth-century churchmen as to man's headship and woman's subjection in marriage, the situations and the specific cases which confronted them were such as to call for an insistence upon the equality of the couple. In correspondence with or within the Franklands, where a double standard of sexual conduct had been until that very age quasi-officially sanctioned, bishops affirmed equal and reciprocal obligations for men and women in marriage. Hincmar used – perhaps misused – Paul in his argument that even if Theutberga were guilty of incest, Lothar had committed adultery by associating with Waldrada after he had married her:

The Apostle says a wife is bound by her husband's law while her husband lives, but when he is dead she is freed from her husband's law. And, by sacred authority, no one can doubt that one is a wife who is legally betrothed, dowered and honored with public nuptials. But the same sacred authority testifies that there is one law in this for husband and wife.[74]

He also began his long discussion on whether Lothar could remarry if he divorced Theutberga (the answer was only after her death, which seemed to obviate the point of the divorce) by asserting 'that there is one law for men and women'.[75] Nicholas I was also careful to specify equality; when, in the passage already quoted, he decreed that the surviving partner of an incestuous couple could marry if he could not contain, he added, 'Which form of indulgence we also wish to be observed for women'.[76] Indeed, Nicholas at one point casually threw out quite a sweeping statement about sexual equality in general. He was telling a newly converted people that both widows and widowers could remarry, and he used as his authority Paul's statement that widows were free to marry again:

What therefore he sanctions for a woman is also to be understood for a man; because, on the other hand, Holy Scripture often speaks of a man when it is no less to be understood of a woman. So, indeed, it says 'Blessed is the man

[73] *PL* 126: 656–7.
[74] ibid., col. 708.
[75] ibid., col. 732.
[76] JE 2841, *MGH, Ep.* VI, p. 642.

who does not walk in the counsel of the ungodly,' and 'Blessed is the man who fears the Lord;' and we firmly believe that not only the man, but the woman, who does not walk in the counsel of the ungodly, and who fears the Lord, is blessed.[77]

Sometimes they went farther. A wife's obedience to her husband was a virtue enjoined by the Pauline Epistles and praised in Church tradition. But when it came to individual cases, it proved – in this period as in others – to be a virtue of very limited scope. It was, in fact, completely ignored or dismissed if it conflicted with any other virtues the churchmen under examination were trying to promote. If a married woman's husband was, by their lights, doing evil or even just impeding good, she was not only allowed but positively encouraged to take an independent path. The most striking example of this even verges on the irresponsible. Theodore the Studite was consulted by a friend of his, a woman whose husband was a high official in the Byzantine government, about her desire to become a nun. Hincmar and Nicholas would have said – they did say to Theutberga – that she could only do this if her husband became a monk at the same time. Theodore knew the texts as well as they did, and started his advice by quoting a patristic authority on obligations in marriage. It was always hard, he said, to enter the religious life:

. . . especially because you are joined to a husband, so that God has linked you together. Who then shall unjoin you, except He Who joined you, in order to bring you to a better commonwealth? For, according to the ordinance of St Basil, you must first look well to what pertains to your husband.

So far, quite conventional. But Theodore then veered off in an original direction:

What is this? To lay bare to him your thoughts about your wish; to show him how empty and dreamlike is the world, and how nothing in it is stable . . . and besides, that there will be an inexorable judgement on those who live passionately in the present life, and not by the precepts of Christ, which are hard to follow in ordinary life. Say these things, urge him, gentle him, so as to persuade him to seize with you the goal of separation; for it says, 'How do you know, wife, if you will save your husband?' And if he goes

---

[77] JE 2812, Letter 99 *MGH*, c. 3. This is his famous *Response to the Consultations of the Bulgars.*

with you, you have no problem; but if not, and if desire for God possesses you so greatly, do what you contemplate doing, even if your spouse is unwilling.[78]

Theodore was an enthusiastic proponent of monastic life and a resister of authority in other areas.[79] But he was not the only one to advise a wife to be her husband's guide or opponent. Nicholas I praised Theodora, widow of the last Byzantine Emperor to support the Icono-clast heresy, for having defied her husband over icons and reversed his policies as regent for their son, the current Emperor Michael III. 'You, seeing that your husband the Emperor was going against the laws of the church, did not fear to witness to health and defend the right. You, I say, persevering in orthodox religion, taught your only son to follow the path not of his father on earth, but of the [Father] above the heavens.'[80] Nicholas was referring to events of a quarter of a century before, but he was perfectly capable, had Theodora's hus-band still been living, of urging her to go against him. He was at this time, in 866, conducting a violent quarrel with the Patriarch of Con-stantinople, and wanted Michael III to abandon his support of the latter; and one of the ways he tried to achieve this was by enlisting Michael's wife Eudocia in the struggle. What he said to Eudocia was expecially interesting because it gave a view of the story of Eve which was a contrast to the better-known part of Christian tradition. Eve, who in the Biblical story precipitates the Fall of Man, was to many Christian writers the paradigm of woman as morally inferior to man, a negative influence on Adam and the cause of evil in the world.[81] Nicholas, however, pointed out Eve's undoubted influence upon Adam's conduct, and implied that such influence of wife on husband – even Eve's – was proper and good. Claiming with a certain amount of hyperbole that the presence of Photius as Patriarch was harming

[78] Letter to the Protospatharia Albenica, *PG* 99: 1261.

[79] He led the resistance to the third marriage of Constantine VI (which marriage so damaged Constantine in public opinion that his mother Irene was able to depose him in 797) and later coordinated the resistance to the Emperors of the second period of Iconoclasm in the 810s and 820s.

[80] JE 2817, *MGH, Ep.* VI, p. 547.

[81] St. Augustine, who appears to have been an exception to the Christian tradi-tion of misogynists who had important friends who were women, gave it as his opinion that God could not have formed Eve for any purpose other than procrea-tion; since a woman was incapable of being a satisfactory friend or companion to a man, she was useless as any other kind of partner.

the world as much as had the Fall of Man, he called upon Eudocia to be an Eve who would save the day:

Christ our God did not vainly make Your Nobility partner in your husband's empire, nor put you in it except to aid His church, watch over its state, help its servants, console the grieving, raise up the oppressed and broken, bring back the expelled and exiled, and with pristine strength remake all that is confused, corrupt, disordered and destroyed; and also so that, like a strong heroine and outstanding helper, you should aid your husband in the innumerable things he must do and decide, holding out the hand of assistance lest he should fall, amidst so many vicissitudes, from the peak of justice. Thus the Lord, at the beginning of the creation of human beings, gave the first-made man a woman to help him, lest the man, being solitary, devoid of counsel, should fall into the depths and rise therefrom only with difficulty.[82]

Nicholas I made one other striking statement on the subject of wifely obedience. If any ninth-century bishop had had a predilection for exalting such obedience into an independent virtue, the case of Lothar and Theutberga would have given him scope to do it. Theutberga was, in fact, obeying her husband when after 865 she pleaded with the pope to let her out of her marriage; she needed all the comfort she could get, and a churchman of different principles might have provided that comfort by acknowledging that she was not responsible for what her husband made her do and therefore dismissing her as an actor in the case and concentrating on swaying Lothar. But Nicholas, in his response to her plea, treated her as one with equal responsibility for achieving the right. Her capitulation to Lothar's wishes was in no way justified by the fact that he was her husband and therefore to be obeyed. Nicholas, in fact, presented Lothar to her in exactly the same terms in which he saw him himself: an enemy to be resisted. With perhaps some concession to human weakness, Nicholas undercut the effect of his main advice by ending it with the statement, already quoted, that he did not believe Lothar would kill her; but the central passage of his letter to Theutberga did no less than invite her to resist even to martyrdom for the sake of other women:

We exhort and vehemently urge you not to put forth your hand against yourself, or kindle the fire of death. It is better for you that another should kill you for speaking truth, than that you should destroy yourself by telling

[82] JE 2818, *MGH*, *Ep.* VI, p. 549. The entire passage comparing Eudocia to Biblical heroines lasts from p. 549 to p. 552.

lies. Remain, therefore, intrepid and steadfast, and above all do not fear to undergo death, which you must experience some day, for the truth. For, since Christ is the Truth, whoever dies for the truth undoubtedly dies for Christ, as John the Baptist, being killed, is known to have been a martyr. And if he was killed while talking of his neighbor's justice, how much less do you need to fear death, talking of God's justice and witnessing to your own truth! . . . We do not accept this confession of yours, which not will but violence extorted; nor will we permit the roots of so much vice to grow, which, unless they are rooted up, will grow to so many evils. For if this is permitted, every husband whose wife has been acquitted by law, if he hates her, will be able to break her with many afflictions, and force from her what is not legitimately offered; or even force her, by inflicting intolerable tortures on her, to confess some mortal crime against herself. For who can do more harm than a domestic enemy? and who can cause greater suffering than a husband to a wife?[83]

Certainly Nicholas in this passage is not making things easy for Theutberga. By modern standards he is inflexible, giving her no way to comfort except through one form or another of martyrdom. But one thing must be admitted: he is treating her with respect for her integrity. He is not patronizing her as a weaker vessel, like Hincmar in his passage on adulterous wives; he is not hinting at any obligation on her part to be subject to her husband, or excusing her compromise with Lothar on the grounds of wifely obedience. He is calling upon her to treat her husband as the enemy he is, and to do exactly what he is known to have done himself: to resist the enemy for the sake of God and of other sufferers.[84] Nicholas I is not speaking to Theutberga, wife of Lothar, as to a lesser limb of a body, whose God-given role is circumscribed and subservient. He is speaking to her as one human being to another.

The ninth century was not radically different from other Christian centuries in the quality of marital advice given by its churchmen to its married people. To a great extent, its value to us simply lies in the fact that the accident of good sources for a few picturesque cases gives us the opportunity to examine the period as an example of how the basic Christian tradition shaped spiritual advice on marriage in general.

[83] JE 2870, *MGH, Ep.* VI, p. 321.

[84] Lothar's brother, the Carolingian Emperor Louis II, invaded Rome in 864 to force Nicholas to revoke his measures against Gunthar of Cologne and the divorce synod. Nicholas led a passive resistance against him which caused Louis to leave without achieving his purpose.

Thus, for instance, the sacramental view of husband and wife as one flesh inevitably meant that the basic goal was to save every marriage, even at the cost, as in the Lotharingian divorce case, of ruining three lives and the independence of a kingdom.

But the Christian centuries do differ in emphasis, and it is this that determines the distinctive flavor of a period. With regard to the two issues which have mainly preoccupied us here, monogamy and wifely obedience or subordination, there are marked differences in emphasis in different periods. The church of the late Roman Empire, with its disgust at the prevalence of sexual temptation in society, gave us the basic pronouncements about the evil and subordinate nature of sexually active women. The seventeenth century, with its emphasis on hierarchy, gave us a housewife–saint, one of whose deeds of heroic virtue was to break off her prayers repeatedly to attend to the trivial wants of her husband. The fourteenth century gave us the awful tale of patient Griselda, whose husband decided to test her wifely obedience, and who meekly and lovingly approved him while he convinced her (falsely) that he had had their children killed, drove her out of his house in nothing but her shift, and called her back as a servant to prepare the house for his pretended new bride.[85] From the cases which have been preserved, we can conclude that ninth-century churchmen had definite predilections on the two issues: they strongly emphasized monogamy, and they had very little commitment to the idea of wifely obedience. The rigid emphasis on monogamy probably stemmed from the fact that in the ninth century it was more than usually imperiled: in the Franklands by the weight of old custom which bishops were struggling to change, and in Byzantium by the needs or whims of Emperors. And as for the attitude of voluntary celibates towards married women, it is notable that in this era neither disgust at feminine corruption nor admiration of wifely subordination *per se* is known to have entered into the calculations of any ecclesiastical marital advisor. There was, it is true, some discussion of husbandly headship, but it seemed to imply responsibility rather than privilege. But women

---

[85] In fairness to the fourteenth century, of course, it must be noted that even the people who told this story were unable to accept it. Boccaccio, in the *Decameron*, depicted the husband's vassals as saying he had gone too far. Petrarch wept copiously at the story and declared that no human being should act so, but made a version of it so that people would know how to act when God – not husbands – sent afflictions. Chaucer, in the *Canterbury Tales*, not only echoed Petrarch's disclaimers but wrote at some length that the proper conduct of wives was really the opposite: they should bully their husbands into submission. Public opinion is not monolithic in any age.

who were resisting actual or potential wrongdoing by their husbands, and who consulted churchmen about it, found not lectures about their duty of womanly deference to their husbands' wills but encouragement in their fights. The basic Christian tradition left some room to maneuver; the ninth-century tendency was to maneuver it in the direction of an egalitarian and reciprocal view of marriage. There have been times in the Christian era (the late Roman Empire was one) when churchmen who had themselves forsaken sexual life let their disgust at its continuation in others stand in the way of justice. But in the ninth century, in which so many of the major issues among celibate clerics had to do with sex and marriage, this was apparently not so. Despite their own predilections, they were able to see past the inevitable sexual component of married women, and treat the individual wives they counselled as human beings.

4

S. Salvatore/S. Giulia: A Case Study in the Endowment and Patronage of a Major Female Monastery in Northern Italy

SUZANNE F. WEMPLE

Without question, one of the most prominent and powerful female monasteries in medieval Italy was that of S. Salvatore, or S. Giulia, in Brescia.[1] Founded in the mid-eighth century, it enjoyed a continuous existence of more than a thousand years, disappearing only in 1797 in the wake of the Napoleonic conquest. Under royal Lombard and then Carolingian imperial patronage, it was able to amass landed and other holdings of considerable size, making it an important

---

[1] Angelica Baitelli, *Annali istorici dell'edificazione, erezione e dotazione del serenissimo monastero di S. Salvatore e S. Giulia di Brescia* (Brescia, 1794). Andrea Valentini, *Codice necrologico-liturgico del monastero de S. Salvatore o S. Giulia in Brescia* (Brescia, 1887). Karl Voigt, *Die königlichen Eigenklöster im Langobardenreiche* (Neudruck der Ausgabe Gotha, 1909; Aalen, 1969). A more modern version of the story is found in *Storia di Brescia*, ed. G. Treccani degli Alfieri, vol. 1 (Brescia, 1963); see especially articles by Gian Piero Bognetti, 'La Brescia dei Goti e Langobardi', pp. 395–446; 'Brescia Carolingia', pp. 449–83; and Girolamo Arnaldi, 'Da Berengario agli Ottoni', pp. 485–517. The *Inventari altomedievali di terre, coloni e reddite* (Istituto Storico Italiano per il Medio Evo, Fonti per la Storia d'Italia, 104, Roma, 1979), includes Gianfranco Pasquali, 'S. Giulia di Brescia', that is the 'Breviaria de curtibus monasterii'. *San Salvatore di Brescia*, 2 vols. (Brescia, 1978), which includes pictures of the monastery and its parts, is a catalog for museums.

The monastery was initially known as S. Michele and S. Petrus (*Historiae Patriae Monumenta*, 13; *Codex Diplomaticus Langobardiae* (Torino, 1873), pp. 36–7, n. 18) (henceforward *HPM* 13); it was also called S. Maria, once the convent had acquired land and a church of that name in Alfiano sometimes before 772 (*HPM* 13, pp. 38–40, n. 19, also 41, n. 1). The royal Lombard founders, however, usually referred to it as S. Salvatore (*HPM* 13, pp. 36–7, n. 18). Finally, in the tenth century, probably under Berengar I in 905 or 906, it came to be called S. Giulia, and henceforth bore the name S. Salvatore or S. Giulia (*HPM* 13, pp. 706–7, n. 419).

economic force in Lombardy during the first five centuries of its history. Curiously, however, S. Salvatore/S. Giulia has attracted less scholarly attention than its prominence and long duration might lead one to expect. In this brief essay, drawing on the body of charters which have survived, I hope to shed some light on the formation and development of the monastery's considerable holdings during the first five centuries of its history.

The monastery was established sometime before January 757 by Ansa, Queen of the Lombards, and was richly endowed by her husband Desiderius and son Adelchis, Kings of Lombardy. Organized according to the rule of St Benedict, it was to be a community of 40 nuns with an elected abbess.[2] The prominent role intended for the monastery from the very beginning was reflected in the fact that its first abbess was the daughter of Ansa and Desiderius, Princess Anselberga. In several histories Ansa is listed as the actual founder of S. Salvatore, and Desiderius and Adelchis as donors.[3] The land on which the monastery was built belonged to Ansa's father, Verissimo, and her two brothers, Arichis the clerk and Donnolo. In constructing the monastery, she was able to honor the entire family. It is reported, for example, that her father and her brothers were buried in the monastery, which was the highest order of recognition accorded to anyone at this time.[4]

When establishing the monastery, the king and queen granted it the curia of Cerpent, today referred to as Serpent, with its laborers and their families, buildings, animals and all movable and immovable property.[5] Together with their son Adelchis, they further endowed the monastery with 'sacred vases and mantles, all things that pertain to the ministry of the altar, . . . gold, silver, bronze, iron, wood and earthen vessels.'[6] The monastery likewise received houses and fishing places on the river Oglio, with lands, vineyards, meadows, pasture, and with the free and servile population living there and some land with livestock near Brescia or along the river Po. A hospital and a

---

[2] *HPM* 13, pp. 40–3, n. 20.

[3] Voigt, *Die königlichen Eigenkloster*, p. 24.

[4] *HPM* 13, pp. 59–62, n. 31, see especially p. 59, n. 1.

[5] *HPM* 13, pp. 36–7, n. 18: 'Cum edificiis, cum bovibus et bubulcis, et operariis cum animalibus utriusque sexus simul cum familiis . . . et omnibus mobilibus et immobilis rebus in integrum . . .'.

[6] *HPM* 13, p. 41, n. 20: 'sacra vasa et pallia, et omnia que ad altaris monasterium pertinent, nec non aurum, argentum, eramenta, ferramenta, lignea, et fictilia omnia . . .'.

basilica in Pavia were also placed under its jurisdiction. The king and queen later added the monastery of S. Maria in Pavia to S. Salvatore's possessions.[7]

Anselberga, the first abbess, played an active role in the beautification of the new community, and the development of its holdings. For example, she commissioned new iron doors for the monastery's church, which not only served a decorative role, but also helped to ensure the security of the jeweled objects her family had donated to the monastery.[8] More important, perhaps, were her economic activities. She planned and constructed a canal system to provide water for the fountains in the convent, acquiring in the process, water rights from several sources.[9] She was undoubtedly a good manager of property; she was effective, for example, in exchanging goods which she had in Lodi for property in Alfiano with the abbess Pelagia of the monastery in Lodi and her sister Natalia and her husband Alechis. She traded lands with Alanus, Abbot of S. Maria in Sabino,[10] as well as with Andrea of Sermione;[11] she bought property from Rotari, Abbot of Monticelli,[12] from Natalia, daughter of the groom Gisulf and Adelberta,[13] and from Stavile, a resident of Brescia. Duke Johannes sold her over 200 acres in Modenese.[14] The Riatorto, a large piece of land near Modena, was obtained from Iobian and his eight fellow fishermen.[15] In all these transactions, Anselberga was treated with respect and confidence.

Her mother, Ansa, also continued to play an important role in expanding the endowment of the monastery. She was responsible, for example, for major properties being willed to S. Salvatore. When Cunimond of Sermione killed one of her husband's military aides, the penalty would normally have been the forfeiture of Cunimond's land. However, Ansa persuaded the king to permit Cunimond to continue to enjoy his holdings, and to will them to the monastery at his death.[16]

---

[7] *HPM* 13, pp. 80-1, n. 42, dated July 771. The document also confirms possession the monastery received from King Adelchis.

[8] *HPM* 13, pp. 43-7, n. 21-3.

[9] *HPM* 13, pp. 48-51, n. 25.

[10] *HPM* 13, pp. 68-9, n. 35.

[11] *HPM* 13, pp. 81-5, n. 43.

[12] *HPM* 13, pp. 69-70, n. 36.

[13] *HPM* 13, pp. 70-2, n. 37.

[14] *HPM* 13, pp. 88-9, n. 46.

[15] *HPM* 13, pp. 64-5, n. 33.

[16] *HPM* 13, pp. 54-5, n. 27.

Cunimond was so grateful to Ansa that he immediately gave some of his property to the church of Sermio, which was already a possession of S. Salvatore.

It is reported that in October 762, the monastery obtained a papal privilege from Paul I, issued at the request of Queen Ansa. In it, the pope prohibited 'any priest of whatsoever church or bishop of whatsoever ministry of spiritual dignity to assume any authority over the aforementioned monastery without invitation from the abbess.' According to the papal order, the abbess and the clerks could be consecrated by the bishop of any city that the abbess chose. Finally, he also granted the abbess license to obtain from any bishop of apostolic standing the chrism for baptism and the oil to perform the divine rites.[17] However, some historians doubt the authenticity of this papal decretal,[18] since it is found with the alleged decree of Sigoaldus, patriarch of Aquileia, which is now believed to have been forged in the early years of the tenth century. We will return to this matter later.[19]

The royal family was the source of by far the largest grants to the monastery. In addition to everything already noted, it is recorded that on 14 June 772, Desiderius gave the monastery two mills located in Brescia,[20] and Desiderius and Aldechis together granted it 4,000 acres of land in the diocese of Capri.[21] All donations to the monastery were confirmed in decrees issued by the kings.[22] Thus, for example, on 24 August 772, Adelchis granted the monastery a charter affirming its possession of the church of S. Maria in Vado Alfiano in the Cremonese.[23] More significantly, on 11 November 773, he issued a con-

[17] *HPM* 13, pp. 52–3, n. 26.

[18] The privilege was suspected by Gius. Brunati, *Leggendario e vita di santi Bresciane* (Brescia, 1834); and Frederico Odorici, *Storie Bresciane* I–IX (Brescia, 1853–65). They are followed by Philip Jaffé (ed.), *Regesta Pontificum Romanorum*, ed. sec. S. Loewenfeldt, K. Kaltenbrunner, P. Ewald (2 vols, Leipzig, 1885–8) Jaffé, 1809; JE 2350. Paul F. Kehr, *Italia Pontificia* (Berlin, 1905–25), vol. 6/1, p. 322, thought it genuine.

[19] *HPM* 13, pp. 90–2, n. 48. The editor, Giulio Porro Lambertenghi, believed it was genuine. But he did not think so of Pope Paul's decretal. In this same document, Adelchis decreed that if a serf of the monastery married an *arimanna*, that is a free woman, he must remain with his wife on the territory of the monastery. Their children would become *aldii* and would be given 6 *soldi* as a sign of their status. Such an order went against the Code of Rothari that punished every serf who married a free woman with the loss of his head.

[20] *HPM* 13, pp. 62–4, n. 32.

[21] *HPM* 13, pp. 86–7, n. 45.

[22] *HPM* 13, pp. 80–1, n. 47.

[23] *HPM* 13, pp. 89–90, n. 47.

firmation of all the gifts to the monastery from his parents. At that time, he affirmed in particular that the following monasteries were subject to the authority of S. Salvatore: Pavia, Sermione, a place called Monte within the limits of Sorianense, S. Cassian in Bologna, Pistoia, Sestuno, S. Vito in Reatina, Intride within the limits of Balbense and S. Liveratore within the limits of Benevento. He also affirmed the possession of some settled lands and fisheries further south in Spoleto, Picino and Abruzzo.[24]

Aldelchis's decree was issued shortly before Charlemagne's invasion of Italy, which resulted in his conquest of Lombardy and the capture and dethronement of King Desiderius in June 774. It is not clear whether Queen Ansa accompanied her husband into captivity in France or joined her daughter Anselberga at her monastery in Brescia. Another daughter Desiderata (or Ermengarta) clearly retired to the monastery after being repudiated by Charlemagne. (The other daughters were safely married, at least for the moment, Adelperga to Arichiso, Duke of Benevento, and Liutperga to Tassilo, Duke of Bavaria.) Her son Adelchis took refuge in Byzantium, where he died shortly afterwards. King Desiderius died in France, and Ansa's life probably ended at Brescia.[25] In Paul the Deacon's funeral inscription for Ansa, he alludes to Anselperga as well:

> Quin etiam aeterno mansit sua portio regi
> Virgineo splendore micans, his dedita templis.[26]

Despite its lovely rhymes, the poem was not to cover the tomb of Ansa. She was not buried at Pavia where the verse was found on a burial tablet. It seems clear, then, that in the time of Ansa, the royal and ecclesiastical powers were working together in the interests of the

[24] *HPM* 13, pp. 93–7, n. 50.
[25] This is the story told in Baitelli, *Annali*, p. 44. For the other three daughters, see *HPM* 13, p. 60, n. 1. However the *HPM* 5, p. 1494, has a different story. Desiderius was transported to Vienne with Ansa and their son and daughters. He returned to Italy before his death and was buried at Vesutanum, in S. Margarite, but his body was stolen and carried to Pavia. This story is tardy, having been composed in 1275. The almost contemporary Frankish account has him proceed with his wife to France; *Annales Alamann, Nazar*, with wife; *Annales Laurissenses Min.*, 7, with wife and daughter; *Annales Lobienses* 744, with wife and children (*MGH, SS* I, 40, 118; II 195).
[26] Paul the Deacon, 'Super sepulcrum Domnae Ansae reginae', 1. 15–16, ed. E. Dümmler, *MGH, Poet.* I, 45–6.

monastery. In the Carolingian period, the situation changed drastic-
ally when a bitter struggle arose as to who should rule the monastery.

Around 781, a document was issued by Charlemagne in his capacity
of King of the Franks and Lombards and Patrician of the Romans
regarding S. Salvatore. He reiterated the judicial immunity of the
monastery, forbidding all bishops, abbots, dukes, counts, officials and
the rest of the faithful to allow a public judge to hear cases, prepare
lodgings or thoroughfares, extract wardships, acknowledge sureties or
require public restitution without having been asked to do so by the
abbess.[27] This charter was later confirmed by Louis the Pious, upon
the request of his wife, Judith, who held the possessions of the monastery as a benefice.[28]

S. Salvatore provides an interesting case study of imperial patronage
of a monastery in the early Carolingian period. The phenomenal
growth of S. Salvatore was largely due to gifts from the dynasty.
Accompanying the royal donations were steps to bring these substantial lands under the control of the family. Judith, the wife of Louis the
Pious, became the official 'owner' of the monastery. Likewise, the wife
of the next emperor, Ermengard (Ermingart) was appointed *rectrix*
of S. Salvatore. She was in turn succeeded by her daughter, Gisla.
However, throughout the evolution of the position of *rectrix*, the
monastery, with one exception, continued to have an abbess as well.
In 833, Emperor Lothar issued a decree in favor of Abbess Amalberga
granting free judgement in the monastery's territory and making provision for the appointment of two abbots as guarantors to assure that
this right was observed.[29] We know that Amalberga was abbess during
the time when Ermengard was assigned the monastery, as well as after
her death when Gisla came to occupy the office of *rectrix* on 16 March
848.[30] Amalberga was still in office three years later on 8 September
851 at the time that Lothar and Louis II issued a confirmation of this
charter, prohibiting all successors from interfering with Gisla's right
of usufruct of all the cells of the monastery.[31]

---

[27] *HPM* 13, pp. 110–11, n. 58. The document was probably issued in 781. The
editor of this volume doubts that it is genuine. He follows L. A. Muratori, *Antiquitates
Italicae Medii Aevi*, 17 vols. (Arretii, 1773–80), vol. 3, p. 85. Girolamo Tiraboschi,
on the other hand, thought it was genuine, *Memorie Storiche Modensi col Codice
Diplomatico Illustrato con Note* (5 vols, Modena, 1793–5), vol. I. *Codex Diplomaticus*,
p. 5. See note 37 below on the abbesses.

[28] *HPM* 13, pp. 188–9, n. 103.

[29] *HPM* 13, pp. 231–2, n. 130.

[30] *HPM* 13, p. 283, n. 166.

[31] *HPM* 13, pp. 294–5, n. 173.

Louis II issued three charters in favor of Amalberga. One of these referred to the property of Ermealdo, a relative of Amalberga,[32] and the others dealt with the privileges and goods to be held by Gisla or Amalberga,[33] the mistress and abbess, respectively of the monastery. One document granted Amalberga the right to sell whatever she wished without payment of tolls.[34] There were also three charters dealing with Gisla: two gave her the right to the monastery's possessions; one was issued in 858, the other on 13 January 861.[35] The last charter, which was dated after the death of Gisla, on 12 January 862, asked the community to pray perpetually for her soul and in recognition of this service, gave the monastery some courts and a fishery.[36]

Gisla's prominence in the monastery of Brescia reflected her royal position (sister of Emperor Louis II and daughter of Emperor Lothar) and consequently her power to exert personal control. Benedict of Aniani had initiated a strong religious movement among monasteries in the ninth century, and more and more houses adopted the Benedictine Rule. Cloistered nuns gave up individual possessions. The initial plan of Louis the Pious was to appoint a female governor, a *rectrix*, at Brescia who would manage the monastery's income as she saw fit, leaving the nuns only what was necessary for their needs. The theory was that this would then free the abbess from unnecessary worldly burdens, so that she could give her full attention to the details of administering monastic life. As might be expected, Amalberga had no time for contesting this diversion of the monastery's income. Immediately following Amalberga's death in 861,[37] Gisla was elected abbess.[38] But Gisla herself died the following year (January 862), and although a new abbess was not elected until 879, the office of *rectrix* was filled promptly by Engelberga (Angilberga) the wife of Emperor Louis II.[39] With Engelberga as mistress (*rectrix*), one wonders whether the income of the monastery was altogether secure in her hands.

[32] *HPM* 13, pp. 324–5, n. 193.

[33] *HPM* 13, pp. 326–7, n. 195.

[34] *HPM* 13, p. 348, n. 211.

[35] *HPM* 13, pp. 325, 348–9, n. 194–212.

[36] *HPM* 13, pp. 368–9, n. 220.

[37] Amalberga was the fourth abbess of the monastery. Anselperga was followed by Radoara and by Eremberga; see Valentini, *Codice*, p. 252.

[38] On the whole subject of Gisla, see Valentini, *Codice*, pp. 253–4.

[39] Ermengard became abbess in 879; she was the sixth abbess of S. Salvatore, see Valentini, *Codice*, p. 254, and *HPM* 13, pp. 471–2, n. 279.

Further evidence of the tensions that were building up with regard to lay interference in the monastery can be evidenced in a decretal of Pope John VIII to Charles the Bold. Issued in 877, it ordered the king to return everything to S. Salvatore taken by Engelberga, his dead half-brother's wife. If Charles failed to comply, he would be excommunicated and regarded as a plunderer of the Church.[40] The other Carolingian charters that have survived are more innocuous. In 879, Carlomann, King of Italy, repeated Charlemagne's guarantee of judicial exemption for the monastery and ceded some additional curias to Abbess Ermengard.[41] In another decree, Charles the Fat ceded territory in Verona to the monastery and confirmed its exemption from public justice.[42] This was done at the behest of Engelberga in 886. With the election of Ermengard, the pope and the emperor came to an agreement concerning Engelberga's superiority at S. Salvatore. She could dominate the monastery, but was unable to alienate its property. In fact, she augmented it whenever she could, as in the case of Verona, possession of which she was able to obtain from the emperor.

These arrangements were continued by Berengar I, King of North Italy, who conceded a small dwelling place in Bescia to the monastery in 889.[43] Berengar of Friuli's reign initiated the age of castles in Italy. His claim to the throne came through his mother, daughter of Louis the Pious and Judith of Bavaria. This would have been enough in the days when the last Carolingian, an illegitimate child, ruled Germany. But Berengar lacked abilities as a strong monarch or an effective administrator. In the first place, he recognized King Arnulf of Germany as the ultimate ruler of Germany. Then, early in 889, he was defeated at the battle of Trebbia by Guido of Spoleto, who was then proclaimed King of Italy by the magnates of Pavia. Cremona was left in Berengar's hands; it was there that he issued his meager gift to S. Salvatore. He disappeared for three years then, and emerged only when Zventibald and his father, Arnulf, went to war with Guido. Fortunately for Berengar, Guido died a few months later and Arnulf became paralyzed, so that rule of northern Italy was shared by Berengar and Lambert, Guido's son. In 898, when Lambert died,

---

[40] Kehr, *Italia Pontificia*, 6/1, p. 322, n. 2.

[41] *HPM* 13, pp. 477–8, n. 283. Not to be confused with Ermengard, the queen, who died in 862.

[42] *HPM* 13, pp. 506–7, n. 298.

[43] *HPM* 13, pp. 574–5, n. 344.

Berengar reunited the kingdom and achieved control over it until his death in 921.[44]

The last 25 years of his rule were preoccupied with the incursions of the Magyars into Italy, and he built new castles and fortified old ones to protect northern Italy. As a part of this program, he issued two decrees in 915 and 916 to his daughter Berta, who by this time had become abbess. First he gave her the right to burn the surroundings of the monastery and to erect whatever was necessary.[45] Then he allowed her to construct a castle with towers, ramparts, trenches and walls in Sclavaria over the river Ticino. Those who resisted her had to pay 100 gold libra, half of it going to the monastic and the other half to the royal treasury.[46] Through these two decrees Berengar enabled his daughter to raise fortifications to ensure her safety from the Magyars. He called the monastery S. Guilia and from this time on it was known as S. Giulia or S. Salvatore.

It was probably in the time of Berengar that a charter, purporting to have been issued by Sigoaldus, patriarch of Aquileia, a contemporary of Desiderius, was drawn up, which is now believed by some to be a forgery. It reiterated the decretal of Pope Paul I but in it Sigoaldus called himself 'servus servorum Dei' and stated that only a priest invited by the abbess could celebrate mass and preach strict observance of the Rule to the nuns. Moreover, the abbess was prevented from selling codices, sacred vessels and any other treasures of the church.[47] The latter clause reflects the continuing Magyar threat, which had so disrupted the economy that the abbess needed to alienate church property to relieve financial pressures. In view of the many treasures that are evidenced in the inventory of the monastery,

[44] Arnaldi, 'Da Berengario', pp. 497–9, and Pio Paschini, 'Le vicende politiche e religiose del Friuli nei secoli nono e decimo di Pio Paschini', *Nuovo Archivio Veneto*, n.s. XI (1911), pp. 61–73.

[45] *HPM* 13, pp. 788–99, n. 456.

[46] *HPM* 13, pp. 809–10, n. 467.

[47] *HPM* 13, pp. 91, n. 48: 'ita ut nisi ab abbatissa monasterii fuerit invitatus, nec missarum ibidem solemnitate quispiam presumet omnimodo celebrare, ut libere liceat sororibus ibidem degentibus regularem normulam inviolabiliter observare ... Nec ... abbatissa ... concedatur codices aut vasa sacrata aut quolibet thesaurum ecclesiae quoquomodo donare aut alienare.' On the authenticity, see p. 90, n. 1, and note 19 above. I accept Arnaldi's argument, 'Da Berengario', p. 506, that it dates from the tenth century. The papal decretal issued by Paul I was found with the decree of Sigoaldus. This does not make Paul's decretal a forgery. See *HMP* 13, pp. 90–2.

it was imperative that S. Salvatore/S. Giulia guarded against transference.[48]

The 'Sigoaldus grant' also dealt with the election of the abbess, repeating what is found in the diplomas issued by Emperors Lothar I and Louis II concerning the free choice of superior within the community.[49] The election of Berengar's daughter, Berta, to the office of abbess raises some interesting questions regarding the issue. Unfortunately, we do not know whether she was a member of the S. Salvatore community before her election. If she was, the charter would simply be confirming this right. If not, then the charter was apparently disregarded. In any case, Berengar also gave Berta the government of S. Sisto of Piacenza, making her as powerful as Engelberga, who likewise had controlled both S. Salvatore and S. Sisto. Berengar had intended his daughter to be as important as the 'consors regni' of Louis II.[50] However, Berta was only the abbess. The title *rectrix* was abandoned with the Carolingians.

It was probably under Berengar, around 905 or 906, that a document was drawn up listing the monastery's properties. The inventory was taken early in the tenth century and it certainly cannot be assigned a time before 879. Damaged by weather and misuse, it has some sections missing. Nevertheless, it does indicate how many people belonged to the 69 curias that are included. The number of prebendary serfs (*praebendarii infra curtem*) is relatively low: 788 men, women and children. The 41 children listed is an underestimated figure; only five curia counted children. In addition, for four curias majors and minors were included. Thus, only for nine curias can we be certain that the children were calculated in the total. In addition, there were 566 *coloni*, 223 serfs, 65 *livellarii*, 121 recommended free men, 20 women in the *gynaeceum*, 20 *aldii*, 67 men whose profession is indicated but status is omitted, 16 whose status is confused, and 136 absent cultivators, bringing the total to 1,234 people. If we add to this list the 788

---

[48] Pasquali, 'S. Giulia di Brescia', p. 93, describes the possessions of the monastery of Sextuna, a locality not identified but probably in Rieti. The monastery had not only precious vases but also several books. Although not as rich as this, in other churches we also find some vessels and missals.

[49] *HPM* 13, p. 91, n. 48: 'non aliunde sed ex eadem congregatione religiosissimae monachae in loco defunctae abbatissae eligant succesorem.' On Emperor Lothar's order, see *HPM* 13, pp. 231–2; on Louis II's decree, see *HPM* 13, pp. 326–7, n. 130, 195.

[50] Arnaldi, 'Da Berengario', pp. 506–8.

praebendarii, we get a total of 2,022.[51] It is unfortunate that we do not know whether the children of all these people were listed. If we assume that the children of the *praebendarii* were listed and of the other workers were not, we end up with approximately 3,250 dependent on the monastery.[52] The data are indeed very limited but sufficient to conclude that the operation was of significant proportions.

Some of the curia produced industrial goods: ploughshares, axes, forks[53] and the iron from which they were made; also rustic cloth,[54] wool[55] and silk.[56] The mention of the eight masters who worked on the walls[57] and the serfs who cut the stone[58] certainly illustrates the scope of the handiwork. The books which were produced in the monastery's *scriptorium* – missals, Gospels, the letters of St Paul, the psalter and various patristic codices, of which usually three or four were present in the chapels[59] – and the sacred vessels, the linen coverings for the

---

[51] Pasquali, 'S. Giulia di Brescia', pp. 52–94; *HPM* 13, pp. 706–27, n. 419. The *HPM* version indicates that on the back is written: 'Inter maiores et minores CIX manentes, inter commendatis et libellariis, aldiones et servos sunt numero MCCCC. Sancti Marini curtem inter maiores et minores XLI, inter manentes et absentes MDCCCLXXXVIII.' The Pasquali version does not have this inscription.

[52] G. Luzzato, *I servi nelle grandi proprietà ecclesiatiche italiane de sec. IX e X* (Pisa, 1910), p. 28, assigns on the average five people per peasant family. I feel that this is somewhat exaggerated, and on the basis of the available figures, I can estimate only 2.5 surviving children per family.

[53] *HPM* 13, n. 419, 706 (Griliano), 708 (Bogonago-Borgonata in the municipality of Corte Franca, Brescia), 711 (Audalvico: perhaps Odolo, Brescia), 712 (Casivico: a place east of Corzano), 714 (Mariano-Mairano, Brescia), 715 (Wassaningus: perhaps Siniga, a place in the municipality of Pisogne, Brescia), 716 (Valcamoniga: curte in Bradellas-Valcamonica, perhaps in Pian Camuno, Brescia). Pasquali, 'S. Giulia di Brescia', pp. 54, 56, 63–4, 69, 71–2.

[54] *HPM* 13, n. 419, 709 (Iseo); Pasquali, 'S. Giulia di Brescia', p. 59; *pannos rusticos*.

[55] *HPM* 13, n. 419, 713 (Nuvoleras); Pasquali, 'S. Giulia di Brescia', p. 66.

[56] *HPM* 13, n. 419, 726 (Chama: probably Como); Pasquali, 'S. Giulia di Brescia', p. 92.

[57] *HPM* 13, n. 419, 720; Pasquali, 'S. Giulia di Brescia', p. 81.

[58] *HPM* 13, n. 419, 710; Pasquali, 'S. Giulia di Brescia', p. 61.

[59] See for example Timoline; Porzano; Castegnato; Tontolfi, a locality not identified perhaps in the vicinity of Goito (Mantova); Marcaria (Mantova); Rivaloro Mantovano; Mantevado, not identified perhaps in the Low Mantovano; Piscilesso, a place in Calvatone (Cremona); Castiglione delle Stiviere (Mantova); Rivalta, not identified; Alfianello; Cigognara, a fraction of Viadana (Mantova); S. Marco, not identified but we know that it was near Bazzano (Bologna); Piacenza; Cinctura, perhaps Centora, a fraction of Rottofreno (Piacenza); S. Pietro Viminario; Kebaharti, either Cellatica (Brescia) or near Alfiano; Sextuna, not identified

altars, and bells that were to be found in the chapels[60] demonstrate the seriousness of the effort. The boats the monastery kept on the various rivers, including military vessels,[61] the harbors it maintained,[62] and the fisheries it exploited also testify to its varied pursuits.[63]

In an enterprise of this magnitude, one might expect a variety of transactions. Abbess Berta in September 916 donated one small curia to Tuetbert and his heirs with the stipulation that each time a mass was said for St Martin, the monastery was to receive from Teutbert and his heirs ten silver *denarii*. If they did not wish to continue to pay this sum, they could terminate the contract by rendering 100 *solidi*.[64] Some transactions were continued throughout the tenth century. For example, Abbess Ata on 4 February 961, under the reign of Berengar II and his son Adelbert, exchanged a small piece of land.[65] Another abbess, likewise called Berta, commuted arable acreage in August 966 with Dominicus, priest of Verona,[66] in 978 with Anonis, son of Norbert,[67] and in 1000 with John, son of Martin.[68] Thus the monastery in the tenth century did not receive significant holdings but engaged in exchanges of land.

The time of uncertainties was by now over and Italy was entering a period of growth. In 997, Emperor Otto III confirmed all the goods, rights and churches in the possession of the monastery of S. Salvatore/ S. Giulia, also called the New Monastery since the days of Louis the Pious. Specifically, Otto III assured the Abbess Berta that he would safeguard:

---

but surely placed in Antrodoco (Rieti); see Pasquali, 'S. Giulia di Brescia', pp. 54, 62, 65, 73–4, 76–81, 84, 86, 89, 92–3. On Sextuna, see also note 48 above; on Tontolfi, see note 60 below.

[60] Pasquali, 'S. Giulia di Brescia', p. 73; in the case of Tontolfi chapel, the following items were in her possession: 'cum altarios III, cu(m) pallias lineas vi, coporturii III, evangeliu(m) I, ebtaticu(m) I, epistulas Pauli, calices stangneos II, patenas II, turibulum ereu(m) I, campana I'; this was a fairly modest chapel.

[61] Pasquali, 'S. Giulia di Brescia', pp. 78, 80–1, 84; *HPM* 13, n. 419, 719–20, 722.

[62] Pasquali, 'S. Giulia di Brescia', pp. 78, 81, 84, 89, 92; *HPM* 13, n. 419, 719–20, 722, 725–6.

[63] Pasquali, 'S. Giulia di Brescia', pp. 61, 75, 80, 84, 86; *HPM* 13, n. 419, 710, 717, 720, 722–3.

[64] *HPM* 13, pp. 812–13, n. 469.

[65] *HPM* 13, pp. 1107–8, n. 643.

[66] *HPM* 13, pp. 1210–12, n. 696.

[67] *HPM* 13, p. 1381, n. 786.

[68] *HPM* 13, pp. 1737–8, n. 987.

... serfs and handmaidens, castles, churches, half free men and women, curias, forests, meadows, pastures, streams running through them, fisheries, mills, clearings with cells and hospices, the monastery that they call Alina, Campora Sextuno, the monastery in Lucca that was built by Duke Allo, the port of Piacensa, Saint Benedict's hospital in Monto Lungo, and the monastery in Sermione.[69]

He also guaranteed that no man, regardless of his stature, should disturb any worker without the permission of the abbess. And that nobody, whether he be 'a duke, archbishop, bishop, marquis, count, vicecount, a judge, or administrator may divest, upset, nor molest, without legal judgement, the abbesses who were ordained at the time.'

During the eleventh century the monastery obtained gifts and confirmations of its possessions from emperors and popes. The first decree was issued in 1014 to the Abbess Rolinda by Henry II and it granted her all the goods that belonged to the monastery and ceded the curia of Grontardo to it, which had previously pertained to Praterio Dalfiano. It also confirmed that no one should disturb the workers of the monastery, unless instructed to do so by the abbess or her faithful delegates, and the abbess herself should not be disturbed under any circumstances. Those who disregarded this order were to pay 1,000 gold pieces, half of it to the emperor and half to the abbess.[70] In 1046, at the request of his archbishop Hermin, Henry III issued a document to the Abbess Otta which stated that all the inhabitants of Castelnouvo, located on Monto Retino in the vicinity of Girda, were exempted from any tax collection. They all were free and immune and should be grateful for this to the monastery.[71] Two years later, in 1048, Abbess Otta obtained confirmation of all rights the monastery enjoyed,[72] and in 1085 Henry IV also verified the proceedings.[73]

A crucial decretal was issued by Nicholas II on 5 (6) May 1060. A very broad, comprehensive document, it stipulated that:

---

[69] *HPM* 13, pp. 1624–5, n. 924. See especially: '. . . cum servis et ancillis, castris, capellis, aldionibus et aldiabus, cortibus, silvis, pratis, pascuis, aquis earumque decursibus, piscationibus, molendinis, stalareis cum cellis et senodochiis, et monasterio quod dicitur Alina, et Campora Sextuno, et monasterio in Luca, quod aedificavit Allo dux, et portu placentino, et hospitali sancti Benedicti in Monte lungo, et monasterio sito in Sermione.'

[70] Baitelli, *Annali*, pp. 61–2.

[71] ibid., p. 63.

[72] ibid., pp. 63–4.

[73] ibid., pp. 67–8.

... priests and other men living in the monastery and inhabiting land belonging to it should not have the highest jurisdiction, power, authority, rule or order above regal power; it confirmed detention of serfs and free men and also tithes and possession of the earliest harvests, as was granted to Ansa by King Desiderius and conceded by the kings and emperors and was corroborated by the pontiffs of the Sacred Roman Church; it confirmed the courts listing them by name; it conceded that the abbess should have the power to build castles and churches wherever she wished in the lands belonging to the monastery; it conceded chrism etc. to be freely dispensed by whatever Catholic bishops as Anselperga, the first abbess, obtained from Paul of Blessed Memory; it advised that wherever the abbess wished to hold or build a market in places of the monastery, no one should contradict her and no one should dare to trespass into the monastery's fisheries.[74]

The decretal was reiterated the same month, with the added stipulation of the free election of the abbess after the reigning one died.[75]

Securing the monastery's rights became ever more important as the investiture controversy influenced attitudes toward women. This occurred during the beginning of the communal period when town governments were capitalizing on the ecclesiastical privileges acquired in previous centuries. The initial legislation concerning the prerogatives of the monastery was promulgated in 1106 when Pope Pascal II issued a decretal to Abbess Ermengard. It specified that 'bishops had no authority in the monastery and it forbade the saying of public masses except with the agreement of the abbess.' It also repeated the points stated in the two previous confirmations.[76] The decretal of Pope Calixtus II to Abbess Ermengard in 1123 contained

---

[74] Kehr, *Italia Pontificia*, 6/1, p. 322, n. 3; 'quorumlibet sacerdotum et omnium hominum in monasterio vel in illius pertinentiis habitantium quamlibet iurisdictionem vel potestatem sive auctoritatem aut ordinationem praeter regiae potestatis culmen habere; confirmat districtum servorum et liberorum et decimas et primitias, vesicut per Ansam reginam a Desiderio rege et regibus et imperatoribus ibidem concessum et a SRE pontificibus corroboratum habetur; confirmat curtes nominatim illustratas; concedit, ut abbatissa habeat potestatem faciendi castella et ecclesias ubicumque voluerit in terris ad monasterium pertinentibus; concedit chrisma etc. a quibuscumque Catholicis praesulibus gratis tribuenda, sicut Aselperga prima abbatissa a Paulo b. m. obtinuit; praecipit, ut ubicumque abbatissa voluerit mercatum constituere vel aedificare in locis ipsius monasterii, nullus ei contradicere praesumat et nullus piscarias monasterii invadere audeat.'

[75] ibid., p. 323, n. 4.

[76] ibid., p. 323, n. 6: 'nec episcoporum quemquam in monasterio ditionem aliquam habere permittit et missas publicas praeter abbatissae voluntatem illic agere prohibet.'

the crucial proviso that the monastery 'was under the protection of the apostolic see and placed under royal defense; it could not be set under any other legal authority.'[77] Pope Innocent II in writing to Abbess Constantina merely repeated Pope Calixtus' decretal in 1133, and Pope Eugenius III in a communication to Abbess Richelda in 1148 followed suit.[78] The imperial office under Lothar II issued a reiteration of the order of 1136 also stating that for the challenging of her claims at the port of Piacenza she was to receive 150 silver pieces.[79]

Breaches of the monastery's jurisdiction occurred nevertheless. The first breach concerned the dispute over the church of Cicognaria between Abbess Richelda of S. Giulia in Brescia and Bishop Obertus of Cremona. Although Pope Eugenius III submitted the case to Alberio, Bishop of Regino, in 1145–52, on 9 June 1152 in Segni, he pronounced his own view that the monastery had jurisdiction over the church according to the privilege submitted by Pope Paul and Innocent II.[80] Pope Alexander III, sometime between 1171 and 1181, confirmed that the monastery of S. Giulia owned the possessions in Cremona that Pope Eugenius III had previously spoken in favor of.[81]

The second dispute was more complicated. It concerned the ownership of the port of Piacenza. The case was opened with the official sentence of Pope Anastasius IV that the Abbess Richelda was the owner of the port on the river Po against the claims of Hugh Speronus and his partners.[82] Hugh, however, was apparently not willing to relinquish his control and it took four decretals, published between 1154 and 1159, of Pope Hadrian IV to deal with the matter. One was directed to the archdeacon of Piacenza excommunicating Hugh and his partners unless they removed a bridge that was blocking the port within 40 days. In the next decretal Peter, Bishop of Pavia, was charged with hearing the case. Then Hugh and his associates were chastized and forced to comply with the sentence of Pope Anastasius. The final decretal was directed to the Bishop of Piacenza and ordered Hugh and his partners to remove a ship that impeded river traffic and to destroy the bridge. If they failed to observe the sentence in 20 days,

[77] ibid., p. 324, n. 7: 'ut mon. b. Iuliae sub apost. sedis protectione et regia defensione submissum nullius umquam alterius iurisdictionibus submittatur . . .'

[78] ibid., pp. 324–5, n. 8 and 11. The decretal of Innocent II issued on 1 May 1133 is a forgery, see ibid., p. 324, n. 9.

[79] Baitelli, *Annali*, pp. 73–4.

[80] Kehr, *Italia Pontificia*, 6/1, p. 325, n. 13–14.

[81] ibid., pp. 327–8, n. 26.

[82] ibid., pp. 325–6, n. 15.

they would be anathematized and the consuls of Piacenza were to desist from refusing to carry out the order.[83]

The case of the Piacenza port, however, continued. The war between Frederick I and the papacy prolonged the affair. Alexander III issued four decretals between 1173 and 1181 to settle the case. First, he transferred the dispute over the port, the bridge and the district to the court of the Archbishop of Milan, Caldinus. The name of the defendant by this time had changed from Hugh Speronus to the commune of Piacenza. Alexander III also sent a decretal to Piacenza declaring that the abbess had right to her claim. The next decretal referred to the order of Emperor Frederick I, concerning the port of Piacenza that he left in the hands of the abbess for 20 silver pieces. On the basis of this order Alexander III asserted that the monastery had paid the full price to the emperor. In 1180 he committed the case to be heard by two churchmen, Peter, *praepositus* of San Antoninus, and Rudolph of Concensius.[84] The definitive order came in Verona on 17 August 1184 when Lucius III gave the Abbess Gatia the corroboration of the orders of Calixtus II, Innocent II and Eugenius III, with the ruling that the port, with the river, the free and servile inhabitants living on its territory belonged with the tithe and the rights to the monastery.[85]

In the meantime the abbess reclaimed the Rioltorti church land in the valley of Galinaria that was allegedly being unjustly held by various individuals. She did the same with some 550 acres of property in Reduto that was held by Albertus, monk of San Silvester of Nonantula.[86] Despite these gains, we know that in 1188 she lost to Sicardus, Bishop of Cremona, a chapel that was constructed on the monastery's allodial land. Sicardus had the chapel razed to the ground.[87]

S. Salvatore/S. Giulia was a powerful institution with a prominent place in Italian church history. It began to experience a decline as the Middle Ages advanced. Not that this diminishing significance was widely noticeable. The monastery remained a strong organization of the Brescian patriciate.[88] Apparently in 1370 the Abbess Mabilia II of the Fabri family had such power that she was able to issue an order to the brothers of San Daniello that began as follows: 'Mabilia by God's grace abbess of the monastery of Santa Giulia . . .'. This form

[83] ibid., p. 326, n. 16–19.
[84] ibid., p. 327, n. 23–5.
[85] ibid., p. 328, n. 27.
[86] ibid., pp. 327–8, n. 21–2.
[87] ibid., p. 328, n. 28–9.
[88] Valentini, *Codice*, p. 258.

of title was only permitted to be used by popes and emperors.[89] But already in 1294 the election became complicated and four capitular deputies were chosen instead of an abbess. In 1315 three regents were selected for the position of abbess.[90] In 1403 Tommasina of Danni and in 1405 Bertolina of Cegoli were elected as abbesses. This did not mean that Tommasina died and Bertolina succeeded her; on the contrary, they represented two separate disputed elections. The difference was finally resolved in 1417 when Bertolina was confirmed by Pope Martin V.[91] In 1449 Elena Masperoni was elected forty-first abbess of the monastery, and after her death in 1483[92] there were only annual abbesses until the monastery was suppressed in 1797 following the French Revolution.[93]

The history of the monastery of S. Salvatore/S. Giulia in northern Italy thus creates an interesting case study in the endowment and patronage of a female monastery. It is apparent that Ansa's design, in founding the monastery and endowing it with its substantial lands and properties, was to create the foremost monastery of the empire. She appears to have had the support of Pope Paul I in her endeavors. There was therefore no split between ecclesiastical and royal interests in Ansa's time. It was only in the Carolingian period that a power struggle arose to decide who should rule the monastery: either the *rectrix*, often a lay person, or the abbess and the ecclesiastical hierarchy. The deciding factor was the papal interference of John VIII, who prevailed and ordered the Emperor Louis II to return everything to the monastery. The issue was further complicated when Berengar of Friuli attempted to carve out a small empire for his daughter, but he was unable to give the kind of donations that were needed to create a block of power. Then, under the Ottonian emperors, the monastery is seen to be protected by imperial proclamation. This is a far cry from the ninth century when Carolingian rulers' wives and daughters dominated the monastery. The investiture struggle, on the other hand, gave rise to papal authority over S. Salvatore/S. Giulia. With the development of the Brescian patriciate, the struggle becomes one between town citizens and the monastery over the rights of the port of Piacenza. Throughout the contest, the rights of the monastery are confirmed. After this point, the history of the monastery is linked with

[89] ibid., p. 260.
[90] ibid., p. 259.
[91] ibid., p. 260.
[92] ibid., pp. 260–1.
[93] ibid., p. 263.

its local competitors and in general its prominence and prestige becomes merely a local affair.

It is hoped that the documentation elucidated in this paper will shed some light on the formation and development of the monastery and its economic and political rise and fall, as well as giving us a sense of its prominence, both in terms of its long history and its position throughout the Middle Ages – as a prize, a pawn and, finally, as an integral part of life in northern Italy.

5

Stephen Langton's *Sermo de Virginibus*

PHYLLIS B. ROBERTS

By the twelfth and thirteenth centuries, a considerable amount of devotional literature had been produced in England for and about women propounding the ideal of the virginal life.[1] In sermons and formal treatises alike, in Latin and in the vernacular, medieval preachers and writers expounded upon this ideal, the supreme model and expression of which was the Blessed Virgin.[2]

The instant sermon of Stephen Langton is representative of the traditional exposition on the Church's view of virginity: the veneration of the virginal state and its embodiment in the person of the Blessed Virgin Mary. The Church, moreover, did more than extol virginity as a state of perfection. By providing the institution of the

---

[1] For an excellent introduction to the subject see John Bugge, *Virginitas: an Essay in the History of a Medieval Ideal* (The Hague, 1975). See also George H. Tavard, *Women in Christian Tradition* (Notre Dame, 1973), especially Part I: 'The Old Tradition', and Jo Ann McNamara, 'Sexual equality and the cult of virginity in early Christian thought', *Feminist Studies*, 3, 3–4 (1976), pp. 145–58, and her book *A New Song: Celibate Women in the First Three Christian Centuries* (New York, 1983).

[2] The literature on the subject is vast and continues to grow. For a beginning and a few examples, see the references to women and to the Blessed Virgin Mary in numerous Old and Middle English homilies, e.g. Richard Morris, *Old English Homilies and Homiletic Treatises of the Twelfth and Thirteenth Centuries*, EETS, 1st ser., 29 (London, 1868); Norman F. Blake, *Middle English Religious Prose* (London, 1972); G. R. Owst, *Preaching in Medieval England: an Introduction to the Sermon Manuscripts of the Period c. 1350–1450* (Cambridge, 1926). For the Latin sermons see Johannes Baptist Schneyer, *Repertorium der lateinischen Sermones des Mittelalters für die Zeit von 1150–1350* (9 vols, Münster Westfalen, 1969–80). Some recently published Marian sermons include John de la Rochelle, *Eleven Marian Sermons*, ed. K. F. Lynch, *Franciscan Institute Publications*, text ser. no. 12 (St Bonaventure, NY, 1961); and R. James Long, 'The Virgin as olive tree: a Marian sermon of Richard Fishacre and science at Oxford', *Archivum Fratrum Praedicatorum*, 52 (1982), pp. 77–87.

cloister and by encouraging women to take the vows of poverty, chastity and obedience, the Church offered women a practical alternative to marriage and a means of attaining the aspired goal of the virginal life.

Among the sermons of Stephen Langton, Archbishop of Canterbury from 1207 to 1228, is a *Sermo de virginibus* which celebrates the feastday of the Blessed Virgin (13.20)[3] and illustrates the traditional view on the virginal life held by this master of theology. Langton, whose career in Paris from 1180 to 1206 included many years of study, teaching and preaching, enjoyed a reputation as a leading biblical commentator of his age. Later, as a distinguished and controversial archbishop of Canterbury at the time of Magna Carta, he was not averse to challenging both king and pope on issues of Church and state.[4]

Stephen Langton had, in numerous sermons, commented on the ideal of celibacy among the male clergy. These sermons generally lauded canons regular, hermits and monks who had given themselves up to religion, forsaking wives, sons and great possessions.[5] In this Marian sermon, however, we have an opportunity to examine Langton's views on the ideal of virginity as applied to female religious.

Our text, *Sermo Magistri Stephani Archiepiscopi de virginibus*, is found in a unique copy in MS Cambridge University Library Ee.6.10, fols. 117^r–121^r.[6] The sermon is one of a series of four texts in the manuscript which are attributed to Master Stephen, Archbishop of Canterbury. The four sermons are of interest because they deal to one extent or other with the regular clergy. Our sermon, however, deals with the subject of the virginal life as an ideal for the women of the cloister.

It is doubtful that the manuscript text represents the sermon as it was actually preached. The language of the sermon, for example, is Latin, but we know that such sermons even when addressed to an audience of nuns would have been preached in the vernacular. In addition, while our text begins with a verse from Scripture, which is the traditional introduction to the medieval sermon, we find no protheme, nor any hint of the complex articulation of parts that were a feature of

---

[3] The number references in parentheses here and throughout the text refer to paragraph and line citations in the Latin text of the sermon given in the Appendix to this essay.

[4] See Phyllis B. Roberts, *Stephanus de Lingua-Tonante: Studies in the Sermons of Stephen Langton* (Toronto, 1968), pp. 1–15.

[5] ibid., pp. 122–3.

[6] On this MS and the sermons in the series, see ibid., pp. 142, 183, 195, 198, 201. For other sermons by Langton on virgins/virginity, pp. 171, 200, 208.

thirteenth-century clerical sermons and that are found in texts as actually preached. The extant text, therefore, may well be a written summary of a sermon prepared either before or after its having been preached on the occasion of the feastday of the Blessed Virgin Mary.[7]

The theme of the sermon is 2 Corinthians 11.2: 'For I betrothed you to Christ to present you as a pure bride to her one husband.' The context is Paul's metaphor of the marriage between the Corinthians and Christ wherein Paul defends his true teachings against the false apostles who would break this marriage bond. This biblical text and the marriage metaphor were not uncommon in medieval preaching on this subject. The theme appears, in fact, in Alain de Lille's model sermon, *Ad virgines*.[8] Langton uses it here in this sermon elaborating on the idea of virginal marriage to Christ and showing himself an apt student of the senses of scriptural interpretation and of the *exemplum* tradition in the preaching art.

There is in the sermon an intermingling of the literal and allegorical senses as these apply to the betrothed, or *sponsa*. The *sponsa* is both faithful soul and the bride of Christ. Thus the preacher Langton compares her vestments and regalia such as the tunic, outer tunic and pallium to the qualities of faith, hope and charity (3.1–4). Also introduced in this section on vestments and ornaments is the story in Genesis 24 of the search for a bride for Isaac in which Abraham's servant Eliezer bestows a gift of earrings and a bracelet on the beautiful Rebecca who offers him and his camels water at the village spring. For the preacher Langton, these gifts are symbolic: 'The earrings represent obedience: one should bend one's ear to God's command and forget one's father's house. The bracelet which adorns the arm represents good works' (3.8–12). A ring is also necessary for a bride (5). Two things are noted by Langton about a ring: its material and form. Its material is gold which signifies *inter alia* chastity; its form, round, which symbolizes eternal beatitude.

Langton then skillfully introduces the biblical *exemplum* in the Book of Esther to illustrate his theme further (7). In the story, the banqueting and slightly tipsy King Ahashuerus sends for Queen Vashti who refuses to come to the king, but instead tarries with her maidservants. The king subsequently finds in the beautiful maiden Esther a more suitable and congenial replacement, and she is promptly

---

[7] For a discussion of sermon construction, language, audiences and methods of transmission, see ibid., pp. 46–62; 75–94.

[8] *Summa de Arte Praedicatoria*, 47 (*PL*, 210: 194–5).

betrothed to the king. The preacher Langton, probably drawing upon St Jerome's book on the interpretation of Hebrew names, discusses the name 'Ahashuerus' which means 'door' (*ostium*). Langton ties this concept to the statement by Christ who said: 'I am the door' (Ioh. 10.9) through which one passes in thought and deed to reach God (7.8–10).

Vashti, in Langton's allegory, is the faithful soul who is led astray by her maidservants: willfulness, vanity and greed. These maidservants prevent their mistress from coming to Christ. The following passage (7.18–9.6) illustrates the way the preacher takes up the initial subject of Vashti and the allegory and moves on, elaborating one feminine image after another of willful disobedience that leads to the devil himself:

Vashti is the faithful soul who in baptism was betrothed to the King of Kings. Instead, she banquets in conviviality with her maids when she busies herself with carnal delights, usury, perjury and pride. Three are the maidservants of the faithless soul, namely willfulness, vanity and greed. These servants keep their mistress from coming to Christ. They are the worst kind of servants since vanity keeps one from Christ; greed [keeps one] from one's neighbor, and willfulness [keeps one] from oneself.

These maidservants cause their mistress to sell her body to the devil. They frequently cross over to the lower depths to consort with black lovers who are evil spirits. Thus does Jeremiah speak shamefully of this disgrace: 'The sons of Memphie have broken the crown of your head.' These servants drag their mistress down to hell after all these delights.

Whence Zacharias: 'Two women were carrying an amphora and a woman was sitting in the amphora, and she is called wickedness; this they carried to the land of Shinar' which is interpreted as stench and the gnashing of teeth. The two women are desire and vanity; the amphora is the mistress over whom wickedness, who is the third maidservant, presides. Accursed is she who, having abandoned her beauteous spouse, kisses the mouth of the serpent.

She embraces the head of the devil who has the sharpest of teeth. Some are incisors, some canine teeth, and others are molars. At first the devil tempts you, and then with his incisors separates you from God. Thus says the Psalmist: 'In the path where I walk they have hidden a trap for me.' Then on the path [the devil] leaps out like a dog, but you should strike at it with the staff of the cross. Finally, [the devil] attacks and then with all its strength bites you with its molars, once it seizes you by the heel.

Furthermore, these three kinds of teeth represent three kinds of attacks: Incisors are persecutors who are responsible for the massacre and death of martyrs. The canines are heretics, and the molars are false brothers who diminish one's life by slander. Of these spoke Job: 'His teeth are terrible round about,' since the just man fears all these things . . .

In the end, Vashti is put aside in favor of Esther who becomes the bride of the king of kings (12.1–2). Langton's skill in turning an Old Testament tale from the Book of Esther into an allegory in which a godly virgin marries Christ was much admired by medieval preachers.

Another *exemplum* in the sermon further develops the theme of Christ the king and bridegroom. Langton tells the story of a king whose unfaithful queen locks the door of the bedchamber in which she cavorts with her lover. In vain does the king knock on the door seeking entry. In the allegory, the king is Christ, the weak-willed queen is the soul, and the lover is the embodiment of sin tearing the soul away from Christ (10.1–8):

A certain king had a very beautiful queen who kept herself absent from the king. She cast her eyes on a certain lover and desired him, so much so, it happens, that having shut the door of the bedchamber, she dallied therein with her lover. The king is Christ; the queen is the faithful soul; the lover is greed or some other crime. Deservedly is he called lover [*contractus*]. The Lord created him standing erect to the heavens, now his back and head are bent [*incurua*] to earthly things. He draws away his arms and extends neither prayer to God nor charity to the poor.

In the course of explicating this *exemplum*, Langton refers frequently to the Song of Songs which had long been used by Christian writers to emphasize the image of the Christian virgin as the bride of Christ.[9] Langton also followed in this tradition.[10] Indeed the twelfth century produced more commentaries on the Song of Songs than had all previous Christendom.[11] Canticles was the subject of a series of sermons by Bernard of Clairvaux, and St Bernard's allegorical treatment of the bridal image in the Song, addressed principally to monks, co-existed in this period with a literal interpretation of the *sponsa* as the Christian virgin who is the bride of Christ.[12]

Thus, the *Hali Meidenhead*, a thirteenth-century treatise on female virginity, expounded upon the idea of the nun or anchoress as the bride of Christ. The work depicts Christ as 'worthiest lover', more handsome and a better provider than an earthly spouse. Indeed, the *Hali Meidenhead* urged marriage to Christ in preference to the physical

---

[9] For a survey of the development of the *sponsa Christi* idea, see Bugge, *Virginitas*, pp. 59–79.

[10] Roberts, *Stephanus de Lingua – Tonante*, pp. 99–100.

[11] Bugge, *Virginitas*, p. 90.

[12] ibid., p. 92.

bond of earthly marriage.[13] At about the same time, this idea of the bride of Christ was influenced by two traditions:[14] the Victorine concept of spiritual marriage and St Augustine's commendation of the 'virginal life as best ensuring the growth and the spiritual liberation of Christian women.'[15]

Langton draws upon the strands of these traditions as he incorporates in his sermon text verses of the Songs of Songs. Thus the king beats on the queen's door and calls out in the words of Canticles (10.8–12):

> Open to me, my sister, my love, my dove,
> my perfect one; for my head is wet with dew,
> my locks with the drops of the night.

In such a manner, says Langton, does Christ appeal to the faithless soul. The drops of dew he compares with the drops of blood which Christ shed as He wore the crown of thorns for the sins of mankind (10.15–24).

The queen, hearing the commotion, says with Canticles: 'I opened to my beloved . . .'. This opening to Christ is the removal of sin through penance. The lover is greed that afflicts all ranks of society (11.1–32):

The bride, on hearing the commotion and pounding on the door, says in Canticles: 'I opened to my beloved.' One opens the bolt who removes sin through penance. However, if the soul does not stir, Christ, like the irate [*sponsus*], smashes the bolt by touching man with the goad of adversity, thereby removing wealth and prosperity. He touched Saul with this goad, but he raised up Paul, saying: 'Saul, Saul, why do you persecute me? It is hard for you to kick against the pricks.'

The king of glory enters therefore, finding the lover with his wife. What should he do? Judge therefore, if some nobleman found a lover in his wife's embrace, he would probably repudiate her or punish her in some way. Not so Christ, however. Nay, he is like a jealous man who would slay the lover, sparing his wife.

Even so is it written in the Book of Kings: 'Dagon fell upon his face to the ground before the ark [of the Lord], and the head of Dagon and both the palms of his hands were cut off.' The ark, i.e. the faithful soul, he preserved. Dagon is interpreted as 'the fish of sorrow' and signifies avarice which through greedy curiosity leads one to eternal sadness. 'Dagon's head is cut off' when one considers that in entering the world one has nothing; 'his hands [are cut off]' when one considers that when the rich sleep, they carry

[13] ibid., pp. 87–9.
[14] ibid., p. 90.
[15] Tavard, *Women in Christian Tradition*, p. 117.

away nothing in their hands. Whence says Timothy: 'For we brought nothing into this world' – this refers to the amputated head [of Dagon]; 'and it is certain we can carry nothing out' – behold the mutilation of [Dagon's] hands.

Although the lord spares his wife and slays the lover, the wife is like one who is crazed and insanely runs 'through the city in the streets' and shouts: 'Where is my lover?' Certain priests, when they hold Christ on high in the mass, call for this lover when they celebrate [the mass] for cash. Princes commit soldiers to war for the sake of this lover; merchants hasten across the sea; burghers count on him at the marketplace; clerics and monks litigate in the courts [for this lover's sake]. Nearly every kind of person toils for the sake of this lover and yet finds nothing except something imperfect which is only transitory. It is remarkable that the rational soul abandons the son of God for such a lover. Sacred virgins put such a lover aside and cling to Christ alone.

The *sponsa*, then, would do well to adopt three different maid-servants. Instead of willfulness, vanity and greed which we saw elaborated earlier in the *exemplum* from the Book of Esther, Langton urges humility, love and chastity. These servants will minister to you the delights of paradise (13.1–3); for these are the gifts of the Blessed Virgin Mary (14.1–13):

The mother of mercy grants three gifts, namely the golden belt of chastity, the gloves of charity, and the robe or hood of humility. Surely, if you were to repudiate the gifts of some great lady, it would be considered for ill. If you do not accept the gifts of the Blessed Virgin, you make her your enemy. Accept, therefore, the golden belt of chastity to bind your loins; receive the gloves of charity lest you burn your hands with the silver that dazzles people. Usurious money changers have black, closed fingers from the frequent counting out of their money. This happens because they do not wear the gloves of charity. Further, if one wears the robe or hood of humility, one would be adorned with other virtues against the flattery of vain glory. The King of Heaven embraces you with loving arms and bestows upon you the kiss of salvation.

Stephen Langton's sermon then is an example of a prominent preacher's traditional views and treatment of the subject of the virginal life. The *exempla* tradition furnished a variety of sources which Langton could elaborate to his homiletical purpose. From the Book of Esther to the verses of the Song of Songs came *exempla* that urged the emulation of the life of goodly virgins who give themselves to the love of Christ. The celebration of the feastday of the Blessed Virgin Mary was

the occasion for this exposition on a theme that was an important
feature of the devotional literature produced for and about women in
the high Middle Ages.

APPENDIX

Sermo Magistri Stephani Archiepiscopi de virginibus

117ʳ   1. 'Despondi enim uos uni uiro uirginem castam exhibere
Christo, etc.'¹⁶ Doctor ecclesie est interloqutor sponsalium inter
animam et Christum. Unde Apostolus: 'Despondi enim uos,
etc.'¹⁷ Quantum quis fuerit per peccatum corruptus, si ad
5   Christum uertitur, sibi desponsat uirginitatem recuperat. Hec
differentia sponsalium: hominum et Christi. Homines integram
corrumpunt, Christus corruptam redintegrat. De nomine uirgine:
uirginem facit ut dicitur: 'Sacre mulieres integre apparebunt in
regno celorum quia neque nubent neque nubentur.'¹⁸ Ieronimus¹⁹
10 uidetur obuiare dicens: 'Cum Deus omnia possit, non potest de
corrupta facere incorruptam i.e. non potest facere quin sit
corrupta, licet possit facere quod sit integra.'
    2. Uideamus de uestibus et ornamentis camerariis et prole istius
sponse. Vestes sunt uirtutes quibus sponsa est munienda: camisia
castitatis quia linum per multas tunsiones peruenit ad candorem,
sic peccator ad castitatem. Unde Ieronimus:²⁰ 'Cum post aspera
5   opera penitentie que feci, caro mea sancta est sicut Ethiops et
*cutis mea aruit*²¹ *et adherebat ossibus.*²² Tamen incentiua libidinis in
me bulliebant.'
    3. De fide designatam per tunicam.²³ De fide: Tunica est fides
contra frigus. Spes, supertunica ut ad caloris²⁴ augumentum²⁵
superadditur, spes eternorum. Pallium, caritas quod omnibus
supponitur, 'quia maior horum est caritas.'²⁶ Salomon in Para-

¹⁶ 2 Corinthians 11.2.
¹⁷ ibid.
¹⁸ Cf. Matthew 22.30.
¹⁹ Cf. *Comment in Matheum* 3. 1827–36 (*CCSL*, 77: 205–6).
²⁰ Cf. Epistles 22.7 (*PL*, 22: 398).
²¹ Job 7.5.
²² Lamentations 4.8.
²³ Rubric in MS.
²⁴ 'calorem *del.*' MS.
²⁵ 'argumentum' MS.
²⁶ 1 Corinthians 13.13.

5   bolis: 'Mulier fortis stragulatam uestem fecit sibi.'[27] Firmam per
constanciam uariam uirtutum picturatam ut circumdata
uarietate quandoque in oratione quandoque in operatione se
exerceat. De ornamentis in Genesi,[28] quando Eliezer duxit
Rebeccam ad Ysaac, dedit ei inaurem et armillam. Per inaurem:
10 obedientiam ut aurem inclinet ad mandata Dei et obliuiscatur
domum patris sui. Per armillam que est ornamentum brachii,
bonum opus intellige. Iterum ornamentum capitis, uelum nigrum
quod significatur per pallium quo se operuit Rebecca uiso
Ysaac.[29] Hoc uelum est claustrum sensuum qui siti sunt in capite /
117ᵛ 15 sicut quatuor muri claustra sunt corporum. Hoc uelum est
nigrum quia omnia exteriora nigra et turpia debent apparere, ut
anima tua in exterioribus renuens consolari cum sponso tuo
gaudeas intrinsecus. Iterum nigrum ut mundo nigrescas et soli
sponso placere desideres. Quedam enim alios non concupiscunt
20 set concupisci desiderant. Set dicit Augustinus:[30] 'Velle con-
cupiscere et uelle concupisci; utrumque est dampnabile.' Unde
prohibet Apostolus mulieres ornari ut placeant hominibus. Ad
Thymotheum: 'Mulieres in habitu ornato cum uerecundia et
sobrietate ornantes se.'[31] Verecundia ne forte attrita sobrietate
25 et ne carnes et uinum oleant.

4. Contra superbum habitum mulierum.[32] Sequitur: 'nec tortis
crinibus non auro uel margaritis uel ueste pretiosa'[33] ubi dicitur
habitus superbus non impetrat nec recte facit de se credi. Si latro
esset statim suspendendus et princeps ei diceret: 'Frater, porta
5   hanc retortam dum uixeris in signum quod es suspendio dignus
et liberaberis,' humiliter portaret neque in ipso gloriaretur.
Mulier quia uirum seduxit, digna fuit suspendio, set princeps
misericors illam non suspendit set retortam i.e. peplum in capud
in signum suspendii concessit. Mirum igitur est quod quedam
10 retortam hanc croco tingunt ut inde superbiant. Similiter
Dominus dedit tunicam pelliceam Ade dicens: 'Ecce Adam factus
est quasi unus ex nobis.'[34] Exprobratio est quasi ecce quale
animal pellicea indutum qui nisi peccasset, nec pellibus nec aliis
indiguisset. Set cui Dominus non sufficit, omnibus indiget.

[27] Proverbs 31.22.

[28] Cf. Genesis 24.22.

[29] Cf. Genesis 24.65.

[30] I have not been able to locate this exact quotation, but see on the subject
Augustine's *De Nuptiis et Concupiscentia* (*CSEL*, 42: 211–319).

[31] I Timothy 2.9.

[32] Rubric in MS. In margin: 'habitu mulierum'.

[33] I Timothy 2.9.

[34] Cf. Genesis 3.21–2.

15 Pelliceam quam Dominus dedit in uerecundiam, conuertimus in
superbiam. Per pellem: penam; per pilos peccatum intellige.
Unde in Leuitico[35] precipiuntur Leuite pilos abradere et nos
peccata tollere.

5. Item sponse necessarius est anulus in quo duo notantur:
materia et forma. In auro quinque notantur, scil. precium quod
significat castitatem quia sicut auro non est metallum preciosius.
Ita ut dicitur in Ecclesiastico 'non digna ponderatio'[36] continentis
5 anime, item gratia super gratiam, mulier sancta et pudica.

118[r]   Forma / anuli rotunda eternam significat beatitudinem quam
premissis operibus reddet Dominus in premium uelud formam
materie. Aurum est ponderosum et significat perseuerentiam ut
non a uento homo rapiatur temptationis sicut palea. Aurum
10 splendet et significat bone opinionis claritatem, quoniam mulieris
bone species in ornamentum domus sue maxime consideratur.
Unde in Ecclesiastico: 'Sicut sol oriens mundo in altissimis Dei,
sic mulieris bone species in ornamentum domus.'[37] Aurum rubet
et significat caritatem que uelut ignis ascendit in altum per
15 dilectionem Dei et dilatatur per dilectionem proximi.

6. Si sic ornata fueris, concupiscet rex decorem tuum; et quam
felix anima que talem habet sponsum qui celum et terram creauit.
Si potentem diligis, ille potentissimus est. Si inquam uidisti
pulchrum[38] quem concupisceres, ille pulcherimus est, suauis-
5 simus, mitissimus rex celi et terre; ergo tu eris regina. Nulla
habent diuisa, ergo regina celi et terre efficieris. Si tali pul-
chritudini[39] sponso placere non studeas, dicit tibi in Canticis: 'Si
ignoris te, o pulchra[40] inter mulieres, egredere et abi post uestigia
gregum tuorum'[41] i.e. sequere motus bestiales, luxuriam, gulam et
10 consimilia. 'Et pasce hedos tuos,'[42] studeas ut per adultationes et
munera ad gloriam collatam; per risus et commessationes
diuitibus uicinis consanguineis qui sunt 'hedi a sinistris'[43] studeas
placere et ualeas. Maledicta sponsa que filium Dei contempnit et
hedos fetidos amplectat et osculatur. Hoc faciunt, Ihesu bone,
15 qui de te loqui et meditari contempnunt set diuitibus episcopis
et huiusmodi pro temporalibus placere affectant. Siue equus,

---

[35] Cf. Leviticus 14.8.
[36] Ecclesiastes 6.15.
[37] ibid., 26.21.
[38] 'pulcrum' MS.
[39] 'pulcritudini' MS.
[40] 'pulcra' MS.
[41] Canticles 1.7.
[42] ibid.
[43] Cf. Matthew 25.33.

siue domus, siue mundus, siue nummus: omne illud in quo
contra Deum gloriaris hedus est quia fetet Deo et te faciet fetere
in inferno.

    7. Exemplum: De rege Assuero.[44] Sequitur: Rex Assuerus
celebrauit grande conuiuium in quo multi erant lecti aurei et
argentei et pauimentum stratum lapidibus preciosis et uariis
118ᵛ   ornamentis. Locus resplendet ut dicitur / in Hester.[45] Et cum rex
5 Assuerus hyllaris esset et uino calefactus, misit propter reginam
Vasti que celebrauit conuiuium cum puellis, et renuit uenire.
Et ideo consilio suorum reprobata, quesita est pulcherima nomine
Hester et regi est deponsata.[46] Assuerus interpretatur hostium et
significat Christum qui dicit: 'Ego sum ostium,'[47] per intrat qui
10 contemplationem et operationem in Deum dirigit. Iste rex
celebrat conuiuium tam in ecclesia militante quam in ecclesia
triumphante. In conuiuio Assueri non erat qui compelleret bibere,
nec in ecclesia militante aliquis compellitur uinum gratie potare.
Non enim ut asini compelluntur intrare in regnum celorum.
15 Unde Psalmista: 'Uoluntarie sacrificabo tibi, etc.'[48] Set pater
dicitur trahere secundum quod dicitur, trahit sua quemque
uoluntas, quoniam quemque amore et uoluntate trahit sibi
Deus. Vasti est anima fidelis que in baptismo fuit regi regum
desponsata. Sed celebrat conuiuium cum puellis quando carnales
20 delicias, usuras, periuria, superbiam exercet. Tres sunt camerarie
anime iniuste, scil. uoluntas, uanitas et cupiditas. Iste camerarie
detinent dominam suam ne ueniat ad Christum. Iste sunt
pessime camerarie quoniam uanitas aufert Christum, cupiditas
proximum, uoluntas seipsum. Iste camerarie faciunt dominam
25 suam prostare diabolo. Iste frequenter transeunt ad inferos pro
nigris amatoribus qui sunt maligni spiritus. Vnde Ieremias de hac
turpitudine turpius ait: 'Filii Mempheos iacuerunt tecum usque
ad uerticem.'[49] Iste camerarie dominam suam post omnes
delicias deferunt in infernum.

    8. Unde Zacharias:[50] 'Due mulieres portabant amphoram et
mulier sedit desuper que dicitur impietas; quam tulerunt in
terram Sennaar' que interpretatur fetor et excussio dentium.
Due mulieres sunt uoluptas et uanitas; amphora est domina

---

[44] Rubric in MS. In margin 'De rege Assuero'.

[45] Esther 1.3–6.

[46] ibid., 1.10–22; 2.1–18.

[47] Ioh. 10.9. See Jerome's interpretation: 'Asuerus atrium eius [i.e. Dei] uel
beatitudo.' *Liber Interp. Hebr. Nom.* 56.1 (*CCSL*, 72: 129).

[48] Psalms 53.8.

[49] Cf. Jeremiah 2.16.

[50] Cf. Zachariah 5.7–11.

5 super quam sedet impietas que est tercia cameraria. Talis
maledicta, relicto sponso pulcherimo, os draconis osculatur.

119ʳ Capud diaboli / amplectitur qui dentes haget acutissimos quorum
quidam sunt incisiui, quidam canini, quidam molares. Diabolus
in principio temptat et tunc dentibus incisiuis separat a Deo.

10 Vnde Psalmista: 'In medio in uia hac qua ambulabam abscon-
derunt laqueum mihi.'⁵¹ Tunc in uia more canis insilit set cum
baculo crucis ipsum percutias. Temptat in fine et tunc cum tota
fortitudine molaribus comminuit quoniam insidiatur calcaneo.

9. Item per tres dentes, tria genera temptationum intellige.
Dentes incisiui sunt persequutores in strage martyrum qui corpus
ab anima separauerunt. Canini sunt heretici; molares sunt falsi
fratres qui alienam uitam per detractionem comminuunt. De

5 istis Iob: 'Circa girum dentium eius formido,'⁵² quoniam iustus
hec omnia timet. Item oculos habet turpissimos sicut in pariete
depingitur. Vnde Iob: 'Inimicus meus terribilibus oculis intuitus
est me.'⁵³ Mirum est quod non abhorret tale capud amplecti tam
fetidum osculari. Talis sponsa merito Vasti que interpretatur

10 finis signatus. Reprobi enim presentia diligentes finalia, penas et
premia non attendunt. Sera que obstant sunt diuitie et delicie.
Disperge igitur diuitias, tolle delicias: frange seram, aufer culpam
et sic uidebis penas quas timeas et premia que desideres.

10. Quidam rex habens pulcherimam reginam que a rege se
absentauit, oculos in quendam contractum proiecit et con-
cupiuit; in tantum processit quod clauso ostio thalami cum
contracto delicias duxit. Rex iste est Christus: regina fidelis

5 anima: contractus est cupiditas uel alia culpa. Merito 'contractus'
dicitur quia quem Dominus creauit erectum ad celestia, dorsum
eius et capud incurua ad terrena. Brachia contrahit ne Deo per
orationem nec pauperi per caritatem extendit. Ueniens igitur
sponsus qui nouit sponsam cum contracto inclusam ad hostium

10 clamat: 'Aperi mihi, soror mea, amica mea, columba mea,

119ᵛ immaculata mea, quia / capud meum plenum est rore, et
cincinni mei guttis noctium.'⁵⁴ Dulcedine uerborum utitur ut ei
citius aperiatur more amantis qui per totam noctem pulsat ad
ostium amice sue donec rore nocturno capud respergatur. Hic

15 Christus per totam noctem paraceues⁵⁵ in contumeliis et uerberi-

---

⁵¹ Psalms 141.4.
⁵² Cf. Job 41.5. The reference here in Job is to the Leviathan, a mythical sea
monster whose scales, jaws, back, eyes, mouth, nostrils, breath and neck offer
evidence of his invincibility. See Job 41.1–34.
⁵³ Cf. Job 16.10.
⁵⁴ Canticles 5.2.
⁵⁵ paraceues = parasceues.

bus ad nichil aliud laborauit nisi ut amica sibi aperiret. Dicit
ergo 'amica mea, aperi mihi' in tantum pulsam 'quod capud
meum plenum est rore.'[56] Et quali rore? Guttis sanguinis quas
noctes i.e. peccatores coronam spineam capiti plectentes effu-
20 derunt. Ihesu bone, quis sic te clamante tibi non aperit? Quis tali
rore perfuso festinanter non occurrit? Anima peccatrix, amore
tui filius Dei, filius uirginis tali rore perfusus est. Ergo aperias,
iter facias illi qui ascendit super occasum i.e. interficit contractum
scil. peccatum quod te cadere facit.

11. Sponsa quandoque tali pulsatione commota, dicit in Canticis:
'Pessulum ostii mei aperui dilecto meo.'[57] Pessulum aperit qui
per penitentiam peccatum tollit. Item anima quandoque non
surgit, set ipse Christus quasi iratus pessulum frangit quando
5 diuitias aut prosperitatem auferendo, stimulo aduersitatis
hominem tangit. Hoc stimulo Saulum tetigit set Paulum erexit,
dicens: 'Saule, Saule, quid me persequeris? Durum est tibi contra
stimulum calcitrare.'[58] Intrans ergo rex glorie inueniens contractum cum uxore, quid faciet? Iudicate si aliquis nobilis
10 contractum inter amplexus uxoris inueniret; forsan ipsam
repudiaret uel aliter affligeret. Christus uero non sic immo quasi
zelotipus, uxori parciter contractum interficit. Sicut dicitur in
Libro Regum: 'Dagon erectum iuxta archam prostrauit, capud
et palmas amputauit.'[59] Archam i.e. fidelem animam conseruauit.
15 Dagon interpretatur 'piscis tristicie' et significat auaritiam que
per curiositatem cupiditatis ad eternam ducit tristiciam. Dagon
120ʳ caput / aufertur cum quis considerat quod in introitu mundi
nichil habuit; manus quando considerat quod diuites cum
dormiunt nichil auferunt in manibus suis. Unde ad Timotheum:
20 'Nichil intulimus in nunc mundum,' ecce capud amputatum;
'haut dubium nichil inde auferemus,'[60] ecce mutilatio manuum.
Set licet dominus sic sponse sue parcat et contractum interficiat,
tamen sponsa quasi demoniata et quasi insana 'per uicos et
plateas'[61] discurrens clamat: 'Ubi est contractus?' Sacerdotes
25 quidam quando erectis Christum in missa clamant contractum
quando celebrant propter nummum. Principes milites pro contracto bella committunt; mercatores trans mare currunt;
burgenses ad campum numerant; clerici et claustrales in foro

---

[56] Canticles 5.2.
[57] Canticles 5.6.
[58] Acts 9.4–5.
[59] Cf. 1 Reg. 5.4. For Jerome's interpretation of 'Dagon', see *Liber Interpr. Hebr.
Nom.* 32.7 (*CCSL*, 72: 99).
[60] I Timothy 6.7.
[61] Canticles 3.2.

litigant. Fere omnium hominum genus pro contracto laborat et
30 tamen nichil inuenit nisi truncum quo ad presens uti poterit.
Mirum ⟨est⟩ quod anima rationalis pro tali contracto filium Dei
relinquit. Sacre uirgines contracto relicto soli Christo adheserunt.

12. Reprobata igitur Vasti i.e. quelibet fidelis anima, efficitur
Hester sponsa regis regum. Hester interpretatur 'abscondita.'
Illa meretur sponsa Christi fieri, que abscondita est ab aura
fauoris humani. Ysaias: 'Erit sicut uir qui absconditur a uento.'[62]
5 In Prouerbiis:[63] 'Cum surrexerint impii, abscondentur homines;
et cum illi perierint, multiplicabuntur ⟨iusti⟩.'[64] Quidam enim
uerbis et operibus apparere desiderant de quibus Gregorius:[65]
'Ipocrita non apud Deum qualiter uiuat, set apud homines
qualiter innotescat excogitat.' Quibus dicit dicens: 'Satis dilatasti
10 fimbrias tuas coram hominibus; ite in tenebras exteriores ubi
nullos de cetero uidebitis ad gloriam. Et claudam os putei ut
numquam exeatis. Sic cum ille perierit, iusti multiplicabuntur in
gloria.'

13. De camerariis Christi.[66] Tres camerarie istius sponse sunt
humilitas, caritas et castitas. Iste camerarie ministrabunt tibi
120ᵛ delicias paradisi. Ascendunt / in celum; celestes milites in solatium
tuum faciunt uenire. Cum filius Dei per ora prophetarum
5 frequenter uocatus fuisset et non uenisset, Beata Uirgo Maria
unam camerariam scil. humilitatem in celum pro ipsa transmisit,
que in tantum ei placuit quod ad preces eius in thalamum
uirginis descendit. 'Quoniam respexit humilitatem ancille sue,
etc.',[67] secure uigilat, secure dormit qui istis camerariis associatur.
10 Iste camerarie sacras uirgines in uariis tormentis confortauerunt
et post certamen in celum detulerunt. Expulsis camerariis
pessimis, has tres acquirere studeamus. Set dicit aliquis: 'Quis
prestabit mihi tam sacras tam dignas puellas?' Domina, cum
cameraria caret, rogat uicinam que habet ut unam sibi accomo-
15 det. Set regina celi dicior est omnibus et benignior, quoniam de
ea dicitur in Prouerbiis: 'Multe filie congregauerunt diuicias, tu
supergressa es uniuersas.'[68] Ergo quia diues accomodare poterit,
quia benignissima negare non poterit. Si non presumis matrem
Domini preces porrigere, roga uirginem cuius hodie celebratur
20 solempnitas et quod uolueris inpetrabis. Immo mater Christi

---

[62] Isaiah 32.2.
[63] Proverbs 28.28.
[64] MS. *om.* 'iusti'.
[65] Cf. *Moral. in Job* 13.36 (*PL*, 75: 975–6).
[66] Rubric in MS.
[67] Luke 1.48.
[68] Proverbs 31.29.

cuilibet has puellas transmittit quam rustica quam maledicta que
illas expellit que illas interficit.

14. De donariis Beate Marie.[69] Mater misericordie tria donaria
cuilibet presentat, videlicet zonam auream castitatis, cerothecas[70]
caritatis, peplum siue capellum humilitatis. Certe si repudiares
munera alicuius[71] matrone, pro malo haberetur. Sic si donaria
5 Beate Uirginis non recipis, ipsam inimicam tuam constitues.
Recipias ergo zonam uaeream castitatis qua renes tuos constringas;
recipias cerothecas caritatis ut argentum quod gentes ardet manus
121[r] tuas non comburas. Usu / rarii camsores[72] digitos suos frequenti
numeratione pecunie nigros habent et aclausos.[73] Hoc contingit
10 quia cerothecas caritatis non habent in manibus. Item si habeat
peplum uel capellum humilitatis, contra aurem uane glorie et
ceteris uirtutibus fueris ornata. Rex celorum brachiis dilectionis
amplectitur te et osculo salutis osculabitur te.

15. Sequitur de prole quia scriptum est maledicta sterilis que
non parit. Et in Canticis: 'Et sterilis non est in eis.'[74] Necesse est
quod sponse Christi prolem habeant. Filii earum sunt bona
opera. Os filios pariunt sponse que a Spiritu Sancto sunt impreg-
5 nate. Tales filii portabunt matres in regnum celorum. Filii
filiorum sunt premia eterna que sponsa Christi uidebit in patria
secundum illud: 'ut uideas filios filiorum tuorum, pacem super
Israel.'[75] Plerique carentes prole carnali filios desiderant qui
parentes perimunt, quoniam propter filios multi usuras, periuria,
10 furta exercent sicut uiperee.[76] Sic filii parentes suos pari lege
perimunt. Item si dolent aliqui quod filios non habent quibus
bona sua reliquant, Christum filium suum et heredem con-
stituant, qui reddet eis centuplum et bene nutriet cum senuerint.
Lumen oculorum et baculus senectutis eorum sicut dicitur de
15 Thobia.[77] Reminiscere faciet in celo cum defecerint. Filius carnalis
frequenter mortem patris desiderat ut in hereditate succedat, set
filius iste hereditatem eterne glorie parentibus preparat. Cum
ueneris ad iudicium non timeas quia filius tuus iudex erit qui
patrem et matrem honorari precepit. Gloria et honore coronabit
20 te. Ihesu bone, digneris nos sic ornare Spiritus Sancti gratia;

---

[69] Rubric in MS.
[70] cerotheca = chirotheca.
[71] 'alicus' MS.
[72] camsores = campsores.
[73] aclausos = clausos.
[74] Canticles 6.5.
[75] Cf. Psalms 127.6.
[76] uiperee = uipere.
[77] Cf. Tobit 11.1–17.

fecundare in thalamo cordis nobis cum habitare; intus amplexus desiderabiles nos recipias Saluator mundi qui cum Patre et Spiritu Sancto uiuit et regnat Deus per omnia secula seculorum. Amen.

ACKNOWLEDGEMENTS

I am grateful to the Syndics of Cambridge University Library for permission to publish Stephen Langton's sermon *De virginibus* from their MS Ee.6.10. I should also like to express my appreciation to Kathleen Greenfield and Jo Ann McNamara for their helpful suggestions.

6

Ancilla Dei: The Servant as Saint in the Late Middle Ages

MICHAEL GOODICH

The female servant as the ready object of abuse and sexual exploitation by her employer has recently drawn the attention of historians of the early modern family. Evidence from both Florence and Venice, drawn from the records of the local 'morals' courts, suggests that sexual escapades outside marriage were widespread, despite official morality; and that young men in particular found a sexual outlet in homosexuality and rape, even of nuns.[1] In fact, as Trexler has shown, in the early fifteenth century unconventional sex had become so widespread in Florence, that the city fathers condoned the opening of bordellos as socially more desirable. The chief competitor of the public prostitute, who often came from afar, was the servant girl, who characteristically came from the surrounding *contado*. While the brothels were frequented by the lower orders, the professional courtesan and servant more often served the high-born and their guests. Trexler notes that in the sixteenth century such establishments were apparently populated by an increasing number of artisans' wives and servant girls, at a time when public prostitution had begun to outlive its original usefulness.

In the Puritan period, the stealthy fornication of master and servant, often under duress, continued to crowd the court calendar.[2] Although

[1] See Richard C. Trexler, 'La prostitution florentine au XVe siècle: patronages et clientèles', *Annales ESC*, 36 (1981), pp. 983–1015; see also Guido Ruggiero, 'Sessualità e sacrilegio', *Studi Storici*, 22 (1981), pp. 751–65; Samuel K. Cohn, jun., 'Donne in piazza e donne in tribunale a Firenze nel Rinascimento', *Studi Storici*, 22 (1981), pp. 515–33.

[2] Edward S. Morgan, 'The Puritans and sex', *New England Quarterly*, 15 (1942), pp. 597–9; G. R. Quaife, 'The consenting spinster in a peasant society: aspects of premarital sex in "Puritan" Somerset 1645–1660', *Journal of Social History*, 11 (1977/8), p. 231.

the servant might work according to a contract, the nearly absolute authority exercised by her employer made his sexual advances almost irresistible. In seventeenth-century Somerset, the most common cases involved premarital sex between an unmarried female servant and a man, married or single, living under the same roof. It seems likely that this same stereotypical relationship of tension and sexual exploitation likewise characterized the master–servant relationship in the Middle Ages, although modified by a counter-image of purity which the Church sought to propagate.

The term most widely used for the female servant – *ancilla* – had a dual meaning.[3] In religious literature, it was traditionally applied to the saintly and cloistered woman, the *ancilla Dei* or *ancilla Christi*, noted for her humble, subordinate, but pious position.[4] In this sense, such a phrase as *ancilla ancillarum Dei* was an appellation of humility akin to the papal title 'servant of the servants of God'. In secular life, in addition to *ancilla*, a variety of other terms were employed, including *famula*, *pedissequa*, *domestica*, *serva* and *domicella*. Here, while maidenhood and youth are implied, immorality, loquacity, treachery and even whorishness were traits often applied to the servant girl. In the early Middle Ages such women were often serfs or slaves, living in concubinage. During the later period, this subordinate condition – the biblical Hagar was regarded as the stereotypical servant *cum* concubine – remained, although the element of bondage had disappeared.[5]

As a means of maintaining the allegiance of this marginal class, often alienated from the ordinary institutional structures of religion, and in order to combat the malevolent effects of the master–servant relationship, the hagiographical genre of the 'servant-saint' found a place in the pantheon of Christian saints quite early on. Although the

[3] The best source for a survey of the various terms denoting service is C. de Fresne Ducange, *Glossarium Mediae et Infimae Latinitatis* (10 vols, Paris, 1883–7), VII, p. 441; III, pp. 161–2; VI, p. 245; I, pp. 242–3. See also R. E. Latham, *Dictionary of Medieval Latin from British Sources* (London, 1975), fasc. 1, p. 83.

[4] G. D. Mansi (ed.), *Sacrorum Conciliorum Nova et Amplissima Collectio* (59 vols, Florence, 1759–1927), XII, p. 263, contains the results of the Council of Rome (AD 721), which anathematized 'monacham, quam Dei ancillam appellamus' for taking husbands.

[5] Pierre Bercheure, *Reductorium Moralis* (Mainz, 1609), p. 72; on the moral qualities of the *ancilla* and the parallels to Hagar. In the canonization trial of Margaret of Hungary (d. 1270), held in 1276, William Franknoì (ed.), *Monumenta romana episcopatus Vesprimiensis* (6 vols, Budapest, 1896–1950), I, pp. 306, 327, 331, 333, 358, several witnesses were asked 'si est libera, vel ancilla'. Their response was often 'serva et libera', which leaves the situation not entirely clear.

early legends are not always reliable, the principal elements of the *ancilla* legend are already present: a grudging, cruel master; charity shown to lepers and the poor; and strength in the face of sexual temptation.[6] To cite merely one example, one of the most popular of such figures was Gunthild of Suffersheim (d. 1057?).[7] Although allegedly of noble birth, she was forced into domestic service at Eichstätt in Bavaria. Her virtues center around acts of charity to the poor, domestic animals and country folk. In one miracle, which recurs in slightly different form in the lives of many other servant-saints, it is reported that when she gave milk to the poor, because her master begrudged the saint this act of charity, all the milk in his tubs and jugs turned to ashes.

By the thirteenth century, the hagiographical motif of the servant girl had already been established, although direct literary filiation between later apotheoses of this genre of saint and its ancient predecessors cannot be proved.[8] It was rather changing social conditions and the need to insure the loyalty of a population increasingly drawn to heresy (particularly women) that demanded revival of a theme attractive to the servant class.[9] Domestics made up a large proportion of the marginal population (including also thieves, prostitutes and the casually employed), which tended to gravitate to the city from the adjacent countryside, particularly in Italy, occasionally in response to

[6] A. C. Dunbar, *A Dictionary of Saintly Women* (2 vols, London, 1904–5), contains brief accounts of female saints. For more detail, see F. Caraffa et al. (eds), *Bibiotheca Sanctorum* (12 vols, Rome, 1961–70) (henceforward *BS*). Most of the contemporary source material is found in Socii Bollandiani, *Acta Sanctorum Bollandistorum (AS)*, rev. ed. (66 vols to date, Paris, 1863–1940).

[7] For the sixteenth-century legend based on earlier sources, see *AS*, 28 September VI, 530–3. Her identity is still somewhat in doubt, *BS*, VII, 532–3.

[8] Baudouin de Gaiffier, 'Les thèmes hagiographiques. Est-il possible d'établir pour chacun d'eux une filiation', *Revue d'histoire écclésiastique*, 77 (1982), pp. 78–81, discusses the rarity of finding 'verbal similarity' in saints' legends, although the influence of one legend on another often appears obvious.

[9] Such servants were likely to adopt the beliefs of their employers, considering their age upon entering service and their familial ties to the family. All of the inquisitorial trials describe the collusion of *ancillae* in heresy. See, e.g., the 1244 trial of the Cathar *perfecta* Arnauda de Lamota of Montauban: '. . . ipsa testis et sociae eius hereticae manebant ibi, Poncius Saquet et Gensers uxor eius, et Raimunda pedisseca eorum, et ibi omnes praedicti pluries adoraverent ipsam testem et sociam eius hereticam.' The witness describes the aforementioned servant Raimunda and the family nurse (*nutrix*) taking part in all the Cathar rituals; Gottfried Koch, *Frauenfrage und Ketzertum* (East Berlin, 1962), pp. 194, 196, 200.

government policy.[10] The dislocating passage from rural to town life is reflected in the parallel rise of the number of saints employed as domestics; for the social origins of the saint tend to mirror the new constituencies which the church sought to attract. The vast majority of such servants came from rural areas, and were often related to their employers. Such employment appeared to have been the best means of solving the problem of female overpopulation and the shortage of dowries. While women with some means might enter a convent, poor girls sought a virtuous solution to their situation through service. Many became domestics at the age of eight or nine, with the aim of marrying under their master's patronage. They perhaps did not receive a salary, but rather a guaranteed dowry and a promise to be married off at the termination of their service. The familiar 'old maid' whose frustrated hopes of matrimony led to bitterness and public abuse, was a medieval invention, reflecting the contemporary preference for marriage or claustration. For purposes of taxation, it would appear that the servant was included in the *familia* along with wives and children, although this is not entirely certain. A privileged position was occupied by the nurse, who in addition to her responsibilities as surrogate mother, might also take charge of the domestic staff. Particular attention was paid to her appearance, morals and diet, although the welfare and whereabouts of the chambermaid were also regarded as the master's responsibility. The innocent young girl fresh from the country sometimes made her way to 'sub-contractors' who were ostensibly engaged in placing country girls in good homes as servants, but instead ran bordellos and hired their girls out as prostitutes. The 'easy virtue' of the serving-maid was even enshrined in law. Florentine legislation (1325) fixing the punishment for rape provides varying fines in accordance with the age, marital status and social position of the victim.[11] The lowest fine of 25 *libri* applies to the rape of

[10] The following is based largely on Bronislaw Geremek, *Les marginaux parisiens aux XIVᵉ et XVᵉ siècles*, trans. Daniel Beauvois (Paris, 1976), pp. 256, 276–7, 282; Christiane Klapisch-Zuber, 'Célibat et service féminins dans la Florence du XVᵉ siècle', *Annales de démographie historique* (1981), pp. 289–302; J. Kirshner and A. Molho, 'The dowry and the marriage market in Early *Quattrocento* Florence', *Journal of Modern History*, 50 (1978), pp. 403–38; David Herlihy and Christiane Klapisch-Zuber, *Les toscanes et leurs familles* (Paris, 1978), pp. 60–2, 153, 161–3, 208, 320–1, 331, 416, 471, 520, 556–9, 597; Johann Plesner, *L'émigration de la campagne à la ville libre de Florence au XIIIᵉ siècle* (Copenhagen, 1934).

[11] R. Caggese (ed.), *Statuti della Repubblica fiorentina: Statuto del podestà dell'anno 1325* (Florence, 1921), III, p. 58.

a *famula* or *pedisseca*. If the girl consented or was a whore, there was no fine. The low fine applied to sexual relations with serving-girls reflects the low repute in which they were held.

Popular and *exempla* literature tend to present a similar picture of the female servant. The housemaid was regarded as easy prey to the lascivious advances of her employer, his sons or of the other servants, more a concubine than a mere domestic. She might serve as a go-between for her mistress, and was often accused of theft, treachery and infidelity. The dissolute maidservant who used her profession as a cover for prostitution was a familiar figure in contemporary literature. Many tales tell of the maid who in collusion with her mistress betrays her master; the most frequent theme concerns the maid who impersonates her mistress in order to test the husband's fidelity, conceals the wife's illegitimate pregnancy or gives her mistress a chance to dally with her lover.[12] Nearly all the female servants who appear in Jacques Fournier's 1323 inquisitorial trial of the residents of Montaillou were involved in sexual escapades. The convicted sodomite Arnold of Vernoille spoke of one maid known for her immorality 'for she is an animal'. Beatrice of Planisolles used her maid as a lookout while she carried on with her lover.[13] The preacher Jacques de Vitry claimed to have known a noble lady who had her maid beaten and thrown in the river for having served as a procuress.[14] A particular object of contempt was the old maid, who would go to any lengths to marry, including consort with the devil.[15]

Male servants were regarded as no less corrupt than their female counterparts, appearing as idle, garrulous, deceitful thieves and corruptors of housemaids. Jacques de Vitry accuses all the servants in Paris of such treachery, a charge which seems to be borne out by the later statistics of the number of domestics among the criminal elements

[12] Marguerite de Navarre, *L'Heptaméron*, ed. Michel François (Paris, 1967), pp. 137–42; Caesarius of Heisterbach, *Dialogus Miraculorum*, ed. J. Strange (2 vols, Cologne, 1851), IV, p. 100; Giovanni Boccaccio, *Decameron*, ed. Vittore Branca (Milan, 1976), IV, p. 10; Pierre Champion (ed.), *Les cent nouvelles nouvelles* (Paris, 1928), no. 35; Agnolo Firenzuola, *Ragionamenti*, in *Classici Italiani*, 83 (Milan, 1802), no. 3.

[13] Jean Duvernoy (ed.), *Le Régistre d'Inquisition de Jacques Fournier, évêque de Pamiers* (3 vols, Toulouse, 1965–6), III, p. 26; I, pp. 255–6.

[14] Thomas Frederick Crane (ed.), *The Exempla . . . of Jacques de Vitry* (London, 1890), p. 106.

[15] For a list of anecdotes concerning the old maid, see Stith Thompson, *Motif-Index to Folk-Literature* (6 vols, Bloomington, Ind., 1954–8), X, 750ff., J. 1811. 1. 1.

in Paris.[16] A stock figure was the servant Maymund, whom John Bromyard says was devoted to his master 'in mensa et prosperitate' but fled 'in bello et adversitate'.[17]

On the other hand, the occasional virtuous maid does appear, who advises her mistress to treat the servants with greater kindness, who rebukes a pilgrim for overeating, heals the sick and drives the devil away with her prayers. Thomas of Cantimpré tells of a maid of noble lineage who succeeded in converting her Jewish mistress.[18] The employment in Jewish homes of Christian servants was a subject which absorbed contemporary rabbinical scholars, who feared the consequences of such employment; although the blood libel charge which flourished beginning in the late twelfth century usually involved the martyrdom of male Christian boys in Jewish homes, rather than female servants.[19]

Humbert of Romans' model *Sermones ad diversos status* describes the reduced spiritual condition of the servant girl, who often did not have the opportunity to attend church or receive religious instruction.[20] At morning mass, her master was responsible for providing some training in the rudiments of the faith, but this seems to have been rarely observed. Jacques de Vitry tells of an unusually good woman who sometimes remained at home in order to give her maid a chance to attend church, and even lent her a cloak; this tale confirms how unusual it was for domestics, except for wet-nurses, to attend church.[21] The chief virtue to be inculcated in such girls was fear, lest they steal or be unfaithful to their masters. Humbert suggests that they were often secretly concubines and involved in carnal sin, readily subject to the temptations of the flesh. Some were ashamed to be employed as public prostitutes, but in private they willingly exposed themselves to sin, losing their virginity to the young men of the house, who preferred their own domestics to the embarrassment of association with public whores. This picture of the debased condition of the chambermaid is confirmed by such encyclopedists as Bartholomaeus Anglicus, who

---

[16] *Jacques de Vitry*, p. 57: 'garciones, serventes scolaribus, que omnes fere latrunculi solent esse . . .'; see Geremek, *Les marginaux parisiens*, pp. 276–7.

[17] *Jacques de Vitry*, p. 85.

[18] Thomas of Cantimpré, *Bonum Universale de Apibus* (Douai, 1827), p. 301.

[19] For a general survey, see Salo Baron, *A Social and Religious History of the Jews* (14 vols, New York, 1962–9), IX, X, *passim*. For a young girl found dead at Pfortsheim in 1261, see *AS*, 20 April V, 834.

[20] Humbert of Romans, *Sermones ad diversos status* (n.p., 1508), I, pp. 76, 98.

[21] *Jacques de Vitry*, p. 93.

notes that in addition to performing such menial tasks as cooking and baking, they often conceive children illegitimately, whose status is open to question. The chief virtue he demands of such girls is humility, lest they be beaten by their masters, who preserve the privileges of the traditional *pater familias*.[22]

This picture of moral debasement and sexual exploitation found in popular literature is balanced by the image of the saintly servant girl, which likewise flourished in the late thirteenth and early fourteenth centuries. Unlike their more elevated sisters, the trans-Alpine servant-saints in particular are survived by little contemporary documentation, and while their legends conform to those of the archetypal saints, little specific can be said about their social origins, the causes of their bondage and the nature of their ministry. They may rather be seen as local apotheoses of a type prevalent throughout Europe. Such a figure, for example, was Teresa (d. 1266), born in the village of Zambujal, who entered the service of the rector of the church of Ourem near Santarem in Portugal.[23] The summary legend alleges that poverty forced her into service, but despite her straitened circumstances, she gave to the poor. Sibillina Biscossi of Pavia (1287–1367), at the age of 12 became a servant to the Dominican sisters of penance as a result of the death of her parents. Much of her life she was blind and sick, living as a recluse with her sister Beatrice.[24] Radegunda of Wolfratshausen, the object of a flourishing cult throughout Bavaria, served as a domestic at the castle of Wellenburg. She likewise gave food from her master's table to the poor, and was eaten by wolves while returning from a local leprosarium where she did good works.[25] The entirely legendary account, much embellished in the seventeenth century on the occasion of the solemn translation of her relics, is lacking sufficient detail, but the main elements of the servant-legend are present.

Two northern European servant-saints, Notburga of Rottenburg and Margaret of Louvain, who have been the objects of somewhat more scholarly attention than most of their genre, have been described as 'true folk heroes' whose lives may be the composite of several figures combining pagan and Christian traditions. The documentation concerning Notburga is sparse, beginning with a brief legend in German,

[22] Bartholomaeus Anglicus, *De rerum proprietatibus*, ed. Georg Barthold (Frankfurt, 1601), VI, p. 11.
[23] *AS*, 3 September I, 786; *BS*, XII, 419.
[24] *AS*, 19 May III, 67–71; *BS*, III, 196.
[25] *AS*, 13 August III, 93–6; *BS*, X, 1352.

which may be linguistically dated to the early thirteenth century, which suggests an earlier lineage for the saint herself.[26] This tale was considerably expanded in the seventeenth century, and contains some similarity to the story of the laborer or ploughman, St Isidore of Madrid. While the original story contains no details of time or place, her cult spread throughout southern Germany, Croatia, Austria, Switzerland, Istria and the Tyrol, centered on the village of Eben. In its purest form, the legend tells of a nobleman's cook who gave leftovers to the poor. Angered by this act of charity, her mistress ordered her to give such scraps to the pigs, and rebuked the poor maid. After she died, the woman returned every night and grunted like a pig in the pigsty. Sometime afterwards, Notburga hired herself out to a peasant with the stipulation that she would not work in the evening. One Saturday, after cutting wheat in the fields, she hung up her sickle, prayed and returned to housework. When she left the peasant's employ, presumably because the contract had been breached, his health and fortune declined. The nobleman then took another wife, who ordered Notburga to return to her former duties. The saint made one request: when she died, the noble should place her body on a wagon drawn by two oxen; he should then follow the wagon, and wherever the beasts should stop, bury her. After she died, he followed these instructions to the letter, and built a chapel in her honor on the spot where the oxen had halted. This tale in its purest form suggests the folklore nature of Notburga's cult, and indeed of the entire 'servant as saint' theme, for the ordinary Christian elements of piety are entirely lacking. Notburga appears more witch than saint in the retribution she wreaks on those who doubt her ministry. The legend notes both Notburga's liberty to choose another employer, and her right to determine her conditions of labor.

The semi-legendary life of little Margaret of Louvain (1207–22/5) is based on a short, nearly contemporary account, along with remarks in the *Dialogus miraculorum* by the Cistercian hagiographer Caesarius

---

[26] *BS*, IX, 1070–3; *AS*, 14 September IV, 717. The best account is H. Bachmann, 'Die historischen Grundlage der Notburga-Legenda', *Tiroler-Heimat*, 24 (1960), pp. 5–49. For iconography, see Louis Réau, *Iconographie de l'art chrétien* (3 vols, Paris, 1958–9), III, 2, pp. 996–7. Notburga's legend has the ring of a folk-tale: 'Es war aines mal ein Edelmann, der het ein gotsförchtige fromme Dienerin: hies mit namen Notburga, die war sein liebe Koechin, und gab armen leuthen zimlich gehrn ihren herrn ohne schaden dass essen, so ybrig bliybe' (Bachmann, 'Die historischen', p. 6).

of Heisterbach.[27] Margaret was born around 1207, probably of rural ancestry, and at the time of her death Brabant was under the rule of Duke Henry I and his wife Marie de France. She was sent to Louvain to serve in the hospice belonging to her kinsman Amando of the Absoloens family, a clan which belonged to the local governing class and supplied consuls to the city. Amando and his wife decided to enter the Cistercian order. On the night of their departure, having gathered all their wealth together, they were visited by eight men, probably members of the guerilla bands hired by the duke, which wreaked depredations on the area. When Margaret was sent to fetch wine, these brigands brutally murdered the innkeeper and his wife, and intended raping the poor maid Margaret. One of the thieves took pity on her, and promised to marry her, but his cohorts refused. Instead they killed the maid, and threw her body in the nearby Dyle river. The next day her body was discovered by some local fishermen, who buried her lest they be blamed for the crime. Lights miraculously appeared that night around her tomb. Her body was exhumed and a chapel in Margaret's honor was erected at the hospice of St George under the patronage of the great Cistercian house of Villers and the Duke and Duchess of Brabant, who took part in the translation of her relics. A monk of Villers allegedly met her master Amando after his death, who reported that while he and his wife had not yet achieved full glory, Margaret was already safely in heaven.

The lives of these northern European servant-saints, despite their legendary nature, share certain common characteristics. Invariably of rural birth, such women served in the city or a local castle. They did not necessarily remain with the same employer throughout their lives. Rather, Notburga had at least two employers, one described as an 'Edelmann' or nobleman, the other as a 'Pauern' or peasant. She also had some control over her conditions of employment. Gertrude of Oosten (d. 1348) of rural stock, also worked at Delft in several places, 'as is the custom among serving maids'.[28] Since domestic service was clearly not a task befitting girls of noble lineage, hagiographical convention requires that, if possible, some case should be made for noble connections: she became a maid because of straitened economic cir-

---

[27] *AS*, 25 September I, 582–95; *BS*, VIII, 777–80; Caesarius of Heisterbach, VI, 34; Marie-Joseph Ollivier, 'La B. Marguerite de Louvain', *Revue Thomiste*, 4 (1896), pp. 592–618. For iconography, see E. Kirschbaum et al. (eds), *Lexikon der christlichen Ikonographie* (6 vols, Rome, 1968–), VII, pp. 504–5.

[28] *AS*, 6 January I, 349: 'more ancillarum ministrare diversis in locis, utpote temporalibus rebus tenuis.'

cumstances, or because she was orphaned, which meant that no dowry was available. Women of a certain class, if at all possible, preferred to enter a nunnery or beguinage rather than domestic service. Thus, when Lutgard of Aywières' father lost her dowry through poor investments, her mother suggested the path which lay before her: 'If you choose a mortal man, you will have nothing but the care of cows.' She thus entered the monastery of St Catherine at St Trond.[29] Another constant element in the lives of these saints is their devotion to the poor, to the extent of stealing scraps from their masters' table to give to the indigent, even in the face of their employers' cruelty. Similar acts of mercy and charity are to be found in the lives of SS. Elizabeth of Hungary, Isidore of Madrid, Medard and others.[30]

The documentation concerning the Italian servant-saints is far more numerous and reliable, but tends to confirm many of the elements in the northern *legendae*. The premier servant-saint was Zita of Lucca (1218?–72), who because of poverty left her native village of Monsegrati at the age of 12 to serve the Faytinelli of Lucca, where she was in charge of domestic affairs.[31] The Faytinelli are described as 'potentes et casatici' of the city, exiled in 1313 as Guelphs, who returned in 1331 during a general amnesty.[32] Like the other saints, despite her meager wages and the opposition of her master, Zita gave liberally to the poor. Her virtue extended to allowing prostitutes (*mulierculas*), pilgrims and the poor to use her bed when in need, to providing food in time of famine and to avoiding the other domestics – the *superstitiones aniles* – who were known for their foolishness and lewdness.[33] She was in no way tempted by the 'scurrilous words and incestuous embraces' of her fellow servants, which suggests that she and the others were related to their employer. Zita purposely scratched her face in order to become more unattractive. The problem of carnal relations between the servants and outsiders seems to have concerned the city fathers of Lucca, who passed legislation providing for fines and whipping for such behavior, in order to prevent pimps or others from enticing young girls to leave their employers. Servants were also prohibited from wearing costly garments. In order to prevent such young women also from turning into concubines, according

---

[29] Thomas of Cantimpré, *Vita Lutgardis*, in *AS*, 16 June IV, 191.

[30] E. Cobham Brewer, *A Dictionary of Miracles* (London, 1884), pp. 418–20.

[31] *BS*, XII, 1483; *AS*, 27 April III, 505: '. . . circa gubernationem domus et familiae utriusque sexus et aetatis eorum'.

[32] Christine Meek, *Lucca, 1369–1400* (Oxford, 1978), p. 190.

[33] *AS*, 27 April III, 505–7.

to the statutes of 1308, such servants were expected to marry.[34] But since Zita's ministry preceded this legislation, it would appear that her virtue was meant as a foil to the otherwise amoral behavior of the average serving-girl.

For morning prayer, Zita generally attended the nearby church of St Fridian, but preferred to avoid the company of the frivolous women who crowded the church. Thus, she was neither talkative nor lewd, two vices often applied to the servant class. Zita's biography, which is based on notarized statements collected in 1278 under the patronage of her employers, describes in some detail the circuit of churches she customarily visited in the region between Lucca and Pisa, which suggests that she possessed considerable freedom to move about.[35] Immediately after her death on 27 April 1272, during the funeral financed by the Faytinelli, a large crowd gathered around and the body had to be moved lest it be dismembered by admiring worshippers in search of relics. All manner of miracles were performed, including cures of blindness, possession, lameness, muteness, infertility, troubled pregnancy and fever, all confirmed by a distinguished professor of law at Pavia, Ugolino de la Fontana. A throng of local noblemen and clergy took part in her funeral, and such miracles occurred sporadically until 1380, when steps were taken to push her case.[36] Among the more notable miracles was that performed on Pietro dei Faytinelli, who fell ill during a trip to Provence (c. 1310); although three physicians attended him, they feared for his life, and he was only saved by prayers to Zita.[37] During her lifetime it is reported that Zita was especially solicitous toward those condemned to death, and when she heard the bells of Lucca heralding an execution, she prayed for the souls of the victims. This charitable nature was confirmed in a *post-mortem* miracle which occurred in February 1300. A certain Checus had admitted under torture to taking part in a theft at Capua and was condemned to death. After he was hanged, Zita cut the rope, while the second man, condemned with him, his alleged accomplice, remained dead, for he was the true criminal. Checus then came to Lucca with the torn rope to testify in Zita's favor.[38] Despite the scepticism of some who may well

---

[34] *Statuto del commune di Lucca dell'anno MCCCVIII* (Lucca, 1867), III, p. 55.

[35] *AS*, 27 April III, 508 ff.

[36] On her cult see E. R. Kemp, *Canonisation and Authority in the Western Church* (London, 1948), pp. 124–5.   [37] *AS*, 27 April III, 514.

[38] *AS*, 27 April III, 515. On this hagiographical motif, see Baudouin de Gaiffier, 'Un thème hagiographique: le pendu miraculeusement sauvé', in *Etudes critiques d'hagiographie et d'iconologie* (Brussels, 1967), 194–226.

have belonged to a faction opposed to the Faytinelli, the city passed regulations for the care of the church of St Martin during the festivities devoted to St Zita, providing men to keep guard and prevent trouble-makers from doing any damage or performing scurrilous acts.[39]

Many of these elements are likewise found in the life of Margaret of Città di Castello (c. 1286/7–1320), which is documented by three nearly contemporary biographies based upon notarized statements testifying to her virtuous life and miracles.[40] Margaret's father Parisio was the castellan of Metola, where she was born, and served as captain of the people at Massa Trabaria. Because of a congenital deformity and blindness she was sequestered in her room by her parents under the care of a nurse. All her biographers are unanimous in berating her family for the cruel treatment accorded her, although at an early age she allegedly devoted herself to religious self-denial. As a child she was taken to the tomb of a Franciscan holy man at Città di Castello in hopes of effecting a cure, and there was abandoned by her parents. After some difficulty the nascent saint was taken in as a servant by the monastery of St Margaret, but her excessive piety led to her expulsion by the sisters. She was then adopted by the kindly Grigia and her husband Venturino, presumably as a servant. While the term *ancilla* is applied to her in the spiritual sense (*ancilla Christi*), it is reported that she was given a small room in the upper part of the house to dwell in. Later tradition describes her as a servant, which seems plausible.[41] Her adopted family seems to have taken an active part in the encouragement of her cult; for two miracles are reported involving members of the house: in one, she saved them from a fire; in another she performed a miracle at the baptism of Grigia's niece.[42] She apparently

[39] Francesco Paolo Luisi, 'L'Anziano di Zita', in *Miscellanea lucchese di studi storici e letterari in memoria di Salvatore Bongi* (Lucca, 1931), 73, n. 1, notes derisive remarks made concerning Zita's alleged miracles. *Statuto . . . di Lucca*, I, 7; IV, 1, on festivities in Zita's honor. Opposition continued to be voiced because her cult was not approved by Rome.

[40] M-H. Laurent, 'La plus ancienne légende de la B. Marguerite de Città di Castello', *Archivum Fratrum Praedicatorum*, 10 (1940), pp. 109–31; 'Vita beatae Margaritae virginis de Civitate Castelli sororis tertii ordinis de paenitentia sancti Dominici', *Analecta Bollandiana*, 19 (1900), pp. 22–36; *AS*, 13 April II, 190–8; see also *BS*, VIII, 756–9; William Boniwell, *The Life of Margaret of Castello* (Dublin, 1955).

[41] Laurent, 'La plus ancienne legende', p. 124. When Margaret was abandoned by her parents, one biographer (*Vita*, 24) says: 'Christus vere pauper sue ancille de hospitio providet.'

[42] Laurent, 'La plus ancienne légende', p. 124; *Vita*, 32–3.

wore the mantle of a Dominican tertiary, the order which encouraged her cult, and was active in spreading the faith among Italy's lower classes. Despite Margaret's miracles, some disagreement seems to have arisen over her claim to sanctity, for while the participants at the translation of her relics demanded immediate veneration, the Church authorities refused. But when a Bolognese professor of civil law, Orlando, spoke in her favor, and a miracle occurred, the council of Città established a commission of inquiry including physicians, clerks and laymen, to examine her heart, which was found to be intact.[43] Her miracles, which included 'driving away demons, curing various illnesses, reviving the dead and predicting the future', were performed mostly on the women or children of local villages. Such miracles differ little from those attributed to other contemporary saints, although Margaret's ministry clearly appealed to a lower social class than contemporary royal or noble figures. Her vision of the divine presence in the Eucharist recalls another orphan-turned-servant, Sibillina Biscossi of Pavia.[44] The initial refusal of the Church to accept her cult and her primarily female, rural constituency, suggests a genuinely popular cult.

In addition to Margaret, Zita and Sibillina, three other contemporary Italian *ancillae* complete the picture of the rural maid forced into service: Veridiana Attavanti of Castelfiorentino (d. 1247?), Oringa or Christiana of Santa Croce sull'Arno (1240–1310) and Jane of Orvieto (c. 1264–1306). Oringa[45] was born to humble parents, was orphaned and mistreated by her brothers, who forced her into service at Lucca after she had rejected entreaties to marry. She then took service with a lady Margaret, went on pilgrimage with her and founded a convent at Florence under Augustinian auspices. After a long illness she died, and her cult was authorized by the commune of Santa Croce. Veridiana took service at Florence with kinsmen who disapproved of her efforts to help the poor during a famine; while Jane was an orphan girl of Carnaiola who refused an offer of marriage and became a seamstress.[46] While these Italian saints share all the motifs common to other servant-saints, they contain some features

43 Laurent, 'La plus ancienne légende', p. 127.

44 *AS*, 19 March III, 67–71.

45 The lives in *AS*, 10 January I, 650–62 were produced in the seventeenth century; cf. *BS*, IV, 324–5.

46 On Veridiana, *AS*, 1 February I, 254–60; Réau, *Iconographie*, III, 3, p. 1311; *BS*, XII, 1023. On Jane, *BS*, VI, 556–7; *AS*, 23 July V, 326; L. Fumi (ed.), *Leggenda della b. Vanna da Orvieto* . . . (Città di Castello, 1885).

peculiar to Italian piety: (a) the greater reliability of the sources, which are based on notarized eye-witness accounts of the putative saint's life and miracles, in accordance with the more rigorous standards laid down by the Church; (b) the obvious role of the saint's employer in supporting her cult, which could improve the clan's political fortunes; (c) the popular enthusiasm immediately following the saint's death; (d) the greater attention devoted to the saint's *post-mortem* miracles, which allow us to identify the largely rural, female constituency of the servant saint; and (e) the appearance of some opposition to the cult, presumably on the part of her patron's political foes.

In addition to these serving-maids who achieved the honors of veneration, the *ancilla* as a hagiographical type appears in several contemporary saint's lives, which allow us to glimpse the relationship between the maid and her mistress, and provide more details concerning the duties she performed. The women who appear in such accounts are usually 'ladies-in-waiting' or inmates of a convent, who perform domestic duties, although the appellations *ancilla* or *pedissequa* are applied. Such figures, along with the many servant girls who themselves witnessed or experienced miracles and who testified at canonization trials, served as a foil to the popular image of the lecherous, talkative, thieving maid. One of the most remarkable sources of thirteenth-century hagiography is the *Libellus* (or *Dicta*) *Quattuors Ancillarum*, the reminiscences of the four maidservants of Elizabeth of Thuringia (1207–31), one of the most popular saints of the period. This document served as the core of her extensive canonization file, and was probably composed in 1236, perhaps by Ulrich von Durne, prior of the Teutonic Knights at Marburg, the site of her relics.[47] These four women remained an inextricable part of the Elizabeth legend, for they were often illustrated alongside her minis-

---

[47] Several editions of this work have appeared. I have used the version in Albert Huyskens, 'Zum 700. Geburtstag der hl. Elisabeth von Thüringen', *Historisches Jahrbuch*, 28 (1907), pp. 810–38. See also P. Diodorus Henniges, 'Prologus et epilogus in dicta IV ancillarum S. Elisabeth Thuringiae Lantgraviae', *Archivum Franciscanum Historicum*, 3 (1909), pp. 464–90. A useful recent article on the relationship between Elizabeth and her servants is André Vauchez, 'Charité et pauvreté chez Sainte Elisabeth de Thuringe d'après les actes du procés de canonisation' in Michel Mollat (ed.), *Etudes sur l'histoire de la pauvreté (Moyen Âge – XVIe siècle)*, 2 vols (Paris, 1974), I, pp. 163–73. A good survey of Elizabeth's sources is found in *BS*, IV, 1110–23.

tering to the sick, carrying a jug, the traditional symbol of service.[48] Although at least two of them may not be classified as mere domestics, their testimony tells us much about the ideal relationship of the servant to her mistress in a noble household. Isentrude is explicitly referred to as a *nobilis femina* closer to the saint than the other servants, although the precise meaning of her nobility may be subject to dispute.[49] These four women remained with Elizabeth after her marriage to Landgrave Louis in 1221 until her death, and thus could testify to the purity of her life and miraculous powers. Guda and Isentrude served the land-gravina as ladies-in-waiting between 1222 and 1228, while the maid-servants Irmegarde and Elizabeth assisted her at the hospital of Marburg between 1228 and 1231.

Both Guda and Isentrude were attached to the saint when she was four and they were five years old, when her father, King Andrew of Hungary affianced her to Landgrave Louis; at 14 she married and began to bear children. They thus served her as playmates, and their childhood games are described in great detail. At this age, Elizabeth observed no social distinctions, frolicking equally with both her chosen companions and poor little girls whom she gave gifts and money. This easy familiarity extended to adulthood, when Elizabeth refused to be addressed as mistress, preferring the familiar form of address.[50] Before her husband's death, Elizabeth lived and worked closely with them, weaving wool for the poor and the Franciscan friars, under whose influence she had fallen.[51] The four women constantly attended her, and were privy to all her secrets.[52] She allegedly always spoke amicably, calling them 'delectas vel amicas'. In fact, the treatment she accorded these women and the other servants was regarded as a prime example of her charitable nature. During meals she allegedly set aside bits of food for her maidservants. (It is not clear whether this refers to the four witnesses, who were surely well-fed, or other less highly placed domestics.) She showed a similar concern for the servants of others.[53]

[48] Reiner Haussherr et al., *Die Zeit der Staufer* (4 vols, Stuttgart, 1977), II, no. 207; I, 404–5.

[49] Huyskens, 'Zum 700. Geburtstag', p. 821: 'nobilis femina plus reliquis pedis-sequis ei familiaris'.   [50] ibid., p. 810.

[51] ibid., p. 816: 'Item viro marito ipsa cum suis ancillis lanam filabat, telam filii faciens, ad vestes fratrum minorum et pauperum.'

[52] ibid., p. 812: 'conscia omnium secretorum eius'.

[53] ibid., p. 814: 'In ancillarum vero penuria plusquam in propria puniebatur, quando non poterat eis iustis bonis ministrare', and 'de serviciis villicorum et quandoque inveniens tantum cibum eicitum dixit ancillis: "modo sunt tantum comeditis".'

Elizabeth's intimacy with these servants is highlighted by her late-night prayers, for the servants were required to waken her in time; they describe the saint's sleeping arrangements with her husband, which led to some embarrassing moments when he was awakened; and they report the penitential beatings they administered to the nascent saint.[54] These women formed a part of Elizabeth's dowry, for when her husband died and she was forced to leave Marburg for a life of mendicancy, they accompanied her. Only when the tyrannical Contrad of Marburg imposed a strict penitential regimen on the saint in 1228, did he forcibly separate her from Guda and Isentrude, which caused the landgravina great grief. Elizabeth was prohibited from speaking to her former companions without his permission, a step which caused much resentment among the servants. Nevertheless, they accompanied her on her ministry to the poor, sick and leprous.

According to eye-witness testimony, several saints of high station, as a sign of their humility, performed the tasks normally reserved for servants, and from such statements we learn the kinds of chores assigned domestics; they thereby achieved the title *ancilla Dei* as a result of spiritual as well as physical labor. Margaret of Hungary (1243–70), daughter of King Bela IV of Hungary, who dwelt in the royal monastery of Veszprem from childhood, and rejected all pleas to marry, willingly carried water, lit the fire, washed dishes and other utensils, and cooked.[55] Margaret's nurse and tutor Olimpiades, who had cared for the saint since she was three and a half years old, likewise describes her performing kitchen duties, including cleaning fish and other unpleasant, but necessary, tasks.[56] Along with the other occupants, she cared for sick and scabrous sisters, making their beds, feeding them and generally tidying up. She also employed an easy familiarity with the domestic staff, which was not always rewarded, striving to become a servant of the poor rather than a daughter of the king; for the new ideal of social service inevitably led to an identification with the domestic class among certain saints.[57] Dauphine of

[54] ibid., p. 815: 'fecit se fortiter, verberari per manus ancillarum'.

[55] Franknoì, *Monumenta romana*, p. 227: 'in sua septimana faciebat coquinam, tulit aquam, et lavabat scutellas et ollas, et accendebat ignem et portabat aquam et alia scundigia faciebat, multum libenter et cum magna humilitate'.

[56] ibid., p. 219: 'libenter faciebat conquinam, lavabat ollas et scutellas, et preparabat pisces, et faciebat alia omnia servitia, que erant necessaria'.

[57] ibid., p. 261: 'Deus, vellem quod ego essem una ancilla pauperis potius, quam filia regis, quia magis possem servire Deo.'; and, p. 219: '. . . libenter serviebat infirmis in omnibus suis necessitatibus, et cum manibus suis faciebat eis ad

Languedoc (d. 1360), wife of St Elzéar of Sabran and herself the object of a canonization inquiry held at Apt in 1360, dwelt for many years in a hospice and allegedly also willingly performed the tasks reserved for servants, including brushing out the sawdust, washing kitchen utensils and dining with the other domestics.[58]

The saint as servant perhaps best embodies the Church's ambivalent attitude toward womankind, at once idealized as Mary, mother of God, and disdained as Eve the temptress.[59] On the one hand, the maidservant was the object of popular humor, despised and distrusted, subject to the sexual exploitation of her masters or fellow employees. At first, as Stephan of Bourbon said, such country girls might be less attractive than their urban kinswomen because of their lack of finery.[60] But once they undertook their new profession, their moral condition declined. As late as the fourteenth century, the encyclopedist Pierre Bercheure, who makes heavy use of Scriptural sources, regarded the servile condition of the *ancilla*, who is occupied with dirty work, wears cast-off clothes and consumes the worst food, as a reflection of her corrupt moral state.[61] She could be treated like a chattel according to both biblical and Roman precedent, and following the example of Hagar, who showed disrespect for her mistress Sarah, she could be expelled and forced to roam about. Only the strictest discipline, he

---

comedendum, et dabat eis comedere et bibere, purgabat et scopabat cameras earum, et necessaria purgabat, quando oportebat, et rasit capita septem in una meridie.' Several witnesses spoke of the kindness she showed the servants.

[58] Jacques Cambell, *Enquête pour le procès de canonisation de Dauphine de Puimichel, comtesse d'Ariano* (+26-XI-1360) (Turin, 1978), pp. 48, 326: 'ipsa domina per multos annos in hospicio habitacionis sue officia vilia et ancillaria sibi assumpsit et illa exercuit, videlicet scobis mundando hospicium, lavando scutellas et ollas et alia vasa in coquina, et cum alia servitrice sive ancilla suarum familiarium, ad mensam ultima sedebat et comedebat; et in omnibus et per omnia sicut ancilla se gerebat, serviebat et faciebat.'

[59] See, e.g., Eleanor McLaughlin, 'Women, power and the pursuit of holiness in medieval Christianity', in Rosemary Ruether and Eleanor McLaughlin (eds), *Women of Spirit. Female Leadership in the Jewish and Christian Traditions* (New York, 1979), pp. 99–130; and 'Equality of souls, inequality of sexes: woman in medieval theology', in Rosemary Ruether (ed.), *Religion and Sexism* (New York, 1974), pp. 213–66.

[60] Etienne de Bourbon, *Anecdotes historiques, legendes et apologues*, ed. A. Leroy de la Marche (Paris, 1877): 'rusticane mulieres, non habentes vestes caudatas, per eos non trahuntur, nec burgenses, sed que dicuntur nobiles'.

[61] Pierre Bercheure, *Reductorium moralis*, I, 10, and *Dictionarium morale*, 175–6, in *Opera omnia* (4 vols, Mainz, 1609).

argued, would reign her naturally animal passions and curb her sensuality. The good maid should be endowed with the virtues of humility, sagacity and diligence.

On the other hand, an anagogical definition of the servant refers to the *ancilla Christi* as the Church itself, and the soul or person who submits himself to God's will, which allows the servant a place among the blessed despite Bercheure's harsh condemnation. The temptations which block the servant's path to perfection are all the more severe when one considers her low condition: orphaned or rejected by her family, buffeted by cruel masters who frustrate her natural charity, subjected to the taunts and lascivious advances of her fellow servants or employers. Her virtuous life and miracles were intended as a solace to others of her class, providing a truly popular saint to one of the most dispossessed and disenfranchised sections of society. However, even such a figure required the patronage of a powerful family to achieve recognition. Although perhaps a later invention, many such women were reportedly associated with the new mendicant orders, particularly the tertiaries. The very virtues embodied by the servant-saint – humility, charity, poverty – were the hallmarks of mendicancy.[62] And the popular enthusiasm generated by a saint like Zita of Lucca was so great, that on the days preceding the translation of her relics, because the streets surrounding the small church of St Fridian were so thronged with pilgrims, the authorities feared for the safety of their charge.[63]

[62] Peter Ferrand, *Legenda sancti Dominici*, I, ed. M-H. Laurent, *Monumenta ordinis praedicatorum historica* (Rome, 1935), XVI, p. 248.
[63] *AS*, 27 April III, 513ff.

7

Prostitution and Repentance in Late Medieval Perpignan

LEAH LYDIA OTIS

'Building brothels is a pious, holy and deserving work, compatible with the holy scriptures, the holy fathers and the sacred canons:'[1] thus, tradition has it, read the signposts throughout Perpignan erected by the Dominicans of that town in 1608, in their effort to collect alms for the reconstruction of the city's medieval center of prostitution. Without entering into a debate on the authenticity of the tradition,[2] it is possible to appreciate this anecdote as a particularly striking though not implausible instance of the persistence into the early modern period, in some minds and in some regions, of the legitimacy which prostitution had enjoyed in the late Middle Ages.[3]

The place of prostitution in late medieval society – the legitimacy which it enjoyed, and the institutions which surrounded it – have only begun to be investigated and understood by medievalists in the past decade or so. Up until the 1970s, which saw a flowering of interest in the history of women, of marginal social groups and of sexuality, prostitution had been a topic of research neglected, one might even say avoided, by 'legitimate' historians. The numerous books and articles

---

[1] 'Edificare lupanaria est opus pium, sanctum et meritorium, consonum sancte scripture, sanctis patribus et sacris canonibus.'

[2] The text is presented by Emile Desplanque, *Les Infâmes dans l'ancien droit roussillonnais* (Perpignan, 1893). He cites no source, but is an author who generally relies on archival documents, and indeed classified the Perpignan town archives.

[3] Although prostitution was officially abolished in France in 1560, the first royal initiative against prostitution in Spain was taken in 1623; Perpignan was under Spanish sovereignty from the late fifteenth to the mid-seventeenth century. For other theological defenses of authorized prostitution in seventeenth-century Spain, see J. M. Guardia, 'De la prostitution en Espagne', in A. J. B. Parent-Duchatelet (ed.), *De la prostitution dans la ville de Paris*, 3rd edn (Paris, 1857), vol. 2.

on prostitution published previously had been largely the work of
littérateurs and of local amateur historians, the former producing
several monumental universal histories of prostitution based on published sources, and the latter a series of monographs which were often
no more than the transcription of local documents. The classic histories
of prostitution, written in the early and mid-nineteenth century,[4]
antedate the most enlightening of these monographs,[5] and as the more
recent histories of prostitution tend simply to recapitulate the earlier
models,[6] the bibliography on prostitution remained diffuse and confusing until the appearance in recent years of several important monographs and a regional study of prostitution.[7] The following discussion
is based on this new research, principally on the regional study of
prostitution in medieval Languedoc.

Tolerated as an inevitable social phenomenon in the high Middle

[4] The best known are *Histoire de la prostitution chez tous les peuples du monde* by
Pierre Dufour (a pseudonym, probably for the prolific *littérateur*, Paul Lacroix), a
six-volume work published from 1851 to 1853, and *De la prostitution en Europe de
l'antiquité jusqu'à la fin du XVIᵉ siècle* by Rabutaux (Paris, 1851). *Histoire de la
législation sur les femmes publiques* by the jurist Sabatier, first published in 1827,
largely recapitulated the relevant pages in Delamare's *Traité de police* (1722).

[5] Some of the more interesting monographs on southern French prostitution are:
H. Mireur, *La prostitution à Marseille* (Paris–Marseille, 1882); L. Barthélemy, *La
prostitution à Marseille documents nouveaux* (Marseille, 1883); L. Le Pileur, *La prostitution: documents tirés des archives d'Avignon* (Paris, 1908); and M. J. Chalande, 'La
maison publique à Toulouse', *Mémoires de l'Académie des Sciences, Inscriptions et Billes
Lettres de Toulouse*, 10th ser., 11 (1911), pp. 65–86. For central Europe, see J.
Schrank, *Die Prostitution in Wien* (2 vols, Vienna, 1886), and for Italy, C. Calza,
'Documenti sulla prostituzione in Venezia', *Giornale italiano delle malattie veneree e
della pelle*, 4 (1869), and A. Fabretti, *La prostituzione in Perugia* (Torino, 1890),
among others.

[6] Probably the best history of prostitution to date is I. Bloch's *Die Prostitution*
(2 vols, Berlin, 1912–25), of which I have only been able to consult the second
volume. One of the most recent and easily available histories is V. L. Bullough's *The
History of Prostitution* (New York, 1964). The same author has published *A Bibliography of Prostitution* (New York–London, 1977), which is far from complete for the
Middle Ages.

[7] The most important monographs are the chapter on prostitution in B.
Geremek's *Les marginaux parisiens aux XIVᵉ et XVᵉ siècles*, trans. Daniel Beauvois
(Paris, 1976); J. Rossiaud, 'Prostitution, jeunesse et société dans les villes du Sud-
est au XVᵉ siècle', *Annales ESC*, 31 (1976), pp. 289–325; and R. C. Trexler, 'La
prostitution florentine au XVᵉ siècle: patronages et clientèles', *Annales ESC*, 36
(1981), pp. 983–1015. See also J. Brundage, 'Prostitution in the medieval canon
law', *Signs*, 1 (1976), pp. 825–45. A regional study of prostitution was the subject of
my doctoral dissertation, L. Otis, *Nisi in postribulo: Prostitution in Languedoc from the
Twelfth to the Sixteenth Century*, presented at Columbia University in 1980. This work

Ages, prostitution in Languedocian towns gradually developed into a veritable institution of late medieval urban society, with its own rules, limits and rights, imposed and guaranteed by municipal, royal and sometimes ecclesiastical authority. The key factor in this transformation of prostitution from a mere social fact to an organized and institutionalized aspect of urban life was the progressive recognition, from the late thirteenth to the late fourteenth century, of official red light districts, in which prostitutes were not only obliged, but authorized to reside. Thus the passive toleration of the high Middle Ages, typical of the Augustinian tradition of resignation to the social evils of an inevitably imperfect world, was replaced by an active interest in the organization and regulation of the business of prostitution. Red light districts were defined, sometimes after collective deliberation of the urban community, and policed by muncipal officers; a code of social behavior for prostitutes was issued and enforced by the municipality.

The intervention of secular authorities in the business of prostitution became more energetic at the end of the fourteenth century, when certain municipalities, apparently unsatisfied with the security and surveillance afforded by the official red light districts, decided to reinforce their control of prostitution by limiting all such activity to one municipally owned brothel. These brothels were protected by royal as well as municipal officers; the king of France was not only willing to grant his safeguard to such houses, but soon became the sole authority able to grant permission for the creation of such centers, from which he sometimes drew certain financial benefits. Almost as zealously as they protected official houses of prostitution, the municipal and royal administration, notably the Parlement of Toulouse, repressed illegal competition, prosecuting procurers and keepers of illicit houses. This system of authorized prostitution flourished in Languedoc until the mid-sixteenth century, when the influence of reforming ideas, combined with other factors, convinced the municipal authorities that the system of municipally organized prostitution should be dismantled.

In most Languedocian towns of the fifteenth century, prostitution was limited to one house, which, if privately rather than publicly owned, was usually the property of one or more of the great *bourgeois*

---

includes an exhaustive bibliography. A revised version of this dissertation is to be published in 1985 by the University of Chicago Press under the title *Prostitution in Medieval Society: The History of an Urban Institution in Languedoc.*

or nobles of the community. Between the private or public owner of the brothel and the prostitutes residing there, stood the middleman who 'farmed' the brothel – that is, who paid the owner a flat yearly fee in exchange for the right to all profits. Conscious of the abuses which could occur in such a system, the municipalities began to regulate the financial dealings between manager and prostitute, fixing maximum rates for room and board, and regulating other aspects of life in the brothel, for example, the admission of customers, the prohibition of procurers and closing during Holy Week. Even in the large Mediterranean towns where a red light district with numerous houses and owners continued to flourish (as in Arles, Avignon and many Italian towns), the municipalities often issued ordinances regulating financial and other relations between the owners and/or managers and the prostitutes.

Closely related to the evolution of prostitution in medieval Languedoc was the growth of communities of repentant sisters in the same period. Stemming from a renewed interest in penitence, such institutions were established in Languedoc by bishops and pious laymen alike throughout the thirteenth and early fourteenth centuries. While some of these convents were under ecclesiastical control, others depended on municipal officers, who appreciated their potential as retirement houses for elderly prostitutes, or as half-way houses for younger prostitutes hoping to be 'reinstated' into the mainstream of society. The fortunes of such communities waned at the same time as institutionalized prostitution was dismantled in the sixteenth century.

Although research on medieval prostitution has made considerable strides in the past decade, much remains to be done before a definitive synthesis of the subject can be undertaken. Essential to providing a sound basis for such a synthesis s ithe continued publication of monographs on medieval prostitution, elucidating the variety of forms this institution took in different cities and regions, and compensating for the sporadic nature of the surviving documentation. Only in a monograph, or in a long-term meticulous regional study, can the historian discover all the miscellaneous documents with a bearing on the history of prostitution. It is the aim of this essay to provide one such monograph, focusing on the very town where the Dominican community of the early seventeenth century continued to defend brothel-building as a pious work: Perpignan, capital of the region of Roussillon.

Catalonian in language and culture, the region of Roussillon, now a part of France, was ruled in the late Middle Ages by the kings of

Aragon and of Majorca.[8] Its largest town, Perignan,[9] like all important centers of commerce in the Mediterranean world at that time, boasted an authorized center of prostitution, and a community for repentant women. Although not quantitatively impressive, the documents concerning these institutions which survive in the archives of Perpignan are qualitatively interesting, casting a new light on certain aspects of these peculiar urban institutions. Dating from the fourteenth and fifteenth centuries, the relevant documents are found in three series: the records of the kingdom of Aragon and the county of Roussillon,[10] a cartulary and a register of the municipality of Perpignan[11] and some charters and papers concerning the convent of St Mary Magalene of Perpignan,[12] some of which have been discussed already by the nineteenth-century Perpignanese historian and archivist Emile Desplanque.[13]

Although there are occasional references to prostitutes from an earlier period,[14] the first text attesting to the existence of an authorized center of prostitution in Perpignan is a royal privilege granted by Peter IV of Aragon to the consuls of the town on their request in 1380.[15] Its presence in the elegant town cartulary testifies to the importance accorded to this aspect of urban life in the Middle Ages, and to the seriousness with which regulations concerning centers of

[8] For the history of Roussillon, see J. Calmette and P. Vidal, *Histoire de Roussillon* (Paris, 1975). The county was under French sovereignty from 1462 to 1493.

[9] See P. Vidal, *Histoire de la ville de Perpignan* (Paris, 1897; reprint. Marseille, 1975). Vidal estimates the population of Perpignan to have been about 24,000 in the 1340s (p. 222).

[10] *Archives départementales de Pyrénées-Orientales* (henceforward cited as *AD P-O*), Series B. B. Alart, *Inventaire sommaire* (Paris, 1868).

[11] *Archives municipales de Perpignan* (henceforward *AM Perp.*) AA 1 and BB 7. Manuscript inventory by E. Desplanque.

[12] *AD P-O*, H 256. Typescript inventory.

[13] Desplanque, *Infâmes*. A further study of prostitution and repentance in Perpignan is justified for many reasons. It will, of course, bring these documents to the attention of a wider audience, whereas the above book is known mainly to regional historians. Desplanque did not, moreover, fully exploit – or explain – the documents he cites, and his conclusions are sometimes debatable or even erroneous. These texts can be better appreciated in the light of recent research in the history of prostitution and repentance, and in the light of other Perpignanese documents not exploited by Desplanque.

[14] A sumptuary law issued in 1308 excuses prostitutes from the observation of certain articles (Vidal, *Histoire de Perpignan*, p. 217). For a text on procurers, see note 42 below.

[15] *AM Perp.* AA 1, 263r°ff.

prostitution were taken by contemporary authorities. In requesting the document, the consuls were principally concerned with maintaining the security of the neighborhood in question and of the town, a recurring theme of the history of prostitution in this period.[16] The privilege authorizes the consuls to fortify the red light district,[17] and to install a system of security. There was to be only one entrance to that district,[18] a gate to be guarded by a strong man, chosen by the consuls,[19] who would refuse entrance to those bearing arms, obliging them, with the authority of the king, to leave him their weapons.[20] Should the gate-keeper prove inadequate, the consuls had the right to remove him and take another man.[21] They were further granted the right to provide for the gate-keeper's salary and the expense of the brothel walls by levying a special tax on the city's public women.[22]

Such a red light district – a fortified town within a town, with tightly controlled entrance and exit – existed in other Mediterranean towns, as is proved for the city of Valencia, for example, by an eye-witness account of 1501.[23] But the privilege granted by Peter of Aragon to the

[16] The consuls sought to avoid '. . . crimina et excessus . . . mala et scandala plurima . . . mutilaciones membrorum, vulnera et alia multa dampna que in bordello ville eiusdem fiunt . . .'. See Otis, *Nisi in postribulo*, pp. 72–3.

[17] '. . . concedimus per privilegium speciale ac licenciam . . . quod consules . . . possint et eas liceat licite et impune dictum bordellum parientibus sive muro claudere sive claudere facere . . .'.

[18] '. . . quod nemo possit vel audeat bordellum ipsum intrare nec exire ab inde, nisi per unicam januam . . .'.

[19] 'Quod in porta eadem sit et stet continue unus homo sufficiens atque bonus pro custodia dicti bordelli et pro preservacione ac conservacione etiam personarum in bordello ipso intrantium ac bonorum et rerum quas et que secum portaverint dicte intrantes persone.' 'Quod dicti consules . . . possint eligere, ponere et tenere perpetuo in porta eadem pro ipsius bordelli custodia unum bonum et ydoneum hominem . . .'.

[20] '. . . quidem homo seu custos possit et debeat auctoritate nostra regia prohibere totaliter ne quis cum armis sive arnesiis intret in dictum bordellum . . .'.

[21] 'Quem hominem . . . casu quo ipsum . . . insufficientem inveniant consules . . . possint consules . . . eorem arbitrio destituere et totaliter removere et alium de novo eligere . . .'.

[22] 'Et ulterius possint et valeant consules . . . tam pro salario scilicet dicti hominis seu custodis quam pro clausura bordelli eiusdem quam etiam pro aliis sumptibus et expensis que et quas premissorum pretextu fieri contigerit quovismodo illud subsidium sive jus quod ipsis consulibus racionabile videbitur atque iustum imponere et statuere in dicto bordello illudque colligere et colligi exigi facere et levari per quemcumque voluerint consules superdicti a mulieribus . . .'.

[23] Antoine de Lallaing, lord of Montigny, describes the place as 'grand comme une petite ville et fermé à l'entour de murs et de une seule porte. Et devant la porte

consuls of Perpignan is not such an account; it is merely the blueprint for a fortified, patrolled center of prostitution, not the proof of the actual existence of such a center in 1380, as Desplanque has tried to claim. Verifying or disproving the realization of such a plan is not an easy matter, given that the archives of Perpignan, so rich in official documents, lack the practical texts detailing the daily functioining of the municipality in the late Middle Ages: neither the deliberations of the municipal council nor the consular account books have survived for that period. In so far as the fortification of the red light district of Perpignan is concerned, one finds no reference to such a wall in the police ordinances of the fifteenth century.[24] The first document to mention walls around the brothel is from 1496, when a resident of the town was granted permission to build extensions onto a house for the use of public women located 'within the walls of the *lupanar* or *prostibulum*'.[25] As to the municipal gate-keeper, it seems unlikely that such an officer was ever employed. Three registers of oaths sworn by town officials survive in the Perpignan archives; they all include oaths of the town gate-keepers, but none mentions a brothel gate-keeper.[26] The only other reference to controlling entrance to a place of prostitution is in the permission granted to a town resident in 1496;[27] but in the latter document, it was the owner of one particular brothel who was to control entrance, not a municipal employee hired to patrol the entire red light district, as Desplanque has implied. Indeed, the fact that such a surveillance was needed for an individual house would imply that it was not provided by the city. There is no mention, more-

---

y est ordonné ung gibet pour les malfaicteurs qui porroient estre dedans; à la porte, ung homme, à ce ordonné, oste les bastons des veuillans entre dedans . . .'; cited by Rabutaux in *De la Prostitution*, p. 102.

[24] See note 38 below.

[25] '. . . intus clausuram lupanaris sive prostibuli inter portalia vulgo dicta de Elna et de Bages dicte ville Perpiniani noviter constructi et edifficati'; *AD P-O*, B 343, 5vᵒ. See note 34 below. This is, in fact, a late sixteenth-century copy of the original. One wonders if the scribe, who changed the original *postribuli* (the late medieval spelling) to *prostibuli* may not also have garbled the noun endings. May it not have been the walls which were newly constructed, rather than the *postribulum*, which was, in fact, not a building, but a street or two of small houses belonging to individuals?

[26] *AM Perp.*, BB 9, 1454–72; BB 10, 1438–48, 1454–9; BB 11, 1444–72.

[27] See note 38 below.

over, in the fifteenth-century police regulations of a tax on prostitutes
to finance a security system for the red light district.[28] The privilege of
1380, while a prime example of the importance accorded to the regulation of prostitution by municipal and royal authorities and an illustration of the concern with public security, cannot be cited as proof of the
existence of the ideal scheme described in its pages.[29]

From the police regulations and notarial acts of the fifteenth century, one learns that the *postribulum* of Perpignan consisted of a cluster
of small houses which were located between the gate of Bages and the
gate of Elne, and which belonged to various owners. In 1404, one of
these owners, Matthew Basset, officer of the household of the king of
Aragon, made donation of three larger and five smaller houses situated
within the brothel of Perpignan[30] to the venerable Dalmatius Canet,
in exchange for an annuity from the same. One of these houses had
been acquired from a noble lady,[31] and the owners of neighboring
property included a noble, a merchant and an officer of the bailiff's
court.[32] In 1490, a royal prosecuter warned three persons to pay their
quit-rents on houses which they owned in the town *lupanar*, under pain
of seizure; among the owners mentioned were a lawyer and a weaver
and his wife.[33] A document from 1496 identifies Peter of Burgos,
sculptor, as the owner of 'two houses with several bedrooms, divided
by a public street, situated within the walls of the *lupanar* . . . of

[28] See note 38 below.

[29] In Albi at the same period, an 'ideal' project for restricting prostitution spatially
(a double brothel, one outside and one inside the town walls) was proposed by the
lord of the town and accepted by the town council, but never put into effect;
Otis, *Nisi in postribulo*, pp. 72–3. The financial difficulties of the late fourteenth century may explain why municipalities sometimes did not complete such plans.

[30] *AD P-O*, B 186, 16r°–17v°. The first three houses are listed individually and
referred to as 'hospitium sive hostal'. The last five are grouped together and identified as 'quinque domos'.

[31] '. . . acquisi de Na Mallorques . . .'. It is perhaps this house ('lupanario vocato
de Na Malorques') which a carpenter and two public women, Alamanda and
Yolanda, rented from Francis Valgarnera in 1411 (Vidal, *Histoire de Perpignan*,
p. 385).

[32] Domimus Macipe; Petrus Andre, mercator perpiniani; Petrus Tixador,
nuntius curie baiuli perpiniani; Pelisser Fabrie de Perpiniano.

[33] Johanis Fulos, causidicus; Guillermus Ban, ? (Desplanque identifies him as a
carpenter); Barrdo Borya, textor et eius uxor. *AD P-O*, B 326, 40r°, February 7,
1490 n.s. This document is incorrectly cited by Desplanque as BB 240. According to
the same, J. Fulos became consul of the town of Perpignan in 1523 (*Infâmes*, p. 104,
n. 4).

Perpignan'.[34] The lieutenant of the king's counsellor granted Peter permission to build a portico over the rooms 'in which the women sinners living there commit illicit relations';[35] a hall on the ground floor of the house 'in which women sinners, procurers [*lenones*] and other persons can and may, as they please, stay, eat and drink';[36] and 'in the walls of the houses, very near the entrance of the *lupanar*, a door by which you may enter the house . . . and another door, and in the hall above that door, a window by which one can give the response to those demanding or wishing to enter the house'.[37] In return for this permission, Peter was to pay 6d. yearly to the king.

King and municipality shared jurisdiction for the 'policing' of the red light district,[38] the primary concern being to oblige all public women to reside within the acknowledged area. According to three of the fifteenth-century police regulations, offenders were subject to a 2l. fine or to 'running' the town, that is, running a fixed path through the town while being beaten.[39] In 1439 and in 1484, however, it was decided that offending prostitutes should be made to 'run' the town

---

[34] 'Petrus de Burgos, ligni faber sive ymaginayre ville perpiniani . . . duo hospitia cum quibusdam *strupratoriis* sive cameris, via publica in medio, scitua intus clausuram lupanaris . . . dicte ville perpiniani.' AD P-O, B 343, 5r°–6v°, June 9, 1496. (My italic, to emphasize this unusually evocative term for a brothel bedroom.)

[35] '. . . in quibus mulieres peccatrices ibidem habitantes illicitum committunt concubitum . . .'.

[36] '. . . in quaquidem aula, mulieres peccatrices, lenones et alie persone possint et valeant, dum eis placuerit, stare, comedere et bibere'.

[37] '. . . et in pariete allius hospicii . . . magis propinqui in gressum dicti lupanaris, unam januam sive portam per quam vos et vestri . . . possint et valeant dictum hospicium ingredi . . . et alteram januam sive portam, et in superdicta aula sive comestorio, videlicet supra dictam januam, unam fenestram per quam possit dari responsum tam postulantibus quam dictum hospicium ingredi volentibus.'

[38] Most of the regulations concerning prostitution are found in the municipal registers, but some are issued in cooperation with the bailiff. Royal ordinances too appear in Series B. The principle ordinances are the following, in chronological order: 1425 (B 232, 105r°), 1432 (BB 7, 259r°), 1439 (BB 7, 289v°), 1443 (BB 7, 303v°), 1484 (BB 7, 373v°). A royal ordinance of 1494 indicates that some public women were customarily allowed to stay in the former Jewish quarter ('les donas publiques . . . acostumanen habitar . . . al call en lo qual solien habitar los jueg'), AP P-O, B 341, papers 10 and 11. The punishment for those who moved elsewhere was confiscation of their goods and beating.

[39] 'Que alguna fembra avol de son cors, cantonera e publicament diffamada no gos star a algun carrer hon sciguen dones honestes, ans hara star al carrer publich o en les cases qui son pres del mur entre lo portal de Bages e d'Elna dins deu dies, sots pena de deu l., o de correr la vila,' 1443. Cf. 1425, 1432.

'without mercy' (*sens alguna merce*), that is to say, without the alternative of paying a fine.

The same ordinances included the prohibition of procuring, giving procurers (*alcavots*) three days to leave the town, after which, offenders were made to 'run' the town without mercy.[40] Sheltering a procurer was also considered an offense, and all brothel-keepers (*hostaler o hostalera*) convicted of offering bed or board to procurers were to pay a 2l. fine.[41] The first measure against procurers dates back, in fact, to 1314, an unusually early date for such a prohibition,[42] but as there is no act between the document of 1314 and the later measures mentioning prostitutes and brothel-keepers as well (beginning in 1425), it would be difficult to argue for continuity.[43] It is evident, moreover, that procuring was not a universally condemned activity in this period. Prostitutes and procurers sometimes made work contracts in front of public notaries, which explains why some police ordinances refer to procurers 'with or without a charter'; Desplanque published one example of such a contract, concluded between a woman and her 'friend' a student, to whom she promises to stay in Perpignan, and who in turn assures her of his protection.[44] It was apparently so common for royal officers to protect procurers from prosecution, that the consuls protested against this practice to the king and queen of Aragon, who

[40] 'Item, que totz alcavots que tenguen fembres en lo carrer publich hagen a desemparer la vila dins tres jorns. . . . E que si algun alcavot sera trovat dins la dita vila, correra la vila sens tota merce,' 1443.

[41] 'Item, que negun hostaler o hostalera del bordell no gos aculhir dins son hostal algun alcavot per jaser ni per menjar ni per beure, sots pena de deu l.,' 1443.

[42] 'Quod omnes lenones et omnes extraney . . . que non vivunt de brassia seu labore corporis sui . . . debeant deservuisse ipsam villam perpiniani . . . [offenders] current publice villam perpiniani et amittent aures suas.' *AM Perp.* BB 7, 54v°, April 1314, on order of the bailiff and the judge. One may note the absence of reference to prostitutes, the allusion to foreigners and to the idle, in addition to the punishment of mutilation, more severe than that prescribed in the fifteenth-century regulations.

[43] In neighboring Languedoc, procuring was still tolerated in the early and mid-fourteenth century (Otis, *Nisi in postribulo*, pp. 196–8). In Castille, however, the *Siete Partidas* (late thirteenth century) prescribed banishment (but not mutilation) as punishment for common procurers (*Siete Partidas* Paris, 1843–4, IV, pp. 638–40).

[44] Desplanque, *Infâmes*, pp. 7–8 (*AD P-O*, B 156, 2r°, 1395). There are also occasional references to procurers, such as in the document of 1496 granting P. Burgos the right to build a hall in his *lupanar*, where prostitutes and procurers (*lenones*) might stay (see note 36 above).

subsequently issued an order in 1433 to their officers to prosecute all procurers, on pain of a 3,000 florin fine.[45]

Two sets of ordinances, in 1415 and in 1442, regulate the financial dealings between brothel-keepers and public women. That the primary aim of this legislation was to protect public women from unbridled exploitation at the hands of brothel-keepers is clearly stated in the introduction to the ordinance of 1415, where the consuls explain that they have decided to intervene as a result of 'complaints by various people' that the brothel-keepers were extorting 'very large and excessive payments' from the public women, which was 'prejudicial to the women and the brothel'.[46] The daily rate was limited to two sous, and any brothel-keeper caught extorting more money, or woman caught paying more, was to be fined 2l. for each offense.[47] It was forbidden for brothel-keepers to exact payment exceeding actual expenses from the women during a period of illness.[48]

The ordinances also provided for the strict control of the brothel-keeper's lending activity. Permission of the bailiff or the judge was necessary for brothel-keepers to lend money to the women on pledges of their clothing. It was also forbidden to lend money to an *alcavot* or any other person wishing to use a public woman as pledge. The punishment for both these offenses was a 100s. fine. The same prohibitions are repeated in the text of 1442, to which is added a prohibition of sheltering procurers, or women keeping the same.[49] The text of 1442 adds two further measures, forbidding brothel-keepers to sell goods belonging to the prostitutes (a 5l. fine) and forbidding prostitutes to

[45] '. . . per part dels consols . . . es estat devant nos exposat . . . vos altres haiats gujats molts dels alcavots dessus dits contre la penia . . . per la qual cosa molts dampnatges, inconveients et scandols . . . se seguexen . . .'. *AD P-O*, B 240, 193r°–v°, 1433.

[46] 'Com diverses clamors sien pervengudes per diverses personas . . . que los hostalers dels hostals del bordel exeguissen de les fembres publiques molt gran e excessiu salari . . . laqual cosa redunda en gran prejudici de les dites fembres publiques e del publich.' *AM Perp.*, BB 7, 223v°–224r°.

[47] '. . . per cascun jorn per menjar . . .', 1415. In 1442, the text reads '. . . per cascun jorn per raho de lur messio cotidiana de manjar, beure e lit, ni salari o loguer de cambra o de hostal, sino dos sous . . .'. The fine is increased to 5 l. *AM Perp.*, BB 7, 308r°.

[48] 'Que los dits hostalers no puguen prendre de les dites fembres malaltes, sino ço que despendran', 1415 and 1442.

[49] 'Que alcun hostaler no gos reculler en son hostal, de nits o de dies, a jazer o menjar ni a beur, alcun alcavot, ne fembra alcuna que tenga amich . . . sotz pena de v l.'

pledge themselves against purchases of clothing and other items.[50] The consuls were clearly seeking to prevent situations in which indebtedness imposed continued prostitution, whether the initiative had come from a manipulative brothel-keeper, an unscrupulous relative or lover, or from an unwise prostitute herself.[51]

A final aspect of the 'policing' of prostitution in Perpignan was the custom of obliging women and brothel-keepers to cease business during Holy Week. Were it not for the single document dealing with this custom which survives in the archives of Perpignan,[52] we would be without information on the practice of this custom in the mid-fifteenth century, not only in Roussillon, but in neighboring Languedoc as well.[53] The document in question is an order to change the place for the yearly retreat of the city's prostitutes. The women had been housed in the preceding period, appallingly enough, in the town leprosarium, a fact which testifies vividly to the tenuous notion of infection and contagion current in the late Middle Ages! The prostitutes were transferred from the leprosarium for reasons, not of hygiene, but of security; as some women had managed to continue plying their trade in the former institution, it was decided to transfer them to the hospital of the poor, where the 'hospitaler' was to keep watch over them. The consuls did not subsidize the 'retreat', but instead ordered the women to pay three *royals* to the works of the hospital as compensation for expenses incurred by their stay. This financial arrangement may provide a possible explanation as to why so few documents concerning these Easter practices have survived. There were probably similar customs in other towns, but only when some towns began to

[50] 'Que alguna fembra publica no gos fer carta de comanda scriptura o altre qualsevol obligatio de sa persona, per divers robes ne bens que prestats o comanats li sien, sotz pena de deu 1.'

[51] While most towns seem to have fixed a maximum daily rate for prostitutes to pay brothel-keepers (Otis, *Nisi in postribulo*, pp. 180–2), the Languedocian archives contain no measures aimed at avoiding continued prostitution through indebtedness. Whereas some Italian cities authorized the contracting of debts by brothel women, the ordinances of some German and Spanish cities in the sixteenth century strictly prohibited such lending activity on the part of the brothel-keeper; Otis, *Nisi in postribulo*, p. 182, and Guardia, 'De la prostitution en Espagne', p. 782.

[52] See Appendix I.

[53] A text from Uzès dated 1357 describes such a custom, but there is no further mention of such practices in Languedoc until the late 1490s; Otis, *Nisi in postribulo*, pp. 188–93.

subsidize such retreats with public money did financial documents appear as proof of their existence.[54]

The *raison d'être* of such Easter retreats was not only to honor the holy time by prohibiting illicit acts, but also, and probably increasingly toward the end of the Middle Ages, to encourage the women to repent from their worldly life. Such a penitent prostitute could 'retire' to the convent of St Mary Magdalene, Perpignan's community of repentant sisters. The first documents concerning this community date from the second decade of the fourteenth century. The priest Berengar Guila was given 15l. a year by King Sancho of Majorca for his services in the chapel of the repentant women in 1316;[55] a legacy to the convent is mentioned in a will drawn up in 1317.[56] No foundation act for the community survives, and not until the end of the fourteenth century does a document allude to Queen Esclarmunda, the wife of James II of Majorca (reigned 1276–1311) as having been the founder of the convent.[57] Whether the early fourteenth-century queen of Majorca founded the convent or not, it is clear that royal initiative remained essential to its functioning; the kings of Majorca and of Aragon continued to nominate its chaplains throughout the late Middle Ages.[58] It was also by royal order that the sisters were obliged to remain in the convent, according to a document dated 1319.[59] Election of the prioress to the head of the convent was to be approved, however, by the bishop of the city.[60]

[54] For example, in Toulouse and Albi; Otis, *Nisi in postribulo*, pp. 189–92.

[55] AD P-O, B 94, 91v°, March 26, 1316: '. . . ordonat per lo senyor rey . . . que lodit Berengar Guila degat cantar en la capeyla de les Rependides de Perpinyan, e que li sien donades cascun any per sa sustenance xv l.'

[56] AD P-O, 3E1 23, 42r°: '. . . mulieribus repentitis . . .'. No mention of such a convent is found in the surviving notarial registers of the thirteenth century; AD P-O, 3E1 1–12. No registers for Perpignan survive from the period 1286–1316.

[57] AD P-O, B 175, 5v°, April 1, 1396: '. . . ex ordinationem serenissime domine Sclarmunde, regine Maioricum ac fundatris dicti monasterii . . .'. Esclarmunda survived her husband, and was still alive when Sancho appointed a chaplain to the convent (see note 55 above).

[58] See notes 55 and 57 above; AD P-O, B 257, H 256 (1456), B 323 (1482 – nomination by the king of France).

[59] AM Perp., BB 7, 69r°, May 1319. Sisters having left the convent were to be banished from Perpignan and from Roussillon on pain of whipping. There are no late documents imposing residence. I have found no similar documents for the repentant communities of Languedoc.

[60] AD P-O, H 256, April 1, 1450. This contrasts with the situation in Montpellier, where the elections of monasterial officers were approved by municipal officials; Otis, *Nisi in postribulo*, pp. 226–7.

The community was referred to as the convent 'of the repentant women' throughout the first half of the fourteenth century.[61] The first attribution to the community of a saint's name is found in a notarial register of 1348, in which two wills included legacies to the 'sisters of Saint Magdalene'.[62] It is by this title that the convent is identified throughout the second half of the fourteenth century, in wills which usually provide for the same sum to be left to each of the city's three women's convents: St Clare, St Saviour and St Mary Magdalene. The devotion to Mary Magdalene is seen in descriptions of the decoration of the convent's chapel, which included a wooden statue of the Magdalene and an altarpiece painted with scenes featuring the saint, both donated to the community by the spice-merchant Peter Pasqual in 1402.[63] The treasury of the convent included a beautiful reliquary of Mary Magdalene.[64]

The community was a small one, usually having about ten sisters. The number seems to have diminished toward the middle of the fifteenth century: there were twelve women in 1394, and eleven or twelve in 1430, but only seven in 1450 and 1455, and just five in 1456.[65] It is generally assumed that most women in the convent had formerly been prostitutes, but there is no direct evidence. The only woman whose social milieu is revealed is one 'Ermengarde of the order of St Mary Magdalene', identified in a notarial act of 1381 as the late mother of a certain Francisca (and presumably the wife of Francisca's late father, James Geli, native of St Hippolyte), who had left her

[61] See notes 55 and 56 above. *AM Perp.*, BB 7, 69r° (1319): 'domus mulierum repentitarum'. Also *AD P-O*, 3E1 25, 32v° (1321), 3E1 56, 11v° (1334), 3E1 57, 33r° (1334), 3E1 88, 10v°, 17r° (1342–3).

[62] *AD P-O*, 3E1 429, 1v° ('sorores sancte Magdalene'), 9v°. One wonders whether the advent of the plague may have had something to do with the sudden devotion to that penitent saint. For the close connection between the cult of Mary Magdalene and communities of repentant sisters in the south of France, see V. Saxer, *Le culte de Marie Madeleine en Occident* (Auxerre-Paris, 1959), pp. 249–50.

[63] The cost of the altarpiece was 70l; *AD P-O*, H 256.

[64] 'Item, lo reliquiari de sancta Maria Magdalena, ab dos angles qui la tenen molt bel'; *AD P-O*, H 256, 1430. The treasury also included relics of the Christ and of St Martha, and of two other saints, St Mary of Bellem and St Mary of Perles (neither of them mentioned in the *Bibliotheca Sanctorum*).

[65] See Appendix II. One cannot be sure that the lists are complete, but as the notarial documents were drawn up in the capitular room of the convent itself, it would seem likely that all the sisters would be present. P. Pansier has noted a marked decline in membership in the repentant convent in Avignon in the fifteenth century, from 40 women in the late fourteenth century to just two in 1489; P. Pansier, *L'oeuvre des Repenties à Avignon* (Paris, 1910).

daughter, wife of the *adventurius* Anthony Genis, a house worth 7 l.[66]
Nothing in the act proves that Ermengarde was (or was not, for that
matter) a prostitute. One may also note the mysterious character Na
Caterineta, identified as a nun of the convent, who appears twice,
briefly, in the testimony of the convent's sisters in 1430, a document
we shall study more carefully in a moment.[67] The title is an abbrevia-
tion of the Latin *domina*, usually reserved for noble or important
people. There is no way of knowing how such a woman ended in a
convent for repentant women, but it is not difficult to imagine a
plausible scenario, such as that of the bereaved widow seeking a suitable community in which to expiate an old sin of adultery.

Another assumption which has been made about convents for repentant women is that they often served as a kind of half-way house for
prostitutes seeking to re-enter 'honest' society; the statutes of some of
these communities indeed reflect that function of the convent.[68] The
community of St Mary Magdalene of Perpignan may also have served
such a purpose, but what is striking in the few lists we have is the
relative continuity of at least part of the personnel of the convent. We
know that Francisca of Elne was prioress of the convent for at least
16 years, from 1381 to 1397. Of the 12 sisters listed in 1394, two were
still there to testify in the investigation of 1430. Two other persons
involved in that investigation were still in the convent in 1450. Of the
seven sisters listed in 1455, three had been mentioned already in 1450,
and were to be listed again in 1456.[69] While for some women a convent
of repentant sisters could be a stepping stone to re-entering respectable
society, for others it was clearly a choice for life.

Although the statutes of the convent have unfortunately not survived, as have those of the repentant sisters of Avignon and of Montpellier, this loss is greatly compensated by several documents which
furnish details concerning the everyday life of the convent. One learns,
for instance, that the women had individual rooms with a dining area,

---

[66] '. . . ordinis sancte Maie Magdelene . . .'; *AD P-O*, B141, 6v°, April 17, 1381.
Du Cange, *Glossarium* (Paris, 1938), defines the *adventurius* as *mercator extraneus*.

[67] See notes 77 and 78 below.

[68] In Montpellier, the women had a tral period of one year during which they
were free to leave the convent. In Abbeville, the women could leave at any time;
Otis, *Nisi in postribulo*, pp. 227–8. The royal order of 1319 of course sanctioned
departures, but as this measure was never repeated, one wonders whether it was
enforced in the fifteenth century (see note 59 above).

[69] From 1455 to 1456 there was a loss of two members, but no additions or
replacements.

although sometimes they slept two to a room.[70] The women were allowed to bring a number of worldly goods with them to the convent, as is seen in the 1430 inventory of the possessions of Sister Beatrice of Monyons, which includes, among other things, tables, chairs, a number of chests, ironware, cooking utensils, bedclothing, cushions, personal clothing, a rosary made of coral and gold jewelry.[71] Permission of the prioress was needed to be able to leave the convent. It was necessary to grant such permission frequently, for the community relied for its sustenance, not only on the legacies and major donations of pious laymen, but also on collections of alms by itinerant sisters in pairs, called the *questa*. Going on *questa* probably necessitated spending several days at a time away from the convent, given that the area covered was considerable (one document shows a pair of sisters on *questa* in Salses, 12 miles north of Perpignan), and the alms donated were often in kind (grain and oil).[72]

These practical documents reveal not only the material facts of life in the convent, but also the ambience of the community, where moral and religious sensibility was not particularly acute. In an act dated 21 November 1394, a notary records that the sisters were called by the sound of a bell to the convent's capitular room to witness an unusua scene: Sister Antonia Richa, on her knees before the assembly, was being questioned by the prioress about the truth of the rumor that while outside the convent she had given birth to a daughter. 'My lady,' responded the accused, 'the truth is that by my sin, while outside the present convent, I conceived and gave birth to a daughter, whose name is Johana, who is the daughter of Berengar Cavenelles, beneficed priest in the church of St James.'[73] Pardon was requested and granted.

The affair of Antonia Richa seems innocent, however, in comparison to that concerning Beatrice of Monyons. So violent and seditious was

[70] See note 90 below.
[71] See note 89 below.
[72] See notes 84 and 86 below.
[73] 'Madona, veritat cosa es que per mon pecat, en estant fora del present monastir, he infantada e hauda une filla, qui ha nom Johana, laqual es filla de Monsenyor Berengar Cavenelles, prevera benefficiat en la sgleya de Sant Jacme.' *AD P-O*, B 157, 16v°. Alart, in the inventory of the Series B, interprets the phrase 'estant foras' to mean *before* entering the monastery. Such is not the only possible interpretation of this imprecise phrase, however. The women, as we have seen, had ample opportunity to leave the convent for days at a time. As the convent's honor, moreover, would not have been compromised by an act committed before entering the convent (such a past was indeed probably not rare among those who were by definition *repentant* women) pardon should not have been necessary.

the latter that an investigation was made into her behavior in March and April of 1430. The majority of the sisters testified to the irascibility of Sister Beatrice and to her lack of loyalty to the prioress and the sisters of the convent. Her aggressions against the sisters, ranging from the petty to the deadly,[74] were continual: 'She is a bad woman and very quarrelsome, fighting constantly with the monks [nuns] of the said convent.'[75] A favorite victim of Sister Beatrice was the by then elderly Antonia Richa, who, forgiven her peccadillo of 1394, had become the subprioress of the convent.[76] Sister Antonia relates three incidents in which Beatrice attacked her. In the first, the elderly subprioress was ordered by the prioress to accompany the mysterious Na Caterineta to the same. But Beatrice intervened, insisting that it was she who should have that honor: 'wishing to lead the said Catherine, the said sister Beatrice grabbed the hand of [Antonia] so hard, throwing her to the ground, that she sprained her hand, and because of the sprain, was under a doctor's care for a month.'[77] The intervention of the prioress saved the poor woman from further violence. A similar incident occurred when Sister Maria of Munts was to accompany the same Na Caterineta, but that time the intervention of the prioress prevented an attack, Beatrice only having had the time to be able to utter a particularly indelicate threat.[78]

On another occasion, Beatrice attacked Antonia with a hoe, and would have landed a blow on the head, had Father F. Paulet, just returning from Elne, not rushed in, retaining Beatrice by the shirt tails.[79] Finally, frustrated from doing all the violence she wished to the poor old woman, Beatrice decided to stalk her prey at the top of the stairway leading to the cloister, club in hand; Sister Francisca's denunciation of the plan to the prioress and the latter's intervention,

---

[74] She was accused of putting excrement into one of the sister's hair ('. . . collats na vella merdosa . . .'). Testimony of Catherina Garcia. In their testimony, the sisters frequently attribute to her the intention to kill; *AD P-O*, H 256, 1430.

[75] 'Que la dita sor Beatriu es mala fembra e molt breguinol, e que tot jorn se barallava ab les monges deldit convent.' Testimony Manda Vilarasa.

[76] Antonia was at the very least in her mid 50s by then, probably older.

[77] '. . . volent s'en menar la dita Caterina, la dita sor Beatriu pregue tant fort la ma della testimoni e lansant la en terra, que la afolla dela ma, delqual affolament ha stat en poder de metge be un mes.' Testimony of Antonia Richa.

[78] '. . . que li fera uxir los budells per la gola,' ('I'll make your guts come out of your mouth!'). Testimony of Maria de Munts.

[79] The testimony of Antonia icha is quoted by Desplanque (*Infâmes*, p. 113, n. 3). Georgia Rabassa and Francisca Foxana also relate the same incident.

accompanying Antonia to her room, prevented possible murder.[80]

Beatrice also attacked another elderly nun, Sister Georgia Rabassa,[81] on Christmas Eve:

Without any preceding cause, the said sister Beatrice threw a stone at Georgia, giving her a great blow on the ear, from which blow she fainted and fell to the ground, and since then, has lost her hearing in that ear. And when Sister Mando Vilarasa, who was present and saw this, asked, 'Why did you do that?' . . . Sister Beatrice responded 'For the fun of it!'[82]

Sister Georgia also testified to having witnessed attacks by Beatrice on Francisca Foxana and Johana Hugueta.[83]

All of the witnesses agree that Sister Beatrice was on numerous occasions rebellious and disobedient to the prioress, threatening to hurt the latter if she tried to punish the accused for her attacks on her fellow sisters. Often when the prioress ordered her to go out seeking alms, Beatrice refused;[84] even when she obeyed, she apparently kept part of the yield for herself.[85] Sister Beatrice was clearly little inclined to respect conventual solidarity, whether material or spiritual; when on *questa* with Sister Violant near the castle of Salses, instead of reprimanding a woman who spoke ill of Sister Francisca, she heartily agreed with the woman.[86] Her ill will toward the prioress was so

[80] The same incident is also related by Francisca Foxana, Violant of St Guillem and Georgia Rabassa, who believed that without the prioress' intervention, Beatrice would have killed Antonia.

[81] She too was already a sister in the community in 1394.

[82] 'E una die que era la vespra del nadal, la dita sor Beatriu, sens causa alguana precedent, lança un cayro a ella testimoni, donant li gran colp ala aurella, del qual colp ella testimoni s'en stavoyda e caygue en terra, e que despuix no es stada sensa del oyr. E quant sor Mando Vilarasa, que aqui era o vehe, digue . . . "Per que ho havets fet?" . . . la dita sor Beatriu respos que "Per solats ho fahia!" '. Testimony of Georgia Rabassa.

[83] Francisca Foxana does not mention the incident, and there is no testimony from Johana Hugueta.

[84] 'La dita sor Beatriu es molt rebele e inobedient ala dita madonna prioressa. Car moltes vegades has vise ella testimoni, que quant madonna prioressa li manava anars ala questa de blats e d'olis, diu que non fara res.' Testimony of Violant de St Guillem.

[85] '. . . se aturava una part . . . dela dita questa . . .'. Testimony of Caterina Garcia.

[86] 'Una vegada que ella testimoni e la dita sor Beatriu exen per la questa al loch de Salses, en lo qual loch una dona disia gran mal de sor F. Foxana, e ella testimoni dix ala dona que mal disia, e que no deya hom mal parlar deles gents en lur absencio,

strong that she attempted to instigate a rebellion to have her thrown out of the convent.[87]

One is hardly surprised to learn that Beatrice's morals were also called into question by her fellow sisters. It was rumored that her entry into the convent was irregular, as she was still under her husband's authority at the time.[88] It was also rumored that Beatrice had a set of 'false' keys, to be able to leave and enter the convent without having to ask the prioress' permission, and that she brought in priests and other people at night.[89] There is no direct evidence of the false keys (it may be for that reason that an inventory was drawn up of her possessions in her room), but Manda Bosonia 'several times saw that Beatrice had opened the doors of the convent', and saw her bring in men, for which reason the scandalized Manda decided to change sleeping arrangements, moving out of Beatrice's room and into the prioress'. When asked whether she could identify any of the accused's nocturnal visitors, Mande responded that she had seen John Vila,[90] a priest who had also been involved in a nocturnal attack on Sister Violant.[91]

The interest of this story lies, not only in the wealth of details concerning the daily material and spiritual life of the convent, but also in the career of Beatrice de Monyons. Although apparently a totally violent, irresponsible and vicious woman, she not only remained in the convent of the sisters of St Mary Magdalene, but by 1450 had been promoted to *vicaria* (second in command) of the community! The behavior of Beatrice, and even of Antonia Richa in her youth, may

---

e lanors ladita sor Beatriu dix a ella testimoni que la dita dona disia ver, e que axit era com ella disia . . .'. When Violant criticized Beatrice's words, the latter attacked her partner, who was save from further violence by the intervention of a citizen of Perpignan. 'E la dita sor Beatriu perde lo vel negre,' presumably as punishment for her acts. Testimony of Violant de St Guillem.

[87] Quoted by Desplanque, *Infâmes*, p. 114.

[88] '. . . que s'es monge ço es quant era en poder de son maryt'. Testimony of Caterina Garcia. This is only hearsay, as Caterina was quoting what Johana Hugueta had told her. There is no testimony from the latter.

[89] Quoted by Desplanque, *Infâmes*, p. 113, n. 3.

[90] '. . . ha vise diverses vegadas que la dita sor Beatriu ha obert les portes del dit monestir . . . vesia com ella los fasia intrar per la qual raho ella testimoni se isque de la cambra de la dita sor Beatriu ab qui jasie lanors, e s'en ana dormer a la cambra de la dita prioressa.' Testimony of Manda Bosonia.

[91] Testimony of Violant de St Guillem. The same John Vila acted as Beatrice's attorney (*eius procurator*) in this case! It is to him that she was handed over by the judge of the baillage on 18 May.

have been exceptional enough to warrant sanctions, but not enough to prevent these women from succeeding in ascending the hierarchy of the convent, a fact which reveals a great deal about the limited spiritual aspirations of these communities.

The documents from the archives of Perpignan amply confirm the legitimacy which prostitution enjoyed in the Mediterranean world at the end of the Middle Ages. Figuring prominently in the elegant town cartulary, regulated by municipal and royal authority, the red light district there consisted of houses owned by members of the best Perpignanese society. The privilege of 1380 provides an illustration of the late fourteenth-century concern with the security and surveillance of places of prostitution; a study of this document serves at the same time as a warning to historians not to confuse ideal schemes of organizing prostitution outlined in privileges or projects with reality. Although the consuls of Perpignan may have aspired to a reserved quarter as sophisticated and well organized as that of Valencia, such a scheme was probably not feasible in the smaller town of Perpignan, where the initiative in matters of policing was finally left to the individual owners. The municipal authorities intervened more actively, however, in regulating the functioning of the center than did their Languedocian neighbors, displaying a precocious, if not consistently enforced, preoccupation with procuring, and prohibiting not only the excessive rates charged by brothel-keepers, but also their leverage over prostitutes in the form of usurious or forced lending, a measure which recalls the brothel regulations of certain Spanish towns. Most significantly, the archives include an important testimony to the practice of the Holy Week 'retreat' of prostitutes in the mid-fifteenth century, filling a lacuna in the information on such customs, and offering an explanation, by way of the financial arrangements involved, of why so few such documents have survived.

Equally, if not more, significant are the documents concerning the community of repentant sisters of Perpignan. Typical in its dependence on secular initiative, this convent was nevertheless distinctive, in this part of the Mediterranean world, for its patronage by monarchs, and especially its putative foundation by a female monarch, Queen Esclarmunda of Majorca. These documents, while far from numerous, are none the less more abundant than in most neighboring towns, supplying precious information on the buildings, decoration, personnel, customs and atmosphere of the convent, revealing an institution with a relatively stable personnel which included noble as well as common women, and with an extremely low level of spiritual aspiration.

The monograph, always a useful exercise for the historian of medieval society, is especially important when dealing with an aspect of social life which has generated relatively sparse and often erratic documentation. Perpignan might seem, at first glance, an inauspicious choice for a monograph on prostitution; the documents are relatively late, and the subject has already been discussed in an old but erudite monograph. Yet as we have seen, the older monograph, accurate but far from exhaustive, provides in fact an excellent springboard for a deeper study of the subject,[92] and the texts from the fourteenth and fifteenth centuries, in addition to verifying certain hypotheses, contain a number of surprising elements, which clarify some problems and call into question certain assumptions which have been made in the past. One hopes that studies of other documents in other towns will do the same, and that, many monographs later, it may at last be possible to build, on the firmest foundations, a reliable synthesis of medieval prostitution, crucial to a better understanding of women and of sexuality in the Middle Ages.

APPENDIX I

AM Perpignan, BB 7, 307v°–308r°. Undated (probably 1442).[93]
Order to transfer the public women of Perpignan from the town leprosarium to the hospital of the poor for their retreat during Holy Week.

Com en tot temps, e en special de santa caresme, e maoirment de la semmana santa, sia prohibit tot acte illicit o deviant de la vida santa de paradis, per la qual raho sia stat e de gran temps ença ordinat e praticcat,

[92] Besides the shortcomings already discussed (see note 13 above), one may note that Desplanque closed his eyes to all that might have shocked contemporary sensibilities, such as the affair of Antonia Richa, and the presence of a noble woman in such a common community. I have already encountered a similar situation in Toulouse, where Chalande's interesting but incomplete monograph (see note 5 above) served as an excellent introduction to a deeper investigation of prostitution in that town, greatly facilitated in that case by the classification of the municipal archives.

[93] The words 'l'any present' probably allude to the preceding document in the register, which is dated 1442. The next dated document in the register (which procedes chronologically) is from 1457. Due to a technical problem, it was not possible to obtain a reproduction of this document, and therefore not possible to have the transcription double-checked; it may include some errors.

que en lo dijous sant de la dita semmana sancta cascun any per los officials reyals de la present vila les fembres publiques meretricants de la dita vila son posades en la casa de sent Latzer, scituada fora e prop lo portal de Canet / de la dita vila, hon acostumane de stare fins e per tot lo divendres sant prop seguent ab custodia de alcuns sags reyals, per deffajir en los dits dies a pecat de carnalitat. Empero per experiencia sia stat vist e praticat que no obstant la dita custodia, los seguexen per les dictes fembres en los dits dies e lechs attes desonests e illicits het alcunes de aquelles posat vullen usure e star degudament son o premudes de pagar moltes messions, tant als dits sags per la dita custodia quant a lurs hostalers. Per tant nos Johan Borro, Bernat Castello, Mallot Cadany, Guillem Anarell, Johan Viador, consols l'any present de la dita vila, volents remediar en los dits fets prece-dents molts colloquis et rahonaments ordinam ab volentat domini Guillem Ribba, spitaler lo dit e present any del spital dels pobres de la dita vila, que daçi avant les dites fembres cascun any en lo dit temps sien posades per los dits officials reyals en lodit spital, en loqual les dites fembres scien sots protectio e custodia del hospitaler e regidor deldit spital, o d aquell o aquells que ell hi deputara en loqual hospital, e dels bens de aquell sien provenhides en los dits dies de beure e menjar rahonablament e de jaure, les quals sien tenguts de donar e pagar ço es cascun dellas en satisfactio de la lur dita provisio a la obra deldit hospital tres reyals,[94] e que no sien tengudes de mes pagar sino com dit es los dits tres reyals.

E mes ordinam nos dits consols que del temps que les dites fembres staran en lo dit hospital no haien ni sien tengudes pagar alcuna cosa als hostalers lurs per salari o loguier de cambra o hostaleria ni per provision o altre quelsevnol fet. E que los dits hostalers no gosen de manar e haver sots pena de retre ho a les dites fembres de 1 [50] s. per cascuna vegada que sera contre fet donadera e aplicadera en ters parts, so es lo terç al fisch del senyor rey e l'altra terça part a la obra del mur de la dita vila e la restant terça part al denunciador.

[94] The French *royal* emitted in 1429 was worth 25s. t. For Aragonese money, see E. J. Hamilton, *Money, Prices and Wages in Valencia, Aragon and Navarre, 1351–1500* (Cambridge, Mass., 1936), which unfortunately was not available to me while I was writing this essay.

APPENDIX II

Sisters of the convent of St Mary Magdalene of Perpignan

(I thank M. Philippe Rosset, Directeur des Services d'Archives des Pyrénées-Orientales, for his aid in deciphering names. † Indicates women appearing on more than one list.)

November 1379 (B 135, 56r° – acquittance of legacy)

> Johana Vidalia, prioress

September 1381 (B 141, 37r°, 6v° – notarial acts)

> †Francisca d'Elna, prioress
> Ermengarde (deceased)

21 November 1394 (B 157, 16v° – notarial act)

> †Francisca d'Elna, prioress
> Selio Vidalia
> Franco Recorda
> Manjo Jordana
> Caterina Fustera
> Ricsen de Bages
> Ricsen Roberta
> ††Jordia Rabassa
> Sclamunda Vidalia
> Johana Pagesa
> Guillelma Beneseta
> ††Antonia Richa

1 April 1397 (B 175, 6r° – nomination of chaplain)

> †Francisca d'Elna, prioress

March–April 1430 (H 256 – investigation of Beatrice de Monyons)

The accused:
  †††Beatriu de Monyons
The witnesses:
  ††Antonia Richa, subprioress
   Maria de Munts
   Violant de Sant Guillem
   Caterina Garcia
  ††Georgia Rabassa (also listed as Jordia)
   Manda Bosonia
  †††Francischa Foxana
   Manda Vilarasa
Mentioned in testimony:
   the prioress (no name given)
   Johana Hugueta
   Na Caterineta

1 April 1450 (H 256 – request for permission to elect new prioress)

  †††Francisca Foxana, prioress (deceased that day)
  †††Beatrix de Monyons, *vicaria*
  ††††Caterina Covilla
   Johana Marchona
  ††††Mundina Yserva
   Barthelomea Bruguera
  ††††Caterina Arayonna

12 May 1455 (H 256 – letter of procuratory)

  ††††Katerina Covilla, prioress
  ††††Mundina Yserva
   Johana Mormorda
  ††††Katerina Arayonna
   Margarita Maslamesa
  †††††Johana Pontilla
  †††††Agnes Flagelle

26 November 1456 (H 256 – nomination of chaplain)

  ††††Katerina Covilla
  ††††Mundian Yserva
  ††††Katerina Aranyona
  †††††Johana Pontilla
  †††††Agnes Fagala

8

Female Imagery: A Clue to
the Role of Joachim's Order of Fiore

STEPHEN WESSLEY

Known today chiefly for his speculations about the future, the age of the Holy Spirit, new forms of religious life and the role of the Antichrist, Joachim of Fiore's (d. 1202) practical accomplishments have received little attention from historians.[1] The historiography has been so dominated, particularly in recent years, by Joachim's influence on subsequent groups such as the Franciscan Spirituals that, in fact, the monastic order he founded, the Florensians, or Order of Fiore, is

---

[1] A good introduction to Joachim of Fiore can be found in Morton Bloomfield's two survey articles: 'Joachim of Flora: a critical survey of his canon, teachings, sources, biography, and influence', *Traditio*, 13 (1957), pp. 249–311, and 'Recent scholarship on Joachim of Fiore and his influence', in A. Williams (ed.), *Prophecy and Millenarianism* (Harlow, Essex, 1980), pp. 21–52. The variety of articles in the two volumes of *Joachim of Fiore in Christian Thought*, ed. D. West (New York, 1975) serves also as a useful approach to the major topics in the field. The bibliography of Joachim and Joachimism by Francesco Russo, *Bibliografia gioachimita* (Florence, 1954), can be supplemented by some of the newer studies: Marjorie Reeves, *The Influence of Prophecy in the Later Middle Ages* (Oxford, 1969); Antonio Crocco, *Gioacchino da Fiore e il Gioachimismo* (Naples, 1976); Henry Mottu, *La manifestation de l'Esprit selon Joachim de Fiore* (Neuchâtel and Paris, 1977); Henri de Lubac, *La postérité spirituelle de Joachim de Flore* (Paris, 1979); and *Storia e messagio in Gioacchino da Fiore, Atti del I Congresso internazionale di studi gioachimiti* (S. Giovanni in Fiore, 1980). Delno West and Sandra Zimdars-Swartz have provided a recent summary of Joachim's thought in *Joachim of Fiore* (Bloomington, 1983). Also much of the important and classic work of Herbert Grundmann on Joachim has been brought together in *Joachim von Fiore, Ausgewählte Aufsätze, Schriften der Monumenta Germaniae Historica*, 25, 2 (Stuttgart, 1977). Two recent surveys: Bernard McGinn, 'Awaiting an end: research in medieval apocalypticism, 1974–81', *Medievalia et Humanistica*, n.s. 11 (1982), pp. 263–89; and Carl Berkhout and Jeffrey Russell, *Medieval Heresies: A Bibliography 1960–1979* (Toronto, 1981), offer a helpful collection of up-to-date material.

generally little known.[2] One reason for this is simply that there are no contemporary Florensians who are tracing their origins. After a not particularly distinguished history, this order was merged with the Cistercians in the late 1500s and early 1600s.[3] And, since Joachim was tainted with the mention of heresy in 1215[4] and, indeed, originally broke with the Cistercians to found the Florensians (as late as 1192 he was ordered to appear before a Cisterian General Chapter or be considered a fugitive),[5] the Cistercians themselves since the 1600s have been ambivalent about their claims to such a legacy as Joachim of Fiore.[6]

While the Florensians were important enough in 1234 for Gregory IX to label them as one of the four pillars of the Church,[7] few of their records survive, their constitutions are not extant and even the source of their name has been a puzzle. Because Joachim himself regarded monastic developments as a key element in the movement to the age[8] of the Holy Spirit, it is unfortunate that Morton Bloomfield (in his second survey of the literature on Joachim of Fiore) could state accurately 'that no one really knows what was being taught and thought in early Florensian circles. In fact not much is known of the inner life and history of the order at any time.'[9]

---

[2] Marjorie Reeves' significant, *The Influence*, and its bibliography illustrate this trend.

[3] Francesco Russo, *Gioacchino da Fiore e le fondazioni florensi in Calabria* (Naples, 1959), p. 246; Marjorie Reeves, *Joachim of Fiore and the Prophetic Future* (New York, 1976), p. 3; Bloomfield, 'Joachim of Flora', p. 293, n. 197.

[4] *Conciliorum oecumenicorum decreta*, ed. J. Alberigo et al. (Bologna, 1973), pp. 231–3.

[5] Joseph Canivez, *Statuta capitulorum generalium ordinis cisterciensis ab anno 1116 ad annum 1786* (Louvain, 1933), I, p. 154.

[6] Reeves, *The Influence*, pp. 116–17; Angelo Manrique, *Annales cistercienses*, 3 (Lyon, 1649), pp. 211, 234.

[7] Reeves, *The Influence*, p. 146.

[8] The term *status*, in fact, would be the most exact and correct term here; see Reeves, *Joachim of Fiore*, pp. 6–8. For a more precise appreciation of the identification of the third *status* with the Holy Spirit see E. Randolph Daniel, 'The double procession of the Holy Spirit in Joachim of Fiore's understanding of history', *Speculum*, 55 (1980), pp. 469–83.

[9] Bloomfield, 'Recent Scholarship', p. 25. This does not mean of course, that work has not been done on the Florensians. In addition to Grundmann and Russo cited above, there is, for example, the noted work of Cipriano Baraut whose articles, 'Joachim de Flore' in *Dictionnaire de spiritualité*, VIII (Paris, 1974), col. 1179–201 and '1. Flore (San Giovanni)' and '2. Flore (Ordre de)' in *Dictionnaire d'histoire et de geographie ecclésiastiques*, 17 (Paris, 1971), col. 513–15, 515–20, provided a recent

In a recent study I demonstrated that Joachim's *Commentary on the Life of Saint Benedict* (1186/7), written in the period just before the founding of Fiore, was an apologia for Joachim's past actions.[10] He wrote this commentary to compare his own life with Benedict's in order to exonerate himself from the charge of abandoning his abbatial duties at Corazzo. In Benedict he found a prototype that justified his own earlier moves and an example to encourage him to climb the Sila plateau to seek solitude and establish a new monastery at Fiore.[11] The *Commentary on the Life of Saint Benedict* tells us about Joachim's preoccupations as he prepared to seek new solitude for his meditation and writings.

The question, however, still remains about those who accompanied Joachim – the early Florensians: how did they view themselves, how did they interpret the new monastic settlement in the Sila? To answer this question we need to look closely at a life of Joachim, the Anonymous' *Vita*, published by Herbert Grundmann in 1960.[12] The leading students of Joachim and the Florensians, such as Grundmann, Marjorie Reeves and Cipriano Baraut, have accepted this *Vita*, despite its convoluted peregrination, as an authentic early thirteenth-century document.[13] Grundmann, in fact, argued that it was not only written

overview and bibliography, and Romano Napolitano, *S. Giovanni in Fiore monastica e civica* (Naples, 1978–81). Also to be consulted for views about Joachim's intentions and the role of the early Florensians are: Antonio Crocco, 'Genesi e significato dell' "età dello Spirito" nell'escatologia di Gioacchino da Fiore', in *Storia e messaggio*, pp. 219–20; Raoul Manselli, 'L' attesa dell' età nuova ed il Gioachimismo', *L'attesa dell' età nuova nella spiritualità della fine del Medioevo*, *Convegni del Centro di studi sulla spiritualità medievale*, III (Todi, 1962), pp. 150–1; Francesco Russo, 'L'eredità di Gioacchino da Fiore. La Congregazione florense', *Archivio storico per la Calabria e la Lucania*, 21 (1952), pp. 132–5; Francesco Foberti, *Gioacchino da Fiore* (Florence, 1934), pp. 148–50.

[10] Stephen Wessley, ' "Bonum est Benedicto mutare locum": The role of the "Life of Saint Benedict" in Joachim of Fiore's monastic reform', *Revue bénédictine*, 90 (1980), pp. 314–28.

[11] ibid., pp. 327–8.

[12] Herbert Grundmann, 'Zur Biographie Joachims von Fiore und Rainers von Ponza', *Deutsches Archiv für Erforschung des Mittelalters*, 16 (1960), pp. 528–39; also reprinted in *Joachim von Fiore, Ausgewählte Aufsätze*, pp. 342–52. This *Vita* has also been edited by Cipriano Baraut, 'Las antiguas biografías de Joaquín de Fiore y sus fuentes', *Analecta sacra tarraconensia*, 26 (1953), pp. 195–232, but without much commentary.

[13] Grundmann, 'Zur Biographie', pp. 477–80; Reeves, *The Influence*, p. 11; Baraut, 'Joachim de Flore', *Dictionnaire de spiritualité*, col. 1179.

shortly after Joachim's death in 1202, but written by a *socius* who had been involved with preparations in Petra Lata and accompanied Joachim to the Sila for the founding of Fiore itself.[14] The author of the *Vita*, Grundmann noted, described the activities and thoughts of an unnamed *socius* of Joachim that only that very *socius* would or could include in such a life.[15]

Since the relationship of this *socius* with Joachim spanned at least 16 years it is understandable that the *Vita*, though written in an awkward style, often echoed Joachim's vocabulary and, in fact, where the *socius* claimed to have distinctly remembered Joachim's speech,[16] the fragments he quoted do fit logically in the broader context of Joachim's commentaries. Because Joachim was the prime mover among these monks, it was only natural that within his lifetime his prophetic vocabulary and symbolism would be taken up by them in one form or another and adopted as part of their own. The Anonymous used Joachim's enigmatic vocabulary to explain the significance of the founding of the Order of Fiore. The comments of the Anonymous about the preparations at Petra Lata and the founding of Fiore were couched in the abbot's biblical imagery of conception and birth. To understand the significance of these comments, Joachim's use of certain biblical women as symbols must be made clear. According to Marjorie Reeves, Joachim's overall use of this symbolism may be seen as a result of his perception of the historical process. She proposed, 'Perhaps because he sees the development of spiritual understanding in history so much in biological terms of germination and fructification, of conception and birth, Joachim returns again and again to this theme of the fertile women in the Bible.'[17] The particular applications of female imagery derive their meaning from the roles and details, as interpreted by the abbot, of various female biblical figures.

In his description of the future of the Church, Joachim of Fiore borrowed examples of conception and birth from the Bible to explain the religious changes he envisioned. Specifically, the pregnancies of Rachel in the Old Testament and Mary in the New were invoked by the Calabrian abbot as vehicles to expound his views on the ideal type

---

[14] Grundmann, 'Zur Biographie', pp. 478–9, 464.

[15] ibid., pp. 478–9.

[16] ibid., p. 536.

[17] Reeves, *Joachim of Fiore*, p. 11; see also Marjorie Reeves and Beatrice Hirsch-Reich, *The 'Figurae' of Joachim of Fiore* (Oxford, 1972), p. 166. For Joachim's use of symbolism see Bernard McGinn, 'Symbolism in the thought of Joachim of Fiore', in A. Williams (ed.), *Prophecy and Millenarianism* (Harlow, Essex, 1980), pp. 143–64.

of religious life to come. Joachim's exegesis mixed traditional elements with his idiosyncratic symbolism and emphasized insignificant details to make his point. Rachel, often taken to represent the contemplative life in contrast to the active life of her rival Leah, gave birth to Joseph, according to Scripture, in the sixth year of her marriage. Since, in Joachim's mind, Joseph stood for the order of spiritual men to be born in the future, the sixth year was interpreted by him to mean that the new spiritual *ordo* will appear in the sixth period in the history of the Church, i.e. just before the third *status*, the age of the Holy Spirit.[18]

Joachim used the symbol of Mary for similar purposes. For him, Mary designated the *ecclesia spiritualis*. And since Mary conceived in the sixth month (the sixth month of her cousin Elizabeth's pregnancy according to Luke) so would the spiritual church of the future be conceived in the sixth period of the Church, and with this would come a new spiritual understanding, also foretold by the abbot.[19] Two of Joachim's drawings in his celebrated *Liber figurarum* present diagrams that show us clearly the relationship he fashioned between the symbol of Mary and the spiritual church in the age of the Holy Spirit. In one drawing the beginning of the age of the Spirit is linked to Mary's name and the age's *fructificatio* linked to the conception of the church

[18] Joachim of Fiore, *Liber concordie Novi ac Veteris Testamenti* (Venice, 1519: Minerva reprint, 1964), 83v–84r; *Expositio in Apocalypsim* (Venice, 1527: Minerva reprint, 1964), 19v, 93v, 12r; E. Randolph Daniel, 'Abbot Joachim of Fiore: the *De Ultimis Tribulationibus*', in A. Williams (ed.), *Prophecy and Millenarianism* (Harlow, Essex, 1980), pp. 179, 187; Reeves, *Joachim of Fiore*, p. 11. Modern editions of Joachim's three main works, *Liber concordie Novi ac Veteris Testamenti, Expositio in Apocalypsim* and *Psalterium decem chordarum* had been promised by Grundmann, and now E. Randolph Daniel's edition of the first four books of the *Liber concordie* has been published by the American Philosophical Society, *Abbot Joachim of Fiore: 'Liber de Concordia Noui ac Veteris Testamenti'*, ed. E. R. Daniel, *Transactions of the American Philosophical Society*, 73 (Philadelphia, 1983), but at the moment it is the Minerva reprints of the early sixteenth-century Venetian editions that are generally available to scholars.

[19] Joachim of Fiore, *Expositio*, 83r–v; Reeves and Hirsch-Reich, *The 'Figurae'*, p. 166. Fuller treatments of Joachim's use of Mary as a symbol may be found in Diego Mario Tallerico, *Maria-chiesa in Gioacchino da Fiore* (Catanzaro, 1982); and Vincenzo Ferrara, 'Maria e la chiesa in Dante e in Gioacchino da Fiore', *Divinitas*, 9 (1965), pp. 259–343. See also Gregorio Penco's short article, 'Maria, modello della vita contemplativa secondo Gioacchino da Fiore', *Benedictina*, 14 (1967), pp. 51–6, and Sandra Zimdars-Swartz, 'Joachim of Fiore and the Cistercian Order: a study of *De vita sancti Benedicti*', in J. Sommerfeldt (ed.), *Simplicity and Ordinariness* (Kalamazoo, 1980), pp. 301, 308, n. 36. Giuseppe Simbula, *La maternità spirituale di Maria in alcuni autori francescani dei secoli XIII–XV* (Rome, 1967) provides a view of later developments which can be studied for comparison.

designated by her.[20] The caption tells us that this *ecclesia spiritualis* was sterile from the time of John the Baptist until the present, but fruitful from the present until the end of time.[21] In another drawing the phrases 'conceptio eiusdem virginis' and 'partus virginis' match stages of the third age or age of the Spirit to symbolize the development of the *ecclesia spiritualis*.[22] There is no doubt that for Joachim of Fiore the stages of Mary's pregnancy represented the development of the *ecclesia spiritualis*.

While the assertions of prophets are generally ambiguous concerning exact dates, Joachim believed his times were ripe for the conception of the *ecclesia spiritualis*. The sixth period of the Church was beginning and, he declared, it was necessary that a virginal, contemplative and continent church be conceived, that is, to have *in utero* (symbolized by Mary's conception of Christ) that holy people who, according to the Book of Daniel, will be given the kingdom under all the heavens.[23] Since Joachim was engaged in monastic reform it is understandable that he also claimed Mary to stand more specifically for Benedictine monasticism.[24] And Joachim foresaw that, as such, Mary would conceive by the Holy Spirit and would carry a son in her uterus, namely again, those holy people who, according to Daniel, would rule until the end of time.[25]

The virtues traditionally assigned to Mary, most importantly chastity, gave Joachim a chance to ascribe certain qualities to the future monks predicted to be 'born of Mary'. In fact, she symbolized not the whole mass of monks but only that monastic group which especially loved the celibate life.[26] The church of the future will be refreshed by

[20] *Il Libro delle Figure dell' Abate Gioachino da Fiore*, ed. L. Tondelli, M. Reeves and B. Hirsch-Reich (Turin, 1953), II, pl. XX. See also Reeves and Hirsch-Reich, *The 'Figurae'*, pp. 164–9.

[21] *Il Libro*, II, pl. XX.

[22] ibid., II, pl. XXI.

[23] *Tractatus super quatuor Evangelia di Gioacchino da Fiore*, ed. E. Buonaiuti (Rome, 1930), pp. 34–5. Criticism of Buonaiuti's editorial skill is found in Ezio Franceschini, 'Il codice padovano Antoniano XIV, 322, e il testo dei *Tractatus super quatuor evangelia* di Gioacchino da Fiore', *Aevum*, 9 (1935), pp. 481–92; and Carmelo Ottaviano, 'Il *Tractatus super quatuor evangelia* di Gioacchino da Fiore', *Archivio di filosofia*, 1 (1931), pp. 73–82.

[24] *Tractatus super quatuor Evangelia*, p. 25.

[25] ibid.

[26] ibid., p. 32, 'Secundum quem intellectum, Maria quoque non universalem ecclesiam, set neque generaliter monastice turbam professionis, set quandam specialem eiusdem monastice professionis ecclesiam, cui datum est a Domino specialius celibem eligere et diligere vitam'.

the silence of hermits. It will be without literary studies or a doctor of ecclesiastical institutions. Here will be found, Joachim opined, simplicity in life, virtue, sobriety, charity arising from a pure heart, and a faith not feigned.[27] Because Mary and her virtues represented religious life of the future, Elizabeth who conceived earlier, represented to Joachim the Church as it existed in his own day. No dispensations, such as were tolerated in the Church of the clerics, designated by Elizabeth – not to speak of the Greek Church – will be granted ever to allow religious men and women to live with members of the opposite sex.[28] Mary's church will be chaste, sober, spiritual and segregated from the world.[29]

The theme of Mary's easy acceptance of the angel's announcement that she would have a child by the Holy Spirit was used by Joachim as a symbol of Christian faith. Contrasted to the unbelief of Zachary, Elizabeth's husband, who symbolized the incredulity of the Jews, Mary was set up as a prototype of the newly converted Gentiles.[30] Expanding on this symbol, Joachim reglossed the verse 'the angel Gabriel was sent by God into a city of Galilee by the name of Nazareth to a virgin betrothed to a man by the name of Joseph.' Joachim's commentary argued that since Mary represented the newly converted Gentiles, Gabriel's coming to Mary at Nazareth was equal to Paul's mission to the Gentiles.[31] According to Joachim's logic, because Mary was already betrothed, so had the Gentiles also already been spiritually betrothed (on the day Peter was sent to Cornelius). And although Mary was indeed betrothed to Joseph, Scripture records that Joseph did not 'know her until the birth of her first-born son', so with the Gentiles the betrothal was completed when the spirtiual order was born.[32] Joachim concluded his gloss by repeating the parallel between Gabriel and Paul, and posited that as Gabriel was sent to Nazareth, so St Paul was sent to the Gentiles to find a 'flos qui proferret fructum gratie spiritualis'.[33] Joachim then proceeded to repeat this phraseology of flowering and producing fruit in his explanation of the meaning of the Annunciation either to indicate what happened in Nazareth as a *topos*: 'Nazareth partem illam gentium que prima floruit', 'floruit in

[27] Joachim of Fiore, *Expositio*, 83r.
[28] ibid.
[29] ibid. and 49r.
[30] *Tractatus super quatuor Evangelia*, p. 27.
[31] ibid.
[32] ibid., pp. 27–8.
[33] ibid., p. 28.

doctrina Christi et protulit fructum spiritualem' or specifically what happened to the virgin: 'quasi florere virginem'.[34]

Joachim of Fiore utilized the Annunciation, Mary's conception of Jesus by the Holy Spirit, to foretell that a new virginal church, a spiritual order following a monastic way of life, would appear in the sixth period of the Church. Judging from Joachim's detailed description of a parallel development in the time of St Paul, one could use the phraseology of flowering and bearing fruit to characterize its genesis. Its hallmark was the celibate life.

Steeped in the vocabulary of Joachim's symbolism, the Anonymous described Joachim's efforts for monastic reform that led to Fiore in terms of the conceptions of Rachel and Mary. These images were meant by him to explain the purpose of Joachim's endeavor and, indeed, were used only after he considered Joachim to be free to found a new form of monastic life. When the Anonymous wrote the history of Joachim's life what he wrote amounted, in a sense, to a history of monastic reform. As a Florensian, however, what was most important to him was the path that led directly to Fiore. The first significant step for the Anonymous was Joachim's decision to return to Calabria after a pilgrimage to the Holy Land and a sojourn in Sicily. His mission was to implement the work of the Holy Spirit, according to the Anonymous, and it was described in the imagery of planting and fertility. By fertilizing with the word and watering through example Joachim was envisioned as helping to bring forth the fruit of the grace of the Holy Spirit in a hitherto sterile land.[35] Later on in Joachim's life the Anonymous established a clear break between the abbot's fruitless reforming efforts in certain areas of Calabria and the new worthwhile work at Fiore; it was demarcated by a judgement from Rome.[36] This turning point arose from an episode at the monastery at Corazzo, which the prophet had tried to affiliate with the Cistercian house. Having become entangled in problems with his monks at Corazzo, Joachim, even though he was their abbot, fled to a place of refuge at Petra Lata. It was here that Joachim wrote his *Commentary on the Life of Saint Benedict* to justify the break with his monks and Cistercian

[34] ibid. and pp. 129, 35, 109.

[35] *Vita b. Joachimi abbatis* in Grundmann, 'Zur Biographie', pp. 529–30. This image happens to echo Joachim's reference to himself as 'qui sum homo agricola a iuventute mea' in *Expositio*, 175r, which generally has been interpreted by scholars to refer to his spiritual work. See H. Mottu, *La manifestation*, p. 13 for literature on the image of Joachim as farmer.

[36] *Vita b. Joachimi abbatis*, in Grundmann, 'Zur Biographie', p. 534.

practices, and even look toward a new form of religious life. The monks of Corazzo would not leave him in peace and the matter was not resolved, according to the Anonymous, until Joachim accompanied the senior monks to the Roman *curia* where he was freed from his abbatial obligations.[37] Noting that Joachim was now exonerated and unfettered, the Anonymous proclaimed that Joachim returned to his haven of quiet at Petra Lata and 'forthwith would begin the copulation of Rachel, the embrace for the propagation of the seed'.[38] Following the symbolism in Joachim's writings, the Anonymous has announced the purpose of Joachim's work: the fertilization of Rachel to produce Joseph, the spiritual, contemplative order of the future.

Petra Lata proved unsuitable for Joachim's design, the Anonymous claimed, because of the constant flow of people coming there.[39] Consequently, Joachim chose to search for a new place of solitude in the Sila mountains and it was in this location in the Sila, specifically in Fiore, that Joachim founded his new order. Although he gives few details of the settlement of Fiore and the origin of the Florensian order, the Anonymous used Joachim's symbolism to present a statement of purpose for the new foundation, an explanation of the new foundation's name and even a confession that the original purpose suffered a delay in fulfillment.

After the Anonymous narrated Joachim's search in the Sila mountains for an appropriate site for his monastic group, he remarked that Joachim finally withdrew from Petra Lata and settled among the mountains 'in Flore, locus in flumine sic vocatus, qui vere inter montes et colles situs est arctaverunt, ut novus in Nazaret fructus Sancti Spiritus nuntiaretur, quoadusque Dominus in omnem terram ex hoc salutem maximam operaretur.'[40] The phrase 'ut novus in Nazaret fructus Sancti Spiritus nuntiaretur' is a crucial line in the Anonymous' *Vita* since it explains the purpose of Joachim's settlement. It is also one that, because of its curious wording, may be quickly skimmed over without a grasp of its meaning. What does this group in the Sila have to do with announcing the *new fruit* of the Holy Spirit in Nazareth? If the Anonymous had even used the phrase 'that the *fruit* of the Holy Spirit may be announced in Nazareth', it could be taken to refer simply to the Annunciation of the conception of Christ to Mary through

[37] ibid.
[38] ibid., '. . . ad Petram Olei rediit ex tunc initiaturus concubitus Rachelis amplexus in propagatione seminis, . . .'.
[39] ibid.
[40] ibid., p. 535.

the action of the Holy Spirit, but the intent might still be a puzzle to us. What purpose of these monks would have to do with the conception of Christ? At any rate the Anonymous specifically used the particular expression 'that the *new fruit* of the Holy Spirit may be announced in Nazareth' and this wording demands interpretation. Since Joachim's own writings proclaim that as a symbolic parallel to the Annunciation in Nazareth, a new monastic order in Joachim's own lifetime would be conceived by the Virgin by means of the Holy Spirit, it is only natural that the Anonymous has employed the phraseology and symbolism, 'to announce the new fruit of the Holy Spirit in Nazareth', to allow for the fulfillment of the abbot's predictions. Joachim's actions, hence, in the Anonymous' description, bring about the annunciation of the new fruit of the Holy Spirit in Nazareth, i.e. enable the new predicted monastic group to be conceived.[41] The very place of settlement, according to the Anonymous, was 'truly located among the mountains and the hills',[42] paralleling Joachim's own remarks of the

[41] Joachim's description of the new order in the third *status* in his *Liber figurarum* included a main oratory named 'Sancte Dei genitricis Marie', *Il Libro delle Figure*, II, pl. XII. Giles Constable, 'Renewal and reform in religious life: concepts and realities', in R. Benson and G. Constable with C. Lanham (eds), *Renaissance and Renewal in the Twelfth Century* (Cambridge, Mass., 1982), pp. 37–67, offers a general background against which Joachim's novel use of traditional imagery can be seen more clearly.

[42] *Vita b. Joachimi abbatis*, in Grundmann, 'Zur Biographie', p. 535. Biagio Cappelli, 'Il titolo dell' Ordine del "Fiore" ', *Archivio storico per la Calabria e la Lucania*, 22 (1953), p. 48, concluded 'che quindi il nome di "Fiore" non deriva dalla originaria toponomastica, . . .'; Antonio Crocco, *Gioacchino da Fiore e il Gioachimismo* (Naples, 1976), p. 22, n. 34, summed up the various conjectures for considering the name Fiore to be strictly symbolic of future developments. On the other hand, Grundmann, 'Zur Biographie', p. 479, inferred from the Anonymous' text, 'ubi Flos Albo flumini iungitur' (p. 535) that *Flos* was a river. While it would have been customary for Cistercian and Florensian monastic sites to be named from a nearby water source, Grundmann had no comment to indicate the significance of his inference for the discussions about the symbolism of Fiore. No other contemporary document, however, mentions a Flos river, and in fact, when in other places the Anonymous specifies the name of a river, he always adds the word *flumen* or *fluvius*. He does not so tag *Flos*. Grundmann's inference stemmed from the verb *iungitur*, which, however, can also be read in the sense of adjoining; see Du Cange, *Glossarium*, 4 (Paris, 1938), p. 449. Contemporary documents relating to Fiore mention other rivers and when these documents refer to their joining together, the verb *miscetur* is used; see Walther Holtzmann, 'Papst-, Kaiser- und Normannenurkunden aus Unteritalien', *Quellen und Forschungen aus italienischen Archiven und Bibliotheken*, 36 (1956), p. 6. Incidently, a seventeenth-century Cistercian, Benedict Conti Soranus, proposed that the name Fiore was chosen by Joachim to hide what was really a

location of Nazareth 'in montanis Galilee'.[43] Finally, not the least to be noted is that according to Jerome's *Interpretation of Hebrew Names*, the source of Joachim's Hebrew etymologies, Nazareth is to be understood as *flos*, a flower of moral purity that is separated and guarded.[44] (Incidently, the significance of *flos* as an interpretation of Nazareth is a theme Bernard of Clairvaux developed in one of his sermons.)[45] Joachim's place of settlement *Flos* or Fiore was to be, consequently, a new Nazareth.

It is curious that in Joachim's writings St Paul, whose mission was described as parallel to Gabriel's in the Annunciation, and who, Joachim claimed, helped to conceive the spiritual order in the early Church, had to search to find the 'flos qui proferret fructum'. Not only did Joachim, according to the Anonymous, search the Sila to find *flos*, but he settled there so that the new fruit would be announced. Hence, there is a concordance in the visionary pattern that pairs Gabriel and the Annunciation at Nazareth, St Paul with his search for the *flos* and the conception of the spiritual order in the new Church,[46] and Joachim himself and the beginning of a new monastic order at Fiore.

These parallels, while they may have been hidden from us, were not lost on commentators of the mid-thirteenth century. In contemporary marginal notations to the thirteenth-century MS Vat. Lat.

Cistercian group from the Cistercian-hating Frederick Barbarossa; see Cipriano Baraut, 'Per la storia dei monasteri florensi', *Benedictina*, 4 (1950), p. 260, n. 22. For information about the destruction of the monastery of Fiore by a fire after Joachim's death and the subsequent construction of a new monastery between 1215 and 1234 in a place originally called *Fara-domus*, but renamed *Flos*, see Holtzmann, 'Papst-, Kaiser- und Normannenurkunden', p. 12; Pietro de Leo, '*Reliquiae* florensi-Note e documenti per la ricostruzione della biblioteca e dell' archivio del protocenobio di S. Giovanni in Fiore', *Storia e messaggio*, p. 400; Romano Napolitano, *S. Giovanni in Fiore monastica e civica* I,1 (1978), p. 77; I,2 (1981), pp. 23, 230, 247–8.

[43] *Tractatus super quatuor Evangelia*, p. 129.

[44] *S. Hieronymi presbyteri liber interpretationis hebraicorum nominum*, *S. Hieronymi presbyteri opera*, I, 1, *Corpus christianorum*, series latina, 72 (Turnhout, 1959), pp. 137, 142; *Tractatus super quatuor Evangelia*, p. 142, L.10, n. 1.

[45] Bernard of Clairvaux, 'In laudibus virginis matris, homilia I', *Sermones I*, *S. Bernardi opera*, ed. J. Leclercq and H. Rochais (Rome, 1966) IV, pp. 16–17. Jerome's etymology of the name Joachim as 'where there is preparation, or the preparation of the Lord' must not have been lost on our abbot, see *S. Hieronymi*, p. 136.

[46] *Tractatus super quatuor Evangelia*, p. 28.

4959, containing the text of the *Super Esaiam,* incorrectly ascribed to Joachim, these parallels were developed in several places. One note pointed out: 'Nazareth is not situated on the sea, but in the mountains of Galilee in concordance with mountainous Calabria. Thus as the angel was directed there to the virgin, here the heavenly doctor was directed to the Cistercian way of life.'[47] Since other sections of the *Super Esaiam* show that this commentary looked to developments beyond Joachim, beyond the new Nazareth to even a second Bethlehem,[48] it is clear that while using Joachim's imagery[49] this commentator built on the earlier tradition represented by the Anonymous.

In all Joachim of Fiore's discussions of the roles of future religious orders a crowning purpose was always conversion.[50] In the *Liber figurarum* Joachim proposed that after the destruction of the Antichrist 'the Lord shall dominate to the ends of the earth . . . Jews and many infidels are to be converted to the Lord.'[51] The abbot's vision has been summed up as 'a purified Church under monastic leadership, embracing all men in an atmosphere of peace, freedom and contemplation.'[52] When the Anonymous asserted that they settled in Fiore so that the new fruit of the Holy Spirit might be announced, he added as no accidental platitude 'in order that the Lord may work the greatest

[47] Rome, Vatican, Lat. 4959, f. 25 recto, 'Nazaret non in marinam sed in montanis posita Galilee cum Calabria montuosa concordat: ut sicut ibi ad virginem dirigitur angelus (Luce I) sic et hic ad religionem cisterci[ense]m doctor celitus dirigitur.' The orthography of this passage follows that in *Super Esaiam prophetam* (Venice, 1517), f. 23v. See Elena Bianca di Gioia, 'Un manoscritto pseudo-gioachimita: Biblioteca Nazionale Centrale di Roma Vittorio Emanuele 1502,' in A. M. Romanini (ed.), *Federico II e l'arte del duecento italiano* (Galatina, 1980), p. 91, for placing the composition of the original text of the *Super Esaiam* as early as 1239, and Reeves, *The Influence,* pp. 521, 154, and Elena Bianca di Gioia, 'Un manoscritto,' p. 94, for the date of the MS Vat. Lat. 4959. Reeves, *The Influence,* summarized her arguments for Florensian/Cistercian authorship of the *Super Esaiam* (and *Super Hieremiam*) on pp. 147–58; and Elena Bianca di Gioia, 'Un manoscritto', pp. 95–6, 100, has restated and supported Reeves' viewpoint.

[48] Vat. Lat. 4959, f. 16 recto.

[49] *Tractatus super quatuor Evangelia,* pp. 68, 51–3, 98–101. (I am at present working on a paper exploring the relationship of the imagery contained in the *Super Esaiam* and its marginal notes to the imagery in Joachim's authentic writings.)

[50] Joachim of Fiore, *Liber concordie,* 85v; Reeves, *The Influence,* pp. 140–4; and especially E. Randolph Daniel, 'Apocalyptic conversion: the Joachite alternative to the Crusades', *Traditio,* 25 (1969), pp. 127–39.

[51] *Il Libro delle Figure,* II, pl. XIV.

[52] Daniel, 'Apocalyptic conversion', p. 138.

salvation on all the earth out of this'.[53] What the Anonymous was proclaiming was Joachim's prophecy that when the new monastic order would appear the world would begin to be converted.

In detailing the first developments of the Florensians, the Anonymous used two symbolic numbers. For the entire summer, according to the Anonymous, the Florensians celebrated while men were drawn to the solitude of Fiore, and they erected 12 huts.[54] In Joachim's writings 12 represented not only the perfect apostolic number but also the number of preachers who were to convert the world in the age of the Spirit. As there had been 12 patriarchs to propagate the synagogue in the Old Testament, 12 apostles in the New for the Church of the Gentiles, so Joachim taught, the age of the Spirit would use 12 to preach the gospel and convert the Jews.[55] These Florensian expectations received a sudden dampening, however, as the passing of the sixth month (the month of the Annunciation) did not see the desired spiritual progress, but, according to the Anonymous, the beginning of a storm (tempestas).[56] Joachim and his monks began to be harassed by royal officials. This so affected them that the Anonymous was forced to conclude that 'the holy seed which had been recently propagated in the summer contrary to the nature of mountains would be delayed and afterwards bear much fruit in the summer'.[57]

The Anonymous' last image worked to complete his general theme. The image of planting recalled Joachim's mission in Calabria, a formerly sterile land. The very wording 'semen sanctum ... seminatum'[58] carried forward his image of fertilization that was begun with the image of 'concubitus Rachel amplexus in propagatione seminis'[59] and also presented more spiritually in the symbol of the Annunciation in Nazareth. It also linked all these images to the foundation at Fiore. At the same time, the confession of a delay, that the fruit would be

[53] Vita b. Joachimi abbatis, in Grundmann, 'Zur Biographie', p. 535; cf. Psalms 73. 12 and Apocalypse 5.6 in Biblia sacra iuxta vulgatam versionem, ed. B. Fischer et al. (Stuttgart, 1975).

[54] Vita b. Joachimi abbatis, in Grundmann, 'Zur Biographie', p. 535.

[55] Joachim of Fiore, Liber concordie, 21v, 57v, 58r; Abbot Joachim of Fiore: 'Liber de Concordia Noui ac Veteris Testamenti', ed. E. R. Daniel, pp. 159–60, 411, 412–13; Reeves, Joachim of Fiore, p. 13.

[56] Vita b. Joachimi abbatis, in Grundmann, 'Zur Biographie', p. 535.

[57] ibid.

[58] ibid.

[59] ibid., p. 534. Cf. the vocabulary Joachim ascribed to the founding of a new group in the ecclesia: 'qui me verbi semine fecundaret', Tractatus super quatuor Evangelia, p. 29.

brought forth later, underlined the sense that the settlement at Fiore did not immediately fulfill the hopes of those whose symbols had promised so much.[60]

In one of Joachim of Fiore's works, the *Tractatus super quatuor Evangelia*, this symbolic vision drawn from the Annunciation is summed up and in his closing remarks Joachim asks the reader if he understands:

According to this concept Mary also designates the church of the continent, which until now, as far as the perfect number of spiritual men, remained sterile like Rachel . . . Her fortunate conception is not from mortal man, but is expected out of the Holy Spirit and the strength of the Almighty. But, when does this take place? 'In the sixth month', it is said, 'Gabriel was sent to Mary.' The first month of the conception of Elizabeth signifies the time of the apostles, the second the time of martyrs, the third the time of doctors, the fourth the time of virgins, the fifth the time of western monks. Then the sixth month in which Gabriel is sent to the Virgin designates the sixth time of the Church, the time of the opening of the sixth seal, according to the Apocalypse, in which it is necessary that the Virgin conceive and give birth a little after the old woman [Elizabeth]. Do you think, O reader, you have understood what I have said, namely that it is necessary that the Virgin conceive and, so to speak, flower, truly to give birth after the old woman? But he easily understands this who at least or in part now knows what may be under the cause of this mystery . . . Thus in the sixth period which we are beginning,[61] it is necessary to conceive a virginal church, continent and contemplative and to have *in utero* that people of this way of life of the saints, to whom, according to Daniel, is given the kingdom under all the heavens, and its birth shall be at the end of time. . . .[62]

[60] This dampening of hopes may have become part of the Florensian legacy and explains partly why they did not assert their claim to a place in the third age as fervently, for example, as the Franciscan Spirituals and why the order of Joachim could enthusiastically receive the Dominicans when the latter first appeared in Calabria. For this aspect of the Florensians see Marjorie Reeves, 'The Abbot Joachim's disciples and the Cistercian order', *Sophia*, 19 (1951), pp. 355–71; and *The Influence*, pp. 72, 145–58.

[61] Mottu, *La Manifestation*, p. 240, interpreted the phrase 'cuius exordia iam tenemus' not as referring to the literal commencement, but ' "l'ouverture" ou "conception" de celui-ci'. Ernesto Buonaiuti, who edited the text, declared in the *Tractatus super quatuor Evangelia*, p. 35, n. 2, that this phrase revealed Joachim's own role in the preparation for the third age: 'Ecco un inciso singolarmente eloquente per far intendere il posto e la funzione che Gioacchino assegna a sè e alla propria riforma monastica nella preparazione della nuova economia spirituale.' See also, ibid., XXV, XXXVII–XLII.

[62] *Tractatus super quatuor Evangelia*, pp. 34–5, 'Secundum quem intellectum Maria quoque designat ecclesiam continentium, que actenus, quoad perfectum spiritalium

I think the Anonymous could answer Joachim's rhetorical question and say he understood perfectly. Not only did the Anonymous cite images relevant to this passage, but he also made it clear that he understood the significance and meaning of Joachim's system of concords or parallel events in the Old Testament, New Testament and contemporary era. Easter was commemorated by the Anonymous as the feast on which the concord (*concordia*) of the Old and New Testament was revealed to the abbot.[63] When it was described in the *Vita* how Joachim used the Old Testament image of Nebuchadnezzar (an interpretation similar to one that occurs in Joachim's *Liber concordie*)[64] to apply to Henry VI and the words of Ezekiel to explain what Henry would do, the Anonymous confirmed that these events were fullfilled by concord, i.e. these events took place 'after three years so that the word of the Lord given to Ezekiel was fulfilled under the mystery of the old events for the prophesying of the new.'[65]

Our Anonymous author, who, according to Grundmann, wrote shortly after Joachim's death in 1202,[66] presented how a Florensian,

---

virorum numerum, sicut et Rachel in sterilitate permansit . . . eius felix conceptus non ex homine mortali, set ex gratia sancti Spiritus et virtute Altissimi expectetur. Set hoc quando? "Mense," ait, "sexto missus est Gabiel ad Mariam". Primus mensis conceptionis Helisabeth tempus significat apostolorum; secundus, tempus martyrum; tertius, tempus doctorum; quartus, tempus virginum; quintus, tempus occidentalium monachorum. Porro sextus mensis in quo missus est ad virginem Gabrihel, designat sextum tempus ecclesie, tempus scilicet apertionis sexti signaculi, secundum Apocalypsim, in quo oportet concipere virginem et paulo post vetulam parturire. Putas, intellexisti lector quid dixerim, oportere scilicet concipere et quasi florere virginem, vetulam vero parturire? Set ille facile hoc intelligit qui saltem vel ex parte iam novit quid sit quod sub eadem causa mysterii . . . Itaque: in sexto tempore, cuius exordia iam tenemus, oportet concipere ecclesiam virginalem, sive etiam continentem atque contemplativam; et habere in utero professionis sue populum illum sanctorum, cui dandum est secundum Danihelem regnum quod est subter omnem celum, eritque partus eius in consummatione seculi . . .'.

[63] *Vita b. Joachimi abbatis*, p. 533, '. . . festum, in quo sibi veteris et novi testamenti fuerat concordia revelata . . .'.

[64] Joachim of Fiore, *Liber concordie*, 126r.

[65] *Vita b. Joachimis abbati*, p. 538, 'Post tres annos, ut compleretur sermo Domini factus ad Ezechielem sub misterio veterum de prophetatione novorum, "Ecce," inquit, "ego adducam ad Tirum Nabucdonasor regem Babillonis ab aquilone, regem regum cum curribus et equis et equitibus et cetu populoque magno" et cetera, que vastationis, direptionis, subversionis eventum ad unumquemque usque singula prosecuntur.'

[66] Grundmann placed it before 1209; see Grundmann, 'Zur Biographie', pp. 464, 479.

significantly one of the original members, would interpret the beginnings and purposes of the order. It happens to be a view that coincides
with Joachim's own written prognostications. Does it present Joachim's
own intentions for Fiore? The answer to this important question may
partly lie in the tract Joachim wrote in 1186/7 just before the founding
of Fiore. If the high hopes and predictions found in the *De Vita sancti
Benedicti et de officio divino secundum eius doctrinam*, written in Petra Lata,
are stressed, it is plausible that Joachim had similar initial intentions.
In Petra Lata, the way station to the mountainous setting of Fiore,
Joachim saw St Benedict's moving to the mountain top to be the great
exemplar of monastic reform and proclaimed that it was the time 'to
uncover Benedict's light and place it high to illuminate everyone.'[67]
Furthermore, in this commentary Joachim prophesied that by the
year 1190 a third order, rejoicing and uninvolved with secular business,
would be established and praised.[68] Could the founding of Fiore and
its settlement have been carried out in the initial flush of Joachim's
enthusiasm, an enthusiasm both necessary for Joachim, comparing
himself to St Benedict, to make a decisive break with his past and also
remarkable enough to leave a definite impression on his first companions? But was it an enthusiasm and confidence that faded with the
realities of reform and everyday administration? Is this what the
Anonymous has alluded to in his mention of Fiore's delay in bearing
much fruit? Perhaps this explains why Joachim's prognostications remained vague, so much so that various subsequent orders saw themselves in his prophecies and the Florensians became deferential to
other religious groups that appeared in Calabria.

A key element in ascertaining Joachim's own intentions for Fiore is
the reliability of the Anonymous, and his text is enhanced by what
seem to be fairly accurate recollections of the language of Joachim.
This can be seen in the Anonymous' summary of a speech given by
Joachim before Tancred, King of Sicily.[69] Joachim's purpose was to
explain why his monastic group must remain at Fiore and not be

[67] Cipriano Baraut, 'Un tratado inédito de Joaquín de Fiore: *De vita sancti
Benedicti et de officio divino secundum eius doctrinam*', *Analecta sacra tarraconensia*, 24
(1951), p. 74.

[68] ibid., p. 97, '. . . circa annum millesimum centesimum et nonagesimum, in
quibus ordo tertius confortatus et auctus, tria cantica suprascripta cum alleluia
cantabit; quia illi soli tria illa cantica cantare nequeunt, qui adhuc occasione aliqua
secularibus implicantur negotiis, sive laici sint, sive clerici quia et plerique non
minus clericos negotiosos videmus.'

[69] *Vita b. Joachimi abbatis*, p. 536.

transferred by the king to the Benedictine monastery S. Maria della Mattina, on lower ground. The text of the speech, as presented by the Anonymous, is really only a catena of scriptural quotes and allusions, but when they are read in the context of Joachim's commentaries a surprisingly full, consistent and, most importantly, thematically relevant speech emerges – a harsh contrast between Joachim's ideals and the present condition of the Church.

Using the example of Sodom, and the imagery of taverns and inebriation, Joachim exhorted the king that his monastic community of the sons of light could not be put together with the temptations of the world. To fight the forced move of his monastery to a less isolated spot, the abbot insisted that to keep his group celibate and out of the range of temptation they must remain in a rustic setting.[70] The biblical quotations as recalled by the Anonymous, 'ut illius etiam elogii recordaremur',[71] back up this theme, and when traced to Joachim's own writings add further dimensions. For example, the Anonymous cited without gloss Genesis 6.2: 'The sons of God saw that the daughters of men were fair, and they took wives for themselves, as many as they wished'. While, as it stands, this citation could simply represent Joachim's need to keep his celibate charges away from temptation, Joachim's own commentary on this text in the *Expositio in Apocalypsim* shows that he equated the sons of God with the clergy, and the daughters of men stood for cities whose riches lured many to fornication.[72]

The question of the authenticity of this speech of Joachim is important because on one hand the themes of celibacy, sobriety, sexual

---

[70] ibid. The images of Sodom and the Pauline community of the sons of light conveyed part of Joachim's message, and his own commentary on the speech's biblical images found in Joachim of Fiore, *Liber concordie*, 76r–v, and *Expositio*, 65r, show us Joachim's stress on celibacy. Other references of the Anonymous, in the *Vita*, pp. 531–2, 533, as the aside that Joachim's retreat at Petra Lata was presented by a man who retained his virginity despite the frequency of temptations placed in his path by his brother, a bishop, and also the condemnation of the monks of Acri who spoke with women inside their monastery, worked to contrast the immorality Joachim perceived in the present Church with the proposed chastity of the new. In his reminiscenses about Joachim, Archbishop Luke of Cosenza, a one-time companion of the abbot, related a tale of Joachim's overcoming the temptation of a lascivious widow and, in general, highlighted Joachim's reputation for chastity in a way that could entitle the abbot to lead the chaste *viri spirituales* of the third age; see Grundmann, 'Zur Biographie', p. 541.

[71] *Vita b. Joachimi abbatis*, p. 536.

[72] Joachim of Fiore, *Expositio*, 194r–v.

purity, rusticity and contemplation, found in Joachim's speech, if they accurately reflect the abbot's own ideas, could represent his ideals for the new Order of Fiore. On the other hand, these also happen to be the same qualities that Joachim in his writings predicted would exist in the monastic group symbolized by Mary and, hence, reinforces the thesis of Joachim as founder of a monastic group that was to play a special role in the third age.[73] The closeness of the Anonymous' to Joachim's own language throughout the *Vita* is obviously an even more significant issue here (and one that requires further study). If the similarity of language is not merely the case of a Florensian appropriating Joachim's texts in a later attempt to enhance the mission of the founder, then the aforementioned themes of Rachel and of Mary's Annunciation might represent Joachim's own intentions and imagery for Fiore. In this instance the clues drawn from the female images suggest that Fiore may have meant for Joachim more of a new beginning than we have been able to prove so far.

[73] Joachim's writings refer often to the qualities of the spiritual men of the future. See *Il Libro delle Figure*, pl. XII; *Short Tract on the Apocalypse*, ed. J. Huck, *Joachim von Floris und die joachitische Literatur* (Freiburg im Breisgau, 1939), p. 304; and Baraut 'Un tratado inedito', pp. 67, 76, for references to some of these virtues (in addition to those noted above) and particularly the celibate life of the new spiritual men. Reeves, *The Influence*, pp. 135-44, provides a large number of citations from Joachim's writings for the qualities of these men of the third age, and Baraut, *Dictionnaire de spiritualité*, col. 1194-6, discusses the qualities found in Joachim's 'true monasticism' as a background for understanding his desire for monastic reform.

9

Queen Sancia of Naples (1286–1345) and the Spiritual Franciscans

RONALD G. MUSTO

Discussing Franciscan events for the year 1334, the *Chronica xxiv generalium ordinis minorum* presents a letter[1] written by Sancia of Majorca, Queen of Naples and wife of King Robert the Wise.[2] The letter is addressed to the Franciscans assembled at the Chapter General of Assisi held in 1334 and incorporates three earlier pieces written by the queen to the order between 1316 and 1331. Sancia presents these letters as a thematic triptych to demonstrate her connections with, and support for, the Franciscan order and for the Spiritual[3] tradition

[1] In *Analecta Franciscana*, 3 (Quaracchi, 1897), pp. 508–14.

[2] Born 1278, d. 1343, son of Charles II, the Lame (1246–1309). The standard works on Robert's life and Angevin Naples include Giovanni Battista Siragusa, *L'ingegno, il sapere e gli intendimenti di Roberto d'Angio* (Turin-Palermo, 1891); St Clair Baddeley, *Robert the Wise and His Heirs 1278–1352* (London, 1897); Walter Wilhelm Goetz, *König Robert von Neapel (1309–1343), seine Persönlichkeit und sein Verhältnis zum Humanismus* (Tübingen, 1910); Romolo Caggese, *Roberto d'Angio e i suoi tempi* (2 vols, Florence, 1922–30); Émile G. Léonard, *Les Angevins de Naples* (Paris, 1954); Paul Audibert, *Histoire des comtes de Provence; rois de Sicile et de Jérusalem* (Villa des Rogations, 1969); and Carlo de Frede, 'Nel Regno di Roberto d'Angio', in *Storia di Napoli* (Naples, 1969) 3, pp. 157–224.

[3] The terms 'Spiritual' and 'Spiritual tradition' are still the subject of some dispute. In this essay they are used to distinguish that group within the Franciscan order combining a Joachite interpretation of Christian history with the strict observance of the Franciscan Rule on matters of poverty. These loyalties led them into conflict with the Conventual majority and eventually to reject obedience to papal bulls perceived as altering Francis' intent. After their condemnations in the 1310s and 1320s the surviving Spiritual groups came to be called Fraticelli. The basic works on the movement are still Franz Ehrle, 'Die Spiritualen, ihre Verhältniss zum Franciscanorden und zu den Fraticellen', *ALKG*, 1 (1885), pp. 509–69; 2 (1886), pp. 106–64, 249–336; 3 (1887), pp. 553–623; 4 (1888); pp. 1–190; and Decima L. Douie, *The Nature and the Effect of the Heresy of the Fraticelli* (Manchester, 1932, reprint. New York, 1978). More recent work dealing specifically with the

within it. The letters provide details of her lineage and family ties to the order, give practical guidance to its members and demonstrate her spiritual kinship with the tradition of Francis and his life of evangelical perfection. This triptych forms a framework for the following discussion of the queen's life, her patronage of the order and her religious and intellectual contributions to the Spiritual Franciscan tradition.

We know little of Sancia's life except for occasional glimpses as she appears within her Majorcan family[4] and behind or alongside her husband. Despite a life that spanned the first half of the fourteenth century, at the center of many of its most important cultural, intellectual and political currents at the court of Naples,[5] there exists no

---

Spirituals includes M. D. Lambert, *Franciscan Poverty* (London, 1961); David Flood, 'A Study in Joachimism', *Collectanea Franciscana*, 41 (1971), pp. 131–40; the collections *Franciscains d'Oc: Les Spirituels ca. 1280–1324*, vol. 10 of Cahiers de Fanjeaux (Toulouse, 1975); and *Chi erano gli Spirituali* (Assisi, 1976); David Burr, *The Persecution of Peter Olivi* (Philadelphia, 1976); Clément Schmitt, 'Fraticelles', *Dictionnaire d'histoire et de géographie ecclésiastique*, 18 (1977), cols. 1063–1108; his 'Fraticelli', *Dizionario degli istituti di perfezione*, 4 (1977), cols. 807–21; and Lydia von Auw, *Angelo Clareno et les Spirituels italiens* (Rome, 1979), the culmination of her fifty years of research on the Spirituals.

4 On the history of the kingdom and dynasty of Majorca during this period see Albert Lecoy de la Marche, *Les relations politiques de la France avec le royaume de Majorque* (Paris, 1892); Guillermo Carbonell y Vadell, *La dinastía de Mallorca. Resumen historico de sus vicisitudes* (Palma de Majorca, 1917); Auguste Störmann, *Studien zur Geschichte des Königreichs Mallorka* (Leipzig, 1918); Antoni Pons Pastor, *Els reis de la casa de Mallorca* (Barcelona, 1957); and *Historia de Mallorca* (6 vols, Palma de Majorca, 1963–70), 1, pp. 91–3; 153–79; Alvaro Santamaría-Arández, 'Mallorca en el siglo xiv', *Anuario de estudios medievales*, 7 (1973), pp. 165–238; Charles-Emmanuel Dufourcq, 'Aspects internationales de Majorque devant les derniers siècles du Moyen Age', *Mayurqa*, 11 (1974), pp. 5–52; and J. N. Hillgarth, *The Spanish Kingdoms 1250–1516* (2 vols, Oxford, 1976–8).

5 Among the basic works consulted were Benedetto Croce, *Storia del regno di Napoli* (Bari, 1925), pp. 46–51; Domenico Ambrasi, 'La vita religiosa', in *Storia di Napoli* (Naples, 1969), 3, pp. 437–574; Francesco Sabatini, 'La cultura a Napoli nell'età angioina', *Storia di Napoli* (Naples, 1974), 4, pp. 17–18, 62–3; *Napoli angioina. Cultura e società* (Naples, 1975), pp. 53–67; and Vittorio Gleijeses, *La storia di Napoli* (Naples, 1974), pp. 331–60. Published registers to the Neapolitan archives, *I registri della cancelleria angioina*, ed. Riccardo Filangieri (Naples, 1950–) have reached 1288 (vol. 29). Bartolomeo Capasso, *Le fonti della storia delle province napolitane dal 658 al 1500*, with notes by O. Mastrojanni (Naples, 1902), pp. 100–68, offers a survey of literary sources. Among these I have found the *Cronaca di Partenope*, ed. Antonio Altamura (Naples, 1974), and the *Chronicon siculum incerti auctoris*, ed. Giuseppe de Blasiis (Naples, 1887), useful.

biography of the queen.[6] Sancia's reign, nevertheless, brought together the influences of Arnold of Villanova[7] and Ramon Lull[8] on the houses of Majorca and Aragon with the more orthodox spirituality of the house of Anjou and the heirs of St Louis,[9] St Louis of Toulouse[10] and St Elizabeth of Hungary.[11] At Naples she and her husband, Robert, provided a haven not only for religious dissenters and reformers like the Spirituals, Fraticelli and Michaelists[12] but also for

[6] Besides occasional references in Gabriel Alomar Estve, 'Iconografia y heraldica de Sancha de Mallorca, reina de Nápoles', *Boletín de la Societat arqueològica lulliana*, 35 (1976), pp. 5–36, I found no entry in any of the standard Spanish, Italian, French, English, Catholic or specialized encyclopedias, including the *Dictionnaire de théologie catholique*, the *Dictionnaire d'histoire et de géographie ecclésiastique* or the *Dictionnaire de spiritualité*. Alomar, 'Iconografia', p. 5, notes that Sancia is unknown even to Spanish and Catalan historians.

[7] On the thought and influence of Arnold of Villanova see J. M. Pou y Martí, *Visionarios, beguinos y fraticellos catalañes, siglos xiii–xv* (Vichy, 1930); Gordon Leff, *Heresy in the Later Middle Ages* (2 vols, New York, 1967), 1, pp. 176–91; Mercedes van Heuchelum, *Spiritualistische Strömungen an den Höfen von Aragon und Anjou während der Höhe des Armutsstreites* (Berlin, 1912), pp. 6–25; Baddeley, *Robert the Wise*, pp. 153–4; and the comments of Ignazio Baldelli in *Chi erano gli Spirituali*, pp. 275–81.

[8] For Ramon Lull see Pastor, *Historia de Mallorca*, 1, pp. 127–34; Allison Peers, *Ramon Lull* (London, 1929); Ray C. Petry, *Late Medieval Mysticism* (Philadelphia, 1957), pp. 142–69; John Moorman, *A History of the Franciscan Order* (Oxford, 1968), pp. 224–5, 230–2, 247–9, 264–5; and J. N. Hillgarth, *Ramon Lull and Lullism in Fourteenth-Century France* (Oxford, 1971), pp. 1–55, 142–9.

[9] Louis IX of France (1214–70) was the brother of Charles of Anjou, first Angevin king of Naples, and thus Robert's grand-uncle.

[10] Robert's older brother, b. 1274, d. 1297, canonized 7 April 1317. See Herbert Thurston and Donald Attwater (eds), *Butler's Lives of the Saints* (4 vols, New York, 1956), 3, pp. 357–9; *Bibliotheca Sanctorum* (12 vols, Rome, 1964–9) (*BS*), 8, cols. 300–7; and Margaret R. Toynbee, *St Louis of Toulouse and the Process of Canonization in the Fourteenth Century* (Manchester, 1929).

[11] As the sister of Yolande of Hungary, queen of James I, St Elizabeth of Hungary (1207–31) was Sancia's great-aunt. She was also the great-aunt of Robert's mother, Marie; see C. M. Previté-Orton, *The Shorter Cambridge Medieval History* (2 vols, New York, 1966), 2, pp. 825, 922; *Butler's Lives of the Saints*, 4, pp. 386–91; *BS*, 4, cols. 1110–23.

[12] For the religious life of Naples during Robert and Sancia's reign see Ambrasi, 'La vita religiosa', pp. 437–574, especially 'Gli ordini religiosi', pp. 487–522. Francesco Russo, 'I Fraticelli in Calabria nel secolo xiv. Fatti e personaggi', *Miscellanea Francescana*, 65 (1965), pp. 349–68, gives detailed information for the southern part of the kingdom.

scholars,[13] artists[14] and poets. Both Boccaccio[15] and Petrarch[16] enjoyed the hospitality of the court of Naples and have left us vivid accounts of events and personalities during the period. Despite this, little is known of the woman herself.

Sancia of Majorca was the eldest daughter of James I of Majorca,[17] the eldest son of James of Aragon, the Conqueror.[18] In 1275 James I had married Sclaramonda of Foix[19] and with her had several sons. These included James, the eldest; Sancho; Fernando; and Philip. James[20] was apparently moved quite early, by meeting Louis of Toulouse, to renounce his claims to the throne for a religious vocation. He left the crown to his younger brother, Sancho, who ruled the kingdom from 1311 and died childless in 1324.[21] Fernando went on to become prince of Achaia and the Morea;[22] while Philip came quite early under the influence of the Spiritual Franciscans, most notably of Peter John Olivi and Angelo Clareno.[23] Under Philip's influence Fernando was later to abdicate his claims to the throne and become a mendicant.[24] Upon the death of Sancho in 1324, Philip took on the regency of the kingdom for his nephew James, Fernando's son.[25] Upon James' majority in 1328–9 Philip resigned his position, renounced the world, and went off to establish a Franciscan house in Naples under the protection of his sister, Queen Sancia.[26]

[13] See notes 2 and 5 above.

[14] See below, pp. 192–3; and Sabatini, 'La cultura a Napoli', pp. 17–18, 62–3.

[15] See, for example, Émile G. Léonard, *Boccace et Naples* (Paris, 1944), pp. 1–28; and Vittore Branca, *Boccaccio* (New York, 1976), pp. 16–40.

[16] See below pp. 198–9.

[17] Born 1262, king from 1278 to 1311. See Pastor, *Historia de Mallorca*, I, pp. 91–3, 153–5.

[18] Born 1208, d. 1276. See Pastor, *Historia de Mallorca*, I, pp. 91–3; J. M. Vidal, 'Un Ascète de sang royale, Phillip de Majorque', *Revue des questions historiques*, 88 (n.s. 44) (1910), pp. 361–4; Alomar, 'Iconografía', p. 7.

[19] Vidal, 'Ascète', pp. 361–4.

[20] Born c. 1275. See Baddeley, *Robert the Wise*, p. 154; Vidal, 'Ascète', pp. 361–4; Pastor, *Historia de Mallorca*, I, pp. 91–3; Previté-Orton, *Shorter Cambridge Medieval History*, 2, p. 825; Ambrasi, 'La vita religiosa', p. 502. Toynbee, *St Louis*, p. 91, places James's birth around that of Louis of Toulouse.

[21] See Vidal, 'Ascète', pp. 361–4, 378; and Baddeley, *Robert the Wise*, p. 64, n. 1.

[22] Vidal, 'Ascète', pp. 361–4, 378.

[23] See Vidal, ibid.; van Heuchelum, *Spiritualistiche*, pp. 53–63; Störmann, *Königreichs Mallorka*; Pastor, *Historia de Mallorca*, I, pp. 177–9; and below pp. 195–6.

[24] See Baddeley, *Robert the Wise*, p. 232.

[25] Störmann, *Königreichs Mallorka*, pp. 6–12.

[26] See below, p. 196.

Within this context of Majorcan dynastic history we can capture a few fleeting views of the infanta's youth. Sancia was born in 1286, most likely in Roussillon, perhaps in Montpieller. She spent most of her early life on the mainland until 1300, after which she traveled with her parents to Majorca.[27]

Sancia grew up in the atmosphere of deep but not always conventional spirituality in the Majorcan court. Franciscan influence there was strong.[28] In a letter of 1316, presented and discussed below, Sancia notes how her mother, Sclaramonda of Foix, was a devoted supporter of the Franciscans;[29] her great-aunt, Elizabeth of Hungary, was a noted patron of the Franciscan order,[30] and all of Sancia's brothers, except for Sancho, abdicated their claims to the Majorcan crown to enter the Franciscans.

Thus for Ambrasi[31] it seems natural that Sancia should make her first acquaintance with her future husband, Robert of Anjou, while the prince was entrusted to the care of the Franciscans in Catalonia. Between 1288 and 1295 Robert was held hostage at various places there[32] along with his brothers Louis and Raymond Berenger[33] as security for their father Charles II, captured by the Aragonese in the wake of the Angevin loss of Sicily in the War of the Sicilian Vespers.[34]

Aside from this Franciscan training, Sancia's future husband was also the product of a religious lineage. Since the conquest of Naples from the Hohenstaufen by Charles of Anjou, the Angevins had stressed their religious mission and connections with the orthodoxy of Rome.

---

[27] Alomar, 'Iconografia', pp. 10–11.

[28] Van Heuchelum, *Spiritualistische*, pp. 44–7.

[29] Ambrasi, 'La vita religiosa', p. 502; see below, p. 208.

[30] Ambrasi, 'La vita religiosa', p. 502; Moorman, *Franciscan Order*, pp. 210–12; and below p. 208.

[31] Ambrasi, 'La vita religiosa', p. 502.

[32] See Caggese, *Roberto d'Angio*, 1, pp. 2–3. Toynbee, *St Louis*, pp. 57–90, traces the young princes' imprisonment in the castle of Moncada, north-east of Barcelona, until 1289, and then for four years at the castle of Suirana, 60 miles south-west of Barcelona, then for a short time with Sancho IV of Castile in 1293, and then to Barcelona in 1293–4, where they enjoyed the freedom of the city before their return to Suirana and their release in 1295. According to Alomar, 'Iconografia', pp. 10–11, Sancia first met Robert in the autumn of 1295 at Suirana.

[33] He took the place of Charles Martel, the oldest brother and heir to the throne.

[34] See Frede, 'Regno di Roberto d'Angio', pp. 157–8; van Heuchelum, *Spiritualistische*, p. 31; Baddeley, *Robert the Wise*, pp. 3–4, 14–17, 153; Previté-Orton, *Shorter Cambridge Medieval History*, 2, pp. 768–72; Gliejeses, *Storia di Napoli*, pp. 331–5.

They had, after all, accepted the kingdom as a fief from the papacy.[35] Robert and his brothers were, in addition, the grand-nephews of St Louis, King of France. Robert's next older brother, Louis, renounced his claims to the Neapolitan throne after their release from captivity and opted for the life of a Franciscan friar. He subsequently became the Bishop of Toulouse and was later canonized.[36] During the hostages' stay in Catalonia the Franciscan influence on Louis was first felt.[37] Robert himself had ample opportunity to be exposed to the influence of both orthodox Franciscanism and to the pervasive influence of Arnold of Villanova and Peter John Olivi.[38] An extant letter written by Olivi to the young princes stresses the approach of the last days and the need to follow the life of evangelical poverty.[39]

Dynastic interests had a more obvious effect in bringing the two houses together. In 1295, in order to secure the newly reached Angevin–Aragonese peace, James II of Aragon married Robert's sister, Blanche. Robert was formally married to Violante of Aragon, the sister of James II and the niece of James I of Majorca, in 1297.[40] At the same time Robert was named Duke of Calabria and Vicar-General of the Kingdom of Naples after the death of his eldest brother, Charles Martel, in 1295.[41] In 1302, however, Violante died, leaving

[35] See Toynbee, *St Louis*, pp. 218–27.

[36] See note 9 above.

[37] See Baddeley, *Robert the Wise*, pp. 16, 153–4. Toynbee, *St Louis*, pp. 56–63, notes that all three were attended and solely educated by the Spiritual Franciscans Francis le Brun and Pietro Scarerii. The two later became Louis' most important friends, heirs and the witnesses to his canonization process. See Toynbee, *St Louis*, pp. 79–85, 103–7, 130–2, 174–85. For Pietro, see below, p. 191.

[38] See Frede, 'Regno di Roberto d'Angio', p. 209; van Heuchelum, *Spiritualistische*, pp. 26–32; Ambrasi, 'La vita religiosa', p. 502.

[39] Dated Narbonne, 18 May 1295. The letter is addressed to Louis, Robert and Raymond Berengar. It explains Olivi's sense of Joachite history, the gradual unfolding of the new age of the Church from the womb of the old, and the need for Christ's disciples to suffer seven tribulations in the great apocalyptic battle to come that would give birth to the great age of evangelical peace. The text is in the Bibl. Vaticana Apostolica, Cod. Vat. Borg. 54, fols. 156va–157vb. It has been edited by Franz Ehsle, *ALKG*, 3 (1887), pp. 534–40, and has been translated into French by M-H. Vicaire in 'Epître aux fils de Charles II de Naples en l'an 1295', in *Franciscains d'Oc*, pp. 127–8. It is discussed by van Heuchelum, *Spiritualistische*, pp. 31–3; and translated into English by Bernard McGinn in 'Peter John Olivi. Letter to the Sons of Charles II', in *Apocalyptic Spirituality* (New York, 1979), pp. 173–81.

[40] Frede, 'Regno di Roberto d'Angio', p. 160; Baddeley, *Robert the Wise*, p. 55, n, 2.

[41] Frede, 'Regno di Roberto d'Angio', p. 158.

Robert with a young son, Charles, later Duke of Calabria.[42]

As the Angevins looked for a new match for Robert they settled on Violante's relatives in the house of Majorca. In its Provençal holdings the house of Anjou was a neighbor to Majorcan fiefs in Rousillon, Perpignan and Montpellier; it was also an ally of sorts against the further designs of Aragon on both the kingdom of Majorca and the kingdom of Naples.[43] In 1304 Sancia therefore married Robert of Anjou.[44] It was a match dictated as much by dynastic policy as by the intellectual and spiritual kinship of the couple, a combination of motives that was to characterize the rest of their life together. In 1305 the link between Majorca and Naples was solidified by the marriage of Sancia's brother Sancho to Robert's sister Marie.[45]

Sancia and Robert remained in the Angevin lands of Provence until the death of Robert's father, Charles II, in 1309.[46] In May of that year at Avignon the pope declared Robert King of Naples.[47] Robert was crowned King and Sancia Queen of Jerusalem and Sicily that September.[48] Sancia accompanied Robert through Italy,[49] and they were in Naples in 1310 when they laid the foundation stone of the Clariss church of Corpo di Cristo, later known as Santa Chiara.[50] Details of Sancia's life are only fragmentary after this. We know that in 1312 the pope had conceded to her the authority to have two Clarisses in attendance on her at all times.[51] Besides this indication of her continuing devotion, little else appears until 1317 when the

---

[42] ibid., p. 160.

[43] Pastor, *Historia de Mallorca*, 1, pp. 159–90.

[44] See Lecoy, *Les relations politiques*, 1, p. 366 and n. 5; Baddeley, *Robert the Wise*, p. 162; and Gliejeses, *Storia di Napoli*, p. 341. The contract is dated 16 June 1304 at Perpignan. See Caggese, *Roberto d'Angio*, 1, p. 23. Sancia attended in person; Robert was represented by Fr Bernard, prior of the Catalonian house of Montserrat. According to Alomar, 'Iconografia', p. 11, the marriage was finalized on 19 September at Colliure in Roussillon.

[45] See Lecoy, *Les relations politiques*, 1, pp. 365–7; Baddeley, *Robert the Wise*, p. 162. The terms of the marriage treaty are given in Caggese, *Roberto d'Angio*, 1, pp. 22–3.

[46] See Frede, 'Regno di Roberto d'Angio', pp. 159–60. See also Luke Wadding, *Annales minorum*, ed. J. M. Fonseca (2nd edn, 19 vols, Rome, 1731), 6, p. 163, 1309.

[47] Baddeley, *Robert the Wise*, pp. 27–8, 55. Charles Martel, Robert's elder brother, had left a son, Charles Robert or Cabobert, since 1309 King of Hungary. Cabobert's claim to the Neapolitan throne was overlooked by the pope. See Previté-Orton, *Shorter Cambridge Medieval History*, 2, pp. 920–1.

[48] Baddeley, *Robert the Wise*, p. 55.

[49] ibid., p. 64; Frede, 'Regno di Roberto d'Angio', pp. 162–6.

[50] ibid., p. 180; Wadding, *Annales minorum*, 7, p. 178, 1310, xix.

[51] Wadding, *Annales minorum*, 6, p. 203, 1312, xv.

queen made the startling request to Pope John XXII for a divorce from Robert and permission to enter a convent.

Historians provide two explanations for the queen's action. Some, including Caggese[52] and Frede,[53] speculate that Sancia was physically or effectively sterile; physically as evidenced by her lack of children; or effectively, arguing that Sancia took her Franciscan ideal of chastity far too seriously.[54] She thus never provided Robert with an heir and preferred to remain in the company of her Clariss sisters. Another view of the incident, however, points to the content of Sancia's letter and to the well-known affair that Robert was then having with Cantelma Cantelmo, widow of Bertrand of Artois, former justiciar of the Terra di Lavoro and governor of Naples, who had died in 1305.[55]

Whatever the interpretation, the queen seemed determined. Pope John apparently had to send two replies to her; one before September 1316,[56] which may indicate an even earlier divorce request, and a second of 5 April 1317.[57] In the latter John refused Sancia's request with an ambiguous and, to the modern ear, somewhat condescending plea to her to remember her earthly as well as her spiritual spouse.[58] The effect, if not the intent, of the letter was to place the blame for the marriage's strain on the queen's religious zeal. Nevertheless, the pope accompanied this with a letter to Robert rebuking him for his philandering.[59] Whoever was to blame, Sancia was ultimately held responsible both for her husband's infidelity and for her own supposed lack of achievement in not producing an heir. In any case, Sancia was allowed her small Clariss community of three,[60] and despite Robert's

[52] Caggese, *Roberto d'Angio*, 1, p. 657.

[53] Frede, 'Regno di Roberto d'Angio', p. 175; see also Léonard, *Les Angevins*, p. 316.

[54] See Baddeley, *Robert the Wise*, p. 162 and n. 2; and Gliejeses, *Storia di Napoli*, p. 357, who concludes that Robert was not 'fortunate' in his choice of wives. Alomar, 'Iconografia', p. 13, asserts that Sancia 'llevaba sangre cátara en sus venas'.

[55] See Baddeley, *Robert the Wise*, p. 136, n. 2 and pp. 162–3. Robert and Cantelma had a son, Charles of Artois, and a daughter, Maria, Boccaccio's Fiammetta; see Gliejeses, *Storia di Napoli*, pp. 557–8; and Caggese, *Roberto d'Angio*, 1, p. 652.

[56] Cited in Caggese, *Roberto d'Angio*, 2, p. 13, n. 3, quoting Arch. Secr. Vat., no. 109, Clt–2, 2t–3t.

[57] Oderico Raynaldi, *Annales ecclesiastici* (Lucca, 1740–59), 5, p. 57, no. xxvi. The letter has also been edited in Baddeley, *Robert the Wise*, pp. 497–8 from Arch. Secr. Vat., no. 109, C 32t, ep. 131.

[58] 'Et licet celesti sponso placere desideres, oculos tamen terreni sponsi non debes offendere, quin pocius servata pudicicia coniugali.' See Raynaldi, *Annales*, 5, p. 57, xxvi.

[59] See Baddeley, *Robert the Wise*, pp. 162–3.

[60] Ambrasi, 'La vita religiosa', p. 502, already confirmed in the bull *Personam tuam*, 12 Kalends Julii, 1312. See Wadding, *Annales minorum*, 6, p. 203, 1312, xv.

liaisons[61] her marriage endured and later seems to have matured into the genuine companionship and spiritual kinship that first appeared possible.

Sancia's influence at court grew steadily, especially after the untimely death of Robert's only son and heir, Charles of Calabria, in 1328.[62] This event seems to have turned the king away from dynastic ambitions and toward a life more in line with Sancia's own sympathies.[63] Ironically, while Robert's worldly concerns waned, Sancia's seem to have grown. Caggese, for example, provides evidence for her direct lordship of several cities in the kingdom,[64] as does Baddeley for her financial dealings.[65] In 1331 she is seen ordering the destruction of houses of the Griffi family as punishment for murder.[66] In 1332, in the midst of his actions against heretics in southern Italy, Pope John warns the queen about her Spiritual sympathies but does so in a tone of deference that suggests fear of her disapproval.[67]

Sancia was directly responsible for the education of Robert's declared heirs, the princesses Joanna and Maria, the daughters of Charles of Calabria.[68] According to the terms of Robert's will,[69] after the king's death on 21 January 1343,[70] Sancia assumed the regency of

[61] Boccaccio uses Sancia's replacement in Robert's affection, even late in the couple's life, as the basis for his story of Philippa of Catania. See *De casibus virorum illustrium* IX, 26, in *Tutte le opere*, ed. Vittore Branca (Brescia, 1969), pp. 982–97. See also Branca, *Boccaccio*, p. 25. The story has been translated into English in *The Fates of Illustrious Men*, trans. and annotated by Louis Brewer Hall (New York, 1965), pp. 234–40.

[62] Frede, 'Regno di Roberto d'Angio', p. 174; Baddeley, *Robert the Wise*, pp. 207–8. The *Cronaca di Partenope (Cron. part.)*, pp. 133, 136, places this event in 1318.

[63] For Robert's patronage of the arts and letters see Frede, 'Regno', pp. 185–7, 213–17. For Sancia's support, see Ferdinando Bologna, *I pittori a la corte angioina di Napoli 1266–1414* (Rome, 1969), pp. 57–8, 131–2, 176–7, 201–12, 276–7 *et passim*.

[64] Including S. Severo in Capitanata, ibid., pp. 290–1; Ruvo, p. 413, n. 2; Potenza, p. 441; Troia, p. 461; and Melfi, p. 473.

[65] Baddeley, *Robert the Wise*, p. 288 and n. 1.

[66] ibid., pp. 163–4, 233.

[67] 'Attende, filia carissima, ne hostis illius astutia te ab ea [ecclesia] valeat separare.' See ibid., p. 233, n. 4, and the other letters edited on pp. 503–7.

[68] See Frede, 'Regno', pp. 174–6.

[69] See Léonard, *Les Angevins*, pp. 335–7. The text of the will appears in Johann Christian Lünig, *Codex Italiae diplomaticus* (4 vols, Frankfurt and Leipzig, 1725–35), 2, p. 1101.

[70] 'Attended to the last by the faithful Sancia'; see Baddeley, *Robert the Wise*, p. 270. Petrarch's epitaph of Robert the Wise is edited in Wadding, *Annales minorum*, 7, p. 295, 1343, xiv. See also p. 297, 1343, v. Sancia's grants to the Franciscans on Robert's death are recorded in ibid., 7, p. 297, 1343, vi.

the kingdom for Princess Joanna, born in 1326 and still a minor.[71] As head of the Supreme Council of the realm she exercised full regal powers[72] and continued to influence her charge, steering her policies against the claims of Joanna's cousin and later husband, Andrew of Hungary,[73] whom Sancia apparently loathed, and against the Hungarian party. She also opposed Maria's marriage to Charles of Durazzo.[74]

Despite her influence, however, affairs in the kingdom seem not to have fared well, at least according to witnesses like Petrarch, who reacted to 'that most unhappy of widows'[75] and her inner circle of Franciscan advisors with outright hostility.[76] The dowager queen's desire to quit the world was evident. On 6 March 1337, during an illness, she had applied to the pope for permission to enter a Clariss house permanently[77] and received papal approval as indicated in a letter of 11 May 1339.[78]

Her desire was compounded by the constant intrigues at court after Robert's death, by family rivalries designed to remove her support for Joanna,[79] and by a papacy anxious to re-establish its feudal suzerainty over the kingdom and to renew its efforts against the heretics and imperialists finding refuge in the south. In May 1344 Naples witnessed the arrival of Cardinal Aimeric de Châtelus who straightway set out to implement papal policy. In August Aimeric pressed his role as papal regent and demanded and received Queen Joanna's renewal of personal homage for Naples, thus effectively removing Sancia from any real power.[80]

[71] Baddeley, *Robert the Wise*, p. 264; Frede, 'Regno', p. 172.

[72] Baddeley, *Robert the Wise*, p. 282.

[73] ibid., p. 299. For the marriage and events of Joanna's early reign see St Clair Baddeley, *Queen Joanna I of Naples, Sicily and Jerusalem* (London, 1893); R. Zenari, *I primi anni di regno di Giovanna I di Napoli* (Massa Marittima, 1925); and *Cron. part.*, pp. 137–44.

[74] *Chronicon siculum (Chron. sic.)*, p. 7, col. 1.

[75] See Franciscus Petrarchus, *Epistolae familiares*, ed. Vittorio Rossi (Florence, 1933–42), vol. 2 (V–XI, 1934), V, 3, p. 10.

[76] See below, pp. 198–9.

[77] Wadding, *Annales minorum*, 7, p. 207, 1337, xii.

[78] ibid., p. 226, 1339, v.

[79] See Baddeley, *Robert the Wise*, pp. 297–8.

[80] See Guillaume Mollat, *The Popes at Avignon* (New York, 1963), pp. 177–8; Baddeley, *Robert the Wise*, pp. 298–9, 304; *Chron. sic.*, p. 9, col. 2; *Cron. part.*, p. 145. Aimeric restored full powers to Joanna on 17 December 1344. See *Cron. part.*, p. 180, n. 23. Mollat dates this 19 November.

On 20 January 1344, after a full year of mourning for her husband,[81] Sancia renounced the world and on 21 January entered the Clariss house of Santa Croce.[82] Here as 'Suor Chiara della Croce'[83] she led a life of rare virtue, piety and humility as a simple Clariss, entrusting her affairs to several of her former advisors.[84] She died on 28 July 1345 and was buried in the same monastery.[85] In June 1352 her body was transferred to Santa Chiara to join that of her husband.[86] In the course of the transfer her remains were found to be 'whole and not decaying, immune from rottenness and stench'.[87] Her successor, Queen Joanna, wrote to the pope that perhaps this was a sign of Sancia's sanctity[88] and claimed this for her guardian on the cenotaph that she had inscribed upon her tomb.[89] The king and queen still rest today in the midst of the restored church of Santa Chiara, itself a memorial to Sancia's life and work in Naples.

It was appropriate that Sancia should find her final resting place next to Robert in the Clariss house of Santa Chiara. The royal couple's devotion to the Franciscan order, from both public policy and personal zeal, is well documented. So too is their adherence to the order's Spiritual wing, even after its fall from grace and the condemnation of

---

[81] 'Die xxi Januarii, expleto anno viduitatis.' Wadding, *Annales minorum*, 7, p. 315, 1344, x.

[82] According to Ambrasi, 'La vita religiosa', p. 504, this was Sta Maria della Croce, a chapel built next to the Castel dell'Ovo on the side of the Echia and attached to the royal chapel by Robert in 1328.

[83] Wadding, *Annales minorum*, 7, p. 315, 1344, x; *Chron. sic.*, p. 9, col. 1 and n. 2, and p. 121. According to Alomar, 'Iconografia', p. 31, the church was destroyed in the Bourbon period.

[84] Including Guillelmus, Bishop of Scala, and the Franciscan Robert of Mileto; see Wadding, *Annales minorum*, 7, p. 315, 1344, x.

[85] ibid.; Ambrasi, 'La vita religiosa', p. 506; Baddeley, *Robert the Wise*, p. 304. Other sources, such as Toynbee, *St Louis*, pp. 218–19; and Paul Blanchard, *Blue Guide to Southern Italy* (New York, 1982), p. 126, say that she died in Santa Chiara. There is some confusion in the accounts. According to Wadding, Joanna had a marble sepulcher built that was similar to Robert's in Santa Chiara behind the high altar. Alomar, 'Iconografia', pp. 12, 20, 31, notes that Sancia found Santa Chiara too opulent and did not have a tomb built in either church.

[86] Ambrasi, 'La vita religiosa', p. 506.

[87] 'Intero, non dissolto ed immune da putredine e fetore.' Ambrasi, ibid., p. 506, does not cite his source.

[88] ibid., p. 506.

[89] Wadding, *Annales minorum*, 7, p. 315, 1344, x. See also Ambrasi, 'La vita religiosa', p. 507.

its positions on poverty and the role of Francis' Rule.[90]

The king's and the queen's family ties to the Franciscans reinforced their own inclinations to the intellectual and religious life. Both ended their days within the order; Sancia was a Clariss from as early as 1319.[91] Robert would often visit Franciscan houses dressed in their habit and was so painted later by Benozzo Gozzoli.[92] Eighteen days before his death he was dressed in the Franciscan habit[93] in which he was buried in the church of Santa Chiara; he was found in it when his body was moved in 1943.[94]

Robert's intellectual bent and scholastic ambitions went hand in hand with his political attempt to establish tranquility, order and morality within his realm.[95] He also used the Franciscan order to bolster his throne against widespread accusations of usurpation and did not hesitate to exploit the sanctity that the order lent his dynasty. Robert pursued and encouraged the canonization and cult of his brother, Louis of Toulouse.[96] In 1317 to mark the bishop's canonization he commissioned Simone Martini to paint a large altarpiece in Santa Chiara depicting him.[97] He later made a special point of receiving the remains of the saint's head for public devotion during the translation of Louis' body.[98] Sancia matched Robert's familial devotion with her own cult of St Elizabeth of Hungary, centered on the church of Santa Maria Donnaregina.[99]

[90] In the bulls *Quorumdam exigit* of 1 October 1317, *Sancta romana* of 30 December 1317, and *Gloriosam ecclesiam* of 6 January 1318. See the works cited in note 3 above.

[91] See Wadding, *Annales minorum*, 6, pp. 540, 542, 1319, cxxix, 5.

[92] Ambrasi, 'La vita religiosa', p. 508.

[93] Wadding, *Annales minorum*, 7, p. 296, 1343, xiv. See also Gliejeses, *Storia di Napoli*, p. 357.

[94] Ambrasi, 'La vita', p. 512.

[95] Baddeley, *Robert the Wise*, p. 152; Frede, 'Regno', p. 209.

[96] Ambrasi, 'La vita', pp. 506–7; Frede, 'Regno', p. 212; Toynbee, *St Louis*, pp. 206, 218–27.

[97] See Alastair Smart, *The Dawn of Italian Painting 1250–1400* (Ithaca, NY, 1978), p. 89; and Toynbee, *St Louis*, pp. 221–2. Alomar, 'Iconografia', pp. 18–19, 27, plate XI, pp. 32–3, notes that Martini's opulence offended Sancia's Franciscan tastes. The queen therefore later commissioned a simpler version for Saint Clair in Aix-en-Provence, which contains her portrait. Alomar reproduces several other likenesses.

[98] Wadding, *Annales minorum*, 6, p. 334, 1319, ii; Toynbee, *St Louis*, p. 222. The inspiration for the cult and this special devotion were Sancia's, according to Toynbee, who adds that 'there were no lengths to which the almost morbid devotion of this lady for her young unknown brother-in-law would not go.'

[99] Frede, 'Regno', p. 212. The church was built by Robert's mother, Marie, the saint's grand-niece.

Amidst the brilliant secular life of art and letters encouraged by the crown, Sancia and Robert's personal routine was rather sober; their court has been described as a 'cenacolo di francescanesimo'.[100] Their protection and patronage of the order extended to all matters 'spiritualia et temporalia'[101] and included gifts, grants, buildings and appointments to such a degree that the Castel Nuovo was eventually 'full of monks'.[102] Sancia took the lead in this regard. Though judging it somewhat less than praiseworthy, Baddeley contends that Sancia's religious influence on Robert was particularly strong and extended even to the support of the Spirituals.[103] Wadding describes Sancia as the order's 'mater, soror, protectrix, patrona et auxiliatrix'.[104] She surrounded herself with Franciscans as chaplains, confessors and advisors.[105]

Among those close to the queen was Pietro Scarerii, Bishop of Rapolla and her confessor. Pietro had been lector to Robert and his brothers during their captivity in Catalonia and was a close friend of Peter John Olivi.[106] The list also included Matteo di Capua, confessor to the duke of Calabria;[107] and Peter of Arquier,[108] confessor both to Sancia and to Delphine de Sabran during her stays in Naples as a member of the community at the Castel Nuovo.[109] Sancia herself

[100] See Ambrasi, 'La vita', pp. 499–506; Frede, 'Regno', pp. 210–12.

[101] Wadding, Annales, 6, p. 243, 1316, iii; as well as 6, p. 542, 1319, lxxix, 5 for further examples of their patronage and protection of the Franciscans.

[102] Frede, 'Regno', p. 209.   [103] Baddeley, Robert the Wise, p. 152.

[104] Wadding, Annales, 7, p. 315, 1344, xi.

[105] See Ambrasi, 'La vita', pp. 502, 508; Frede, 'Regno', p. 223; Wadding, Annales, 6, p. 334, 1319, iv.

[106] See McGinn, 'Peter John Olivi', p. 180 and p. 302, n. 37; Toynbee, St Louis, pp. 63, 76–85, 103–7; 130–2, 174–85, et passim; Conrad Eubel, Hierarchia catholica Medii Aevi (Münster, Regensburg, 1913–14, reprint, Rome, 1960), 1, p. 412; and P. B. Gams, Series episcoporum ecclesiae catholicae (Graz, 1957), p. 915.

[107] Ambrasi, 'La vita', p. 502.

[108] See Wadding, Annales, 7, p. 183, 1335, xiv; Ambrasi, 'La vita', pp. 506, 508.

[109] See ibid., p. 507; Wadding, Annales, 6, p. 334, 1319, iv; BS, 4, cols. 540–1; Butler's Lives of the Saints, 3, pp. 661–2; Marthe Dulong, La vie provençale de sainte Delphine (Paris, Thesis, École des Chartes, 1928); Jacques Campbell, Vies occitanes de saint Auzias et de sainte Delphine (Rome, 1963); and Enquête pour le procès de canonisation de Dauphine de Puimichel, comtesse d'Ariano (+26-XI-1360) (Turin, 1978); Cecily Hallack and P. F. Anson, These Made Peace (Paterson, NJ, 1957), pp. 98–106; and André Vauchez, 'La place de la pauvreté dans les documents hagiographiques à l'époque des Spirituels', in Chi erano gli Spirituali, pp. 125–53, for the political motivations of her canonization. Sancia invited Delphine to join her several times. She finally came to Naples from 1326 to 1331 and from 1332 to 1336. See Campbell, Vies occitanes, pp. 190–1.

makes much of her role of mother to the order in her letter of 1334[110] and makes no effort to disguise her influence over and patronage of the Franciscans. By 1333 this control had become so strong that the pope took specific action to restore control of the Clariss houses of the kingdom of Naples to the Franciscan minister general.[111]

The record of Sancia's patronage of the Franciscans is clear, extending from the foundations of Santa Maria Egiziaca,[112] Santa Maria Maddelena[113] and other houses in Naples and various parts of the kingdom[114] to the house of Santa Clara in Majorca[115] and the church of Saint Claire in Aix-en-Provence.[116] As titular rulers of the Holy Land [117] Sancia and Robert also provided support and protection to the Franciscan houses of the Holy Sepulcher in Jerusalem and on Mt Sion[118] and received concessions from the Sultan of Egypt to this end.[119]

Most impressive of all was the royal couple's devotion to the building project for the church of Santa Chiara. Most sources agree that the inspiration and energy for the completion of this Angevin shrine was Sancia's.[120] The project was begun in 1310[121] and entrusted to the

---

[110] See below, pp. 207–9.

[111] Wadding, *Annales*, 7, p. 148, 1333, xvi; see also Sancia's protest (xvii) and Robert's (xviii), pp. 148–9. Ehrle, *ALKG*, 4, pp. 83–7, cites a papal letter of 18 April 1333 denying permission to exempt Santa Chiara from the control of the minister general because of Sancia's support of several excommunicated Franciscans there, including Andreas de Gagliano, her chaplain.

[112] Ambrasi, 'La vita', p. 506; Wadding, *Annales*, 7, p. 182, 1335, xiv.

[113] Ambrasi, 'La vita', p. 506.

[114] Wadding, *Annales*, 6, pp. 538–9, 541, 1319, lxxix, 5, 7; 7, p. 207, 1337, xi; Ambrasi, 'La vita', p. 504.

[115] Alomar, 'Iconografia', pp. 22–5.

[116] Ambrasi, 'La vita', p. 502.

[117] Wadding, *Annales*, 7, p. 149, 1333, xix; Moorman, *Franciscan Order*, p. 436.

[118] Wadding, *Annales*, 7, p. 260, 1334, xvii.

[119] Wadding, *Annales*, 7; pp. 260–1, 1342, xviii.

[120] See, for example, Ambrasi, 'La vita', p. 504; Caggese, *Roberto d'Angio*, 1, p. 642 and n. 2; Wadding, *Annales*, 6, p. 542, 1319, lxxix, 5; Frede, 'Regno', p. 180. The *Cron. part*, p. 132, gives responsibility to Robert. For that matter, the chronicler completely ignores Sancia except for a fleeting reference on p. 137. For general histories and descriptions of the church see B. Cercano, *Guida della monumentale chiesa di S. Chiara in Napoli* (Milan, 1913); Aldo De Rinaldis, *Santa Chiara* (Naples, 1920); and T. Gallino, *Il complesso monumentale di Santa Chiara in Napoli* (Naples, 1963). For a brief account see Vittorio Gliejeses, *La nuova guida storica, artistica, monumentale, turistica della città di Napoli e dintorni* (Naples, 1973), pp. 182–4. The church was also referred to as Corpo di Cristo or S. Eucarestia, according to Ambrasi, 'La vita', p. 504.   [121] *Chron. sic*, p. 10, col. 1.

architect Gagliardo Primario. Sanca laid the foundation stone in that
year; work began in earnest in 1313. In 1330 John XXII personally
presided over the dedication of the first altar.[122] Between 1328 and
1334 Giotto was commissioned to complete a cycle of frescoes for the
church that were white-washed in the seventeenth century[123] and are
now destroyed.[124] In 1338 the foundation stone for the famous campanile was laid by Sancia, Robert, Andrew of Taranto and other
members of the royal family.[125] The church was consecrated in 1340;
and in 1343, just in time to receive Robert's remains, work was completed on all but the campanile.[126] The project thus spanned the years
of Sancia's life in Naples. She lavished funds and attention on every
stage of the building,[127] the courses of its stones reflecting the gradual
work of her reign on behalf of the Franciscan order.

Several students have tried to describe the Franciscan piety of the
royal couple;[128] one has even attempted to contrast Robert's intellectual spirituality with the purely emotional devotion of the queen.[129]
Upon close examination, however, such distinctions yield no useful
results. For both the king and the queen, attachment to Franciscanism
combined the practical issues of political influence and patronage
with a sincere, deep and intelligent appreciation of the movement.

Though Dante mocks the pedantic style and interests of Robert's
'sermons'[130] apparent in a work like his *Apophtegmata* on biblical texts
in honor of the monastic life,[131] the king's *De paupertate* of 1332 was a
capable and rigorous defense of the Spiritual position on poverty and
the immutability of the Rule[132] written at a low point in the fortunes

---

[122] Gliejeses, *Nuova guida*, p. 183.

[123] Karl Baedeker, *Southern Italy and Sicily* (New York, 1930), p. 57.

[124] ibid., p. 57. See the comments in Bruce Cole, *Giotto and Florentine Painting
1280–1375* (New York, 1976), p. 12; and Vasari's *Lives of the Artists* (Baltimore,
MD, 1968), pp. 68–9.

[125] *Chron. sic.*, p. 10, col. 1. The *Cron. part*, p. 140, dates it to 1328. A Giottoesque
frescoe in the refectory still contains traces of portraits of Robert, Charles of
Calabria, Sancia and Joanna; see Alomar, 'Iconografia', pp. 28–9.

[126] Ambrasi, 'La vita', p. 504; Caggese, *Roberto d'Angio*, 2, pp. 397–402.

[127] ibid., 2, pp. 397–402.

[128] See, for example, Ambrasi, 'La vita', pp. 502–12.

[129] Van Heuchelum, *Spiritualistische*, pp. 45–6, states: 'Für ihn war auch die
Religion, zum guten Tiel wenigstens, Sache des Intellekts, vernunftgemässer
Reflexion, ihr war sie durchaus eine Angelegenheit des Herzens.'

[130] Dante, *Paradiso* VIII, 145–8.

[131] See Ambrasi, 'La vita', p. 510.

[132] The work is contained in Paris, Bibl. Nat., Ms. Lat. 4046. It has been edited
in Siragusa, *L'ingegno*, Appendix V, pp. xiii–xxviii. See also Caggese, *Roberto d'Angio*,

of the Spirituals.[133] Robert and Sancia continued their adamant support of the Spirituals[134] and granted protection to refugee Fraticelli after their condemnation.[135] Both defended the radicals' positions even when faced with the ire of Pope John XXII and his successors and stood up for individuals like Michael of Cesena, the renegade minister general,[136] and less important friars like Pietro de Cadeneto[137] or Sancia's chaplain, Andreas de Gagliano.[138] They ultimately banished Michael of Cesena's successor, Gerald Odonis, from their presence for his harsh stance toward the Michaelists and his perceived shift from the pure Franciscan tradition.[139]

Sancia's own relations with the Spirituals and later Fraticelli are complex. Her knowledge of the Franciscan tradition and its sources was wide and deep.[140] We know that she was familiar with the Franciscan Rules,[141] with the *Vita I* and *II* of Thomas of Celano,[142] with Bonaventura's *Legenda maior*,[143] and at least with the tradition of the *Legenda trium sociorum*.[144] Certain passages in the letters discussed below

---

2, pp. 123 and 365–8. The tract has been analyzed in Felice Tocco, *La quistione della povertà nel secolo xiv* (Naples, 1914), pp. 284–5; in Baddeley, *Robert the Wise*, pp. 155–6; Frede, 'Regno', p. 168; and Ambrasi, 'La vita', p. 510.

[133] By 1323 the pope had condemned the *usus pauper* and ended the debate on Apostolic Poverty in the bull *Cum inter nonnullos*; see Douie, *Heresy of the Fraticelli*, pp. 153–66.

[134] See Baddeley, *Robert the Wise*, pp. 145–61, 230–1; Ambrasi, 'La vita', pp. 499–502, 504; Frede, 'Regno', p. 209; Léonard, *Les Angevins*, pp. 256–7.

[135] See Russo, 'Fraticelli'; Ambrasi, 'La vita', p. 508; Frede, 'Regno', p. 223, notes that all in attendance at Robert's deathbed, except for his almoner Pietro Baudet, were Spirituals. Alomar, 'Iconografia', plate XV, pp. 32–3, reproduces a miniature from the *Trepas du Roy Robert de Sicile*, Paris, Bibl. Nat., Ms. Fr. 1049, fol. 14v, that also, and erroneously for propaganda purposes, includes Andrew of Hungary.

[136] Baddeley, *Robert the Wise*, pp. 156–7; Ambrasi, 'La vita', p. 504; Wadding, *Annales*, 7, p. 84, 1328, xvii; 86, xxi; Gliejeses, *Storia di Napoli*, p. 360. See also Ehrle, *ALKG*, 4, pp. 65–9, for several of Pope John's letters condemning the Spirituals in Naples and their royal support.

[137] Ambrasi, 'La vita', p. 508.

[138] See below, pp. 199–200.

[139] See Baddeley, *Robert the Wise*, p. 233 and n. 4.

[140] These have been analyzed by van Heuchelum, *Spiritualistische*, p. 46.

[141] See below, pp. 210, 213.

[142] See below, pp. 211, 213.

[143] See below, pp. 211, 212–13.

[144] See below, p. 212.

are also reminiscent of the *Prophesies* of Francis,[145] the *Speculum perfectionis*[146] and works of Ubertino da Casale[147] and Angelo Clareno.[148]

We have already noted the strong ties between Sancia's family and Ramon Lull, Arnold of Villanova and Peter John Olivi.[149] Among her family's counselors was Adhemar de Mosset, the knight of Roussillon who was later tried for his adherence to the heresy of the Fraticelli.[150] Adhemar was also the close friend and protegé of Sancia's younger brother, Prince Philip of Majorca,[151] in whom we have one of the strongest links between the Spiritual tradition and Sancia's circle at Naples. He and several others close to the queen at Naples merit detailed examination in order to illuminate the context within which Sancia acted and thought. These persons include the Neapolitan Franciscans Robert of Mileto[152] and Andreas de Gagliano.[153]

Prince Philip was a long-time friend and disciple of the Spiritual Franciscan leader Angelo Clareno.[154] The prince first met the friar at

---

[145] See below, p. 213

[146] See below, p. 212.

[147] See below, pp. 210–12.

[148] See below, pp. 210–13.

[149] See above, p. 184 and note 38.

[150] Pou y Marti *Visionarios*, pp. 165–89; Douie, *Heresy of the Fraticelli*, pp. 253–7; and J. M. Vidal, 'Procès d'inquisition contre Adhémar de Mosset, noble rousillonais, inculpé de béguinisme (1332–1334)', *Revue d'histoire de l'église de France* 1 (1910), pp. 555–89, 682–99, 711–24.

[151] On Philip of Majorca's life and thought see Störmann, *Konirgeichs Mallorcka*; van Heuchelum, *Spiritualistische*, c. 4; Vidal, 'Ascète'.

[152] See below, pp. 197–9.

[153] See below, pp. 199–200.

[154] Born *c.* 1250 near Fossombrone in the March of Ancona; d. 1337 at Santa Maria del Aspro in Basilicata. The most recent work on Clareno includes Bernard McGinn's translation with notes of Clareno's *Epistola excusatoria* in *Apocalyptic Spirituality*, pp. 149–72; Raoul Manselli, 'Spirituali missionaria: L'Azione in Armenia e in Grecia. Angelo Clareno', in *Espansione del Francescanismo tra Occidente e Oriente nel secolo xiii* (Assisi, 1979), pp. 271–91; von Auw, *Angelo Clareno*; and *Angeli Clareni, Epistole* (Rome, 1980), released by the Istituto Storico in Rome; Olga Zorzi Pugliese, 'Il "Chronicon" di Angelo Clareno nel Rinascimento volgarizzamento postillato da Girolamo Benivieni', *AFH*, 73 (1980), pp. 514–26; P. Jean Gribomont, 'L'espositio d'Ange Clareno sur la Regle des Frères Mineurs et de la tradition monastique primitive', *Letture delle fonti francescane attraverso i secoli: Il 1400* (Rome, 1981), pp. 388–424; R. G. Musto, *The Letters of Angelo Clareno (c. 1250–1337)* (New York, Dissertation, Columbia University, 1977); 'Angelo Clareno's "Preparantia Christi Iesu habitationem', *AFH*, 73 (1980), pp. 69–89; and 'Angelo Clareno, O.F.M.: fourteenth-century translator of the Greek Fathers. An introduction and a checklist of manuscripts and printings of his "Scala Paradisi" ', *AFH*, 76 (1983), pp. 215–38, 589–645.

Vienne during the winter consistory of 1311–12.[155] The two immediately formed a friendship that was to withstand the years of trial of the
Spiritual party. Philip probably also helped spread Peter John Olivi's
influence among many royal and noble supporters, including Robert
the Wise, Louis of Anjou, Frederick III of Sicily, James II of Aragon,
Giacomo and Pietro Colonna and Napoleone Orsini.[156] As early as
1317 Philip had joined his brother-in-law, King Robert, in writing to
John XXII on behalf of the Spirituals during the final debate and
definitions of the poverty issue.[157] In 1329 the prince completed his
regency for his nephew, James II of Majorca, and promptly left the
kingdom for Naples.[158] Angelo Clareno's correspondence reveals that
the Franciscan Spiritual leader was in constant contact with his royal
follower during this period[159] and probably helped him make his final
decision to join Sancia in the city. In Naples Philip promptly attracted
a circle of Spiritual followers, many from France and Spain, referred
to as the 'fratres fratris Phillippi de Majorci'.[160] They were soon established, under Sancia's protection, at Santa Chiara[161] and within the
Castel Nuovo.[162] The group included Sancia's chaplain, Andreas de
Gagliano, and Robert of Mileto, later an influential member of the
royal court vividly, if maliciously, described by Petrarch.[163]

[155] See Musto, *Letters of Angelo Clareno*, pp. 254–5; von Auw, *Epistole*, pp. xxxviii–
xlviii; and *Angelo Clareno*, pp. 107–12.

[156] E. Randolf Daniel, *The Franciscan Concept of Mission in the High Middle Ages*
(Lexington, KY, 1975), p. 86, n. 30.

[157] Vidal, 'Ascète', p. 373.

[158] Baddeley, *Robert the Wise*, p. 154 and n. 1, citing Arch. Secr. Vat., John XXII,
Anno 15–16, Reg. 8, fol. 91, Epist. 426.

[159] See Musto, *Letters*, VI, p. 326, n. 3 and 6. Nine of Clareno's 78 extant letters
are addressed to Philip and date from spring 1316 to 1334. See Musto, *Letters*,
XXVIII–XXIV, pp. 307–43; and XXIV–XL, pp. 367–98; and von Auw,
Epistole, pp. xl–xlvii.

[160] Ambrasi, 'La vita religiosa', p. 510; and F. Ehrle, 'Die verschiedenen Gruppen
der Spiritualen und ihre Schicksale', *ALKG*, 4 (1888), p. 100. Vidal, 'Ascète',
pp. 367–9, 374, reports that Philip had requested permission to form his own order
as early as 1317–18 but was refused and offered instead the bishopric of Mirepoix
and the archbishopric of Tarragon. Philip's repeated requests were all refused; see
Wadding, *Annales*, 7, p. 238, 1340, xxii; Ehrle, *ALKG*, 1 (1885), p. 67; *Bullarium
Franciscanum (BF)* ed. J. Sbaralea and C. Eubel (Rome, 1759–1904), 5, p. 490, n. 1;
Vidal, 'Ascète', p. 389. Philip finally took matters into his own hands, see Wadding,
Annales, 7, pp. 239–40, 1340, xxiv.

[161] Frede, 'Regno', p. 223.

[162] Wadding, *Annales*, 7, pp. 238–40, 1340, xxii–xxiv; Baddeley, *Robert the Wise*,
pp. 154, 231–2.

[163] See below, pp. 198–9.

Philip's impact at court was considerable. Shortly after his arrival we hear of his public sermon, probably written in collaboration with Andreas de Gagliano,[164] against the pope. So popular was the prince that evidence exists of a movement, supported by Sancia and Robert, to have him elected pope.[165] Philip appears in later Fraticelli literature as the prophesied Angelic Pope of the Last Days.[166] Pope John strongly opposed this conjunction of Spiritual forces in Naples and wrote to King Robert in December 1330 protesting Philip's presence there.[167] In January 1331 the pope again wrote and attempted to gain control over Philip by ordering him to join an approved order.[168] Though little is known of the prince after this date, he apparently retained close connections with Clareno during the latter's refuge from the Inquisition in the kingdom of Naples after 1334 and played some part in the collection of Clareno's letters after his death in 1337.[169] He may even have been the 'frater Philippus' who assisted the aged Spiritual at his deathbed in Basilicata.[170]

We know for certain that another member of Sancia's circle at Naples was present at Clareno's death and immediately took steps to protect the Spiritual's remains, to record his last days and death and

[164] Andreas later denied any such involvement; see F. Ehrle, 'Der Process gegen Fr. Andreas von Galliano, den Kaplan der Königen Sanctia von Neapel, von 1338', *ALKG*, 4 (1888), pp. 82–95, especially p. 94. For the text of the sermon see Felice Tocco, *Studi francescani* (Naples, 1909), pp. 297–310.

[165] See Marjorie Reeves, *The Influence of Prophecy in the Later Middle Ages* (Oxford, 1969), p. 219.

[166] See L. Fumi, 'Eretici e ribelli nell' Umbria dal 1320–1330', *Bollettino della regia Deputazione di storia patria per l'Umbria*, 5 (Perugia, 1899), pp. 411–14; Reeves, *Influence of Prophecy*, pp. 212–13, 411, n. 2.

[167] See *BF* 5, p. 486, no. 891, 12 December 1330; Musto, *Letters of Angelo Clareno*, XXXVI, n. 2, p. 378; and von Auw, *Epistole*, pp. 183–6. John may also have feared the consequences of the Neapolitan court's protection and support for William of Ockham, who had escaped from Avignon in 1328 and had headed for Italy; see Moorman, *Franciscan Order*, pp. 319–24.

[168] Ehrle, *ALKG*, 4 (1888), pp. 67–8.

[169] See Musto, *Letters of Angelo Clareno*, pp. 71–81; and von Auw, *Epistole*, pp. xxviii–xxxiii.

[170] See Clareno's *Miracula*, collected after his death, extant in Florence, Bibl. Naz. Cent., CL. XXXIX, 75, fol. 214v–219v, fol. 219v. This has been edited by Daniel Papebroch, 'De Beato Angelo Clareno', *AS* 3 (Paris–Rome, 1867), pp. 574–6; see p. 566, col. 1; and by F. Ehrle, *ALKG*, 1 (1885), p. 534.

to collect his letters and his *miracula*.[171] Robert of Mileto[172] appears as early as 1329 as the recipient of Clareno's translation of the *Rule* of St Basil.[173] He is connected with Philip of Majorca in a letter written to him by Clareno from Subiaco *c.* 1330.[174] According to Ambrasi, Robert brought his report of Clareno's death and *miracula* to the court of Naples immediately after leaving the Spiritual's deathbed in June 1337.[175]

In the 1330s Robert of Mileto's influence at Sancia's court seems to have grown rapidly. In 1331 he was named a witness to a transcription of testimony against Sancia's chaplain, Andreas de Gagliano.[176] He is also recorded as the recipient of payments from the queen.[177] Much of our information on his later years and connections with Sancia and the court comes from Petrarch. The poet made two visits to Naples, one in February/March 1341 in preparation for his coronation as poet laureate;[178] the second in October/November 1343 on behalf of the pope to secure the release of the imprisoned Pepini.[179] Petrarch describes Robert, already an old man when the poet first saw him, in a

---

[171] See Musto, *Letters of Angelo Clareno*, pp. 75–9; and von Auw, *Epistole*, pp. xxviii–xxxiii.

[172] Identified by Lorenzo Berardini, *Frate Angelo da Chiarino alla Luce della storia* (Osimo, 1964), p. 245, as a relative of Tommasso da San Severino, lord of Marsico. Clareno, Letters XLI and XLII, in Musto, *Letters of Angelo Clareno*, pp. 399, 403; von Auw, *Epistole*, pp. 201 and 203, addresses Robert as 'dominus', a title he is known by in the preface to the *Miracula* and in the process against Andreas de Gagliano; see Edith Pásztor, 'Il Processo di Andreas da Gagliano (1337–38)', *AFH*, 48 (1955), p. 267. This has led to the assumption that Robert may have been a layman. Russo, 'Fraticelli', p. 364, n. 51, argues that he remained a layman throughout his life. Evidence presented by Petrarch and others seems to point against this, however. See also Vincenzo Forcellini, ' "L'horrendum tripes animal" della lettera 3 del libro V delle familiari di Petrarca', in *Studi di storia napoletana in onore di Michelangelo Schipa* (Naples, 1926), pp. 167–99; and Sabatini, 'La cultura a Napoli,' pp. 17–18, 62–3.

[173] Musto, *Letters of Angelo Clareno*, XLI, pp. 399–402; von Auw, *Epistole*, pp. 201–3; Musto, 'Angelo Clareno: fourteenth-century translator'; and Frede, 'Regno', p. 216.

[174] Musto, *Letters of Angelo Clareno*, LXII, pp. 403–9; von Auw, *Epistole*, pp. 203–7.

[175] Ambrasi, 'La vita religiosa', p. 510.

[176] Pásztor, 'Il Processo', p. 267.

[177] Wadding, *Annales*, 7, p. 315, 1334, x; Baddeley, *Robert the Wise*, p. 302, n. 1; Russo, 'Fraticelli', p. 365.

[178] See Ernest Hatch Wilkins, *Life of Petrarch* (Chicago, 1963), pp. 26–7.

[179] Wilkins, *Petrarch*, pp. 39–44.

famous letter from the *Familiares*.[180] According to Petrarch, Robert's influence was all pervasive, evil and corrupting. This deformed and vicious old hypocrite was chief among the pack of wolves who controlled the court.[181] Though exaggerated by personal hostility, apparent lack of sympathy for Robert's ideals and the failure of his own mission to Naples, Petrarch's portrait of the old man gives us some idea of the influence that Sancia allowed Robert to bear.[182] According to Baddeley, he served as both the queen's confidant and as confessor to Prince Andrew of Hungary.[183] As Sancia's henchman he supported her unorthodox ideas and aided her in her encirclement of the young Queen Joanna.[184] Even after Sancia's renunciation of the world, Robert continued as her trustee and as the head of the ministry of the Clariss community at Santa Chiara,[185] a post he held even after Sancia's death.[186]

The case of Andreas de Gagliano offers another excellent insight into the circle of personality and opinion at Sancia's court. Appointed chaplain of the monastery of Santa Chiara in 1329,[187] Andreas quickly became the 'familiaris' of the royal couple.[188] Although little is known of his early life,[189] he was associated with Philip of Majorca soon after the prince's arrival in Naples.[190] He quickly rose in the queen's esteem to become her 'consilarius, capellanus et secretarius'.[191] He acted as Sancia's liaison between the court and the various groups of Fraticelli within the kingdom[192] and apparently fully shared their views. In October 1331 Andreas became the target of a preliminary process of inquisition. Testimony was gathered from his fellow Franciscans that would eventually form the basis of the process launched against him

[180] He was Petrarch's 'horrendum tripes animal' of *Familiares* V, 3, 9–15.

[181] *Familiares* V, 3, 13–14.

[182] Wilkins, *Petrarch*, p. 41; Baddeley, *Robert the Wise*, p. 305 and n. 1.

[183] ibid., pp. 301–3.

[184] ibid., p. 300, n. 2.

[185] Wadding, *Annales*, 7, p. 315, 1344, x. See also Ambrasi, 'La vita religiosa', p. 510.

[186] Wadding, *Annales*, 7, p. 316, 1344, xii.

[187] Pásztor, 'Il Processo', pp. 274–5. The Inquisition accused Andreas of harboring Franciscan rebels in the convent; see also Ehrle, *ALKG*, 4 (1888), pp. 92–3.

[188] Pásztor, 'Il Processo', p. 254.

[189] *BF*, 5, p. 513, no. 945; p. 537, no. 1001; pp. 544–7, no. 1016–17.

[190] See above, p. 197 and note 164. He may, in fact, have arrived in Naples with Philip.

[191] Pásztor, 'Il Processo', pp. 294–5. For his ready access to Santa Chiara see pp. 374–5.

[192] ibid., p. 263.

in 1337–8. Among the major charges[193] were his repudiation of obedience to both Pope John XXII and the minister general of the
Franciscan order[194] on the grounds that neither pope nor minister
general could alter the Franciscan Rule[195] as revealed to Francis by
Christ.[196] In so doing they had shown themselves to be neither pope
nor minister general. As later revealed in the process of 1337–8,
Andreas did not consider Gerald Odonis the legitimate minister
general but a usurper in place of Michael of Cesena, who had been
forced from office for his devotion to the Rule.[197]

Finally, the inquisition cited Andreas' close ties with both Philip of
Majorca, a known leader of the Fraticelli, and to Queen Sancia herself.[198] This last accusation is significant. It reveals what already
appeared obvious: that the papal inquisition was using the process
against Andreas not as an end in itself but as an oblique method of
getting at Sancia. King Robert took it as a personal offense to the
queen.[199] The royal couple would have been all too familiar with this
technique; it had already been used by James II of Majorca against
his uncle Philip in instigating the process against Adhemar de
Mosset.[200]

The royal response was predictable. At Sancia's urging,[201] the
king set out to interfere with the movement and publication of all
Franciscan communications concerning Andreas.[202] Gerald Odonis
was banished from the royal presence.[203] On 28 January 1336 Robert
wrote to Arnald, Cardinal of Sant 'Eustachio, defending the queen's
chaplain in order to prevent the inquisitorial process against him.[204]
In 1338 Benedict XII ended the proceedings at Robert' isnsistence.[205]

[193] The following account is based on Ehrle, *ALKG*, 4 (1888); and Pásztor, 'Il
Processo'.
[194] Pásztor, 'Il Processo', p. 281.
[195] ibid., p. 282.
[196] ibid., p. 256.
[197] ibid., pp. 296–7; Ehrle, *ALKG*, 4 (1888), p. 90.
[198] Pásztor, 'Il Processo', p. 256.
[199] *BF*, 5, p. 1016; and Pásztor, 'Il Processo', p. 257.
[200] See Vidal, 'Procès'; Douie, *Heresy of the Fraticelli*, pp. 253–7.
[201] She was so accused by John XXII in a letter of 2 September 1332. See
Baddeley, *Robert the Wise*, p. 158, n. 1.
[202] ibid., pp. 157–8.
[203] ibid., p. 233.
[204] Pásztor, 'Il Processo', pp. 277–9 and 278, n. 1.
[205] Ambrasi, 'La vita religiosa', p. 510; Léonard, *Les Angevins*, p. 334. No doubt,
Benedict's attempts to retain Robert's alliance against Lewis of Bavaria aided the
king's chances of success. See Mollat, *The Popes*, pp. 221–2.

The cases of Philip of Majorca, Robert of Mileto and Andreas de Gagliano are telling. One might be tempted to argue that the queen's presence in Naples and her tolerance created an ideal situation for these zealous, and perhaps exploitive, men to work their wills.[206] On the other hand, the fact that Sancia chose to surround herself with courtiers like these, that she attracted her brother to the Castel Nuovo, provided a safe haven in the kingdom for Clareno and his followers and made her court the center of their activities, strongly suggests that she was a major protagonist in the later history of the Spirituals.

Sancia waged a running struggle of words and wills against John XXII's attempts to bring the Fraticelli in the kingdom within his grasp.[207] She repeatedly blocked both inquisitors and papal legates in their struggle against Michael of Cesena, Philip of Majorca and Angelo Clareno.[208] In the spring of 1331 the pope demanded an accounting of all those preaching the heretical doctrines of evangelical poverty and other disturbing ideas, including the equality of all pastors and bishops with the pope, the denial of Peter's singular commission and the negation of the Church's coercive powers.[209] Sancia's reply was to request such evidence of heresy from the Neapolitan Franciscans and, indeed, to find none.[210] John later warned Sancia explicitly against her support of the heretical doctrine of apostolic poverty and her favoring 'schismaticis et hereticis apostatis dicti ordinis'.[211]

By 1332–3 Sancia and Robert had taken the offensive against the pope. Using the condemnation of John's theological views on the condition of the soul before the resurrection as their opportunity, they proposed the pope's deposition and the election in his place of Philip of Majorca. No one knows how far they would have been willing to pursue this action. John died in 1334, and the plan was quickly dropped.[212] The episode, though inconclusive, is instructive. Philip seems to have been very much the pawn in the royal game, despite the couple's affection for his person and agreement with his principles. This suggests the queen's ability to master those in her following for

[206] See Pásztor, 'Il Processo', p. 263; Frede, 'Regno', p. 210.

[207] Baddeley, *Robert the Wise*, pp. 157 and 233, n. 2–3, sees Sancia as the main force behind the royal struggle against John.

[208] See Frede, 'Regno', pp. 203, 209–10.

[209] Pásztor, 'Il Processo', pp. 268–9.

[210] ibid., pp. 269–73.

[211] See Raynaldi, *Annales*, 5, p. 536; Pásztor, 'Il Processo', p. 255 and n. 3; and Baddeley, *Robert the Wise*, p. 233, n. 1.

[212] Frede, 'Regno', p. 210; and Léonard, *Les Angevins*, pp. 267–9, 333–5.

her own political ends and her willingness to use power on behalf of her spiritual ideals.

This, however briefly outlined, is the background to the three letters written by Sancia to the Franciscans and incorporated into her letter to the Chapter General of Assisi in 1334. The chapter general had assembled that year in the penumbra of the poverty debate, the destruction of the Spiritual party and the revolt of Michael of Cesena.[213] Sancia's intent, therefore, was both to remind the order of her very tangible material support and to rally the spirit of its lingering strict adherents.

As the letters appear in the *Chronica xxiv generalium*,[214] a brief introduction presents them as illustrative of Sancia's steadfastness to the Franciscan ideal. The text of the queen's letter to the chapter general follows. It begins with a brief *proemium* in which the queen establishes her ties with the Franciscan order through her family and marriage and declares her devotion to the Franciscan ideal. She then goes on to present the text of the three letters written by her on various matters affecting her relationship with the order.

The first, dated 10 June 1316,[215] was written by the queen from the Castel Nuovo at Naples to Michael of Cesena, then minister general, during the Chapter General of Assisi held in that year.[216] It reminds the minister general of Sancia's affections for, and support of, the order. The queen then requests the confirmation of certain privileges and masses for her during her life and after her death to be offered in the province of Terra di Lavoro. She then asks that the minister general see to it that the same offices be confirmed through all Franciscan provinces, chapters and convents. Sancia concludes with a prayer for Michael's continued rule over the Franciscans.

The second letter was written in Naples, by the queen's own hand, and dated 15 March 1329.[217] It is addressed to the Franciscans attend-

---

[213] See Moorman, *Franciscan Order*, pp. 324–5.

[214] *Analecta Franciscana* (*AF*) 3, pp. 508–14. The letters follow the diplomatic forms of those indexed in Filangieri, *I Registri*, 20, p. 2; and Bartolomeo Capasso, R. Rinaldi and G. Sellitto, *Registri angioini. Inventario cronologico-sistematico dei registri angioini* (Naples, 1894), pp. liv–lvi.

[215] *AF*, 3, pp. 509–10. The letter is discussed in Ambrasi, 'La vita religiosa', p. 500.

[216] See Moorman, *Franciscan Order*, p. 360; and Armando Carlini, 'Constitutiones generales Ordinis Fratrum Minorum anno 1316 Assisii conditae', *AFH*, 4 (1911), pp. 269–302.

[217] *AF*, 3, pp. 510–12; also edited in Wadding, *Annales*, 7, pp. 97–8, 1329, vi, who cites his source as 'Ex Reg. 5 Franc. c. 1'.

ing the Chapter General soon to be held in Paris. The letter comes in the wake of John XXII's arrest of Michael of Cesena at Avignon in December 1327, the deposition of the minister general at the Chapter General of Bologna and his flight from Avignon to Lewis of Bavaria in May 1328, and his final deposition by the pope that June.[218] Sancia's letter thus had to compete for the friars' attention with one from the pope outlining his final condemnations of the Michaelists for the heresy of evangelical poverty and denial of papal authority to alter the Rule[219] and one from Michael himself still claiming to be minister general.[220]

In her message[221] Sancia employs a theology of Francis and of the Rule that by the 1320s had become a hallmark of the Spirituals. She urges the assembled brethren to remain true to Francis' foundation of the Rule upon the Holy Gospel, marked by evangelical poverty and chastity. She reminds them that this observation was symbolized by Francis' stigmata, the sign of the saint's imitation of Christ impressed upon his very person. These stigmata are also Christ's seal upon the new order. Francis himself had prophesied the order's election, its future tribulations and the perseverance of his true disciples who follow his vestiges.

Sancia reminds her readers that she is among this group willing to suffer martyrdom for their devotion to the Rule. In obvious defiance of the pope she then appeals to the assembled brothers to follow the path of Francis and let the pure principles of the Rule and the order guide them in their selection of a future minister. Finally, after commending her husband and the members of her family and household to the brothers' prayers, she makes a claim to the divine inspiration of her words, probably a conscious allusion to Francis' own inspiration in founding the Rule. This also suggests a mystical aspect of the queen's spirituality that she repeats in the last letter and that is reinforced by the structure of the general letter, a point that is discussed further below.

Sancia's last letter is dated from the Castel Nuovo on 18 April 1331.[222] It is addressed to Gerald Odonis, the new minister general of

---

[218] See Moorman, *Franciscan Order*, pp. 318–22. The chapter general had been summoned by Bertrand de Tour, the papal vicar-general of the order.

[219] *BF*, 5, pp. 388–97 for the condemnations.

[220] See Moorman, *Franciscan Order*, p. 321.

[221] See below, pp. 210–12, for the text of the letter.

[222] *AF*, 3, pp. 512–14. See also Wadding, *Annales*, 7, p. 120, 1331, vii.

the order,[223] and to the Franciscans about to assemble at the Chapter General of Perpignan in May 1331.[224] Once again, Sancia's letter reinforced an appeal by Michael of Cesena, who still regarded himself as the true minister general, to repudiate the policies of John XXII.[225] Gerald Odonis' control of the proceedings and of the order appears to have been firm, however. The Statutes of Perpignan, issued at this chapter general, show a further, dramatic shift away from the strict observance and scarcely mention the issue of poverty.[226] It is, there-fore, all the more revealing of Sancia's support of the now heretical Spirituals that her letter makes its strongest appeal for Francis' original ideal.

The queen begins immediately at the point,[227] admonishing Gerald and the brethren not to deviate from the *vestigia*, the path laid down by Francis, the 'standard-bearer of Christ', whose Rule had been twice directly inspired by Christ and sealed with the stigmata, the visible symbol of Francis' true imitation of Christ. Sancia makes it clear that, although many brothers now say that the strict observance of the Rule cannot possibly be followed, this observance has been confirmed explicitly by Pope Innocent III with the specific ban of blasphemy against anyone who impugns the observance of evangelical perfection. Sancia goes so far as to say that the individual Franciscan who denies the Rule is a blasphemer and encourages the friars not to support Gerald Odonis in his attempts to move away from it. She calls up a standard Spiritual theory of authority and disobedience in support of her plea: anyone who tampers with the Rule, changing even one iota, is no longer a pastor, but a mercenary and, by implication, not worthy of obedience.

Sancia then comforts the Franciscans with Christ's promise to sup-port his followers, once again recalling the prophecies of the true Franciscans then attributed to Francis himself but more probably the product of the Spirituals.[228] She reiterates her determination to follow

[223] Elected at Paris in 1329. See Moorman, *Franciscan Order*, pp. 321–2 and n. 10. He was still banished from the royal presence. See Baddeley, *Robert the Wise*, p. 233.
[224] See Moorman, *Franciscan Order*, pp. 360–1.
[225] ibid.
[226] These have been published in S. Mencherini, 'Constitutiones generales O.F.M. a capitulo Perpiniani anno 1331 celebrato editae', *AFH*, 2 (1909), pp. 269–92, 412–30, 575–99.
[227] See below, p. 212.
[228] These appeared in Luke Wadding's *Beati patris Francisci Assisiensis opuscula* (Antwerp, 1623), and were subsequently included in most editions of Francis' works into the twentieth century. Paul Sabatier's checklist in his *Vie de S. François d'Assise*

the *vestigia*, even to martyrdom if necessary, and repeats Francis' familiar exhortation, long a Spiritual rallying cry, for the plowman to remain steadfast at the plow and not to turn back from his task. She then reminds the friars of the inspiration provided the Apostles in their time of trial at Pentecost and to the Franciscans gathered to hear St Anthony preaching at Arles soon after Francis' death. Finally, Sancia reveals the source of her own strength: the literal observance of Christ's direct inspiration to her, alone in prayer in the middle of the night at Castel Nuovo in Naples. For those in doubt she provides the exact date and duration of the event. She concludes with her normal commendation of her husband, family and household to the prayers of the brethren.

The collection of letters ends with a brief restatement of Sancia's claim to be called the mother of the Franciscan order. She finishes the collection by characterizing her attachment not only as the love of a mother for her physical son, but also as a bond of love as great as spiritual love is greater than physical love. The general letter is dated at the royal villa at Quisisana near Castellamare di Stabia[229] on 25 July 1334 and is signed with Sancia's secret seal.

This series seems an odd assortment of unrelated items, written at widely differing times and touching peripherally on the same themes only as occasion dictated, unified only by the queen's obvious affection for the Franciscan order. One might be tempted to speculate that the compiler of the *Chronica xxiv generalium* simply placed them together under a thematic or chronological heading for the Spiritual debate, adding a spurious cover letter from the queen that artificially binds them together. The independent appearance of Sancia's cover

---

(Paris, 1894) excluded these prophecies on textual grounds, as did Walter Goetz in his *Die Quellen zur Geschichte des Franciscus von Assisi* (Gotha, 1904). John R. H. Moorman's study in *Sources of the Life of St Francis of Assisi* (Manchester, 1940) rejected the prophecies authenticity. They are now believed to have been a product of the Spiritual Franciscan tradition. For a study of the relationship between the prophecies and Angelo Clareno's *Historia septem tribulationum ordinis minorum* see Alfonso Marini, 'Una fonte italiana su San Francesco del secolo xiv', *AFH*, 73 (1980), pp. 3–68.

[229] The pleasure villa of Quisisana or Casasana on the Bay of Naples, approximately 18 miles south of the city, built by King Robert in 1310; see Blanchard, *Blue Guide*, p. 142; Gliejeses, *Nuova guida*, pp. 369–70.

letter in Wadding's *Annales minorum*,[230] however, makes this speculation unlikely.

The version of the letter that Wadding presents contains both the *proemium* and the conclusion included by the compiler of the *Chronica*.[231] It then goes on to enumerate three reasons why Sancia considers herself a mother to the order. As also presented in the *Chronica*, these reasons are spelled out in three rubrics but without the accompanying letters. These reasons are first, *since a mother is one with her dear son*; secondly, *a mother loves her sons*; and thirdly, *a mother gives counsel to her sons and assists them*.[232] The rubrics appear as an integral part of Sancia's general letter to the Chapter General of Assisi.

They are in fact Sancia's own thematic comment on her three letters written years apart, added either when she collected the letters together or when she made reference to them to the Chapter General, knowing full well that the order would have already received them from her and would have retained copies, as is evidenced by their independent survival in the *Chronica* and in Wadding's *Annales minorum*.[232]

In these rubrics we have Sancia's unifying principle for this small collection and her own, very personal, interpretation of her relationship with the Franciscan order and the Spiritual party within it: her role as a mother. This role unfolds in a triad of ascending importance from the mother's physical bond to her son, to the mother's earthly love for her son, and finally in the mother's counsel, or spiritual love, for her son. Thus Sancia sees her relationship as a progressive union rising from the carnal ties of blood relation and physical parentage, to the earthly affection and loyalty of the later parental role, to the intellectual and spiritual bond that unites similar souls on the highest level.

This is, of course, a common theme in late medieval spirituality,[233] explicitly called upon by Sancia at the conclusion of her collection as she summarizes her bond to the Franciscans: 'I do not call you servants, but intimate sons, as if you were born from my own body and

---

[230] Wadding, *Annales*, 7, pp. 172–3, 1334, xxxii. The letter is reprinted in van Heuchelum, *Spiritualistische*, p. 45. See also Vidal, 'Ascète', pp. 262–3; Ambrasi, 'La vita religiosa', p. 502.

[231] *AF*, 3, pp. 508–9, 514.

[232] Wadding, *Annales*, 7, p. 172.

[233] Most forcefully formulated within the Franciscan tradition in Bonaventura's *Itinerium mentis in Deum*. The Quaracchi edition of 1891 has been revised by Wilhelm Nyssen (Munich, 1964).

as more as spiritual love is greater than physical love.'[234] Though
certainly not proof of any real mysticism in the strict sense of the
word,[235] Sancia's words must be taken along with her claims to divine
revelation. She was certainly familiar enough with the Franciscan
tradition to realize the import of her words and of her thematic
structure in this collection. This compendium letter, then, succeeds
in combining the disparate facts and themes of her life: the familial
ties to the Franciscan order and its saints, the everyday facts of political
patronage and influence, and the most elevated ideals of loyalty to
the pure observance of the Franciscan Rule and to its beleaguered
adherents. This letter is a synthesis of practical political power,
idealistic spirituality and intellectual fervor that we have already
seen at work in all the queen's dealings with the order. In this triptych
of letters we therefore see Sancia as she saw herself and as she wanted
to be seen: as a staunch and realistic supporter of the Franciscan ideal
and as the person who was key to the fortunes of its strict observance
in the kingdom of Naples.

APPENDIX

Queen Sancia's Letter[236] to the Chapter General of Assisi of 1334[237]

Around that time Lady Sancia, Queen of Sicily and Jerusalem, sent certain
letters of sweet good will towards our order carried to the brothers gathered
at the Portiuncula at the time of sacred indulgence. In this letter she proved
herself to be a true mother of this religious order through various letters
previously sent by her. I have not judged it unworthy to include these letters
in this compilation just as she herself dictated them in order better to show
her affection for the order. Here the careful reader may see how great this
lady's steadfastness was for the Rule when the petty brethren wavered in
fear.

Letters of Lady Sancia, Queen of Sicily and Jerusalem

To the venerable fathers and brothers and sons, the Friars Minor coming
to the holy indulgence of Santa Maria de Angelis, so called from antiquity

---

[234] See below, p. 214.

[235] As defined by Dunstan Dobbins, *Franciscan Mysticism* (New York, 1927);
Elmer O'Brien, *Varieties of Mystic Experience* (New York, 1964), pp. 27–43, 65–72,
112–27, 175–80; and Evelyn Underhill, *Mysticism* (New York, 1961), pp. 95–124,
167–265.

[236] The following translation is based on the text in *AF*, 3, pp. 508–14.

[237] See above, p. 202.

but now named Santa Maria de Portiuncula, where our common father, Francis, began the order and ended his life and blessed the brothers present as well as future and commended them to the glorious Virgin; I, Sancia, by the grace of God queen of Jerusalem and Sicily, the humble daughter and servant of blessed Francis, send greetings in Jesus Christ crucified.

Know, fathers, that for this God caused me to be born into this world from such a lineage and family tree,[238] just as was Lady Sclaramonda of holy memory, my lady mother, queen of Majorca and true daughter of blessed Francis. He also caused that my firstborn brother, namely Friar James of Majorca, my dearest brother, renounced royal power for the love of Jesus Christ and became a son of blessed Francis and entered his order. He also caused me to be a descendent of blessed Elizabeth, who was such a true and devoted daughter of blessed Francis and a mother of his order. She was the blood sister of the lady mother of my father, Lord James, well remembered king of Majorca. He also caused me to have as a husband the most illustrious lord, my lord Robert, king of Jerusalem and Sicily, who was the son of Lady Marie, the well-remembered queen of these realms and of Hungary. She was also the true daughter of blessed Francis and bore a son, blessed Louis,[239] who refused and renounced royal power for the love of Jesus Christ and became a Friar Minor.

I also firmly believe that God and blessed Francis ordained that my lord – who was the third brother[240] – would be king and would have all the virtues that were proper for him and more wisdom and knowledge than have been known of any prince of the world since the time of Solomon;[241] and this knowledge he gathered from the friars of the order[242] so that he – and I with him – might defend the order of blessed Francis.

I myself have recounted these things so that you may see how much I am held to be, and ought to be, a servant of so great a father and of his order. If I consider the example of those who preceeded me in both my own and and in my lord's family, I can accept that passage in John[243] when our Lord Jesus Christ said to his disciples: 'For I call you not servants but sons.' That passage I can also say myself to you and to the entire order as a mother, and a true mother, for three reasons.

---

[238] See above, pp. 182–3.

[239] St Louis of Toulouse; see above, p. 181 and note 10.

[240] After Charles Martel and Louis; see above, p. 184. The translation follows the variant reading in *AF*, 3, p. 509, n. 2. Other variants have also been used below.

[241] See the *Cron. part.*, p. 132, 'lo quale Re Roberto fo lo più savio omo in sapienza che fosse in terra da lo tempo di Salamone.' Caggese, *Roberto d'Angio*, 2, p. 427, n. 2 cites Benvenuto da Imola's *Epistolae metricae* I–II, ep. vi for the same description.

[242] Probably a reference to his education by the Franciscans while in captivity in Catalonia; see above, pp. 183–4.

[243] John 15:13.

I. First, *since a mother is one with her dear son*, and I am one in soul with any Friar Minor, as appears in the letter that I have from the Chapter General of Naples[244] that was written by Lord Brother Cardinal Bertrand de Tour,[245] then minister of the province of Aquitaine, in the holy convent of Assisi by order of Brother Michael,[246] appointed minister general, and also in the letter that I myself sent to him, the tenor of which is such:

Reverend and venerable father in Christ, Brother Michael, minister general of the Order of Friars Minor, Sancia, by the grace of God queen of Jerusalem and Sicily, humble and devoted daughter of blessed Francis and of his order, sends herself with humble and devoted commendation.

Let it be known to you, dearest father, that the brothers of your order, who lately in the Chapter General of Naples remarked our devotion and most sincere affection with which we embrace the order itself singularly among all the estates of the Church, by unanimous vote and in perfect concord favorably conceded and wished that certain things be confirmed through your office that we had humbly and devoutly sought from them for the salvation of our soul and the prosperity of our realms. For we had asked that the salvation of our soul and of our lord be firmly impressed upon the hearts of all the brothers and that our soul be one with the soul of each one of them in the unity of the spirit, and that through the bond of charity we might be partners fully in the benefits that are combined for you through individual brothers wherever on earth the clemency of the savior deigns to work, so that any brother whatever might accept our soul as one with his own in the full participation of all merits. The brothers ought to do this since our soul is better in the order, which it loves most justly, than in our body, which it gives life and informs.

Furthermore, since that chapter general will have set aside for us – at our humble and affectionate petition – one mass for the living in every convent of the entire order for every day that we live and likewise, after our death, one mass for the dead forever wherever it is to be celebrated through the entire order, we devoutly and humbly beseech your reverend paternity that you deem to confirm all the abovesaid and that you embark to transmit under your seal those things confirmed for us through the minister of Terra di Lavoro to all the ministers so that they might be bound to announce in their provincial chapters and in each convent of their provinces those things conceded through you and through them to us and to bind each brother to all of the aforesaid.

We, for our part, beyond our person and our realm, offer as much as we can for the honor and utility and defense of your order. We also intend

---

[244] The Chapter General of Naples in May 1316; see Lambert, *Franciscan Poverty*, pp. 206–7, 210–11; Moorman, *Franciscan Order*, p. 309. The chapter met under the patronage of Sancia and Robert.

[245] Bertrand de Tour, later named Vicar-General; see above, p. 202.

[246] Michael of Cesena; see above, pp. 202–4.

always to persevere in this course with the help of God. May the Almighty deign to keep your venerable person on behalf of this holy order for a long time to come.

Dated in the castle at Naples, tenth day of June, fourteenth indiction.[247]

II. Second, *a mother loves her sons*, and so I love my sons, the Friars Minor, as appears in the letter that I sent to the chapter general to be held in Paris,[248] whose tenor is noted below:

Venerable brothers and sons, the Friars Minor of the Chapter General of Paris to be held soon; Sancia, by the grace of God queen of Jerusalem and Sicily, your humble and devoted daughter sends greetings in the Lord Jesus Christ.

You know how our common father, blessed Francis, founded your Rule upon the holy Gospel,[249] and you know your wish, which is 'namely to observe the holy Gospel of our Lord Jesus Christ by living in obedience without any property and in chastity';[250] and you know what are the commands and what are the admonitions of your Rule. I ask you [this] humbly, and I admonish you through our Lord Jesus Christ crucified, who by his precious stigmata deigned to mark his servant, our said common father, blessed Francis,[251] about whom one reads in the Epistle to the Galatians: 'Brothers, God forbid that I should glory save in the cross of our Lord Jesus Christ, through whom the world is crucified to me, and I to the world.' Later he adds in the same epistle: 'and whoever would follow this rule, peace and mercy upon them and upon the Israel of God. Henceforth let no man give me trouble, etc.'[252] because you follow the vestiges of our father.[253]

---

[247] In 1316.   [248] In 1329. See above, pp. 202–3.

[249] The theme of the Gospel as the foundation of the Rule is basic to Franciscan life; see *Opuscula Sancti patris Francisci Assisiensis*, ed. Kajetan Esser (Grottaferrata–Rome, 1978). It is stated explicitly in the Testamentum, 14; RegNB, Prol. 2; 2, 10; 3, 13; 22, 21; less explicitly in RegB 1, 1; 3, 14; 12, 4. These abbreviations follow those in Esser's edition.

[250] See RegB 1, 1.

[251] On the theme of the stigmata as the seal of Christ impressed upon Francis see Bonaventura, *Legenda maior* 4. This has been edited in *AF*, 10. See also the English translation in Ewert Cousins, *Bonaventure* (New York, 1978), pp. 177–327. This is also a major theme in Spiritual literature; see, for example, Ubertino da Casale, *Arbor vitae crucifixae Jesu Christi* (Venice, Andrea de Bonettis de Papia, 1485. Facs. ed. Charles T. Davis, Turin, 1961), V, iiii, 435, 1–2; 437, 2; Musto, *Letters of Angelo Clareno*, pp. 23–4, 182, 396, 553–4; von Auw, *Epistole*, pp. 60, 99, 297. See also Burr, *Persecution of Peter Olivi*, pp. 19–20.

[252] 6:14, 16–17. The Pauline text continues: 'for I bear the marks of the Lord Jesus in my body'.

[253] The notion of following the *vestigia* is a major Franciscan theme; see, for example, Ep. Fid. II: 13, RegNB 1, 1; 22, 2. For its use among the Spirituals see Musto, *Letters of Angelo Clareno*, pp. 15–16, 630; von Auw, *Epistole*, pp. 341–2.

Have no doubt that such a rule is founded upon such a foundation, namely the holy Gospel, and is signed with such signs, namely the wounds of our Lord Jesus Christ, impressed upon the person of our said common father. No one could, nor can, nor will be able to break it. May our Lady – in whom our common father himself began and fulfilled your order in Santa Maria de Angelis and in his death especially commended himself to her – defend and govern you, unless, God forbid, it be your fault by which you stray from the way of the father.

Also remember the word that the father himself spoke at his death: 'Farewell, all my sons, in the fear of the Lord and remain in it always. And because the future tribulation approaches, happy are they who will persevere.'[254] Thus may no past or present or future tribulation terrify you, recalling the word of the Apostle in the Epistle to the Romans: 'Who shall separate us from the love of Christ? Shall tribulation or distress or hunger or persecution or nakedness or danger or the sword? Even as it is written, "For thy sake we are put to death all the day long. We are regarded as sheep for the slaughter." For I am sure that neither death, etc.'[255]

I myself hope in the Lord Jesus Christ, who gave grace to his Apostle, that he will give to you and to me and to those who intend to follow the vestiges of our father that charity and happy fortitude of the above words, unless, God forbid, your or my fault impede it. As your devoted daughter, I offer to expose myself and my interests and my body to death, if necessary, for the defense of your Rule, which was sealed in the person of our common father by the stigmata of our Lord Jesus Christ.

Finally, in the election of the future minister general we warn and remind you to keep God before your eyes and not favor or reward. Let no individual allegiance seduce you in this election, but may you choose a person who will be prepared to follow the vestiges of our father and the words of the Apostle quoted above. I commend to you my lord husband, the king of Jerusalem and Sicily, father and brother, everyone in his household, my dearest son of good memory, the duke of Calabria,[256] and all the deceased from the royal household and myself, your devoted daughter, and all those

[254] See I Celano II, 7. This has been edited in *Vita prima, Vita secunda, Tractatus de miraculis S. Francisci, AF*, 10 (1926–8), pp. 1–117, 127–268, 269–331. See also Bonaventura, *Legenda maior* 14; and Cousins, *Bonaventure*, p. 319. On the theme of the approaching tribulations of the last days see Olivi's letter to the sons of Charles II, note 39 above; Ubertino da Casale, *Arbor vitae* V, iiii, 443, 1; and its classic formulation in Angelo Clareno's *Historia septem tribulatioum ordinis minorum*. This has received several partial or complete editions of varying usefulness. The standard edition is by Ehrle, *ALKG*, 2 (1886), pp. 106–55, 249–336. For a complete list of manuscripts and editions see Musto, *Letters of Angelo Clareno*, pp. 652–3; and von Auw, *Angelo Clareno*, pp. 207–37, which examines these in great detail.   [255] Romans 8: 35–8.

[256] Charles of Calabria, the son and heir of Robert, who died in 1328; see above, p. 187 and note 62.

from our household of Majorca, living as well as dead, and all others both living and dead to whom I direct my thoughts.

Written in Naples by my own hand and dictated through us without any other assistance except divine[257] on account of your merits, fifteenth day of March, twelfth indiction.[258]

III. Third, a *mother gives counsel to her sons and assists them.* So I have given counsel and aid to my sons the Friars Minor as is declared in the letter that I sent to the Chapter General of Perpignan,[259] which begins thus:

To the venerable brother in Christ, Gerald,[260] minister general of the Order of Minors, and to the brothers assembled in the Chapter General of Perpignan; Sancia, queen of Jerusalem and of Sicily, your humble and devoted, albeit unworthy, daughter of blessed Francis and of his entire order, sends greetings in the Lord Jesus Christ.

I ask and admonish your paternity that you do not stray from the vestiges of so great a father who is the standard-bearer of Christ,[261] our common father, blessed Francis. I have heard that some of your brothers say that your Rule cannot be served, which Rule was revealed by God twice to our holy father Francis and ornamented with those five seals that are the precious wounds of Christ ensealed upon the body of the nourishing confessor.[262] Let the brothers remember what the venerable father, Lord John of Saint Paul,[263] Bishop of Sabina, and what the vicar of Christ, Lord Innocent III of holy memory, said when he confirmed the Rule: 'For if anyone were to say that the intent and observation of evangelical perfection contained anything harmful or irrational or impossible to observe, he is guilty of blaspheming the author of the Gospel himself.'[264] Do not believe

---

[257] Here and in her letter of 1331, p. 213 below, the queen invokes her direct, divine inspiration. This may be an allusion to Francis's own claims in Testamentum 14.   [258] 1329.

[259] See above, p. 204 and note 224.

[260] See above, pp. 203–4 and note 223.

[261] See Ubertino da Casale, *Arbor vitae* V, iiii, 437, 1–2.

[262] The theme of the immutability of the Rule based on divine revelation and marked by the stigmata is central to Spiritual thought. The Spirituals saw their position justified in Francis' own Testamentum 14 and 39. They repeat it in the *Speculum perfectionis* 38, I, 1, edited by Paul Sabatier, *Le Speculum perfectionis ou Mémoires de Frère Léone sur la seconde partie de la vie de Saint François d'Assise*, British Society of Franciscan Studies, vol. 13 (Manchester, 1928), and vol. 17 (Manchester, 1931). See also Ubertino da Casale's *Arbor vitae* V, v, 445, 2; and Musto, *Letters of Angelo Clareno*, pp. 24–6. It also appears in Bonaventura's *Legenda maior* 4, 9–11. See also Cousins, *Bonaventure*, pp. 213–17.

[263] See Moorman, *Franciscan Order*, p. 18.

[264] Bonaventura, *Legenda maior* 3, 19; Cousins, *Bonaventure*, p. 205; *Legenda trium sociorum* 12, in Rosiland B. Brooke (ed.), *Scripta Leonis, Rufuni et Angeli sociorum S. Francisci* (Oxford, 1970).

them at all, since they are not sons of the father except in name only. If, God forbid, your father the general wishes to change anything one single iota, do not support it. Because if he were to tamper with it, he is not a pastor but a mercenary, and as such should you hold him.[265] Know for certain and do not doubt that God and the Blessed Virgin will govern and defend you who wish to be true sons of the father. Also remember the words that the Lord Jesus Christ said to the father: 'I have called, I shall serve, and I shall feed, and I shall choose others for those falling away, so that if they were not born, I shall cause them to be born. And by whatever shocks this poor little order may be battered, it shall always remain safe in my protection.'[266]

I myself offer myself with all my ability to governing those who will wish to follow the vestiges of our own and your common father all the way to the death of the cross. I also consider it the greatest grace if God causes me to die and to be a martyr for this cause. May that blessing descend upon you and me and all those who are or will be of this most holy will that the father gave in the Chapter of Arles, when blessed Anthony, brother and father, was preaching on the chapter of the cross and on that grace that on Pentecost day[267] came over the Apostles. May it not turn away because of our sins, as is written in the Gospel and in your Rule: 'No one having put his hand to the plow and looking back is fit for the kingdom of God.'[268]

Since I am a sinner and insufficient and unlettered, and I speak literally,[269] I know nothing except from the grace and intimacy of God, and I trust nothing of my own, on Thursday, the eighteenth day of April, I entered the small chapel next to my chamber in the Castel Nuovo in Naples where well through three candles before daybreak, with the door closed, alone with the body of Christ, which was upon the altar, I commended

---

[265] The theory of disobedience to those who tamper with the Rule had been formulated in the 1320s and 1330s by the Spirituals in response to papal and conventual decisions. It found its chief expression in Angelo Clareno's theory of the rejection of unjust authority expressed in his *Apologia pro vita sua* of 1330, edited by Victor Doucet, 'Angelus Clarinus ad Alvarum Pelagium, Apologia pro vita sua', *AFH*, 39 (1946), pp. 63–200. See especially the chapter 'De obedientia', pp. 171–200.

[266] From Prophetia VI. The same text appears in Musto, *Letters of Angelo Clareno*, XIV, pp. 203–4; von Auw, *Epistole*, p. 75; and in *Letters*, LXXV, p. 626; von Auw, *Epistole*, p. 339. See note 228 above and II Celano III, 90.

[267] See Bonaventura, *Legenda maior* 4, 10; Cousins, *Bonaventure*, p. 215; I Celano 48. The scene is the subject of frescoes by Giotto in the Bardi chapel in Santa Croce, Florence and by the St Francis painter in Assisi. See Cole, *Giotto*, pp. 105, 114 and 152.

[268] Luke 9:62; RegB 2: 13; RegNB 2: 10; Adm. 3: 10.

[269] Sancia's rhetorical self-deprecation may also be an allusion to Francis' own claims to being 'idiota' in the Testamentum 19.

myself to him and afterward began to write as the Lord directed me, without any counsel, human or earthly.

I commend to your prayers the lord king, my reverend husband and your father and special son, and all his household both living and dead, and especially the well-remembered duke of Calabria,[270] that God may give his glory to him and to me and to all our people living as well as dead and to those to whom I direct my thoughts, and especially Lord Fernando, my dearest brother, who was the father of the king of Majorca who now reigns, my dearest nephew and my son.[271]

Written by my own hand on the aforesaid day in the Castel Nuovo, indiction . . ., in the year 1331.

Although I am not worthy on my own, nevertheless through the grace of God I can be called the true mother of the order of blessed Francis in several ways, not only in word or writing, but by works that I have performed continuously and that I intend to do with his help all the days of my life. For, although I feel that I have nothing on my own except sin, nevertheless I can accept the word of the Apostle: 'What I am, I am by the grace of God.'[272] And later it continues: 'No longer do I call you servants, because the servant does not know what his master does . . ., but all things that I have heard from my father I have made known to you.'[273] And like a mother I can say to you and to the whole order: I do not call you servants, but intimate sons, as if you were born from my own body, and as much more as spiritual love is greater than physical love.

Dated in Quisisana near Castellamare di Stabia with my own secret ring on the twenty-fifth day of July, fourteenth indiction.[274]

ACKNOWLEDGEMENTS

I would like to thank Donn Michael Farris of the Divinity School Library, Duke University, Sig. Josep Segura i Salado of the Societat Arqueològica lulliana of Majorca, and Dr Eileen Gardiner of New York City for their help with this project.

[270] See above, p. 211, note 256.
[271] See above, p. 182.
[272] I Corinthians 15: 10.
[273] John 15: 15.
[274] 1334 at the Villa Quisisana. See above, p. 205, note 229.

10

'Of the Gift of her Husband': English Dower and its Consequences in the Year 1200

JANET SENDEROWITZ LOENGARD

The widow, particularly the widow with young children, has been seen to be in need of special consideration by most societies, and often enough this has been echoed in law codes and customary practices. One arrangement for the well-being of the woman who lost her husband was what late twelfth-century England called *dos*, dower, the gift from the husband to the wife upon their marriage 'because of the burden of matrimony . . . for the maintenance of the wife and the nurture of the children when they are born, should the husband predecease her.'[1] The gift at marriage from husband to wife was known in England both before and after the Norman Conquest; a great deal has been written about its origins, and efforts have been made to ascertain its early scope and effect.[2] But examples – most of them

---

[1] Bracton, *De Legibus et Consuetudinibus Angliae*, ed. George E. Woodbine, trans. with revision and notes by Samuel E. Thorne (4 vols, Cambridge, Mass., 1968–77) (henceforward Bracton), f. 92 (2: 265).

[2] See, for example, the useful summary of dower and other property rights of the Anglo-Saxon woman, together with a valuable bibliography, by Marc A. Meyer, 'Land charters and the legal position of the Anglo-Saxon woman', in Barbara Kanner (ed.), *The Women of England from Anglo-Saxon Times to the Present: Interpretive Bibliographical Essays* (Hamden, Conn., 1979), pp. 57–82. References to work done on the background of Anglo-Saxon dower were earlier collected by F. Joüon des Longrais in *La conception anglaise de la saisine du XIIᵉ au XIVᵉ siecle* (Paris, 1924), pp. 315–17; and George L. Haskins, 'The development of common law dower', *Harvard Law Review*, 62 (1948), pp. 42–3. An informative early article setting out nineteenth-century scholarship on the Continental Germanic background of English dower, as well as discussing the Anglo-Saxon and Anglo-Norman periods, is Florence Griswold Buckstaff, 'Married women's property in Anglo-Saxon and Anglo-Norman law and the origin of the common law dower', *Annals of the American Academy of Political and Social Sciences*, 4 (1893–4), pp. 233–64. Other references to

gleaned from wills and charters – are relatively few for the Anglo-Saxon and Anglo-Norman periods, while laws are cryptic and offer little evidence of how, or if, they operated. The surviving pipe roll of the reign of Henry I and the rolls of Henry II present a mosaic of evidence for the existence of dower, often tantalizing in its incompleteness. It is only with *Glanvill* in the 1180s and the first survivals of plea rolls and feet of fines in the 1190s that large quantities of material exist setting out in detail the theory and practice of dower and permitting examination of the social and economic problems it presented.

In 1200, *dos* in England shared little more than a Latin name with the Roman law institution familiar on the European continent. It was provided by the husband, not by the father of the bride.[3] It resulted

---

Anglo-Norman materials are included in the bibliography appended to Ruth Kittel, 'Women under the law in Medieval England, 1066–1485', in Kanner, *Women of England*, pp. 134–7.

[3] The land which the bride brought to the marriage as the gift of her own family was called the *maritagium*, the marriage portion. The term may have come to England with the Normans; I have not seen it in the Anglo-Saxon law codes but it meant Roman-law dowry in eleventh-century Norman usage. See Emily Zack Tabuteau, 'Definitions of feudal military obligations in eleventh century Normandy', in Morris S. Arnold, Thomas A. Green, Sally A. Scully and Stephen D. White (eds), *On the Laws and Customs of England: Essays in Honor of Samuel E. Thorne* (Chapel Hill, NC, 1981), p. 47, n. 102. English jurists were well aware that it corresponded to Roman-law *dos*; *Glanvill* explains at the beginning of Book VI that '*Dos* has two meanings', that in England it means the gift by the husband to the wife at the time of the marriage, and in Book VII that 'In Roman law the word *dos* has a different meaning: there *dos* is properly used for that which is given with a woman to her husband, which is commonly called *maritagium*, a marriage portion'; *Tractatus de legibus et consuetudinibus regni Anglie qui Glanvilla vocatur*, ed. and trans. G. D. G. Hall (London, 1965), VI, 1; VII, 1 (henceforward *Glanvill*). F. Joüon des Longrais comments on the insularity of the usage of *dos* to mean the gift *propter nuptias* by the husband in 'Le Statut de la femme en Angleterre dans le droit commun mediéval', *La Femme*, 12, II (Receuils de la Société Jean Bodin, Brussels, 1962), p. 184. Bracton, describing English law in Roman terms, says in one of his discussions of English dower that it is 'of two kinds, profectitious and adventitious: profectitious is that given by a father ... when the agreement for marrying a daughter is made; The land so given ... may be called her *maritagium* or patrimony ...' and goes on to discuss the gift *propter nuptias* given by the husband on the day of the marriage as that which is 'properly called the wife's *dos* according to English custom ...'; Bracton, *De Legibus*, ff. 92–92b (2: 266). See also the comments by George E. Woodbine in his edition of *Glanvill* (New Haven, 1932), pp. 215–16. The wife's interest in her dower and her interest in her *maritagium* were in the same position while her husband lived in that she had in each an interest protected after her husband's death but in neither case controlled the property involved (and could not prevent its alienation) while he

in a life estate for the widow, but no more; on her death it did not pass to her heirs but rather to the heirs of her husband. It was valid only within rigidly controlled upper limits and it could be created only under defined conditions. Rules were hammered out, sometimes apparently with knowledge, perhaps indirect, of canonists' and civilians' pronouncements on an issue, more often without obvious reference to them.[4] There could be dower only in a valid marriage; it was lost if a marriage was dissolved for consanguinity, even though a child of that marriage was his father's heir.[5] It was lost if a woman was separated from her husband because of her own 'shameful act'.[6]

---

lived. The question, 'dower or *maritagium*', was an issue in a number of cases related to the interest held in land by an ancestress; see below, pp. 242-4. But I have seen only one entry in the plea rolls which suggests any confusion between the two on the part of the woman endowed; a widow says that her husband married her 'without land with money', afterwards acquired land, and gave it to her in *maritagium*; *Rolls of the Justices in Eyre at Bedford, 1202*, ed. G. Herbert Fowler, Bedfordshire Historical Record Society, vol. I (Aspley Guise, 1913), no. 73. The plea, and the gift if there was one, may have been a deliberate attempt to circumvent the prevailing rule that there was ordinarily no dower in property acquired after the marriage and that the bride who accepted money at the church door was thereafter foreclosed from claiming against her husband's lands upon his death (*Glanvill*, VI, 2).

[4] See, for an assessment of the influence of canon law, Michael M. Sheehan, 'The influence of canon law on the property rights of married women in England', *Medieval Studies*, 25 (1963), pp. 109-24, esp. p. 114. Both *Glanvill* and Bracton show familiarity with at least the terminology of Roman and canon law (see note 3 above and note 6 below), but I have not found important points on which either law prevailed when there was a conflict with English practice concerning dower. See comment in Sir Frederick Pollock and Frederic William Maitland, *The History of English Law before the Time of Edward I*, 2nd edn, reissued with new introduction and select bibliography by S. F. C. Milsom (2 vols, Cambridge, 1968), 2, pp. 374-5 (henceforward P&M).

[5] *Glanvill*, VI, 17; Bracton, *De Legibus*, f. 304 (3: 377).

[6] On the 'shameful act': *Glanvill*, VI, 17. Mr Hall has noted that the meaning of *turpitudo* is not clear and that in the thirteenth century the passage was glossed to mean fornication or blasphemy 'ut dic' aug' mag', which Maitland believed to be a reference to Augustine by way of Gratian's *Decretum* (*Glanvill*, p. 68, n. 1). Maitland discussed the gloss in his article 'Glanvill revised', *Harvard Law Review*, 6 (1892), pp. 1-20; also found in H. A. L. Fisher (ed.), *The Collected Papers of Frederic William Maitland* (3 vols, Cambridge, 1911), 2, pp. 266-89. While *Glanvill* speaks only of the divorce for consanguinity or *turpitudo*, Bracton explains that there is a loss of dower after a divorce for any reason; Bracton, ff. 92, 92b, 302 (2: 266-7; 3: 372). Both Joüon des Longrais (*Saisine*, pp. 366-7, n. 6) and Professor Thorne (Bracton, 2: 267, n. 1) have noted the echo of Roman or canon law here. *Glanvill* probably is not

It could not result from even a valid secret or deathbed marriage because, according to *Glanvill*, it was to be given at the church door at the time of the wedding.[7] It was a gift, but it was a gift which a free man was bound to give, says *Glanvill*, 'by secular and ecclesiastical

---

suggesting that divorce for other causes did not mean loss of dower; it is more likely that the treatise's author simply had not thought of other causes for divorce. There is support, if belated, for the *Glanvill* glossator; the Statute of Westminster II (1285) c. 34 denied dower to the adulterous wife.

[7] *Glanvill* is quite clear that all dower, nominated or the unnamed third, is given at the church door: 'In common English law usage it means that which a free man gives to his wife at the church door at the time of his marriage ... When a man endows his wife either he nominates certain property as dower or he does not ...' (*Glanvill*, VI, 1); see also Bracton, ff. 92, 304b, 305 (2: 266; 3: 378–9) and especially ff. 303b–304 (3: 376). This is a troublesome point. Joüon des Longrais believed that the requirement that dower be given at the church door on the day of the marriage was related to ecclesiastical sanction of the marriage as well as guaranteeing publicity (*Saisine*, pp. 317–18); in his later work, he emphasized the latter function ('Statut de la femme', p. 186). Maitland declared emphatically that publicity was the purpose (P&M, 2: 375), but commented on the influence of dower given at the church door on the validity of a marriage. Yet long before the end of the thirteenth century, dower at the church door had become only one of several possible forms. Only *dos nominata* was appointed there and it accounted for a small proportion of all dower. The question then arises whether the statements of Bracton and even *Glanvill* reflect actual practice. Bracton's period falls outside the scope of this paper, but I am convinced that *Glanvill* is accurate for the end of the twelfth century. Admittedly, most plea rolls for the years around 1200 mention neither the day of the marriage nor the church door in the statement of the widow's claim. An entry commonly reads 'X, who was the wife of Y, asks against Z the reasonable dower which pertains to her of the free tenement which was Y, her former husband's, in Such-and-Such' or 'asks from Z so much named land in Such-and-Such as the dower which pertains to her of the gift of Y, her former husband'. I have seen fewer than two dozen instances in which the sentence continues, 'on the day on which he married her'; *Abbreviatio Placitorum* (Record Commission, 1811), pp. 4, 8, 28; *Rotuli Curiae Regis*, ed. Francis Palgrave (2 vols, London, 1835) (henceforward *RCR*), I: 20, 167, 439; *RCR*, II: 32; *The Earliest Lincolnshire Assize Rolls AD 1202–1209*, ed. Doris M. Stenton (Lincoln Record Society, 1926) (henceforward *ELAR*), vol 22, nos. 216, 428, 513; *Curia Regis Rolls* (London, 1922–) (henceforward *CRR*), vol. I: 85, 150, 155, 160, 228, 322, 323, 363; *Three Rolls of the King's Court in the Reign of King Richard the First*, ed. Frederick [*sic*] William Maitland, Pipe Roll Society (London, 1891), vol. 14, pp. 7, 131. And even fewer entries allege endowment at the church door; one is the celebrated 'broken knife' case of Michaelmas term, 2 John, in which a widow asserted endowment *ex assensu patris* with a transfer of seisin made by a certain knife broken at the church door; *CRR*, I: 213, 323, 361 and *Select Civil Pleas*, ed. William Paley Baildon, Selden Society (London, 1890), vol. 3, no. 16. Better examples, because less extraordinary in their facts, are the cases at *RCR*, II: 264;

ELAR, nos. 230, 428; and *CRR*, I: 419, also in *Staffordshire Suits*, ed. George Wrottesley, William Salt Archaeological Society (London, 1882), vol. III, p. 72.

But I think that the inclusion or omission of 'die qua eam desponsavit' and/or 'ad hostium ecclesie' has no substantive significance. In 1200, neither the writ of right of dower nor the writ *unde nihil habet* mentions the time and place of endowment; see *Glanvill*, VI, 5, 15 and the 1199 writs of dower *unde nihil habet* of Geoffrey fitz Peter, as Justiciar, to the sheriff of Suffolk; *Pleas before the King or his Justices, 1198–1212*, ed. Doris M. Stenton, Selden Society, vols. 67 (London, 1953), 68 (1952), 83 (1967), 84 (1967), I, nos. 3511, 3543 (henceforward *PBKJ*). Indeed, even in the 1220s apparently neither the writ of dower *unde nihil habet* nor the writ used when dower was *ex assensu patris* stated the circumstances of endowment, nor was there any distinction in that respect made between nominated dower and the 'third'; see the 'Irish Register' (British Museum Cottonian MS Julius D II, ff. 143b–147b, 150a) and the Register in Cambridge University Library MS Ii vi 13, ff. 56a–62b, both edited by G. D. G. Hall and Elsa de Haas in *Early Registers of Writs*, Selden Society, vol. 87 (London, 1970), pp. 7, 8, 16, 30. Neither Register sets out a writ of right of dower but a rubric following the writ of right in the Cambridge University Library MS says, 'Or thus: which they claim as appurtenant to their free tenement which they hold of you in dower in the same vill by free service' (p. 18).

That it was unimportant whether the phrases 'ad hostium ecclesie' and 'die qua eam desponsavit' were included or omitted is also demonstrated by several cases which appear in more than one entry. There are two reports of the 'broken knife' case; one states that the events recounted took place 'die quo [*sic*] ipsa desponsata fuit' (*CRR*, I: 361), while the other adds that they occurred 'ad hostium ecclesie' (*CRR*, I: 323). An entry for Hilary term, 1 John, reports that Cecilia, widow of William [le] Palm[ier] asked a third part of a virgate in Besinton 'ut illam quam Willelmus vir suus ei dedit in dotem die qua eam desponsavit' (*CRR*, I: 142); another entry concerning the same case, in Trinity term, 2 John, says that Cecilia asked the third part of the half virgate 'qua eam contingit ex dono W. viri sui etc.' (*CRR*, I: 192). Joia de Bolinton, widow of Luke, alleged by attorney in 1199 that she sought 'rationabilem dotem', stated in terms of acreage, against four men; in 1200, against a fifth man, she asked half a virgate of land as the dower 'que eam contingit ex dono Luce quondam viri sui et unde eam dotavit die qua eam desponsavit . . .' (*CRR*, I: 102, 160). She could not, obviously, have been endowed on the day of her marriage with only a portion of her dower.

Nor, whatever the later practice, have I seen any clear correlation between the fact that dower was nominated and the allegation that it was given on the wedding day. There are cases which seem to deal with *dos nominata* which do not specify either the time or place of endowment; see, for example, *CRR*, I: 166, 277, 325 (specified money rent); *RCR*, I: 80 (specified money rent); 81, 416 (specified money rent). Again, this may reflect the wording of the writ; in 1200, there was no distinction between nominated dower and the 'third' in either the writ of right of dower or the writ *unde nihil habet*, although later, when a writ for nominated or 'assigned' dower appeared, it included 'ad hostium ecclesie quando eam desponsavit'; see the Register in Bodleian Library, Oxford, MS Rawlinson C 292, ff. 9a–104a, in *Early Registers of Writs*, p. 246. S. F. C. Milsom, *The Legal Framework of English Feudalism* (Cambridge, 1976), p. 143, n. 5, has suggested that the existence of a statement setting out the circumstances of endowment is related to whether the dower was *ex assensu patris* and that seems in part borne out by the cases. Five of the entries which law'.[8] In 1200, it would often be specifically nominated property; otherwise it could be an endowment of a third of the land of which the husband had seisin on the day of the marriage. In either event, it could attach only to land held in free tenure.[9] If specifically nominated, dower could be less than a third, but it could not be more and the action of admeasurement lay to reduce the widow's share in such case. Nominated dower was not limited to land; it could also consist of money, rents, services or chattels.[10]

---

include such a statement involve dower *ex assensu patris*, although there are cases which do not, e.g. *ELAR*, nos. 253, 490; *PBKJ*, II, no. 490; *Memoranda Roll for the Tenth Year of King John together with the Curia Regis Rolls of Hilary 7 Richard I (1196) and Easter 9 Richard I (1198)*, ed. R. Allen Brown, Pipe Roll Society, n.s. vol. 31 (London, 1957), p. 107 (henceforward *Pipe Roll Society* n.s. vol. 31). Moreover, while in the 1220s the writ for dower *ex assensu patris* did not mention either time or place of endowment, by the 1260s it did; see the 'Luffield Register' (Cambridge University Library MS Ee i 1, ff. 194a–211a) in *Early Registers of Writs*, p. 82.

But none of this goes to the question of what the demandant widow had to plead, let alone prove, in order to win her case. The plea roll entries make clear that the time and place of endowment were in fact crucial factors. There are too many cases for it to be otherwise, cases in which the defense to a claim of dower is based on just such an endowment or lack of it. The most common argument was that endowment at the wedding was of land other than that now claimed; see *ELAR*, no. 230; *RCR*, I: 145 (also *Abbreviatio Placitorum*, p. 21); *RCR*, II: 264; *CRR*, I: 260, 419. In *CRR*, I: 260 and *RCR*, I: 145, the phrase 'ad hostium ecclesie' is not used, but there is mention of producing 'sectam que interfuit sponsaliciis' (*CRR*, I: 260) and 'que interfuit desponsacioni' (*RCR*, I: 145, *Abbreviatio Placitorum*, p. 21). Mention of the wedding appears in cases of dower *ex assensu patris* when the widow offers to produce witnesses to prove the father-in-law's presence and/or the endowment at the wedding; see *PBKJ*, II, no. 129; *Pipe Roll Society* n.s. vol. 31, p. 107; *CRR*, I: 22; *RCR*, I: 365. The wedding was obviously equally significant when the defense was that the demandant had not been married; see *CRR*, I: 322. See also the (successful) offer to produces witnesses 'who were present at her wedding' to prove a husband's seisin on the day of the wedding, in *RCR*, I: 359, and other cases collected at notes 22 and 58 below, all of which assume dower appointed at the church door.

[8] *Glanvill*, VI, 1.

[9] ibid.; Bracton, f. 92 (2: 265). There are cases on the point in *PBKJ*, III, no. 853; *Abbreviatio Placitorum*, p. 26; *CRR*, I: 313, also in *Select Civil Pleas*, no. 14; *RCR*, II: 89.

[10] *Glanvill*, VI, 2; Bracton f. 94 (2: 271). There is a writ for dower in money in the mid-thirteenth-century Register of Writs in Cambridge University Library MS Ee i 1, ff. 194a–211a, the 'Luffield Register', in *Early Registers of Writs*, p. 83, and it appears in registers thereafter. Widows sued for dower in rents in a number of cases around 1200; examples are to be found in *CRR*, I: 99, 146, 189, 325; *RCR*, I: 80, and other cases in which rent was taken into the king's hand in a dower action for non-appearance of the tenant. For a case of dower in labor services, see *Feet of Fines of the*

The nature of the interest a new wife took upon endowment was not entirely clear and has led to speculation.[11] Certainly she acquired

---

Reign of Henry the Second and of the First Seven Years of Richard the First, 1182–1196, Pipe Roll Society, vol. 17 (London, 1894), no. 99 (henceforward *Fines Henry II and Richard I*). By the beginning of the fifteenth century, judges were declaring confidently that English dower had never permitted dower in chattels; see materials collected on the point by Woodbine in his notes to his edition of *Glanvill*, p. 217. For a discussion of dower in chattels and the objections to it, see Joüon des Longrais, 'Statut de la femme', pp. 193–4.

By the end of the thirteenth century, unnamed dower had expanded to include a third of all lands held in seisin by the husband at any time during the marriage; the change may have been signalled by the language in Magna Carta (1217 and later issuances) c. 7 ('Assignetur autem ei pro dote sua tercia pars tocius terre mariti sui que sua fuit in vita sua, nisi de minori dotata fuerit ad hostium ecclesie.') The 'que sua fuit in vita sua' does not seem to have been the practice; Bracton repeats *Glanvill* (f. 92; 2: 265) and there is at least one post-Magna Carta case in *Bracton's Note Book* which follows the older rule; *Bracton's Note Book*, ed. F. W. Maitland (3 vols, London, 1887), no. 970 (henceforward *BNB*). Moreover, dower had ceased to be a matter of agreement between the parties and was held to arise by operation of law; the old endowment at the church door was only one option among many. In the fifteenth century, Littleton knew five kinds of dower, with no restriction on that nominated at the church door, although common law dower was one-third of the land of which the husband was seised during the marriage; *Tenures*, ed. Eugene Wambaugh (Washington, DC, 1903), V, §§37, 51 (pp. 16, 21).

[11] The question, like many others, probably descends from Bracton's language on the point. His distinction between *dos nominata* and *non nominata* suggests that some undefined right passed to the woman immediately upon the constitution of named dower; she will have *ius*, *dominium*, which her husband's act cannot impair; ff. 93b–94 (2: 270), 299b (3: 365), 300b (3: 368), 310 (3: 392). Maitland, commenting, says that in Bracton's day named dower seemed to involve 'true proprietary rights' while unspecified dower was 'a charge on all the husband's lands' (P&M, 2: 423). The nature of the wife's rights has, however, been variously interpreted. In 1924, Joüon des Longrais insisted that in nominated dower the constitution of the dower conveyed seisin of the tenement: 'PAR SON DON IL PERD CETTE SAISINE ET LA FEMME L'ACQUIERT' (*Saisine*, p. 331; capitalization his). It was one of the premises of his treatment of dower. He reiterated his position in 1962, adding that 'the real right' was transferred but that it had two distinctive traits: it was conditioned on the wife's survival of her husband and it ended automatically upon her death ('Statut de la femme', p. 199). Later in the article, he commented that seisin in named dower passed upon endowment but that seisin in the undifferentiated 'third' did not (pp. 214–15).

Others have been more hesitant. George Haskins wrote of 'immediate rights' in nominated dower ('The development of common law dower', p. 50) and, in a case dating from half a century later than the period discussed here, he found an instance in which there was a present transfer of seisin although one conditioned on the bride's survival (p. 44, n. 12): a difficult concept. But the case may not be a useful precedent for its own or an earlier period. It was dower *ex assensu patris*, the great exception to the rule requiring seisin in the husband on the wedding day and one, not surprisingly, productive of uncertain results. It is equally unsurprising, then, that the case involved a charter which spelled out the grantor's intentions. In 1200 also, charters were not uncommonly involved in dower *ex assensu patris* in an attempt to protect the new wife's interest; see *ELAR*, no. 490; *CRR*, I: 87; *RCR*, I: 365; *RCR*, II: 102. But for the most part their exact language and provisions are uncertain; they are not transcribed into the entries of the cases in which they figured. In any event, no doweress in 1200 appears to have received a charter which she interpreted as transferring immediate seisin to her. Indeed, only in one of the several reports of one case, in which there was no charter, does a widow appear to allege that on the wedding day she received seisin of named property appointed *ex assensu patris*. The account in *CRR*, I: 323 says that Amicia, now wife of Gilbert Avenell, asked land which her father-in-law had given and conceded to her first husband on their wedding day for the purpose of endowing her, so that her husband was seised of it 'et eam inde dotavit et per quendam cultellum fractum . . . ad hostium ecclesie inde ei saisinam fecit.' But there are two reports, and they do not seem to agree; the second reads 'et saisinam inde fecit filio suo per quendam cultellum . . .' (*CRR*, I: 361).

Certainly widows claiming dower do not appear to have regarded themselves as having been in seisin, even of nominated dower, from the time of their wedding. Emma de Pirefield asked half the vill of Pirefield as her dower 'of the gift of Robert de Lose, her former husband, and of which he endowed her', and then added enigmatically, 'unde ipsa post mortem ejus saisita fuit' (*CRR*, I: 166). Cunegard, widow of Adam de Mandevill, asked a virgate of land 'as that which her husband gave her in dower on the day when he married her' and went on to explain that 'her husband was seised of it on the day when he took the road for Jerusalem, where he died' (*Abbreviatio Placitorum*, p. 8).

Moreover, the writ of right of dower itself does not suggest present seisin in the widow, whether dating from the wedding or from the husband's death. Like the writ of right itself, it is in terms of a claim to land of which one does not have seisin. One does not base the claim on one's own prior seisin but on that of another, in this case the dead husband. The writ for dower does not resemble the writ for the assize of novel disseisin and there is no record, at the end of the twelfth century, of anyone trying to use novel disseisin for the purpose. (There is a possible exception: in 1194, 'Hawise the widow' brought an assize against Simon le Taneur and his wife for disseising her of her dower in Benford. The *juratores* who came 'said that they did not disseise her' and she was in mercy; *Three Rolls of the King's Court*, p. 69. But she could, of course, have been in seisin of the dower land long before the acts of which she complained; there is no way of knowing whether the *juratores* were saying that such acts did not happen or did not constitute a disseisin of the land she held, or that dower not yet allocated by the heir did not carry seisin and so was not a subject for the assize.) Nor have I seen an assize of novel disseisin, brought by a husband for land specified to have been previously appointed by him as *dos nominata*, in which his wife joined as plaintiff. Reading a draft of this paper, my husband took the reasoning one step further and asked whether the fact that land was the subject of inchoate nominated dower was ever used as a bar by a third party in an action of novel disseisin by a husband alone; so far as I can tell, it was not. It is of course possible that none of the relevant records survives, but the conclusion otherwise seems clear.

Yet this is not to deny any present interest in the wife. Long before Bracton – and despite *Glanvill*'s comments about the wife's powerlessness to object to her husband's acts (VI, 3) – there was recognition of what Maitland might have called the wife's present proprietary right in even inchoate *dos nominata*. There is a charter from Henry II in 1153–4, when he was still Duke Henry, which illustrates the point: it runs to Nigel fitz Arthur and it confirms a grant made to him earlier by Robert of Gloucester of land which Nigel then appointed to his wife in dower; there is no statement as to evidence or circumstance of endowment. It reads in part, 'And I have conceded to him and to his wife and their heirs all that land . . .'; for the charter, Nigel gave the Duke 40 marks silver and his wife gave 'an *anulus* of gold because the thing was of her dower'; *Regesta Regum Anglo-Normannorum*, vol. III, ed. H. A. Cronne and R. H. C. Davis (Oxford, 1968), no. 115.

S. F. C. Milsom, on the other hand, would more severely restrict the wife's interest; indeed, he would give even the widow with nominated dower only a right to be seised against her husband's heir, if that; *The Legal Framework*, pp. 42–3, but see p. 145. He has also suggested that dower was simply an internal arrangement, an allocation by the husband, albeit one which the son as heir was obliged to honor, a 'dependent tenure within the inheritance'. Endowment meant that the woman, on her marriage, received dower 'in a ceremonial sense'; S. F. C. Milsom, 'Inheritance by women in the twelfth and early thirteenth centuries', in Morris S. Arnold et al. (eds), *On the Laws and Customs of England*, pp. 60, 76, 83. One might quarrel with this view if it were to be taken to its extreme limit; an allocation, internal or otherwise, which when it matures can be enforced in a law court should probably be seen as more than ceremonial.

But then the question remains: in 1200, exactly what interest did a wife have in her dower, nominated or otherwise, during her marriage or immediately following her husband's death? Not seisin, for all the above reasons. Not a present proprietary right in land, certainly not in the undifferentiated 'third' and probably not in *dos nominata* in a period when *Glanvill* could threaten a wife with eventual loss of her dower if she opposed her husband's sale of nominated lands. Professor Milsom was probably accurate when he saw the interest as a right to seisin upon the husband's death rather than as a right in land. What a wife had, functionally, was closest to a modern contract right, alien as the concept would have been to her or her husband or a court in 1200. If a man stands on the steps of a public place in the presence of witnesses and says to a woman who is about to marry him or who is in the process of marrying him – Littleton, in the fifteenth century, says it is 'after affiance and troth plighted between them' (*Tenures*, I, V, §39; p. 17), but endowment at the church door was rare when he was writing and much of what he says in the paragraph was not true in the late twelfth century – 'Because you are marrying me, and provided that you remain married to me so that you survive me as my wife, then on my death you shall have Blackacre for the rest of your life', then, so long as the woman remains married to him – and absent statutory or other provision to the contrary – she has the right to believe that she is fulfilling her part of an agreement which will eventually give her Blackacre.

The analogy is imperfect for many reasons and must not be carried too far. It provides a frame of reference for us; it would have meant little in 1200. No one in 1200 thought of dower rights in terms of contract, even though there was as yet no

some right or rights, but they meant little either in theory or practice so long as her husband lived. *Glanvill* says flatly that a wife, being 'plene in potestate viri', had no right of alienation and could not protest the sale even of previously nominated dower land. He declares, in a chapter which seems to have been ignored even in the 1190s, that if she did protest, she lost the right to claim the land from the purchaser after her husband's death.[12] Otherwise, of course, she could make such a claim; *Glanvill* explains that if a husband sold his wife's dower to another and then died, 'his heir must, if he can, deliver that dower to the woman and must give to the purchaser reasonable lands in

theory that dower arose automatically from the fact of marriage by operation of law. Indeed, it would not have been possible for anyone to think of contract since a married woman could hardly have continued to be a party to a contract with her own husband; they were 'one person' for such purposes and he was the person. Moreover, the action of covenant was not and could not have been brought for dower even in the period when specific performance was a possible remedy in that action, early in the thirteenth century. (On the question of remedy in the action of covenant, see A. W. B. Simpson, *A History of the Common Law of Contract* (Oxford, 1975), pp. 13–14.) For *Glanvill*, dower was simply a gift, albeit an obligatory one (VI, 1); to us that seems self-contradiction but his definition must be accepted. Yet that provides no answer to the underlying question, for the problem remains: a gift of what? Professor Donald Sutherland has suggested to me that the answer is that dower created something analogous not to a contract right but to a 'life estate if and when'; in other words, again by analogy, that endowment resulted in something close to what would later be called a contingent future interest, although he is careful to point out that the term was never applied to dower even in the following centuries when both the concept and the law based on it developed. His reasoning has force as to *dos nominata* in particular although, again, the analogy must not be pushed too far.

[12] *Glanvill*, VI, 3. Joüon des Longrais has noted that Bracton repeats the statement at f. 95b (2: 275). He comments several times on Bracton's archaic attitudes about dower ('Statut de la femme', pp. 196, 209), but actually, in the passage cited, Bracton appears to draw a distinction between his own time and some earlier unspecified period: 'Today, if the husband aliens it, though against the wife's will, she will have it after his death . . .'. Joüon des Longrais accepts *Glanvill*'s statement as representing law for *Glanvill*'s period, despite the fact that, as he points out, the result is paradoxical: the widow will be able to attack after her husband's death only those acts of his which she did not oppose in his lifetime (p. 209). *Glanvill*'s remark is also accepted at face value by Florence Buckstaff, although she considers the result a 'very exceptional state of things' ('Married women's property', pp. 252, 259). But I have not seen a case, or discussion in the rolls about a case, for the period under consideration, in which a wife's opposition to the alienation of her dower during her husband's lifetime was made the basis of a defense to her later claim to the dower.

exchange . . .'.[13] As was true of her own inheritance or her *maritagium*, it was only on the death of her spouse that the widow could hope to treat the dower lands as hers in any meaningful sense. When her husband died, she could enter upon nominated dower lands at once if they were vacant.[14] If some nominated lands were not vacant, or if she had been appointed a 'third' and was assigned less than a third of the lands of which her husband had had seisin on their wedding day, she required a writ to her warrantor – her dead husband's heir – directing him to 'do full right without delay' to her concerning the dower land. As in any writ of right, the plea in the writ of right of dower was held initially in the court of the doweress' lord, her warrantor. From there, again as in other writs of right, it could go to the county court and then to the king's central court at Westminster or elsewhere. If an endowed woman received no dower at all on the death of her spouse – because she had been given a third of her husband's free tenements of which he had seisin on their wedding day and none had been apportioned to her after his death by the heir, or because she was kept out of all the nominated lands – she could bring the *praecipe* writ of dower *unde nihil habet*; as with all *praecipes*, the action so initiated began in the king's court.[15]

Assuming that the matter appeared there sooner or later, and this essay is concerned only with cases which did,[16] the usual procedural

---

[13] *Glanvill*, VI, 13. He does not distinguish between nominated dower and the gift of a third, but the language suggests a specific previously identified endowment. He may have been assuming it because he considered it the more common arrangement. Certainly the rule enunciated here was later the rule for nominated dower; see Bracton, ff. 93b–94 (2 : 270) and note 20 below.

[14] *Glanvill*, VI, 4. The passage is not entirely clear; *Glanvill* says she needed the heir's consent to remain in the land and he probably meant to include the initial entry under the same rubric.

[15] ibid., VI, 14. Joüon des Longrais believes the writ *unde nihil habet* to have been 'en 1184, une innovation encore assez récente' (*Saisine*, p. 363); he has restated the position in 'Statut de la femme', p. 222.

[16] It is useful to keep in mind several points which necessarily limit the scope of this essay. First, the essay deals with no cases settled in feudal or county courts. Secondly, it deals with no cases which went to borough courts or to the mayor and aldermen of London. Thirdly, and related to the first two, it deals almost exclusively with dower in land held by knight tenure. Land held in socage could carry dower of one-half; see Bracton, f. 93 (2 : 268) and P&M, 2 : 422. Land held in gavelkind also carried dower of a half; for collected authority see Thomas Robinson, *The Common Law of Kent or the Customs of Gavelkind*, new edn by J. D. Norwood (Ashford, Kent, 1858), pp. 95–6. Borough custom varied as to amount; see *Borough Customs*, vol. II, ed. Mary Bateson, Selden Society (London, 1906), vol. 21, pp. 120–9. Littleton says

delays came to the fore. A tenant or warrantor might essoin, although the rule was that the essoin of bed sickness did not lie in dower.[17] Defendants frequently delayed proceedings by asking a view.[18] Worse,

---

'By custom of some town or borough she shall have the whole' (*Tenures*, V, §37; p. 16). But tenure in gavelkind yielded dower only so long as the doweress remained unmarried and chaste; evidence of a new husband or a child born of another than the dead husband meant its loss. See Robinson, *Common Law*, pp. 96–101 (with lurid examples for the proposition). *BNB* includes a case from Trinity term, 1218, in which the *juratores* spelled out the limitations on a doweress in some detail (*BNB*, no. 9). As to socage, the same is probably true; see P&M, 2: 422. I have seen no evidence on the point for the period before 1200. By borough custom, varying conditions were imposed on the widow; some are collected at Bracton, ff. 308b–309 (3: 388–9). Only a very small proportion of these cases can have come to the king's courts; see the entry in *BNB* involving Emma, widow of Hummedew Scissor, who asked one-half messuage in Oxford. The bailiffs of Oxford appeared in court to say that no one should plead about tenements in Oxford outside it and to ask their liberty, which they got (*BNB*, no. 577). See also *CRR*, I: 138 (borough of Northampton) and *CRR*, I: 344 (Bishopric of Durham) for successful claims of jurisdiction over cases which appear to involve dower. One pipe roll entry from 7 Richard I looks as if it is invoking a local custom; it is from Yorkshire and it reads that Beatrix Fossard owes ten marks to have her reasonable dower of the land of William Fossard, her husband, which he held on the day he died.' Nor is the entry a mistake; it reappears the next year; *Pipe Roll 7 Richard I*, ed. Doris M. Stenton, Pipe Roll Society, n.s. vol. 6 (London, 1929), p. 91; *Chancellor's Roll 8 Richard I*, ed. Doris M. Stenton, Pipe Roll Society, n.s. vol. 7 (London, 1930), p. 178. In a case in Hilary term, 2 John (1201), a group of named jurors was asked of what a man could have dowered his widow 'following the law and custom of the city of Carlisle'; they said in their verdict that they did not know of what the particular widow had been endowed but that the husband could have endowed her 'de purkaciis suis secundum consuetudinem Karduil' (*CRR*, I: 388). For comparison with yet another kind of tenure, there is an interesting if brief discussion of the dower rights of the peasant's wife in Lady Doris Mary Stenton, *The English Woman in History* (London, 1957; reprint. New York, 1977), pp. 76–7, 80.

[17] *PBKJ*, I, no. 2470; *RCR*, I: 272; *Pipe Roll Society*, n.s. vol. 31, p. 112. Bracton, f. 296b (3: 357) says the rule is true for the writ of right of dower and implies that it is not for the writ *unde nihil habet*. There is a case on the point: Emma de Peria brought an action for dower against Geoffrey fitz Robert. Unfortunately, the membrane was damaged and the entry is incomplete, but it reads in part, 'non videtur curie quod langor debeat esse de Dote quando domina nichil dotis habet et do . . . per consili . . .' and ends with the land in dispute being seized into the king's hand for default, as it would have been in a suit brought by the writ of right of dower; *Three Rolls of the King's Court*, p. 29.

[18] They seem to have had an absolute right to do so; see Bracton, f. 297 (3: 359). Sometimes, when they asked a view defendants explained that they had lands in the vill in addition to the ones in dispute; see e.g. *CRR*, I: 15, 450.

they simply failed to appear at all, although that could eventually cause judgement by default; an earlier unexcused non-appearance meant that the land would be seized into the king's hand, but it could be replevied.[19] Once plaintiff and defendant – demandant and tenant in the language of the action of dower – were both in court, the widow, or her attorney if she had appointed one to stand in her place, made her claim. She would be met with an admission of it, a denial of it or the reply that the tenant was not the heir of the widow's former husband; in the last instance, the tenant would either vouch the heir to warrant his ancestor's grant or else refuse to answer until the heir was summoned to warrant the dower. If the heir warranted both, he had the obligation in the instance of nominated dower to recover the property for the widow and compensate the tenant or, if he could not do so, to make exchange to the widow by giving her other lands equal to the ones lost to her, if he had sufficient land; where dower was the unspecified third, possibly the widow had no right to specific lands and the heir was free at once simply to assign her lands of the appropriate value.[20] If the heir, when summoned, denied the widow's claim, the dispute became a matter between them just as it was when he was originally named in the writ. The issue could be settled by one of several means of proof. *Glanvill* specifies battle, but in the plea rolls I have seen only one mention of duel in an action for dower and indeed, in 1202, a court refused to allow combat in such a case: 'duellum non fit de dote'.[21] Again and again in the entries, parties ask for a *jurata* of

---

[19] *Glanvill*, I, 7. The defaulting party had two weeks to replevy the land.

[20] Bracton gives this as the rule (ff. 93b–94; 2: 270 and ff. 299b–300; 3: 364–5) but it may not have been true earlier in the century. S. F. C. Milsom has collected a number of cases dating from the period around 1200 in which the later grantee got *escambium* even when the dower claimed was the unspecified third; *The Legal Framework*, p. 43, n. 1.

[21] *Glanvill*, VI, 11. A plaintiff offered battle in a suit concerning dower in Michaelmas term, 1194. Maud, widow of Walter fitz Robert, demanded the manor of Swereford as dower of which her former husband, Henry de Oilli, had endowed her on the day they were married and of which he had been seised on that day. She produced Henry's son, who warranted the dower 'as his right and inheritance' and offered to prove it by one of several named men willing to prove the matter by their bodies. Defendants denied his right, explained why, and put themselves on the grand assize. Henry's son then offered to produce suit to prove that they saw Henry seised on the relevant day, taking esplees, and put himself on an assize. The entry ends with the notation that Maud was granted a writ for a recognition to say whether Henry de Oilli was seised on the day she married him or not. There seems to have been more than a little confusion as to what the parties thought they were litigating (*RCR*, I: 20; see also *CRR*, I: 173, 176, 376 for Maud's appointment of attorney and

the neighborhood, of the country, of lawful men, to decide the issue. They bring their *secta*, the witnesses to the endowment at the church door.[22] Occasionally, they produce charters setting out the endowment and sometimes the *testes*, the witnesses to them.[23] Even more rarely, a

---

for a day given the parties to hear the will of the king as to whether he wished there to be a grand assize. Two interim postponements are recorded, *RCR*, II: 132, 183). In 1202, Walter de Barthon asked, for himself and his wife, two bovates of land as his wife's dower from her former husband, Lambert fitz Dinant. Dinanz de Pincebech, the tenant, answered that Lambert had not been seised of the land on the day he married. Walter offered to prove by his body that the husband had been seised and had taken the esplees of the land. The court declared that the duel did not lie in dower and nonsuited Walter because he had not produced sufficient proof that Lambert had been seised (*ELAR*, no. 513). If in fact Dinanz de Pincebech was the father of the dead Lambert, he may have been significantly older than Walter de Barthon but he did not decline battle on those grounds and the court's decision goes to the nature of the claim, not the condition of the parties. Certainly the duel was not a possibility in dower actions by the time of Bracton; see f. 296b (3: 357).

[22] Demandant puts herself 'upon the good men [*probos homines*] who were there when she was therein dowered, and besides that on a jury of the country' (*ELAR*, no. 498); tenant offers proof by those present at the church door and if that is not enough he will put himself on the good men who were there, while demandant produces suit from among those there and puts herself on a jury of the country (*Abbreviatio Placitorum*, p. 21); demandant produces two witnesses who offer to prove the matter as the court orders, and tenant puts himself on an assize (*Three Rolls of the King's Court*, p. 131); demandant produces five witnesses who were at the wedding (*Pipe Roll Society*, n.s. vol. 31, p. 107); demandant has witnesses but if they are not enough she will put herself on the verdict of the neighborhood (*veredictum visneti*) (*CRR*, I: 85); demandant produces *secta* who were at her wedding and so know she was dowered and *testes* to the fact that her husband was seised on the wedding day (*RCR*, I: 359). The most remarkable use of witnesses was in the case of Richard and Eustacia de Kamville, who brought suit for Eustacia's dower against Nicholas de Verdun. Nicholas said that Eustacia, on her wedding day, had held herself content with the land she now held as dower, i.e. had accepted less than a third, and he produced suit who were at the wedding in the persons of six men; he said he could have more there on another day. Eustacia said she had not so held herself content and she produced eight men who had been present at the wedding; she also could have more on another day. The justices told them to come before the king in the Octave of Hilary with all the witnesses then present and enough others who had been at the wedding 'for the purpose of hearing the truth of the thing' (*CRR*, I: 260; also in *Staffordshire Suits*, ed. George Wrottesley, William Salt Archaeological Society, vol. III (London, 1882), p. 71. Unfortunately for finding the truth, the parties settled the dispute by a fine (*Staffordshire Suits*, p. 170).

[23] Especially in suits against a father-in-law, in cases of dower *ex assensu patris*; see *CCR*, 1: 87; *ELAR*, no. 490; *RCR*, I: 365 and *RCR*, II: 102. Plaintiffs tended to reinforce their position by bringing the charter and 'putting themselves' on the wit-

party wages his or her law on a point[24] or puts himself or herself on the rolls of the king's justices.[25]

So much is black-letter law, neatly laid out if not permanently settled. *Glanvill* was uncertain on some points, many of them to be answered long after 1200, some earlier. What is the proper way to compel the heir to come to court when he is vouched to warranty; can he be distrained by his fee?[26] Is a widow, endowed by her husband of lands held in seisin by his father but with that father's consent, entitled

---

nesses to it. Perhaps the most spectacular use made of a charter was by the Countess Gundreda, wife successively of Hugh Bigod, first Earl of Norfolk, and Roger de Glanvill, Rannulf's brother. When Robert de Crec, second husband of her second husband's heir, said he had already given her a third of the lands which were the subject of her suit for dower, she replied calmly that she had never claimed a third 'but all the land which they hold, as the charter of Roger de Glanvill testifies' (*RCR*, II: 135). For a discussion of Gundreda, the case and her other holdings and lawsuits, see S. J. Bailey, 'The Countess Gundred's lands', *Cambridge Law Journal*, 10 (1948), pp. 84–103.

[24] I have seen one such case. The defense in a long-drawn-out action for dower was that tenant had given demandant 60 marks silver for a quitclaim of the dower. She denied taking the money and the court ordered that she defend herself with 12 hands, i.e. defend the statement that she had not done so (*CRR*, I: 100). There is another entry suggesting a wager of law concerning a dower action, but it is in an essoin and is not entirely clear: John de Causton essoined against Estrilda de Itringham in a plea of dower 'and the plea is touching law waged' (*PBKJ*, II, no. 1189). It could simply be in connection with the denial of summons, where wager of law was commonly used. Other entries concerning the suit do not add further information; see *CRR*, II: 150, 262.

[25] In 1201, Margery, Countess of Warwick (Maud de Percy, widow of William, the third earl, was still living and styling herself by the same title and Waleran, William's brother and the fourth earl, was still alive) brought suit against the Bishop of Winchester for the advowson of the church at Cnoel, which she claimed as dower together with the manor there. She explained that she had already deraigned her right in the court against the bishop's predecessor and put herself on the rolls of the king's court at Westminster (*CRR*, I: 402). In Michaelmas term, 6 Richard I (1194), Lucy, widow of Robert de Cauz, exhibited a chirograph made pursuant to a court decision in 33 Henry II to substantiate her claim that she had proved her dower against her warrantor. He had later made a fine quitclaiming the land to William de Spineto: could one make a fine on a fine? Since William did not show that the decision on which the first fine was based was false, Lucy held her dower (*RCR*, I: 83 and *Abbreviatio Placitorum*, p. 4). It is the earliest case I have seen involving dower in which a party relied on a fine made in the king's court as proof.

[26] *Glanvill*, VI, 10. By the 1190s, it was common for the land to be 'taken into the king's hand' for the heir's default.

to dower if her husband predeceases his father?[27] May a widow with dower marry without the consent of her warrantor and yet retain the dower?[28] Should a widow be bound by a husband's act which has resulted in the loss or release of dower rights – often, in practice, the act of a second husband and the dower from a first?[29] *Glanvill* offers opinions, some of them not received into later law. But he sketches in the outlines of both the action and the underlying right more or less as they seem to have been in the 1190s, when the plea rolls and the fine rolls start.

Outlines deal in generalities. For *Glanvill*, there were widows, there were heirs, there were hypothetical facts with rules to settle the disagreements that might arise upon them. *Glanvill* does not claim to be

---

[27] ibid., VI, 17. It was one of the most vexed questions involving dower and was litigated frequently in the late twelfth and early thirteenth centuries; *BNB* has ten cases of dower *ex assensu patris*. It was clear by the 1190s that the courts would enforce the father-in-law's charter against him on behalf of a daughter-in-law, as in the case of Margaret, widow of Henry of Bodiham, who in two instances showed her father-in-law's charter conceding land to his son to appoint to her as dower. In one suit, the father denied that the son ever held the land or had seisin when he married, but he did not deny the wedding nor the charter and Margaret got the dower (*RCR*, I: 365). Quaere whether she would have prevailed against a third party if the father-in-law had sold the land in the interim; see *BNB*, no. 18 (1219), where a demandant lost in such a situation. In Margaret's other suit, the father-in-law pleaded that the land in question was the *maritagium* of his wife and so could not be granted by him as dower, but the charter specifically named it and Margaret prevailed (*RCR*, II: 102).

[28] *Glanvill* says she cannot (VII, 12). A tenant-in-chief's widow apparently could not; see the case of Alice de Nonant in 1186; *Pipe Roll 33 Henry II*, Pipe Roll Society, vol. 37 (London, 1915), p. 146. See Joüon des Longrais, 'Statut de la femme', pp. 233–4 for discussion of the point.

[29] *Glanvill*, XI, 3. The treatise comes to no definite conclusion. It was particularly a problem when her husband acted fraudulently. Bracton has a series of writs for the widow whose second husband alienated her dower (f. 322b–323; 4: 34). The Statute of Westminster II (1285) c. 4 attacked the problem by granting an action in those cases where the husband gave up land to an adversary by covin or default. But the feeling that the widow should not lose her dower in such situation was reflected at a much earlier date; in Easter term, 9 Richard I (1198), Eudes fitz Miles complained that Margery, widow of Robert le Poer, unjustly disseised him of custody of the person and lands of the heir of Augustine fitz Miles and that she had unjustly taken certain chattels 'about which he made a fine with Robert, her husband'. Margery (or Margaret; the entry has both names) acknowledged the fine but said she was dowered of the land by her first husband and took it as her dower after the death of her second. She put herself on the consideration of the court whether she ought to lose her dower of her first husband by reason of the gift of her second. The court decided she should hold her dower (*Pipe Roll Society*, n.s. vol. 31, p. 98; *CRR*, I: 48).

founded on case law; there is non of Bracton's familiar 'as it happened in the case of. . .''. For the writer of the treatise, issues were not clouded by difficulties of proof. Mistake, anger, dislike and affection played no role because they had no bearing on theory, but of course they had a great deal to do with practice. Dower was not claimed as an abstract right. It was not even an arm's-length business transaction. It was a family affair, and it was as much subject to mistake, anger, dislike and affection as any other intra-family arrangement. Often it had repercussions affecting not only the heir but also his siblings; sometimes it had consequences for more than one generation. It is the purpose of this essay to explore some possible consequences and so to offer an explanation for the frequency, often noted, of dower-related actions in the earliest plea rolls.[30]

In those actions, one is often watching a family quarrel; sooner or later dower litigation drew in people related, however distantly, by blood or marriage, although the relationship is not always obvious to the outsider reading the plea roll. There are actions stated to be between mother and son, both for dower withheld and for admeasurement. Sometimes pleadings show that the litigants are brother and sister-in-law; presumably the dead man and his wife had no surviving descendants and as a result his brother was his heir. I have seen no suits between a mother and a daughter acting alone; the circumstances necessary for such an action could not have arisen often, given the restrictions on women's control of land, although there are examples of a daughter's acting as her mother's warrantor.[31] The more predictable litigation is between a mother and her son-in-law acting for

---

[30] For example, see G. D. G. Hall's review of *Curia Regis Rolls of the Reign of Henry III: 9–10 Henry III* (London, 1957) in *EHR*, 74 (1959), pp. 107–10. 'The most casual reader must be struck by the number of actions of dower . . . In Michaelmas 9–10 Henry III nearly 200 entries or about 20 per cent of the business related to dower' (p. 108). *Curia Regis Rolls*, vol. I has some 150 entries definitely relating to dower; the number includes appointments of attorney and in many instances two, three and even four entries record the progress of a single action. On the other hand, some of the pleas 'about land' and involving widows probably concerned dower; see, for instance, the matter of Agnes de Sumeri, who claimed lands against Henry de Pinckney and his wife. There are six entries about it and only one specifies that the plea is 'de dote' (*CRR*, I: 232, 237, 339, 347, 355, 356).

[31] For an action to be between a mother and a daughter, both would have had to be widows who had not remarried. An unmarried girl without a father would have been in the custody of her guardian and a married woman would have been joined in the action by her husband. But a husband could not, of course, warrant for his wife.

himself and his heiress wife in respect of land he held in her right; even that is not frequent. Still more predictable is the action against the dead man's lord when the lord is also guardian of the minor heir. But the most predictable adversary is the stepson. Second marriages significantly complicated the economic and social relationships within a family and such complications understandably led to litigation. In fact, the number of actions explicitly stated to be between a stepmother and her stepson is not exceptionally high – although the relationship is specified more often than any other one, including brother-in-law/sister-in-law or father-in-law/daughter-in-law – but it becomes clear from the rolls that clerks frequently did not include the fact of relationship, particularly when they were recording essoins, appointments of attorney or other routine process.[32] The number of second (or third) wives litigating with sons of first wives is significantly greater than is obvious at first sight, judging from clues given in the pleadings. Second wives also tended to mean both stepbrothers and half-brothers and again, while the rolls frequently do not specify their status, there are cases involving men who must on the facts be so related, cases founded in dower lands held by a second wife. Obviously, twelfth-century marriage patterns accounted in part for the frequency of the action of dower.

Anglo-Saxon England had expected that the widow would not remarry immediately and had apparently accepted the possibility

---

[32] One example: Rose de la Pomeray [Pumerai] brought an action against her stepson, Henry, for dower and, at Easter term, 1199, he essoined against her as his *noverca* (*RCR*, I: 274). But when at a later time the clerk noted that he had already essoined once before, in the preceding Hilary term, the entry gives both names but mentions no relationship (*RCR*, I: 374). And Rose's remarriage soon after did not make matters clearer; in the concord between them, she is not only not identified as his stepmother, she is called 'Rose, wife of John Russell' (*Abbreviatio Placitorum*, p. 26); the jurors reported there that agreement had been reached between Henry de la Pomeray and John Russell and Rose, his wife. Claims which are specifically stated to be by or against a stepson or stepdaughter and those in which the facts clearly indicate the relationship include those in *ELAR*, nos. 238, 426; *PBKJ*, I, nos. 2669, 2853; *PBKJ*, II, nos. 463, 547; *PBKJ*, III, no. 55; *RCR*, I: 145, 274, 282, 289, 290; *RCR*, II: 100; *Feet of Fines of the Seventh and Eighth Years of the Reign of Richard I, 1196–1197*, Pipe Roll Society, vol. 20 (London, 1896), no. 167 (henceforward *Fines 7–8 Richard I*); *Feet of Fines for the County of Lincoln for the Reign of King John, 1199–1216*, ed. Margaret S. Walker, Pipe Roll Society, n.s. vol. 29 (London, 1954), no. 157 (hereafter *Lincoln Fines, John*). Other cases may well involve stepmothers, but the facts given do not reveal the relationship of the parties.

that she would not remarry at all.[33] The *Leges Henrici Primi* simply followed earlier provisions;[34] more important in showing the Norman ideal, although perhaps tempered by Anglo-Saxon thought, is the coronation charter of Henry I, which declared that a childless widow was to have her dower and that the king would not bestow her in marriage except as she wished, while the widow with children was to have her dower 'dum corpus suum legitime servaverit' and was also not to be married against her wishes.[35] But Henry did not allow his charter to prevent him from using both dower and remarriage as a source of income and rewards. The sole remaining pipe roll from his reign shows widows fining for their dower and for the right to marry or not to marry, as well as listing the fines men paid to secure marriages with them.[36]

[33] V Aethelred 21¹ and VI Aethelred 26¹ in *The Laws of the Kings of England from Edmund to Henry I*, ed. and trans. A. J. Robertson (Cambridge, 1925), pp. 85, 99; II Canute 73¹, 73a¹ §1, ibid., p. 211. See also comment by Michael Sheehan on the widow as a *miserabilis persona* and the canonists' attitude toward her remarriage ('Influence of canon law', pp. 111–12). Theoretically, they gave her the best of all possible worlds; she could remarry at will without waiting for a given period but she was not obliged to do so.

[34] *Leges Henrici Primi*, ed. with translation and commentary by L. J. Downer (Oxford, 1972), cc. 11,13–11,13b (p. 113).

[35] Coronation Charter of Henry I, c. 3 §2; c. 4 in *Laws of the Kings of England*, pp. 277–9.

[36] Fines for dower: Emma, wife of Robert fitz William, 15 marks (p. 14); Alan Lescures [de Scuris], £15 for the dower of his wife (p. 26); Agnes, wife of Geoffrey Talbot, 2 marks gold for dower and *maritagium* (p. 67); Basilia, wife of Odo de Danmartin, 60 marks (p. 94); Maud, wife of Reginald de Argentom, £8 10s 8d for dower and *maritagium* (p. 95); Hugh de Walterville, £21 13s 4d for dower of his wife (p. 96); Robert fitz Fulcher, 2 marks gold 'for the dower of his daughter' (p. 122). Fines not to marry: Wiverona, wife of Euerwacrus de Ipswich, £4 and 1 mark (p. 96); Lucy, Countess of Chester – and possibly daughter of Algar, the Saxon Earl of Mercia; see G. E. Cokayne, *The Complete Peerage*, vol. 7, rev. edn, H. A. Doubleday and Lord Howard de Walden (London, 1929), pp. 743–6 – 500 marks 'not to take a husband within five years' (p. 110). Fines 'for' a widow with her dower: William Girbert, 20 marks (p. 21); Robert de Venuiz, 16s 8d (p. 37); Mainerus [Maynard?] de Waipred, 10 marks (p. 43); William de Hocton, £200 for the wife of Edward Sar [Salisbury?] 'with her land for the use of Payn, his son' (p. 81); William Flanders, 32 marks (p. 83); Geoffrey de Tailli, 300 marks silver, 2 marks gold and four horses 'for the wife of Roger de Kamville and to have custody of Roger's land until Roger's son is 20 years old' (p. 88); Aluric son of Wihenoc, 19s (p. 136); Hervey de Veceio [Vesci?], £10 (p. 142); William fitz Richard, £52 11s 8d for the wife of Fulbert de Dover 'cum dote et maritagio suo' (p. 158). Fines 'to lead in marriage' a widow with her dower: Ralph de Pinkeni [Pincheneio], 20 marks (p. 81); Ralph fitz Geoffrey, 4 marks (p. 82); William de Hocton, 10 marks

Widows' dower and remarriage were built into the economic and political policy of Henry II and his sons. Henry's pipe rolls show that widows of tenants in chief paid both to have their dower and not to remarry.[37] Richard's methods were no less direct; witness the entry in the pipe roll for the sixth year of his reign that the sheriff had rendered account of 115 pounds 16 pence 'of the stock of the Countess of Aumale, sold in the first year of King Richard because she was unwilling to marry William de Forz', while an earlier entry, from 2 Richard I, makes clear that the said stock was part of the countess' dower from an even earlier marriage.[38] And Richard's sweep of eligible widows in

gold for the widow of Geoffrey de Fauarc 'with her land and her son in custody until he is able to be a knight and then the son to hold his land of William' (p. 94); Hamo de Saint Clare, 135 marks 'for his wife with dower and maritagium' (p. 139); *Magnum Rotulum Scaccarii vel Magnum Rotulum Pipae de Anno Tricesimo-Primo Regni Henrici Primi*, ed. Joseph Hunter (Record Commission, 1833) (henceforward *Pipe Roll 31 Henry I*).

[37] Entries became more frequent as the reign progressed. For example, I have not found any fines stated to be for remaining unmarried in the pipe rolls for either 13 or 14 Henry II; *Pipe Roll 13 Henry II*, Pipe Roll Society, vol. 11 (London, 1889); *Pipe Roll 14 Henry II*, Pipe Roll Society, vol. 12 (London, 1890). Dower-related fines are not always clear. There is one entry in 14 Henry II 'pro habenda dote sua' (p. 29), but other entries may bear on dower; see p. 38, where a widow gives 20 marks for right of a house and land; and p. 118, where a woman gives 40 shillings for right of land 'quod nundum habuit'. By contrast, the roll for 31 Henry II has four entries stated to be 'pro habenda saisina de dote sua' or similar wording, four 'ne capiat virum contra voluntatem suam' or words of like import, and two for a widow with her dower; *Pipe Roll 31 Henry II*, Pipe Roll Society, vol. 34 (London, 1913), pp. 15, 65, 76, 84, 111, 115, 145, 175. There are also payments which appear to be for writs or other intervention in dower litigation, e.g. 'three marks for a recognition about the dower of his wife against Reginald de Roudecliva' (p. 187); 'to have her reasonable part of the land and chattels of Ralph, her husband, against John fitz Martin and John nephew of Ralph and Luke his brother' (p. 212). The Assize of Northampton (1176) c. 4 provides that a freeholder's wife shall have her dower but it does not specify the terms; *Select Charters*, ed. William Stubbs, 9th ed. rev. by H. W. C. Davis (Oxford, 1962), pp. 179–80.

[38] *Pipe Roll 6 Richard I*, ed. Doris M. Stenton, Pipe Roll Society, n.s. vol. 5 (London, 1928), pp. xxxiv, 163. The entry identifying the stock as dower is in *Pipe Roll 2 Richard I*, ed. Doris M. Stenton, Pipe Roll Society, n.s. vol. 1 (London, 1925), p. 2: 'Et de iiii li et viii s et ii d de instauramento terre de Cunton et de Stralega dote comitisse de Albem' vendito'. Lady Stenton, in her introduction to the edition of the pipe roll for 6 Richard I commented, 'By such methods was that marriage made' and on the 'crying need' for Magna Carta c. 8 (*Pipe Roll 6 Richard I*, p. xxxiv). She chronicles the career of the countess more fully in *The English Woman in History*, pp. 35–6. The number of fines not to marry or to marry as one chose fluctuated

the last year of his reign appears to have been little less than an act of extortion.[39] John's habits regarding the forced remarriage of widows are too well known to require much comment, although in this as in other instances he seems in part to have reaped the whirlwind sowed by his father and brother.[40] The fact is that Magna Carta (1215) c. 7 and c. 8 were a much-needed corrective to the behavior of all three Angevin kings.[41]

during the reign of Richard I. In the roll for 6 Richard I there are four for widows (pp. 64, 142, 147, 238); the roll for 7 Richard I has eight, not all new (pp. 5, 72(2), 82, 179, 190, 234, 240). The number falls back to four, again not all new, in the roll for 9 Richard I; *Pipe Roll 9 Richard I*, ed. Doris M. Stenton, Pipe Roll Society, n.s. vol. 8 (London, 1931), pp. 10, 43, 82, 124.

[39] The Pipe Roll for 10 Richard I has no fewer than 39 entries, all but a few of them new, showing fines paid by women not to marry or to marry as they chose. Several women added that they had 'vowed chastity' (pp. 93, 210); Richard's net caught up everyone; *Pipe Roll 10 Richard I*, ed. Doris M. Stenton, Pipe Roll Society n.s. vol. 9 (London, 1932), pp. 7, 16, 42, 43, 72, 76, 93, 94, 107, 111, 118, 125, 138, 146, 147, 155, 159, 160, 164, 165, 195, 210, 213, 222. Fines ranged from Sybil de Bolebec's 1 mark (p. 146) to 100 pounds for the Countess Gundreda (p. 94); of the others, several were for 100 marks.

[40] One example: at Michaelmas, 10 Richard I (1198), Maud, Countess of Warwick owed £276 5s 4d of her fine for the land of her father, i.e. her inheritance; the right to her dower; and the right not to remarry if she did not so choose (*Pipe Roll 10 Richard I*, p. 28). Her husband had died in 1184 and the first notice of her fine, for 700 marks, appears in the roll for 31 Henry II (*Pipe Roll 31 Henry II*, p. 76); she had not yet paid the entire fine when she died in 1204. *Early Yorkshire Charters*, vol. XI, ed. Sir Charles Travis Clay, Yorkshire Archaeological Society Record Series, Extra Series vol. IX (Wakefield, 1963), gives some idea of the extent of her inheritance and dower, esp. pp. 4–5, 48, 49, 85–8. J. C. Holt sees some of the proffers concerned with remarriage of widows as a step forward: 'One of the first great stages in the emancipation of women is to be traced in the emergence of the proffer that they should not be distrained to marry for a second time without their consent'; J. C. Holt, *Magna Carta* (Cambridge, 1965), p. 46. The implication is that the king's willingness to entertain such offers indicated recognition of a kind of independence on the part of the widow. Holt also points out that acceptance of proffers not to remarry or to remarry at the widow's will actually represented a threat to royal power in that John's acceptance of such offers was 'to admit the justice of the claims of widows' and so to encourage the barons' demand for justice in other areas (*Magna Carta*, pp. 114–15). Whether it was a step forward in the emancipation of women would seem to depend at least in part on the size of the fine! Lady Stenton has suggested that Magna Carta c. 8 was 'a tentative beginning of the emancipation of English women from the legal subservience which had followed the Norman conquest' (*The English Woman in History*, p. 51).

[41] Magna Carta (1215) c. 7 reads in part, 'A widow after the death of her husband shall at once and without difficulty have her marriage portion and inheritance, nor

But the attitude underlying their behavior was probably shared by most male members of the English nobility in 1200: a woman in control of her own land was an anomaly in a system based on military tenure.[42] Two entries in the pipe roll for 2 John indicate that at least one great magnate followed the same practice of marrying off his tenants' widows. In one entry Maud, widow of Roger de Sumervill, fined that she not be distrained to marry since she held nothing of the king nor of the Earl of Chester, who gave her to William de Chaucumb; in the other, Nicole, widow of Robert de Burun, gave two marks for seisin of land of which she had been disseised 'because the Earl of Chester married her to another without the assent of the king, although she was in the king's gift.'[43] Magna Carta c. 8 is worded to curtail the

---

shall she give anything for her dower, nor for her marriage portion, nor for [her] inheritance. . .'. Magna Carta c. 8, not amended in later reissuances of the Charter, provides that a widow shall not be compelled to remarry so long as she prefers to remain without a husband, but that she shall give security not to marry without the consent of the king if she is the widow of a tenant-in-chief or of her immediate lord otherwise. For discussion of the provisions in detail, see William Sharp McKechnie, *Magna Carta* (Glasgow, 1905), pp. 253–61. Evidence that before 1215 dower was sometimes a widow's single bargaining tool - and of the difficult position of even a woman of means when her husband died – is afforded by a plea roll entry of 1200. Maud de Bussy, co-heir of her brother, Walter, and widow of Hugh Wake of Bentham, Berkshire, came into court to concede her dower to Hugh de Nevill, 'so long as he shall have custody of her son and heir'; Hugh, in turn, was to pay 40 marks of the 80 which Maud had offered King John 'pro pace habenda de se maritanda'. That seems reasonable, but there is the further provision that 'when the heir comes of age, he will recover that dower as his inheritance so that the said Maud has nothing to recover' (*CRR*, I: 265). In fact, the heir apparently never came of age; Maud was succeeded by her daughter; I. J. Sanders, *English Baronies* (Oxford, 1960), p. 133.

[42] Attitudes based on the demands of military tenure filtered down to affect land not so held. For an example of a great lord's activities in the matter of remarriage of widows among his tenants, who held in villein tenure, see Lady Stenton, *The English Woman in History*, pp. 83–4.

[43] *Pipe Roll 2 John*, ed. Doris M. Stenton, Pipe Roll Society, n.s. vol. 12 (London, 1934), pp. 19, 185. The earl married her to Anketinus de Brikeward; earlier in the same year Nicole had offered 2 marks silver for an inquisition to determine whether she held land of the king in chief and was, therefore, in his gift when the earl had married her off, and whether she had been disseised of named land by reason of the marriage. The sheriff of Derbyshire was ordered to inquire into the matter and inform the king; *Rotuli de Oblatis et Finibus in Turri Londinensi Asservati Tempore Regis Johannis*, ed. Thomas Duffus Hardy (Record Commission, 1835), p. 47 (henceforward *Rotuli de Oblatis*). The answer must have been that she held of the king and was in his gift. Robert de Burun, who appears several times in the plea rolls, is a

barons' use of compulsion as well as the king's; before 1215, it was a general principle, not an attitude unique to the monarchy, that, as J. H. Round noted, 'a dowered widow was rarely allowed to remain unmarried.'[44]

That principle needs no further comment here. It is mentioned because, royal assumptions and accepted practice notwithstanding, second marriages must have had painful emotional and economic repercussions. The difficulties of the personal relationship can only be guessed at, but there is enough evidence of the economic bases for resentment. The son by the first wife could not think generously of his dead father's second wife who had since remarried; she and her new husband were, after all, two strangers enjoying property which should be enriching his own family. The second wife's son – a stepbrother or even a half-brother to the heir – was less an object of affection than someone else to be provided for at best and, at worst, a possible usurper of the inheritance. The son of a later husband was a particular threat and doweresses, especially before Magna Carta, did not necessarily stop with two husbands. Round has also pointed out that widows 'in favorable circumstances' tended to live longer than the general population and that a widow's successive spouses gave her 'the chance of accumulating fresh dower in the course of her career';[45] that, in turn, heightened the possibility of her bringing several of her families into court.

But stepsons were not unique in their attitude and second marriages were not the only underlying cause of conflict. Economic repercussions were more widely felt; dower, after all, always meant less for the warrantor, whatever his relationship to the widow. Against that loss there were generally no compensating benefits. A brother-in-law, himself married and with children to provide for, had no ties of

---

somewhat mysterious figure; he may have been the son and heir of Roger de Burun, lord of Horsley, Derbyshire, but in some way he lost the Burun barony; see Sanders, *English Baronies*, p. 123, n. 1. If he had held it, he would have been a tenant-in-chief and his widow would certainly have been in the king's gift. The land of which she was disseised was probably her dower; it was four virgates in Offerton and four in 'Eston'. The Earl of Chester may have been Robert de Burun's lord for yet another holding.

[44] *Rotuli de Dominabus et Pueris et Puellis de XII Comitatibus*, ed. John Horace Round, Pipe Roll Society, vol. 35 (London, 1913), p. xxxviii (henceforward *Rotuli de Dominabus*). The collected *Rotuli* are the record of sworn returns made to the justices in eyre in 1185.

[45] ibid., pp. xxxvii, xxxviii.

affection prompting him to encumber even an unexpected inheritance on behalf of a dead older brother's wife. The guardian of the infant heir and his lands saw the value of the wardship diminished by dower lands carved out of the inheritance for a period extending in most cases well beyond the heir's minority. The father-in-law, having already lost his eldest son, perhaps without gaining a grandchild, now watched an important part of his lands fall into the hands of a young woman, possibly herself still a child, whom he perceived as a stranger; and he realized that a daughter's or a second son's chances for a good marriage had been correspondingly lessened. Only when her husband's heir happened to be her own fully grown son could the widow hope for good will on the part of her warrantor, and even then she might find herself facing a suit for admeasurement.

A doweress could mean lands outside family control for as much as 70 years. The sworn inquiry of 1185 designed in part to inform the king of the value of widows in his gift reports on Maud de Bidun. Maud, the daughter of Thomas fitz Bernard and Eugenia Picot, was married to John de Bidun, the minor heir of his father (lord of Lavendon, Buckinghamshire) at an age young enough that she was widowed at the age of ten. She survived into her eighties and, remarried, held her dower throughout her life.[46] The list of widows in the 1185 inquest holds none to match Maud, but even if the ages given there are only inexact estimates, what must it have meant to a family that 'the

---

[46] ibid., pp. xxxvii, 55, 87. The age to which a husband must survive before his wife could claim dower, and the age to which his wife must attain before his death to claim dower, seem to have been questions of interest to the thirteenth and later centuries. *Glanvill* says nothing on the subject. Bracton says at one place that a male, although a minor, may endow a wife 'though she is under age, provided that she may merit dower and is mature enough to take a husband' (f. 92; 2: 265); and at another, where he is treating exceptions to dower, that one exception is that the wife was of such tender age that she could not receive a husband (f. 302; 3: 372). Fleta chooses the age of nine and a half (*Liber Quintus*, c. 23) 'ita fieri poterit cuilibet foeminae cujuscunque fuerit aetatis ultra aetatem 9 annorum et dimidii ... nec obstabit mulieri petenti minor aetas viri'; *Fleta* (London, 1685), p. 340. Britton thought the husband had to have been of an age to consent to the marriage; *Britton*, ed. Francis Morgan Nicholas (Washington, DC, 1901), V, X, 5 (p. 553), but that does not seem to have been the rule. Littleton queried, in cases of endowment at the church door and *ex assensu patris*, whether the wife should have dower if she were not nine when her husband died and declared that in other cases she could not; *Tenures*, Book I, V, §§36, 42 (pp. 16, 18). Cases are collected in Fitzherbert, *La Graunde Abridgement* (London, 1577) under dower (ff. 257–66).

mother of Ralph de Humestain ... is more than 70 years old. She has two bovates of land in dower, which return her annually one-half mark.' or 'Alice de Essex ... is 80 years old and holds Clavering ... with 40 pounds with these beasts ...' or 'Margaret de Tony is 60 years old', with other records showing that she had held her dower, worth 24 pounds a year, since at least 1164.[47] And what could a family look forward to when the widow was 29, like the widow of Earl Hugh of Chester (d. 1181), or 24, like the widow of Simon de Crevequor, or 20, like Alice, widow of Thomas de Beaufoe [de Bello Fago], who had one and a half knights' fees held of her by two men 'whose service was given in dower' to her.[48]

The immediate concern of a family with one vested doweress must have been that they would acquire another. Few families could afford two women, each claiming a third of the property of which her husband had been seised on the day of marriage or even a nominated dower. In 1185, it was reported that one heiress, aged ten, held one-half hide of land of the king in serjeanty; it was worth 12 shillings unstocked and 19 with stock, but she had only one virgate in demesne because her mother 'and a certain other lady' (probably a grandmother) held the rest in dower.[49] The case of Herbert de Bolebec can be followed to its relatively happy ending. In 1185, Herbert was 18 and in custody of William de Jarpenville. He held land worth ten pounds and more, but 'in the land there are two ladies in the king's gift, one 70 and one 40, and they have two parts of the said vill. William had the third part with the boy in wardship.'[50] William de Jarpenville, who held a hereditary office, did not profit mightily from his wardship. But in 1190, he married a daughter to Herbert.[51] His faith was justified; some seven years after that Richeut, either Herbert's mother or his grandmother, released her dower to him for 16 shillings rent and four acres of meadow, although she retained a tenant and

---

[47] *Rotuli de Dominabus*, pp. 16, 76, 77.

[48] ibid., pp. 15, 18, 25.

[49] ibid., p. 43.

[50] ibid. It is probably one of these two ladies who paid a mark to the king for leave not to remarry, in 1198; see note 39 above.

[51] The license to do so is in *Pipe Roll 2 Richard I*, p. 145. William was master of the hawks in right of his wife, as was his other son-in-law, Thomas fitz Bernard, according to an entry in *Pipe Roll 6 Richard I*, p. 250: Albreda, William's widow, offered 200 marks 'ut Tomas f. Bernardi ... habeat marescalciam avium domini R quam idem Willelmus habuit. . .'.

certain income.[52] Even if the other lady mentioned in the 1185 inquiry still held hers, Herbert had at least two-thirds of his inheritance in demesne by the time he was 30 years old.

The effect was severe when the women were of different generations, but it was even worse when they were not. The death of two married brothers in rapid succession could cripple a family for more than a generation, perhaps permanently. Witness the Pinels of Wycombe, Buckinghamshire. Roger Pinel died in 1180, leaving a widow aged 20 and no child. His brother and heir, David, died four years later leaving a widow aged 17 and two very young children, a boy and a girl. In 1185, it was reported, the Pinel holdings were one-half hide worth 30 shillings a year stocked, together with a virgate held for one *hospitium* a year, an acre held for two shillings a year, and half an acre held for 12 pence and worth two shillings a year. Roger's widow held one-third hide as her dower; David's widow, Basilia, had custody of the children and held the other two-thirds. After the death of David Pinel, the two widows and the children lived 'vix de exitibus terre' on a total of something exceeding 34 shillings a year income. There was nothing left over for the crown.[53] When the unnamed boy came of age, he would have had an aunt in her early forties and a mother in her mid-thirties, each likely to be unmarried because of the unattractiveness of her financial position, between them entitled to a majority of the half hide for life. Unless one or both renounced her dower, he would start his adult life holding in demesne land from which he drew income of less than 15 shillings a year, and with little prospect of any alteration of the situation in the immediate future.

Yet all these examples are the result of an uncomplicated although perhaps ill-affordable transfer to a doweress of lands unencumbered by other claims. As warrantor of his ancestor's grant, the heir might in fact find himself faced with conflicting rights and thus with the necessity of making undesirable exchanges with either grantee or doweress. The classic example is the case, or the cases, of Alice, widow of Ralph fitz Hugh, who has attracted attention simply by the volume of her litigation. In Trinity term, 2 John (1199), she very effectively sued twelve men, her son and the grantees of her former husband. Her son, the heir, had to warrant both her dower and his father's grant in

---

[52] The fine is printed in *Fines 7–8 Richard I*, no. 135 and in *Fines sive Pedes Finium*, ed. Joseph Hunter (2 vols, Record Commission, 1835, 1844), I, p. 156, where the lady's name is spelled 'Richent'.

[53] *Rotuli de Dominabus*, p. 37.

six cases, although he protested in one of them that too little of the land remained for him to do the king's service from it. His mother got her dower, the land she was asking, and the son somehow found exchanges for at least five men.[54] In 1195, when Margery de Appleby asked dower of Nicholas de North and they came to an agreement, the fine recited the land, messuages and tofts, houses and crops she would receive. But the men who held the land and their chattels were to remain with Nicholas, and he agreed to remove them from it. Five men and their possessions were uprooted and were found new housing and lands elsewhere.[55] Fines more often recited that one party would receive land after the death of a doweress, frequently with the provision that for so long as she lived the grantee would receive an annual sum, presumably equivalent to the income from the holding. In such cases, then, the effect of dower was to postpone the final settlement of competing claims to the land or the division of the land of co-heiresses.[56] Even when the doweress died the settlement was not immediate because her land did not automatically return to the heir. The pipe rolls and oblate rolls contain enough entries to make clear that late-twelfth

---

[54] *RCR*, I: 406–9. For comment on the heir's obligation, see Milsom, *The Legal Framework*, pp. 126–7.

[55] *Fines Henry II and Richard I*, no. 88.

[56] See e.g. *CRR*, I: 79, 183; *PBKJ*, II, nos. 467, 969; *Feet of Fines for the County of Norfolk for the Reign of King John 1201–1215 and for the County of Suffolk for the Reign of King John 1199–1214*, ed. Barbara Dodwell, Pipe Roll Society, n.s. vol. 32 (London, 1958), no. 330 (henceforward *Norfolk–Suffolk Fines*); *Feet of Fines of the Ninth Year of King Richard I 1197–1198*, Pipe Roll Society, vol. 23 (London, 1898), no. 123 (henceforward *Fines 9 Richard I*); *Fines Henry II and Richard I*, no. 184 (provision for division of holdings as doweresses die). The fine in *Fines 9 Richard I* involved Jollan de Amundeville, who here agreed to give one Elias de Aringes 40 shillings a year. Jollan's father had given Elias' father land which Agnes de Amundeville, Jollan's aunt, later proved to be her dower and Agnes was still holding it. Agnes stayed put and Jollan made the exchange. The Amundeville family history is somewhat complex, in part due to Agnes' childless marriage to William de Amundeville and her second marriage to Theobald Hautein. The dower from that first marriage was at the root of litigation long after Agnes' death; see the fine made in 1214 between Margery Hautein and her son (*Lincoln Fines, John*, no. 341). A good example of dower postponing final division of land to co-heiresses can be found in *Early Yorkshire Charters*, XI: 85-9. When William Percy II died before Easter, 1175, leaving two daughters, his lands were apportioned between their husbands. But Percy's second wife and widow, Sybil de Valoignes, had extensive dower holdings in them and as a result a number of interim arrangements, intended to last for her lifetime, were made for Jocelin de Louvain, one of the sons-in-law. In fact she outlived him; she and Agnes de Percy, William's daughter and Jocelin's widow, can be seen acting together to recover both their interests in an advowson in 1198 (*ibid.*, p. 75).

century tenants-in-chief, at least, paid well to get it back; fines ranged
from 5 marks to 60 pounds.[57] Moreover, one might have to prove to
the king that the land had indeed been held as dower.[58]

All the above assumes some certainty about the size and terms of the
doweress' holdings. But the longevity of widows and the consequent
duration of dower arrangements could easily obscure the original
nature of such arrangements. Endowment, after all, needed no writing
to be valid. When it was made at the church door only the men who
had stood around that door might remember the relevant facts years
later. When arrangements had existed for a generation and more, the
precise events became more murky in men's memories as time passed;
eventually even a recognition might not afford an accurate answer.
And, as a result, land might be lost permanently to a family. A commonly litigated question was whether land held by an ancestress had
been held in dower or in a descendible estate, usually *maritagium*. But
sometimes the questions were so involved and the decisive events so
far in the past that plaintiffs and defendants alike must have despaired
of finding the truth. One instance which can be followed to its end
involved William de Solvesdon who at Easter term, 1200, brought an
action asking one and a half knights' fees in Beaufield from William
de Badelesmer 'sicut ius suum et hereditatem', of which Wielard, his
great-uncle, had been seised as of right and fee in the time of King
Henry I. Wielard, William alleged, had married one Denise, to whom
he gave the land in dower and who held it after his death. Denise
remarried and had a son, Thomas, whose son in turn was the defendant. William de Solvesdon alleged that William de Badelesmer had
had entry into the land through his father, who in turn had had entry
through his mother, who had had the land in dower. William de
Badelesmer replied that Denise had held the land not in dower but in

---

[57] See e.g. *Pipe Roll 31 Henry I*, pp. 25, 38, 65, 156; *Pipe Roll 31 Henry II*, pp. 127,
232. The debts appear in succeeding rolls throughout much of the reign of Richard I.
Other entries in the rolls cited may have been similar payments or may have been
for the king's intervention in a disputed claim; the intent of the offer is not always
clear.

[58] In 1201, Robert fitz Adam offered the king 10 marks to have full seisin of all
the land in which seisin had been given to his mother, Maud, by order of the king
that she have her dower. But the king wished to be certified by those who were
present at Maud's marriage that she was so endowed at the church door (*Rotuli de
Oblatis*, p. 120). Robert must have found the witnesses, because in the next year he
paid the 10 marks for seisin of the land and was quit; *Rotulus Cancellarii vel Anti-
graphum Magni Rotuli Pipae Tertio Anno Regni Regis Johannis*, ed. Joseph Hunter
(Record Commission, 1833), p. 69 (henceforward *Chancellor's Roll 3 John*).

maritagium and he traced an equally complex history of its descent, ending with the allegation that a fine settling the question had been entered into between William de Solvesdon's grandfather and Denise and her son 'in the court of St Augustine' (Canterbury), whereby Beaufield went to Denise and Thomas. Apparently no fine was produced and William de Solvesdon denied its making; the entry ends with the direction that an inquiry be made by lawful men to find out whether Denise held the land in *maritagium* or in dower.[59] In Michaelmas term, 1200, a jury came to answer the question and both men restated their positions. William de Badelesmer said as well that William de Solvesdon had drawn him into a plea by writ of intrusion which had not been terminated (the inquiry ordered at Easter had been scheduled for Trinity term, but in the Octave of Trinity William de Badelesmer essoined and the Michaelmas date was given; the 'writ of intrusion' must refer to an even earlier proceeding) and asked consideration whether the jury should proceed. There was a postponement to hear judgement before the king wherever he might be in England, and it was decided that the recognition should be taken. The jurors declared that the land was the *maritagium* of Denise; William de Badelesmer was to hold in peace and William de Solvesdon to take nothing.[60] Was the decision correct? Henry I had died on 1 December 1135, almost precisely 65 years before the recognition took place, and Wielard had held the land, whether in right of his wife or otherwise, during that reign. Moreover, sometime after that Denise and her son may have been unsure enough of their claim to have made a fine with Wielard's brother. But there was a final answer. The land did not belong in the family of William de Solvesdon, wherever it had once come from.

Admittedly, most questions turning on the nature of a woman's holding did not wait so long for resolution. Antagonists were, more typically, stepbrothers: Arthur marries Cecily and Bernard is born. Cecily dies and Arthur marries Denise. Arthur dies and Denise marries again and has a son, Edward, who after Denise's death wishes to

---

[59] *RCR*, II: 237. William de Solvesdon's offer, at Michaelmas, 1200, of 20 marks 'pro habenda inquisitione' is at *Pipe Roll 2 John*, p. 215. He also asked that if the inquisition said the land was dower he be awarded full seisin of it.

[60] The record that a day was given them to hear judgement whether the assize should take place before the lord king wherever he might be in England is at *CRR*, I: 281. The record of the assize is at *CRR*, I: 254. William de Badelesmer's essoin is at *RCR*, I: 241. A similar suit, apparently between the grandson of a first wife and the son of a second, appears at *RCR*, I: 317.

inherit her land as her son and heir. But Bernard is poised to enter the land as the heir of his father, Arthur, who, he says, granted it to Denise in dower. A variation is that after Cecily dies, Arthur marries Denise, who has previously been married and who already has a son, Edward. Arthur dies and Denise holds certain lands after his death. She dies and Edward wishes to inherit, opposing Bernard's claim. In a textbook illustration dating from 1200, William de Brisewurd gave the king two marks for an inquiry whether Gunnora de Gillingham had had other entry into 30 acres of land at Gillingham except as dower of her first husband, whose heir William claimed to be. The land was then held by Robert de Gillingham, son and heir of Gunnora and her second husband, 'in which he had no entry, as the said William says, except that the same Gunnora had them [the acres] in dower.'[61] The inquiry was duly held in Hilary term, 2 John (1201), but was put into respite until Easter term because none of the recognitors came. In the interim, a view was to be made. There was a further adjournment for the same reason at Easter term, and the case disappears from the records at that point.[62]

Sons of other marriages were not the only possible claimants. Second husbands, too, posed a threat to heirs. The pipe roll for 3 Richard I includes a note that Robert de Buxstead owed 15 marks of an amercement 'because he intruded himself into the land at Otrepol' after the death of his wife who held it in dower and was unwilling to leave for the serjeant of the sheriff.'[63] He was one of many. Walter de Baskervill was implying that land had been his wife's *maritagium* or inheritance when he offered the king 50 marks 'to have seisin of the land of Emma, his wife . . . and that he not be disseised except by judgement.'' The money was not accepted; the king had already returned the land to Geoffrey de Longchamp, Emma's son by her first husband, as the inheritance for which he, Geoffrey, had been prudent enough hastily to offer a fine.[64] The only explanation is that the land was Emma's dower. Both Ascelina de Waterville and William Pichard brought suits against Richard de Lecton in Easter term, 1198. William's was

---

[61] *Rotuli de Oblatis*, p. 91. William's debt for the inquiry is at *Pipe Roll 2 John*, p. 148.

[62] *CCR*, I: 404, 466.

[63] *Pipe Roll 3 and 4 Richard I*, ed. Doris M. Stenton, Pipe Roll Society, n.s. vol. 2 (London, 1926), p. 145. The entry appears in the rolls for 4, 5 and 6 Richard I, apparently until Robert's death; the roll for 7 Richard I notes that the amount is to be asked of Robert's son-in-law (*Pipe Roll 7 Richard I*, p. 3).

[64] *Pipe Roll 7 Richard I*, p. 181.

simply for land which Richard had held on the day his wife, Agnes, died; Richard acknowledged that the land was the right and inheritance of William and quitclaimed to him all right and claim in it. In return, William agreed that Richard could keep all the chattels he had taken from the land up to the day of the agreement, with certain exceptions.[65] Ascelina's suit, more involved, makes the nature of the claim clearer. She asked the land at La More which belonged to Hamo Pichard of which, she alleged, she ought to have had custody together with the custody she had of the heir to the land. Richard, then holding the land, had had no entry into it except through Agnes, his wife, who had held it in dower of her first husband, Hamo. Richard essoined, but eventually they reached agreement: Richard would return to Hamo's heir all the land claimed and Ascelina and the heir quitclaimed to him 'omnia dampna et omnes prisas quas fecerat in terra illa.'[66]

Deliberately or otherwise, a doweress could by her own act make it difficult for an heir to assert his claim. Since she held a life estate, she could alienate it for the term of her own life by lease or by pledge. If she did no more than that, she was not acting improperly and in fact a widow sometimes acted with the knowledge and consent of her warrantor.[67] But the result could still be questions answerable only in a lawsuit, particularly when uncertainties about the nature of a transaction arose later, after the doweress' death. In Hilary term, 1 John (1200), Richard de Garwinton asked land of Theobald de Tuitham as his right and inheritance of which his great-grandfather had been seised on the day Henry I died, 65 years earlier. He alleged that Theobald had had no entry into the land except through one

[65] *Fines 9 Richard I*, no. 176.

[66] *Pipe Roll Society*, n.s. vol. 31, p. 102.

[67] The Statute of Gloucester (1278) c. 7 reads that 'if a woman sell or give in fee or for term of life the land that she holdeth in dower, ... the heir ... shall have present recovery to demand the land by a writ of entry made thereof in the Chancery.' At first reading, it would seem to prevent the doweress from granting an estate for her own life but that does not seem to have been the intent; Fitzherbert, in the *Nouvelle Natura Brevium* (London, 1581), says specifically that a writ of entry at common law will lie where a tenant in dower aliens 'en fee, ou a terme dauter vie, ou en taile ...' (f. 207b). And the statute of 11 Henry VII (1495) c. 20, which makes certain alienations of dower by a widow void, ends 'Provided ... that it shall be lawful to every such woman ... after the death of her first husband, to give, sell or make discontinuance of any such land for term of her own life only, after the course and use of the common law before the making of the present Act'; there follows a reference to the Statute of Gloucester.

Hawise, the second wife of his own great-grandfather, who had pledged the land to Theobald's father for a term.[68] Theobald answered that the land was his in gavelkind and that he had held it for more than 60 years; he was unwilling to respond to Richard's claim unless the court so ordered. The matter became somewhat confused and ended with Richard's offering a mark for a jury to say whether his great-grandfather had pledged the land to Theobald's father after the death of Hawise! He apparently changed his theory (unless the report is confused) but the *jurata* was granted without comment. When the jurors came, in Trinity term, 2 John (1200), they declared that the land was Theobald's inheritance; he was to hold in peace.[69]

Widows, like others, could use the fine as a means of effective conveyance. In October 1200, Helewise de Curzon [Curcun] made a fine with Henry Chamberlain [Camerarius] about one-third hide of land in Culundon which she claimed as dower. Henry recognized the land as her dower and Helewise granted it to him from the Sunday after the feast of St Luke the Evangelist (October 18) for 14 years for the service of 3 shillings a year. If she survived, the land was then to return to her to be held as her dower. The fine does not include a statement as to what was to happen if Helewise died during the term, but by acknowledging the land to be her dower, Henry was in fact acknowledging that his rights under the agreement would end with her death.[70] When the interest was intended to outlive the doweress, the prudent thing was, of course, to get both doweress and heir as parties to any conveyance. There are fines showing that it was done. In 1202 Elena, the widow of Geoffrey de Papurth, and her daughter and heir, Agnes, agreed with Peter del Homme that he and his heirs would hold one-half virgate from Elena for her life, since it was her dower, and then from Agnes, for the service of 3 shillings a year and forinsec service. In addition, Agnes got two marks.[71]

[68] The 'term' for which Hawise was alleged to have pledged the land was probably her own life; there is no suggestion that she was acting in bad faith.

[69] *CRR*, I: 158, 220. Earlier procedural problems faced by Richard are noted in *RCR*, I: 306 and *RCR*, II: 46.

[70] Hunter, *Fines*, I: 196.

[71] ibid., p. 48. Elena had sued for the land as her dower; Peter asked for a view before they compromised (*CRR*, II: 51). See also *Feet of Fines for the County of Norfolk for the Tenth Year of the Reign of King Richard the First 1198–1199 and for the First Four Years of the Reign of King John 1198–1202*, ed. Barbara Dodwell, Pipe Roll Society, n.s. vol. 27 (London, 1952), no. 441 (henceforward *Norfolk Fines, Richard I and John*): three men, who may have been grantees of the doweress' husband, reach an agreement with her and her son whereby they will hold land from her for her life and then from her son and his heirs for the same service.

But either a doweress' careless handling of the heir's rights or an unscrupulous lessee could mean disaster. The most extreme case I have seen is set out at length by C. A. F. Meekings in his 'Notes on the de Abernon family before 1236'.[72] Sometime in the twelfth century, Roger de Clere, who died about 1183, married and endowed his wife, Hawise de Gurnay, with the manor of Lasham in Hampshire. Hawise, after his death, 'conveyed this estate to Ingram de Abernon'. The conveyance was the source of litigation which lasted for seven years: what estate did Hawise grant Ingram? Litigation began in 1200, with an action brought by Hubert Walter as guardian of Roger de Clere's nephew (Roger had died childless) against the de Abernons. He argued that the lease had been for the term of Hawise's life, by charter which he produced. There would seem to have been no defense, for there was no argument that Hawise had held the land other than as dower or that the charter was fraudulent. But the surviving de Abernon brothers pleaded that Ingram, then dead, had granted them each one-third of Lasham to hold in fee of him and they produced charters to that effect. After an incredible series of adjournments, essoins and failures by the brothers to produce their warrantor, the dispute disappears from the records until 1205, when the Clere heir came of age. Then, in a series of moves breathtaking in their audacity, two de Abernon brothers brought, respectively, a writ of entry and a mort d'ancestor against Ralph de Clere – the action of 1200 must therefore have ended eventually with his being put into possession of the land – and there were two more years of litigation before a cirograph was taken in May 1207. By it, Ralph de Clere and Walter de Abernon partitioned Lasham. The case must have sent shudders down the spine of every heir in England with dower land outstanding. It also helps explain some otherwise inexplicable settlements found in the plea and fine rolls: a tenant having more gall than right might convince the heir to take half a loaf lest all be lost.[73]

Hawise's alienation was in good faith, if her charter is to be believed. Doweresses did not always act in good faith any more than any other group of tenants did. The problem of the widow who wrongfully alienated more than her interest in land was perhaps as serious as the

[72] C. A. F. Meekings, *Studies in Thirteenth-Century Justice and Administration* (London, 1982), XV, pp. 159–60, 162.

[73] See e.g. *Norfolk Fines, Richard I and John*, no. 432 (dead father's daughters compromise with sons of their stepmother on future tenancy of land which she is holding in dower).

problem of the husband who attempted to terminate the doweress' interest. While *Glanvill* says nothing of it, Bracton gives a whole series of writs for use in both situations.[74] That the problem was seen as serious in the thirteenth century is attested by provisions in both the Statute of Gloucester (1278) and the Statute of Westminster II (1285) dealing with it; the provisions made for protection of the doweress were in effect turned on end to protect the heir.[75] But in the last decade of the twelfth century, such abuse does not yet seem to have become significant, although the conclusion can be only tentative since the evidence for it is the silence of the plea rolls on the point. There is one exception, the matter of Osbert and Henry de Hinton and their wives, which appears in three separate records: the pipe roll for 2 John (1200), the oblate roll for the same year and the curia regis roll for Easter term, 2 John (1201). The wording of the first two entries is the same, except for added details in the oblate roll. Osbert, Henry, Maud and Margery asked that John de Winchcombe and Nicole, his wife, respond to them to explain why they were asking Robert Wandard for Nicole's dower, which they had already recovered from Robert's father, William, and which Nicole had then sold to William, quitclaiming it in perpetuity, 'whereof the aforesaid Osbert and Maud and Henry and Margery complain that this was done unjustly and to the decrease and diminution of the dower of the said Maid and Margery.'[76] The curia regis roll adds the result of the writ: John and Nicole did not come, neither did they essoin themselves. They were to be taken by pledges, but they were not found.[77] It is difficult without further information to reconstruct the facts: did Nicole de Winchcombe's release of her dower injure the dower rights of the two Hinton wives and if so how; why did they have standing to sue? But their allegation – in all three entries it reads 'quod hoc factum fuit iniuste et ad decrementum et diminucionem dotis' – together with the Winchcombes' apparent flight may suggest a wrongful alienation of her dower by Nicole, although it is possible, of course, that Nicole's original claim against William was the unjust act complained of, or

---

[74] Bracton, ff. 322b–323 (4: 34).

[75] Statute of Gloucester (1278) c. 7; Statute of Westminster II (1285) c. 4. But the Statute of Gloucester gave the heir greater protection than the doweress had when a husband alienated her dower; the heir could enter on a grantee of a doweress at once rather than waiting for her death.

[76] *Pipe Roll 2 John*, p. 184; *Rotuli de Oblatis*, p. 96.

[77] *CRR*, I: 462.

that it was the commencement of the second action by the Winch-combes.[78]

Sometimes neither a doweress nor her own child was at fault when land was wrongfully kept from an heir; sometimes a husband had made a wrongful endowment of his second wife. Most commonly, he had used land he held only in curtesy, his first wife's *maritagium* or inheritance. Such a situation involving Gunnora, second wife and widow of the Lincolnshire baron, Robert de Gaunt, was significant not only because of Robert's position but because the heir in question, Robert's grandson through his daughter by his first wife, was in custody of the Bishop of London. It, too, appears in the oblate, pipe and plea rolls.[79] William de Ste Mère Église, Bishop of London, and until 1201 one of the king's justices, offered a sum variously recorded as 10 marks, 20 marks and 20 pounds for a recognition at Westminster in Trinity term, 1200, to say whether Nicholas de Stuteville and his wife, Gunnora, had had entry into the vill of Saltby other than as Gunnora's dower from Robert; dower, it was alleged, which Robert had had no right to give because he had had no right in the land except as curtesy. Saltby had been the inheritance of his first wife, Alice; she had died before 1181 but her husband had retained her lands until his own death in 1191.[80] The bishop's ward, Maurice son of Robert the Younger, was the son of Alice's daughter and heir, Avice, and her husband, Robert fitz Robert fitz Harding (who complicated the genealogy by taking the name Robert de Gaunt) who died in 1194.[81]

[78] Sometimes, of course, it was convenient for an heir to characterize an ancestress' conveyance as invalid because involving dower, as a means of ending an inconvenient arrangement. This seems to have been the case in an action from Trinity term, 5 Richard I (1194). A much-damaged entry records that two men were ordered to take the homage of a third for a free tenement which he held from them, which he had deraigned against one Maud in the king's court, and 'about which he had made an agreement with her that he would receive the land after her death'. The defenders replied that Maud had been unable to make such fine since she had only dower in the land, but it was shown that an assize had been summoned, bearing on that point, in earlier litigation. Judgement was that plaintiff hold in peace, with defendants ordered to take his service. The decision was cemented by a concord for which plaintiff gave 1 mark (*Three Rolls of the King's Court*, p. 43).

[79] *Pipe Roll 2 John*, p. 153; *Rotuli de Oblatis*, p. 61; *CRR*, I: 288.

[80] Sanders, *English Baronies*, p. 55.

[81] There can be no better illustration of the problem of second marriages. Robert's own heir was Gilbert III de Gaunt. The original entry shows a *jurata* in Michaelmas term, 2 John (1200) put into respite for default of jurors; the sheriff was to show on the Quindene of Michaelmas why he had not had the recognitors present (*CRR*, I:

Another dower grant open to challenge was one made by a husband from land in which he or his grantor held only a guardian's interest, one of the relatively few situations involving dower which turned on feudal rather than family relationships. A mort d'ancestor against Maud de Lousted in 1203 brought the usual reponse that she claimed only dower; her under-age son, Warin, was her warrantor. The plaintiff argued that he should not have to wait until Warin attained his majority because the boy's father had entered the land through one Roger, who had had it in wardship as plaintiff's guardian. The assize was ordered to go forward, apparently in part on the grounds that Warin had an older brother, unheard of for seven years, who might or might not be living but who, if alive, was of full age.[82]

Finally, of course, a husband might simply have been in possession of land in which he had no right at all, as by dissesin or intrusion, on the day he married; then, long after the rightful tenant had successfully regained his tenement, he might have to contend with a widow's dower claim based on her recollection that her husband had, at the relevant time, been in possession of it, or even that he had specifically endowed her with it.[83]

---

288). On the morrow of St Martin (November 10), the king ordered by his writ to the justices at the bench 'that they put into respite the assize concerning the land of Saltby between Nicholas de Stuteville and Gunnora his wife and Maurice son of Robert "de Berkeley" until he shall order them to the contrary' (*CRR*, I: 335). In Easter term, 2 John (1201), Gunnora appointed one Robert de Edenham her attorney against Maurice in a plea 'of land' (*CRR*, I: 428). Thereafter the matter disappears from the records. Maurice de Gaunt came of age *c.* 1205 (Sanders, *English Baronies*, p. 55).

[82] *CRR*, II: 139, 219; also *Select Civil Pleas*, no. 156. Another case, in which the facts are not entirely clear but which appears to involve a grant of dower by a guardian from the lands of a minor heir of whom he held the wardship, is in *PBKJ*, II, no. 917.

[83] Such a case is described in detail in the introduction to *Norfolk–Suffolk Fines*, p. xxv. H granted land to Y who granted it to Z. Later H seized the land and still later he married. Litigation between H and Z finally ended in a concord whereby Z regained the land, more than ten years after the original grant and after the marriage. H died and his wife claimed dower in the land. The case is in *CRR*, VI (London, 1932), 215–16. See also the reference in *RCR*, I: 443, where a defendant pleads that land is held in dower by one who proved her right to it in court against plaintiff's father and plaintiff replies that he knows the doweress holds the land 'but unjustly, and through one who neither has nor had any right in it'. There are, of course, any number of reasons why the doweress' husband and/or her warrantor might have had no right in the land.

Doubtless, twelfth-century heirs had heard such stories of endless litigation and property loss arising from dower rights. The plea rolls, the pipe rolls and the fine rolls show that they tried to protect their interests in two different but related ways: they attempted to defeat or whittle down dower rights and they made a record of them. Given the evidence of the rolls, there are cases in which it is not possible to be certain which course was being followed. It is unclear whether these actions were begun because of a conflict between the parties, or primarily for the purpose of making a record in the rolls of the court or even as the basis for a fine, itself a record. Often the mort d'ancestor brought by the heir seems to have been brought for the latter purposes.[84] There are dower claims by the widow which look as if they served a similar function, but for the period before 1200 at least, it is usually not possible to be sure that a real dispute, although quickly resolved, did not lie behind them. Some brief plea roll entries reporting the resolution of a suit certainly must reflect out-of-court agreement on seriously contested claims; others may simply be the fruit of a warrantor's concern that the nature of the interest of his stepmother, sister-in-law or even his mother be made clear.[85] Fines could serve the

[84] Of course, the plea rolls recorded court decisions which could be used later when a party to an action 'put himself on the rolls of the justices'. But both the pipe rolls and the plea rolls were also used to record agreements between parties, particularly before the commencement of the fine rolls. Many of these agreements were certainly in compromise of litigation; others may have been purely for record purposes. See *Pipe Roll 7 Richard I*, p. 111 (touches dower only as part of a larger settlement); *Pipe Roll 2 John*, p. 51; *RCR*, I: 81; *RCR*, II: 130, 153; *CRR*, I: 271, 285, 313, 410, 416 (settling action for admeasurement). Nor was it only heirs who wanted protection; see the anxious widow who in 1200 gave half a mark to have it written in the pipe rolls that her husband gave her as dower and confirmed to her by charter certain specified lands and that it had been done with the will and assent of Ralph, his son and heir (*Pipe Roll 2 John*, p. 91). She was almost certainly Ralph's stepmother. The most obvious use of the plea rolls to provide a record is set out in *Abbreviatio Placitorum*, p. 35, where Maud de Cauz, widow of 'Robert fitz Stephen', is reported to have come into court and acknowledged that she held Winterborne with appurtenances of Richard Wall as dower and that after her death it ought to revert to Richard and his heirs. I have seen no record of prior litigation between the parties. The 'Maud, widow of Robert de Cauz' who appears in 1202 litigating with John de Cauz about her dower (*ELAR*, no. 230) was this Maud's mother and herself the daughter of Richard Basset. The Maud de Cauz of the acknowledgement was the daughter of Robert de Cauz, married to Ralph, not Robert, fitz Stephen, the chamberlain, as her second husband (*Sanders English Baronies*, p. 77; *Rotuli de Dominabus*, p. 13).

[85] See *Rolls of the Justices in Eyre at Bedford, 1202*, p. 181; *ELAR*, os. n135, 490; *CRR*, I: 322; *PBKJ*, III: nos. 836, 865; *RCR*, I: 406; *RCR*, II: 243; *Staffordshire Suits*, p. 170.

same purposes, whether they ended the assize of mort d'ancestor or the action for dower. Attempting to reconstruct the events leading up to a fine is a tricky business; one is attempting to reconstruct complex but often informal intra-family relationships and one is doing so for a period when the plea rolls, which might contain an entry explaining the events leading up to an agreement, are incomplete. It is hard to believe that there was a serious dispute behind certain of the final concords recorded at the end of the twelfth century; affection between the parties coupled with a desire to clarify holdings seems much more likely as a motivating factor.[86] But picking out such fines is not to suggest on the one hand that all other fines settled actual dower litigation nor, on the other, that most dower litigation was commenced with a view to compromise. Fines were certainly a way of arranging the affairs of a family, whether or not there was affection present, and dower would have made a prime candidate for such arrangement.[87]

---

[86] *Fines Henry II and Richard I*, no. 152; *Fines 7–8 Richard I*, nos. 44, 113; *Feet of Fines of the Tenth Year of the Reign of King Richard I (1198) and a Roll of the King's Court in the Reign of King Richard I*, Pipe Roll Society, vol. 24 (London, 1900) (henceforward *Pipe Roll Society*, vol. 24), no. 28; *Norfolk Fines, Richard I and John*, no. 458; *Norfolk–Suffolk Fines*, no. 330. See also the releases of dower referred to in *Rotuli de Dominabus*, pp. 28, 42; the latter, 12 years after the inquest, was by fine recorded in *Fines 9 Richard I*, no. 93.

[87] It was pointed out by Barbara Dodwell in her introduction to *Norfolk–Suffolk Fines* that in matters of dower, as well in establishing the order of succession to a holding or the partible share of heiresses, 'the aristocracy and the country gentry found the final concord of great value', not so much because they conveyed land by it but because they used it to arrange family holdings among parties who were or might be in conflict (p. xxv). The introduction to *Norfolk Fines, Richard I and John*, points out that mort d'ancestor was 'outstandingly popular' as an original writ to open proceedings which ended in a fine, representing nearly three-quarters of all concords, while the action for dower itself provided nine fines (p. xxv). A similar conclusion is reached in the introduction to *Lincoln Fines, John* (p. xviii). When it is considered that a number of the assizes of mort d'ancestor involved dower, the estimated percentage of dower cases ending in a fine rises significantly. Against the fairly sanguine view adopted by the editors of the fine rolls, it should be noted that Joüon des Longrais considers that most fines at the end of the twelfth and the beginning of the thirteenth centuries reflect the weakness of the doweress' position ('Statut de la femme', pp. 215–16). Assuming that he held the better bargaining position, there are good financial reasons for the heir's interest in entering into a fine concerning dower holdings. If the doweress did not pay any rents or services to the heir nor perform forinsec service, the dower was a double drain: while he got no benefits from the land, the heir was obliged to acquit it of all services due his own lord and/or the king. Naturally, it was helpful if a fine ended in a doweress' paying an annual sum for her land and it was even more so if she could be made responsible

But the plea rolls make clear that many or most dower actions were begun in earnest and were vigorously litigated. Where a claim was truly hostile, tenants or heirs did not hesitate to press any objection or employ any delaying tactic in an attempt to intimidate, discourage or defeat the widow. Defenses that she had never been married to the dead man, or had married him only on his deathbed; that she had not been endowed of the land claimed at the church door; that her husband, although absent, yet lived; that her husband had been outlawed; that she had quitclaimed her dower for money; that the land she asked was held in villeinage, and many others are found in the rolls, some frequently and others less so.[88] They were designed to bar the claim once for all. Objections such as the allegation that the widow had a (second) husband who had not joined in the writ and the familiar demand that she produce her warrantor were sometimes only delaying maneuvers, as was, often, the request for a view. The common response that the widow had been assigned other dower at the church door, usually less than the amount now claimed, frequently looks like an attempt to force a compromise on terms disadvantageous to the doweress. She was in a peculiarly vulnerable position. Doweresses were virtually the only women in society whose claim to land was not to the benefit of a man (unless, of course, they had already remarried); unmarried widows were the only women who could in

for the forinsec service. Many fines take account of forinsec service, either expressly or by implication; a few examples must suffice. A doweress is to pay a named rent service 'for all service except forinsec' (*Fines 9 Richard I*, no. 175). She is to give 6 pence a year 'for all services except forinsec service' (*Lincoln Fines, John*, no. 158). She is to hold one-half virgate for half a pound of pepper per annum for all services except forinsec (Hunter, *Fines*, I: 184). Or she is to hold for life by service of 23 pence a year for all services (*Norfolk Fines, Richard I and John*, no. 236). Or for the service of 5 shillings a year for all services (*Pipe Roll Society*, vol. 24, no. 62). Occasionally, scutage is mentioned and the burden of it thrown on the doweress as in *Norfolk Fines, Richard I and John*, no. 449; the doweress is to hold in the name of dower by free service of 24 shillings for all services 'and towards scutage 20 shillings 18 pence and if more, more and if less, less'. Or, more generously, for 1 penny a year for all services except those owed the king: 5 pence towards 20 shillings scutage and if more, more and if less, less (Hunter, *Fines*, I: 265).

[88] By far the most common defense for the years before and including 1200 was that the wife could not have been endowed with certain land because her husband did not have it as a free tenement in demesne at the time of the wedding; he held it only for a term of years, or in service, or in villeinage, or as pledge, or he had already alienated it or he did not yet have it. See, for examples, *CRR*, I: 140, 150, 152, 161, 166, 192, 449; *RCR*, I: 20, 359, 415, 416; *RCR*, II: 32, 254.

any real sense call their land their own. When Maud de Percy, Countess of Warwick, spoke in one of her charters about giving and confirming land 'in viduitate et in legali potestate mea', she was not simply using a figure of speech.[89] But as such, widows were often without a male ally to give support to their cause; they could perhaps be frightened or bought off more easily.[90] Many heirs were willing to make the attempt.

Nor should it come as a surprise that such tactics were employed. Philosophically and theoretically, dower invoked conflicting sentiments. It was proper that a woman should have enough to live on and to bring her children up with after her husband died, but there must be limits on how much her rights should be allowed to inconvenience or injure the heir and through him, the family. By its nature, dower ran counter to a strong desire, countenanced by the family structure of feudal England, to keep landholdings undivided and in the hands of the heir.[91] When philosophical objections were buttressed by economic considerations and sharpened by the existence of relative 'outsiders' as doweresses, dower must often have seemed to have been an unwarranted imposition on essentially family resources. The frequency of dower-related litigation in the early plea rolls, then, does not necessarily point to greed on the part of widows, as some modern commentators have suggested.[92] It is, rather, the result of a cluster of constant, pre-existing circumstances. The first is the economic importance of competing claims to land; a claim of dower was a claim

[89] *Early Yorkshire Charters*, XI: 64.

[90] In connection with this, it is interesting to note whom widows appointed as their attorneys, assuming they had not remarried. Brothers were named most often, but there are a number of sons, some of them not the sons of the husbands from whom the widows derived the claimed dower, some of them younger brothers of the heir.

[91] There is a fair amount of literature on the tensions between the family's desire to consolidate its holdings, on the one hand, and both the institution of dower and the attitudes of Henry II's judges who, after all, enforced dower rights, on the other. See, for example, P&M, 2: 424; Joüon des Longrais, *Saisine*, pp. 325–30; Sidney Painter, 'The family and the feudal system in twelfth century England', *Speculum*, 35 (1960), pp. 1–16, esp. at 4, 12–13; George Haskins, 'Development of common law dower', pp. 47–9 and references collected there.

[92] There has been some suggestion to this effect on the part of modern scholars, although I have not seen it mentioned in either cases or contemporary treatises. See G. D. G. Hall's review of *Curia Regis Rolls of the Reign of Henry III, 9–10 Henry III*, p. 108; S. J. Bailey, 'The Countess Gundred's lands', pp. 88, 89, 98; S. J. Bailey, 'Warranties of land in the thirteenth century (contd.)', *Cambridge Law Journal*, 9 (1945), 83.

to the very basis and measure of wealth. Next is a social pattern which at the least encouraged remarriage by widows; second and third marriages all too frequently put a chunk of family land firmly outside family control for a prolonged period and tended to produce accompanying step-siblings and half-siblings, through their mother a threat to the eventual recovery of dower land by the heir. And third is the very procedure so rigidly prescribed for the valid appointment of dower: there would have been a high possibility for mistake and potential for fraud about rights which had been established by oral declaration, sometimes half a century earlier. It is not surprising, given all these factors, that endowment, even at the church door with the neighbors looking on, was not really so definitive of the widow's rights as either she or her bridegroom might have believed it would be, 'die qua eam desponsavit'.

ACKNOWLEDGEMENTS

I am grateful to Professor Sue Sheridan Walker of Northeastern Illinois University for reading an early draft of this paper and to Professor Donald Sutherland of the University of Iowa for his comments on a later version.

11

Wives' Claims against Insolvent Husbands in Late Medieval Italy

JULIUS KIRSHNER

The goods and monies conveyed between husband and wife in late medieval Italy have been the subject of numerous monographs during the past decade. Recent studies have drawn upon, but also depart from, the standard accounts of legal historians, notably Brandileone, Ercole, Pertile and Bellomo.[1] Where previous scholarship was pre-occupied with the historiographic issue of the survival and revival of Roman law and institutions, recent scholarship has been preoccupied with charting the demographic, social and ideological history of the medieval family and the role women played within and between families.[2] Although their perspectives and aims differ, both previous and recent scholarship concur that a momentous shift was underway in the twelfth century: the re-emergence of the Roman dowry (*dos*) –

[1] A. Pertile, *Storia del diritto italiano* (2nd edn, Turin, 1894), vol. 3; F. Brandileone *Scritti di storia del diritto privato italiano* (Bologna, 1931); F. Ercole, 'L'istituto dotale nella practica e nella legislazione statuaria dell'Italia superiore', *Rivista italiana per le scienze giuridiche*, 45 (1908), pp. 191–302; 46 (1910), pp. 167–257; 'Vicende storiche della dote romana nella practica medievale dell'Italia superiore', *Archivio giuridico* (1908), 80–1 (1908), pp. 393–490, pp. 34–148; M. Bellomo, *Ricerche sui rapporti patrimoniali tra coniugi* (Milan, 1961). For an overview of the literature, see G. Vismara, 'I rapporti patrimoniali tra coniugi nell'alto medioevo', in *Settimane di Studio del Centro italiano di studi sull'alto medievo, XXIV: Il matrimonio nella società altomedievale* (Spoleto, 1977), II, pp. 633–91.

[2] See D. O. Hughes, 'From brideprice to dowry in Mediterranean Europe', *Journal of Family History*, 3 (1978), pp. 262–96, and the bibliography cited therein; D. Herlihy, 'The medieval marriage market', in *Medieval and Renaissance Studies*; Duke University, 6 (Durham, NC, 1976), pp. 3–27; Karl Schmid, 'Heirat, Famili-enfolge, Geschlechterbewusstsein', *Il matrimonio nella società altomedievale*, II, pp. 103–37; Robert Fossier, 'Les structures de la famille en occident au Moyen-Age', *XVe Congrès International des Sciences Historiques, Rapports*, II (Bucharest, 1980), pp. 115–32.

the goods, monies or estates a wife brought to her husband in marriage – and the concomitant decline of the Germanic *morgengabe*, a gift the groom gave his bride on the consummation of marriage. The victory of the Roman dowry over the *morgengabe*, it is also agreed, had enormous consequences for social relations and economic activities as well as for the disposition and devolution of property.[3]

Accompanying the victory of the Roman dowry was the development of the norms, rules and procedures regulating the dowry's constitution and disposition. This essay investigates a single, remarkable medieval legal development which has received scant attention: the reaffirmation and enforcement of the remedy that Roman law made available to wives whose husbands were verging on insolvency (*vir vergens ad inopiam*). To prevent the dissipation and loss of the wife's dowry and patrimony, she was granted express sanction to reclaim her dowry or to lay claim to an equivalent amount of her husband's goods during marriage (*constante matrimonio*). And she was allowed to perform all the actions necessary to defend her claim against her husband's creditors.

This essay begins with an outline of Roman legal prescriptions governing the disposition of the dowry during marriage. Next, it presents a critique of Manlio Bellomo's celebrated thesis on the radical transformation of these and related prescriptions in the twelfth and thirteenth centuries. The heart of the essay is an investigation of civil law doctrine and jurisprudence which not only warranted the wife's action against an insolvent husband but extended this remedy to myriad situations not envisioned by the compilers of the *Corpus iuris civilis*.

Under the rules promulgated by Justinian in the *Corpus iuris civilis*, the husband was vested with ownership of the dowry during

---

[3] The victory, however, was far from universal. Lombard law and custom persisted in Apulia well into the sixteenth century and in Lombardy well into the fourteenth century: F. P. De Stefano, 'Romani, longobardi e normanno-franchi dalla Puglia nei secoli XV–XVII', *Ricerche sui rapporti patrimoniali fra coniugi fino alla prammatica 'de antefacto' del 1617* (Naples, 1979); C. Storti Storchi, 'La tradizione longobarda nel diritto bergamasco: i rapporti patrimoniali tra coniugi (secoli XII–XIV)', in *Diritto comune e diritto locale nella storia dell'Europa, Atti del Convegno di Varenna 12–15 giugno 1979* (Milan, 1980), pp. 481–554. Christiane Klapisch-Zuber, in a provocative article, has argued that the gifts lavished upon Florentine brides by grooms and their families perpetuated the role that the *morgengabe* had played; 'Le complexe de Griselde. Dot et dons de marriage au Quattrocento', *Mélanges de l'Ecole Française de Rome*, 94 (1982), pp. 7–43.

marriage.[4] He was also vested with responsibility for administering dotal goods and for applying its fruits to support the burdens of matrimony. And he was entitled to receive compensation for the risks and necessary expenses incurred while discharging his moral and legal obligations. The husband's ownership and administration of dotal property was both ambiguous and restricted. The statement of the Roman jurisconsult Tryphoninus is worth recalling: 'Although the dowry is counted among the husband's goods, it nevertheless belongs to the wife' (*Digesta* 23.3.75. *Quamvis in bonis*). Should he wish to alienate dotal property consisting of land, he was prohibited from doing so without first seeking his wife's consent. However, his ability to alienate movable goods whose value had been fixed by agreement was unrestricted. The wife had an implied hypothec or security over all her husband's goods for the restitution of the dowry. As the wife's security over these goods was automatically established by law (*hypotheca tacita*), it was deemed privileged and took precedence over other hypothecs.[5]

The husband's ownership of the dowry terminated upon dissolution of marriage. He or his heirs were compelled to restore dotal goods or their equivalent value if that had been fixed, except in the case where the wife divorced her husband without justifiable cause. Restoration of the dowry, upon the husband's predecease, to the wife's *paterfamilias* or to anyone else was prohibited without her consent. Upon the wife's predecease, her husband was obligated to restore the dowry to her *paterfamilias* if he had been its donor. Anyone other (*extraneus*) than the paternal ascendant who provided the dowry could claim it upon the wife's death, if there had been an express agreement for its return. In the absence of an express agreement, the husband was obligated to return the dowry to his wife's heirs. When circumstances were such that the husband was under no obligation to return the dowry to his father-in-law or to anyone else, and when there were surviving children, the husband received a qualified usufruct over the dowry, while formal ownership devolved upon the children.

These legal niceties would, of course, be pointless unless there remained dotal goods or their equivalent to be restored. The Roman

---

[4] On the Roman law regarding marital property, see P. F. Girard, *Manuel élémentaire de droit romain*, 8th edn (Paris, 1929), pp. 1007–24; P. E. Corbett, *The Roman Law of Marriage* (Oxford, 1930), pp. 147–210; C. A. Cannata, 'Dote (dir. rom.)', *Enciclopedia del diritto* (Milan, 1965), vol. XIV, pp. 1–8.

[5] A hypothec was a form of real security carrying no obligation to transfer to the creditor either money or possession.

jurisconsults recognized the necessity to protect the wife's patrimony during marriage against loss owing to her husband's insolvency. In an opinion of the jurisconsult Ulpian, cited in *lex Si constante* (*Digesta* 24.3.24), a wife was permitted during marriage to initiate a suit to reclaim her dowry when her husband became insolvent. Before she could act, however, it had to be established that his assets were clearly insufficient to restore the dowry, presumably upon the dissolution of marriage (*soluto matrimonio*).[6]

Another *lex*, *Ubi adhuc* (*Codex* 15.12.29), established that where the husband had fallen into insolvency during marriage, his wife can provide for herself by taking physical control of her husband's goods, which had been secured, as well as his prenuptial donation (*donatio ante nuptias*) and other goods which belonged to her (*res extra dotales*). She was to be treated as a preferred creditor and was permitted to defend her claim to her husband's goods against any other creditor. This rule referred to situations in which her husband's creditors held goods pledged for the dowry as well as situations in which the wife herself held these goods. Two legal actions were available to the wife. She could exercise her claim through the *actio rei vindicatio*, which permitted an owner to reclaim goods held by someone else; and the *actio hypothecaria*, which permitted someone who has a security over goods to claim them. The capacity to exercise these remedies was restricted to the wife who was emancipated (*sui iuris*) at the time of the action. If she was under the paternal power, it was her paternal ascendant who, with the wife's consent, initiated the action as co-plaintiff. The rights and claims of creditors against the husband for any property he subsequently acquired were unimpaired. Whatever separate agreement the wife and husband had concluded about the disposition of the dowry upon dissolution of marriage continued to be in force.[7]

[6] *Digesta* 24.3.24 in the *Corpus iuris civilis*, eds T. H. Mommsen, W. Kroll, P. Krueger and R. Schoell (3 vols, Berlin, 1928–9) (henceforward *Digesta*): 'Si constante matrimonio propter inopiam mariti mulier agere volet, unde exactionem dotis initium accipere ponamus? et constat exinde dotis exactionem competere, ex quo evidentissime apparuerit mariti facultates ad dotis exactionem non sufficere.'

[7] *Codex* 5.12.29 in *Corpus iuris civilis*, eds T. H. Mommsen, W. Kroll, P. Krueger and R. Schoell (3 vols, Berlin, 1928–9) (henceforward *Codex*): 'Ubi adhuc matrimonio constituto maritus ad inopiam sit deductus et mulier sibi prospicere velit resque sibi suppositas pro dote et ante nuptias donatione rebusque extra dotem constitutis tenere, non tantum mariti res ei tenenti et super his ad iudicium vocatae exceptionis praesidium ad expellendum ab hypotheca creditorem secundum praestamus, sed etiam si ipsa contra detentatores rerum ad maritum suum pertinentium super isdem hypothecis aliquam actionem secundum legum distinc-

Since by definition, the dowry's purpose was to sustain the burdens of marriage, the wife was prohibited from alienating the restored dowry during marriage. Like her husband, she was charged with the duty to use dotal fruits and income to support herself, her husband and children. A Justinianic constitution (*Novellae* 97.6. *Illud quoque sancire*) admonished the wife, whose husband was mismanaging his affairs and squandering his own goods, to act to recover the dowry and to administer it competently and prudently. Otherwise she would be held to blame, if when threatened with the loss of her dowry, she failed to act while she still had the opportunity.[8]

The prescriptions set forth in the *Corpus iuris civilis* regarding ownership, administration and restitution of dowries were vigorously debated, modified and even reversed by medieval jurisprudents.[9] By

---

tionem moveat, non obesse ei matrimonium adhuc constitutum sancimus, sed ita eam posse easdem res vindicare vel a creditoribus posterioribus vel ab aliis, qui non potiora iura legibus habere noscuntur, ut potuisset, si matrimonium eo modo esset dissolutum, quo dotis et ante nuptias donationis exactio ei competere poterat: ita tamen, ut eadem mulier nullam habeat licentiam eas res alienandi vivente marito et matrimonio inter eos constituto, sed fructibus earum ad sustentationem tam sui quam mariti filiorumque, si quos habeant, abutatur. Creditoribus scilicet mariti contra eum eiusque res, si quas postea forte adquisierit, integra sua iura habentibus: ipsis etiam marito et uxore post matrimonii dissolutionem super dote et ante nuptias donatione pro dotalium instrumentorum tenore integro suo iure potituris.'

[8] *Novellae* 97.6 in *Corpus iuris civilis*, eds T. H. Mommsen, W. Kroll, P. Krueger and R. Schoell (3 vols, Berlin, 1928–9) (henceforward *Novellae*): *Illud quoque sancire*: 'Quia enim dedimus mulieribus electionem et constante matrimonio, si male res maritus gubernet, et accipere eas et gubernare et secundum decentem modum et sicuti nostra constitutio dicit, si quidem suae potestatis et perfectae aetatis mulier est, sibimet culpam inferat, cur mox viro incohante male substantia uti non percepit et auxiliata est sibi. . . .'

[9] For what follows, see Bellomo, *Ricerche*, pp. 61 ff. See also Bellomo's *La condizione giuridica della donna in Italia: Vicende antiche e moderne* (Turin, 1970). The privileging of the husband's claims to the dowry must be seen in a broader European context, in which the tracing of descent and the transmission of property by inheritance in the eleventh century became exclusively determined by the ideology of patriliny, whereas in the early Middle Ages patriliny and matriliny co-existed in practice as well as in theory; Georges Duby, 'Structures de parenté et noblesse dans la France du nord au 11e et 12e siècles', (1967), reprinted in his *Hommes et structures du Moyen Age* (Paris, 1973), pp. 267–85. David Herlihy has offered a cogent summary of the historical conditions which made this transformation possible: 'The Church's now effective insistance on monogamous marriage was a precondition, but surely not the principal cause of this realignment of elite families around patrilineal lines. The crucial factor seems to have been diminishing opportunities and resources available

the fourteenth century, they unanimously affirmed that ownership of all dotal goods and properties during marriage was without qualification vested with the husband (*maritus est dominus rei dotalis*), though the wife retained a residual ownership rooted in natural law. No longer could a wife act during a marriage to recover dotal goods alienated to third parties. This prerogative was vested in the husband as *dominus*. Alienation of dotal goods became infinitely easier through loopholes given juristic sanction and the near universal custom of giving dowries a pecuniary valuation (*dos estimata*). Not only was the wife's claim to her dowry attenuated; the rule compelling a husband to restore the dowry to his father-in-law upon his wife's predecease was also overturned. The husband, with surviving children, was now allowed to retain the dowry. Preference for the husband's claim to dotal property was strengthened and even expanded by the statutes of Siena, Pisa, Pistoia and Florence, which established that widowers with or without surviving children could retain from one-third to the whole dowry.

A number of explanations have been advanced to explain the conspicuous reversal of Roman rules which had favored wives and their kinsmen. Manlio Bellomo, in his classic study of marital property, pivots his explanation on the political sociology and psychology of the medieval Italian commune. Survival of families in the political struggles which characterized communal life made it incumbent upon the *capo di famiglia* to control his wife's goods without interference from her kinsmen. As a son he expected to receive a share of his mother's dowry; as a father he was expected to transmit this bundle of dotal rights to heirs within his patriline. The interdependence of patrimony and political rank, the obsession with continuity of the patriline and the identification of family fortune with the fortune of its patrimony, were defining features of the Italian commune of the twelfth and

---

for the support of elite households. The establishment of more stable feudal principalities, the partial pacification of European life, reduced the profits of pillage, save along the distant frontiers. The chief remaining resource was the landed patrimony. Elite families struggled to preserve the extent and integrity of their holdings. They forced their younger sons to delay or eschew marriage, or sent them forth to make their fortunes. Daughters did not enjoy even this option. Their fathers or brothers gave these girls – some girls – the dowries they now needed for marriage, but this represented the extent of their claim upon the family patrimony. The position of women, central in the cognatic system of the early Middle Ages, clearly weakened within the patrilineal line.' This quotation is taken from Herlihy's forthcoming paper, 'The making of the medieval family: structure, symmetry and sentiment', which he kindly allowed me to read and cite.

thirteenth centuries, the historical setting in which the rights of widows and their heirs were curtailed. The *capi di famiglia* not only enacted legislation to avoid restitution of dowries, but also resorted to other tactics: refusing outright or delaying restitution, alienating dotal goods and properties through fictitious sales, constraining wives to renounce their hypothecary rights and insisting that widows receive supplements to their dowries (*alimenta*) only if they forgo remarriage and remain with the surviving children in their husbands' houses and in the orbit of his patriline. Just as daughters were excluded from inheritance once they were endowered, widows and their legitimate heirs were denied the recovery of dowries. Viewed from the vantage point of men in authority, women were little more than minor actors in a social drama scripted and directed by men.

Bellomo's thesis, forcefully argued and presented with technical finesse and formidable erudition, has justifiably attracted adherents.[10] That Roman legal rules were radically transformed in the context of medieval political, social and economic developments is an intransigent fact that cannot be denied. Nor can one deny the difficulties with which widows and their heirs had to contend in recovering their dowries or other goods to which they were entitled. The financial plight of this group in fifteenth-century Florence (where one in every four adult women was a widow) has been put into bold relief by Herlihy and Klapisch-Zuber.[11] Petition after petition was presented to the Signoria in Florence, in which widows, their heirs and descendants solicited governmental intervention in settling disputes over the disposition of dotal goods.[12] The ability of husbands, moreover, to

[10] T. Izbicki, 'Two *consilia* on widow's rights', *Bulletin of Medieval Canon Law*, 8 (1978), pp. 47–50; J. Larner, *Italy in the Age of Dante and Petrarch, 1216–1380* (London, 1980), pp. 68–9; C. Violante, 'Alcune caratteristiche delle strutture familiari in Lombardia, Emilia e Toscana durante i secoli IX–XII', in G. Duby and J. Le Goff (eds), *Famiglia e parentela nell'Italia medievale* (Bologna, 1977), pp. 46ff; and in the same volume, P. Cammarosano, 'Aspetti delle strutture familiari nelle città dell'Italia comunale: secoli XII–XIV', pp. 109–24.

[11] D. Herlihy and C. Klapisch-Zuber, *Les toscans et leurs familles: Une étude du catasto de 1427* (Paris, 1978), pp. 610–11; C. Klapisch-Zuber, 'The "cruel mother"': maternity, widowhood and dowry in Florence of the fourteenth and fifteenth centuries', forthcoming in her collected papers, *Women, Family and Ritual in Renaissance Italy* (Chicago, University of Chicago Press, 1985). In the same vein, see the older but useful study of L. Zdekauer, 'Le donne nella Lira senese de 1297', *Bolletino senese di storia patria*, 10 (1903), pp. 91–106.

[12] An analysis of these petitions is included in the forthcoming study on the *Monte delle doti* or Dowry Fund of Florence which I am preparing with Anthony Molho and Alan Morrison.

alienate dotal property during marriage, which served the requirements of liquidity in the nascent market economy, clearly jeopardized
the wife's chances of recovering a dowry threatened by impending
insolvency. And bankruptcy itself became an endemic feature of urban
life, not only because of the constant volatility of the market economy,
but also because of oppressive tax burdens.[13]

Despite its obvious merits, Bellomo's thesis postulating a general
deterioration of women's legal capacities remains unidimensional and
must be modified. It places excessive emphasis upon the husband's
and his kinsmen's dominance over the wife and her patrimony, while
neglecting to take seriously the emotional and material bonds that
persisted between a married woman and her own kinsmen.[14] It over-
emphasizes the inevitable conflicts between the wife's and husband's
kinsmen, between her heirs and his, while neglecting to consider
common bonds forged by ties of *parentado*. It places too much weight
upon the figure of the *capo di famiglia* as a domestic predator of both his
wife's and his mother's dowry, while failing to take seriously the figure
of the 'husband–father', who dutifully provided for the well-being of
his wife in widowhood and his daughter in marriage. It gives undue
emphasis to formal prescriptions and androcentric texts, ignoring the

[13] On bankruptcy, see G. Cassandro, *Le rappresaglie e il fallimento a Venezia nei
secoli XIII–XVI con documenti inediti* (Turin, 1938); U. Santarelli, *Per la storia del
fallimento nelle legislazione italiane dell'età intermedia* (Padua, 1964); on taxation, see
W. M. Bowsky, *The Finance of the Commune of Siena, 1287–1355* (Oxford, 1970);
G. Luzzatto, *Il debito pubblico della repubblica di Venezia dagli ultimi decenni del XII
secolo alla fine del XV* (Milan, 1963); C. Violante, 'Imposte dirette e debito pubblico
a Pisa nel medioevo', in his *Economia, società, istituzioni a Pisa nel medioevo* (Bari,
1980), pp. 101–69; A. Molho, *Florentine Public Finances in the Early Renaissance,
1400–1433* (Cambridge, Mass., 1971).

[14] For what follows, see C. Klapisch-Zuber, 'Parenti, amici, e vicini: Il territorio
urbano d'una famiglia mercantile nel XV secolo', *Quaderni storici*, 33 (1976), pp.
953–82; F. W. Kent, *Household and Lineage in Renaissance Florence. The Family Life of
the Capponi, Ginori and Rucellai* (Princeton, 1977); S. Chojnacki, 'Patrician women in
early Renaissance Venice', *Studies in the Renaissance*, 21 (1974), pp. 176–203;
'Dowries and kinsmen in early Renaissance Venice', in S. M. Stuard (ed.), *Women
in Medieval Society* (Philadelphia, 1976), pp. 173–98; G. Forchieri, 'I rapporti
patrimoniali fra coniugi a Genova nel secolo XII', *Bollettino ligustico per la storia e la
cultura regionale*, 2 (1970), pp. 3–20; D. O. Hughes, 'Domestic ideals and social
behavior: evidence from medieval Genoa', in C. Rosenberg (ed.), *The Family in
History* (Philadelphia, 1975), pp. 115–43; E. Riemer, *Women in the Medieval City:
Sources and Uses of Wealth of Sienese Women in the Thirteenth Century* (New York University Dissertation, 1975), pp. 6ff.; J. Kirshner, *Pursuing Honor while Avoiding Sin.
The Monte delle Doti of Florence* (Milan, 1978); T. Kuehn, 'Women, marriage and
patria potestas in late medieval Florence', *Revue d'histoire du droit*, 49 (1981), pp. 127–47.

possibility that women may have played an influential backstage role in domestic life. It lends too much importance to the curtailment of the wife's dotal rights by statutory codifications, while ignoring statutory and legislative remedies designed to safeguard her patrimony. Florentine petitions cited above not only testify to the affliction of widows, but also the willingness of the Florentine government to alleviate their plight. Above all, Bellomo's thesis places too much emphasis upon legal mechanisms which may have weakened the wife's dotal privileges, such as renunciation of hypothecary rights to her husband's property, while ignoring the enforcement of guarantees and remedies set forth in dotal contracts for the restoration of the dowry and prenuptial donation to the wife and her heirs.

Another shortcoming of Bellomo's thesis is his failure to come to terms with the disparities between legal doctrine and local statute and custom. How did jurists resolve disputes over the disposition and devolution of the wife's property when the common law (*ius commune*) – the Roman and canon law and the teachings and opinions of civilian and canon lawyers – and local statutes collided? Was legal doctrine and jurisprudence simply disregarded, was it devoid of all practical significance? Such questions are not addressed by Bellomo, for he believes that, with few exceptions, both common law and local statutes privileged the claims of husbands and their kinsmen. He also believes that by the mid-fourteenth century the contributions of jurisprudents to these issues had become passive regurgitations of traditional doctrine and opinion. However, the intellectual energies of jurisprudents such as Bartolo (d. 1357) and Baldo (d. 1400) and their disciples were, as we shall see, far from spent.[15] Their exegesis of the constitution, disposition and devolution of the wife's property (*bona mulieris*) constitutes a veritable stockpile of model cases and solutions drawn from experience and deductive argument, which were employed by jurists who felt no qualms about defending the patrimonial interests of wives and their relatives.[16] Given the problems arising from statutory ambiguities and lacunae and from conflicts between statutes, jurisprudents had ample opportunity to practice their technical expertise on the triangular relationship between common law, local customs

[15] See J. Kirshner and J. Pluss, 'Two fourteenth-century opinions on dowries, paraphernalia and non-dotal goods', *Bulletin of Medieval Canon Law*, 9 (1979), pp. 64–77; T. Kuehn, *Emancipation in Late Medieval Florence* (New Brunswick, NJ, 1982), pp. 143ff.

[16] J. Pluss, *Baldus de Ubaldis on Dowry Law* (University of Chicago Dissertation, 1983).

and dotal agreements, as witnessed by hundreds of extant legal opinions (*consilia*) involving dowries.

These jurisprudents were, moreover, rendering their *consilia* in a setting starkly removed from the robust commune of the twelfth and thirteenth centuries as depicted by Bellomo. By the mid-fourteenth century the position of the consortial family had suffered political, economic and demographic erosion. Recurrent visitations of the plague threatened the continuity and biological existence of patrilines. In this new setting, the disposition and devolution of the wife's property upon dissolution of marriage was not only determined by local statutes, jurisprudential mediations, strategies and counter-strategies of wives, widows, widowers and their respective kinsmen and heirs, but also by chance. The devolution of the wife's property was neither entirely predictable nor unidirectional; its course must be tracked on multiple roads and byways. Those who journey this road are advised to leave behind stereotypical verities about the subordination and oppression of women, about the squalid indignity of their lives (we know little about what motivated women, what they experienced and thought across the social and economic spectrum of late medieval Italy) and instead explore the terrain of partial and complementary truths.

Let us now turn our attention to the legal recourse of the wife when her husband was verging on bankruptcy. For Bellomo, her legal recourse was limited to the realm of theory, representing little more than a reassuring fantasy. He acknowledges that the prescriptions enunciated in *Si constante* and *Ubi adhuc* were reaffirmed in the twelfth century by the author of the *Summa trecensis* (c. 1160), and by Azo (d. c. 1270).[17] This reaffirmation, in his view, was not intended to

---

[17] *Summa Trecensis*, ed. H. Fitting (Berlin, 1894), p. 145; Azo, *Summa codicis* (Lyon, 1557), to 5.12 (*De iure dotium*), f. 127rb: 'Et dicetur deduci ad inopiam vel vergere ad inopiam, cum erit evidentissimum mariti facultates sufficere non posse ad exactionem dotis et aliorum onerum quae imminent viro: ut ff. soluto matrimonio, 1. Si constante (*Digesta* 24.3.24). Hodie tamen videtur quod fiat exactio statim ex quo maritus inchoat sua substantia male uti: ut in authen. de aequalitate dotis. § aliud quoque (*Authentica* 7.8). Et puto hoc exaudiendum secundum opinionem, vel famam communem, quia dicunt homines eum male agere factum suum, argum. ff. de fundo instructo lega., 1. cum. delanionis. § Asinam. (*Digesta* 33.7.18). Sed licet dixerim exigi posse dotem, et soluto matrimonio et quandoque eo constante, aliter tamen et aliter fit exactio: nam soluto matrimonio ita fit exactio ut mulier de dote exacta faciat quicquid velit, eo constante, si exigat, non habet licentiam alienandi eas res vivente marito, sed fructibus earum verum potest abuti ad sustentationem sui et mariti et filiorum communium: ut infra eodem, 1. ubi (*Codex* 5.12.29).' A similar view was expounded in the Provençal paraphrase of the

encourage wives to exercise their legal recourse. Rather, it was intended to pledge allegiance to the dowry system's fundamental
objective: to support the burdens of marriage.[18] Whatever the intentions we may attribute to these twelfth-century jurists, it is no less
remarkable that the privilege enabling a wife to act against her husband in the case of insolvency was neither questioned nor reversed by
medieval jurisprudents, as were other Roman rules and privileges.
During the century spanning the compilation of the *Glossa ordinaria* by
Accursius (d. 1260) and the magisterial analysis of *Si constante* by
Bartolo (d. 1357), the leading doctors of civil law – Odofredo (d.
1265), Iacopo d'Arena (d. 1296), Jacques de Revigny (d. 1296), Dino
del Mugello (d. *c.* 1303), Jacobus de Belvisio (d. 1335), Cino da
Pistoia (d. 1336), Iacopo Bottrigari (d. 1347) and Alberico da Rosciate
(d. 1360) – unqualifiably and unhesitatingly sustained the privilege
enabling the wife to take legal action against a husband verging on
insolvency to lay claim to or recover not only her dowry but also her
trousseau (*paraphernalia*) and her husband's premarital donation
(*donatio propter nuptias*) during marriage.[19] This fundamental legal

Codex Justinianus of the twelfth century known as *Lo codi: Lo codi in der lateinischen
Übersetzung des Ricardus Pisanus*, ed. H. Fitting (Halle, 1906), pp. 163–4: 5.11.2,
5.14.1–3; and *Lo codi: eine Summa Codicis in provenzalischer Sprache aus dem XII.
Jahrhundert*, ed. F. Derrer (Zurich, 1974), pp. 119, 121.

[18] Bellomo, *Ricerche*, pp. 147–9. Bellomo stresses the wife's incapacity to alienate
the dowry restored to her and the requirement that the dowry be used to support the
burdens of marriage, while ignoring the *mens legis* of *Si constante*, *Ubi adhuc* and
Illud quoque sancire, one that was endorsed by all jurisprudents to prevent the total
loss of her dowry and patrimony.

[19] *Glossa ordinaria*, to *Digesta* 24.3.24, *Si constante* (Venice, 1591), p. 22b; *Codex*
5.12.29, *Ubi adhuc*, p. 708ab; *Novellae* 97.6, *Illud quoque sancire* v. *inchoante* (=*Authentica*
7.8), p. 263ab; Odofredo, to *Digesta* 24.3.24 (Lyon, 1552), f. 10b–va; Jacques de
Revigny, to *Codex* 5.12.29, *Lectura super prima parte Codicis* (attributed to Petrus de
Bellapertica) (Paris, 1519), f. 230v–231r; Dino del Mugello, to *Digesta* 24.3.24,
Apostillae super infortiato, Vatican, MS Urb. lat. 156, f. 68vab; Borgh. lat. 274, f.
22rb–va; Vat. lat. 1416, f. 4rab; Vat. lat. 1420, f. 4rb; Vat. lat. 2514, f. 6rb; Jacobus
de Belvisio, *Lectura super IX collationibus authenticorum*, Coll. VII, tit. 8, *De equalitate
dotis et propter nuptias donationis*, v. *Illud quoque* (Lyon, 1511), f. 54vb; Cino da Pistoia,
to *Codex* 5.12.29 (Frankfurt am Main, 1578), ff. 307a–308vb; Iacopo Bottrigari, to
Codex 5.12.29 (Paris, 1516), f. 152b–va; Alberico da Rosciate, to *Codex* 5.12.29
(Venice, 1576), ff. 256vb–258rb; Bartolo, to *Codex* 5.12.29 (Venice, 1570–1571),
f. 174v; to *Digesta* 24.3.24, f. 16a–20a. The opinions of Iacopo d'Arena are reported
by Alberico and Bartolo. There are several of Iacopo d'Arena's glosses (*Codex*
5.12.29) in Vat. lat. 1428, f. 133vab. For subsequent treatments, see Baldo, to *Digesta*
24.3.24 and to *Codex* 5.12.29 (Lyon, 1498), unfoliated (I have used a copy of this

privilege was also sustained by the preeminent canonists, Hostiensis (d. 1271), Guillaume Durand (d. 1296), Giovanni d'Andrea (d. 1348), Antonio da Budrio (d. 1408), Pietro d'Ancarano (d. 1416), Francesco Zabarella (d. 1417) and Niccolò de' Tedeschi (Panormitanus, d. 1445).[20] The legal remedy against such insolvent husbands was also endorsed by leading religious authorities in their *summae* or manuals of conscience, which had enormous influence upon penitential practice.[21] And it was enshrined in Rolandino dei Passaggeri's *Summa artis notarie* (1255–6), the principal textbook for notaries during the late Middle Ages.[22]

At the same time, jurisprudents, especially civilians, vigorously debated the various meanings of *inopia* and cognate expressions, and established juridical tests and procedures to identify and verify the

---

edition found in the Old Library, Queens College, Cambridge); Angelo degli Ubaldi, to *Digesta* 24.3.24 (Lyon, 1548), f. 8vb–9a; Bartolomeo Saliceto, to *Codex* 5.12.29 (Lyon, 1515), ff. 19v–20v; Lodovico Romano, *Consilia* (Lyon, 1565), cons. 462, f. 205r; to *Digesta* 24.3.24 (Lyon, 1547), ff. 44v–49ra; Paolo di Castro, to *Digesta* 24.3.24 (Lyon, 1553), ff. 22a–23b; Alessandro Tartagni, to *Digesta* 24.3.24 (Venice, 1595), ff. 41b–44a; Giovanni da Imola, to *Digesta* 24.3.24 (Lyon, 1502), ff. 13va–15ra; Raffaele Cumano, to *Digesta* 24.3.24 (Lyon, 1549), ff. 12rb–13ra; Pier Filippo Corneo, to *Codex* 6.20.5, *Dotis quidem* (=*Authentica* 7.8, *Quod locum*).

[20] Hostiensis, to the *Decretals* of Gregory IX 4.20.7, in *Corpus iuris canonici*, ed A. Friedberg (Leipzig, 1881) (henceforward cited as *X*), *Per vestras, In quartum Decretalium librum comment.* (Venice, 1581); f. 47a; Guillaume Durand, *Speculum iudicale* 4.4 tit. *De donat.* n. 18–24 (Frankfurt am Main, 1592), f. 464–5, with additions by Giovanni d'Andrea; Antonio da Budrio, to *X*.4.20.7, *In librum tertium Decretalium comment.* (Venice, 1575), f. 62r; Pietro d'Ancarano, to *X*.4.20.7, *Super quarto Decretalium facundissima comment.* (Bologna, 1580), ff. 159r–165v; Francesco Zabarella, to *X*.4.20.7, *Commentaria super primo (-quinto) decretalium* (Venice, 1502), fol. 27b; Niccolò de' Tedeschi, to *X*.4.20.7, *Super quarto Decretalium* (Lyon, 1521), ff. 50r–v.

[21] Johannes de Erfordia, *Summa confessorum, De dote*, ed. N. Brieskorn (Frankfurt am Main, 1980), vol. 2, p. 337; Bartolomeo da San Concordio, *Summa Pisanella*, *s.v. dos* (Venice, 1479); Sant'Antonino, *Summa Theologica*, Tit. 1, c. 23, *De dotibus et donationibus propter nuptias*, n. VII (Verona, 1740), p. 113; Angelo Carletti da Chivasso, *Summa Angelica*, *s.v. dos*, n. 14 (Venice, 1569); Bartolomeo Fumi, *Summa Armilla*, *s.v. dos*, n. 23 (Venice, 1554), f. 144v.

[22] *Summa totius artis notariae Rolandini*, I, 1 De dotibus (Venice, 1587), f. 69ab: 'Sed tunc de necessitate restituitur quando maritus ad inopiam vergit, ut C. de iure do., 1. Nisi [*sic*], scilicet cum incipit dilapidare bona sua et substantia propria male uti, ut Authen., de aequalitate do. § illud quoque (*Authentica* 7.8; *Novellae* 97.6), et hoc forte, quia ideo vir suspectus est, quod dissipaturus dotem sit;' cf. Salatiele (d. 1280), *Ars Notarie*, lib. IV, rub. *Instrumentum receptionis dotis*, ed. G. Orlandelli (Milan, 1961), vol. II, p. 267.

circumstances considered responsible for producing insolvency. They also debated which persons other than the husband the wife could sue to recover her dowry (for example, the husband's father and creditors), which persons other than a wife could reclaim the dowry during marriage (for example, her father and her children), which goods besides the dowry were subject to reclamation, and which legal actions could be initiated. They also paid considerable attention to the legal effects arising from reclamation with respect to the husband, his heirs and, especially, his creditors. Their teachings provided the repertoire of authoritative guidelines and strategies for litigants, notaries, lawyers and judges from the late-thirteenth century onward.

Si constante made the wife's actions for reclamation of the dowry contingent upon the husband's insolvency (*propter inopiam mariti*) and its obvious and predictable result: that his resources would be insufficient to satisfy his wife's claims (*facultas ad dotis exactionem non sufficere*). It was obvious and predictable to jurists of the thirteenth century that a wife's chances of actually reclaiming her dowry under this law were minimal. It was fully recognized that *Si constante* could serve, against its intent, as a means for delaying and frustrating the wife's legitimate claim. To avoid this harmful consequence, *Si constante* was reformulated, and the grounding text of its reformulation was a model case presented by the *Glossa ordinaria*.[23] Titia gave a dowry to her husband Seius, who began to mismanage his assets (*maritus inchoat male uti substantia sua*), and it is asked whether during marriage she can bring a suit against her husband to reclaim the dowry. Yes, the *Glossa* replied, if the wife witnessed her husband's mismanagement of his assets, the consequence of which would be that if he satisfied his other creditors, he would not be able to satisfy his wife's claims. The husband, therefore, is no longer required to be factually insolvent, as he was in *Si constante*, before his wife could take legal action. The formula, *maritus inchoat male uti substantia sua*, was not original but intertextual, that is, imported from *Illud quoque sancire* in the *Authentica* (the medieval designation of the *Novellae*). As Odofredo reminded his audience, 'today by virtue of the law of the *Authentica*, where the husband begins

---

[23] *Glossa ordinaria*, to *Digesta* 24.2.24, *Si constante* (*casus*), p. 22rb: 'Titia dedit dotem Seio marito suo; maritus inchoat male uti substantia sua, quaeritur utrum constante etiam matrimonio mulier contra eum posset agere ad dotem? Et dicitur, quod sic, si mulier viderit eum ita male uti et ita male usum circa substantiam suam; quod si satisfaciat aliis creditoribus non possit satisfieri mulieri'; see also *Glossa ordinaria*, to *Codex* 5.12.29, *vv. Ad inopiam*, p. 708a.

to mismanage his assets, a wife can demand her dowry or initiate a hypothecary action.'[24]

The differences among *Si constante*, *Ubi adhuc* and *Illud quoque sancire* became a source of contention, and may have been exploited by creditors or other parties opposing wives who sought to reclaim their dowries. Bartolo denied that these laws contradict or detract from each other; they are, he insisted, complementary, and a wife was fully entitled to reap the privileges and benefits provided by each law.[25] *Si constante* fully (*plene*) permits a wife to act when her husband's condition is so lamentable that, after having deducted his debts, his goods no longer suffice for the reclamation of the dowry. The wife, however, could not bring suit unless her husband sank into *extrema miseria*. As she was not permitted to institute an hypothecary action under *Si constante*, the wife was limited to the reclamation of her dowry.[26]

Ubi adhuc provided fuller (*plenius*) latitude to the wife. Even though the husband's goods may be sufficient to satisfy his wife's claim, still, if he inclines toward insolvency (*laborat ad inopiam*), she can demand the return of her dowry. For example, a nobleman may have enough goods to satisfy his creditors as well as his wife, yet he must spend everything he has in order to live honorably. This set of circumstances is considered tantamount to someone inclining toward insolvency. Excessive expenditures for the maintenance of honor were incurred, ironically, by husbands of well-to-do and socially prominent families who lavished gifts of jewels, ornaments and fine clothing upon their new brides. In former times, Bartolo related, a wife was not able to reclaim her dowry when her husband's resources were sufficient, but today she could in accordance with *Ubi adhuc*.[27]

---

[24] Odofredo, to *Codex* 5.12.29, *Ubi adhuc*, f. 277ra, n. 4: '. . . sed hodie iure authenticorum ex quo maritus incipit uti male substantia sua, potest exigere dotem vel agere hypothecaria; ut infra, de coll. 1. dotis in Authen. quod locum' (*Codex* 6.20.5, *Dotis quidem*, *Authentica* 7.8).

[25] Bartolo, to *Digesta* 24.3.24, *Si constante*, f. 16ra, n. 1: 'Mihi autem videtur quod circa hoc sunt tria iura, scilicet ius digestorum, et hoc providet mulieri plene. Ius codicis, et hoc providet plenius. Et ius authenticorum, et hoc providet plenissime, et nullum alteri derogat, immo diversis casibus loquuntur.'

[26] ibid.: 'Nam secundum haec iura digestorum mulier tam poterat agere, cum vir erat in illa extrema miseria, quod bona sua non sufficiebant ad exactionem dotis deducto aere alieno, nec ante poterat agere, et istud est solum in dote.'

[27] ibid.: 'Sed per ius codicis provisum est plenius, quod licet bona mariti sufficiant ad exactionem dotis, tamen si maritus laborat inopia: puta, quod sit nobilis homo et habet in bonis parum, tamen habet in bonis tantum quod sufficit creditoribus et doti; tamen quia oportet eum vivere honorifice, omnia expendit, et mulier peteret

Illud quoque sancire provided the fullest (*plenissime*) latitude to the wife. Under this law, the wife was allowed to take legal action to recover her dowry, even if the husband's resources were sufficient to satisfy his creditors, his wife and his desire to live well. She can act when there is reason to believe that the husband is verging on insolvency because he is mismanaging his assets.[28]

Although *Si constante, Ubi adhuc* and *Illud quoque sancire* gave life to the normative metaphors which would mark the insolvent husband from the late twelfth century onward, they were silent on the procedural mechanisms by which the husband's financial condition would be ascertained. Roman jurists typically focused their attention on the circumstances giving rise to particular actions and lacked interest in developing procedures for the resolution of disputes. To discover the extent of her husband's assets or alleged insolvency in a contemporary divorce suit, a wife would have to resort to a variety of time-consuming and expensive procedures, involving lawyers, accountants, property appraisers, pension experts and court stenographers. Our jurists, with few exceptions, taught that the husband's public reputation (*vulgi opinio*) should be the cardinal test in ascertaining his financial condition.[29] This would be achieved by making inquiries among his

---

necessitatem, secundum ista tempora mulier non poterat agere, sed hodie potest, per dictam legem Ubi (*Codex* 5.12.29). . . .' On the 'gifts' presented to the wife, which by law reverted to the husband and his heirs, see Bartolo, to *Digesta* 24.3.66, *In hiis* § *Servis uxoris*, ff. 30vb–31ra; cf. C. Klapisch-Zuber, 'Le complexe de Griselde', pp. 7–43.

[28] ibid. n. 4: 'Item per ius authenticorum est provisum plenissime. Ecce, vir habet tantum, quod sufficit creditoribus et doti, et est dives et habet tantum quod potest bene vivere; tamen est dubium quod vergat ad inopiam, male utitur substantia sua et secundum ista iura mulier non poterat agere, sed hodie est sibi provisum plenius, ut etiam tunc possit agere. Unum ergo ius non corrigit aliud, sed addit alteri iuri plenius providendo.'

[29] *Glossa ordinaria*, to *Codex* 5.12.29, *vv. Ad inopiam*, p. 708a: '. . . hodie autem constat prius et post posse agi, scilicet quando vir cepit male uti sua substantia, ut authen., de aequa. dot. § illud collat. VII (*Authentica* 7.8), quod inspiciam secundum opinionem vulgi, argum. ff. de fun. instruc., 1. cum delanionis § Asinam (*Digesta* 33.7.18).' Rolandino dei Passaggeri, *Summa*, f. 69va: 'Sed sufficit ad hoc ut mulier possit agere, et sibi de dote providere, maritum inchoasse male uti sua substantia, ut praealega. § illud quoque (*Authentica* 7.8), quod inspicitur secundum opinionem vulgi seu famam communem, ut quia dicunt homines eum incepisse male agere factum suum vel dicunt talis incepit navigare, et poterit mulier in praedicto casu agere personali actione contra maritum, et accipere de bonis suis in solutum si non satisfacit sibi;' Jacques de Revigny, to *Codex* 5.12.29, *Ubi adhuc*, f. 230va: 'Dico quod

neighbors, who presumably know his affairs best. 'If there are men under the sun who know their neighbor's secrets,' Odofredo quipped, 'they are neighbors.'[30] A notable exception to the common doctrine was the teaching of Iacopo Bottrigari, which stressed that the husband's mismanagement of his assets was not proved by public reputation, but by witnesses who testify that he is a gambler, swindler or negligent in the administration of his goods. He did admit that the teaching of the *Glossa ordinaria* was true with respect to *Ubi adhuc*, where *vulgi opinio* constituted sufficient proof of the husband's inability to pay his legal debts.[31] This issue, as Bartolo demonstrated,

---

nos recurremus ad vulgi opinionem: unde quando erit opinio in civitate de seipso quod ipse male administrat res suas et male facit que habet facere, tunc dicemus cum male uti re sua, ut de ff. questionibus, 1. de minore (*Digesta* 48.18.10) et ff. de. fundo instruc., 1. cum delanionis § Asinam (*Digesta* 33.7.18).' Jacques de Revigny's opinion is reported by Cino da Pistoia, to *Codex* 5.12.29, f. 307a, n. 3. Dino del Mugello's opinion is reported by Bartolo to *Digesta* 24.3.24, *Si constante*, n. 6, f. 16rb: 'Dynus dicit quod probabitur secundum vulgi opinionem . . .;' and is found in glosses (MS Vat. lat. 1416, f. 4ra) to *Digesta* 24.3.24, *Si constante, vv. evidentissime apparuent:* 'per oppinionem vulgi, ut infra, de questionibus, 1. de minore ult. (*Digesta* 48.18.10) et de fundo instruc., 1. Cum delanionis § Asinam (*Digesta* 33.7.18), dy.'

[30] Odofredo, to *Codex* 5.12.29, n. 4, f. 277bv: 'Sed quero, quando maritus dicitur inchoare male uti substantia sua, et certe non eo ipso quod propter solitum ordinem duos denarios expendit. Sed ex quo vulgi opinio est, quod mittit in navem vel male faciat facta sua: nam si sunt homines sub sole qui sciunt secreta vicinorum suorum, sciunt vicini et in talibus vulgi opinio spectat, ut ff. de questionibus, 1. de minore penul. (*Digesta* 48.18.10), et de fundo instru. 1. cum delanionis (*Digesta* 33.7.18).' An early example of *vulgi opinio* at work occurred at Siena on 1 April 1253, where Benvenuta di Ildebrandi was assigned and took possession of real estate and personal property from her insolvent husband's (Maestro Domenico's) estate: 'Omnibus pateat evidenter quod, cum adhuc matrimonio constituto inter dominam Benvenutam, uxorem magistri Dominichi quondam Dietauti, iidem Magister Domenicus male uti sua substantia incohasset et ad inopiam deveniret, sicut vulgi sui populi ecclesie Sancti Gilii oppinio publice testabatur, quia se multis creditoribus pro se et aliis obligavit, ita ut si eis primitus solveretur, facultates ejusdem non sufficerent ad dotes easdem expediendas, et inanes plerosque alios sumptus fecit, volens eadem mulier uti legis consilio et forma conventionis inite inter se et magistrum Dominicum supradictum, ne dotibus suis et lucro donationis propter nuptias sibi facto a dicto viro suo indebite fraudaretur . . .'; ed. L. Zdekauer, *La vita privata e pubblica dei senesi nel dugento* (Siena, 1896), pp. 96–7.

[31] Bottrigari's opinion is reported by Alberico da Rosciate, to *Codex* 5.12.29, n. 2, f. 257ra: 'Contrarium tamen tenet Iacobus Butrigarius et dicit quod maritus male utatur substantia sua, non probari per vulgi opinionem, set opus sit probari per testes, qui deponent, quod sit lusor, baratator, vel negligens in administratione

did not admit a simple solution. He denied that the circumstances triggering the wife's action – the husband's insufficiency of goods, his destitution and mismanagement of his assets – are interchangeable, just because the *Glossa ordinaria*, Dino del Mugello and other doctors held that each circumstance can be proved in the same manner, namely, by common opinion.[32] Arguing *pro et contra*, he first put forward the thesis that the husband's worth must be fully authenticated by documents and witnesses; it must be fully proved that his assets remain insufficient to pay off his debts; and the husband must be allowed the opportunity to prove that in fact he has many goods.[33] The principle behind Bartolo's thesis is that cases whose outcome might produce great damage (*magnum praeiudicium*) require full proof (*plena probatio*) and formal proceedings. Swiftly reversing his course, Bartolo acknowledged that only partial proof (*semiplena probatio*) based on *vulgi opinio* and summary proceedings were required, since any damages suffered by the husband would be moderate or little. The reasoning animating his counter-thesis is that the husband would suffer only minor damage, since his wife must use income earned from the dowry now in her control for their mutual support.[34] Partial proof based on the husband's public reputation and summary procedure were also valid, Bartolo instructed, in ascertaining and establishing the husband's mismanagement of his assets and the extent of his insolvency.[35] Should the wife wish to bring suit against a third party

---

rerum suarum. Opinionem tamen gl. dicit veram quoad legem codicis, quia tunc opus erat probare, maritum ad inopiam vergere, quia cum ista probatio sit mere negativa, scilicet probare aliquem non esse solvendo, sufficiat probari per vulgi opinionem.'

[32] Bartolo, to *Digesta* 24.3.24, *Si constante*, n. 6, f. 16r: 'Ista verba videntur invenere, idem esse, bona ad dotis quantitatem non sufficere, et virum esse inopem, et male uti substantia sua, cum eodem modo videantur probari. Sed ego praedicta posui supra ut diversa, ideo singulariter examinemus.

[33] ibid., n. 7.

[34] ibid., n. 9–10, f. 16va: 'Cum ergo ex hac sententia quae fertur in hoc iudicio ipso marito fiat modicum praeiudicium, ideo dotem esse tantam mulier probat plene: quia si de hoc dubitaretur fieret plenum praeiudicium aliis creditoribus, sed non esse tot bona quae sufficiant debitis computatis ad exactionem dotis, probatur per vulgi opinionem, quia summaria et semiplena probatio per famam videtur haberi. . . . Nam haec sententia parum praeiudicat viro, cum fructus deserviant oneribus matrimonii. . . . Quod puto verum quando agitur contra ipsum virum.'

[35] ibid., n. 13–16. Bartolo's thesis was sustained by Baldo (to *Codex* 5.12.29, and to *Digesta* 24.3.24), Pietro d'Ancarano (to *X*.4.20.7, *Per vestras*, n. 23–5, pp. 161–2); Raffaele Cumano, to *Digesta* 24.3.24, f. 12vb; and Bartolomeo Saliceto, to *Codex*

holding the husband's goods, full proof of the husband's financial condition was necessary.[36] Bartolo urged judges presiding over cases of insolvency to be aware that its determination is contingent upon social rank and material circumstances. A knight or nobleman worth 1,000 (pounds) is considered poor, while a rustic worth less is considered rich.[37] After recommending to his audience Bartolo's theses, Baldo proffered this advice:

I say that the discerning judge not only ought to make inquiries about the husband's reputation but also about the reasons for his reputation. Let us assume that he is reputed to be a spendthrift [*prodigus*]. The judge ought to examine the reasons which prompted those asserting that he is a spendthrift, and they ought to come forth with their reasons: for example, they witness him daily acting wastefully and spending way beyond what his resources can bear.[38]

The wife can also act against her husband, Bartolo instructed, when his reputation as a prosperous merchant is belied by the fact that he is actually verging on insolvency. He has in mind a wealthy husband who becomes a merchant, travels overseas, performs his profession with skill, but begins to suffer heavy losses and impoverishment. His neighbors and acquaintances back home remain ignorant of his plight, believing that his goods are sufficient to satisfy both his creditors and his wife. Technically, under these conditions, the wife is barred from enlisting *Si constante* to buttress her claim. Likewise, she is barred from enlisting *Ubi adhuc*, because even though the husband is in fact verging

---

5.12.29: 'Opinatur enim vulgus iuxta proverbium antiquum quo dicitur in vulgari nostro: "Richezza maldisposta a poverta se acosta." In latino: "Divitie male disposite pauperitati sunt proxime." Cum enim hoc non posset bene et necessario concludentur probari, sufficit probari verisimiliter et secundum opinionem vulgi, quia non in duorum vel trium testium iudicio hoc consistit, sed in opinione et iudicio vulgi.'

[36] Bartolo, to *Digesta* 24.3.24, *Si constante*, n. 10: 'Sed si ageretur contra extraneum, tunc credo quae deberet probari plene . . .'.

[37] ibid., n. 14: 'Arbitrabitur autem hic iudex diversimode secundum diversitatem personarum et factorum, unde miles vel nobilis homo habens mille in bonis est pauper; unus rusticus habens minus est dives.'

[38] Baldo, to *Codex* 5.12.29: 'Ego dico quod discretus iudex non solum debet interrogare de fama sed de ratione fame. Pone enim quod fama est quod aliquis est prodigus, debet interrogare iudex qua ratione moveantur isti dicentes quod iste est prodigus et tunc debent assignare rationem: verbi gratia, quia vident eum quotidie dilapidare et valde ultra expendere quam portent sue facultates.'

on insolvency, he is popularly reputed to be wealthy. Finally, she is barred from enlisting *Illud quoque sancire*, because even though the husband suffered business losses, his business career commenced profitably. Thus the requirement that the husband began to mismanage his assets would not, literally speaking, be met. Rejecting a literal and strict interpretation of these laws, Bartolo asserted that the wife is able to act in this case in order to prevent the loss of her dowry.[39] It does not matter when a husband verges on insolvency, whether at the time he commences his business or at a later date, he remains subject to his wife's suit.

Opinion was divided over whether a wife can act to reclaim her dowry during marriage, if from the beginning of marriage her husband was already insolvent. Dino, Alberico da Rosciate and Baldo were flatly opposed to the wife's action.[40] Both Jacques de Revigny and Cino opined that if a wife knew that her husband was insolvent at the time of marriage, she was prohibited from acting; if she was ignorant, on the other hand, she was permitted to act.[41] Bartolo believed that a wife was always entitled to her dotal benefits and privileges during marriage. *De iure*, a wife who gave a dowry to an insolvent husband has not entered into an implied agreement to forfeit her future right to take legal action. Even if she so desired, she is not entitled to renounce these benefits and privileges by an antenuptial agreement, tacit as well

---

[39] Bartolo, n. 17, f. 16vb: 'In proposito ergo favore dotis ne mulier possit perdere dotem, si vir pervenerit ad perfectam paupertatem, utroque modo intelligam, ut sive vir male inchoaret respecta initii sive male exitum habeat, consuletur mulieri. . . .'

[40] Dino del Mugello, to *Digesta* 24.3.24 (MS Urb. lat. 156, f. 68va): 'In principio huius legis. Constante matrimonio exigitur dos, id est, si evidenter appareant facultates viri non sufficere ad quantitatem dotis et hoc dicit. Quid si ab initio non erat solvendo? Dic non habere locum remedium huius legis, ar. infra, ut (MS: si) in pos., 1. si is a quo § fi. (*Digesta* 36.4.3)'; Alberico da Rosciate, to *Codex* 5.12.29, n. 5, f. 257ra; Baldo, to *Codex* 5.12.29.

[41] Jacques de Revigny, to *Codex* 5.12.29, f. 230vb: 'Ego concedo quod si mulier dedisset dotem marito inopi quod non allegaret ignorantiam. Ipsa non haberet constante matrimonio dotis repetitionem. Sed si contraxit cum eo credebat eum divitem et solvendo, tunc ego dico quod proest ac si postea esset factus non solvendo . . .;' Cino da Pistoia, to *Codex* 5.12.29, n. 9, f. 307vb: 'Pone, quod mulier accepit maritum inopem et dedit sibi dotem, nunquid habebit tunc remedium huius legis? Dico distinguendum, aut mulier scivit talem et accepit eum, quia forte placuit sibi persona propter formam; tunc imputet sibi, ut ff. ut in possess. leg., 1. si is a quo § ultimo (*Digesta* 36.4.3). Aut ignoravit et tunc perinde est, ac si de novo fieret egenus . . .'.

as express.[42] The contrary opinion, Bartolo stressed, produces noxious results. 'It would impede marriage for someone who is destitute and has mismanaged his affairs, since he would not find a wife with a dowry, and consequently women would witness themselves, with the aid of these laws, abandoned. This our opinion is beneficial to marriages and therefore is to be upheld and accepted.'[43] Baldo did not clarify the issue by espousing contradictory opinions. He advised his audience (to *Ubi adhuc*) that Dino's negative opinion was preferable. His reasoning: an agreement in which a wife renounces her right to act during marriage, does not nullify the functional purpose of the dowry, and is in all respects valid. Yet, in his commentary on *quod locum (Authentica* 7.8), he upheld Bartolo's teaching.[44]

Although these competing opinions were frequently cited by fifteenth-century jurists, I have not yet found actual disputes involving wives who were prevented from bringing suit on the grounds that their husbands were insolvent at the start of their marriage. Less academic and certainly more conspicuous were cases in which wives sought to reclaim their dowries from husbands who were placed under a ban for commiting a civil wrong or a crime and from husbands who were actually exiled.[45] The plight of Florentine wives whose husbands were placed under the ban – Gemma di Manetto Donati (Dante's wife),

---

[42] Bartolo, to *Digesta* 24.3.24, f. 17ra, n. 23: 'Ego credo quod semper mulier habeat tale beneficium. Primo, quia ante contractas nuptias mulier non potest aliquod pactum facere expresse, per quod longiori die repetatur dos, ne conditio eius fiat deterior . . .'.

[43] ibid.: 'Praeterea sententia praedicta esset nuptiis impedimento, nam pauper et qui male facit facta sua non invenerit uxorem cum dote, eo quod mulieres viderent se auxilio istarum legum destitutas. Ista autem nostra sentent a nuptiis est favorabilis et ideo est tenenda et admittenda . . .'.

[44] Baldo, to *Codex* 5.12.29 and to *Digesta* 24.3.24: 'Sed quid si ab initio vir non erat solvendo, utrum mulier habebit beneficium istius legis, et dicit Dynus quod non . . . Bartolus dicit contrarium, quia si mulier velit expresse renunciare beneficio huius legis non posset . . . Tu tene opinionem Dyni et Petri [Jacques de Revigny], quia istud pactum est secundum naturam dotis quod non agatur constante matrimonio et omnino valet pactum . . .'; to *Codex* 6.20.5, *Dotis quidem* § *quod locum (Authentica* 7.8). Bartolomeo Saliceto adhered to Bartolo's teaching (to *Codex* 5.12.29, n. 11, f. 20rb), while Lodovico Romano returned to the teaching of Dino del Mugello (to *Digesta* 24.3.24, f. 46vb).

[45] On banishment and exile, see D. Cavalca, *Il bando nella prassi e nella dottrina giuridica medievale* (Milan, 1978); P. R. Pazzaglini, *The Criminal Ban of the Sienese Commune, 1225–1310, Quaderni di Studi Senesi*, 45 (Milan, 1979); R. Starn, *Contrary Commonwealth. The Theme of Exile in Medieval and Renaissance Italy* (Berkeley, California, 1982).

Lisa di Monte (Matteo Villani's wife) and the remarkable Alessandra Macinghi Strozzi, to name only the famous – was a source of enormous domestic tension as revealed in private letters and diaries. According to Bartolo, if all the goods of a *bannitus* are confiscated by public authority, no doubt exists that his wife can take legal action to recover her dowry, for the husband is now considered to be completely insolvent. She can also take legal action if only part of his goods is confiscated, even though, in theory, he would appear to have sufficient resources to cover the claims of both his wife and creditors. Yet the cruel realities of banishment and exile were otherwise. Exiles customarily suffered a host of legal disabilities: they were forbidden from communicating with their family, relatives, neighbors and business associates, and were barred from doing business within the jurisdiction of their cities. The life of an exile was thus fraught with a series of hardships, often leading to insolvency. It was this reality which lay behind Bartolo's determination that the wife of an exile, whose goods were not confiscated, could none the less sue to recover her dowry on the grounds that her husband has begun to mismanage his assets.[46] Bartolo's determination quickly became the *communis opinio*.[47]

The ability of wives to lay claim to the goods of husbands placed under the ban was a political as well as legal issue. Governments were as obsessed with confiscating the goods of *banniti* as were wives with recovering their dowries. Where the *ius commune* favored the interests of the wife, statutory law tended to favor the interests of governments. This tension is illustrated in the following dispute which occurred in late fourteenth-century Florence during her war with Milan, a period

---

[46] Bartolo, to *Digesta* 24.3.24, ff. 16v–17r, n. 18–20.

[47] Cf. Nello di San Gimignano (b. 1373), *De banniti* (*Tractatus universi iuris*, Venice, 1584, XI, 1, f. 369v): 'Titius satis dives sumpsit uxorem et ab ea recepit dotem cum promissionibus consuetis, deinde bannitus est. Queritur, an uxor possit petere sibi dotem consignari per legem Si constante vel per legem Ubi adhuc . . . Bartolus in lege Si constante (*Digesta* 24.3.24) in quarta quaestio primae quaestionis concludit quod si omnia bona publicantur, nulla est dubitatio. Potest enim tunc petere per remedium 1. Si constante. Item, etiam dicit si pars bonorum est publicata, 1. Si marito, eo tituli (*Digesta* 24.3.31). Si vero retinet omnia bona sed exulare cogitur, tunc quia cepit uti male substantia sua, potest petere consignationem per d. §. illud (*Authentica* 8.7).' However, Nello added this qualification: 'Sed hoc ultimum intelligo in bannito personaliter vel in tanta quantitate, quod dici possit eum male cepisse . . . Si vero sit bannitus in parva quantitate, puta in 200 libris, et habet magnam substantiam, tunc licet non solvat vel quia non vult vel quia absens ignorat, non puto tale quid considerandum;' Lodovico Romano, to *Digesta* 24.3.24, f. 46vb; Giovanni da Imola to *Digesta* 24.3.24, f. 13va.

of heavy taxation.[48] In 1397 Tommaso di Rosso de' Ricci was condemned to death for not satisfying his forced loan assessments (*prestanze*), a sentence that would be carried out should Tommaso not pay up within a specified period. The commune and his neighborhood (*gonfalone*), which was responsible for levying these assessments, were planning to confiscate Tommaso's goods, when his wife Francesca claimed that they were secured for her dowry. She sought to recover a dowry of 1500 florins so that she could support herself (*se alere possit*), on the technical grounds that her husband was verging on insolvency and was mismanaging his assets. Four local jurists, Rosello dei Roselli, Rosso di Andreozzo Orlandi, Riccardo di Francesco del Bene and Giovanni de' Ricci, were engaged to decide whether superior rights to Tommaso's goods were vested in the commune and *gonfalone* or in his wife.

If the case were decided solely on the basis of the Florentine statutes, Roselli pronounced in the lead opinion, there can be no question that Francesca's claim should be quashed. Her action appears to be blocked by two statutes, one prohibiting a wife laying claim to her husband's goods, while he is alive, against his creditors; another prohibiting restitution of dowries except when the husband's death is due to natural causes. Since Tommaso was not yet dead, and since his future fate, if the sentence were carried out, would be a civil death, the statutes prevailed against Francesca's claim. Reversing his course, Roselli argued that these statutory prohibitions were outweighed by reasons anchored in the *ius commune*. First, the dowry was given and Tommaso's goods were obligated for its return in 1390 and 1392 respectively, that is, *before* he was assessed for *prestanze*. Consequently, the wife's rights are preferred to those of the fisc (*iura fisci*). Secondly, Tommaso's goods remain secured for his wife's support (*alimenta*). This reason allowed Roselli to circumvent the two Florentine statutes cited above. They do not prevail here, because they do not expressly prohibit the wife from demanding support from her husband's goods. Thirdly, 'a great iniquity' would result if creditors, with weaker legal privileges than the wife, were allowed to seize her husband's as well as her own goods.[49] For these reasons, Roselli concluded, the wife can demand and secure support from her husband's goods for the amount

---

[48] Florence, *Biblioteca Nazionale, Magliabechiano*, XXIX, 117, ff. 100r–103v.

[49] ibid., f. 100r: 'Iniquitas magna esset quod alii creditores qui non sunt tam privilegati possint cupere bona viri et uxoris . . .'.

of her dowry and in conformity with their social rank.[50]

Roselli's opinion was roundly approved and buttressed on 2 May 1399 by Rosso di Andreozzo Orlandi. Citing *Ubi adhuc, Illud quoque sancire* and Barolo's commentary on *Si constante*, he stated that Francesca had an unquestionable claim to be assigned an amount not exceeding her dowry from her husband's goods, and that in this case the *ius commune* prevailed over the *ius municipale civitatis Florentie*.[51] Francesca's victory was not solitary.[52] Between 1375 and 1431 the government of Florence recognized the claims of 90 wives whose husbands had been condemned and exiled as rebels. They received amounts equivalent to their dowries from the properties which had been confiscated and from the proceeds of confiscated property which had been sold.[53]

Husbands who become insolvent through no fault of their own (owing to an accident such as a shipwreck), Cino, Baldo and others taught, were not open to legal suit. Wives were admonished to share their husband's losses and stand firmly by them in times of adversity and misfortune.[54] Bartolo was pointedly silent on this particular issue, but it is difficult to believe that he would have agreed with either his mentor, Cino, or his disciple, Baldo. Whatever the cause, the hus-

[50] ibid.: 'Concludo igitur quod dicta domina Francischa usque ad quantitatem alimentorum sibi debitorum secundum quantitatem sue dotis et qualitatem personarum dicti Tommasii et ipsius domine Francische secundum que considerantur alimenta . . . debet preferri comuni Florentie in predictis prestantiis et hominibus dicti gonfalonis habentibus iura a dicto comuni Florentie.'

[51] ibid., f. 102r: 'In proposito ergo potest indubitanter dicta domina Francischa petere sibi de bonis dicti Tomasi assignari usque ad quantitatem dicte dotis ex predicta causa ut dictis iuribus et in eis habet prima et potiora iura quam comune Florentie vel vexillum predictum, ut in rationibus et iuribus per prefatum patrem et dominum meum supra allegatis. Et hoc sine dubio verum est de iure comuni. Nempe vero predictis obstare videtur ius municipale civitatis Florentie.'

[52] Francesca was assigned properties in lieu of her dowry on 17 August 1401. The list of properties (*bona assignata pro dote domine Francisce uxoris Tommasii de Riccis*) is found in *Archivio di Stato di Firenze* (henceforward *ASF*), *Capitane dei parte* 50 (numero rosso rep.), f. 121r.

[53] Starn, *Contrary Commonwealth*, p. 114.

[54] Cino da Pistoia, to *Codex* 5.12.29, f. 308ra, n. 15; Alberico da Rosciate, to *Codex* 5.12.29, f. 257vb, n. 13; Baldo, to *Codex* 5.12.29: 'Secundo vero casu principali quando mulier est sollicita quia adverso casu maritus laborat inopia, ut quia flumen portavit podere suum vel naufragium est passus, tunc non habet locum quod mulier possit conqueri constante matrimonio, que debet esse particeps infortunii mariti, ut ff. so. ma., 1. si cum dotem § Sin autem in sevissimo (*Digesta* 24.3.22)'; Bartolomeo Saliceto, to *Codex* 5.12.30, *In rebus dotalibus* § *omnis autem*, f. 21va.

band's evident insufficiency of assets to meet his wife's dotal claims was, for Bartolo, sufficient grounds on which to institute legal action. Only in the exceptional case where the wife was considered mentally incapable (*furiosa*) of administering her own affairs in a responsible manner, did Bartolo permit the dowry to be sequestered on her behalf. He advised that a judge acting on her behalf in the name of equity should sequester what remained of the dowry from a husband who was illegitimately squandering it. The dowry was not to be restored to the wife, but to a third party enjoined to administer it in the mutual interest of husband and wife.[55] Civilian jurists tended to follow Bartolo's lead, teaching that with few exceptions the dowry should be directly restored to the wife.[56] If canonists respectfully acknowledged the authority of civil law in cases of insolvency, they tended to follow the lead of Pope Innocent III's decretal *Per vestras* (*X*.4.20.7) of 1206.[57] They taught that the husband can furnish his wife security for the dowry rather than the dowry itself; and that the dowry can be safe-

[55] Bartolo, to *Digesta* 24.3.24, f. 16rab, n. 5 and to *Digesta* 24.3.22 *Si cum dotem* § Sin autem in saevissimo, f. 14va. Alberico da Rosciate shared Bartolo's position; to *Codex* 5.12.29, f. 257va, n. 13: 'Sed salva pace tantorum virorum contrarium communiter in iudicio vidi servari, ut si maritus vergat ad inopiam culpa sua, vel sine culpa, locus sit exactioni dotis, secundum formam huius lex. Nam prael. illud (*Authentica* 8.7) favore mulierum inductus est, ut non expectetur inopia viri, sed sufficiat eum male uti substantia sua, ergo in mulierum laesionem non dent retorqueri, et quia legum coerctio vitanda est, maxime dotium favore, et hoc satis innuit text. in d. § illud.'

[56] Paolo di Castro, to *Digesta* 24.3.24, f. 22rb, n. 7; Alessandro Tartagni, to *Digesta* 24.3.24, f. 42rb, n. 6. One exception was the wife who herself contributed to the dissipation and mismanagement of the dowry. Alberico da Rosciate, to *Codex* 5.12.29, f. 257rb, n. 6: 'Sed quid si maritus et uxor sunt ambo dissipatores et male utentes substantia sua, nunquid habebit locum haec lex? Vidi terminari quod non, quia tunc cessant rationes et mens huius legis, quia dos non esset in tuto et dissipari posset, et ideo deponenda est dos in aliquo tuto loco. . . .' Giovanni da Imola counseled that when both husband and wife are suspected of dissipating the dowry or the husband's assets, these goods ought to be sequestered and placed with a merchant for the purpose of producing licit profit; to *Digesta* 24.3.24, f. 14rb.

[57] See references in note 20 above. The decretal *Per vestras*, sent to Genoa in 1206, resolved a case between an insolvent husband, his wife and a third party, Master R, with whom she had invested her dowry. The pope commanded the husband to furnish security that he would safeguard the dowry or to commit it to some merchant, 'so that from honest gain the husband can sustain the burdens of matrimony'. For a discussion of the contribution of *Per vestras* to the debate over usury, see J. T. Noonan, jun., *The Scholastic Analysis of Usury* (Cambridge, Mass., 1957), pp. 136–7; J. Baldwin, *Masters, Princes and Merchants. The Social Views of Peter the Chanter and his Circle* (Princeton, 1970), I, pp. 280–1.

guarded by placing the insolvent husband's remaining assets in trust with a merchant. As it provided canonists from the thirteenth century onward with an opportunity to contribute to the general doctrinal analysis of principles and procedures to be applied to cases of insolvency, *Per vestras* was certainly an influential decretal. Its practical significance is difficult to assess, since wives' suits against insolvent husbands were, as far as we know, resolved in accordance with the civil law. However, civilian jurists alleged *Pers vestras* when they doubted the wife's ability to administer her dowry, or conversely, when they sought to justify the placement of cash, which the wife received from her husband in lieu of her dowry or from the husband's creditors in lieu of his goods, with a reputable merchant.[58] The potential conflict between canon and civil law must not obscure the collective desire of all jurists, many of whom were *doctores utriusque iuris*, to keep intact both dowry and family.

A father-in-law who received the dowry, an altogether conventional occurrence when his son was not yet emancipated, was liable to be sued for its return, if he himself was inclining towards insolvency. The *Glossa ordinaria* admitted that the daughter-in-law's action was not sanctioned by the *Digest*, and it filled the lacuna with a doctrine that won rapid approval in subsequent jurisprudence. The dowry could be reclaimed from the father-in-law when he was inclining toward insolvency on the grounds that equity, which furnishes the rationale for action against an insolvent husband, also furnishes the same rationale for action against an insolvent father-in-law.[59] Bartolo, in another classic text, laid down a series of distinctions and guidelines for determining the father-in-law's legal responsibilities regarding his son's dowry. When he received the dowry in his name only, the father, not the son, is obligated for its restitution. However, when he received

---

[58] See Angelo degli Ubaldi, to *Digesta* 24.3.24, f. 99; and p. 290 below.

[59] *Glossa ordinaria*, to *Digesta* 24.3.24, *v. mariti*, p. 22b: 'Quid in socero, si ipse vergat ad inopiam, et receperit dotem? Hoc quidem vel alibi non exprimitur, nisi de marito vergente ad inopiam, et alias generaliter et prohibetur agi constante matrimonio, ut C. de praesci. 30 an., 1. cum notissimi § illud (*Codex* 7.39.7); puto tamen idem in socero quod in marito servari: quia eadem ratio aequitatis intervenit, scilicet ut mulieri consulatur, ut C. ad leg. Fal., 1. fi. (*Codex* 6.50.19)'; Rolandino dei Passaggeri, I, 1, f. 69rb; Odofredo, to *Codex* 5.12.29, f. 277b, n. 5; Jacques de Revigny, to *Codex* 5.12.29, f. 230vb; Cino da Pistoia, to *Codex* 5.12.29, f. 307vb, n. 6; Jacobus de Belvisio, to *Authentica* 8.7, *Illud quoque* f. 54vb; Giovanni d'Andrea, *additiones* to Guillaume Durand *Speculum iudicale* 4.4. tit. *De donat. viro* (Frankfurt/ Main, 1592, f. 464); Bartolo, to *Digesta* 24.3.24, f. 17ra, n. 25; Baldo, to *Digesta* 24.3.24.

the dowry in the name of his son and with his consent, the obligation for restitution falls on the shoulders of the son, not the father. When the father receives the dowry in his own name with his son's consent, both are obligated for restitution. A son who received the dowry without his father's consent undertakes full responsibility for restitution. In the most customary situation, where the son received the dowry with his father's approval, both are obligated for its restitution.[60]

That both father and son were obligated for the dowry was beneficial for the wife, but could she undertake legal action if only one of them was verging on insolvency? Under *Si constante*, she was without legal recourse, since, in principle, there remained sufficient assets to secure her dowry. The *Glossa ordinaria* disagreed, explaining that legal action was justified because her dowry was undeniably in danger as a result of being administered irresponsibly.[61] Although this doctrine, too, rapidly gained a foothold in subsequent jurisprudence,[62] there was opposition from jurists like Jacques de Revigny and Pierre de Belleperche (d. 1308), who contended that the dowry remained secure so long as one co-debtor possessed sufficient resources.[63] While Cino da Pistoia reproved the reasoning of the *Glossa*, he taught that the wife is authorized by *Si constante* and *Ubi adhuc* to act against the solvent co-debtor because, he contended, 'it is in our interest to have many debtors'.[64] Bartolo held deep reservations about the logic and propriety of permitting actions against the party not verging on insolvency. The doctrine of the *Glossa* and the opinion advanced by Cino,

---

[60] Bartolo, to *Digesta* 24.3.22, *Si cum dotem* § *Transgrediamur*, f. 15ra.

[61] *Glossa ordinaria*, to *Digesta* 24.3.24, *v. mariti*, p. 22rb: 'Item quid si maritus et socer tenentur, et alter tantum ad inopiam vergat? Respon. secundum has leges non posse agi constante matrimonio, quia utriusque vel alterius bona sufficiunt, et ideo non agitur, ut hic, sed hodie agetur, quia negari non potest coepisse male geri pro dote adstricta.'

[62] Rolandino dei Passaggeri, I, 1, f. 69rb; Odofredo, to *Codex* 5.12.29, f. 277b; Iacopo d'Arena, to *Digesta* 24.3.24, f. 90rb; Iacobus de Belvisio, to *Authentica* 8.7, *Illud quoque sancire*, f. 54vb.

[63] Jacques de Revigny, to *Codex* 5.12.29, f. 230vb. I have not had an opportunity to examine the MSS containing Pierre de Belleperche's treatment of the issues relating to *inopia*, but his influence is recorded by Alessandro Tartagni (to *Digesta* 24.3.24, n. 3, f. 41v): 'Sed ultramontani post Petrum tenent contrarium etiam si sint duo rei debendi, videlicet quod non possit agi contra vergentem ad inopiam, nec etiam contra alium, quia divitie unius supplere debent pro inopia alterius.'

[64] Cino da Pistoia, to *Codex* 5.12.29, n. 7, f. 307rb: 'Pone, quod socer et maritus ambo receperunt dotem, et obligaverunt se. Modo incipiat alter ad inopiam vergere, nunquid tunc erit locus huic legi? Glossa breviter dicit quod de iure isto non, sed per ius novissimum sic, quo iure statim, cum male incipit uti substantia sua, locus est

he believed, was pernicious and against all laws where husband and
father-in-law were not implicitly or expressly obligated as co-debtors
(*duo rei*).[65] In the end, he did accept the fundamental teaching of the
Glossa that the solvent co-debtor, whether husband or father-in-law,
can be sued by the wife, but he added, only when it can be shown that
they originally intended to undertake a joint obligation for the dowry's
restitution.[66]

The authority of the *Glossa ordinaria* and Bartolo on determining the
liability of co-debtors for restitution of the dowry in cases of insolvency
extended into the sixteenth century. This is amply illustrated by a
consilium of the Florentine jurist Antonio di Vanni Strozzi (d. 1523)
drafted in 1504 on behalf of Vaggia di Giovanni Vernacci.[67] These are
the bare facts of the dispute. Vaggia's husband Marco de' Tempi,
together with his father Alberto, formally acknowledged receipt of
Vaggia's 1050 florin dowry, and undertook the customary obligation
for its restitution, that is, any one of them would be liable in the event
of restitution for an amount equivalent to the whole dowry (*in solidum
et in totum*). Marco became insolvent and destitute, while his father
reamined both solvent and sufficiently wealthy to fulfill his obligation
for the dowry. Anxious about losing her dowry and thus without the
means to support herself and her family, Vaggia took legal action to
recover her dowry from her husband and father-in-law, described
here as co-debtors (*duo rei*). The legal issue to be resolved is whether

---

auxilio, sicut hoc est in uno male utente, sic est in duobus ex quo alter male utitur
eodem ratione adversitatis. Glossa salva reverentia sua male sentit et male loquitur.
Dico enim quod de iure isto locum habet huius legis auxilium, ex quo unus ex
obligatis incipit esse non solvendo, quia interest nostra, plures debitores habere. . . .

[65] Bartolo, to *Digesta* 24.3.24, n. 33, f. 17rb: 'Aut sunt obligati ambo, non tam'
quam duo rei, ut in casu nostro, et supra eodem 1 . si cum dotem § Transgrediamur
(*Digesta* 24.3.22): puta, quando mulier dedit uni dotem contemplatione utriusque,
vel ubi obligati sunt ambo, non tamen tamquam duo rei, quia unus cogitavit de
obligatione alterius, et sic non est actum tacite vel expresse quod sint duo rei, et
tunc non credo quod propter inopiam alterius possit agi contra alium, quia est
contra omnia iura.'

[66] ibid.: 'Ratio diversitatis est quando sunt duo rei et quando non sunt, quia
primo casu debet imputari sibi quod alterius obligationem participavit, unde eius
inopia sibi noceat. Secundo casu nihil potest sibi imputari, unde alterius inopia
nihil debet nocere, ut no. Dy. in cap. mora. in fi, extra, de regu. iur. lib. VI.' Cf.
Dino del Mugello, *Commentarius in regulas iuris pontifici* (Cologne, 1578), p. 251, reg.
mora.

[67] *ASF, Carte Strozziane*, III *serie*, 41, vol. 14, f. 574–6.

Vaggia's action is valid, when one co-debtor is insolvent, while the other's wealth suffices to meet the wife's claim.[68]

Although Strozzi's *consilium* was devoid of doctrinal originality, it does contain a valuable compendium of references on this specific issue, and allows us to view the state of the question in the early sixteenth century. After setting forth the opinions of the *Glossa*, Bartolo and later jurists in favor of the wife's claim, Strozzi went on to cite opposing opinions. He cited the opinions of French jurists who opposed the wife's claims, where the resources of one co-debtor make up for another co-debtor's insolvency.[69] He cited the brothers Baldo and Angelo degli Ubaldi, who restricted the wife's action to only the insolvent co-debtor, an opinion seconded by Raffaele Cumano (d. 1427).[70] He cited the opinion of Alessandro Tartagni who instructed that the opinion of Baldo has more validity than Bartolo's and is thus preferred, though he reluctantly conceded that the wife can act against both husband and father-in-law if they undertook a common obligation as *socii*.[71] He cited the opinion of Paolo di Castro who validated the wife's action against a co-debtor on condition that he not only be verging on insolvency, but also be the party responsible, for her support (*alimenta*), usually but not always the husband.[72] And, finally, he cited the opnion of Lodovico Romano (d. 1439) who contended against Bartolo that the wife had no legal action where one co-debtor was solvent.[73]

[68] ibid.: 'Viso instrumento dotis in quo Marchus filius Alberti et Albertus pater dicti Marci, et quilibet dictorum Marci et Alberti in solidum et in totum se obligando fuerunt contenti habuisse et recepisse in dotem domine Vaggie uxoris dicti Marci florenos 1050 modis et formis de quibus in dicto instrumento continetur. Et viso qualiter dictus Marcus maritus deductus est ad inopiam et paupertatem ita quod domina Vaggia non potest alere se et suos ex dote sua; et attentis dictis testium pro utraque parte examinatorum, est videndum an sit locus repetitioni dicte dotis ex eo quod probetur Marcum maritum vergere ad inopiam, non obstante quod facultates soceri ad dotem obligati sufficiant, et non obstante quod non asseratur Albertus socer vergere ad inopiam: et sic an sola paupertas mariti – dato quod socer sit facultatibus ideoneus, faciat locum repetitioni.'

[69] See note 63 above.

[70] ibid.: 'Baldus autem et Angelus in d. 1. Si constante, volunt quod possit agi contra illum tantum qui sit factus inops, non contra alterum, quia non est inconveniens quod ex post facto surgat inequalitas in duobus reis, 1. eandem, Si quis, ff. de duobus reis (*Digesta* 45.2.9).' Cf. Baldo, to *Digesta* 24.3.24; Angelo degli Ubaldi, to *Digesta* 24.3.24, f. 9ra, n. 1. I have not been able to locate Raffaele Cumano's text.

[71] Alessandro Tartagni, to *Digesta* 24.3.24, n. 3, f. 41va.

[72] Paolo di Castro, to *Digesta* 24.3.24, n. 8, f. 22va.

[73] Lodovico Romano, *Consilia*, cons. 462, f. 205rv; to *Digesta* 24.3.24, f. 45rab.

For Strozzi, the path leading out of this thicket of contrasting and conflicting opinions was paved by the *Glossa* and its adherents:

From the above citations it is apparent that on this difficult question the doctors have declared in various ways and have issued opposing opinions. Nevertheless, the opinion of the *Glossa* is more common and is supported by many greater authorities. For as was stated above, Cino, Riccardo Malombra, Odofredo, Alberico, Bartolo, Jacobus de Belvisio, Giovanni d'Andrea, Iacopo Bottrigari and [Giovanni] da Imola hold the opinion of the *Glossa*. There are thus nine doctors who follow the *Glossa*, and their collective opinion is more than common, since others [in opposition] have few opinions with less authority, and especially since we have the *Glossa* sustained everywhere by this command: that we must not depart from its opinion in matters of legal deliberation and judgement, according to Baldo.[74]

Strozzi's quantitative argument and his deft manipulation of Baldo's texts carried the day: it was on the basis of his *consilium* that Vaggia's claim was vindicated.[75]

What role did the wife's father play in the case of insolvency? Was paternal consent required before the wife could undertake legal action? In theory, it would seem that paternal consent was necessary if the father furnished the dowry (*dos profecticia*) and if his daughter remained unemancipated. In practice, it was in the interest of the wife to act in concert with her father to prevent the loss of her patrimony. However, under *Illud quoque sancire* the wife alone was permitted to recover her dowry (*a*) when it represents a great sum and her action

---

[74] ibid., f. 575v: 'Ex predictis apparet quod in hac difficultate doctores vario modo locuti sunt et sunt in diversis opinionibus. Tamen opinio glo. est magis communis et pluribus et maioribus auctoritatibus fulcita. Nam ut dictum est supra, illam tenuit Cy., Ricar. Mal., Odofr., Alberi., Bart., Iaco. de Bel., Io. An., Iaco. Butr. et Imol., et sic sunt novem doctores post glo., et ista opinio est plusquam communis, cum alie opiniones habeant paucos et minoris auctoritatis, maximus cum habemus glosam ubique hoc tenore, a cuius opinione in consulendo et iudicando non est recedendum secundum Bald. in 1. precibus, C. de impub. et ali. sub. (*Codex* 6.26.8), quia in dubiis non possumus adherere meliori opinioni, Bald. in 1. II, C. de Sen. que si. cer. 9 (*Codex* 7.46.2), et cum glosa non potest errari secundum Bald. in 1. f. §. si necessitatem, C. de bo. que lib. (*Codex* 6.61.8), cuius auctoritas ceteris antecellit secundum Bald. in 1. cum hereditas, C. deposit. (*Codex* 4.34.9).' Giovanni da Imola (to *Digesta* 24.3.24, f. 13vb) adhered to the opinion staked out by the *Glossa*. I have not been able to track down the opinions of Riccardo Malombra and Iacopo Bottrigari, whose works were unavailable to me.

[75] ibid., ff. 575v–576r: 'Et secundum istam opinionem ego consilui. Et fuerunt late omnes sententie in favorem domine Vaggie, pro consilio meo.'

thus prevents serious loss, and (*b*) when her father is himself unwilling to lay claim to the dowry or refuses to allow his daughter to do so. The wife can also act without paternal consent, Bartolo added, when her dowry is small and her father is destitute, since, should the dowry be lost, he would not be able to supply another one.[76] When she was unable to obtain paternal consent owing to her father's absence, the doctors unanimously awarded the wife the right to take legal action. Conversely, the father was permitted to recover the dowry when it was imperiled by the husband's insolvency and when the wife herself was unwilling or legally incapable of acting. His action was permitted, the *Glossa ordinaria* reasoned, because he bears the risk and responsibility of endowing his daughter a second time if her dowry is irretrievably lost.[77] For the very same reason, according to Alberico da Rosciate, he can seek to recover the dowry, even without her consent, if the wife fails to act out of negligence when her husband is verging on insolvency.[78] A father who successfully recovered the dowry was forbidden to use if for his self-enrichment and was legally bound to employ dotal fruits for the benefit of his daughter and son-in-law's common household.

Under no circumstances could a third party (*extraneus*) – someone other than the wife or her father – act to recover the dowry during marriage. This doctrine applied to the circumstance in which a third party gave the dowry on behalf of the wife, and stipulated that restitution be made to him. The *Glossa ordinaria*, followed by a legion of jurists, ruled that such stipulations were valid only upon termination

---

[76] Bartolo, to *Digesta* 24.3.24, n. 47, f. 17va.

[77] *Glossa ordinaria*, to *Digesta* 24.3.24, *v. Mariti*, p. 22: 'Item quid si non mulier, sed pater eius velit agere? Respon. idem, cum et ipse teneatur eam denuo dotare.' Note Bartolo's qualification (to *Digesta* 24.3.24, n. 50, f. 17va): 'Adverte, hoc dictum intelligo si filia sibi consentit, vel causam condicendi non habet. . . .' See also the comments of Paolo di Castro, to *Digesta* 24.3.24, n. 9–10, f. 22va, and Alessandro Tartagni, to *Digesta* 24.3.24, n. 4, f. 41va. An example of an insolvent husband returning the dowry to his father-in-law is found in *ASF, Notarile antecosimiano*, G 570 (19 September 1420), unfoliated. Here, Angelo di Balducci Angelli of Cortona had received a dowry of 75 florins paid on behalf of his wife Margherita by her father Matteo Santucci. Angelo returned the dowry to his father-in-law because '. . . videmus et cognoscens quod dictus Angelus se vergere ad inopiam, paupertatem, calamitatem et miseriam et quasi omnia sua bona consumpsisse et se incepisse male uti rebus. . . .'

[78] Alberico da Rosciate, to *Codex* 5.12.29, n. 13, f. 257rb: 'Quid si mulier est negligens in utendo beneficio huius lex, nunquid pater eius uti poterit? Dic quod sic, ut d. 1. Si constante, in prin., ff. so. ma. et ibi no.'

of marriage. The third party's action was denied on the grounds that it would divert funds intended and necessary for the wife, husband and their children, and thus violate the dowry's *raison d'être*, and that in point of law true restitution of the dowry was triggered by the dissolution of marriage, not the husband's insolvency.[79] For the same reason, the wife was prohibited from ceding her claim against her husband's goods in the case of insolvency to a third party. There was no question, however, that a third party who received the dowry in lieu of the husband or his father was liable to be sued for its return if he himself was verging on insolvency.[80] Only the wife or her father could initiate suits against third parties.

Bartolo extended the remedies furnished by *Si constante* to children whose mother had died and whose father's incipient insolvency endangered their mother's dowry. Permitting children to take legal action against their father to recover their mother's dowry was in clear violation of *Si constante* and cognate laws. Under Roman law, as Bartolo himself taught, an administrator must be appointed to manage the spendthrift or insolvent father's assets (*curator prodigi, curator bonorum*). But where the father has squandered or lost his deceased wife's dowry and his acts have resulted in the ruin of his own patrimony, Bartolo advised that judicial intervention is necessary to save the dowry for the children.[81] Instructive here is an arbitrated agreement concluded in Florence between Francesco di Arnaldo Manelli and his daughters Papera and Tita. In May 1413 Manelli formally acknowledged receipt of a dowry of 880 florins on behalf of his wife Ginevra di Lorenzo Gualterotti. As was customary, he promised to restore or consign the dowry to Ginevra or her heirs in those cases in which he was legally required to do so. About 1423, Francesco was sent by the Florentine government to Alexandria, Egypt, where he

---

[79] *Glossa ordinaria*, to *Digesta* 24.3.24 v. *Mariti*, p. 22b: 'Item quid si extraneus dedit pro muliere et est sibi pactus? Videtur pactus in casum soluti matrimonium tantum. . . . Item iam non esset unde alerentur ipsa et vir et filii, quod est quando ei redditur . . .;' Rolandino dei Passaggeri, fol. 69vb; Odofredo, to *Codex* 5.12.29, n. 5, f. 277rb; Jacques de Revigny, to *Codex* 5.12.29, f. 230vb; Jacobus de Belvisio, to *Authentica* 8.7, *Illud quoque sancire*, f. 54v; Cino da Pistoia, to *Codex* 5.12.29, n. 12, f. 308ra; Bartolo, to *Digesta* 24.3.24, n. 55, f. 18ra; Baldo, to *Codex* 5.12.29.

[80] *Glossa ordinaria*, to *Digesta* 24.3.24, v. *mariti*, p. 22b: 'Item quid si alius recepit dotem et se obligavit, quod fieri potest? . . . Resp. idem, quia eadem aequitas'; Rolandino dei Passaggeri, f. 69vb; Odofredo, to *Codex* 5.12.29, n. 5, f. 277rb; Cino da Pistoia, to *Codex* 5.12.29, n. 13, f. 308ra; Bartolo, to *Digesta* 24.3.24, n. 60, f. 18ra.

[81] Bartolo, to *Digesta* 24.3.24, n. 62–3, f. 18rb; Baldo, to *Codex* 5.12.29; Giovanni da Imola, to *Digesta* 24.3.24, f. 14rb.

served as consul. Owing to circumstances beyond his control, he was forced to remain in the East. Meanwhile, his wife had died, Papera had reached marriageable age, and as a result of his prolonged absence from Florence his assets were imperiled. In the words of the agreement of 3 September 1429, reached between the father's procurator and the administrator of the daughters' affairs, Francesco Manelli 'incepit male uti substantia sua et ad inopiam versit et vergit'. To protect their marriage prospects as well as their welfare, his daughters requested their mother's dowry plus 20 florins they had already expended for their support (*alimenta*). As Manelli's estate was bereft of cash, ownership of properties in the city and in the countryside (*contado*), estimated to be worth 900 florins, was transferred to Papera and Tita. If, when the properties were alienated, the price recovered was below 900 florins, Manelli remained obligated to pay the difference.[82]

By the mid-fourteenth century, a consensus had been reached on the series of legal actions a wife could undertake against her husband who was squandering the dowry and who was verging on insolvency.[83] She could undertake a personal action (*actio personalis de dote*), which applied to situations in which the husband squandered the actual dowry he received. She could undertake an action to recover goods not identical with the actual dowry (*actio utilis in rem* and *rei vindicatio utilis*). This action especially applied to goods and property purchased by the husband with dotal monies and goods. These actions also applied to a dowry or a component of the dowry whose value had been established (*dos estimata*) at the time the husband acknowledged its receipt. If the value of the dowry was not fixed (*dos inestimata*), Bartolo opined, the wife could petition legal officials that it be sequestered and held in safekeeping. The wife could also employ the *rei vindicatio*, laying claim to dotal goods that belonged to her as owner (*domina*) but were in her husband's or another's possession. These overlapping actions, though important, may have had limited application in practice. The major component of dowries in urban centers like Florence, Siena, Pisa and Bologna was cash. Dowries were liquid and thus highly disposable. The likelihood that a wife would recover the actual dowry which had been given at the time of marriage was more apparent than real.

---

[82] *ASF, Notarile antecosimiano* G 212, ff. 431r–432v.

[83] Cino da Pistoia, to *Codex* 5.12.29, n. 14–15, f. 308ra; Bartolo, to *Digesta* 24.3.24, n. 70–3, f. 18va; Baldo, to *Codex* 5.12.29; Alessandro Tartagni, to *Digesta* 24.3.24, n. 1, f. 41rb; Guillaume Durand, *Specul.* (De donat., n. 21), pp. 464–5.

The most effective weapon in the wife's arsenal was the hypothecary action (*actio hypothecaria*). Here the wife has an implied (*tacita*) and privileged claim over her husband's personal goods and real property commensurate with the amount of her dowry, trousseau and her husband's premarital donation. Her hypothec extended to rights (*iura*) and claims the husband held, for example, to rental income, annuities and credits in the public debt. One category of goods exempt from the hypothecary action was merchandise that a businessman had previously sold. Merchandise remaining in his possession was considered to be obligated for the dowry.[84] This distinction was clearly a practical necessity to protect merchants who had purchased merchandise in good faith and who were ignorant of the husband's financial condition. The wife was required to initiate the hypothecary action against her husband before acting against a third party who was in actual possession of the dowry. Her claim, the jurists unanimously argued, is preferred to the general hypothecs of all her husband's creditors, even if theirs had come into existence at an earlier date. The suspension of the venerable Roman rule, *qui potior est tempore, potior est in iure*, was part of the bundle of privileges which, it was envisioned, would allow the wife to recover and preserve her dowry.[85]

There was considerable controversy over the wife's claim to those of her husband's goods which had been specifically pledged (*hypotheca expressa*) to his creditors *before* her own implied hypothec took effect, that is, before he received the dowry. One opinion, associated with Martinus (fl. 1150), was that goods formerly and expressly pledged to a third party were not exempt from the wife's claim. This opinion was endorsed by Iacopo d'Arena and Cino da Pistoia and Iacopo Bottrigari.[86] The French jurists, Jacques de Revigny and Pierre de Belleperche, opined that the wife's implied hypothec was valid except

[84] Cino da Pistoia, to *Codex* 5.12.29, n. 22, f. 308va; Bartolo, to *Digesta* 24.3.24, n. 73, f. 18va; Baldo, to *Codex* 5.12.29; Alberico da Rosciate, to *Codex* 5.12.29, n. 13, f. 257rb; Bartolomeo Saliceto, to *Codex* 5.12.29, f. 20va; Lodovico Romano, to *Digesta* 24.3.24, f. 47rb–47va; Alessandro Tartagni, to *Digesta* 24.3.24, n. 27, f. 43va.

[85] This was the *communis opinio*: *Glossa ordinaria*, to *Codex* 5.12.29, p. 708a (*casus*): 'An constante matrimonio, vir ad inopiam vergat, mulier dotem repetere possit, quaeritur? Dicitur quod sic et si tenet res mariti, adversus creditores mariti agentes habebit exceptionem. Si non tenet, aget adversus creditores qui tenent res viri, si ipsa sit prior tempore seu posterior, modo priores non sint privilegio aliquo muniti, et hoc in prima.'

[86] Iacopo d'Arena, to *Codex* 8.17(18).12, *Assiduis*, n. 3, f. 55b; Cino da Pistoia, to *Codex* 5.12.29, n. 26, f. 308vb; to *Codex* 8.17(18).12, n. 8, f. 495rb–va; Iacopo Bottrigari, to *Codex* 8.17(18).12, f. 73va.

against creditors whose claims to her husband's goods were even more preferable and privileged than hers.[87] Finally, there was the opinion associated with Bulgarus (d. 1166), which flatly prohibited the wife from laying claim to goods formerly and expressly pledged to her husband's creditors. It was Bulgarus' opinion, reincarnated in the teachings of the *Glossa*, Odofredo, Dino del Mugello, Alberico da Rosciate, Bartolo, Baldo, Paolo di Castro and others, which eventually triumphed.[88] This triumph, in turn, most likely stimulated counter measures by which the wife and her family demanded that the husband pledge specific assets as security for the dowry.[89]

There were times when the husband's hypothecary creditors were unwilling to restore to the wife the goods and properties of her husband in their possession. Restoration might result in financial loss: for example, when the hypothecary creditors had increased the value of her property through improvements or when they would be prevented from enjoying rental property for which they had paid in advance. In these situations hypothecary creditors could exercise the *ius offerende pecunie*, the right to pay the prior hypothecary creditor (the wife) the amount owed by the common debitor (the husband), and thus retain the property. Although this legal option was sanctioned by the *ius commune*, it was declared inoperable in the *casus inopie* by the *Glossa*, Cino da Pistoia and Bartolo.[90] The wife's dependence upon a stable income base for support, it was reasoned, would be endangered if the husband's creditors were allowed the *ius offerende pecunie*. Baldo, in a key text, dissented. He limited the teachings of the *Glossa* and Bartolo to those cases in which the wife seeks the return of her dowry (including dotal goods that had in some way been altered) that were in the

---

[87] Jacques de Revigny, to *Codex* 5.12.29, ff. 230v–231r. Pierre de Belleperche's opinion is cited, *inter alia*, by Cino da Pistoia.

[88] *Glossa ordinaria*, to *Codex* 8.17(18).12, *Assiduis vv. hypotheca* and *licet anterioris sint*, pp. 1283–4; Odofredo, to *Codex* 5.12.29, n. 4, f. 277ra: '. . . et ideo vos dicetis mulier prefertur posterioribus, ut infra qui po. in pig. ha., 1. i et ii (*Codex* 8.17(18), 12, 1 and 2); anterioribus habentibus expressas hypothecas non prefertur, ut ibi; anterioribus habentibus tacitas, sic. . . .' Bulgarus' opinion is cited by Alberico da Rosciate, to *Codex* 8.17(18).12, n. 4, 5, f. 151rb: 'In iudiciis communiter vidi servari opinionem Bulgari . . .;' Bartolo, to *Codex* 8.17(18).12, n. 3 and 7, f. 106va; Baldo, to *Codex* 8.17(18).12 and Paolo di Castro, to *Digesta* 24.3.24, n. 2, f. 21v.

[89] Hundreds of examples of this practice in Florence are analyzed in our forthcoming study on the *Monte delle doti*.

[90] *Glossa ordinaria*, to *Codex* 8.17(18).10, *Cum tibi* (*casus*), p. 1281; Iacopo d'Arena, to *Codex* 8.17(18).10, n. 1, f. 55rb; Cino da Pistoia, to *Codex* 8.17(18).10, n. 3, f. 494ra; Bartolo, to *Digesta* 24.3.24, n. 88, f. 19ra; Alberico da Rosciate, to *Codex* 8.17(18).10, f. 150vb.

hypothecary creditor's possession. When the wife instituted a simple hypothecary action to reclaim her husband's goods, there was no question in Baldo's mind that the *ius offerende pecunie* was operable, especially in cases where the hypothecary creditors actually possessed the husband's goods.[91] Paolo di Castro, Rafaelle Cumano, Giovanni da Imola and Alessandro Tartagni took Baldo's opinion one step further. Citing the model fact case established by *Per vestras*, they maintained that it was entirely legitimate for the hypothecary creditor to exercise the *ius offerende pecunie*. It was left to a judge to arrange for the cash payment to be placed with a merchant, thereby providing a secure haven for the cash as well as a source of income.[92] This doctrine, which was intended to afford security to the husband's hypothecary creditors, prevailed over the teachings of the *Glossa* and Bartolo.

Did a wife inadvertently renounce her right to act during marriage if, when the dowry was transferred to the husband, it was expressly stipulated that restitution to her and her heirs would occur only in the event of dissolution of marriage *(soluto matrimonio)*? This was not a pseudo-problem, since dotal instruments invariably carried such stipulations in accordance with notarial formularies. Did the omission of reference to restitution during marriage *(constante matrimonio)*, there-fore, constitute evidence that the wife had renounced her claim in the event that her husband became insolvent? The *Glossa ordinaria* did not tackle this issue, while Dino del Mugello left it unresolved. Jacques de Revigny and Iacopo d'Arena argued that the wife had forfeited her rights during marriage, but they were opposed by Cino da Pistoia, who allowed the wife to act because her demand that the dowry be returned during marriage in the case of insolvency does not constitute genuine restitution. Cino's opinion was reaffirmed by a legion of jurists, including Bartolo, who reiterated that by law the wife cannot re-

[91] Baldo, to *Digesta* 24.3.24; to *Codex* 6.20.5, *Dotis quidem* § *quod locum* (=*Authentica* 7.8). See also the opinion of Angelo degli Ubaldi, who is said by *quattrocento* jurists to have shared his brother's view on this issue, but whose opinion, as far as I can tell, remains inconclusive; to *Digesta* 24.3.24, f. 9ra.

[92] Paolo di Castro, to *Digesta* 24.3.24, f. 20rb; Raffaele Cumano, to *Digesta* 24.3.24, f. 12va; Giovanni da Imola, to *Digesta* 24.3.24, f. 14vb; Alessandro Tartagni, to *Digesta* 24.3.24, n. 31, f. 44rb. The opinions of these jurists were cited in a *consilium* of the Florentine jurist Luca Corsini, who defended the right of the husband's hypothecary creditor to pay the wife cash in lieu of the husband's goods in his possession (*ASF, Carte Strozziane*, III, 41, vol. 11, f. 223r).

nounce the benefits and remedies granted her by the *Digest, Code* and *Authentica*.[93]

Similarly, was the wife banned from acting during marriage if the statutes of the community make restitution contingent upon dissolution of marriage, a condition appearing in almost all of the *Statuta* I have examined for northern and central Italy. That condition does not appear to have been an important doctrinal issue, as jurisprudents, judges and codifiers were unanimous that restoration of the dowry in cases of insolvency did not count as true restitution and that in the event of conflict the *ius commune* would prevail over local statute. Bartolo's dictum, *casus inopie remanet in iure communi*,[94] most likely accounts for the omission of the *casus inopie* in the majority of *Statuta* dating from the late thirteenth and fourteenth centuries. Notable exceptions are Arezzo, Ravenna and Vicenza and the university towns of Pisa and Bologna, whose statutes expressly sanctioned a wife to sue her insolvent spouse and lay claim to his goods.[95]

One city which did witness disputes over statutory prescriptions regarding restitution of dowries was Florence. The *Statuta* of the Podestà redacted in 1325 made restitution conditional upon dissolution of marriage due to the husband's natural death.[96] Sometime after this redaction, Iacopo Bottrigari was asked to resolve a dispute pitting

[93] Jacques de Revigny, to *Codex* 5.12.29, f. 230vb; Cino da Pistoia, to *Codex* 5.12.29, n. 10, f. 307vb. The opinions of Dino and Iacopo d'Arena are reported by Bartolo, to *Digesta* 24.3.24, n. 53, f. 18va: 'Teneo cum Cino: quia si mulier ab initio voluisset expresse huic repetitioni renunciare non potuisset, ut iam dixi;' Baldo, to *Codex* 5.12.29; Alberico da Rosciate, to *Codex* 5.12.29, n. 8, f. 257rb.

[94] Bartolo, to *Digesta* 24.3.24, n. 55, f. 18ra. Towns whose statutes apparently omitted the *casus inopie*, but where wives were none the less laying claim, on the basis of the *ius commune*, to their insolvent husbands' goods, were Siena (see note 30 above) and Florence (*Documenti dell'antica costituzione del comune di Firenze*, ed. P. Santini [Florence, 1895], pp. 303-4, document of 1244), Volterra (*ASF*, Notarile Antecosimiano, G576, unfoliated [3 Dec. 1439]), and Verona (University of Chicago, Department of Special Collections, Rosenthal MS 310).

[95] *Statuto di Arezzo (1327)*, ed. G. M. Camerani (Florence, 1946), p. 173; *Statuti inediti della città di Pisa (1286)*, ed. F. Boniani (Florence, 1870), I, lib. I, rub. 130, p. 237; A. Tarlazzi, *Appendice ai monumenti ravennati* (Ravenna, 1869-76), II, pp. 82-4, n. 64 (year: 1271). For Bologna, see P. Torelli, *Lezioni di storia del diritto italiano: La famiglia* (Milan, 1947), p. 130; Vicenza, Biblioteca Bertoliana, MS Gonzati 566, *Liber Statutorum communis Vincentie (1311)*, lib. II, rub. 5. (I owe this reference to Professor James Grubb.)

[96] *Statuta della Repubblica Fiorentina: Statuto del Podestà (1325)*, ed. R. Caggese (Florence, 1921), lib. II, rub. 17, p. 99: '... nec ad restitutionem teneatur aut compelli vel cogi possit ratione mortis alterutriusque coniugum vel aliqua alia ratione vel causa, nisi ratione mortis naturalis tantum.'

a certain Caterina against her insolvent husband's solvent co-debtors (*correi*), who claimed that they were not open to suit because of the wording of the *Statuta*. The dotal contract, they also claimed, specified that their obligation to perform restitution took effect only upon dissolution of marriage. Bottrigari, in his opinion, admitted that Caterina has no legal claim against her husband's co-debtors under the wording of the *Statuta*.[97] In complete restitution the wife would be free to use and alienate the dowry as she saw fit. In this case, the dowry is inalienable and must serve the common benefit of her family. None the less, Bottrigari continued, her action is sanctioned by the *ius commune*, namely *Ubi adhuc, Si constante* and *Illud quoque sancire*.[98] And it is sanctioned by equity which removed the statutory prohibition and which 'regulates the meaning of statutory words, as it is neither fitting for, nor will equity allow, a wife to be without a dowry and for the same reason, her husband and children.[99] Finally, the *casus inopie* is by virtue of the *ius commune* exempt from dotal pacts making restitution conditional upon dissolution of marriage. For these reasons, Bottrigari concluded, the dowry can be restored to the wife during marriage, notwithstanding stipulations to the contrary.[100]

---

[97] MS Vat. lat. 8067, f. 294r: 'Questio proponitur ex facto. Quidam Fence per se vel per procuratorem constituit dotem domine Caterine sue filie, et eius constitutionem confessi fuerunt, scilicet maritus et quidam cum eo, habuisse dictam dotem et ad eius restitutionem se in solidum obligaverunt. Modo marito ad inopiam vergente aliis correis existentibus solvendo. Queruntur duo: Primo de restitutione dotis, an possit advocari ab ipsis qui solvendo sunt? Aliud dubium sive questio: cessante restitutione dotis, an possit agi ad alimenta? Et circa primam questionem insurgit dubium ex forma statuti quo restitutio et repetitio dotis denegatur, nisi in casu mortis naturalis, et in hoc ponderandum est quod statutum sic conceptum de restitutione deneganda et repetitione in casu mortis vel alia ratione, nisi in casum [*sic*] mortis naturalis. . . .'

[98] ibid.: 'Sed hec non est plenaria restitutio que fit per casum inopie, cum adhuc vir cum uxore habeat in promiscuo usu et res est facta quasi dotalis et inalienabilis et sic deserviens matrimonio tam marito quam uxori et liberis eius, et per hoc impropria est restitutio eius, et sic non comprehenditur forma statuti communis Florentie et eius prohibitione, sed remanebit sub iure communi quo restitutio fieri debet in casu inopie, et habet locum 1. Ubi adhuc, C. de iure dotium (*Codex* 5.12.29), 1. Si constante, ff. solu. ma. (*Digesta* 24.3.24). . . .'

[99] ibid., f. 294v: 'Probat equitas, que modificat verba statuti, non est conveniens et equitas non patietur quod mulier careat dote et ideo ipse et liberi eius. . . .'

[100] ibid.: 'Et per hoc concluditur ad premissa quod dos de qua queritur veniat mulieri reddenda et restituenda, non obstante stipulatione vel pacto tertii. Et per consequens non obstante statuto communi Florentie eadem ratione assistente; et hoc quantum ad restitutionem dotis.' Bottrigari's opinion was cited approvingly by

In Florence as elsewhere, husbands and their sureties promised to restore and repay the dowry and premarital donation in every instance that they were required to do so. The question arose whether this contractual obligation to perform restitution could serve to block the wife's suit against an insolvent husband. Put in another way, did the formulaic guarantee 'restituere, solvere, et pagare in omnem eventum restituende dotis et solvende dotis' encompass restitution during marriage. Lodovico Romano counseled yes, boasting that his opinion triumphed.[101] He conceded that the dowry was intended to support the burdens of marriage and so remained inalienable. But these burdens, he contended, continue after the husband's death, and consequently it was imperative that the wife's dowry be restored in expectation of her second marriage. Ingenious and unorthodox, Romano's argument at least recognized two significant facts of Florentine life: Florentine husbands tended to predecease their wives and young widows with dowries could and did remarry.[102] Romano also denied the conventional argument that true restitution cannot occur during marriage. Restitution, he explained, is defined as the transfer of possession of a thing and its fruits. This is exactly what happens when the dowry is retrieved by the wife from the insolvent husband. As for the supposition that the words 'solvende' and 'reddende' are excluded from the definition of restitution, Romano replied that these words, which are customarily employed in dotal instruments, are understood to include the return of the dowry 'constante matrimonio'.

It was only in the *Statuta* redacted in 1415 that Florence formally recognized the right of wives to recover their dowries from insolvent husbands.[103] Meanwhile, wives and their kin took legal precautions to strengthen dotal rights in the event of the husband or his co-debtors

---

Baldo, to *Codex* 5.12.29: '. . . non tamen ista vera restitutio dotis sed magis in tuto posita secundum 1a [cobum] Buttrigarii qui consuluit quod si statutum dicit quod mulier non possit petere restitutionem dotis constante matrimonio, quod hec verba non extenduntur ad hanc in tuto positam, quia non est propria restitutio. Et sic statutum intelligeretur solum secundum ius commune. . . .'

[101] For what follows, see Lodovico Romano, to *Digesta* 24.3.24, f. 45rb–45va.

[102] C. Klapisch-Zuber, 'The cruel mother'.

[103] *Statuta populi et communis Florentiae*, I, lib. II, rub. 74 (Fribourg, 1778–83), p. 161: 'Viro vero vergente ad inopiam, mulier agere possit in bonis viri, et ea petere secundum formam iuris communis usque ad quantitatem et rotham suae dotis et donationis et augmenti, et ea defendere contra quoslibet creditores, facta prius extimatione secundum formam statuti. . . .'

becoming insolvent during marriage. Numerous dotal contracts stipulated that the husband and all other parties would be obligated for the dowry's restitution *during* marriage as well as upon its dissolution.[104]

Jurists also argued that a husband could not forestall his wife's action by merely acknowledging his obligation in a written document (*carta*) that would serve as evidence in litigation. Nor could he forestall her action by providing sureties, that is, guarantees issued by third parties that they will perform the husband's obligation in the event he is incapable. Such sureties were common and considered operable, but only upon dissolution of marriage. Given the imminent danger to the dowry and to the well-being of the family, jurists plugged what they believed was a loophole through which the husband would be able to frustrate the wife's legitimate claims. They reasoned that a written promise, no matter how solemn, is easily broken and that it is safer to have something in hand rather than a written guarantee.[105]

---

[104] Some examples: *ASF, Notarile Antecosimiano*, A 849, unfoliated (September 1343): '. . . predictus Laurentius fuit confessus habuisse in dotem a dicta domina Katerina uxore sua libras centum XXV . . . promisit eidem domine etc. dictas dotes et donationes . . . restituere et solvere et pagare in omnem eventum restituende dotis et solvende donationis, constante matrimonio vel soluto, in Civitate Florentie, Pistorii, etc.;' (5 November 1343): '. . . dictus Pierus fuit confessus habuisse in dotem a predicta domina Bartola uxore . . . libras quinquaginta . . . promictens dictas dotes et donationes . . . reddere, solvere et pagare in omnem eventum dicte dotis restituende et donationis solvende, constante matrimonio vel soluto, in civitate Florentie, etc.;' *Not. Antecos.* A 206, unfoliated (3 May 1353): '. . . quam dotem et donationem prenominatus Tendi promisit . . . reddere, solvere, pagare et restituere in omnem casum et eventum dotis reddende et donationis solvende, constante matrimonio vel soluto . . .;' *Notarile antecos.* B 191 (31 July 1394): '. . . predicti . . . promiserunt et solempni stipulatione convenerunt . . . eidem domine Tommase et suis heredibus dictam dotem reddere, dare, solvere et restituere in omni casu et eventu dicte dotis restituende constante matrimonio vel soluto . . .;' (23 April 1409): '. . . quas dotes et donationes predicti Gherardinus et Stefanus . . . in totum et in solidum promiserunt dicto Zenobio . . . reddere, dare, solvere et restituere in omni casu et eventu dicte dotis restituende et donationis solvende, constante matrimonio vel soluto, in civitate Florentie, Pisarum, Bononie, Ianue, Venetiarum etc.' Such guarantees are found in dotal pacts after 1415 as well.

[105] *Glossa ordinaria* to *Codex* 5.12.29 vv. *Ad inopiam*, p. 708a: 'Sed pone in nostro casu virum velle dare fideiussorem de dote restituenda uxori soluto matrimonio, nunquid evitabit exactionem dotis ad praesens?. . . sed dico contra, quia infra dicit quod retinere debet ad sustentationem sui et uxoris;' Rolandino dei Passaggeri, f. 69vb; Odofredo, to *Codex* 5.12.29, n. 5, f. 277rb; Cino da Pistoia, to *Codex* 5.12.29, n. 8, f. 307vb: 'Praeterea cum maritus vergit ad inopiam, est obligatus ad dotis restitutionem, nec potest dando fideiussores liberari. Praeterea cautio fragilis est, et tutius est habere rem quam fideiussores;' Alberico de Rosciate, to *Codex*

Canonists, as we have seen, permitted the husband to offer his wife solemn promises and guarantees to serve in lieu of restitution. Their collective opinion may have carried weight in ecclesiastical courts, but not in the civil law arena, where the *casus inopie* was customarily played out.

The inherent incapacity of the wife to alienate her insolvent husband's properties as well as her own dowry raised serious doubts about her ownership (*dominium*) during marriage. Yet, by permitting the wife to undertake the *actio rei vindicatio*, jurists were, in theory, acknowledging her capacity to act as *domina* with respect to her own dowry.[106] A more vexing issue was whether she became *domina* of the husband's goods and properties assigned to her by a judge.[107] Looking backwards from the perspective of the fifteenth century, it is clear that the teachings of Bartolo, endorsed by Baldo, formed the core doctrine on this contested issue. For Bartolo, ownership was dependent upon the specific type of legal action undertaken by the wife. When her suit was based on the husband's wrongdoing (*actio in personam*), she acquired ownership of goods paid to her in lieu of the actual dowry. When she sued to recover specific goods and properties in her husband's possession, claiming, for example, that she was their lawful owner (*actio in rem, rei vindicatio*), she was obviously not *domina* by means of a transfer of ownership (*traditio*), but by reason of the civil law. However, when she instituted a hypothecary action, it was certain that under *Ubi adhuc* she did not acquire ownership of the assigned goods and properties,

---

5.12.29, n. 4, f. 257ra; Baldo, to *Codex* 5.12.29; Alessandro Tartagni, to *Digesta* 24.3.24, n. 19, f. 43rb: 'Teneo communem opinionem, maxime per rationes allegantur per Cynum in d. 1. Ubi, quia non est equum mulierem se committere fragilitati cautionis. . . .'

[106] Cino da Pistoia, to *Codex* 5.12.29, n. 15, f. 308ra: 'Hodie vero, ubi maritus dissipat, sit mulier de subdita domina.' Cf. *Glossa ordinaria*, to *Codex* 5.12.29, vv. *Eas res*, p. 708b.

[107] Bartolo, to *Digesta* 24.3.24, n. 92, f. 19rb: 'Secundo quaero, an mulier hoc casu consequatur dominium rerum assignatarum pro dote? Quidam quod sic, quando agitur personali, nam tunc res dantur in solutum, et mulier consequitur dominium. Ita videtur Gl. in d. 1. Ubi. . . . Alii, ut Ubertus de Bobio, tenet contrarium, quod probant ex dicta 1. Ubi, nam ibi prohibetur alienari, dicit ipse, ergo non dantur sibi in solutum; ergo nec transfertur dominium. . . . Credo glossa bene dicere, et videtur casus in Authen. de aequal. do. § illud ibi, sic eius habitura erat in collationis ratione proprias res, et cetera.'

but only a real security (*pignus*).[108] Here, transfer of possession, not ownership, takes place. The meaning of the word 'to assign' (*assignare*), Bartolo observed, is equivocal, signifying both the transfer of possession as well as ownership.[109] Under ordinary circumstances, *assignare* is presumed to signify transfer of possession. But in the exceptional case of insolvency, he hesitantly concluded, *assignare* is presumed to signify transfer of ownership.[110]

In practice, it may well have been to the husband's advantage to transfer ownership as well as possession of the goods and properties assigned to his wife. As owner, it was the wife, not the husband, who would bear the responsibility and risks of administering dotal goods. Should the value of these goods diminish during her administration, the loss was entirely hers. The husband's voluntary transfer of ownership was also universally recognized as a stratagem for protecting property threatened by his creditors. As a privileged creditor, the

[108] ibid.: 'Aut mulier agit hypothecaria, et tunc certum est quod non consequatur dominium, sed pignus tantum: dicta 1. Ubi. Aut actione in rem, et tunc dominium non consequitur per traditionem, sed suum esse ex legis ratione declaratur dicta 1. In rebus, C. de iure do. (*Codex* 5.12.30). Aut agitur in personali, et dantur sibi res in solutum, et consequitur dominium, ut dictum est.'

[109] ibid.: 'Aut dubitatur, verbi gratia: mulier petit de rebus viri sibi assignari usque ad dotis quantitatem, et iudex in sententia assignavit. Modo istud verbum assignare est dubium, potest nam intelligi per translationem dominii. . . . Item poterit se habere loco pignoris, ut loco custodie.'

[110] ibid.: '. . . unde in dubio non praesumitur causa donationis, sed causa custodiae: hic secus;' Baldo, to *Codex* 5.12.29: 'Extra quaero, pone quod constante matrimonio: quia vir male utebatur substantia sua, hoc liquidato, et viro legitime citato. Iudex dixit ita tibi mulieri assigno tale predium viri tui pro dote tua. Numquid per ista verba significat translationem dominii in mulierem, an vero possideat solummodo iure pignoris? Dicit Bartolus in 1. Si constante (D. 24.3.24) quod verbum assigno quandoque significat iuris translationem quandoque non, secundum quod ratio iuris patitur, et hec doctrina est vera ex qua infert quod in casu dotis restituende, ista assignatio intelligatur facta loco restitutionis et sic cum translatione dominii.' After citing Baldo's opinion, Lodovico Romano stated: '. . . que probat quod verbum| assigno actioni adiectum a iudice prolatum, denotat ipsius actionis translationem. Dum autem circa vult quod per hec verba, assigno tibi dotem, a iudice prolata: in dubio intelligitur in mulierem translatum dotis dominium'; to *Digesta* 24.3.24, f. 48ra. In an opinion of uncertain authorship preserved in a collection of *consilia* of Mariano and Bartolomeo Sozzini, we read: '. . . nam ista communis conclusio doctorum quod ubicumque agitur ad dotis consignationem actione personali, tunc consignatio operatur dominii translationem, ut concludit Bartolus in d. 1. Si constante . . .'; *Consilia* (Venice, 1579), I, *cons*. LXI, ff. 113va–115va. See also the critical discussion of these texts by Alessandro Tartagni, to *Digesta* 24.3.24, n. 32–33, f. 43v.

wife's claim to the assigned goods and properties was preferred to all other creditors. Fearing collusion between husband and wife, jurists not only opposed voluntary transfers, but also voluntary confessions of insolvency made by husband and wife together or by the husband alone. Both Dino del Mugello and Cino da Pistoia presumed voluntary confessions of insolvency to be fraudulent and the ensuing assignment of goods to the wife tantamount to an illegitimate donation that damaged creditors.[111] Cino conceded the validity of such confessions when made in a legal forum where evidence and testimony attest to the husband's insolvency. To win their claim against the husband, his creditors would not only have to prove that they suffered damages, but equally that the husband alone or husband and wife in concert acted with intent to defraud. Those couples who were intent on defrauding creditors would probably have made their confession quietly, in the presence of a judge-notary (*judex ordinarius*) or extrajudicially in a document, beyond the glaring notoriety of public legal proceedings. Dino and Cino ruled that in this case the husband's creditors could lay claim to his goods by merely showing that they had suffered damages. Their ruling, which eliminated the requirement to provide evidence of fraudulent intent, was clearly advantageous to creditors seeking to assert their claims against the husband's assets.

Bartolo, on the other hand, favored the wife and husband.[112] The voluntary confession was valid, he contended, in so far as it conformed to truth: that the husband was indeed verging on insolvency. The assignment of goods to the wife effected by a voluntary confession made by a genuinely insolvent husband before a judge-notary, or even extrajudicially, was not revocable. Bartolo's teaching rested on the premiss that any contract made between husband and wife which served to improve the condition of the dowry, and at the same time did not impoverish the husband, is licit. Creditors wishing to contest the confession and the assignment must go to court and prove both that the confession was made with fraudulent intent and that they suffered damages. Bartolo did agree with his predecessors that any amount assigned to the wife exceeding the value of the dowry which the husband originally acknowledged receiving (another common

---

[111] For what follows, see Cino da Pistoia, to *Codex* 5.12.29, n. 19, f. 308rb–va; who followed the opinion of Dino, while rejecting 'quidam moderniores dicunt, quod est casus quod confessio non praeiudicat. . . .' See also Alberico da Rosciate, to *Codex* 5.12.29, n. 18, f. 258ra.

[112] Bartolo, to *Digesta* 24.3.24, n. 95–100, f. 19v.

strategy to defraud creditors) was an illegitimate and revocable donation.

Whatever their doctrinal differences, all jurists, as well as notaries and legislators, recognized that the remedy provided by the *ius commune* to safeguard the wife's dowry and patrimony, unleashed the baleful consequence of providing husbands and wives with a golden opportunity to defraud creditors. The line dividing a fraudulent from a legitimate assignment of goods to the wife, either owing to her petition and suit or to the husband's voluntary confession, was often barely perceptible. In practice, it was relatively easy for the husband, with his wife's collusion, to conceal assets. Even when the wife petitioned for the restoration of her dowry and the assignment of her husband's goods before a judge-notary, there was no certainty, given the delays in the redactions of documents and the loss of notarial documents during periods of plague, that this act would inevitably become public knowledge.[113] This state of affairs damaged the husband's creditors at the time of the assignment, as well as unfortunate potential creditors who remained ignorant of the husband's insolvency. Not only was the smooth functioning of the market place at stake, but also the integrity of the communal fisc whose tax revenues were jeopardized by fictitious insolvency.

It was left to local governments to deter the abuse of this legal remedy by bringing insolvency to the attention of the public. Public notification would alert creditors, and, by heaping shame upon the insolvent husband and his kin, may have served as a deterrence. In Pisa, assignments of monies and goods to the wife were required to be registered in a special chartulary conserved in the chancery. In Vicenza, a wife was forbidden to receive the assignment of her husband's goods, unless a formal announcement of her husband's insolvency and the impending assignment was made in the Great Council and by heralds in customary public places. In fifteenth-century Florence, cases of insolvency were enmeshed in a web of red tape, and petitions for the assignment of the insolvent husband's goods to the

---

[113] D. Herlihy has pointed out that, at Pisa from 1100 onward, 'increasing demands for the notary's services were causing extensive delays in redaction. Sometimes notaries might die before they had formally redacted all their rough drafts...'; *Pisa in the Early Renaissance* (Yale, 1958), p. 4 and c. I: 'The notarial chartulary'. Cf. G. Costamanga, 'La triplice redazione dell' "instrumentum" genovese', *Studi di paleografia e diplomatica* (Rome, 1972), p. 241ff.

wife required prior approval of the *Signoria* and legislative councils.[114] By making governmental approval mandatory before assignment of the husband's goods could take place, the laws of Florence violated the spirit and the letter of the *ius commune*. It must be stressed, however, that regulations and procedures crafted on the local level were not designed to eliminate the wife's legal remedy, but only its abuse. Although it is impossible at present to discern whether these measures mitigated the incidence of fraud, public registration and notification of insolvency has furnished the modern historian with abundant evidence that recourse to this legal remedy was very common indeed. In Florence, 460 cases are recorded between 1435 and 1535 in which women were awarded their dowries or their equivalent during marriage.

Insolvency, though often chronic, was not necessarily a permanent condition. The issue of temporary insolvency and its legal consequences were raised by jurists in the following model case. A husband verging on insolvency returns the dowry or assigned goods to his wife in accordance with the law. Later, either by inheritance or some other means, he becomes wealthy, and now wishes to recover what he returned or assigned to his wife. Does the husband have a legal action to reverse the restitution made to his wife? Since the *Corpus iuris civilis* did not give any guidance on this issue, it was left to the *Glossa ordinaria* to fill the void. The *Glossa* categorically opposed the husband's action, as the payment made to the wife had been made for a just reason (*ex iusta causa*). By logical extension, the wife recovered her dowry or acquired her husband's property in good faith and thus has just title to them.[115] Odofredo and Jacques de Revigny seconded the *Glossa*'s defense of the wife.[116] Dino held that the dowry should remain with the

[114] For Pisa and Vicenza, see references in note 95 above. For Florence, see *ASF*, *Provvisioni*, 126 (9 March 1435), f. 430ff.; ibid., 128 (23 December 1437), f. 215ff. These and related documents will be fully analyzed in our forthcoming study on dowries in Renaissance Florence. This legislation was part of a sweeping campaign against the fraudulent abuse of emancipation, repudiations of inheritance and the like: see Thomas Kuehn, '*Multorum fraudibus occurrere*: legislation and jurisprudential interpretation concerning fraud and liability in Quattrocento Florence', *Studi Senesi*, 93 (1981), pp. 309–50.

[115] *Glossa ordinaria*, to *Codex* 5.12.29, *v. abutatur*, p. 708b: 'Quid autem si maritus efficiatur dives, an recipiet dotem? Resp. non, secundum H., ex causa iusta est soluta.'

[116] Odofredo, to *Codex* 5.12.29, n. 2, and Jacques de Revigny to *Codex* 5.12.29: 'Sed queritur ponamus maritus vergit ad inopiam et sic mulier dotem exegit constante matrimonio, deinde maritus factus est dives et solvendo, nunquid ergo recuperabit dotem a muliere? Videtur quod sic, quia cessante causa cessat effectus.'

wife as it would if the marriage had dissolved.[117] Riccardo Malombra and Oldrado da Ponte sided with the husband. Malombra reasoned that, owing to the husband's change in fortune, the cause, *inopia*, precipitating restitution to the wife ceases to exist. In consequence, the dowry can be returned to its former state, that is, to the husband. Similarly, Oldrado opined that the husband's newly acquired wealth – an *ex post facto* event – removed the impediment blocking the husband's action.[118] Before deciding on this issue, Iacopo d'Arena asked whether the goods recovered by the wife resulted from an hypothecary action or from a payment for her dowry. In the first instance, the husband can recover his goods, because they are not considered to be in the wife's permanent possession; they remain with her only as long as the husband remains insolvent. In the second instance, the husband cannot act to recover what he paid to the wife because it belongs to her. The husband, Iacopo observed, has no cause to complain, since by law his wife must use the dowry for their common benefit.[119]

In the fourteenth century, the *Glossa*'s position was championed by Cino da Pistoia, Bartolo and Baldo, whose teachings would constitute the *communis opinio*. After reviewing earlier opinions *pro et contra*, Cino advised that the path to be followed is the one which is safer and more

---

Videtur contra, nam ex quo dos iusta de causa reddita est; videtur quod non debeat de cetero reddi marito, ut ff. qui satisda. cog., 1. Sciendum, in fi. (*Digesta* 2.8.15) quod dicit, vult quod quilibet habet salva sua pacta in casum suum.'

[117] Dino del Mugello (Urb. lat., 156, f. 68va): 'Sed quid si restituta dote maritus factus est dives postea, an dos redibit in pristinum statum? Videtur quod non, ut 1. Sciendum § ult., supra, qui satisdare co. (*Digesta* 2.8.15) et 1. Ubi adhuc, circa fi. (*Codex* 5.12.29); ar. contra, infra, de operis novi nuntiatione, 1. Praetor (MS: Plane) ait (*Digesta* 39.1.20) cum lege equivalente et de inoff. te., 1. Eum qui (*Codex* 3.28.14) et 1. Contra maiores (*Codex* 3.28.16), supra, qui satis co., dy. Videtur non audiendus maritus postea, quia perinde habetur ac si matrimonium esset solutum, ut 1. Ubi; sed dic favore dotis conservandum non subeuntem, dy.'

[118] The opinions of Riccardo Malombra and Oldrado are reported by Baldo, to *Codex* 5.12.29: 'Sed contra glossam facit ff. ut in pos. le., 1. si pecunie § fi. (*Digesta* 36.4.6) et 1. hoc amplius, de dam. infe. (*Digesta* 39.2.9), ubi dicitur quod id tollit rem iam factam ex post facto superveniens quod impedit ab invito interveniens secundum Old[radum]. Idem tenet Ri[ccardus] Mal[ombra], quia cessat causa restitutionis: ergo in primum statum debet dos reponi, ff. de condi. sine cause, 1. si fullo (*Digesta* 12.7.2).'

[119] Iacopo d'Arena's opinion is reported by Alberico da Rosciate, to *Codex* 5.12.29, n. 17, f. 268ra.

beneficial for the dowry. And Cino was inclined to believe that the dowry was safer in the wife's possession, since any goods acquired by the husband after having made restitution to his wife, were subject to the legitimate claims of his creditors.[120] Bartolo, too, placed a premium on the dowry's security. The husband's supervening wealth, he contended, did not erase the cause of restitution: to provide security for the wife. Indeed restitution and the husband's supervening wealth were not contradictory but complementary, because both produced the desired result of furnishing security for the wife's dowry. For this reason, the restitution cannot be overturned.[121] Baldo considered the opinion of the *Glossa ordinaria* to be 'truer' than the opinion of Malombra and Oldrado. He reasoned that once the dowry is restored to the wife, she becomes its permanent owner, which consequently prevents her husband's action. At the same time, her right to act against her husband regarding the dowry is, in every respect, extinguished (*consummatus*). Should the dowry revert to her husband, the wife would have no legal recourse either upon dissolution of marriage or if he became insolvent once again. It is implicit in Baldo's logic that the certain injury the wife would suffer from the dowry's reversion to the husband must be avoided.[122] Multiple insolvencies and reclamations, for our jurists, was a nightmare which they chose not to contemplate.

It should be evident by now that, contrary to Bellomo's thesis, medieval jurists not only inherited and reaffirmed, but also amplified, the Roman law remedy that allowed wives to reclaim their dowries and other goods from insolvent husbands during marriage. Their chief contribution, certainly, lay in the domain of procedure, in fashioning institutional measures for the practical implementation of the remedy.[123] Cumbersome and time-consuming proceedings were discouraged in favor of summary procedure. There was a pervasive

[120] Cino da Pistoia, to *Codex* 5.12.29, n. 24, f. 308va.

[121] Bartolo, to *Digesta* 24.3.24, n. 107–8, ff. 19vb–20ra: 'Ego sustineo gl[ossam] et sic probo ... haec restitutio facta est ad securitatem mulieris et divitiae supervenientes tendunt ad eundem effectum, scilicet ad securitatem mulieris, ergo non tollit restitutio iam facta.'

[122] Baldo, to *Codex* 5.12.29. For the *communis opinio*, see Angelo degli Ubaldi, to *Digesta* 24.3.24, n. 5, f. 9ra; Alessandro Tartagni, to *Digesta* 24.3.24, n. 39, f. 44ra; Giovanni da Imola, to *Digesta* 24.3.24, f. 15ra; Pietro d'Ancarano, to *X*.4.20.7, *Per vestras*, n. 66, p. 166a; Antonio da Budrio, to *X*.4.20.7, n. 8, f. 62r.

[123] Their contribution is not surprising, given the creation and extensive development of the science of procedure in the Middle Ages; R. C. Van Caenegem, 'History of European civil procedure', in *International Encyclopedia of Comparative Law*, XVI, 2 (Tübingen, Paris and New York, 1973), pp. 16–23.

belief, corroborated by professional experience, that delay would blunt the remedy's effectiveness. The paramount challenge facing these jurists was to make the remedy operable in a world criss-crossed by local jurisdictions with their volatile market economies, a world radically different from the one which confected the *Corpus iuris civilis*. The challenge was met; conceptual and practical obstacles were overcome. Indeed the validation and enforcement of the wife's action was so overwhelming that the remedy was seized as an opportunity by unscrupulous couples to defraud creditors. In practice as well as in theory, wives were not merely passive victims incapable of preventing the loss of their dowries, but were also agents endowed with the legal capacity of taking action to preserve what rightfully belonged to them.

The jurists who constructed the texts through which we have traversed were great problem-solvers. They did not contribute substantially to the Roman legacy of cultural and moral postulates which made the remedy conceptually possible. As the Roman jurisconsults before them, their ideal of marriage was an affectionate and trusting union, whose welfare depended upon marital prestations, especially the dowry. Insolvency directly assaulted this transcendent ideal, undermining the legitimacy of the androcentric universe. The purpose of the wife's remedy was to assure the welfare of the family, whose *sine qua non* was the dowry; to insure that the wife would have her patrimony so that she could live honorably; and to assure that the dowry would be duly transmitted to legitimate heirs, namely her children. There is no trace here of a concern for female rights or female control over the dowry. The dominant focus of their texts was the orderly and eternal circulation and devolution of dowries among mothers, wives, daughters, fathers, husbands, sons and their kinsmen. So conceived, property was not a matter of individual claims over a material object, but an instantiation of claims between persons in relation to something charged with pecuniary and symbolic value. Their texts confirm the sociological insight that property is not a natural artifact but a constellation of cultural meanings. Their texts also lend confirmation to the Marxist insight that law favors groups who control property, even when it does nothing more than permit them to keep what they have. And finally, their texts confirm the anthropological perception that our own insights into another society, past or present, will not result from true or false tests, but from investigations of shifting contexts yielding partial and complementary truths.

ACKNOWLEDGEMENTS

The research for this essay was generously supported by the National Endowment for the Humanities. I am grateful to Professor Alan Watson and my colleague, Constantin Fasolt, for their critical reading of my essay.

12

On the Status of Women
in Medieval Sardinia

JOHN DAY

The favorable if far from privileged status apparently enjoyed by
Sardinian women in the Middle Ages derived from marriage and
inheritance customs which tended to place them on an equal footing
with men with regard to property ownership and succession. Marriage
custom, as codified in the statutes of Sassari (1316)[1] and the *Carta de
Logu* of Arborea (*c.* 1392),[2] recognized the dowry as well as the community systems, but the former, as the expression 'in the Pisan
manner' (*a sa pisanesca*) indicates, was borrowed from Continental
practice and it seems to have been confined largely to the foreign
merchant and landed classes and to members of the ruling dynasties
with strong Pisan and Genoese connections. An early example concerns in fact the testament of a certain Gottifredo d'Arborea, probably a son of the 'judge' Pietro I, who had resided in Pisa and was
married to a Pisan woman. At his death in 1253, the bulk of his considerable property in lands, villages, serfs and livestock was left to a
minor daughter to provide for her dowry (*pro se dotanda*), to three
individuals, whose ties of kinship with the deceased are not stated,
and to the Church. His widow recovered her marriage portion of
£300 Pisan money, plus £15 in interest disguised as a legacy, but did
not, in line with the strict principles of the dowry system, share in the
inheritance.[3] In the statues of Sassari and the *Carta de Logu* on the
other hand, doubtless out of deference to local custom, the widow in

---

[1] G. M. Diaz (ed.), *Il codice degli Statuti del libero comune di Sassari* (Cagliari, 1969).
[2] E. Besta and P. Guarnerio (eds), *Carta de Logu* (Sassari, 1904). I have used the
edition of R. Carta Raspi in *Mariano IV d'Arborea* (Cagliari, 1934), pp. 217–82.
The Pisan statutes of Villa di Chiesa make no reference to the community system;
C. Baudi de Vesme (ed.), *Codex Diplomaticus Ecclesiensis* (Historiae Patriae Monumenta, XVII) cols. 5–456.
[3] F. Artizzu, *Pisani e Catalani nella Sardegna medioevale* (Padua, 1973), pp. 25–38.

such cases retained the right to a substantial portion of her husband's estate[4] which tended to compensate for the basic inequity of a strategem intended to preserve the patrimony from excessive fragmentation at the expense of female siblings.[5]

In the case of indigenous marriage custom 'in the Sardinian manner' (*a sa sardesca*), the two spouses retained separate title to their respective inheritances, but any property acquired subsequent to marriage was owned in common and could not be disposed of in part or in whole except by mutual consent.[6] In the statutes of Sassari, the wife was responsible for half of any debts contracted by her husband for their common benefit.[7] But she was not permitted to sell, transfer or hypothecate her own property, except in cases of obvious necessity, without his consent.[8] These restrictions did not, however, rule out her participation in joint conubial undertakings like the farming of ecclesiastical revenues (the example is from 1345).[9]

Despite that fact that she remained under the lifelong economic tutelage of her father, husband, kinsmen or (male) neighbors, a woman's inheritance was to all intents and purposes inviolable.[10] It could not be alienated by her husband without her consent and on the advice of her father, collateral kin or men of good repute.[11] It was not subject to seizure for crimes committed by her spouse, or for harboring

---

[4] *Statuti di Sassari*, I, 104; *Carta de Logu*, c. 98.

[5] G. Rossi, 'Le statut de la femme dans l'histoire du droit italien', *La Femme* (Recueils de la Société Jean Bodin, XI, Brussels, 1959–62), II, p. 121. Cf. E. Cortese, *Appunti di storia giuridica sarda* (Milan, 1964), pp. 65–117.

[6] The formulae found in the monastic records of the twelfth and thirteenth centuries are, depending on the case, 'cun boluntate dessa mugere', 'cun boluntate dessu maridu', 'cun boluntate de pari', 'ambos unpare'; see A. Marongiu, 'Aspetti della vita giuridica sarda', in his *Saggi di storia giuridica e politca sarda* (Padua, 1975), pp. 36–9; and, in general, E. Besta, *La Sardegna medioevale* (Palermo, 1908–9), II, pp. 170–80; Cortese, *Appunti*, pp. 65–117; A. Marongiu, 'Nozze proibite, comunione di beni e consuetudine canonica', in *Saggi di Storia giuridica e politica sarda* (Padua, 1975), pp. 163–83.

[7] 'Si cussu depitu siat torratu ad utilitate comunale' (*Statuti di Sassari*, II, 8).

[8] As determined by the Great Council in the presence of the chief magistrate (*podestà*) and at least three of her kinsmen; ibid., I, 49.

[9] F. Artizzu, *L'Opera di Santa Maria di Pisa e la Sardegna* (Padua, 1974), pp. 111–12.

[10] The two conditions were obviously related: 'Si les intérêts (de la femme romaine) sont de mieux en mieux protégés, c'est précisément parce qu'on la tient pour faible et parfois pour incapable'; J. Gaudement, 'Le statut de la femme dans l'empire romain', *Le Femme* (Recueils de la Société Jean Bodin, XI) (Brussels, 1959–62), I, p. 192.

[11] *Statuti di Villa di Chiesa*, III, 64; cf. III, 68; *Statuti di Sassari*, III, 1.

family members who were fugitives from justice (*homini isbandidu*).[12] As a final precaution against marital pressure, married women were required to seek the advice of their fathers or kinsmen in drawing up their wills, and were forbidden to name their husbands as beneficiaries for more than half of their estate.[13] In practice this solicitude for the property rights of the wife and her blood relations tended to preserve the status quo in the case, for example, of a poor man married to a wealthy woman.[14]

Sardinian custom provided that all children regardless of sex share in their parents' inheritance on an equal basis. In the *Carta de Logu*, even a dowered daughter had a right to a full share, after deducting for the dowry, if the father died intestate.[15] The insistence on perfect parity in the division of the patrimony led to the extreme pulverization of rural property and doubtless explains the frequent references in medieval texts to collective exploitation (*pro indiviso*) of fields, vines, fruit trees and pasture by two or more individuals, often of different sexes.[16]

If the rural population in particular persisted in its attachment to the community system it was not out of respect for women's rights but because the overwhelming majority of parents lacked the means to provide their female issue with marriage portions.[17] At the same time, the strict application of the principle of partible inheritance helped to counter extreme manifestations of sibling rivalry in a society

[12] *Statuti di Villa di Chiesa*, II, 29; *Carta de Logu*, c. 1, 7; *Statuti di Sassari*, III, 1.

[13] Or for more than £10 at Villa di Chiesa. *Statuti di Villa di Chiesa*, III, 64; *Carta de Logu*, c. 100; *Statuti di Sassari*, II, 1. Cf. Besta, *La Sardegna medioevale*, II, pp. 181–5; A. Solmi, *Studi storici sulle istituzioni della Sardegna nel medio evo* (Cagliari, 1917), p. 181.

[14] Marongiu, 'Aspetti della vita giuridica', p. 39. Cf. Cortese, *Appunti*, p. 78. The example is in E. Besta and A. Solmi (eds), *I condaghi di S. Nicola di Trullas e S. Maria di Bonarcado* (Milan, 1937) *CSMB*, no. 62.

[15] *Carta de Logu*, c. 198.

[16] R. di Tucci, *La proprietà fondiaria in Sardegna* (Cagliari, 1928), pp. 105–8; F. Artizzu (ed.), 'Rendite pisane nel Giudicato di Cagliari', *Archivio Storico Sardo*, XXV (1957–8), pp. 1–98 (1316); 'Liber fondachi', *Annali delle Facoltà di Lettere* (Università di Cagliari), XXIX (1961–5), pp. 215–99; 'L'Aragona e i territori pisani di Trexenta e di Gippi', *Annali delle Facoltà di lettere* (Università di Cagliari), XXX (1966–7), pp. 309–415, for examples.

[17] See J. Day, 'La Sardegna e i suoi dominatori dal secolo XII al secolo XIV', *Storia d'Italia*, vol. X: *La Sardegna* (Turin, 1984).

notoriously prone to violence.[18] There is nothing to suggest that either of these institutions underwent significant modifications under Italian influence, contrary to the 'undeniable legal trend' in the thirteenth and fourteenth centuries toward increasing control over the wife's property by her husband or his heirs.[19]

'The principle of equality pushing up from below'[20] does not seem to have encountered serious obstacles in Sardinia until it reached the very summit of society where the dowry system combined with male primogeniture to preserve the unity of the realm and the integrity of the royal domaine. The judge Ugone II of Arborea, who died in 1335, provided for dowries for two daughters, appointed two younger sons provincial governors and named the eldest his successor and universal heir.[21]

A Sardinian princess, even in the absence of male heirs, could not succeed to the throne in her own right. The title of queen, or *giudicessa*, bestowed on famous personages like Adelasia of Torres, Benedetta of Cagliari or the national heroine, Eleanora of Arborea, was purely honorific.[22] The fierce competition for the hand of royal heiresses in the Pisan–Genoese period is explained by the curious right they enjoyed in Sardinian law, subject to the assent of the high court (*corona de logu*), to convey sovereignty from their father to a husband or son.[23]

At the bottom of the social pyramid, by contrast, the status of female serfs[24] did not differ in most respects from that of their male counter-

---

[18] 'The manner of splitting property', writes Jack Goody, 'is a manner of splitting people; it creates (or in some cases reflects) a particular constellation of ties and cleavages between husband and wife, parents and children, sibling and sibling'; J. Goody, J. Thirsk and E. P. Thompson (eds), *Family and Inheritance. Rural Society in Western Europe, 1200–1800* (London, 1978), p. 3.

[19] J. Kirshner, 'Two fourteenth-century opinions on dowries, paraphernalia and non-dotal goods', *Bulletin of Medieval Canon Law*, IX (1979), pp. 65–77.

[20] J. Thirsk, 'The European debate on customs of inheritance, 1500–1700', in *Family and Inheritance*, p. 183.

[21] P. Tola (ed.), *Codex Diplomaticus Sardiniae* (Historiae Patriae Monumenta, X), sec. XIV, no. 68. His widow's dowry of £500 was returned to her.

[22] A. M. Oliva, 'La successione dinastica femminile nei troni giudicali sardi', *Miscellanea di studi sardo-catalani* (Cagliari, 1981), pp. 9–43. The one exception was the Catalan Agulbursa, queen consort of Barisone I of Arborea who assumed the prerogatives of sovereignty at his death.

[23] ibid.; Day, 'La Sardegna e i suoi dominatori'.

[24] Serfdom, following a long agony, was finally abolished in Sardinia in 1452; B. Anatra, 'Di barone in barone', *Almanacco della Sardegna* (Cagliari, 1973), pp. 9–13.

parts.[25] The chief distinction seems to have been that the traditional devaluation of feminine labor extended, in the case of female serfs, to their persons. In the statutes of Sassari, the damages for taking the life of a female serf were set at £25 compared to £50 for a male,[26] with the predictable advantage of reducing a woman's redemption dues for labor services to half those of a man.[27] In certain cases female serfs were expressly exempt from masculine tasks. The act of donation of a family of serfs to S. Maria de Bonarcado by the judge of Arborea provided that the women, except at harvest time, devote themselves to such activities as making bread, washing, spinning and weaving.[28] In another donation involving the semi-servile inhabitants (*liberus de panilu*) of several villages ceded to the Church by the judge of Cagliari, married women were not required to join in the reaping.[29] As a rule, however, serfdom like poverty had a leveling effect in the negative sense. Serfs of both sexes at Sassari could be beaten, mutilated or killed by their masters with equal impunity.[30]

Children born of a freewoman married to a serf, even if she was of high estate (*libera maiorale*), did not necessarily inherit their mother's condition at the 'age of division'.[31] The problem was complicated by the fact that serfs were routinely divided into halves, quarters and even smaller fractions according to the number of days of labor services per week or per month assigned to their different masters. The general rule, probably inspired by inheritance custom, seems to have been that of partibility. Thus, if two children were born of a mixed marriage, one was serf and one was free, while a single child might be half serf and half free. In the early thirteenth century, the abbot of S. Michele de Salvennor complained that 'female serfs married free-

<hr>

[25] R. Carta Raspi, *Le classi sociali nella Sardegna medioevale. II. I servi* (Cagliari, 1938); Marongiu, 'Aspetti della vita giuridica sarda'; A. B. Unali, 'La servitù in Sardagna dall' XI al XIII secolo', *Critica Storica*, X (1973), pp. 222–42; Besta, *La Sardegna medioevale*, II, pp. 46–55.

[26] *Statuti di Sassari*, III, 1.

[27] *Statuti di Villa di Chiesa*, III, 63; E. Baratier, 'L'inventaire des biens du prieuré Saint-Saturnin de Cagliari . . .', *Studi storici in onore di F. Loddo Canepa* (Florence, 1959), II, pp. 70–1.

[28] *Condaghe di S. Maria di Bonarcado*, no. 131.

[29] '. . . et non fazant messas mulieres issoru.' (Solmi, *Studi storici*, appendix I, doc. 1, pp. 393–4 (a. 1070–80).

[30] *Statuti di Sassari*, III, 1.

[31] Marongiu, 'Aspetti della vita giuridica sarda', pp. 27, 39 (*CSMB*, no. 25); G. Bonazzi (ed.), *Il condaghe di San Pietro di Silki* (Sassari 1900), no. 120. Cf. Marongiu, 'Aspetti della vita giuridica sarda', p. 34.

men and male serfs freewomen and the church of S. Michele as a result lost [its claims to] their offspring.'[32]

Because of universal doubts about female candour and common sense,[33] the statutes of Sassari stipulated that a woman's testimony in criminal cases was 'not to be believed' if uncorroborated by a man's and, elsewhere, that two female witnesses should count as one male witness.[34] In recompense, the fines imposed for minor crimes were invariably lighter if the offender was female, at least in principle.[35] In practice, to judge from the accounts of the Catalan *veguer* (magistrate) of Cagliari in the fourteenth century, the administration of criminal justice tended to be even handed. In the periods 1341–2, 1366–8 and 1375–9, 110 women of different nationalities (one out of four offenders) were condemned for crimes and infractions ranging from murder and bigamy to immoral conduct and disturbing the peace. A housewife, for example was fined for throwing water into the street; a Jewess, for working on a Christian feast day with her door ajar; a Greek fortune-teller for 'dreaming of S. Helena'; two prostitutes for seating themselves bareheaded among honest women at mass. The sentence in all these cases seems to have been determined by the nature of the offense and the ability to pay, irrespective of sex or country of origin.[36]

In Sardinia, as elsewhere, the husband exercized the *ius corrigendi*, the right to castigate anyone who 'ate at his table' (*qui starit a pani et a vino*), including his spouse, without incurring the usual sanctions for physical injury.[37] Outside the home, however, the protection of women against violence was a major preoccupation of Sardinian law-makers. Penalties were graduated according to the victim's status and condition.[38] For rape, these ranged from decapitation if the

[32] R. di Tucci, 'Il condaghe di San Michele di Salvennor', *Archivio Storico Sardo*, VIII (1912), no. 24.

[33] 'Nam varium et mutabile testimonium semper foemina producit' and 'in foemina minus est rationis'; Rossi, 'Le statut de la femme', p. 118.

[34] *Statuti di Sassari*, III, 8, 33.

[35] ibid., III, 6, 7, 13, 33 etc.; *Statuti di Villa di Chiesa*, II, 20, 21, 23. The principle involved here is 'propter sexus fragilitatem'; Rossi, 'Le statut de la femme', p. 128.

[36] P. Roqué, *L'infraction de la loi à Cagliari au XIVe siècle. Une société et sa justice* (MA thesis, University of Paris, VII, 1979).

[37] The *ius corrigendi* was unrestricted in the statutes of Sassari and the *Carta de Logu*. In the statutes of Villa di Chiesa, the husband could only use his bare hands and must not draw blood (*Statuti di Sassari*, II, 3, 13; *Carta de Logu*, c. 9; *Statuti di Villa di Chiesa*, II, 32).

[38] Cf. *Statuti di Sassari*, III, 3.

woman was married to a modest fine in the case of a female serf.[39] In the statutes of Sassari, the rape of a virgin was a capital offense unless she agreed to marriage.[40] In the *Carta de Logu*, the same crime was punished by a huge fine of £500 or the loss of a foot. The fine was reduced to £200, however, if the victim was nubile and agreed to marriage of her own free will ('si est sença maridu et plaquiat assa femina') or, failing that, if the accused provided her with a marriage portion suitable to her station.[41]

The rigor of sexual mores is reflected in the fact that the penalty for violating a woman who was neither married nor nubile was a simple fine (£10–25 at Sassari; £25–50 at Villa di Chiesa).[42] Contrary to a famous passage in Dante on the promiscuity of Sardinian women,[43] there was no middle way, as Francesco Alziator writes, between virtue and vice, and no redemption in this life for the sins of the flesh.[44] Infidelity was punished by flagellation in the *Carta de Logu* and, if the act occurred in the woman's own home, by the confiscation of all her property.[45] In the cosmopolitan city of Cagliari in 1367, a husband and his two accomplices were let off with a fine for the murder of an unfaithful wife.[46]

Murder and bigamy were capital crimes in the case of women as well as men.[47] So too, at Sassari, was the curiously innocuous offense of entering the public baths on the days reserved for the opposite sex. Women were usually burned at the stake, a form of execution evidently considered more appropriate to female nature than hanging or decapitation.[48]

Medieval sources shed very little light on such basic demographic structures affecting the feminine condition as age at marriage and size of household. In the eighteenth century, the notoriously low birth

---

[39] ibid., II, 31.

[40] ibid.

[41] *Carta de Logu*, c. 21. Cf. *Statuti di Villa di Chiesa*, II, 12.

[42] *Statuti di Sassari*, III, 31; *Statuti di Villa di Chiesa*, II, 12.

[43] '. . . ché la Barbagia di Sardigna assai nelle femmine sue più è pudica che la Barbagia [i.e. Florence] dov'io la lasciai' (*Purg.* xxxiii, 94–6).

[44] F. Alziator, *Il folklore sardo* (Cagliari, 1978), p. 39: 'Al di là del confine vi è la fama di essere una donna disonesta. Ma tra bene e male, tra onestà e disonestà, tra purezza e colpa non vi sono ponti. Chi ha peccato non ha redenzione.'

[45] *Carta de Logu*, c. 22.

[46] Roqué, *L'infraction de la loi*.

[47] At Cagliari in 1368, a woman accused of bigamy was let off with a fine of £12 because the offense was not proved [*sic*] (ibid.).

[48] *Statuti de Sassari*, III, 1, 50; *Carta de Logu*, c. 1, 5; *Statuti di Sassari*, I, 160.

rate in Sardinia was blamed on late marriage; late marriage on rural poverty. A peasant girl, before she could marry and start a family, was expected to make her own trousseau in the little time she could spare from domestic chores and furnish her future home with meager earnings from outside work.[49] Parents moreover were reluctant to sacrifice 'that modicum of profit' represented by their daughter's labor at home and in the fields and tended to withhold their consent as long as possible. The result, 'to the immense detriment of propagation', was that most girls did not marry until they were well past puberty.[50] In the village of Solarussa, not one of the 22 married women and widows on a list of plague victims in 1653 was under the age of 24.[51] Late marriage, combined with high infant mortality, severely reduced the size of families, especially among the poor.[52] At Sanluri, families of six or more constituted barely 20 per cent of the total in 1611 and 1643, and less than 3 per cent following the plague of 1652–5. The average size of households for the rural population as a whole in the period 1688–1751 was about 3.8 members.[53]

[49] C. F. Leprotti, 'Liber primo delle cagioni dello spopolamento della Sardegna', in L. Bulferetti (ed.), *Il riformismo settecentesco in Sardegna* (Cagliari, 1966), pp. 105–6; A. Bongino, 'Relazione dei vari progetti sovra diverse materie che riflettono la Sardegna', ibid., p. 224. The same situation obtained until recently: 'Le ragazze provenienti da famiglie di piccoli proprietari di artigiani di lavoratori dipendenti, devono provvedervi (all'arredamento della casa, corredo compreso) in prima persona. A tal fine si occupano come giornaliere in campagna, nei lavori di zappatura, diserbatura, spigolatura e in genere di raccolta; o si si recano al fiume a lavare la biancheria, impegnandosi con una o più famiglie per uno o più anni. Spesso l'anno precedente il matrimonio, investono un pò dei denari così guadagnati nell'acquisto di un maialino . . . [oppure] si impegnano come domestiche in casa dei grossi o medi proprietari' (village of San Sperate); L. Orrù, 'Donna, casa e salute nella Sardegna tradizionale', *Quaderni sardi di storia*, I (1980), p. 171.

[50] Leprotti, 'Liber primo', pp. 105–6.

[51] *Archivio di Stato*, Cagliari, FG – busta 13, ff. 60–4.

[52] Bongino, 'Relazione', p. 229: Allattati da madri quasi consonte dalla fame, lasciati esposti nella loro educazione alle ingiurie dei tempi ed a cielo scoperto, non farebbero che una comparsa effimera. Infatti vediamo al lume della esperienza che questi teneri figliuoli . . . chiudono ben soventi li giorni suoi nella culla per difetto della cura dovuta nell'allevarli, e si suppone infatti che il numero di questi sia eguale e forsanche maggiore di quegli altri che sopravvivono.'

[53] B. Anatra and G. Puggioni, 'Considerazioni su alcune caratteristiche socio-demografiche della popolazione di Sanluri . . .', *Problemi di utilizzazione delle fonti di demografia storica* (CISP), Rome, 1972–73, II, pp. 257–79; F. Corridore, *Storia documentata della popolazione di Sardegna* (Turin, 1902).

Paradoxically, the 'civil' marriage of female children, sometimes formalized by notarized contract, was also current in many parts of the island, at least in the seventeenth and eighteenth centuries. In 1770, there were so many child brides between seven and ten years of age cohabiting with their 'husbands' in the village of Orotelli that the viceroy felt obliged to denounce the scandal in public assembly.[54] This method of disposing of (and providing for) unwanted female offspring did not preclude recourse to infanticide by exposure to the elements and to sheepdogs ('a form of homicide') in the case of illegitimate infants or because the parents were hopelessly poor.[55] But it seems to have been practiced indiscriminately on newborn babies of both sexes, at least to judge by the nearly perfect parity between males and females in the demographic statistics of the seventeenth and eighteenth centuries.[56]

Given the general precariousness of human life, female heads of families were certainly numerous in the Middle Ages, but since women, regardless of their situation, were exempt from personal taxes, it is impossible to estimate their numbers. At Sanluri, a village of several hundred inhabitants in 1611–71, between one in ten and one in five heads of families were women.[57] The proportion could be even greater in small isolated communities like Bosove near Sassari where three out of seven servile families in 1339 were apparently headed by women.[58]

The rites of courtship and marriage in the Middle Ages probably did not differ significantly from those described by modern ethnologists. Matches were arranged between families after long and delicate negotiations conducted by a *trattadore*, or match-maker, sometimes preceded by the secret inquiries of a 'spy' (*s'uspia*) who had been charged by the suitor to determine the girl's availability and her parents' intentions. The culmination of the process was a reunion of all concerned in the home of the bride's father which opened with

[54] F. Loddo Canepa (ed.), 'Relazione della visita del vicere Des Hayes al regno di Sardegna (1770)', *Archivio Storico Sardo*, XXV (1958), pp. 188–9. Loddo Canepa describes it as 'an ancient Sardinian custom'.

[55] B. Anatra, 'I "Quinque Librorum" nei sinodi sardi', *Le fonti della demografia storica in Italia* (Atti del seminario di demografi storica, 1971–2), I, pp. 71, 73, 76.

[56] *Archivio di Stato*, Cagliari, FG – busta 13, ff. 60–4. Corridore, *Storia della popolazione*.

[57] Anatra and Puggioni, 'Sanluri'.

[58] F. Artizzu, 'Un inventario dei beni dell'Opera di Santa Maria di Pisa (1339)', *Archivio Storico Sardo*, XXVII (1961), pp. 65–80.

the following exchange: Father: 'Why have all these people assembled in my house?' *Trattadore*: 'To conclude the matter we have agreed on'. Father: 'What is it we have agreed on?' *Trattadore*: 'The marriage of . . . and . . .'. The bride and bridegroom sealed the pact with a ritual kiss which was followed by an exchange of gifts, a wedding feast and a festive procession to their new home.[59] These proceedings satisfied the twin criteria of legitimate marriage in the eyes of the populace; that it be public[60] and consentient.[61] The religious benediction was usually dispensed with. As early as 1204 a judge of Torres was condemned by the Church for deferring to the 'perverse customs' of the island in abstaining from matrimony *in facie ecclesiae*.[62]

The ecclesiastical authorities continued to fulminate against cohabitation 'more uxorio', described as a scourge and a plague, for centuries.[63] In 1595, public penance was demanded of the guilty couples who were ordered to attend a nuptial mass bearing lighted candles, the men barefoot, the women bareheaded, their hair unbraided.[64] The problem was compounded by the fact that the priests themselves often set the example. A visiting Jesuit in 1568 noted that Sardinian priests commonly observed local marriage customs in taking a concubine, including a marriage contract *a sa sardesca* and a wedding procession through the streets. The woman was regarded by her neighbors as the priest's legitimate spouse, 'indeed as the first lady of the village'.[65] The churchmen condemned the female partners in non-religious marriages as 'public concubines' or 'women friends' and blamed the practice, as was their wont, on ignorance, superstition and concupiscence. It seems to have persisted longest in the pastoral communities and among the poor. In 1777, it was said that

[59] E. Espa, 'S'uspia e su trattadore considerati nel matrimonio in Sardegna,' *Studi Sassaresi*, II (1971), pp. 215–20.

[60] 'By daylight and by torchlight' (. . . kertiat fuit coiuuata sa mama issoro a cclaru et a facke'); Bonazzi (ed.), *Il condaghe di S. Pietro di Silki*, no. 373. Cf. Besta, *La Sardegna medioevale*, II, 172.

[61] According to the principle 'consensus facit nuptias'; A. Marongiu, 'Unioni e convivenze "more uxorio" in Sardegna prima e dopo il concilio tridentino', *Rivista di Storia del Diritto Italiano*, LII (1979), pp. 5–17; 'Nozze proibite, comunione di beni e consuetudine canonica . . .', *Saggi di storia giuridica*, pp. 163–83.

[62] Besta, *La Sardegna medioevale*, II, 177, n. 44.

[63] F. Sechi, 'Matrimonio nei riflessi canonici e civili in Sardegna', *Studi Sassaresi*, II (1971), pp. 221–30; M. A. Aimo, 'Istituto matrimoniale e società in Sardegna', ibid., pp. 203–11; Marongiu, 'Unione e convivenze'; Anatra, 'Quinque Librorum'.

[64] Sechi, 'Matrimonio'.

[65] Marongiu, 'Unioni e convivenze'.

many peasants 'attempt to postpone the marriage ceremony for a protracted period on the pretext of poverty',[66] and as late as 1935, the village of Lodé counted 35 illicit couples who insisted that they lacked the 'capital' (*su gaudale*) to start an independent family (*ponner domo*).[67]

Medieval law was chiefly concerned with three conditions of women: nubile (or virgin), married and widowed.[68] In the statutes of Sassari, however, one encounters 'women without husbands' who could be sentenced to work off their debts in the service of their creditors at the rate of 12s per year plus upkeep, or 24s if they practiced a trade.[69] The only distinctively female trades mentioned in medieval sources are domestic servant, laundress and prostitute.[70] But women also sometimes materialize as street-sellers and tavern-keepers.[71] Since any task performed outside one's own home was considered degrading, or in any case a sign of inferior status, independent working women naturally occupied the bottom rung of the social ladder.[72]

The precarious situation of unwed women in a country of unextended families and strict sexual mores is reflected in the attitude of the Church toward consanguinous marriage. In 1708, eight out of ten situations that were judged to warrant dispensation concerned young women who were otherwise unmarriagable because they lived in isolated communities, were bereft of 'dowries', had attained a certain age or whose honor had been compromised ('propter infamiam et scandalum').[73] The same preoccupation, coupled with the force of tradition, also helps to explain the curious indulgence of the Church toward clerical marriage. If married priests were better than no

[66] Anatra, 'Quinque Librorum', pp. 74–5, 83, n. 23.

[67] Aimo, 'Istituto matrimoniale', p. 210, n. 6.

[68] R. Metz, 'Le statut de la femme en droit canonique médiéval', *La Femme*, II, p. 96. At Villa di Chiesa the 'taulito' of the church of S. Clara was reserved for virgins, wives and widows (*Statuti di Villa di Chiesa*, II, 74).

[69] *Statuti di Sassari*, II, 8.

[70] ibid., II, 8; III, 38; *Statuti di Villa di Chiesa*, III, 20; *Carta de Logu*, c. 22; Roqué, *L'infraction de la loi*. One out of five women involved with the law at Cagliari were prostitutes.

[71] ibid. In the village of Quartu in 1323, seven out of 17 tavern-keepers were women; F. Artizzu, 'Rendite pisane nel Giudicato di Cagliari', *Archivio Storico Sardo*, XXV (1957), p. 407 ff.

[72] Orrù, 'Donna, casa e salute'.

[73] Anatra, 'Quinque Librorum', pp. 67–8.

priests at all,[74] the status of priest's concubine was doubtless preferable to that of spinster.

There are those who discern in certain features of Sardinian peasant society today the survivals of an ancient matriarchal system. Women usually control the purse and are responsible for running the household in their husband's absence, sometimes, in the pastoral communities, for weeks at a time. It has also been pointed out that, in contrast to Sicily and southern Italy, so-called crimes of honor, which are regarded as symptomatic of female servitude, are extremely rare in Sardinia. On the contrary, women themselves tend to play an active role in fomenting violence by instigating vendettas for murdered kin.[75]

Most serious observers, however, question this thesis. In actual fact, Sardinian women are, or were until recently, subject to a rigid code of conduct that assured their complete subservience to male authority. Gavino Ledda, himself the son of an autocratic shepherd 'patriarch',[76] remarks that the woman's domain was limited by the four walls of her home. In her husband's absence she was left in charge, but the moment he set foot inside the house again he was the absolute master.[77] For Francesco Alziator, the submission of women to masculine mores expresses itself in their 'unnatural' repression of outward signs of tenderness and affection except toward very young children.[78] The jurist and novelist Salvatore Satta considers women in traditional Sardinian society as the invisible objects of a silent cult, in practice little better than slaves to their husbands.[79]

---

[74] '... cum sciat expedire uxoratos potius quam nullos habere sacerdotes et ministros' (pastoral letter of the Archbishop of Cagliari, 1570, cited by Marongiu, 'Unioni e convivenze', p. 11).

[75] See especially, M. Pitzalis Acciaro, *In nome della madre. Ipotesi sul matriarcato barbaricino* (Milan, 1978).

[76] G. Ledda, *Padre Padrone, L'educazione di un pastore* (Milan, 1975).

[77] In M. Brigaglia, *Gavino Ledda dopo Padre Padrone* (Cagliari, 1978), p. 44.

[78] Alziator, *Il folklore sardo*, p. 106: 'La posizione [della donna] è sovente quella di chi deve obbedire, lavorare ed avere solo per sé le lacrime e i patemi d'animo. Da ciò deriva quella sorta di amore asciutto, senza espansioni, senza affettuosità esteriori che lega i membri della famiglia sarda. Solo ai bimbi sono riservate le carezze e le moine; con l'età anche essi diventeranno i sudditi di un silenzio regno senza tenerezza.'

[79] S. Satta, *Il giorno del giudizio* (Milan, 1979), pp. 50-1: 'Per il Sardo ... la donna, la moglie era come l'oggetto di un culto silenzioso, esposto alle vicende della vita, strumento delle esigneze della vita, e quindi anche delle esigenze del marito e

If medieval records do not leave one with this impression of universal female servitude[80] it may be because the status of Sardinian
women actually deteriorated during the four centuries of Spanish
domination under the influence of Iberian–Islamic laws and customs
which tended to isolate them more and more from dangerous contacts
with the outside world.[81]

---

della famiglia, ma come rarefatta, esterna a quello che è il dominio dell'uomo, cioè
al governo del piccolo stato familiare. In questo governo non poteva né non doveva
entrare, più di quanto non possa entrare la regina nel governo del re.'

[80] 'Sapevo e avevo anche visto di donne che si sono ribellate al marito, e anche di
donne che commandavano loro ... La "ribelle" c'è sempre anche nell'immensa
enorme servitù della donna'; Gavino Ledda, in Brigaglia, *Gavino Ledda*, p. 44.

[81] Alziator, *Il folklore sardo*, pp. 38–9.

13

Anthonius Guainerius
and Medieval Gynecology

HELEN RODNITE LEMAY

One of the most important developments in women's studies during the past decade has been the growth of scholarship on the history of women and health care. Feminist analysis of the role played by male and female healers and of the effects of male medical care on women's lives, especially with reference to their reproductive faculties, has brought a new dimension to our understanding of women's health today. This investigation up to now has been confined mostly to the modern period. In their studies of childbirth practices, doctors' advice, women physicians and the women's health movement, Donegan,[1] Wertz and Wertz,[2] Ehrenreich and English,[3] Walsh,[4] and Ruzek[5] have given us a new perspective on the history of women and medicine.

The purpose of this essay is to explore the implications of this feminist analysis for the Middle Ages and the Renaissance. To what degree can one adopt the methods of these historians without imposing twentieth-century standards on medieval source material? Indeed, what kinds of source material do we even have to work with? So far, no firsthand account of a patient's medical treatment has been discovered for the twelfth century similar to Charlotte Perkins Gilman's *Yellow Wallpaper* which describes her experience in the 1880s following

---

[1] Jane B. Donegan, *Women and Men Midwives* (Westport, Connecticut, 1978).

[2] Richard W. Wertz and Dorothy C. Wertz, *Lying In: A History of Childbirth in America* (New York, 1979).

[3] Barbara Ehrenreich and Dierdre English, *For Her Own Good: 150 Years of the Experts' Advice to Women* (Garden City, New York, 1979).

[4] Mary Roth Walsh, *Doctors Wanted: No Women Need Apply* (New Haven and London, 1977).

[5] Sheryl B. Ruzek, *The Women's Health Movement – Feminist Alternatives to Medical Control* (New York, 1978).

her doctor's prescription for a rest cure.[6] We do not even have, to my knowledge, a good record of a medieval woman's encounter with gynecological surgery. I propose that we can nevertheless make profitable use of medieval medical source material to provide a better understanding of the experiences of women during this period.

Certainly a central focus of our study of these sources should be to define the role of the physician, both in relation to his patients and to other practitioners. Historians have addressed themselves to this problem, exploiting legal records, natural-philosophical and medical treatises, and a manuscript account of folk practices in the course of their research. From a Bern codex of the late eleventh or early twelfth century, Lucille Pinto concludes that male physicians did not treat women in intimate matters concerning their reproductive systems,[7] and Beryl Rowland's recent translation of an early fifteenth-century gynecological handbook provides further evidence of an awareness that the special problems of women required that they be treated by practitioners of their own sex.[8] Thomas Benedek, too, cites the fourteenth-century physician Guy de Chauliac to the effect that midwifery was as a rule practiced by women, and concludes from the account of Jacoba Felicie's trial in 1322 that only women were allowed to examine women's private parts. This posed a special problem when midwives were required to obtain licenses in the sixteenth century, and a system was instituted whereby male doctors with little practical knowledge acted in a supervisory capacity over them.[9]

This material suggests, of course, that the concept of a feminist analysis of the medieval physician's role in dealing with women patients is meaningless, for his contacts with women were almost nonexistent, and that the most we can do toward defining his relations with other practitioners is to repeat the statement that from the sixteenth century on men began to replace women in the lying-in chamber. A closer examination of medieval source material, however, indicates that the task of finding male physicians treating medieval women is not a hopeless one. Edward Kealey notes, for example, that

[6] See Ehrenreich and English, *For Her Own Good*, pp. 101–2.

[7] Lucille B. Pinto, 'The folk practice of gynecology and obstetrics in the Middle Ages', *Bulletin of the History of Medicine*, 47 (1973), p. 521.

[8] Beryl Rowland, *Medieval Woman's Guide to Health: The First English Gynecological Handbook* (Kent, Ohio, 1981), pp. 14, 59.

[9] Thomas G. Benedek, 'The changing relationship between midwives and physicians during the Renaissance', *Bulletin of the History of Medicine*, 51 (1977), pp. 550–64.

no female practitioners appear in the records of Norman England, although they must have existed,[10] and that we have documented evidence of the presence of Dr Fauritius of Abingdon at the birth of Queen Matilda's first child in 1101.[11] Ynez Violé O'Neill provides us with a careful study of Giovanni Michele Savonarola's fifteenth-century vernacular treatise on gynecology, obstetrics and child care addressed to the women of Ferrara, and demonstrates clearly that the court physician actually treated women with gynecological and obstetric problems. In addition, Savonarola did much more for mid-wives than simply to supervise them by quoting Galen: he made available to them a significant amount of medical learning and practical experience.[12] Further, the substantial sections of Beryl Rowland's fifteenth-century vernacular gynecological handbook that include opinions by medical authorities provide additional evidence of inter-action between learned doctors and practically trained midwives in the Middle Ages.[13]

If male doctors did indeed treat female patients, and if they had more than remote contact with practicing midwives, we need to probe more deeply into the nature of these relations. If, for example, doctors prescribed treatments for women's gynecological problems, what results did these medical ministrations have for the patients' lives? Do we have examples of iatrogenic disease in medieval documents? Thomas Benedek does refer to sixteenth- and seventeenth-century complaints about 'the various errors and mistakes which the midwives commit on parturient women',[14] but little has been published on gynecological and obstetrical malpractice in the preceding centuries.[15]

Doctors do more than treat disease, however; they prescribe how we should deal with aspects of our daily lives. The 'medicalization' of

[10] Edward J. Kealey, *Medieval Medicus: A Social History of Anglo-Norman Medicine* (Baltimore and London, 1981), p. 35.

[11] ibid., pp. 66–7.

[12] Ynez Violé O'Neill, 'Giovanni Michele Savonarola: an atypical Renaissance practitioner', *Clio Medica*, 10 (1975), pp. 77–93.

[13] Rowland, *Medieval Woman's Guide*, pp. 85, 103–5, 121–3.

[14] Benedek, 'Changing relationship', p. 563.

[15] See, for example, Madeleine Pelner Cosman, 'Medieval medical malpractice: The dicta and the dockets', *Bulletin of the New York Academy of Medicine*, 2nd series, 49 (1973), pp. 22–47, which gives an example of one case concerning a woman, although her disease does not involve her reproductive organs. References to mal-practice by female practitioners are found in Rowland, *Medieval Woman's Guide*, pp. 13–14.

childbirth is one of the main themes of modern feminist scholarship: during this century parturition and other natural biological events in women's lives, such as the menopause, have been transformed into medical events requiring a doctor's supervision and treatment. Similarly, in the Middle Ages menstruation[16] and sexual intercourse were topics about which doctors felt it necessary to give instruction. If these directions were followed, or if they were heard but ignored, certainly there were consequences for women patients.

Finally, we need to know what assumptions about women were behind the doctors' prescriptions. Maryanne Cline Horowitz, Vern Bullough, and Ian Maclean are among the scholars who have examined this question with respect to antiquity and the Middle Ages.[17] Women have been considered inferior to men, oversexed, unclean and this opinion has certainly affected their medical treatment. A central question in feminist studies of women and medicine has been to what degree the complexion of the womb was regarded as the explanation for woman's physical and mental well-being. A glance at Hippocrates or at nineteenth-century medical literature will confirm the central role of the uterus in medical explanations for such diverse symptoms as convulsions and writer's cramp,[18] and certainly a foray into medieval sources has a good chance of yielding similar information. Sex stereotypes play an important role in gynecologists' attitudes, diagnoses and treatments, and must therefore be examined carefully in any study of medieval women and medicine.

It is the purpose of this essay to demonstrate how a medieval medical source, Anthonius Guainerius' *Tractatus de matricibus*, can be used to address these questions. Although Guainerius represents 'academic' medicine, since he was a professor of medicine at the University of Pavia during the early fifteenth century, his *Treatise on the Womb* reflects actual practice to a much greater degree than most writings of this genre. The author's constant references to his personal experience indicate that his prescriptions were applied in his own treatment

---

[16] On this topic see Charles T. Wood, 'The doctors' dilemma: sin, salvation and the menstrual cycle in Medieval thought', *Speculum*, 56 (1981), pp. 710–27.

[17] Maryanne Cline Horowitz, 'Aristotle and woman', *Journal of the History of Biology*, 9 (1976), pp. 183–213; Vern Bullough, 'Medieval medical and scientific views of women', *Viator*, 4 (1973), pp. 485–501; Ian Maclean, *The Renaissance Notion of Woman* (Cambridge, 1980).

[18] See, for example, John S. Haller and Robin M. Haller, *The Physician and Sexuality in Victorian America* (Urbana, Illinois, 1974), pp. 8–9.

of patients, although since fifteenth-century Pavian gynecological case histories are not available, the historian is not in a position to know exactly to what degree the recommendations of the *Tractatus* were generally followed. Guainerius is interesting because he is conventionally trained and respects the standard medical authorities, yet prefers to rely on tried-and-true methods.

Guainerius appears to have achieved a certain importance during his lifetime. Even though he did not make much of a mark on academic medicine, as we can conclude from the absence of citation of his opinions, he nevertheless was a reasonably prolific writer with a prominent audience. His most famous work, a treatise on pest and poisons, was dedicated to Filippo Maria, Duke of Milan, and he addressed treatises on pleurisy and fevers to the physician of the Duke of Savoy.[19] What, then, can we learn about his relations with women patients?

The *Tractatus de matricibus* makes it very clear both that Guainerius saw an important role for the physician in the treatment of female illness and that he played this role actively during his lifetime. His treatise records his personal experience with patients and his relationship with other contemporary practitioners, as well as his reading of medical authorities. Guainerius was consulted by women, discussed with them their symptoms and examined them. He exchanged ideas with midwives, used them to carry out his prescribed treatments and was familiar with astrology, the practices of soothsayers and peasant beliefs. He was, therefore, very much in touch with the practice as well as with the theory of medicine.

Guainerius was consulted for a number of female maladies, and was therefore required first to make a diagnosis. He relied heavily on the testimony of the patient; the Italian doctor evidently questioned his clients closely on their symptoms. In his discussion of hemorrhoids of the uterus, for example, he states that these excrescences appear either in the neck of the womb or deeper inside, and that they often cause intense pain. They may be perceived by touch or by sight, he continues, or 'more decently, by the testimony of the patient from whom the doctor should inquire studiously as to their form'.[20] Similarly,

---

[19] Lynn Thorndike, *History of Magic and Experimental Science* (New York, 1934), IV, pp. 215–16.

[20] 'Excrescentias igitur tales apparentes tactu ac visu vel honestius ut dixeri[m] ex infirme relatu comprehendes de quarum forma etiam inquiras studiose et talia tibi signa demonstrativa erunt.' Anthonius Guainerius, *Tractatus de matricibus* in *Opera Omnia*, Pavia, 1481, f. x8va.

humidity of the womb can be diagnosed by inspection of the bloody discharge or from the description by the sick person of its color and texture.[21] In order for the physician to identify most of the illnesses listed in the *Tractatus*, the patient must set forth her complaints and answer questions on her menstrual flow, perception of heat or cold in the womb, pain and even her appetite for sexual intercourse. There is no record in this treatise of an intermediary between doctor and patient at this point in their encounter.

These passages would lead us to believe that Guainerius did not perform physical examinations and that he respected the patient's ability to describe her symptoms. Neither of these conclusions is entirely warranted. Although the doctor probably engaged only rarely in direct inspection of a woman's genitals, he nevertheless normally did at least carry out the examination far enough to palpate the abdomen. When instructing the physician on how to distinguish between a false pregnancy (or tumor known as a *mola*) and a true one, he states that if the hand is placed with some violence on the *mola*, the tumor moves aside and returns to the original place when the hand is taken away, whereas a fetus might move or might stay in the same place.[22] Similarly, a womb that has moved out of place may be detected by the doctor's touch; if the uterus has migrated upwards a round mass may be felt in the abdomen.[23] Guainerius does allude to the possibility of a doctor conducting a pelvic examination on a female patient, however. In the chapter on sterility, he states that if examination is permitted to the physician, he can determine whether sterility is caused by exceeding narrowness, width or tortuosity of the mouth of the womb.[24]

Guainerius' recommendations for physical examination normally do not extend this far, however. Both in the case of prolapse and in the

---

[21] 'An sanguinee flegmatice colerice aut melancholice fuerint ex earum colore cognosces. Nam si albe flegmatice, citrine colerice [colorice], rubee sanguinee et fusce seu nigre melancholice erunt quod ex ipsarum inspectione aut infirme narratione comprehendes et hec tibi signa demonstrativa sint.' Guainerius, f. y3ra.

[22] 'Quintum quandocumque impressio violenta in mola cum manu fit movetur et amota manu locum ad pristinum redit fetus autem quandoque ex compressione tali movetur quandoque vero minime.' Guainerius, f. 2z5va. (Following series 'z', the next quire is marked simply '2'. It will be referred to here as '2z'.)

[23] 'Intrinsecarum vero si sursum matrix non prefocans ascendit dolor ac gravedo ab umbilico supra sentitur. Ibidem quoque rem rotundam tactu percipies videtur. . . .' Guainerius, f. y1rb.

[24] De strictura vero nimia sive amplitudine aut oris tortuositate ubi certificare cupias tu ipse ubi phas sit experire. . . .' Guainerius, f. 2z1ra.

event of suffocation (where the womb moves upwards toward the diaphragm and impedes the flow of breath) the treatment seems to involve a female assistant, or midwife (*obstetrix*). First, fumigation is used to induce the womb to give up its corrupt seed or venomous humors and to return to its original place. This involves the midwife's administering through the nose or genital opening foul odors which have medicinal value in this disorder. After outlining other procedures to be carried out by the midwife in both of these cases (e.g. vomiting), Guainerius states specifically that for prolapse Avicenna's directions should be followed. The midwife is to anoint her hands, have the afflicted woman lie on her back with her thighs elevated, and gently introduce the womb. Then she is to apply to the vulva a woolen cloth that has been soaked in vinegar and wrung out, and to have the patient stretch out to rest before taking an hour-long therapeutic bath.[25] In the case of suffocation, the *obstetrix* is to bring the woman to orgasm, so that the womb will expel its venomous humors. Guainerius instructs the operator to anoint her hands and the mouth of the vulva, and then to introduce a finger and rub continuously the neck of the womb until it ejects the corrupted seed or humor. He comments that the midwife will be more successful in this procedure if the patient is not a virgin, although it is not necessary if she is married, for in this case her husband should possess her roughly, taking care that she assumes the bottom position, and bring on orgasm in this fashion.[26]

Guainerius' awareness of social factors affecting treatment of women is not limited to his recommendations on physical contact between doctor and patient. Although he recognizes the necessity for the doctor to rely on the patient's description of her complaint, he remains skeptical about her ability to make an accurate observation. Since Guainerius thinks that suffocation of the womb is caused by vapors generated in it from corrupt seed, he concludes that the fumes often travel upwards toward the head, causing pain. When women feel pain in the esophagus, in the head or in the medulla from these fumes, he tells us, they think that the womb has actually crept up to that place. 'If you say the opposite of this,' he continues, 'they will call

[25] Guainerius, f. y2ra.

[26] 'Ostitrix deinde os vulve perungat iniuntumque digitum si corrupta fuerit quanto plus poterit immitat matricis collum fricando [fricatio] continue sperma eius corruptum seu humorem quamvis alium venenosum talem per fricationem matrix evomit. Cumque suppositio in hoc casu prevaleat si maritum habuerit eam supponat gagliarditer quia nihil supra et hec in peroxismo fienda sunt.' Guainerius, f. x4rb.

you a stupid doctor.'[27] Not only did he mistrust women's testimony, then, but he realized that tact and restraint were required in a doctor's dealings with his patients.

Guainerius drew a clear line between the health professional and the public, and he did not think that women should be told too much. Just as he was willing to keep silent on the topic of the wandering womb to avoid an insult and its professional implications, so he believed in keeping trade secrets. In his chapter on superfluity of menses, Guainerius gives a prescription for a potion made from menstrual blood, myrtle syrup and water of plantain which the patient is instructed to drink. The author comments, 'This [formula] is healthy, and unless the flow comes from an ulcer of the womb I have never found an error in such a medication.' However, he continues, 'You should take care not to reveal this to women, and instead have a trustworthy apothecary who will affirm that this syrup has been made from conjugal substances, and see to it that he sells it at a high price so that it commands greater faith. You will have to make up for this sin in another way, however.'[28]

Guainerius is consciously deceiving his patient and he is aware that this deception is morally wrong. Nevertheless, he often remarks on the secrecy of recipes and the high price of drugs. For example, he describes an ointment for the cure of excess bleeding caused by hemorrhoids of the womb and similar conditions, and states that in Italy it is called 'unguent of the countess' and is of such great virtue that many apothecaries price it so high that they will reveal the formula only in exchange for gold.[29]

If we attempt to assess standard medieval protocol in treatment of

[27] '. . . fumus quoque ab illa materia corrupta resolutus matricem sursum pellit que ad dyafragma ascendens ipsum coartat multum et si deinceps ad caput fumos raptum habere contingit matricem in caput devenisse mulieres non dubitant unde a matricis mala dispositione vexate dolorem aliquo in loco dum presentiat illuc matricem repere aiunt sive in gula capite nuca alio sive quovis in loco fumi illi perveniant cuius oppositum si dixeris te medicum stolidum predicabunt.' Guainerius, f. x3va.

[28] 'Et ne hoc mulieribus reveles cave fidum imo habe apotecarium qui preciosum hunc esse sirupum ex maritis confectum rebus affirmet et ut fidem maiorem adhibeant precio magno vendatur in aliis tamen propter peccatum precium reconpensando.' Guainerius, f. y5ra.

[29] '. . . et fiat unguentum vel facias sic et est quod in ytalia unguentum comitisse appellatur et est tante virtutis ut apotecarii nonnulli tantum caripendant ut receptam pro auro darent. . . .' Guainerius, f. y5vb.

diseases of the womb by today's standards, we may certainly characterize it as 'interventionist'. Women were treated very aggressively for most of the illnesses Guainerius lists, although the intervention was not often surgical in nature. An example of a typical regimen is the treatment for retention of the menses when it is caused by a phlegmatic complexion. The doctor should begin with the six things non-natural,[30] aiming in this case to restore heat and dryness to the woman's disposition. This normally involves vomiting and purging of the patient, who afterwards receives a medicinal bath. She is then put to bed, anointed with oil of lily and told to consume a potion. Fumigation follows; extremely odiferous fumes are applied at the genital opening, and the doctor is cautioned not to allow them to penetrate the nose because of their terrible smell. Phlebotomy is next, for in order to induce blood to flow from the vagina blood-letting is recommended. Finally a pessary is applied, preferably in the first quarter of the moon, and if this does not work the process is repeated in the second quarter.[31] Although this procedure seems to be a harsh one, Guainerius' motivation seems to be simply to do what he can to bring relief to the patient. He realizes that the doctor cannot cure all disease; however, he believes that if a physician exerts effort, he can relieve pain and help the patient get well.[32]

One central point made by feminist interpreters of the history of medicine is that the lay healer's approach has traditionally been gentler to the patient, and more respecting of her natural body processes. Much of this is attributed to woman's instinctive understanding of the workings of the female body, and a male doctor's alienation from it. If we compare the above cure with what we learn about wise women's cures, however, we see little difference in the procedures. In Beryl Rowland's fifteenth-century English gynecological handbook, for example, treatment for retention of the menses is almost identical with the one described by Guainerius,[33] and we have seen that the Italian doctor made use of female operators in carrying out his aggressive procedures.

[30] The six things non-natural are: (1) air, (2) food and drink, (3) sleep and watch, (4) motion and rest, (5) evacuation and repletion, (6) passions of the mind. These categories determine health or disease depending upon their use or abuse; see L. J. Rather, 'The "six things non-natural": a note on the origins and fate of a doctrine and a phrase', *Clio Medica*, 3 (1968), pp. 337–47.

[31] Guainerius, f. w7vb–x1ra.

[32] See, for example, Guainerius, f. x8va.

[33] Beryl Rowland, *Medieval Woman's Guide*, pp. 61–75.

This willingness on the part of medical practitioners of both sexes to subject women to painful, often debilitating, treatments has been connected by feminist historians with a valuation placed on women as lesser beings. Although men, too, have submitted to 'heroic' measures such as blood-letting and purging, the history of women and medicine has been marked to a much greater degree by harsh treatment directed especially at the reproductive system. Female fertility has been so prized historically, and women's sex organs have been so undervalued, that procedures such as 'splitting the womb', oophorectomy[34] and radical mastectomy have caused unnecessary anguish to substantial numbers of women. Women as well as men have accepted the cultural assumptions that led women in the Middle Ages to submit to fumigation and phlebotomy and that induce them today to undergo unnecessary hysterectomy and to take the birth control pill.

Guainerius demonstrates a heavy reliance on female healers in his treatise, and not simply as assistants for the sake of propriety. Midwives' recipes often form an important part of his recommendations; in the case of superfluity of menses, for example, he gives directions for the preparation of a plaster for, as he says, 'I put more faith in plasters than in any other medicine.' The one he describes, he informs us, is used by old women of the region, and is so efficacious that it can stop a miscarriage that has already begun.[35] Similarly, in the case of suffocation of the womb, Guainerius notes that 'women who are learned in these things' immediately apply to the nose of a woman so afflicted any fetid odor such as burned hair or feathers in order to stimulate the expulsive power.[36] Sometimes he will recommend that a cure be left entirely to the midwives. For example, if sterility is caused by exceeding length or shortness of the penis, he states, 'you should leave the cure to old women who are expert in this.' In this case, the 'cure' involves the old woman giving instructions to the wife

---

[34] On this topic see G. J. Barker-Benfield, *The Horrors of the Half-Known Life: Male Attitudes Towards Women and Sexuality in Nineteenth-Century America* (New York, 1976), c. 10 and 11.

[35] 'Et in istis partibus vetule sic faciunt et nedum menstrua restringunt verum iam inceptum aborsum prohibent . . . Bone deus ab his emplastris discedere nescio et hoc est quia magis creditum quam alii medicamini.' Guainerius, f. y6ra.

[36] 'Et sic mulieres in his docte omnes quecumque fetida naribus [nares] applicant statim ut omnium animalium incensas plumas et perdices maxime hominis capillos, canis quoque pilos, ac hirci filtrum etiam ac corium quodlibet ungulas pariter ac cornu quodcumque.' Guainerius, f. x4ra.

on how to place herself during sexual intercourse so that she can receive the penis more or less.[37]

Peasant beliefs even figure in the *Tractatus de matricibus*. In the chapter on false pregnancy, we read about fleshy growths that are sometimes generated in place of a fetus. Enunciating the principle that nature always chooses the best of all possible actions, Guainerius declares that such masses of flesh are caused by the effect of a constellation or by an indisposition of matter. The peasants in Apulia once told him about a toad that was born to a woman along with her baby, and he explains that the male seed in this case acted on the purer portion of matter in the womb to form the child, and on the more corrupt matter to form the creature, for it was the best nature could do under the circumstances. Toads and other poisonous animals are often generated along with a child, he continues. Sometimes they kill the fetus before birth from their gassiness, but more frequently the two are born together, but the creature destroys the baby at birth with its venomous bite.[38] Therefore we see Guainerius taking seriously stories he has heard from the peasants and providing a scientific explanation for them.

Despite his reliance on midwives and popular lore, Guainerius clearly recognizes the necessity of distinguishing himself from the lay healer. When reporting that old women apply burned hair and feathers to the nose of a patient who is suffering from suffocation of the womb, he recommends that the doctor use instead other odiferous substances 'in order to establish a difference between yourself and vulgar practitioners.'[39] Professional decorum required that he should not associate himself too closely with the unlearned.

[37] 'Brevitatis autem virge seu longitudinis curam expertis vetulis derelinquas quia in actu coitus mulierem diversimode situando plus et minus de virga suscipiunt.' Guainerius, f. z2rb.

[38] 'Facit enim natura de possibilibus semper quod melius est. Nonne etiam constellationis ac dispositionis materie cum fetu simul frustrum carnis seu aliud quoddam in apulia generari sepe ab incolis narratum mihi fuit, ut bufo vel consimile aliud. Nam tunc virile [verile] semen in puriorem menstrui partem agens, in eam formam humanam inducit; et, sui in superfluam materie corrupte actionem continuans, perfectorum qua potest forma eam informat. Et hoc modo ex materia illa ad recipiendum humanam formam indisposita cum fetu bufo aut consimile venenosum quoddam animal generatur cuius venenositate fetus ipse in matrice inficitur sepe ac moritur. Frequentius tamen cum fetu ipso nascitur simul in cuius exitu ipsum mordet interdum ex quo venenoso morsu infelix fetus moritur statim.' Guainerius, f. z6vb–z7ra.

[39] 'Sed ut inter te et vulgares differentiam ponas aliquam utere assa fetida castoreo albano . . . et similibus.' Guainerius, f. x4ra.

It is not only their lack of university training that causes Guainerius to remain aloof from lay healers, however. The doctor refers many times in the course of his treatise to the incompetence, ignorance and sometimes even the evil of these individuals. He cautions, for example, against the *trovantuli*, local persons who use a woman's urine as a kind of crystal ball to determine whether she is pregnant, whether she has ever conceived before, how many times she has given birth, whether she has previously been married and whether her parents are alive. These individuals so impress people that many come from afar to consult them. Guainerius states, however, that in his opinion nothing about pregnancy can be concluded from the urine, and he rejects the *trovantuli* and their determinations.[40]

Guainerius sees the doctor as a scientist (*vir scientificus*) who should leave aside incantations in favour of natural remedies.[41] However, despite this modern-sounding statement, he is actually ambivalent about the powers of soothsayers and witches. He tells us, for example, of cases he is familiar with in which men and women were bewitched and rendered sterile as a result, and he suggests that in this instance the afflicted individual can consult an old woman, seeking a cure by contrary incantations. Although Guainerius feels obliged to repeat his statement that he has no faith in these practices and to cite Avicenna on the natural cause of bodily afflictions, he does admit to some hesitancy on the topic. Since Ptolemy states in the *Quadripartitum* that a certain celestial configuration in an individual's nativity will give that person the ability to cause evil spirits to move from place to place, Guainerius reasons, it is no wonder that cursed old women offering tribute to demons do incredible things. Thus he advises the person who has been bewitched that if he wishes he may have recourse to these healers.[42]

[40] 'Trovantuli tamen in istis partibus ex urinis impregnationem non modo cognoscere affirmant sed verum et si mulier conceperat unquam ac natorum numerum maritum alium an habuerit pater atque mater vivat ne et plurima talia. Propter quod homines taliter infamant ut a remotissimis partibus non credenda ad eos copia continue confluat. Sed his missis trovantulis ad propositum redeundo, ego ipse nihil ex urina super impregnationem posse concludi, certi quiquam persuadere volui nunquam.' Guainerius, f. 2z5va–b.

[41] 'Tu tamen vir scientifice incantationes istas trovantulis derelinque, cum in medicaminibus naturalibus . . . [the rest of this sentence is missing from the text]. Guainerius, f. y6vb.

[42] 'Praecantationes quoque fascinationes per contrarias praecantationes curentur, de quibus ad vetulas sortilegitas recursum habeas. Verum et si his fidem nullam adhibeam non credenda tamen quotidie istis in partibus audio ubi anno isto ob haec

There was a clear distinction between astrology and other arts of divination during the Middle Ages, and this difference plays an important part in the *Tractatus de matricibus*. Unlike necromancy, which was classified with the occult, astrology was taught at the university as a respectable science.[43] Guainerius quotes astrological authorities at length and with considerable respect, and yet stops short of accepting their opinions without question.

In his chapter on the generation of the embryo, Guainerius outlines the method of computing the time from conception to birth. He first presents Avicenna's formula, which involves doubling the time until motion is first perceived by the pregnant woman and adding this to the period before movement to arrive at the time of birth. This is followed by the astrological method found in the pseudo-Ptolemaic *Centiloquium*, which determines the moment of birth from the configuration of the heavens. Guainerius comments, however, that 'although the procedure is indeed true of the stars, as Ptolemy, such a great man, affirms,' nevertheless differences in the agents and the matter cause this rule to be fallible. The doctor maintains that a robust, sanguine woman fertilized by a powerful seed will give birth sooner than a weak, phlegmatic one impregnated by feeble sperm, even though the astrological formula states otherwise. 'Therefore,' he says, 'I think it is better to leave the question to the masters in astrology.'[44]

---

cremate sunt plurime. De his tamen Ptolomei sententia quarta parte Quadripartiti capitulo 3° me hesitantem interdum facit. Inquit enim quod si in nativitate alicuius domini dispositores operis fuerint in Sagitario vel Piscibus, talis per mortuos divinabit et malignos etiam spiritus, de loco ad locum moveri coget; et si in Virgine fuerint aut Scorpione nigromanticus et astrologus iudicabit occulta et predicet futura. Ecce ergo secundum Ptolomei sententiam qualiter sub tali constellatione natis demones obediunt. Nimirum igitur si ille maledicte vetule demones tributa prebentes non credenda faciant. Avicenna tamen vehementi affectioni in quarta Sexti Naturalium hoc attribuit et tu praecantatus ad tales recursum habeas si libet.' Guainerius, f. z1rb.

[43] See Richard Lemay, 'The teaching of astronomy in medieval universities, principally at Paris, in the fourteenth century', *Manuscripta*, 20 (1976), pp. 197–217.

[44] 'Astrorum merito et si precedens regula [dupla] forsan vera sit, ut Ptolomeus vir tantus affirmat, tamen agentis particularis diversitate quam etiam materie fallacem illam inveniri sepe puto. Posito etiam quod eodem instanti mulier sanguinea ac robusta ex semine valde potenti concipiat, et debilis flegmatica ex debili semine, cetera ponendo paria, ad nativitatis usque tempus sanguinea citius pariet cum materia in ea obediens sit magis; particulare agens fortius et virile ut suppono. ... Ex quo bene sequitur quod si precedens regula astrorum merito vera sit, ratione particularis agentis ac materie fallax reperire debet sepe. Istam igitur dominis astrologis dimittere melius puto.' Guainerius, f. 2z3vb–2z4ra.

Although Guainerius claims to reject the astrological opinion, we
see that he refers to Ptolemy with reverence. His studies in the faculty
of medicine have included astrology as part of the curriculum, and
thus, in accordance with this training, he proceeds to set down a
detailed account of the influence of each of the planets on the formation of the fetus, which he states that he has collected here and there
in different books of astrology.[45] Similarly, he gives the astrological
as well as the medical explanation for why the child born in the
eighth month cannot live, and states that the astrologers make a perfect case, if you can live with their reasoning.[46] Thus, although he
maintains a certain independence, Guainerius nevertheless pays due
respect to the astrological interpretation.

The *Tractatus de matricibus* gives ample discussion of iatrogenic disease,
most of it caused by midwives. If Italian university-trained physicians
caused harm to their patients through their treatments, Guainerius
does not provide us with testimony to this effect.

Contrary to the practices of later centuries when midwives assisting
at birth let nature take its course, some of the women we learn of in
Guainerius' treatise intervened too aggressively, and injured the
patient. Others, as one would expect, did not act when they should
have. Of course, it would be natural to find evidence of complications
in the doctor's account of his experience; normal cases would never
have come to his attention. Abscess of the womb is one of the results
of insufficient skill of the midwife; this is defined as a tumor in the
womb's substance which can be generated by unnatural and difficult
birth, and by the defect of an ignorant midwife who does not know
how to give aid to the childbearing woman.[47] Prolapse of the uterus,
on the other hand, is caused by unnecessary intervention. If the birth
assistant attempts to extract the secundines violently, the organ is
often injured.[48]

[45] '. . . ut in diversis astrologorum libris sparsim recollegi'. Guainerius, f. 2z4rb.

[46] 'Patet ergo secundum medicos quare in octavo natus non vivat. In septimo
vero sic. Quod si hac cum astrologorum ratione convixeris quesiti perfecti causam
habebis.' Guainerius, f. 2z5ra.

[47] 'Apostema matricis est tumor in substantiam eius a quavis causa preter
naturam perveniens. A privativa quod contingit ipsum generare sepe ut partu
innaturali difficultate parienti, aborsu, et obstetricis defectu parienti succurrere
nescientis.' Guainerius, f. x4va.

[48] 'Ex descriptione autem cause precipitationis matricis manifeste tibi fiunt. Nam
quedam extrinsece ut . . . secundine ab obstitrice violenta extractio.' Guainerius,
f. y1ra–b.

We have already seen that Guainerius fears the powers of the old women, and that he believes they are capable of causing sterility by incantations. The doctor claims as well that he has seen a number of cases where their medical attention designed to induce fertility led to the opposite result. Men have had a plaster of opium applied to their testicles, for example, and women have had it administered in a pessary. Other hot substances have also been applied to the womb, which have had the effect of extinguishing its natural heat and causing sterility. Indeed, Guainerius states that he has even seen some die from these procedures, ending their lives with 'great pain and cruel suffering'.[49]

The *Tractatus de matricibus* gives us little information on the results for women of Guainerius' cures. We can assume that his 'heroic' prescriptions must often have been difficult to take; vomiting, purging and blood-letting cannot have been pleasant procedures. We can conclude as well that Guainerius' patients did not often have to undergo surgery; the physician rarely recommends surgical intervention in gynecological disorders. Finally, we receive somewhat of a glimpse of what 'rest' involved when he describes the treatment for superfluity of menses attributed to hemorrhoids of the womb, cold veins, sharp blood and other causes: quiet above all things, climbing ladders to be prohibited entirely, more sleep than usual and coitus to be avoided 'like a mortal enemy'.[50]

Guainerius' advice on how a healthy woman is to conduct her affairs is also limited, although he does indicate what behavior can cause disease. Probably his most extended recommendation which does not involve illness is his description of the proper procedure for performing sexual intercourse, more elaborate than the conventional medical directions, which he inserts as an 'addition to the text'. His purpose here is to inform the reader what substances cause delight in coitus and 'excite sleeping Venus' because the pleasure of both man

---

[49] 'Ab extra quoque ut testium cum iusquiamo opio vel consimili emplastrato et in mulieribus cum eisdem pessarizatio. Sepe et cum hoc mulieres calidarum rerum fumum ut concipiant suscipiunt vel ex eisdem nastalia suppositoria encautisanta balnea vel stufas conficiunt que sua caliditate matricis calorem naturalem exterminant. Et ego plurimas ob hoc steriles factas vidi ac non nullas que cum magnis angustiis et doloribus credelissimis vitam cum pietate terminaverunt.' Guainerius, f. y8ra–b.

[50] 'Super omnia quies iniungatur et scalarum ascensus omnino prohibeatur. Somnus aliquantulum solito longior et ingens gaudium devitet coitem vero velut inimicum mortalem fugiat. . . .' Guainerius, f. y4va.

and woman is a great help to conception. It is clear from Guainerius' account that the initiative is up to the man. He is instructed first to place himself in the familiar embrace of the woman, to give many kisses with sweet sucking of the lips and to utter tender words that bring on ardor. He is then to handle the nipples delicately with his fingers, and, 'because in such an act it is right to do all things' he should lightly rub the area between the anus and the vulva. Guainerius notes that 'the authors' attest that this friction offers the greatest delectation to many women. When he perceives that the woman's eyes shine, and that she speaks with shortened words because she is too tired to finish them, he should immediately chew pepper and lubricate the penis with the saliva he has produced. He may also use the bile of a she-goat or the dust from the seed of a stinging nettle for this purpose. This procedure is designed to bring pleasure to the *woman*, who will receive 'incredible delight' from these substances. At this point she is instructed to place herself with her head lowered, her hips elevated, her left foot under her hip and her right leg extended. Then, 'having diligently observed these precepts, they should strenuously resolve their debt to the lady Venus, taking care to emit their seed in the same instant.'[51] It should be noted that Guainerius' entire two chapters on the subject are designed to enable the man to overcome whatever problems he might have and to give pleasure to his partner. Aphrodisiacs such as the testicles of a wild boar, the excrement

---

[51] 'Delectatio in actu coitus quam vir similiter et mulier capiunt magnum immo maximum ad conceptionem iuvamentum prestat. Ea de re non nulla coitum delectantia et aliqua a proprietate sopitam venerem ex[c]itantia que ab extra approximanda sunt in presenti capitulo describam. Antequam igitur ad coitum vir accedat in mulieris amplexibus familiariter se ponat et cum suavi labiorum succione oscula det plurima, verba dulcia et amorem inducentia proferat, mammillarum papillas digitis leviter pertractet. Et quia in actu tali omnia facere fas est locum inter anum et vulvam leviter confricet. Ea eam fricatio, ut autores ferunt plurimi, in muliere delectationem affert maximam. Sepe ut venereum actum perficiat operam det donec tandem mulieris oculos scintillare percipiat eum interrumpet semper. Cumque mulieris scintillant oculi ac verba truncata loquitur sic quod in medio suorum verborum lassata sistit et in motibus suis modum habet nullum tunc vir statim piper aut cubebas masticet et cum saliva ex tali masticatione causata virgam illiniat vel idem cum felle capre et pulvere seminis urtice faciat vel pulverem satirionis in modum ung[u]enti cum melle conficiat cum quo tunc virgam inungat. . . . In actu enim coitus ex his mulieri incredibilis delectatio sequitur. Que tunc taliter situanda est cum demisso capite scilicet et anchis elevatis sinistrum pedem sub ancha reponat dextrum autem extensum teneat et sic in tali situ et dictis diligenter observatis domine veneri debitum finale persolvant obnixe studendo ut in eodem instanti spermata simul emittant.' Guainerius, f. z4va–b.

of a sparrow, powder from the heel bones of a pig 'move the man to the venereal act so powerfully that when the woman leaves him, if she is not satiated, she is at least tired'.[52]

Guainerius' treatise shares with other medical writings the assumption that the character of a woman is determined by the state of her uterus. Just as the womb was a central focus in explaining the feminine disposition in Hippocrates' works and continues until today to provide for physicians the reason behind women's behavior, Guainerius looked to this organ for the source of a woman's nature. 'It is useful to you', he tells the reader, 'to know the complexion of the womb.'[53] A woman with a hot womb can be recognized, for example, by her abundance of pubic hair, quick emission of seed and yellowness of her menstrual flow. Just as her uterus is hot, her character is hot. She takes great delight in sexual intercourse, is energetic and moves quickly. Similarly, a cold-wombed woman is fainthearted and lazy; a woman with a dry womb finds little pleasure in life; and a humid woman is not grateful to her sexual partner.[54] Female character also varies with the time of the month. In the first stage of menstruation women are hot and humid, and this gradually changes until the fourth when they are cold and wet.[55] Thus the menstrual cycle is another important determinant of a woman's disposition.

Sexual stereotypes underlie Guainerius' thinking on human generation as well. It is clear that the male sex is superior and is produced by finer human beings. The man who will generate a son is robust and of fine figure; his testicles are large with prominent veins, especially the right one, and he has an abundance of hot seed. A woman who will bear males has a joyful face and a refined menstrual flow. When she is carrying the child her color is good, her appearance happy and

---

[52] 'Hoc enim calorem naturalem restaurant, seminis materiam adauget ac ad venereum actum hominem adeo potentem efficit ut ab eo mulier etsi non saciata tamen lassata recedit.' Guainerius, f. z6va.

[53] 'Et quia in sequentibus matricis complexionem noscere perutile tibi est. . . .' Guainerius, f. w6ra.

[54] Guainerius, f. w6ra–b.

[55] 'Ex his scilicet lune etatum diversitatem diversam mulieribus complexionem attribui liquet nam in prima menstruationis etate calide dicuntur et humide esto magis humide. In secunda calide et sicce, calide tamen magis. In tertia frigide et sicce, sicce quamvis plus. In quarta frigide et humide, magis tamen humide et hoc per accidens.' Guainerius, f. w5vb.

her step agile.[56] The opposite is true if she has conceived a daughter, for a female child is carried in the colder part of the womb.

This type of thinking extends to the sex organs and to the seed itself. Male seed is to be active, female passive. A monster, for example, is generated because of the weakness of the male seed or the rebelliousness of the female seed.[57] The female sex organ, usually referred to by the single word *vulva* with little distinction as to its parts, is susceptible to much unpleasantness. We learn in the chapter on the suffocation of the womb, for example, that the mouth of the vulva is always ready to be anointed with anything odiferous,[58] and as a result will respond well to fumigation with fetid substances.

Probably the most pervasive assumption made historically by doctors about female diseases is that women cause their own illnesses by failing to follow the proper feminine role. This has been particularly characteristic of medical opinion on reproductive disorders. The reasoning as seen in the nineteenth century, for example, was that if girls exceeded their natural capacities and undertook to receive the same educational training as boys, their reproductive organs would atrophy instead of developing normally.[59] Guainerius does not concentrate on female education, but he does adopt the 'blame the victim' approach to many feminine disorders. Retention of the menses, for example, can be caused by 'superfluous exercise' or 'immoderate accidents of the soul – exceeding wrath, excessive sadness or worries'.[60] Emotions have an effect on sterility as well, although in this case men are also responsible. Guainerius attests that he has 'never seen a woman or man who continually bears sadness or rancor in her/his heart conceive or generate'.[61] Men bear the blame in certain cases of

[56] 'Vir enim habitudinis bone robusti corporis ampiarum venarum testium magnorum cuius dexter ab adolescentia usque maior fuerit continue ac quod multi et calidi seminis existit. . . . Femina vero que bone fuerit habitudinis venarum apparentium et gaudentis aspectus. Cuius menstrua digesta sit et non cruda. . . . Attende ergo quod mulier impregnata masculo colorata magis ac mediocris faciei semper erit leta quoque agilis levis. . . .' Guainerius, f. z6ra–b.

[57] 'Insuper propter virilis seminis debilitatem aut menstrui rebellitatem seu utriusque impotentiam in humana specie monstra generantur sepe.' Guainerius, f. 2z6vb.

[58] 'Prestantissimum quoque est os vulve ex aliquo odorifero inungere. . . .' Guainerius, f. x4rb.

[59] See Haller and Haller, *The Physician and Sexuality*, c. 1 and 2.

[60] '. . . accidentibus anime immoderatis ira maxime excessiva tristicia seu sollicitudine et exercitio superfluo. . . .' Guainerius, f. w6rb.

[61] 'Mulierem virumque tristem rancorem in corde aliquem continue qui defert concipere seu generare vidi numquam.' Guainerius, f. y8ra.

excess menstrual flow; among the extrinsic causes of this disorder is a rupture of a vein in the neck of the womb caused by jumping, by a blow, a fall, a woman lifting a burden not proportional to her strength or a 'raging male penis entering her and disrupting the vein because of its magnitude'.[62]

For the most part, women cause their own disorders, however. Priapism, or constant excitation and itching of the womb resulting in a continually greater appetite for coitus and eventual death, can be prevented by leading an abstemious life. If a woman fasts regularly, she will never get priapism 'since without Ceres and Bacchus Venus grows cold'.[63] Similarly, women should be married and have regular intercourse with their husbands. Guainerius accepts the Galenic theory that seed must be released periodically or it will poison the womb and cause suffocation, and he states that a woman subject to this suffocation is one who lives a gay, sumptuous, leisurely life and lacks a male companion.[64] It is clear that women should be married and avoid luxury.

Guainerius' account of the social consequences of disease reveals his ideas about woman's role in society. Women exist to bear children; the stated purpose of the *Tractatus de matricibus* is to provide information on the cure of disorders that prevent conception.[65] In order to become pregnant, a woman must be attractive to men; humidity of the womb is considered by Guainerius as a particularly serious disorder not only because it affects the woman's fertility but also because it makes the victim unclean. This displeases her husband, and thus, the doctor tells us, conception is impeded multiply.[66] Women should be virgins before marriage and arrive at their wedding night with their hymens intact. He recommends that abscess of the womb be treated with a medicated

[62] 'Extrinseca quidem ut ruptura vene in collo vel ad intra matricem existentis a saltu percussione casu oneris sue non proportionalis virtuti levatione a virili virga furibunde ingrediente et pre magnitudine venam disrumpente. . . .' Guainerius, f. y3vb.
[63] 'Et cum sine cerere et bacho frigeat venus cum pane et aqua macerantia ieiunia sepe faciat.' Guainerius, f. y8rb.
[64] 'Si spermatis retenti vitio hoc fiat invenis delicata erit laute jocunde at in otio vivet consotio quoque caret. . . .' Guainerius, f. x3vb.
[65] 'Tractatus huius intentio est tam ex parte viri quam ex parte mulieris conceptionem causas impedientes curandi doctrinam dare verum mulierum proprie egritudines hoc efficiunt sepe.' Guainerius, f. w4vb.
[66] 'Ob has mulieres immunde fiunt et maritis per consequens non bene grate et sic ob hoc conceptio multipliciter impeditur.' Guainerius, f. y3va.

pessary, except in the case of an uncorrupted woman who should receive a bath and a plaster.[67]

From the *Tractatus de matricibus*, we learn that Anthonius Guainerius, a university-trained physician, was actively engaged in the practice of obstetrics and gynecology in fifteenth-century Italy and therefore had direct contact with women patients. In the course of his career he performed physical examinations, which only rarely involved direct inspection of a woman's genitals. For the more intimate procedures he employed female assistants to carry out his recommendations, and these often included very aggressive medical treatment of gynecological disorders.

Guainerius drew a clear distinction between doctor and patient, often mistrusting the patient's observations. The notion of 'informed consent' was alien to him; he was on occasion willing to deceive his clients. He was wary as well of lay healers. In his opinion, they caused iatrogenic disease and cast spells which caused women to lose their fertility and sometimes even their lives. Yet despite his suspicions, Guainerius recognized the value of many folk recipes and incorporated them into his treatise. Astrology, too, was accorded great respect, although the doctor did not always accept all of its teachings.

Although Guainerius devotes considerable effort to describing how sexual intercourse can be made more pleasurable for women, men are clearly superior in his opinion, and a woman's character is determined by the complexion of her womb and her menstrual cycle. Women should marry, bear children and avoid excess in food, drink, exercise or emotion. When they do not follow these recommendations, he believed, they cause their own gynecological disorders.

Nevertheless, Guainerius was sympathetic to his patients. He expressed concern about their pain, and stated clearly that the physician must exert every effort to relieve it. He referred often to the women he treated as *pauperculae*, in the sense that their suffering had made them poor souls, and devoted his life to providing aid and comfort to those under his care.

---

[67] 'Mulieri non corrupte aut pessarizari volenti ex infrascriptis balneum ab umbilico infra fieri iubeas ex quibus etiam emplastra fieri possunt.' Guainerius, f. x5va.

14

The Problem of Feminism in the Fifteenth Century

BEATRICE GOTTLIEB

A number of women who lived in earlier times have been called feminists, and among them is Christine de Pisan, the prolific writer of French verse and prose who lived from 1364 to about 1430 and did most of her work in Paris. Christine could not, of course, be called a feminist before the word existed. As a matter of fact, she was virtually unknown before the time of the French Revolution. It was then that she was discovered by a kindred soul, a learned and prolific writer and translator named Louise de Keralio, who between 1786 and 1789 issued a 14-volume edition of works by women.[1] This marked the first appearance in print of many of Christine's works, but as interest in medieval and Renaissance literature intensified, Christine became better known. As early as 1838 her contributions to the polemical literature on women were recognized,[2] although she was most often regarded as one of those *monuments historiques* of which the French are so proud. I do not know who first labeled her a feminist, but in 1886 a politically liberal literary critic in Great Britain called her a 'woman's rights person' in an article entitled 'A champion of her sex'.[3] A few years later he would probably have said 'feminist'; the *Oxford English Dictionary* reports that the word first appeared in print in 1894.[4] A

[1] Mlle de Keralio (ed.), *Collection des meilleurs ouvrages français composés par des femmes* (14 vols, Paris, 1786–9).
[2] Raymond Thomassy, *Essai sur les écrits politiques de Christine de Pisan* (Paris, 1838).
[3] William Minto, 'A champion of her sex', *Macmillan's Magazine*, LIII (February, 1886), pp. 264–75.
[4] *The Oxford English Dictionary* (Oxford, 1933) gives only an early and 'rare' use of 'feminism' as 'the quality of females'. Its *Supplement*, however, catches up with the late nineteenth century, stating that the word is no longer rare and that, by way of

scholarly edition of her poetry meanwhile began to appear, and is still
the most authoritative available presentation of her work.[5] Her
reputation as a feminist was based on her prose works, however,
which remained, for the most part, in manuscript. As scholars, especially women scholars, read them, they kept being struck by something
they characterized as feminism. Christine's feminism is a common-
place today. The author of a recent biography for a general audience
may be somewhat cautious: 'That kind of feminism which claims that
women are the equal of men in every way was far from her. Her ideas
on the subject were much more reasonable.'[6] But an even more recent
article names her as the first of the 'early feminist theorists' who resisted 'the cultural and social colonization of women by men'.[7]

Interesting questions are raised by this application of a modern
term to a fifteenth-century person. Feminism is not easy to define in
spite of its free use by its present-day proponents and attackers.
Though it is sometimes used today to refer to a general sensitivity
about women and a concern with their plight, many who share that
sensitivity and concern shy away from the label. This has been true
from the word's first appearance. French dictionaries say it was first
used by the Utopian Socialist Charles Fourier, and it has never
completely lost its radical associations. Almost the whole history of
women's movements in the nineteenth and twentieth centuries can
be written in terms of those who took a radical stance, thinking of
themselves as feminists, and those who did not. It is a complicated
history because notions about what is radical have changed over the
years. Broadly speaking, radical proponents of women's rights in the
nineteenth century (those most likely to call themselves feminists)
believed in the complete equality of men and women and wanted to
end what they regarded as the demeaning restriction of women to the

---

French *féminisme*, means 'the opinions and principles of the advocates of the extended recognition of the achievements and claims of women; advocacy of women's
rights.' The earliest reference for the word 'feminist' is an 1894 newspaper article
about a political group in France.

[5] *Oeuvres poétiques de Christine de Pisan*, ed. Maurice Roy (3 vols, Société des
Anciens Textes Français 24, Paris, 1886–96; reprinted New York and London,
1965).

[6] Enid McLeod, *The Order of the Rose; the Life and Ideas of Christine de Pizan*
(Totowa, NJ, 1976), p. 73.

[7] Joan Kelly, 'Early feminist theory and the *Querelle des Femmes*, 1400–1789',
Signs, VIII (1982), p. 28.

domestic sphere. Less radical activist women spoke not of equality but of women's special qualities, qualities they believed should be recognized and used to benefit all of society. One curious feature of this history is that the demand for suffrage began as an extremely radical issue and gradually became absorbed into the program of the non-radicals. Feminism, if not perfectly easy to define, was in those early days a movement, and it had a program.

Today the label of 'feminist' may be more widely accepted, but its meaning seems to have become more diffuse. There are self-styled feminists who still hold something very similar to the radical nineteenth-century women's-rights position. They are concerned about equal pay for equal work, the Equal Rights Amendment, affirmative action, the availability of legal abortions and a number of other essentially political matters. They no longer think of themselves as terribly radical, of course. Those who now call themselves radical feminists have moved into different areas. They have taken up matters connected with domestic arrangements and sexual identity, some even suggesting that heterosexuality is inherently oppressive to women. Equality with men is almost beside the point for them. Somewhere in the middle are feminists who support the generally agreed upon political positions but have a 'raised' consciousness of the larger implications of being a woman in our society and see some value in recognizing male and female differences. It is probably still true that to regard oneself as a feminist of whatever stripe it is not enough to think certain thoughts: one needs a sense of sharing those thoughts with others, of being part, even if not a particularly active part, of a movement.

I cannot claim to have exhausted the subject of modern feminism. On the contrary, the subject has almost exhausted me. 'Feminism' has too many interests and factions to be briefly defined, except in rather reductionist terms. If it has a common shared meaning, it is that it is the opposite of 'not feminism', which is not a movement, of course, even if some of us are convinced we could paint a picture of it. Feminists are opposed to a wide variety of ideas and conditions, not a single enemy, and they are commited to a fairly wide variety of remedies. Here, then, is a complex concept belonging to our age, and there is a fifteenth-century woman. Is there any justification for bringing the two together?

There is an obvious danger in doing so, a danger that Lucien Febvre went so far as to call a sin. The name of the sin (the cardinal sin for a historian, he said) is anachronism. I have just spent some time translating Febvre's *Problem of Unbelief in the Sixteenth Century*,[8] the book in which he makes his most eloquent and elaborate attack on this sin, using what he regards as the only effective procedure for a historian. He amasses detail upon detail of the context in which the ideas under scrutiny existed. The question he deals with is whether it is appropriate to call Rabelais an atheist and, beyond that, whether atheism, as we usually understand the term, could even have existed in Rabelais' time. It was only natural that, being immersed in Febvre's approach to the mental life of the past, I would respond to Christine de Pisan's alleged 'feminism' with some sensitivity to the possibility of anachronism.

What follows is an attempt to do in very modest terms something analogous to what Febvre did for the problem of atheism in the sixteenth century. Unlike his *magnum opus*, what I can produce on this modest scale is only a first foray into the problem of feminism in earlier times. It suggests some appropriate questions and possible answers. Febvre's basic axiom was that the changes over the past centuries have been considerable and it is therefore dangerous to assume that words carried the same load of meaning in the sixteenth century as in the twentieth. Utterances of the past should never be taken at face value, because 'face value' more often than not means current value, the value derived from a twentieth-century context. As historians we are prepared to find modes of thought in the fifteenth century that are no longer with us. For example, a tendency to think in hierarchical terms, to see both the physical world and society as naturally existing in layers arranged in something like a pyramid, a tendency to explain things by what we call supernatural causes (whether emanations or sympathies or miracles), and a tendency to think allegorically and use symbols not as arbitrary literary devices but as expressions of a real correspondence between different spheres of being. It is not a world we can be truly at home in, even if we are trained historians. We have to put on a pair of fifteenth-century eyeglasses (as Febvre would say) and make a special effort to keep them on. We have to be prepared to deal with dead literary conventions that can easily tax our patience, at the same time trying to imagine them striking contemporary listeners as fresh, natural and compelling. Their listeners, of course, not their readers. Even after the introduction of printing, as Febvre loved to

---

[8] Lucien Febvre, *The Problem of Unbelief in the Sixteenth Century; the Religion of Rabelais*, trans. Beatrice Gottlieb (Cambridge, Mass., 1982); original: *Le Problème de l'incroyance au XVIe siècle; la religion de Rabelais* (Paris, 1942).

point out, most information came through the ears, not the eyes. In the end, we have to ask how much is a matter of surface style and how much a reflection of something very deep that we have to reckon with.

There is one obvious difference between the problem of atheism and the problem of feminism. The word feminism did not exist, while the word atheism did, and was used a great deal. Some may consider this to be the end of the discussion: there is no problem, feminism is clearly an anachronism and it is foolish to waste time. Of course, there was no term for anything remotely resembling feminism, but that is not really where the problem lies. The problem is linked to the larger problem of women's history. Our history, the history of the history books, has until very recently been one from which women have been absent. They have been absent much as peasants have been absent. Women and peasants could be fitted into 'larger' events and structures, but they were not themselves considered worth focusing on. Now that our eyes have been opened to the fact that women were not absent (opened very slowly, I would say), we see that all history has to be rewritten. The contributors to this volume have been rewriting history, most of them having gone back over 'womanless' material and found that there were women there all along if only they had had the eyes to see them. The problem of feminism in the fifteenth century is not the simple-minded one of whether Christine de Pisan had the same ideas as Gloria Steinem. That would be what Febvre called a *question mal posée*. The problem is more complex. How was it possible to think about women and how in fact did women think about themselves in the fifteenth century? For a serious historian, furthermore, this does not mean a search for heroines and inspiring precursors, years ahead of their times. Precursors, as Febvre demonstrated, are dubious historical personages. Let us be content if we can see what women were like in their own times. I hold this to be a goal of self-evident importance. But reaching it is not easy.

For a woman to write for a wide audience (as audiences went) and to deal specifically with the subject of women was extremely rare in the fifteenth century. Christine de Pisan dealt with the subject many times. Her *Book of the City of Ladies* was entirely devoted to demonstrating the worth and talents of women, and its sequel, *The Book of the Three Virtues*, was a sort of instruction manual for women. Her other works contain frequent references, both direct and indirect, to the situation of women. There is no doubt that she gave the subject a lot of thought.

As a remarkable woman herself, who had managed to establish herself as a literary craftsman with a distinguished patronage, she also thought about her own situation and related it to that of women in general.

Most of her explicit utterances about women were defenses against attacks and abuse. She saw these as coming from two sources, misogynistic books and men's behavior. In addition, in comments on her own life and in some passages in *The City of Ladies* she made the particular point that women had at least as much capacity for learning as men did.

The strain of misogyny is strong in the Western literary tradition, and although it is often glibly referred to as Christian, Christine apparently saw it as older and not distinctively Christian. She particularly took Ovid to task. Juvenal was perhaps a likelier target among the ancients, but she was clearly concerned with what her contemporaries might be reading and hearing, and Ovid, who was widely available in vernacular translations, was known for his advice on seduction. She referred in a general way to a multitude of nameless misogynistic 'clerks', but singled out for special mention two works, *The Romance of the Rose* and *The Lamentations of Matheolus*. Jean de Meun and Matheolus, the authors of these popular works, were almost proverbial in Christine's time as denigrators of women.

What did misogyny mean to Christine? What exactly was she defending women against? We can get an answer from a poem, 'L'Epistre au dieu d'amours', from the letters she contributed to the war of words over *The Romance of the Rose*, and from the introduction to *The Book of the City of Ladies*. In brief, misogynists called women lascivious, fickle and incompetent. They complained that women could not keep faith and could not be trusted with confidences. Women were depicted either as evil seductresses or as passive quarry for sexual predators, an inconsistency of outlook that Christine seems to have enjoyed pointing out. Inferior is hardly the right word: women were seen as utterly vicious and worthless, an afterthought in cosmogony and a mistake in biology. 'A great unhappiness and sadness welled up in my heart, for I detested myself and the entire feminine sex, as though we were monstrosities in nature...'[9]

Christine does not cite chapter and verse, and we may not feel that she has to. But since she chose to refer by name to Jean de Meun

[9] Christine de Pizan, *The Book of the City of Ladies*, trans. Earl Jeffrey Richards (New York, 1982), p. 5.

and Matheolus, it may be useful to take at least a cursory look at what disturbed her.

The Lamentations of Matheolus, written in Latin around 1300 and translated into French some 70 years later, seems to be the impassioned outpourings of an unhappy husband. To a modern reader it is likely to convey more passion than sense, in spite of the impressive array of authorities it cites. The writer bewails the fact that when younger and vulnerable he fell in love with a widow and married her; as a result, he is now saddled with a wife who is no longer attractive, who has burdened him with children and household cares, and who is a constant nuisance. On top of that, by marrying a widow he has lost the privileges and prospects he used to have as a member of the lower orders of the clergy. The message of the poem at first glance seems to be that marriage is a trial and women are to be avoided – a plea for chastity, in other words, for those lucky enough to be able to manage it. But no, at second glance it appears that women should not be avoided. Men are inevitably going to be attracted to them, and others must simply try to avoid falling into the same trap as Matheolus. Poor Matheolus. I think I might have been able to sympathize with him if he had only stuck to his own case. But instead he reaches out in all directions for stories and sayings about the failings of women in general. It may have been some comfort to him that such material existed in abundance. At any rate, it was no doubt for marshalling and recounting it with such zest that he gained the reputation of being a hater of women.[10] Christine did not go into any detail about Matheolus, but her choice of an example of misogyny seems uncannily perceptive if, as may be the case, the impulse toward misogyny arises from the inability of men to come to terms with their own sexuality.

Jean de Meun is better known but more difficult to understand. Literary scholars today treat him with great respect as a master of subtle irony, and the misogynistic passages tend to get explained away. Since *The Romance of the Rose* is a tissue of speeches by the various allegorical personages who populate the work, we are told to be wary about assuming that any of them speaks for the author. Among the passages that excoriate women are a speech within a speech, the words of a jealous husband to his wife, quoted by the character Friend to the Dreamer who narrates the poem. Written shortly before *The*

[10] For the text of the *Lamentations* and much other information, see A. G. Van Hamel (ed.), *Les Lamentations de Mathéolus et le Livre de Leesce de Jehan le Fèvre, de Resson* (2 vols, Paris, 1892, 1905).

Lamentations of Matheolus, it goes over some of the same ground ('Ah! If I had believed Theophrastus, I would never have married a wife . . . By Saint Denis! Worthy women, as Valerius bears witness, are fewer than phoenixes . . . .')[11] Another passage is the speech of The Old Woman, who says that since all men are sensualists who betray and deceive women, women should be deceivers in return.[12] And there is a passage in which Genius, starting with references to Virgil, Solomon and Livy, shows how women cannot be trusted, especially with secrets. ('Fair lords, protect yourselves from women if you love your bodies and souls'.)[13] The whole poem, of course, is about how to win over a woman, but its literary merit is said to lie in complex levels of meaning and a panoramic view of contemporary life and learning. One side in the early fifteenth-century debate on the poem seems to have agreed with this assessment. A modern French scholar feels that misogyny may actually be held up to ridicule in the poem, and an American woman, writing in 1917, said that Jean de Meun was 'in many ways . . . in advance of his times in his attitude towards women . . . The most abusive passages . . . are put in the mouth of those whose cavil is slight reproach.'[14] I am willing to grant a work of literature its complexity, and I do not know enough about this particular giant of a work to enter the debate on its meaning, but it must be pointed out that the cumulative effect of all those passages was to convince many fifteenth-century readers that Jean de Meun had a low opinion of both women and sexual morality.

As I have said, Christine wanted to defend women not only against what was written about them but also against how men treated them. She started where The Old Woman in *The Romance of the Rose* did, with a conviction that many men wanted only to trick women into sleeping with them. They lied to these women, and if they were un-successful they told lies about them. Men were promiscuous as a matter of course and falsely accused all women of being the same. They boasted of their conquests after having promised to guard their mistresses' honor. In 'L'Epistre au dieu d'amours', Christine says such behavior was readily observable in France.

---

[11] Guillaume de Lorris and Jean de Meun, *The Romance of the Rose*, trans. Charles Dahlberg (Princeton, 1971), pp. 157, 159.

[12] ibid., pp. 229ff.

[13] ibid., p. 279.

[14] Daniel Poirion (ed.), *Le Roman de la Rose* (Paris, 1974), preface; Mary Morton Wood, *The Spirit of Protest in Old French Literature* (New York, 1917; reprinted 1966), p. 182.

Christine's defense against both literary attacks and shabby treatment was, first, to deny the truth of what was said. She could see with her own eyes that women were not what they were said to be. If some women were vicious, it was unjust to say that all were. The bad examples found in books were isolated cases, and they could be countered with at least as many good examples. *The Book of the City of Ladies* is essentially a long list of such examples. She implied that men's judgement was warped because they were slaves to lust and, even worse, poor losers. Her defense also moved onto another plane, where in effect it became an attack, in which she claimed that women had special qualities that made them superior to men. They were gentle, sweet, kind and by their very nature loyal. Women did not cause wars and mayhem, as men did. And they had a monopoly on one of the most wonderful things in the world, motherhood. Men, she said, should try to be loyal, considerate and truthful to women because they were 'elles de qui tout homme est descendu', and there was no joy for men in this world without women: 'C'est sa mere, c'est sa suer, c'est s'amie.'[15]

On the subject of education, Christine also took the stance of a defender. Not allowing women to study implied a lack of capacity that she denied. Again, she used examples, among them herself by implication. The fact is that she had few enough real examples, so she resorted to fable. She is more interesting when she occasionally gives up argument and demonstration and falls back on observation. Her father had educated her, and she had learned to love books as much as any man could. She looked around and saw women who seemed to possess all the mental ability that was needed. Her most moving passages are those in which she seems to plead for a fair chance, as in her dialogue with the allegorical figure of Reason, who assures her that 'if it were customary to send daughters to school like sons, and if they were then taught the natural sciences, they would learn as thoroughly and understand the subtleties of all the arts and sciences as well as sons . . . [Women] have minds that are freer and sharper whenever they apply themselves.' Christine pretends that she cannot believe her ears. 'My lady, what are you saying?' she cries. 'Certainly men would never admit this answer is true, unless it is explained more plainly, for they believe that one normally sees that men know more than women do.' Reason does explain: 'Without the slightest doubt, it is

[15] 'Epistre au dieu d'amours', ll. 725, 733, in Maurice Roy (ed.), *Oeuvres poétiques*, II, pp. 23-4.

because they are not involved in many different things, but stay at home, where it is enough for them to run the household, and there is nothing which so instructs a reasonable creature as the exercise and experience of many different things.'[16] Christine's advice in *The Book of the Three Virtues* is kept within cautious bounds. In the exercise of ordinary housewifely duties, she suggests, an educated mind is no hindrance, and a knowledge of literary graces and practical skills is a great help in running a noble household. There is even more urgency for widows to have the great treasure of education, not only for the consolation it could provide (here she is autobiographical) but also for its practical value in protecting themselves from being defrauded and mistreated (also probably autobiographical).

In the light of all this, I can detect in Christine what we today would call a feminist consciousness. Here was a woman who, pained and outraged by reading and hearing that women were inferior and evil, refused to suffer in silence. She did not defend herself as an individual but made common cause with all women. She thought about women's lives and how they might be improved. We have no idea whether she talked about any of this with other women since there are few hints in her writing or in any writing of the period of what women said to each other, but it is tempting to think that she did, even that women had been saying such things to each other for a long time. 'Such things' were not a modern feminist program. There were no demands for equal rights or political power, there was no hint of women forming organizations, there was not even a modest proposal that regular schooling be available for women. Still, to see that women as a group shared common problems that not only differed from men's problems but also somehow stemmed from men's defects, and to refuse to accept insults and contempt in silence – this is a plausible kind of feminism. There is too much that is recognizable in it for us to ignore it.

There is much more to say about Christine de Pisan. She had many sides, and we need to see what they were before we can understand this plausible feminism more fully.

She was perhaps the closest thing to a career woman in the fifteenth century. I have already suggested that what she had achieved in her own life was one of her implicit arguments when she wrote about women's capacities. She had shown that a woman who had been married at 15 and had had several children could at 25, when her

---

[16] *The City of Ladies*, p. 63.

husband died, galvanize her energies and resources to support herself and her family without any loss of dignity or respect. She must have been a strong and enterprising person, to say nothing of her intelligence. She did what had to be done to be a successful writer in those days. That is, she gained patrons by cultivating her acquaintance among the rich and highly placed, some of whom were women. She seems to have been very good at keeping her patrons, both by being personally ingratiating and by producing works that pleased them. Her reputation as a writer was excellent, and she was admired for her personal qualities. A fifteenth-century manuscript of one of her poems refers to her as 'a lady distinguished for her birth and her character'.[17]

Her output was tremendous and astonishingly varied. She wrote more than a hundred poems, on many subjects. She was the official biographer of Charles V and wrote a long work on warfare (*The Book of Feats of Arms*) that later so impressed Henry VII of England he asked William Caxton to translate and publish it. She wrote works of moral counsel, political theory, patriotic exhortation and philosophical reflection. All in all, it was a prodigious display of literary energy and versatility that would have been equally impressive in a man.

She seems to have played the role of woman of letters to the hilt, even initiating a controversy that has become famous as probably the first literary *querelle*. This was the famous debate on *The Romance of the Rose*, which Christine apparently triggered by a letter to a distinguished scholar who had written in praise of the *Romance* after reading it for the first time. A number of other people entered the fray later, most notably Jean Gerson, who shared Christine's dislike of Jean de Meun. It was Christine who was most responsible for pursuing and preserving the debate, since she collected the letters that were exchanged and had them published in a single manuscript. It is a complicated story. Scholars disagree about the sequence of events and what the fight was really about, but the episode's main interest may be that it shows the different ways in which educated readers of the time responded to immorality and sexual explicitness in literature. Christine and Gerson both felt that the *Romance* was disgustingly lubricious, an inducement to adultery and fornication. We know that Christine thought it was particularly insulting to women, but that was not the focus of the debate, although she herself pursued the point.

[17] 'Domina praeclara natu et moribus.' See Christine de Pisan, *Ditié de Jehanne d'Arc*, ed. Angus J. Kennedy and Kenneth Varty (Oxford, 1977), p. 2.

It is also true that Christine was not treated with much respect by the brothers Gontier and Pierre Col, the chief defenders of Jean de Meun, and that she vigorously defended the right of a woman to participate in such a discussion. Still, it is not clear whether she thought that Jean de Meun's chief offense was against women or against propriety. As far as the merits of the arguments go, modern critical judgements of the *Romance* tend to agree with Christine's antagonists, who believed that words were not in themselves lascivious or immoral and that a work had to be seen in its entirety. Gerson's *Treatise Against the Romance of the Rose*, which supported her side of the debate, was a strict moralist's indictment of love literature as frivolous, hedonistic and destructive of the institution of marriage (he did not say anything about its being demeaning to women). From the distance of so many centuries we have no way of knowing what he thought of Christine's love poetry.

As a writer, Christine's favorite voice, especially as she grew older, was that of moralist and patriot. She frequently bewailed the decline of moral standards, especially in the relations between men and women. She saw this moral decline as part and parcel of France's perilous condition. She lived in turbulent times (the midpoint of the Hundred Years War), and eventually, when the Burgundians occupied Paris in 1418, when she was about 54 years old, she had to leave her home and her whole way of life, effectively ceasing to be a writer. Eleven years later she broke her silence with her last work, a poem in praise of Joan of Arc's triumphs over France's enemies. One of her preoccupations in all her writings was individual morality, how to live a virtuous, useful and honorable life. Her method of handling the subject, as she dealt out advice to her son, to statesmen, to young men in general, to women at all levels of society, to princes and to soldiers, was the approved medieval one of combing the authorities and restating what had already been said and had stood the test of time. We should not expect her to be an original thinker on all these subjects, and we can only guess which attitudes reflected her deepest convictions. But if frequent repetition means anything, she thought life was a serious matter and that doing one's duty was more important than personal enjoyment. Princes and rulers were the guardians of order, and to rebel against authority was to destroy the fabric of society. After all, she had before her very eyes the spectacle of a legitimate king defied, with dire results for France. The morality she expressed was the conventional morality of her day, and she wrote much more about the plight of France than she did about the plight of women.

Christine also had another voice, that of a fashionable court poet, especially at the beginning of her career. For some modern scholars, this is the most interesting part of her work; it was certainly what caught the fancy of nineteenth-century Frenchmen. She turned out ballades, virelays and rondeaux by the dozen, with what looks like considerable skill at rhyming and meter. The subject matter of her poems was precisely what these verse forms were normally associated with: the beauty of spring, the power of love, praise of the beloved, the sorrow of lovers' parting, the capriciousness of Fortune, pleas for reassurance. She had begun by writing some particularly sorrowful poems about the loneliness and misery of widowhood, but she soon shifted to the more conventional melancholy of lovers' addresses. There has been some speculation whether these were poems addressed to a real lover, but for our purpose this hardly matters. Whether the lover was real or imagined, the language and outlook came from the courtly love tradition, the tradition of Guillaume de Machaut before her and of her contemporaries Alain Chartier and Charles d'Orléans.

What emerges from a consideration of Christine's life and work as a whole is a picture of a strong person who was not a rebel, who succeeded by applying her talents to activities that, while unusual for a woman, were considered admirable, and who conformed to the dominant values of the world around her. Her ideas about women should be seen in this light. They were the ideas of an upper-class fifteenth-century woman about fifteenth-century women. To focus on her outrage and concern without seeing the context of values that underlay them is to miss an opportunity to get a little closer to what things were really like for women then.

Christine de Pisan wrote poems that placed love in a special realm with its own rules and values. It was a realm that often seemed to exist only in literature and the imagination, but its influence was none the less great for that. Everyone familiar with the secular literature of the Middle Ages knows what I am talking about, and I shall not attempt to describe it fully or minimize its complexities and contradictions. One of its characteristics was surely the high place it gave to women. According to the rules, women were in command and men existed to serve and honor them. The complaint to Cupid in Christine's 'Epistre au dieu d'amours' was that too many men were no longer doing this, that they pursued women to satisfy their lust and that they made their conquests, real and pretended, a matter of public knowledge instead of preserving the silence that the rules of love required.

The Book of the Duke of True Lovers, a long poem by Christine, depicts the special realm of love in a particularly uncompromising form. It is one of several long poems she wrote exploring the nature of love, but it seems more definitive than the others, claiming as it does to tell the story of someone who is without irony called a True Lover.[18] He is depicted as a paragon of a lover of a married woman. He falls in love when he reaches a point in his life when the desire to be in love overcomes him, as though in love with love itself. He then thanks the god of love for providing him with a lady to serve, a lady who is again and again called 'perfect'. There follows a long narrative about letters, go-betweens, secret meetings, a jealous husband, etc. Suffice it to say that this perfect love affair continues for ten years as a demanding and absorbing relationship in which nothing more physical than a kiss passes between them. At one point a startling, jarring note is sounded when the lady receives a letter from an older woman friend advising her to avoid the snares of such love affairs. 'Consent not, for the sake of any foolish pleasure, to be forgetful of your soul and of your honour,' she cautions, saying that lovers' promises to behave honorably cannot be trusted and that even innocent behavior can lead to loss of honor. 'From such faithless rascals keep you free,' is the refrain of the ballade appended to the letter. The lady is deeply disturbed, but the True Lover is equal to the challenge. Assuring her that it would be impossible for him ever to give up his total dedication to her, he offers to 'go beyond the seas to end my days'. This makes her see she was wrong to doubt him, and before long the affair resumes its perfect and honorable course, ending only when the inevitable slander – though they have still not given any carnal expression to their love – becomes too great.

As we read this story we may very well think it is simply too ridiculous to be taken seriously. Yet it is imbued with a deeply serious, quite passionate tone. We may therefore understandably resort to the kinds of exclamations and questions Febvre peppered his writing with. This is astonishing! Did people think such behavior was possible? Did they admire it? Why do we find a criticism of love in the middle of a work that seems to be celebrating it? Why was love a god anyway? What did Christine really think? And what does it tell us about her thoughts on women?

These questions go to the heart of important differences between

---

[18] Christine de Pisan, *The Book of the Duke of True Lovers*, trans. Alice Kemp-Welch, with verse trans. by Laurence Binyon and Eric R. D. Maclagan (London, 1909).

the fifteenth century and the twentieth century. Final answers are impossible, but let us engage in a little speculation, based in part on two distinguished works of scholarship, Huizinga's *The Waning of the Middle Ages* and Febvre's *Amour sacré, amour profane*, his book about Margaret of Navarre (see the references at the end of this chapter for both of these books).

Love was a god because he wielded power over people. This was an inescapable conclusion based on the observation of human behavior. He took possession of men and women and inspired them to acts of passion, unreason, brutality – and incredible selflessness. He was a god of a sweet and bitter mystery, impossible to ignore and difficult to come to terms with. The religion of love that formed the subject of court poetry was one way of dealing with this importunate deity. It was an elaborate structure for taming a force often perceived as uncontrollable. In its obsession with rules and refinements it was clearly disjunctive with the rest of fifteenth-century life. Everyone knew that. It contradicted the experience of most men and women in their sexual encounters, and it contradicted the precepts of the Christian church. The fifteenth century confronted the god of love with a mixed legacy of attitudes.

Christine was aware of these contradictions. The letter from the perfect lady's friend shows that. What is more, Christine later used the letter again in almost the same form in a prose work of advice to women, *The Book of the Three Virtues*. And yet she apparently remained attached to the values of love's religion. She thought some men misused the rules to imperil women's immortal souls, but the rules could bring out the best in men, encouraging them to treat women with proper respect. Christine was an enthusiastic supporter of the new chivalric orders that required their members, among other things, to adhere to the rules of the courtly religion of love. She wrote an approving poem, 'Le Dit de la Rose', about such an order, dedicated, so she said, to the honor of 'the female sex'. Her main complaint in 'L'Epistre au dieu d'amours', remember, was that too many men in France were unmindful of the old codes of behavior and no longer seemed to know how to act toward ladies. She cared as much as anyone of her time about 'honor', a value intimately associated with chivalry. Much ink has been spilled on the subject of honor, but I suspect there is more to be said, now that historians are asking new questions about women. Christine, at any rate, accepted the prevalent notion of honor as good reputation achieved at almost any cost. She said, for example, that a maid had such an overriding duty to guard her mistress' honor that if the lady strayed from virtue and bore an illegitimate child the maid should claim the child as her own.

I doubt whether Christine ever resolved the contradictions connected with the god of love. *The Book of the Duke of True Lovers* can be seen as an attempt, one that I find interesting for all that it is feeble and far-fetched. The scorn expressed for the chivalric code in the letter to the True Lover's lady bears a slight resemblance to the scorn of Jean de Meun for those who do not recognize the earthy reality behind lovers' fine words, but it really comes out on the side of Jean Gerson, who emphasized the huge gap between the demands of Christian morality and the concerns of love's devotees. The True Lover makes himself almost blameless in Gerson's terms, even though he devotes his life to loving a married woman. He does not threaten her virtue because he never tempts her to actual adultery. His love is totally pure, almost saintly in its spiritual magnificence. His conduct is a most reassuring fantasy, a lovely daydream in which Cupid and Christ are reconciled.

Did Christine think the story was ridiculous? Did it occur to her that all this idealizing of ladies might be denigrating to women? We have no way of knowing, but she seems to have liked what I would regard as an exaggerated veneration of women. It certainly could have been welcome as a refuge and relief from the harsh denigrations of the everyday world and the painful attacks in misogynistic literature. Did women belong on a pedestal? Christine's answer might have been, 'Why not?'

In the everyday world most men and women were husbands and wives, and the realm of marriage was very different from the realm of love. The connection between love and marriage is another complex subject, which again I will only touch on. Broadly speaking, there were two opinions. Either love was a force too powerful to be contained by marriage (with its requirements of fidelity, its involvement in the trivia of ordinary living and its subordination of free choice to financial and political considerations) or it was too ephemeral and unreliable a basis for a permanent relationship on which both Church and society made heavy demands. The married state as described in the writing of Christine's time is a far cry from perfection. It is often a battlefield or a vale of tears. Christine herself said a great deal about married women, including herself. She tells us that she loved her husband very much, but in her advice to women she says that marrying for love is a bad idea. An admirable husband inspires love to develop in his wife. As for a husband who is not admirable, his wife has a duty to care for him tenderly and try to improve him with tact and gentleness. Of cruel and unfaithful husbands she wrote that their wives needed to learn how to cope with them. They might, after all, eventually repent, if only on their deathbeds, and leave them well provided for as widows.

As Christine knew, and not only from her own experience, one of the commonest consequences of marriage was widowhood. Therefore a woman needed an education, not only because she often helped her husband to run household and estate but also because the day might come when she would be left to deal with these matters alone in a hostile world. Christine said she had known nothing about her husband's financial situation before he died. Learning to fend for herself had turned her into a man, and she had had to remain so ever since. Are there, by the way, feminist implications in such a statement? At the very least it suggests that widowhood revealed resourcefulness in women that was ordinarily hidden, and that only outside their tightly confined 'normal' roles could women find opportunities to develop wider skills. It is a suggestion some of us are likely to fasten on, but I think we should not overlook Christine's tone. It is ambiguous, if not downright sorrowful. Turning into a man (whatever that means) was a misfortune. On the other hand, Christine urged widows not to re-marry. This may have been a conventional Christian attitude or a deep conviction about the opportunities of widowhood – she only said remarriage was not necessary for survival.

There was a conventional ideal picture of marriage, which played down conflict and omitted passion. It highlighted the virtues of loyalty and obedience, just as the chivalric code did, except that the lines of authority ran in almost exactly opposite directions. The head of the household was the man, and the wife owed him complete obedience. This was a view Christine never directly opposed (we can speculate whether anything in her love poems implied opposition). She praised women's capacity for humility, which was a kind of moral superiority, related to women's natural gentleness and other maternal qualities. It was the wife who guarded the peace of the household and its honor (that is, its reputation, even if it meant covering up a husband's misconduct). The ideal view of marriage included loyalty, kindness and wisdom on the man's part, but Christine implied that it was women's responsibility to make marriage what it should be. There is an exaggerated depiction of the ideal wife's virtues in the story of patient Griselda, which Christine retold with as much loving attention to the details of the poor heroine's sufferings at the hands of her capricious husband as did Chaucer and other male writers.

This ideal view of marriage embodied Christian values. Christine, who was not what could be called a religious poet, was nevertheless mindful of religion at every turn. Her ideas on women at their most explicit were suffused with religious ideas and feelings. She said women's characteristic virtues were those most highly valued in Christianity: humility, fidelity, charity. Her response to the attacks on women's lustfulness was to say that men blamed women for a problem that was their own, and that in fact most women were naturally chaste. The crowning 'argument' in *The City of Ladies* is that God chose the Virgin Mary as his spouse 'from among women' and therefore 'not only should men refrain from reproaching women but should hold them in great reverence'. This did not mean that women should succumb to the sin of pride. Christine urged them to:

. . . follow the example of your Queen, the sovereign Virgin, who, after the extraordinary honor of being chosen Mother of the Son of God was announced to her, humbled herself all the more by calling herself the handmaiden of God . . . So, my ladies, be humble and patient, and God's grace will grow in you, and praise will be given to you as well as the Kingdom of Heaven.[19]

The goal of an individual on this earth was to live a Christian life, not to pursue happiness or self-fulfillment. Needless to say, any improvement in women's conditions that met Christine's approval would have to be in harmony with Christian virtues.

Not only did Christine inevitably look to God for the moral basis of life but she also saw the hand of God in most social and political arrangements; hence her acceptance of a hierarchical structure in the state and the family and her belief that men and women have separate spheres of activity ordained by God. Like so many of her contemporaries, Christine welcomed hierarchical rank as a guaranty of order, regarding rebellion against authority as a form of sinful self-indulgence with no possible redeeming value. This was, after all, long before democracy stopped being a term of disapproval. Her thinking about women took place in this hierarchical framework with its religious sanction. 'God has . . . ordained man and woman to serve Him in different offices and also to aid and comfort one another, each in their ordained task, and to each sex has given a fitting and appropriate nature and inclination to fill their offices,' she says in the book that

[19] *The City of Ladies*, pp. 218, 254–5.

comes closest to being her feminist manifesto. 'Though God has given women great understanding – and there are many such women – because of the integrity to which women are inclined, it would not be at all appropriate for them to go and appear so brazenly in the court like men, for there are enough men who do so.'[20]

One of the things that made Christine so much a person of her time is the feeling she conveys of being on good terms with God. She was in awe of His power, but she was not afraid of His justice and she relied on His mercy. She believed that the learned men who cited chapter and verse to defame women were simply wrong about God's intentions. They either misread God's works or they followed the opinions of evil men. When Christine defended women from misogynistic attacks she usually went back to the same authorities used by the misogynists, and it was in Christian texts that she found the greatest consolation. Though her works do not especially sparkle with wit, there is an amused irony in her triumphant display of the ways in which God evidently approved of women much more than his creature, man, did. The best example of this is her poem on Joan of Arc. At first glance it seems to be a poem in praise of an outstanding woman, and has been called part of her 'defence of the feminist cause'.[21] Read a little more skeptically, it is an expression of love for France and praise to God. What was remarkable about Joan was that she was a mere girl – not only a woman but also young and lowly – and God miraculously transformed her into a warrior more triumphant than any man. It was something only God could have done, since it was 'chose fors nature'.[22] In a way, Christine agreed with Joan's prosecutors, but they gave the credit to the devil. Christine said that, in exalting Joan, God demonstrated his love for France – and, of course, his love for women. 'What an honor for the female sex!' Christine exclaims.[23] Some feminist irony is surely there. But the praise goes to God, who guides every victor, whether male or female. The example of Joan was an encouragement to religious and patriotic fervor, not to acceptance of women's aptitude for the military arts.

Christine's thinking about women can hardly begin to be understood without reference to her period's attitudes toward love and religion. Her ambivalence about love and sexuality was not unlike

---

[20] ibid., p. 31.
[21] *Ditié de Jehanne d'Arc*, p. 16.
[22] ibid., p. 34 (l. 274).
[23] ibid. (ll. 265–6).

that of her contemporaries, and it colored her view of women as both refiners of manners and innocent victims. Her concern with the relationship of women to God, while low-keyed, was constant. It was impossible for her to speak of moral values without referring to God, and she found consolation for her sex in the fact that it had always been assumed by Christians that the arrangements of the City of Man ultimately did not matter. Each soul, even if downtrodden on earth, was in touch with God.

The Book of the City of Ladies may have started the *querelle des femmes*, a series of loosely related texts to which many European writers, mostly male, contributed in the course of the fifteenth and sixteenth centuries, and even to some degree into the eighteenth century. An individual writer usually took up a position on one side or the other: women were bad or women were good. The many-sided debate on women in Castiglione's *Courtier* is sometimes considered part of the *querelle* because it makes use of familiar arguments from both sides. The method of argument was almost always the same, and Christine de Pisan had shown the way: examples and authorities, organized by topics. Except for the interspersed conversations between Christine and the allegorical visitors who instruct her, her book is a list of names and an anthology of exemplary tales. There is a pervasive tone of hyperbole. To modern tastes the genre is repellent. This should make us wonder why it was so popular, and I am sure an investigation of this would be a real contribution to the history of *mentalité*. For our present purposes it is enough to recognize that with an obsolete literary form we can never be sure we are reading it correctly. We cannot tell whether Christine's marshalling of examples from every kind of source and her uncritical inclusion of goddesses and mythical characters were intended to convince by force of authority or to overwhelm by force of numbers. Or was her aim to charm and amuse, making a serious point along the way? I know I am not alone in finding the method unconvincing. The argument seems forced, even desperate, no matter how much a modern reader may share her conviction about women's worth. To be sure, the inhabitants of Christine's *City of Ladies* have much in common with the guests at Judy Chicago's *Dinner Party*,[24] so a potpouri of legend, fiction and history may not be as out of date as I think. Out of date or not, it is none the less hyperbolic and naive.

[24] A recent multimedia art work consisting of a dinner table of huge proportions with distinctive place settings for 39 famous women from many periods and spheres of activity.

Christine was undoubtedly sincere when she said that women were unfairly maligned, that the vices of a few did not apply to all, that the distinctive qualities of women were admirable and that there have been outstanding women in past and present. Whether the later contributors to the *querelle des femmes* were equally sincere is another question. No difference in tone is detectable when a man argues that women are inferior to men and another man argues that men are inferior to women. It is all too easy to assume that men only meant it when they said men were better. Furthermore, one and the same man often took both positions in the *querelle*. The translator of the terrible Matheolus, Jehan le Fèvre, wrote a work in typically fulsome praise of women, called *Le Livre de Leësce*, as a kind of answer to Matheolus. Its method was not unlike Christine's. The *querelle* ran its zigzag course through the fifteenth century. To mention a few of the works that have survived: John Lydgate translated *De coniuge non ducenda* into English; an anonymous author wrote *La Malice des femmes*; another wrote the sardonic *Quinze joyes de mariage*; on the other side were Martin le Franc's *Champion des dames*; Pierre Michault's *Procès d'honneur fémenin*; and Philippe Bouton's *Miroir aux dames*. The *querelle* picked up steam at the beginning of the sixteenth century with Cornelius Agrippa's *Nobility and Excellence of Womankind* and continued on its way, including among its productions an English poem with the all-encompassing title *In Praise and Dispraise of Women*. For purposes of political polemic, John Knox borrowed from the *querelle* for his *First Blast of the Trumpet Against the Monstruous Regiment of Women*, but most of the contributors were literary men. The *querelle* was an approved means for displaying learning, ingenuity and writing skill, and we are probably right to be suspicious that so many of the praisers of women were seeking the patronage of women rulers. In a word, it was a literary game, a game with a popular subject and one that was capable of turning serious. It was not till the end of the seventeenth century that the form of the argument changed and both hyperbole and traditional authorities disappeared. Poulain de la Barre called his 'Cartesian discourse' *De l'égalité des deux sexes*. The title alone says a great deal. Its aim was to reason dispassionately, and its unflamboyant conclusion was that neither sex was better or worse.

But that was in the distant future. The first hundred years of the *querelle* showed little movement, going over the same ground again and again. We can get a sense of how familiar it was to literate people when we read the Third Book of *The Courtier*. When women are praised it is always for 'womanly' qualities of sweetness, beauty and chastity, and they are said to be capable of learning, which is to be put to 'womanly' uses. If we think we detect a plausible feminism in Christine de Pisan, can we detect it in male writers who sometimes wrote the same sorts of things she did? If not, what is the difference? The answer would seem to lie only partly in the writing itself. It is true that the sense of outrage that comes through in Christine's writing is mostly absent from the others. But the fact that a woman was doing the writing, that she was speaking for herself and for other women, conditions the effect of what she wrote.

If other women had written about women in that period would the effect have been the same? That is a hard question to answer, since we have almost nothing to go by. If we wait for about a hundred years to pass, however, we come upon a woman of equal literary stature who had something to say on the subject.

Although Margaret of Navarre never wrote a full-dress defense of women as Christine did, I find striking similarities in their attitudes. Margaret has also been called a 'feminist', and it is interesting to compare the two. The most obvious difference is that Margaret did not quote authorities or tell exemplary tales drawn from history and legend, although the *querelle des femmes* was flourishing when she lived. She adopted instead the manner of the Erasmian dialogue, something unknown to Christine a century earlier, and her reflections emerge from the freewheeling conversations of the storytellers about the stories told and heard in her *Heptameron*.

What concerns Margaret in these conversations are the private relations between men and women. The answer Margaret gives to any general condemnation of women is the one Christine gave: all women should not be judged for the evil of a few. Like Christine, Margaret complains that men deceive and betray women to achieve sexual gratification. Chivalric ideals are a front for seduction, and a truly loyal 'servant of love' is almost never found. Men who commit adultery are outraged if their wives do the same; like Christine, Margaret says that men condemn women for their own failings. Margaret's advice to women was similar to Christine's. Since women were naturally more chaste, they could help refine the behavior of men and make relations between the sexes less brutal. As wives they had a right to be loved and cared for, but if their marriages were unhappy they still had a duty to preserve the peace and stability of the home. Women had always to be on guard to keep their honor (the same honor Christine wrote about). Above all, women needed to exercise great patience and accept the conduct of bad husbands with resignation.

Like Christine, Margaret was abundantly aware of the power of God. Unlike Christine, she wrote religious poetry and carried on a correspondence with distinguished theologians. In the *Heptameron* her strong religious feeling plays an interesting counterpoint to her depiction of a world in which the god of love holds everyone in thrall. Love – and Margaret was less reticent than Christine in showing that love was inseparable from sexual passion – is part of the human experience, causing both men and women to behave irrationally and sinfully. Only God could rescue them. He could help them avoid the temptation of that other powerful deity, and His justice, not human vengeance, was to be relied on when a lover or a wife was betrayed or abused.

Margaret was probably not influenced by Christine. She was simply reflecting on similar subjects a hundred years later, when things had not changed very much with regard to those subjects. She was as sensitive as Christine to the plight of women, although she was perhaps less outraged by it because of her deeper acceptance of human fallibility. She thought men always tended to deceive women, and she had no nostalgia for some chivalric code that men supposedly used to follow. We can almost hear Christine and Margaret talking to each other across the chasm of years. The poet and the queen had a lot in common. They were both well-educated, both had been buffeted by fate, both had been widowed when young. They shared a yearning for better treatment of women by men and a sense of their own superiority to many men, which they expressed indirectly in their writing but might have talked about openly if they had come face to face, the remarkable accomplishments of the one reinforcing those of the other. As the scene unfolds in my imagination, I wonder whether it would have culminated in the laughter and tears of newly found comradeship or with Christine and Margaret on their knees before God.

If feminism means thinking about women and feeling that they deserve better in the world, then Christine was a feminist, Margaret was a feminist, and I have no doubt that many mute women whose thoughts we will never know were feminists. So were the men who sang the praises of women in the *querelle des femmes*, if we are to judge from what they wrote. But if feminism means a belief in the equal capacities of men and women, if it means wanting sweeping changes, if it means demanding equal opportunities for women to be educated and trained for careers, if it means women organizing to get what they want, if it means having *any* kind of program – well, then feminism obviously did not come into existence until the nineteenth century. That does not have to be proved.

The questions that are raised when we look for the glimmerings of feminist consciousness in earlier centuries are not about similarities but differences. We know – or we should know – that women were not worse off in the nineteenth century than in the fifteenth. If suffering alone caused revolutions there would have been a radical feminist movement in the fifteenth century. The nineteenth-century women's movement did not come into being because things had become more and more unbearable. On the contrary, one of the preconditions of all revolutions is an atmosphere of rising expectations. I leave it to others to delineate the atmosphere of the late eighteenth and early nineteenth centuries. We need to remind ourselves why it may have taken so long to develop.

There were important changes between 1400 and 1800 in politics, economic conditions and thought. Certain key notions of the fifteenth century had faded considerably by the nineteenth century. Conversely, it is easy to recognize that many of the notions most taken for granted today were absent in the fifteenth century. They include the belief in equality, in the autonomy of the individual and in the right to self-government. Could anyone, much less women themselves, have thought it possible to change the conditions of their lives before they learned to be familiar with the idea of political action? The idea of inalienable human rights in the secular realm came before the idea of women's rights, and the idea that all men were equal came before the idea that men and women were equal. There is no need to labor this, but the danger of anachronism lurks in an unwillingness to recognize the role played by this cluster of ideas. Those embryonic feminists of the past may have smarted at the injustices done to women, but they issued no calls to action. They issued instead what may seem to us like calls to inaction. What we find in Christine and Margaret is something akin to quietism or stoicism. An individual woman was to make her own peace with the world by doing what the world was supposed to admire most profoundly: living a good Christian life. Historical research has shown that women were engaged in all kinds of enterprises and that widows in particular sometimes achieved considerable independence. But these facts were hardly mentioned by the writers we have been talking about, and never as models or goals. For them the ideal woman was a competent, virtuous, devout wife, whose merits they wanted to be recognized. Beyond that, they suggested that the greatest consolation to women should be the fact that they had no less an inside track to God than men did. If we are looking for an element of subversion in a supposed early feminism, it is hidden in the religious message. The traditional church made the male priest the intermediary between God and the rest of the population, just as men were the intermediaries between secular authorities and the members of their families, but at the same time women could pray directly to God, and the experience of women saints and mystics showed that God did not always communicate through men. Christine often reminded her readers of this, and it is a large part of the message of her poem about Joan of Arc. Margaret, in her less flamboyant, evangelical way, said something similar.

What did women really talk about? We wish we knew, since we have good reason to believe they took comfort from each other, even if they never organized for action. The topics discussed by Christine and Margaret offer some clues. They may have talked about the travails of love, about their resentment of their husbands' petty tyrannies and about the unfairness of misogyny. Did they also talk about their secret feelings of superiority, especially their special aptitude for Christian living? Did they consciously see religious devotion as a wonderful opportunity for women, in the perspective of the values they held most dear? A long line of fifteenth- and sixteenth-century women mystics and martyrs suggests that women took advantage of the opportunity. Reform movements seemed to offer particular promise, as one women wrote in a letter to Margaret of Navarre, urging women to be active in the Reformation, partly to support a worthy cause, partly to vindicate women, 'hoping to God that from now on women will not be so despised as in the past'.[25]

To want to know about women in the past is a feeling all historians – if they are motivated by curiosity about humanity's endless variety and resourcefulness – should share. To know them piecemeal, however, is not enough. Historians cannot understand the past if they admit only the bits and pieces of information that correspond to their present concerns, even if their questioning of the past necessarily begins with those concerns. Avoiding anachronism is always hard when historians care deeply about an issue, but they have an overriding commitment to be fair to the people of the past, to stretch their

[25] 'Esperant en Dieu que doresnavant les femmes ne seront plus tant mesprisées comme par le passé.' In a letter of 1539 by Marie Dentière, wife of Antoine Froment, cited in Emile Telle, *L'Oeuvre de Marguerite d'Angoulême, reine de Navarre, et la querelle des femmes* (Toulouse, 1937; reprinted Geneva, 1969), pp. 377–8.

own vision to take in what may no longer matter but used to matter very much. Women historians may very well feel a special obligation to the women of the past, but that is all the more reason to be fair and to shun anachronism. At the same time, we should also be fair to ourselves. For what we have to do as women in the second half of the twentieth century we do not need women of the fifteenth century, as embryonic feminists or as anything else. We should give ourselves credit for recognizing our own problems, which are not the same as theirs, partly because the world has changed and partly because perceptions have changed. We are dealing with different conditions and different options. If we need fifteenth-century women, it is not for guidance or inspiration, but simply because history is a poor thing without them.

REFERENCES

Agrippa of Nettesheim, Henry Cornelius, *Of the Nobilitie and Excellence of Womankynde*, trans. David Clapham (London, 1542).

Bell, Susan Groag, 'Christine de Pizan (1364–1430): humanism and the problem of a studious woman', *Feminist Studies*, III (1976), pp. 173–84.

Castiglione, Baldesar, *The Book of the Courtier*, trans. Charles S. Singleton (New York, 1959).

Chafe, William H., *The American Woman; Her Changing Social, Economic and Political Roles, 1920–1970* (New York, 1972).

Degler, Carl N., *At Odds; Women and the Family in America from the Revolution to the Present* (New York, 1980).

Favier, Marguerite, *Christine de Pisan; muse des cours souveraines* (Lausanne, 1967).

Febvre, Lucien, *Amour sacré, amour profane; autour de l'Heptaméron* (Paris, 1944).

—— *The Problem of Unbelief in the Sixteenth Century; the Religion of Rabelais*, trans. Beatrice Gottlieb (Cambridge, Mass., 1982).

Golenistcheff-Koutouzoff, Elie, *L'Histoire de Grisélidis en France au XIVe et au XVe siècle* (Paris, 1933).

Hicks, Eric (ed.), *Le Débat sur le 'Roman de la Rose'* (Bibliothèque du XVe Siècle, XLIII, Paris, 1977).

Huizinga, Johan, *The Waning of the Middle Ages*, trans. F. Hopman (New York, 1949; paper 1954).

Kelly, Joan, 'Early feminist theory and the *Querelle des Femmes*, 1400–1789', *Signs*, VIII (1982), pp. 4–28.

Keralio, Mlle de (ed.), *Collection des meilleurs ouvrages français composés par des femmes* (14 vols, Paris, 1786–9).

Knox, John, *The First Blast of the Trumpet Against the Monstruous Regiment of Women*. In *The Works of John Knox*, ed. David Laing (6 vols, Edinburgh, 1846–64), IV, pp. 363–420.

Laigle, Mathilde, *Le Livre des trois vertus de Christine de Pisan, et son milieu historique et littéraire* (Bibliothèque du XVe Siècle, Paris, 1912).

Langlois, Ernest, 'Le traité de Gerson contre *Le Roman de la Rose*', *Romania*, XLV (1918–19), pp. 23–48.

Lorris, Guillaume de and Jean de Meun, *Le Roman de la Rose*, ed. Daniel Poirion (Paris, 1974).

—— *The Romance of the Rose*, trans. Charles Dahlberg (Princeton, 1971).

McLeod, Enid, *The Order of the Rose; the Life and Ideas of Christine de Pizan* (Totowa, NJ, 1976).

Marguerite de Navarre, *L'Heptaméron*, ed. Michel François (Paris, 1967).

Matheolus, *Les Lamentations de Mathéolus et le Livre de Leesce de Jehan le Fèvre, de Resson*, ed. A. G. Van Hamel (2 vols, Bibliothèque de l'Ecole des Hautes Etudes, Sciences Historiques et Philologiques, XCV, XCVI, Paris, 1892, 1905).

Minto, William, 'A champion of her sex', *Macmillan's Magazine*, LIII (February 1886), pp. 264–75.

Phillips, James E. jun., 'The background of Spenser's attitude toward women rulers', *The Huntington Library Quarterly*, V (1941–2), pp. 5–32.

Pisan (or Pizan), Christine de, *The Book of the City of Ladies*, trans. Earl Jeffrey Richards (New York, 1982).

—— *The Book of the Duke of True Lovers*, trans. Alice Kemp-Welch, with verse trans. by Laurence Binyon and Eric R. D. Maclagan (London, 1909).

—— *Ditié de Jehanne d'Arc*, ed. Angus J. Kennedy and Kenneth Varty (Medium Aevum Monographs, New Series IX, Oxford, 1977).

—— *Oeuvres poétiques de Christine de Pisan*, ed. Maurice Roy (3 vols, Société des Anciens Textes Français 24, Paris, 1886–96).

Richardson, Lulu McDowell, *Forerunners of Feminism in French Literature of the Renaissance; from Christine de Pisan to Marie de Gournay* (The Johns Hopkins Studies in Romance Literature and Language, 12, Baltimore and Paris, 1929).

Rigaud, Rose, *Les Idées féministes de Christine de Pisan* (Neuchâtel, 1911; reprinted Geneva, 1973).

Seidel, Michael, 'Poulain de la Barre's *The Woman as Good as the Man*', *Journal of the History of Ideas*, XXXV (1974), pp. 499–508.

Telle, Emile, *L'Oeuvre de Marguerite d'Angoulême, reine de Navarre, et la querelle des femmes* (Toulouse, 1937; reprinted Geneva, 1969).

Thomassy, R., *Essai sur les écrits politiques de Christine de Pisan* (Paris, 1838).

Utley, Francis Lee, *The Crooked Rib; an Analytical Index to the Argument About Women in English and Scots Literature to the End of the Year 1568* (Columbus, Ohio, 1944).

Wood, Mary Morton, *The Spirit of Protest in Old French Literature* (Columbia University Studies in Romance Philology and Literature, XXII, New York, 1917; reprinted 1966).

Select Bibliography of the Writings of John H. Mundy

Reviews have not been included in this bibliography.

1943 'John of Gmunden', *Isis*, 34, pp. 195–205.

1954 *Liberty and Political Power in Toulouse, 1050–1230* (New York).

1955 *Essays in Medieval Life and Thought Presented in Honor of A. P. Evans*, edited and contributed to by J. H. Mundy, R. W. Emery and B. N. Nelson (New York).

1956 'Un usurier malheureux' in *Hommage à M. François Galabert* (Toulouse), pp. 117–25.

1958 *The Medieval Town*, historical essay by J. H. Mundy and readings by P. N. Riesenberg (Princeton).

1961 *The Council of Constance: The Unification of the Church*, trans. by L. R. Loomis; edited, annotated and introduced by J. H. Mundy and K. M. Woody (New York).

1961 'European society in the Middle Ages', in *Chapters in Western Civilization* (New York), I, pp. 91–138.

1963 'On Henri Pirenne and the medieval town', in H. Pirenne (ed.), *Early Democracies in the Low Countries* (New York), pp. ix–xxvi.

1966 'Charity and social work in Toulouse, 1100–1250', *Traditio*, 22, pp. 203–87.

1967 'La croisade albigeoise et l'interdiction de l'usure à Toulouse', *Archéologia*, 19, pp. 28–34.

1972 'The Western Middle Ages', in J. A. Garraty and Peter Gay (eds), *Columbia History of the World* (New York), pp. 363–415.

1973 *Europe in the High Middle Ages, 1150–1309* (New York).

1974 'Noblesse et hérésie – Une familie cathare: les Maurand', *Annales: ESC*, pp. 1211–23.

1976 'The origins of the College of Saint Raymond at the University of Toulouse', in E. P. Mahoney (ed.), *Philosophy and Humanism: Essays in Honor of Paul Oskar Kristeller* (Leiden), pp. 454–62.

1977 'Henri Pirenne: a European Historian', *The Journal of European Economic History*, 6, pp. 473–80.

1981 'Village, town, and city in the region of Toulouse', in J. A. Raftis (ed.), *Pathways in Medieval Peasants* (Toronto), pp. 140–90.

1981 'The farm of Fontanas at Toulouse: two families, a monastery, and a pope', *Bulletin of Medieval Canon Law*, 11, pp. 29–40.

1982 'Kirche und religiöses Leben', in *Propyläen Geschichte der Literatur*, II (Berlin), pp. 39–62.

1982 'Urban society and culture: Toulouse and its region', *Renaissance and Renewal in the Twelfth Century*, ed. R. L. Benson and Giles Constable, with C. D. Lanham (Cambridge), pp. 229–47.

1983 'The financing of the Cistercian Order', *The Journal of European Economic History*, 12, pp. 203–9.

1985 *The Repression of Catharism at Toulouse: The Royal Diploma of 1279*, forthcoming from the Pontifical Institute of Medieval Studies in Toronto, Canada.

Contributors

JANE BISHOP holds a doctorate from Columbia University in Medieval, Byzantine and Roman History, and is a member of the Institute for Research in History. She is author of the forthcoming book *Pope Nicholas I and the First Age of Papal Independence*.

JOHN DAY is Research Professor at the Centre National de la Recherche Scientifique and Lecturer in Economic History at the University of Paris VII. His recent publications include *La Sardegna e i suoi dominatori dal secolo XI al secolo XIV* (1984) and *Etudes d'histoire monetaire* of which he is editor.

MICHAEL GOODICH is chairman of the Department of History at the University of Haifa in Israel. His chief interests are medieval social and ecclesiastical history; his recent publications include *Vita Perfecta: The Idea of Sainthood in the Thirteenth Century* (1982).

BEATRICE GOTTLIEB is writing a book on the family in pre-industrial Europe and America. Her translation of Lucien Febvre's *Problem of Unbelief in the Sixteenth Century; the Religion of Rabelais* was published by Harvard University Press in 1982. She is affiliated with The Institute for Research in History.

JULIUS KIRSHNER is Professor of History at the University of Chicago and editor of the *Journal of Modern History*. His previous publications include *Pursuing Honor While Avoiding Sin: The 'Monte delle Doti' of Florence* (1978). At present he is working on a study of matrimony and patrimony in Renaissance Florence.

HELEN RODNITE LEMAY is Associate Professor of History at SUNY Stony Brook. She has published a number of articles on medieval scientific ideas on human sexuality. At present she is studying the manuscript sources of medieval gynecology and obstetrics.

JANET SENDEROWITZ LOENGARD is Professor of History at Moravian College. She has published articles in English legal history and is currently completing work on early sixteenth century London viewers' certificates.

JO ANN MCNAMARA is Professor of History at Hunter College, City University of New York, and a founding member of the Institute for Research in History. Her publications include *A New Song: Celibate Women in the First Three Christian Centuries* (1983).

BERNARD MCGINN is Professor of Historical Theology and of the History of Christianity at the Divinity School of the University of Chicago. His publications include *Visions of the End, Apocalyptic Spirituality*, and the forthcoming *The Calabrian Abbot: Joachim of Fiore in the History of Western Thought* (1985).

RONALD G. MUSTO is a writer and editor in New York City. He has taught at Columbia, NYU, and Duke University. His research focuses on fourteenth-century reform spirituality. Previous publications include *Angelo Clareno, O.F.M.: Fourteenth-Century Translator of the Greek Fathers* (1983).

LEAH OTIS is lecturer at the University of Montpellier I. Her publications include several articles on late medieval social history and *Prostitution in Medieval Society: The History of an Urban Institution in Languedoc* (1985).

EUGENE RICE is William R. Shepherd Professor of History at Columbia University. His publications include *The Foundations of Early Modern Europe* (1970) and *The Prefatory Epistles of Jacques Lefevre d'Etaples and Related Texts* (1972).

PHYLLIS B. ROBERTS is Professor of History at the College of Staten Island and the Graduate Center, City University of New York. Her previous publications include *Studies on the Sermons of Stephen Langton* (1968) and *Selected Sermons of Stephen Langton* (1980). She is currently engaged in research on the cult of Thomas Becket in the medieval Latin preaching tradition.

SUZANNE FONAY WEMPLE, Professor of History, Barnard College, Columbia University. Her *Women in Frankish Society; Marriage and the Cloister, 500–900*. Philadelphia, University of Pennsylvania Press, 1981, received the 1981 Berkshire prize. At present she is working on a Female Monastic Repertory and Bibliography, Italy and England to 1500.

STEPHEN WESSLEY teaches history at York College of Pennsylvania. His current research centers on *Joachim of Fiore*.

Index

Toulouse, Parlement of, 139
Tractatus de matricibus (Guainerius), 317–36
Tractatus super quatuor Evangelia (Joachim of Fiore), 174
Trebbia, battle of (889), 92
Trexler, Richard C., 119
Tryphoninus, 258
Tuetbert, 96
Tuitham, Theobald de, 245–6

Ubaldi, Angelo degli, 283
Ubertino da Casale, 195
Ubi adhuc, 259, 265, 269–73, 281, 295
Ugolino de la Fontana, 129
Ugone II, judge of Arborea, 307
Ulpian, 259
Ulrich von Durne, 132

Varro, 9
Vashti, Queen, 105–7
Vaticinium Sibyllae Erythraeae (or *Prophecy of the Erythraean Sibyl*), 30–5
Venturino, 130
Veridiana Attavanti of Castelfiorentino, 131
Verissimo, 86
Vernacci, Vaggia di Giovanni, 282, 284
Vincent of Beauvais: *Mirror of History*, 20
Violant, Sister of St Guillem, 154, 159
Violante of Aragon, 184
Virgil: *Aeneid*, 9; Fourth Eclogue, 14, 18

virginity, 103–4 *see also* celibacy
Vita Sanctae Rictrudis, 37

Wadding, Luke, 191: *Annales minorum*, 206
Waldrada, 55, 66, 70
Waltar, Hubert, 247
Wandard, Robert, 248
Warwick, Maud de Percy, Countess of, 254
Waterville, Ascelina de, 244
Whiston, Prof. William: *A Vindication of the Sibylline Oracles*, 7
widows: remarriage of, 234–7, 255; *see also* dower, English
Wielard, 242–3
Williams, Charlotte (later Mundy), 2
Willindane, 48
Winchcombe, John de, 248
Winchcombe, Nicole de, 248
witchcraft, 67–8, 328
women: ambivalent attitude of church to, 135; assumptions *re*, 320, 326, 333–6; biblical as symbols, 164–74; as Devil's gateway, 57; history, 341; as naturally or morally inferior, 59, 76, 80; old maid syndrome, 122, 123; rights, 338, 360; role *re* family, 256, 262; status in medieval Sardinia, 304–16
Wonders of the City of Rome, 21

Zabarella, Francesco, 267
Zita of Lucca, 128–30
Zventibald, 92